HABEAS CORPUS

PAUL D. HALLIDAY

Habeas Corpus

From England to Empire

THE BELKNAP PRESS OF
HARVARD UNIVERSITY PRESS
Cambridge, Massachusetts
London, England
2010

For Angie and Bob Halliday

Library of Congress Cataloging-in-Publication Data

Halliday, Paul D. (Paul Delaney), 1961–
    Habeas corpus : from England to empire / Paul D. Halliday.
        p. cm.
    Includes bibliographical references and index.
    ISBN 978-0-674-04901-7 (cloth : alk. paper) 1. Habeas corpus—Great Britain—
History. 2. Extraordinary remedies—Great Britain—History. 3. Habeas corpus—
Great Britain—Sources. I. Title.
    KD7612.H35 2010
    345.42′056—dc22   2009035482

Contents

Acknowledgments

I planned to write a very different book when I set out. That I finally learned what kind of book I should write resulted from the kindness of many people who helped me see things more clearly. None of them is responsible for those things I still fail to see.

I should begin by thanking those who made it possible to do the research for this book. The staff of the Conservation Department of the National Archives in London kindly opened scores of recorda files whose thongs—which had bound them together since they were made—were so tight as to make them unreadable. This allowed access to thousands of writs I could never have read otherwise. I am also grateful to the staff of the library of the University of Virginia Law School—especially Kent Olson and Cathy Palombi—and to Lew Purifoy and all the people who make LEO roar, delivering library books and articles with astonishing efficiency.

For commenting on large portions of the manuscript, I owe particular thanks to John Baker, Eric Freedman, Thomas Green, Cynthia Herrup, James Oldham, Catherine Patterson, Wilfrid Prest, David A. Smith, Philip Stern, and the anonymous readers for the press. I am grateful to Lauren Benton, Mary Bilder, Allen Boyer, Christopher Brooks, Richard Cust, Jonathan Hafetz, Daniel Hulsebosch, Krista Kesselring, Mark Kishlansky, Hope Metcalf, Tim Stretton, and Robert Travers for illuminating discussions. I also want to thank kind hosts and audience members for their ideas in university history faculties at Cambridge, Durham, Harvard, Oxford, and Virginia; and in the law faculties of Boston College, Georgetown, Harvard, Michigan, New York University, Queen Mary College, London, and Virginia. I especially appreciate Kathleen McDermott of Harvard University Press for all her hard work getting this off my desk and into print, and Julie Carlson for doing so much to make the result more readable.

For anyone writing legal history that crosses many time zones, the University of Virginia provides a wonderful place to work. My colleagues, current and former, have taught me so much about their fields, answered scores of questions, and offered support in so many ways, especially Brian Balogh, Rich Barnett, Lenard Berlanstein, Brandon Garrett, Risa Goluboff, Patrick Griffin, Maya Jasanoff, John Mason, Allan Megill, Erik Midelfort, Joe Miller, Peter Onuf, Duane Osheim, Sophie Rosenfeld, and George Van Cleve. Elizabeth Meyer was very generous with comments on an early sketch of this project, as was Chuck McCurdy, who has offered unstinting encouragement. Neeti Nair patiently reduced my ignorance of South Asian history, while Ted White helped me understand American law better during a fruitful collaboration together. Brian Owensby has provided warm friendship and plenty of good ideas for years. I also want to thank graduate students who helped with aspects of the research, namely Brian Dudley, Jason Eldred, Jessica Otis, and Heather Weidner. And though few may realize it, the questions many wonderful undergraduates have asked over the years show their imprint across the book.

For funding to allow time for writing, I am grateful for a fellowship from the National Endowment for the Humanities and to the American Council of Learned Societies for a Frederick Burkhardt Fellowship. A Franklin Research Grant of the American Philosophical Society helped to fund an early stage of the research. I am grateful to successive deans of the College of Arts and Sciences at the University of Virginia for funding summer research trips and for a semester's leave from teaching, which permitted completion of this book. For putting up with my absences from home and in the study, I offer my family all my love and the promise of more time together now that we are all released from this book. Finally, no one has been more generous with hospitality that made this work possible from beginning to end than Richard Linenthal and Larry Wallace. Thank you for all the weeknights in London, and for the relaxing weekends that helped keep me going.

This book is for my parents, who taught me to hear the sighs of others.

A Note on the Text

Spellings and punctuation have been modernized in quotations from early modern texts, except for book titles and where doing so might alter meaning. Words and phrases originally in law French have been silently translated. Words that have been added or deleted in order to clarify meaning are noted respectively with brackets or ellipses. Standard abbreviations for money amounts have been used throughout: £ for pounds sterling, s. for shillings, and d. for pence. The place of publication of works printed before 1800 is London, unless noted otherwise. Biblical quotations are from the 1611 King James Version.

Before 1752, all dates are given in old style, though the year is taken to have begun on January 1 rather than March 25. After 1752, dating is according to modern usage. As a general rule, when practices used in the principal common law court in Westminster Hall are discussed, that court is called King's Bench. It is referred to as Queen's Bench only when discussing an episode during a period when a queen reigned (1553–1558; 1558–1603; 1702–1714; 1837–1901) or as the Upper Bench when there was no monarch (1649–1660). The court's meetings were organized into four terms each year: Hilary (winter), Easter (spring), Trinity (summer), and Michaelmas (autumn). The periods between terms were referred to as vacation.

Hearing the Sighs of Prisoners

Let the sighing of the prisoner come before thee . . .
PSALMS 79:11

Prisoners sigh throughout the Bible, held in real or figurative chains, captive in body or soul. Their fate reveals the workings of justice, human and divine. Scriptural stories about prisoners recount the persecution of the righteous and the damnation of the unrighteous. Such stories demand that we learn how to distinguish the two.

But judging well is not a matter of faith. It is a matter of legal practices by which right judgment might be assured. A Roman magistrate taught this lesson to St. Paul. Festus, governor of Judea, explained to him, "[I]t seemeth to me unreasonable to send a prisoner, and not withall to signify the crimes laid against him" (Acts 25:27). An English judge sixteen centuries later, Sir Edward Coke, transposed his Roman predecessor's words, making them divine: "[B]y the law of God, none ought to be imprisoned, but with the cause expressed."[1] For millennia, judges and prisoners have understood that knowing the difference between right and wrong when ordering imprisonment is a legal imperative because it is a moral and spiritual imperative. Discovering the difference between right and wrong requires that the human judge, like God, hear "the sighs and groans of his poor oppressed and distressed prisoners," as the political prisoner John Lilburne wrote from his Tower cell in 1648.[2]

The writ of habeas corpus has served in Anglophone legal cultures for more than four centuries as the judicial practice by which we hear those sighs. Its purpose was and is to bring a prisoner before a judge in order "to signify the crimes laid against him," and thereby to ensure

1

that law is honored in holding or releasing him. But the writ's history has traditionally been approached as something grander, told as the tale of liberty: "the Great Writ of Liberty," as we have called it for three hundred years.[3]

As such, its past has been written less as a history than as an exercise in legal narcissism. Through our celebrations of habeas corpus, the Anglo-American liberal mind has praised its uniqueness.[4] It proclaims itself the result of an inescapable process, begun in a misty past, carried through Magna Carta, past a tyrannical king or two, and finally to its triumph: the realization of all that the writ portended with the help of democratic impulses working through statute-making bodies, whether British Parliaments, colonial assemblies, or American Congresses. This makes an appealing story, in part because we believe—or hope—that it arrives in us.

Rather than write of past ideas and practices as if their purpose was to make our own, I have approached the writ's history from within ways of thinking and living quite foreign to ours.[5] By doing so, I hope we can reach a position from which to understand when, how, and why it became possible to hear the prisoner's sighs, what it has meant when we have done so, and what it has meant when we have not.

This is a history of England and of its empire. It can and must be a history of nation and empire in order to be a history of habeas corpus, because no other part of law touched so much of life. No legal instrument dealt equally with things so public as treason and so personal as insanity. No other writ provided opportunities to think through the political threat posed by religious dissent while at the same time considering the social meaning of fathering an illegitimate child, of whore-mongering, or of sodomy. And no other writ issued simultaneously to church leaders, mayors and sheriffs, professional societies, violent husbands, and military officers. Well before 1800, jailers in imperial outposts around the globe answered the writ's demands. Using it, judges inspected the performance of all kinds of administrators and magistrates as they collected tithes and taxes, monitored sewers and the debts of bankrupts, held prisoners of war, and imprisoned the queen's enemies as well as those mistakenly supposed to be her enemies. Given this range, and given the high quality of judicial records, habeas corpus provides an otherwise unavailable means to follow political dislocations and cultural transformations of all kinds over centuries and across the globe. Writing the writ's history permits—even requires—uniting disparate historical fields: social and religious history, the history of the state, histories of politics in thought and action, the history of empire, and the history of law. The presence in this book of each of these varieties of historical explanation makes all the others intelligible.

My hope has been to engage historians in all these fields, especially those who do not usually read in that dry-as-dust place called legal history. Given the fragmentation of early modern English and imperial historiography, law provides the one site at which religious history, social and political history, the history of ideas and the history of people's actions—in England and far beyond—may be brought into a single frame. By putting the king's prerogative rather than the usual liberal ideas at the center of habeas corpus, I am asking historians of political thought to consider again how talk of "liberties" operated in the sixteenth century and beyond. By emphasizing the power of judges in supervising all other authorities, I ask that we do more to incorporate law, courts, and their personnel into our thinking about the early modern state. By writing across many centuries, I am looking past traditional chronological barriers—the civil wars of the 1640s, the Revolution of 1688, the adoption of the U.S. Constitution in 1789—that block our analytic vision. By bringing empire to the fore in exploring what has long been taken to be a fundamentally English practice, I am suggesting how students of empire and of nation may learn from each other in order to promote a different way of doing legal or constitutional history.

Lawyers, too, might find much here to interest them. While writing about one legal instrument, I offer by my practice an implicit essay on what constitutes a properly historical analysis of law's past, and on the sources and methods we might use to produce such an analysis. This matters not only to the validity of the claims historians make about what law "was" in any given past. It matters because such claims are often put to work in legal problem solving, especially in the United States. We read Coke, Blackstone, and a handful of printed reports, then claim that we know what the law "was" in 1789 or some other moment. If we do that while countless parchment court records and case reports surviving only in manuscript lie unread in archives, then we have been derelict as historians. If we act upon such claims in our courts, we may be derelict in our jurisprudence, our claims resting on hollow foundations.[6]

My intention has been to offer a history of habeas corpus that is better grounded empirically and broader conceptually than the one still routinely invoked in courtrooms and public debate. The final chapters explore aspects of the nineteenth and twentieth centuries, but I make no attempt to draw lines out of the past to arrive on one moment or set of issues, nor do I want to suggest where the writ might or must go from here. Rather than seeing law's past moving with a logic that requires it to resolve on a particular point, the book concludes by highlighting the paradoxical ways that the writ does and does not work—the many human values that law does and does not realize in operation. I address recent epochs simply to show the writ's astonishing geographical diffusion and the variety of purposes it serves. This diffusion and variety manifest the same principles that informed the making and using of the writ from the sixteenth century to the nineteenth. It must remain for lawyers and jurists to decide, through practices appropriate to their profession, whether such principles should inform judicial decisions in the dozens of countries that use habeas corpus today. But if lawyers and judges want to act on claims about history, we must first make a fully contextualized reclamation of those past principles. Only then might history serve law: not as a grab bag of poor analogies, but as an otherwise unseen position from which to think anew about the questions that law must answer.

Historical analysis requires a search for the ideas and concerns of others. How and where can we find them? A central premise informing this book is that actions convey ideas as well as—perhaps better than—words. My approach has been to read the deeds of judges before reading their words.[7]

Doing this required learning about patterns of use before attempting to explain any single writ. I thus began in the archives of the court of King's Bench, England's greatest common law court and the court to which most prisoners went for habeas corpus. Supporting the entire book is information gained from a quadrennial survey of habeas use from 1500 to 1800, made possible by examining the records of King's Bench. The court's writs, rolls, and rulebooks have been little studied before, yet they are rich with information that we can find nowhere else about the ideas and actions of prisoners and judges. They are indispensable for situating habeas corpus in the worlds of law and living that constituted England and the empire.

In all, 2,757 prisoners used habeas corpus in the survey years. Basic multiplication suggests that at least 11,000 people across three centuries resorted to the writ, although given variations in record quality over three centuries, the actual number was probably much greater. In addition to the survey years, I have explored the files and rolls comprehensively for periods known to contain important developments: the 1590s to the 1610s, when the writ was made an instrument of great judicial force; the 1640s and 1650s, when the court responded to one political crisis after another; 1678 to 1715, a period of plotting and revolution, of invasion scares and abortive rebellion; and the years of imperial war after 1756. From writs in both survey and nonsurvey years, we have information on over 4,800 prisoners, more than 40 percent of the total who used habeas corpus.

This book is quietly undergirded rather than driven by the numbers. Aggregating thousands of cases allows us to establish the patterns against which we can make serious claims about the meanings of lone cases: were they singular or exemplary, points on a trajectory, or points around which practice turned? Individual cases are literally meaningless without the contexts—social and cultural, as well as those provided by other cases—through which we can hope to understand them. By tracing patterns, we also learn where we must look more closely to explain how people thought about law. These patterns will pull our gaze repeatedly to certain eras—especially the one between roughly 1590 and 1615—and to the work of certain justices: Popham and Fleming; Bacon, Hale, Holt, and Mansfield. Only after identifying the patterns and their moments of transformation will we be in a position to make sense of the words that people spoke and wrote.

But to work on words, we must do more than read printed case reports.[8] Many more reports of habeas cases survive only in manuscript. Extensive use is made of these, as well as of manuscript treatises or readings from the Inns of Court. Learning stored and conveyed in manuscript was central to law's life before 1800. The ideas of some of the most influential lawyers of their day survive only in this form. To make sense of the central concepts informing their work with habeas corpus, we must reach beyond texts of law, to political pamphlets, sermons, letters, newspapers, and more. Other archive materials—for instance, King's Bench affidavits—allow us to see how and why so many thousands turned to habeas corpus for help. The letters of captains in the Royal Navy and the fee books of minor attorneys reveal the small details that often had enormous consequences in shaping what law could do and for whom it could do it.

With all this in hand, how then to write a history of habeas corpus? There are three approaches we might take, beginning with the narrative mode, a chronologically ordered story that makes the writ a hero—"the Great Writ of Liberty"—in the unfolding of modern liberal ideals.[9] In legal history, we do such work by lining up a string of cases found in the expected place: the canon of printed case reports. By adding resounding dicta from a great judge or two, and, for the benefit of American readers, some nostrums from Founding Fathers and Framers, we give our story poetical and patriotic as well as narrative force. Like a tone poem's hero, such a tale resolves exactly where its composer decides it must: in tonic chords, fortissimo. This produces a heartening story that hits on comfortably familiar notes, but not a history, the point of which is to discomfit us with the significance of the unfamiliar.

A second approach might take us through categories of modern legal practice. One might write a chapter on each procedural rule shaping the writ: one on evidentiary restrictions, another on standing, a third on territorial ambit and sovereignty. We might organize chapters by jurisdictions: one each on Chancery, justices of the peace, and the Privy Council. Or we might work around the varieties of wrongs for which prisoners were held: felony, misdemeanors, and so on. There is much to recommend this approach. But doing so obscures many of the most important concepts we must understand, many of which came from outside law. It can also drive a search for things that were not there. All the matter in these categories is considered in this book. But to bring out their significance requires a different approach.

If narrative is like a tone poem, then this book has been written as a fugue. Admittedly, fugues, like tone poems, end as their composers design. But in the fugue, we encounter more surprises along the way. Take a theme, then repeat it, layering on new themes while playing them all against each other. Doing so brings out revealing dissonances. After all, the writ's past involved disappointed expectations as often as realized ones.

Four motifs run throughout the book's three sections and nine chapters, which are organized around concepts and practices rather than particular periods or strict chronology. The first motif is the writ's core principle: *that* the judge judges. Histories of habeas corpus traditionally focus on how they judged. This book, too, considers how judges made judgments. But underlying modes of judgment was the central fact of habeas corpus: that a judge should hear the sighs of all prisoners, regardless of where, how, or by whom they were held.

Second, this power to judge arose not from ideas about liberty, but from sovereignty as it was understood three and four centuries ago: as embodied in an actual person. The king is the traditional villain in the history of habeas corpus. Here, however, we shall see that the power to use the writ came from the prerogative, that part of legal authority peculiar to the king. The prerogative explains how, during periods of instability or war, the writ met new forms of constraint generated by fear. It also illuminates how the writ responded as cultural change prompted new questions about old forms of constraint, from the abuses of husbands to slavery. In the years around 1600, judges took the prerogative into their own hands so that they might oversee the work of all other courts and officers whenever they detained a subject's body. After listening to the prisoner's sighs, and considering "the crimes laid against him," the judge spoke in the sovereign's name to order release or a return to jail.

Third, what constituted liberties was the result rather than the starting point of judicial decision-making. Habeas corpus became an effective instrument of judicial oversight of all other jurisdictions in a world that did not conceive liberty as a quality inhering in morally autonomous individuals: the modern liberal ideal. Such ideas arose outside of law. As they did, they came to law looking for refuge. Sometimes they found it, though not always. John Lilburne learned this in his sufferings after England's civil wars. So did Granville Sharp, a tireless champion of slaves and impressed sailors a century later. English law could never do all that lay morality demanded of it, especially when legislation made in assemblies from Westminster to Jamaica to Auckland hemmed in the writ that judges had made.

Finally, statute and empire, often acting together, revealed both the limits and possibilities of habeas corpus. The 1679 Habeas Corpus Act and other statutes suggest a legislative impulse to improve the writ's capacities, though their results were more mixed than is often appreciated. Other statutes had a more negative influence on habeas corpus, which could do nothing about detention forms generated by legislation. Many statutes, such as those that shaped impressment, arose in response to empire. Colonial legislators, like those in Westminster, exalted liberty, then passed acts creating chattel slavery or declaring martial law, which all but eradicated the writ. But imperial experience also shows the vastness of subjecthood and of the writ's territorial range. From its work in the earliest acquisitions of the king outside his English realm (Ireland, Calais, Berwick) to the latest (Barbados, Quebec, Ceylon), the common law writ of habeas corpus would find its way. Only by investigating the writ's work across the king's global dominions will we appreciate fully what the writ was as English and imperial law circulated through, and thereby transformed, each other.

By the eighteenth, nineteenth, and twentieth centuries, wherever the writ was named, it provided a way for lawyers and nonlawyers alike to talk about the moral ends they hoped to achieve through law. They called habeas corpus the "palladium of Liberty": the icon of a wise goddess, a well-armed protectress. It is a striking image. People's liberties, like their physical selves, needed protection. Throughout its history, the central purpose of habeas corpus has been to provide the means by which the judge might find the place at which liberty and physical security could be protected simultaneously by ensuring that subjects were imprisoned only according to law.

From the end of the seventeenth century, and especially from the late eighteenth century on, war or rebellion, overseas and at home, provoked fears. When channeled through ostensibly representative legislatures, these fears squelched the writ. For all that the palladium has been adored, she has sometimes disappointed those who have worshiped her. To Ireland and South Africa, to Barbados, Australia, the United States, and elsewhere, the writ would spread, making it possible to hear the prisoner's sighs all over law's empire. When they have not been heard, it has not been for lack of effort by the very judges who made the writ and put it to work.

PART I

Making Habeas Corpus

Habeas corpus did not evolve. Judges made it, transforming a common device for moving people about in aid of judicial process into an instrument by which they supervised imprisonment orders made anywhere, by anyone, for any reason. The justices considered the writ's work to be so important that when jailers refused to answer commands made to them by habeas corpus, the court sometimes jailed the jailer himself.

In the decades to each side of 1605, the justices responded to a host of political and cultural forces, making the writ into the means by which they took the survey of all other magistrates. By looking closely at their work as evidenced in the archives of King's Bench, we can see how they achieved this judicial supremacy and how they put it to work in the centuries following. By subjecting each clause in habeas corpus to a close reading—as in Chapter 2—we consider the writ's origins and how it worked.

The most important force driving the writ was the idea at its foundation: the prerogative, those aspects of legal authority possessed only by the monarch. As a prerogative writ, habeas corpus expressed the king's concern to know the circumstances whenever one of his subjects was imprisoned. By taking the idea and language of the prerogative into their own hands, the justices made a writ of majestic, even equitable, sweep that made it possible to protect the king's subjects.

CHAPTER 1

The Jailer Jailed:
1605 and Beyond

Walter Witherley suffered terribly, drinking his own urine by the time his ordeal ended. So he must have heard the news that his own jailer had been imprisoned with the pleasure that comes from seeing one's tormenter paid in kind.

Sometime in 1604, the Council in the Marches of Wales had ordered its jailkeeper, Francis Hunnyngs, to confine Witherley "in little ease" for his disobedience to their commands. Witherley had repeatedly shown his legal ingenuity in the long property battle he had fought before the council. Now in prison, Witherley made his boldest move yet: he asked the justices of King's Bench to send for him by a writ of habeas corpus so that they might investigate the reason for his detention. King's Bench sent the writ, then nothing happened. So the court sent a second writ to the jailer, along with an attachment for contempt against him for his failure to answer the first one. Silence still. More orders followed, each containing nastier threats than the last should Hunnyngs continue his refusal to return the writ, and Witherley's body with it.

By February 1605, Witherley had been released and was in London, where, on his oath, new attachments issued against the jailer.[1] Hunnyngs was brought to London and examined by King's Bench attorneys. The justices concluded that the jailer's disobedience of their writs amounted to a contempt of their court. Afraid of what might happen next, Hunnyngs wrote to the Earl of Salisbury, the king's secretary and, as head of the king's Privy Council, the most powerful man under the throne. The jailer pleaded for support "in defense of the royal prerogative": a shrewd move.[2] Hunnyngs must have reasoned that the king's leading advisers would want to defend his actions, taken as they were on command of the Welsh Council, which was an offshoot of the king's own Privy Council. Edward, the Baron Zouche and, as Lord President of the Council in the Marches, Hunnyngs's ultimate superior, also sought support for the Welsh Council's claims for immunity from the writs and orders of King's Bench. Perhaps it was the self-pitying tone of Zouche's letters. Perhaps it was because powerful figures were aligned against Zouche: Attorney General Sir Edward Coke and Lord Chancellor Ellesmere, among others. No help came. The Privy Council—probably with the king's permission—left Zouche, Hunnyngs, and the Welsh Council to their fate at the hands of the justices of King's Bench.[3]

Attorney General Coke happened to be in Westminster Hall when the justices discussed how to handle the "great abuse" that Hunnyngs had shown to them and their writs.[4] Turning Hunnyngs's prerogative pleas against him, Coke asked if he might "plead a little for the prerogative of the king, the jurisdiction of this court, and the benefit of all the king's subjects." This made sense: the jurisdiction of King's Bench rested on the prerogative—powers unique to the king—as did the benefit of the king's subjects. Some lawyers, Coke explained, believed that King's Bench did not have power to send writs of habeas corpus for anyone imprisoned by the king's Privy Council or by any of the special courts that had grown from it, including the Welsh Council. This "is a great error," he said. After all, he argued, Magna Carta demanded that none be imprisoned unless "by the law of the land." Only by inspecting imprisonment orders using habeas corpus could King's Bench ensure this was so.

But there was a more potent line running through Coke's argument, one concerned more with the court's power than with the prisoner's body.

All courts of justice within the dominions of the king are subordinate, this court alone excepted, in which the king is always by law intended to be present, and which is restrained to no place but extends to all his dominions. Thus this court will have the examination of all other courts of justice, and when the king gives authority by his commissions, or the law by act of parliament, to anyone to execute justice, still the examination of them will be by such authority that will remain in the absolute and supreme power of the king and in his bench, which is his proper seat of justice.

Chief Justice Sir John Popham could only agree: disobedience to their writs was indeed "a derogation of the royal prerogative of the king." Justice Yelverton elaborated: "[W]hen anyone is brought into this court with his cause [of imprisonment] by habeas corpus, this court must examine the cause and may remand, bail, or discharge him as his cause deserves, which is much for the liberty of the subject." Neither Popham nor Yelverton picked up on Coke's remark about Magna Carta, grand flourish though it was. Just what was the law of the land? Answering that would be work for another day. On this day, the prerogative—the king's concern for his subjects' liberty, as pronounced through his justices using habeas corpus—provided quite enough to do what needed doing. Witherley was free and his jailer had been jailed for contempt, with a £100 fine to drive the point home.[5]

We cannot tell Witherley's tale in the heroic verses traditionally used to recount imprisonment stories ended by writs of habeas corpus. Witherley had not confronted the king; rather, he took the king's name in his own cause. We never hear Witherley speak for his liberty. His was a silent role, played in the opening scenes that set in motion the main events: a struggle between two great courts and many great egos; a struggle in which both sides invoked the king's prerogative in hopes of prevailing. But if Witherley was no hero, Hunnyngs was simply pitiful. He had done his job, perhaps too well. He had obeyed his superiors, imprisoning one who had disobeyed their commands. Hunnyngs then became a prop, used by the justices of King's Bench to show their resentment and thereby to teach a lesson not to Hunnyngs, but to his superiors and to everyone else who heard his story.

The attorney general and justices had the best lines, humbling the Council in the Marches of Wales, condemning its "manifest contempt of the king, and his court, and his prerogative."[6] Using the prerogative, they made all other courts so many lesser jurisdictions, even those, like the Welsh Council, that derived their authority from the king's prerogative.[7] About Witherley and Hunnyngs, we know nothing more. About the justices of King's Bench, however, we have thousands of writs and much more that tell us everything: they had made themselves great.

Getting to 1605

In 1605, we discover, as Francis Hunnyngs did, the conceptual impetus behind habeas corpus. The king's prerogative would thrust habeas corpus outward in the centuries following in a vast jurisdictional and geographical reach. The writ's history, we find, was less a matter of the development at law of "liberty"—in the singular—as if the history of English law and the history of modern liberal ideas involved the same actors and ideas working in harness together. Instead, habeas corpus was fundamentally an instrument of judicial power derived from the king's prerogative, a power more concerned with the wrongs of jailers than with the rights of prisoners. Only fitfully would it become the means by which aspirations external to law, concerned with liberty claims, might be realized. To see how King's Bench made a sharp weapon with a long reach, let us begin where popular ideas locate the writ's origins to see if we can get from there to 1605.

A cardinal of the Roman Church—the sort of person English Protestant lawyers would revile four centuries later—took the lead in 1215. With him stood the cream of England's knighthood and nobility, along with London's merchant leaders. Across the field stood King John. He had demanded much in recent years: patience, treasure, blood. While spending all this with abandon, John did the one thing a medieval king must not do. He failed in battle, repeatedly. Loss of wealth and loss of face had brought England into civil war. The time had now come to negotiate an end to it. Long lists of grievances were debated; articles were drawn, discussed, and redrawn.[8]

Magna Carta did not grant liberty; it granted liberties, lots of them. The cardinal out front, Archbishop of Canterbury Stephen Langton, made sure that the first and best went to God. John thus opened his charter by explaining that he agreed to it "out of reverence for God and for . . . the exaltation of holy church." With the treaty's preamble done, the king proclaimed "that the English church shall be free, and shall have its rights undiminished and its liberties unimpaired." The church thus gratified, John continued: "We have also granted to all free men of our kingdom . . . all the liberties written below." Then followed the most varied list imaginable: terms honoring widows' interests, powers and protections for barons and merchants, restrictions on the capacity of Jews to collect debts from those same barons and merchants, and limits on fishing weirs. Among the biggest winners were the men from the king's greatest city: "London shall have all its ancient liberties."[9] Those who visited London but who did not live there knew well how urban liberties imposed mightily on anyone not lucky enough to have been born to them.[10] Many were the liberties made by the king's gift, even if the liberties of some constrained the liberties of others.

Tucked into the middle of Magna Carta was one of many clauses—number thirty-nine of sixty-three—whose language had been left vague. "No free man shall be arrested or imprisoned . . . except by the lawful judgment of his peers or by the law of the land."[11] There were no explanations: a very big problem. Nonetheless, the king and his foes, following Christ's example and medieval custom, exchanged the kiss of peace. Three months later, the deal was dead, the kiss hardly worth remembering. Soon John was dead, too.

Magna Carta failed as a peace treaty, but it survived in new packaging. Some clauses were removed and others combined so that the thirty-ninth chapter became the twenty-ninth, by which number its words would usually be known in centuries to come. In this form, the charter was reissued in 1225, confirming the gift of so many liberties made ten years earlier. Thus it took its place as what has been counted since as the first English statute.[12]

Magna Carta is as close to scripture as English law comes. Its meanings are every bit as elusive. Many liberties were given. But nowhere do the words "habeas corpus" appear. That did not stop law's high priesthood four centuries later from finding in the charter what they would proclaim were evanescent traces of the writ. Habeas corpus, argued Sir Edward Coke, John Selden, and their allies during the 1628 House of Commons debates on the "liberty of the subject," was the means implied in the charter by which English law could ensure that "the law of the land" was rightly used. By this brilliant sleight of hand, they fused Magna Carta and habeas corpus together for the purposes of political argument. For all the scholarship then and since that shows just how novel those claims were at the time, habeas corpus remains firmly, if incorrectly, joined to the charter in the popular imagination.[13] Like the ideas conveyed by scripture, belief, not empirical demonstration, continues to hold them together.

Despite the force of this belief, connecting the thirteenth century to the seventeenth along a single story line has always proved difficult. So much awkward silence separates them that some authors have thrown up their hands.[14] Others have filled the silence with inferred lineages sprinkled with words of praise, borrowing heavily from nineteenth-century historians like Henry Hallam, who in turn accepted Coke's claims of the late 1620s as gospel truth.[15] Those historians who do not rely on Magna Carta nonetheless sometimes resort to vague notions of "the unconscious forces of constitutional law."[16] Accounts of habeas corpus written in the nineteenth and twentieth centuries thus serve as durable examples of what Herbert Butterfield long ago called "whig" history. As Butterfield remarked, "the whig historian can draw lines through certain events . . . to modern liberty." In doing so, the historian "begins to forget that this line is merely a mental trick."[17] A linear approach to the writ's past that starts in 1215 fit nicely with a high Victorian impulse to write histories drawn in bold story lines with clear points of origin and arrival. But for all the power of such narratives, they do not amount to a history.[18]

Perhaps we might begin in the registers of writs rather than at Runnymede. Nothing in Magna Carta spoke to a specific process to prevent imprisonment contrary to "the law of the land." But many court instruments from the thirteenth century might seem to resemble ancestors of the later habeas corpus in its *ad subjiciendum* ("to undergo") form, which is the form that concerns us in this book. Medieval English courts used many different forms of words, some containing the phrase "habeas corpus," to bring people before them. Ad hoc letters of command to sheriffs or abbots ordered them to produce named persons at a particular place in order to prosecute or answer criminal accusations, to provide evidence, or to hear that evidence as jurors.[19] But none of these thirteenth- or fourteenth-century devices share enough characteristics that we may see them cohering around overlapping ideas and practices. Generally, these medieval writs did not display any impulse to make a vigorous review of the circumstances underlying an imprisonment order made by other magistrates. And this was the point of habeas corpus *ad subjiciendum:* it would be less concerned with moving bodies—many writs did that—than with inspecting the thinking and actions of those who confined bodies.

Other possible antecedents to the *ad subjiciendum* writ considered by historians were the writs *de homine repligiando, de odio et atia,* and mainprise. We can find these as early as the twelfth century, when they were used to check the poorly used discretion of sheriffs, the most powerful local officers of the day.[20] Some sheriffs extorted prisoners who desired bail. In other cases, whether an alleged wrongdoer might be bailed was simply unclear. *De odio*—used for checking malicious prosecutions by the private process of appeal for homicide—had generally fallen out of use by the end of the fourteenth century. Mainprise, a form of bail, was used little from the sixteenth. *De homine,* which released one on bail pending trial where bail had been wrongly refused, did not open the facts of detention to a searching enquiry.

None of these three writs could be considered means for scrutinizing the behavior of other jurisdictions in the intensive manner associated with the later writ of habeas corpus. To find antecedents, we need to be less concerned with the capture and release of bodies than with the location of ultimate supervisory authority among the kingdom's magisterial institutions. The location of that authority was just the thing that King's Bench explained so clearly to Francis Hunnyngs in 1605.

Consider other possible antecedents to this kind of judicial behavior. The medieval royal Council—precursor to the Privy Council and, like King's Bench, always attendant on the king—was as much a court as an advisory body. Little surprise then that the Council summoned prisoners from other jurisdictions by a form of habeas corpus.[21] The court of Chancery had a similar practice. By the writ of *corpus cum causa,* fifteenth-century chancellors called prisoners before them from other courts, especially urban ones. Closely related to the *cum causa* writ were two others. By certiorari, records of proceedings in other courts were called into Chancery; by subpoena, commands might be made for people to do as Chancery required. As we shall see in Chapter 2, the King's Bench writ of habeas corpus *ad subjiciendum* would fuse these elements: the calling of a body and an account of its detention from another court, along with the kind of "do so, or else" clause that Francis Hunnyngs had disobeyed, much to his dismay.[22]

By the early fifteenth century, Chancery *cum causas* were sometimes returned into King's Bench as well as into Chancery.[23] In the latter part of that century, we can observe a number of practices by which the justices of King's Bench, perhaps in imitation of Chancery, used writs with the expressions "habeas corpus" and *"ad subjiciendum"* to call prisoners, most often accused felons, into their court, usually as a prelude either to sending them to trial, bailing them pending trial, or discharging them altogether when the accusations seemed unfounded.[24] Perhaps following conciliar or Chancery practice, King's Bench sent writs outside England, too, showing that it possessed the authority to enact justice for the king's subjects without regard to territorial bounds. Thus King's Bench sent for prisoners by habeas corpus to Berwick, Bordeaux, and Calais: all places outside the king's realm and where other aspects of English law did not pertain.[25] From the beginning, habeas corpus was thus used to manage the relationship among otherwise legally distinct dominions held by a single king. We can also find the writ used for a few people arrested by the king's Council, a church court, or some other special jurisdiction, but such cases remained so rare in the mid- to late-fifteenth century that they form no pattern, no trajectory. Even in the first half of the sixteenth century, little evidence survives in the writ files to suggest the existence of a great power, lodged in one court, enabling it to inspect all other jurisdictions, thereby making it the final arbiter of what counted as the subject's liberties.

No single line runs through the Middle Ages to the writ that was newly invigorated in the decades around 1605. To understand the writ's past, we must drop our expectation that there is a long story to tell, one statute, writ, or judgment begetting another from 1215 forward. Rather, habeas corpus was made into a powerful writ by judges responding to the volatile mix of social, religious, and political controversy present in the decades just before and after 1605. So let us examine life in England in this period, then see where law and lawyers fit into that life.

England, circa 1605

With Elizabeth I's death in 1603, the last Tudor was gone. That a foreign king succeeded her without violence—Scotland's James VI now became England's James I—indicates the stability of England's monarchical state. Such stability was remarkable given the forces arrayed against it, many of which arose from the dramatic population growth of the previous two or three generations. The 1590s had been one of the worst decades for poverty in English history. Illegitimate births were at an all-time high. Successive harvest failures set many people on the road, looking for work and sustenance. And most roads led to London. Long the realm's greatest city, London's growth during these years was astonishing, especially given the numbers of people pulled in only to be killed off: urban mortality rates, especially for rural immigrants, were stunning.[26]

In London and beyond, the aftershocks of religious controversies since the 1530s continued to shake individuals and institutions. Queen Elizabeth would later be famous for her "settlement" of the Church. But the 1559 Act of Uniformity and the Thirty-nine Articles of 1563 generated nonconformity in the process of defining uniformity. There was a single form of worship: a Book of Common Prayer for a land with an ostensibly common law. And there was a theology that charted what some hoped might be a middle way between Roman Catholicism and those zealous Protestants who thought the English Church in need of further reform.[27] English religion had a center. Whether it would hold remained to be seen.

To keep these and other centrifugal forces from blowing society apart, English parliaments passed a steady stream of new statutes. And per capita litigation rates rose like never before during the last decades of Elizabeth's reign.[28] Four courts, all located in Westminster Hall, occupied the center of English law. Common law courts such as Queen's Bench and Common Pleas were busy, though few could help noticing that the increasing business in Queen's Bench far outpaced that of Common Pleas. Queen's Bench actually did two kinds of work on its two "sides," handling civil complaints on its Plea Side and criminal and regulatory disputes on its Crown Side. The courts of Chancery and of the Exchequer likewise had split personalities, operating by common law on one side of each, and on the other side in each, by equity.

Hundreds of local and church courts dotted England and Wales. Many rural and urban courts followed rules known only to them: local custom sometimes had little contact with that law which was common. The church courts covered matters ranging from contests over wills to contests over marriage. They policed clerical behavior and sexual behavior—sometimes the same problem—and punished defamatory words and other misdeeds that broke the charity among neighbors that Christians were supposed to maintain.[29] They followed the civil law, which in turn looked to Roman canon law principles. The Court of Admiralty, which dealt with international commercial disputes, also followed civil law.[30] The queen's Privy Council, in addition to its advisory and administrative roles, served as a court when it heard complaints brought before it by petition. And the courts of Star Chamber and Requests—conciliar courts that had been spun off from the Privy Council and that grew rapidly in importance during the sixteenth century—were popular owing to their speed, their equitable approach to problem-solving, and the hope that only they could give to poorer litigants.[31]

Informing the vibrant, troubled society of turn-of-the-century England was a polyglot law.[32] The question Queen's Bench hoped to answer by new uses for habeas corpus in the last decades of Elizabeth's life was whether one court could monitor all that was said in so many ways by so many different magistrates. Perhaps. But there would always be one court higher than Queen's Bench: the Queen-in-Parliament.

Henry VIII famously said it to one of his Parliaments, but every early modern monarch must have felt it:

> [W]e at no time stand so highly in our estate royal as in the time of Parliament, wherein we as head and you as members are conjoined and knit together into one body politic.[33]

A few points leap out from Henry's remarks. First, a Parliament was "an event and not an institution."[34] In the seventeenth century, Parliament became less of an event—a gathering to do the king's business—and more of an institution, especially after 1640, and more so after 1689. As this transformation occurred, Parliament's impact on habeas corpus would grow. Second, Parliament knit together head and members, king and people. Henry's language underscored hierarchy, but also mutual dependence. A Parliament was the kingdom writ small.

In the House of Lords, Parliament produced judgments acting retrospectively on deeds already done by some person or persons, just as King's Bench or an assize court might do. Parliament also produced prospective judgments: legislation that anticipated rather than reacted to problems. In these two capacities, King-in-Parliament stood as the highest court in the land. As such, it was the only court that could review judgments of King's Bench. And by making statutes, Parliament was the only court that could shape the operations of King's Bench, even in the use of its most important writ. Crown and Parliament, king and legislature, judges and legislators: thinking in modern binaries like these is a habit to avoid if we want to understand the world that made habeas corpus and set it to work. All these things constituted one another, merged as they were in King-in-Parliament. Parliament would shape the possibilities and limits of habeas corpus across the centuries, and ultimately, around the globe.

The late Elizabethan statute book testifies to a powerful hope that the assignment of new powers to magistrates, special commissioners, and other courts by statute might soften the blows of social dislocation and religious controversy. Granting new powers and redefining old ones through legislation might even diminish the need for litigation in the courts, or at least, help it move more expeditiously. In the decades around 1605, laws already on the books controlling Catholic priests, people who would not swear allegiance to the queen, and those who interrupted sermons were supplemented by sterner statutes. Poverty and vagrancy became objects of parliamentary attention. Given a mobile population, we can little wonder that one of the first items added to the Jacobean statute book appointed new powers to deal with plague.[35] All these statutes, and many more, gave someone a power to jail someone else, though the language used to describe that power was not always as precise as might be desired.[36]

Not all statutes were well penned, but there were plenty of books to explain them to the people who had to apply them. These years marked the first great age of legal publishing. Particularly popular were treatises written for justices of the peace, those workhorses of the law scattered across the counties of England and Wales and among the nearly two hundred incorporated towns. JPs, as they were known, did everything: determining whether to hold accused criminals for trial; taking bonds to keep the peace from minor troublemakers; and implementing laws that regulated everything from ale-making to witchcraft. In their quarter sessions, a county's JPs sat together in judgment on cases of statutory and other misdemeanors.[37] JPs accepted appointment by the king's commission precisely because it was the king who appointed them. This was less a recognition of political status than of social standing: being named in the king's commission was a sign of one's eminence, an honor compensating the otherwise unpaid work one performed. And it could be demanding, sometimes confusing work, especially since many JPs had little if any legal training. At their sides, most kept a copy of one or both of the most well-thumbed law books of the seventeenth century: recently published justicing manuals by William Lambarde or Michael Dalton.[38]

Everywhere we look in the years around 1605, we find potential crises met by innovation: social problems on a startling scale; religious disputes generating political fears; more litigation and statute-making than ever before; and all this legal work performed by old courts or officers exercising new powers.[39] Little wonder that in the decades at the end of one dynasty and the start of another we should see a pressing need for one authority to police relations among the many jurisdictions that addressed these problems.

Habeas Corpus, circa 1605: Three Lawyers, Three Judges

Sir John Popham sat as chief justice of King's Bench in 1603, when Scotland's James VI became England's James I. Appearing often before Popham to represent the king were the attorney general, Sir Edward Coke, and the solicitor general, Sir Thomas Fleming. Fleming would succeed Popham in King's Bench when he died in 1607. Coke, in his turn, would succeed Fleming in 1613, only to leave the bench under a political cloud in late 1616. Coke is by far the best known of these three today. But his two predecessors in King's Bench did more to transform habeas corpus from an instrument for moving around bodies as part of routine court business into an instrument for controlling other jurisdictions. They did this by capturing the king's prerogative for their own, then defending this capture with procedural innovations.

To see the difference three lawyers made, consider two prominent commonalities in their pre-judicial careers: all served as recorders of major English towns; and all served as attorney general, solicitor general, or both before rising to the bench.[40] By examining these commonalities, we can observe how all varieties of law—criminal and civil, common law and equity, secular and church law—intersected in their work. We can also watch the interaction of law with politics and policy, and thus appreciate how the overlap of jurisdictions in England's pluralist legal culture provides the key to understanding the operation of habeas corpus.

A recorder was the chief legal officer of an incorporated town. Such corporations managed virtually every aspect of urban life. By the charters that created corporations, urban fairs and markets were given their own courts. Most incorporated towns also had their own JPs, appointed in their charters and independent of those in the county around them. All corporations held property, some of it by common law norms, but much of it according to the equitable assumptions used to manage charitable trusts.

Three features about lawyering on behalf of borough corporations stand out as training for future justices. First, an urban corporation represented in microcosm the variety of jurisdictional features found in the national legal landscape. Towns had courts that addressed criminal wrongs and civil complaints; their operating norms came from common law and equity alike, usually with a heavy overlay of local custom; and their charters empowered them to make ordinances regulating urban ills ranging from the swill that butchers left in markets to endemic poverty. Second, if there was one thing town leaders and their recorders understood, it was that their legal liberties—in the form of various kinds of jurisdiction—were franchises: gifts of the crown, granted by royal charters, and thus dependent on the good graces of the monarch.[41] Finally, no town's laws lived in a vacuum. The key to the successful operation of law within the town was managing the overlap of jurisdictions in town and outside it. Most towns encountered an occasional run-in with the legal officers of the counties in which they were situated. Cathedral cities—like Winchester, where Fleming served as recorder—faced the added problem of the relationship between secular and sacred authorities.[42] As a major port, Bristol, where Popham had been the recorder, would have had citizens involved as often in admiralty courts as in others. All these circumstances created possibilities for jurisdictional contests. A recorder needed to be a legal diplomat, able to maintain good relations among many jurisdictions whether within the town or far beyond.

Experience as a recorder was useful to an attorney or solicitor general. Both officers were in charge of negotiating, drafting, and redrafting the terms put in urban charters before they passed the great seal, the symbol of the queen's authority. By such letters patent, as charters were also known, the queen distributed franchisal authority to corporations or to special commissioners. Service as one of the queen's law officers thus meant applying in a higher realm the same insights and skills one needed in order to manage the jurisdictional relationships overseen by recorders.

But the queen's law officers did much more. As attorney or solicitor to the queen, Popham, Fleming, and Coke advised the Privy Council on every conceivable legal problem, from minor trespasses to high treason: experiences that prepared them well for their role as members of the Privy Council when they became judges. Scanning the business coming across the Council's table and then delegated to the monarch's law officers, we can appreciate the variety of problems they were asked to solve: litigation at common law and equity; legal management of the queen's role as supreme governor of the Church of England, from settling disputes over church property to the control of clerical opinions and practices; and representation of the queen in private suits. All three men prosecuted criminal wrongs, both at common law, where the penalty could involve death, and in the Court of Star Chamber, where it could not.[43] All three had roles to play in the great state trials of the age, most notably in 1601 against the Earl of Essex, the aging queen's erstwhile favorite turned absurdist traitor.[44] All participated vigorously in the legal attack on Catholics made possible by statutes passed in Elizabeth's reign. All were complicit—at least—in the use of torture as they performed this role. This would not be the only time when Coke's later and better known comments about law's nature would differ from the understanding he showed while the queen, and then the king, were his principal clients.[45]

By examining a single writ of habeas corpus, we can observe the intersection of these careers and the personal and operational connections between the queen's Council and Queen's Bench. Thomas Manock was a Catholic gentleman in Essex. In June 1597, local officials picked up Manock and other suspected Catholics who had gathered ominously on horseback in a field near Colchester. Manock was found to have dozens of bows and sheaves of arrows at home. Though they did not indict him, Essex JPs sent Manock to London, along with a number of depositions, for examination by the Privy Council. On that Council sat the chief justice of Queen's Bench: Popham. The attorney and solicitor general—Coke and Fleming—provided legal advice. The Council referred Manock to these two law officers for further questioning. On the first of July, after Manock had already spent weeks in custody, Attorney General Coke finally signed a warrant for Manock's confinement in Westminster's Gatehouse. By law, that warrant should have been made at the time of his arrest. The warrant simply stated that he was to be held by the command of the Privy Council, without specifying any cause. Coke and Fleming continued to question Manock, who remained in prison long after these examinations apparently ended. Only in November of the following year did Chief Justice Popham's court issue a writ of habeas corpus to bring Manock before them. Having waited so long for the writ to issue, and given that the chief justice and the attorney and solicitor had all been involved in the process up to this point, we might guess—surviving Privy Council registers are silent on Manock's case—that the order to bail him at last had come only after discussion of the matter in the Council.[46] We can only note here that Sir Edward Coke signed a warrant without expressing any cause of detention, an irony that will become more apparent in later chapters.

Serving as attorney or solicitor general acquainted one with the full range of England's jurisdictional life and with the many ways that law could be activated to confront society's problems. It is hard to imagine better job experience for those who would develop and use habeas corpus to manage relationships among England's many jurisdictions. By understanding their service to the crown, and by seeing how it reveals the overlap in the work of the queen's Council and Queen's Bench, we can imagine how action on the problems raised by the management of jurisdictional relationships migrated between these two institutions as these lawyers did. This migration was not coherent, intended, or unidirectional. Nor did it usually produce confrontation, even though an assumption of conflict between Privy Council and court—between "executive" and "judiciary"—so often underpins histories of habeas corpus.[47]

While Popham, Fleming, and Coke served as the queen's leading law officers, the Privy Council remained the final clearing house for delicate matters in the relationship among jurisdictions. The Council could serve this role so effectively in a case like Manock's because the important legal officers and judicial figures were all there. But as we saw in the case of Walter Witherley, the location of that ultimate authority would begin to move in the seventeenth century. Change in the varieties of habeas corpus usage during this period points to the same conclusion: on this writ, the court of King's Bench was beginning to assume the role of final arbiter by taking part of this function from the Council. Cases like Witherley's suggest that this happened because the alignment of forces within the Privy Council allowed, perhaps even encouraged, the supremacy of King's Bench over other tribunals.

As more writs of habeas corpus were sent from King's Bench to ever more jurisdictions, the Privy Council did nothing to stop the court. Why should it? The authority of court and Council flowed from the same fount: the prerogative. As successive chief justices, Popham, Fleming, and then Coke were members of the Council. This helps explain why there was only one institution in the early seventeenth century that could return habeas corpus without showing a cause for imprisonment: the Privy Council. Privy Council and King's Bench shared the function of supervising England's many jurisdictions, even as the Council appears to have allowed King's Bench to take up such work. This symbiosis would only end in the transformed political circumstances of Charles I's reign, after 1625, and especially after the dramatic Five Knights' case of 1627. In the generation after that, Privy Council imprisonment orders—like those of other jurisdictions—would come largely, then entirely, under the scrutiny of King's Bench. But from the late 1620s to the 1660s, as King's Bench vied off and on with the Council, another jurisdiction would do much more to undermine the court's ability to inspect imprisonment orders to protect the liberty of the subject: Parliament.

Between 1604 and 1607, Popham's last years, there were many signs of innovation in the processes used to impose the will of King's Bench on other magistrates. A handful of innovations stand out as having been used for the first time or with greater vigor in these and surrounding years: process by attachment for contempt and the insertion of subpoena clauses in writs to impose obedience; issuance of writs requiring immediate return, sometimes to individual justices in chambers; and the issuance and return of writs during vacations. Novel procedures like these—explored in Chapter 2—made using habeas corpus easier, faster, and more effective for King's Bench and its clientele: other courts' prisoners. In a similar vein, writs of restitution—prototypes of the prerogative writ of mandamus—issued for the first time in 1605–1606. This development, which arose simultaneously with these other practices, was no coincidence.

By developing new practices, Popham's court showed less interest in putting down other jurisdictions than in watching them work. The goal was to ensure both that they followed their own rules and that local customs regarding imprisonment were not repugnant to common law and common weal. Habeas ensured that the king's subjects were imprisoned only in accordance with "the law of the land." As Popham remarked of the sometimes controversial High Commission in 1607, King's Bench would "not oppose any court of the king in their ordinary course, because the forms of courts differ, and where it will seem to us to be irregular, still, where that appears to be the course of that court, it will not be opposed."[48]

Popham's words, like Witherley's case, undermine traditional narratives of habeas history that emphasize conflict between King's Bench and other tribunals. Jurisdictional motion circa 1605 did not result from a contest between "executive" and judicial bodies, a contest in which one court was consistently "versus" others.[49] As we watch the relationship among King's Bench, the Privy Council, and Parliament move from the sixteenth century to the nineteenth, we must not see these as coordinate—much less checking and balancing—institutions. Indeed many of the king's servants would serve in all three simultaneously: witness Popham, Fleming, and Coke. Sir John Popham at the opening of the seventeenth century, or Sir John Holt at the opening of the next century: each of these chief justices sat in Parliament and on the Privy Council at the same time that he sat on the bench. Each served the monarch, wherever he happened to sit.

Examining this three-way relationship will show that the Council, especially after 1660, played a much smaller part in the story of habeas corpus than we often imagine. And because our own democratic assumptions have encouraged us to imagine Parliament as the court's partner in the development of habeas corpus, the fact that the court's work was more seriously restricted by Parliament than by any other institution is often overlooked. The symbiosis achieved among court, Council, and Parliament in the decades around 1605 would falter—especially during the late 1620s, the 1640s, the 1650s, and the end of the

1680s—as authority shifted among them. But the balance was never entirely lost as each tinkered with the possibilities of the others. By appreciating this interplay, we can make sense of some surprising developments in the centuries after 1605: the power of Parliament to imprison without showing cause; the power of Parliament to suspend the use of habeas corpus; the capacity of King's Bench to continue innovating on a common law writ if not a statutory one; and the movement outward of all these impulses as an empire expanded. To see this, let us put the years around 1605—when judges made the writ—into a longer view in order to see what the writ meant for prisoners as they used it.

A Narrative of Habeas Usage

The period ten or twenty years to each side of Walter Witherley's day in court was pivotal for the development of habeas corpus. Social dislocations, religious controversies, and political novelties brought to Westminster by the needs of creative litigant-prisoners gave the justices of Queen's Bench the opportunity to transform the writ in dramatic ways. In the centuries following, habeas business would wash across England in waves, each flowing over a different part of society and over the different legal problems found there. The writ's use left evidence of the new anxieties confronted from one generation to the next: crime in one era; control of personal behavior, sexual or spiritual, in another; regulation of family life; and the maintenance of imperial stability.

Between 1500 and 1800, more than 11,000 people used habeas corpus. We know this because the court's records survive: the writs themselves, returns to those writs, enrolled copies, rulebook entries of court orders, and affidavits sworn to gain the writ's issuance. These records, especially the bundled writs and returns, have lain largely untouched since they were made. We have repeatedly written the same history of habeas corpus from the same limited, and accidental, canon of printed sources.[50] The writs and returns, often filthy and rumpled, contain stories of painful detentions we can find nowhere else. These stories recount legal usages and ideas we have not been able to see before. Without reading them, we would not know about the fate of prisoners like Francis LaPierre and Daniel DuCastre. And we certainly would not be able to consider how these "alien enemies and spies" not only used the writ in 1697, but also were released from custody.[51] Without these records, and without manuscript case reports—which survive in greater quantity and quality than printed ones—we could not have read the story of the jailer jailed. Only by opening the archive can we write a full history of the common law's most important judicial instrument.

For now, rather than read stories, let us aggregate them by exploring a survey of King's Bench Crown Side records.[52] Evidence from the survey years—every fourth year from 1502 to 1798, inclusive—yields information on the detention of 2,757 people. A projected total of 11,028 users is certainly an undercount, given variations in record quality across the centuries. Significantly, the average rate of dismissal for all prisoners who used habeas corpus across three centuries was 53 percent. Deviations from this norm, and others like it, may suggest changing purposes for, and conceptions of, habeas corpus.

Until roughly 1500, habeas corpus had been used as an instrument for bringing the prisoners of prominent abbeys to King's Bench for bail or trial.[53] At least until the death of Queen Mary, in 1558, 90 percent of prisoners using habeas corpus had been charged with felony or treason. The writ operated like other instruments of felony process: moving prisoners forward in the proceedings rather than looking backward to review earlier magisterial decisions. Consider one spectacular example: in 1554, Queen's Bench used two writs to bring ninety-seven of Thomas Wyatt's companions to trial for their rebellion at the outset of Mary's reign. In the margin of the enrolled copies of their writs we can still read the clerk's simple notes that they should hang, then endure all the other horrors performed on the bodies of traitors.[54] It is unlikely any of the prisoners thought of habeas corpus as a writ of liberty as they approached their executioners.

From about 1590 on, felony steadily declined as a proportion of habeas business as the writ addressed the growing number of nonfelony offenses created by legislation. These included acts defining religious uniformity or regulating firearms, bastard bearing, and alehouses.[55] Habeas corpus was bringing an ever more varied group of alleged wrongdoers into Queen's Bench so that the novel statutory norms by which they had been imprisoned might be reviewed. Statutory innovation inspired judicial innovation in reply.

As the kinds of wrongs subject to habeas corpus broadened, so too did the kinds of jurisdictions covered. But even as conciliar courts, church courts, and other non–common law tribunals came under increased scrutiny, they always generated a minority of the imprisonment orders inspected by habeas corpus. Though the writ's history has traditionally been written around a presumed contest between King's Bench and the king's Privy Council, a look at the jurisdictions covered by the majority of uses of habeas corpus suggests how we must rethink this emphasis. If the history of habeas corpus concerns law's capacity to prevent oppression, then the potential oppressor was not the king or his minions in far away Whitehall. Rather, the oppressor was probably a justice of the peace who lived nearby, a legal amateur empowered to imprison using summary conviction process every time Parliament passed a statute defining a new regulatory misdemeanor.[56]

As more cases on nonfelony imprisonment orders came into Queen's and King's Bench from the end of the sixteenth century, the number of prisoners released by habeas corpus increased. The widening range of wrongs covered signaled more aggressive supervision of imprisonment. Before the 1590s, rates of prisoner release on habeas corpus ran consistently below the three-century average of 53 percent. Then, for two decades after 1590—when Popham, and then Fleming, led the court—release rates increased dramatically.

By contrast, after 1613, when Sir Edward Coke took the reins in King's Bench, the tendency to release prisoners fell below average. Intriguingly, for all his fame for speaking out against arbitrary imprisonment during the late 1620s, Coke's years presiding in King's Bench (1613–1616) marked a significant retreat from the vigor of his two predecessors.[57] Who led the court mattered to how the court conceived and performed its work.

During the seventeenth and eighteenth centuries, supervising wrongs created by statutes formed most of the writ's business. In the 1640s, Parliament created novel authorities to wage war against the king. Special commissioners raised troops and money. Some parliamentary leaders took it upon themselves to reform the nation's conscience as they reformed its governance, imposing more restrictive ideas about legitimate Protestant belief. Whether raising money to pay troops or raising consciousness to promote national redemption, many used imprisonment orders to convince the unconvinced. King's

Bench met them head on: from the war's beginning in mid-1642, through its conclusion in 1646 and until the political crisis at the end of 1648, King's Bench released nearly three-quarters of prisoners brought before it.[58] In the case of Thomas Ridyard, London mayor Isaac Pennington ordered imprisonment without showing any cause at all: the same practice used by the Privy Council, of which Pennington and his compatriots had long been critical.[59] The court's independence—measured by rates of release on habeas corpus—declined with the purge of Parliament in late 1648, the trial and execution of the king early the next year, and the resulting transformation of King's Bench into the Upper Bench during the Interregnum of the 1650s.[60]

Especially after the Restoration of monarchy in 1660, nervous members of Parliament, operating on the assumption that political uniformity required spiritual uniformity, passed more statutes imposing penalties on those who did not attend their parish church or who met elsewhere for worship.[61] Those who violated the Five Mile Act, the Conventicle Acts, or the Test Acts—which attempted to control preaching, worship, and office holding by Protestant dissenters—often received a sympathetic hearing when habeas brought them into King's Bench.[62] Rising rates of dismissal for those brought in on religious wrongs suggest the justices' dislike of such imprisonment orders and the legislation on which they were based.[63] The justices could never declare such statutes void, but by construing their terms as narrowly as possible, they could effectively void them as they applied to particular prisoners.[64]

The most dramatic use of the writ to police imprisonment for alleged political wrongs came after the Revolution of 1688–1689. At the time, William and Mary's England battled on two fronts: against the erstwhile King James II, who led an effort from Ireland to recapture his throne; and against France's Louis XIV, an ally of James who had his own ambitions to humble the Dutch prince who had been declared England's king in early 1689. Throughout the 1690s and Queen Anne's reign (1702–1714), as war persisted with only minor interruption, hundreds were jailed on suspicions of treason, seditious libel, or the vague charge of "treasonable practices." Though appointed to the bench by William and Mary and serving on their Privy Council, Chief Justice Sir John Holt would show astonishing energy in his use of habeas corpus.

Under Holt, from 1689 to 1710, more than three-quarters of those using the writ were released. Moreover, Holt's court handled the most sensitive cases in a time of political anxiety: a period begun in late 1688 by an invasion, a palace coup, and a revolution, followed by two decades of foreign war, persistent invasion fears, and incipient rebellions at home. The year 1689 also marked the first time that the use of habeas corpus would be suspended by Parliament. But once that suspension lapsed at the start of Michaelmas term, in October of that year, Holt's court showed just how well it could distinguish real traitors from those conjured by fertile official imaginations. Well over half the habeas corpus cases in 1690—the year with the highest recorded writ use before 1800—concerned wrongs against the state: treason, seditious words, or treasonable practices. King's Bench released four out of five of these most frightening prisoners.[65] Holt's court made clear that habeas corpus could do the very thing that members of Parliament doubted it could do every time they suspended the writ's operation. The results of 1690 were not isolated. Writ usage remained vigorous during the war-torn decades that followed.[66] The use of habeas corpus for "prisoners of war" was hardly an oddity, nor was the release of some POWs surprising given the hundreds of other cases found in the court's files.[67]

By the middle of the eighteenth century, fewer prisoners jailed by justices of the peace were brought into King's Bench by habeas corpus.[68] By then, a crucial change had occurred: the writ was being used to inspect those forms of detention that involved no allegation of wrongdoing. Beginning in the 1670s, and increasingly across the next century, habeas was used to adjudicate family custody contests. As we shall see in Chapter 4, such cases were few but conceptually significant, because they widened the scope of work that habeas corpus could do.

Naval impressment cases, by contrast, were both numerically and conceptually significant. The Seven Years' War and the American Revolution, during which the use of habeas to question naval impressment skyrocketed, were nothing if not imperial wars, the challenges of which were met with parliamentary innovation. Statute multiplied the forms of status by which some might be impressed while others were not. Habeas corpus saved many from such servitude, especially foreigners. Alien status, far from barring habeas use, provided the chief grounds by which hapless Portuguese sailors picked up in Caribbean ports escaped such servitude.[69] In all, nearly a thousand unfortunate seamen probably used habeas corpus to challenge their impressments during the final four decades of the eighteenth century. Many more began habeas proceedings but were released without a struggle before the writ issued.[70]

Watching this profound shift in the forms of detention policed by habeas corpus, we might conclude that allegations of wrong had nearly disappeared from the writ's work, to be replaced by claims of right. But these rights claims were not premised on ideas about one's condition as a human according to the decrees of God or nature, nor as an Englishman according to English law. They were premised on ideas about status: of husband and wife, of parent and child, of "seaman" as defined by statute. The application of habeas corpus to detentions that contained no element of wrong in them indicates less a change in conceptions of rights than it indicates the impact of individual justices. That family custody questions were first raised by habeas corpus in the 1670s, when Sir Matthew Hale was in charge, was no accident. Similarly, the surge in impressment cases subject to habeas corpus after 1756 resulted from the work of another energetic justice with a grand conception of his role: Chief Justice Lord Mansfield.

From his earliest days in King's Bench, Mansfield tended to innovate. Appointed on November 8, 1756, Mansfield issued his first writ for a sailor five days later. This was during the early stage of a war fought on multiple oceans. The Royal Navy was scrambling to man the ships. Nonetheless, once Mansfield got John Backas and his captain into court, he discharged the sailor from serving aboard HMS *Princess Royal*.[71] Impressment cases provide some of our favorite stories of justice done, of habeas corpus freeing those who had done nothing wrong. But for all the sailors released from impressment, we must ask: why did some have to serve in the king's navy when others could show, in habeas corpus proceedings, that they were not similarly obliged? The answer is that statutes generated new status distinctions among the king's subjects.

Parliamentary interference with the writ's work—statutory forms of detention—came in many forms, reflecting a transposition of ultimate authority in the polity from Privy Council and King's Bench to Parliament over the course of the seventeenth and eighteenth centuries. One form this transposition took was the passage of legislation meant to aid the work of habeas corpus: for instance, the so-called Habeas Corpus Act of 1641, more properly known as the Star Chamber Act.

That act imperfectly assisted a judicial move toward ending the practice of Privy Council imprisonment orders that did not contain a legally identifiable cause for imprisonment. The better-known Habeas Corpus Act of 1679 had a more mixed effect.[72] Many of the practices it prescribed had long been used in King's Bench.

Other statutes tightened the bounds of habeas use. In particular, some suspended bail and mainprise—what we usually call the suspension of habeas corpus—in times of war or rebellion. From 1689 to 1747, Parliament used a consistent set of practices when suspending the writ: alleged traitors were taken from the supervision of King's Bench and given over to the Privy Council, the very body whose discretion Parliament had curtailed during the seventeenth century.

Suspension statutes broke the protective bonds of subjecthood that tied subjects to their monarch, whose laws were to ensure their liberty. Britons living in North America learned this lesson between 1777 and 1783, but many more would learn it in other places in the decades following.[73] Suspension was not the only statutory practice that excluded some from the benefits of subjecthood in the eighteenth and nineteenth centuries, nor did such statutes come only from Westminster. As the king's dominions proliferated around the globe, so too did lawmaking assemblies. Their enactments—for instance, colonial statutes that made slavery possible—curbed habeas corpus even as the writ set forth from England on its imperial wanderings.

No dominion of the king was exempt from habeas corpus, even those palatinates or other special places within the British Isles and far beyond them, where process from King's Bench normally did not go. Habeas corpus and the other prerogative writs—mandamus, certiorari, quo warranto—went everywhere not because they protected "rights," a modern conceit, but because they addressed the wrongs committed by those who acted according to the king's franchise: specific powers the king granted to others so long as they were not abused. By the prerogative writs, King's Bench made the instruments it needed to ensure proper behavior by all who acted in the king's name. Over time, new superior courts created in new dominions would take up this work, in explicit imitation of King's Bench. The imperial dimension—operating from Berwick-upon-Tweed to Bengal—reveals better than any other the peculiar geographical and conceptual reach of habeas corpus owing to this franchisal notion of its purpose.

As an instrument of jurisdictional management, habeas corpus covered a wider space and a wider range of people than we often appreciate, pulling many who were not the king's "natural" subjects into the benefits of subjecthood. "Alien" and "subject" is a modern binary, not an early modern one. A "subject" was not the early modern synonym of the modern word "citizen," as if the only difference in conception is to remove the king from the formulation and replace him with a president. Subjecthood was a condition one entered by coming into a particular kind of relationship with the king: his protection. By using the writ, the king, through his judges, ensured the liberty of the subject, a being of many kinds found in many places.

More than any other part of law, habeas corpus threatened to make one legal zone—the empire—out of what was otherwise a legally polyglot gaggle of dominions. But in the end, the experience of empire would fracture law even as it carried the writ outward. By the late 1770s and 1780s—as people learned in Barbados and Boston—statutes would multiply the variety of subjects, limiting the perquisites of subjecthood for some while widening them for others. A writ that went forth on the king's prerogative was broken into pieces by Parliament and by the decrees of colonial legislatures and governors. This is precisely what suspension had done in the generations after 1689. It is what was done by statutes that put some people on His Majesty's Ships while leaving others undisturbed at home. And as the eighteenth century turned into the nineteenth, the use of martial law or of special powers of detention from Ireland to Ontario and from Jamaica to New Zealand would make the writ all but irrelevant except in a persistent triumphal rhetoric that celebrated the writ as the palladium of English liberty. Such developments would converge in the late eighteenth century and beyond as statutes and the demands of empire broke apart the protections for subjects' liberties that judges like Popham and Fleming had made two centuries earlier. There was only so much that justices, who had made themselves mighty by taking up the king's prerogative, could do. Their day had passed.

The Chief Justice and the *Princess Royal*

If one hundred and fifty years had not separated them, Francis Hunnyngs would have had plenty to tell Captains Edward Barber and

John Falkingham, successive commanders of His Majesty's Ship the *Princess Royal*. It would have been good for them to hear the story of the jailer jailed, for Barber and Falkingham detained many more subjects than Hunnyngs ever did. Like other guard ships, the *Princess Royal* spent 1759 and 1760—the height of Britain's first great imperial war—as a clearinghouse, holding hundreds of impressed sailors until they were sent to the vessels on which they would serve at sea. The question a few of these sailors asked was whether their bodies were indeed Barber's and Falkingham's to detain on His Majesty's behalf.

Lord Mansfield issued writs for Booy Booysen and John Jurgenson Brandt, a pair of Danes aboard the *Princess Royal,* in April 1758. In sending the writs, Mansfield had apparently answered the petition of Frederick Franks, the owner or captain of the merchant vessel from which the hapless sailors had been taken. But it was Frederick's wife, Mary Franks, who tried to serve the writs on Captain Barber, only to fail when the guards around his cabin stopped her. Undaunted, she returned the next day, when she was introduced to Lieutenant Crisp instead. She handed him the writ and explained what it was. Crisp paused, then dropped it and walked off, perhaps to avoid any claim that he had received it. As if a filthy rag, various crew members picked it up, only to drop it again, until one of the seamen—apparently by an officer's command—kicked it overboard.[74]

Mansfield was certainly not the sort to accept such rudeness. He immediately issued an attachment against Barber for contempt. This got the attention of the Admiralty's solicitor, Samuel Seddon, if not of Barber himself. Seddon could hardly endorse Barber's behavior. He suggested that Barber would be "answerable for all the consequences." On Seddon's advice, the two Danes were dismissed from the king's service. Barber was told to yield, which he quickly did. By offering to pay all court costs, Seddon hoped the Admiralty might smooth things over with the chief justice.[75] Barber thus avoided the ultimate consequences of attachment for contempt.

Perhaps Barber told Captain Falkingham nothing about this episode when he handed over command of the *Princess Royal.* Little more than a year later, the ship's new commander found himself in the same trouble, perhaps worse, for he feared imminent imprisonment of just the kind Hunnyngs had endured. What happened when Mansfield's tipstaff came out to the *Princess Royal* was a matter of dispute. But the tipstaff was certainly not treated with the respect that a messenger of King's Bench should expect when boarding one of the king's ships. Falkingham denied that he asked any of his crew to impress those who rowed the tipstaff's skiff to the ship's berth at the Nore.[76] Luckily for Falkingham, his evasions left enough doubt that he was not jailed.

A year later, in late 1760, Falkingham found himself again facing the prospect of imprisonment for neglecting to return habeas corpus. He begged the Lords of the Admiralty for help, asking that they order the discharge of those for whom the writs then in dispute had issued. Again, the Admiralty came to Falkingham's rescue, and ordered the sailors released.[77] The Admiralty board even agreed to pay the £160 costs of the dispute. But they balked when Falkingham asked that they pay the £10 fine imposed on him for not returning the writs in the first place. "As his behavior drew the censure of the court upon him, he cannot expect any more relief than what he has already had," the board responded.[78] The Admiralty had bowed to King's Bench; so too must the captain.

Like the Council in the Marches of Wales, the Admiralty folded, though not before one of its servants had done his utmost to uphold the navy's honor under considerable pressure applied by King's Bench. Once the lesson had sunk in, Falkingham behaved better, returning later writs without much ado.[79] And in the years following, Solicitor Seddon rarely suggested that the Admiralty dispute any of the hundreds of writs that issued for sailors in navy custody.[80] Nearly all would be released. Like Francis Hunnyngs and the lords of the Council of Wales, Captain Falkingham and the lords of the Admiralty had learned who was in charge: the lords justices of King's Bench.

In 1758, using habeas corpus for impressed sailors was relatively new. By this time, older uses of the writ had fallen into disuse. The writ's purposes had changed along with the society it served. That it could change resulted from the one aspect of the writ that had not changed: the judicial force that drove it outward to every jurisdiction and to every corner of the king's realm, his dominions, and beyond. This was a particularly powerful piece of parchment. Old too: its form, if not its uses, had not changed since 1628, even if its text was now written in English rather than Latin.[81] Whatever the language, that text still carried all the force of the king's prerogative. Captain Barber, or men in his command, had dropped habeas corpus on deck and even kicked it overboard. But habeas corpus always seemed to kick back, especially under the direction of chief justices like Mansfield. What made these bits of parchment so powerful? The words written on them.

CHAPTER 2

Writing Habeas Corpus

On October 11, 1605, an unknown clerk in the Crown Office of King's Bench dipped his quill into iron gall ink, then began to write on a parchment scrap barely one inch by ten. Working hastily, in a tight court hand, he wrote in the name of James, by the grace of God king of England, Scotland, France, and Ireland, before greeting the lord mayor, aldermen, and sheriffs of London. With the formalities common to all writs out of the way, the clerk wrote on:

> We command you that you have the body of Nicholas Lowe, who is detained in our prison under your custody, as it is said, together with the cause of his detention, by whatever name the aforesaid Nicholas is charged, before us at Westminster on Saturday next after eight days of Saint Michael, to undergo and receive whatever our court should then and there happen to order concerning him in this behalf, and this in no wise omit, upon the peril that may befall, and have there this writ. Witness, Sir John Popham, at Westminster, the eleventh day of October in the third year of our reign in England, France, and Ireland, and in Scotland, the thirty-ninth.

Here, at the end, appeared the *teste:* the witnessing of the writ in the name of the chief justice, signaling the authority on which it issued.[1]

The writ commanded London's leaders to bring Nicholas Lowe before the justices of King's Bench the following day, along with an explanation of why they had imprisoned him in Woodstreet Counter. Their answer: Lowe had violated their trading privileges. The justices quickly decided that this was insufficient reason to imprison some-one, and ordered Lowe bailed. A few months later, King's Bench discharged him altogether from his bail. We do not know whether Lowe continued to make guns and crossbows in his Holborne shop without being a City freeman.[2] We do know that he had used the writ of habeas corpus *ad subjiciendum* to great effect.

"We command you that you have the body": this was the least distinctive phrase in Lowe's writ. Sheriffs everywhere received many writs known by other names—attachment, *capias,* and others—that contained such words. After all, courts deal routinely in bodies. Bodies institute prosecutions and answer them; they testify to facts in those prosecutions; and as jurors, bodies declare the truth or not of such facts. All the courts of Westminster Hall, and courts across England, issued commands in the king's name for the appearance of certain bodies in certain places, for certain reasons.[3]

In addition to these writs containing this command but known by other names was a group of writs known then and since by the name "habeas corpus." These, too, took many forms. Habeas corpus *ad prosequendum* required a body already in prison on a criminal charge to be brought into court to pursue specified private pleadings.[4] The *ad testificandum* form of habeas corpus summoned witnesses from their jail cells to give evidence. Habeas corpus *ad deliberandum et recipiendum* was actually two writs: the first a message to one jailer to deliver a body in his custody to another jailer, who was instructed by the second writ to receive the prisoner.[5] Another writ known colloquially as "habeas corpus" was a day pass from London jails for those held for debt. Upon payment of 2s. 6d., a prisoner might use this "day writ," which "giveth liberty to the prisoner" to attend to business.[6] The most common writs of habeas corpus supported civil proceedings: habeas corpus *ad respondendum* and habeas corpus *ad faciendum et recipiendum* both moved a body from one court into another in a private cause.[7] Clerks' signatures at the bottom show that the *ad faciendum* writ issued almost uniformly from the Plea Side of King's Bench—the side concerned with private pleadings—though it was sometimes returned into the Crown Side, where the court addressed criminal wrongs.[8] By the middle of the seventeenth century, use of *ad faciendum* writs to bring criminal matters into King's Bench was criticized and the practice, already rare, ended.[9] Writs of habeas corpus of various kinds issued from local courts, too, especially to require the appearance of jurors.[10]

When we use the unmodified phrase "habeas corpus" today, we think of none of these writs. Instead, we refer to the writ of habeas corpus *ad subjiciendum et recipiendum:* to undergo and receive. But throughout the sixteenth and seventeenth centuries, when lawyers said "habeas corpus" without further description, they almost always referred to habeas *ad respondendum* or *ad faciendum,* which were used in civil process. Practice manuals of the period are full of information on how to use the forms of habeas corpus concerned with private pleadings, while virtually none addressed the *ad subjiciendum* writ.[11] This might seem surprising, given the later fame of this writ. But criminal and civil liberties law did not pay the bills; private litigation did.

It is tempting not to read a writ, and instead rush ahead to read the often marvelous stories told in the returns jailers made to them. We might glance at the writ's language, call it "formulaic," then move on. But the power of the writ as the king's command, and the significance of small variations in formula, suggest that we must start where all habeas proceedings began: with the words written by court clerks each time they made out a writ of habeas corpus. We must explore the writ's text as we would a rich passage from a novel or poem. By holding one writ next to others, we can think not only about authorial intent, but also about sources of authorial influence. For this writ was made by judges and their clerks. It was they who wrote the text, and they who used and interpreted it. To understand how Nicholas Lowe got out of jail, we must attend closely to the words written by a King's Bench clerk four centuries ago.

The Custodian's Franchise

The pronouns matter. Nicholas Lowe was "in *our* prison under *your* custody." This construction recognized that anyone who held the bodies of the king's subjects was empowered by the king to act in his name. It was in the king's prison, but in someone else's care, that the king's subject Nicholas Lowe languished.

A prison or jail was a franchise. James Morice, in his 1578 reading on the prerogative, called a franchise, including the franchise to keep a jail, "a flower of [the king's] crown."[12] Sir Francis North, attorney general and then lord keeper a century later, elaborated:

> Franchise is a general denomination for all privileges, exemptions, capacities, and interests, which are claimed either by grant from the king . . . and are distinct from all specific estate or title in lands, tenements, or chattels . . . [P]ublic franchises are all but parts of the king's ordinary government, detached and entrusted to particular persons, for his ease and the people's convenience.[13]

Inherent in all franchises was the need to supervise their use for the common weal. Legal investigation of alleged abuses of franchises was made using the information in the nature of quo warranto. As North put it, liberties or franchises "are forfeitable either by nonuser or by abuser, they having a condition in law annexed to them, that if they are used so as to turn to the public prejudice . . . they are forfeit."[14] It was no accident that in the very period when habeas corpus came to be most closely attached to the king's prerogative, use of quo warranto skyrocketed.[15] Nothing showed better the impermanence of the possession of franchises—given and taken by grace—than the repeated entries in Crown Side rulebooks that liberties from the crown should be seized "into the hands of the king" after they had been found to be misused.[16] But quo warranto was a blunt instrument whose work concluded with recognition or seizure of franchises. Habeas corpus was more subtle, though it operated on much the same principle: that by the prerogative, King's Bench might inspect the use of the specific franchise to imprison. If the franchise was misused, a prisoner would be released rather than the franchise destroyed. This helps us see the significance of the writ's mode of address: to jailers, as the king's franchisees.

As the justices explained, habeas corpus "shall always be directed to him who hath the custody of the body."[17] That "him" was often identified by location: for instance, the custodian of Colchester Castle. But it was to the custodian, not the castle, that the writ issued. The rationale behind one's use of habeas arose from his personal relationship to the king, his status as the king's subject. The rationale behind the direction of the writ likewise lay in a personal relationship: that between the king and his franchisee, to whom the king had delegated authority to hold people in his name so long as he did so according to the king's laws. People, not places, were the objects of the writ's supervision, a point we shall revisit when we consider the writ's imperial reach.

Given this emphasis on individual responsibility, addressing the writ incorrectly might render it ineffective. But determining the proper recipient could be difficult, especially when a single prison held people committed by different magistrates or tribunals. At the Bocardo in Oxford, for example, prisoners might be in the custody of either the university's vice chancellor or the mayor and sheriff of the city. Directing the writ to the vice chancellor for one in the sheriff's custody would fail for misdirection.[18] Likewise, care had to be taken in deciding whether to direct a writ to a jailer—who generally served under the sheriff of his county or town—or to the sheriff himself. Commitments to jail came in different forms. Prisoners committed by court process were legally in the sheriff's custody. Those committed by one or two JPs pending trial for felony or on summary conviction for misdemeanor were held by the jailer. In 1700, Chief Justice Holt explained that the writ should not be addressed simultaneously to both or either: "habeas corpus, being directed in the disjunctive to the sheriff or gaoler, was wrong." In the case then in question, commitment on a writ of *excommunicato capiendo* meant that the prisoner was in custody of the sheriff alone, and not in the custody of "the gaolorress of Worcester, Eleanor Hemmings." The writ directed to either was quashed.[19] Sending the writ properly depended on knowing just who was responsible, in the king's name, for keeping the subject's body.

In 1671, the court began to move beyond the franchise view of habeas corpus as it issued the first writ for a wife confined by her husband. The justices sent the writ for Lady Howard on the last day of term, making it returnable immediately: a sign of its concern about her husband's violence. The writ brought her into court so that she could swear articles against him, by which the judges then required that he give a bond to keep the peace toward her. How did they justify this novelty?

Part of the answer has to do with the particular justices on the bench. Sir Matthew Hale, who consistently pushed the writ's possibilities, had become chief justice three weeks earlier. Justice Sir Thomas Twisden likewise showed in his discussions of another prerogative writ—mandamus—a tendency to look past inchoate public/private distinctions that might otherwise have made the court balk at Lady Howard's request.[20]

Perhaps ideas about the king as *parens patriae* explain why the court soon broadened this usage for spouses to consider child custody.[21] Or maybe patriarchal ideas so common in seventeenth-century political thought were influential: that husbands and fathers, like kings, were masters of their households, yet accountable to the king for the exercise of that authority.[22] Little patriarchal language survives in reports of the Howard case or other family disputes investigated using habeas corpus. Nonetheless the justices did show their concern about husbands' or fathers' abuse of their authority under the law, just as they did about the abuses of jailers as the king's franchise holders.

These cases also show a further element: a concern for wrongs done to wives and children and for ensuring the availability of the king's protection to all his subjects. As we shall see in Chapter 3, ideas about the king's protection enacted by his justices were just as fully grounded on the prerogative as were ideas about the franchisal responsibilities of jailers.

Going into the middle of a family clearly made the justices nervous: using habeas seemed "a strong process to disturb a man in the lawful government of his wife." But the lawfulness of the husband's governance was precisely the issue. By using habeas corpus and bonds to keep the peace, the court extended the protection of the king's laws and made effective his prerogative interest in his subjects' liberties, including their freedom from violence and fear.[23] The most famous case of this concerned Mary Countess Ferrers, in 1757. The affidavits made by her siblings detailed the Earl Ferrers's violence against her. When the earl heard that his wife's brother intended to help her use habeas corpus, the earl declared that he would kill her rather than allow her to be "put under the protection of a court of judicature."[24] Nonetheless, King's Bench sent the writ. Once in court, Lady Ferrers was able to swear the peace against her husband, a form of protection she sought again the following year, "through fear of death." In 1760, Ferrers would earn further infamy when he murdered his steward, for which he was hanged and then—as statute required—dissected at Surgeon's Hall. His wife looked on as the cart carried him to the gallows at Tyburn, dressed in his wedding clothes, his waistcoat embroidered with silver.[25]

Nicholas Lowe's writ pronounced the king's concern to ensure the proper behavior of every jailer whenever he detained one of his subjects "in our prison under your custody." Writs in family cases contained distinctive language: the 1751 writ to John Hinson, for example, asked that he bring "the body of Mary Hinson, your wife, detained in your custody."[26] In cases like Hinson's, we can see how habeas use from the 1670s forward showed how deeply intertwined were notions of public and private. The writ issued in any case, because anyone detained by someone else might resort to the court for the king's protection at the judges' hands.

Getting the Writ

Why had Lowe's writ been sent? Because someone—perhaps Lowe himself—told a story suggesting that his body was detained contrary to law. Again, the precise wording matters. "As he says" *(ut dicit)* appears in many types of writ, pointing to a story told by a known person who desired a writ's issuance. But in habeas corpus, the language is vague, even passive: "as it is said" *(ut dicitur).*[27] Someone, somehow, had made a claim both that Nicholas Lowe was being detained and that he should be brought before the court with an explanation of his imprisonment because his detention rested on soft legal ground.

Anyone could tell a story about someone else to touch off the writ's issuance. Typically a barrister would do so. This was probably how Lowe gained his writ when it was "prayed" on his behalf.[28] Or someone else altogether might tell the story to have another person's body brought before the court. The motion for the writ might be made at the request, or for the benefit, of the person to be produced in court. But habeas corpus could be used against the wishes of a body as well as for it. This was sometimes the case in family disputes: for instance, when a husband tried to use the writ to have a wife, who may have fled out of fear, returned to his custody. Such efforts always failed. It was also done when the attorney general used habeas corpus to bring a body into King's Bench for arraignment for major crimes. Thus habeas corpus brought Edward Coleman, former secretary to the Duke of York and a Catholic conspirator, to his arraignment, and thence to a traitor's doom, in 1678.[29] And though the writ would often be used in the eighteenth century by sailors to escape impressment, it might also be used by a master to retrieve an apprentice who had volunteered to serve aboard one of His Majesty's Ships to escape his master's custody.[30] "As it is said," rather than "as he said," is apt; any person, regardless of his or her social standing, could tell a story to justify the court's concern that it should learn more about a person's confinement by anyone, anywhere. Who told the story mattered little, if at all.

How was this story told? In most cases, especially before the seventeenth century, the court was moved to act by an oral motion in court, by which a barrister recounted details of a person's imprisonment.[31] Individual judges, too, might hear such stories and grant the writ, especially when the court was not in session. Tracing this usage is difficult since Crown Side rulebooks do not record activity between terms or in chambers. But evidence of vacation writs or others granted in term by individual justices appear everywhere from the fifteenth century to the eighteenth. In term, an oral order from the bench set the process moving. When working out of term or in chambers, the judge sent a written fiat to the court clerks to make out a writ according to his instructions. The fiat would also contain details about when and to whom the writ should be returned: often to the same justice in his chambers on an appointed day, and perhaps at an appointed hour.[32] Justices might even command that returns be made to them while on assize or at home in the country.[33]

Stories were also told in affidavits, only occasionally before 1689, but commonly thereafter, an increase due in part to a statute that appointed attorneys for taking affidavits in the country.[34] By the early eighteenth century, the use of affidavits as ground for the motion for the writ was all but assumed, especially in noncriminal detentions.[35] The affidavits themselves make moving reading. When Thomas Cooke gave an affidavit to support motions for a writ to free his sister, Catherine Marsden, he substantiated the pitiful story he told by enclosing in his affidavit a letter in which Catherine poured out the miseries she had endured at her husband's hands. Edmund Marsden had abandoned her for another woman eight years earlier. In January 1722, Catherine, by then destitute, had learned that Edmund was living in Essex, so she began proceedings in the church courts in hopes that he would be ordered to pay maintenance to support her and their children. Edmund replied by luring Catherine to Essex, saying that he desired a reconciliation. When she arrived, he locked her in a hayloft. Somehow, Catherine managed to slip word out through a sympathetic friend. "O com quickle to my relef," she begged. They did: her brother, sister, and a friend swore an affidavit before Chief Justice Sir John Pratt at his chambers in Serjeants' Inn, and the writ was soon issued.[36]

Affidavits like that by Catherine's supporters do not survive from before 1689. But many signs point to their earlier use. These were sworn in open court, before a single justice, or before specially commissioned attorneys. Rulebook orders as early as the 1620s and reports from midcentury show judges issuing habeas corpus based on information provided by affidavit.[37] Affidavits might initially have been used when one could not gain direct access to a barrister or to the court. Two of the earliest uses of habeas corpus by wives against violent husbands were begun by affidavits. In each case the wife had been kept, like Catherine Marsden, from nearly all contact with the world. Lady Howard prayed the writ in 1671 through her daughter, who made an affidavit that Sir Philip had "dragged her upstairs himself, taking her by the neck and his servant by the heels, and had locked her up in a room and there [kept] her for two days with only bread and water."[38] As Francis Hunnyngs, jailer of the Council in the Marches, knew well, affidavits were also used from the late sixteenth century to provide evidence that a writ had been served and thereby to hold the recipient responsible for its nonreturn.[39]

If gaining the writ depended on a story told in writing, the process may have been like that for issuing *corpus cum causa* out of Chancery. There, one made a petition or bill to the Chancellor laying out the grounds for the writ.[40] Chancery's *corpus cum causa*, like the King's Bench writ, was issued because, "as it is said" (*ut dicitur*), some unnamed person wrongly held another. Chancery bills were more elaborate than King's Bench affidavits, and substantive and procedural likenesses may not be taken as evidence of imitation. Nonetheless, both Chancery bills and King's Bench affidavits provided evidence to justify court action: in Chancery, by issuing *corpus cum causa* and perhaps an injunction, a writ of subpoena, or a certiorari to commence proceedings; and in King's Bench, by issuing habeas corpus or other related judicial writs by which the court might learn more about the complaint sworn before it.[41]

"As it is said": the need for a story highlights a central aspect of habeas corpus. It was a judicial writ, issuing at the justices' discretion. Issuance was not to be had just for the asking or simply by paying cursitors (officers of the court) a few shillings to write one, as one did when purchasing original writs.[42] As Sir John Maynard explained, "Where a court has power to grant a habeas corpus, 'tis never granted before that court is informed of the merits of the cause."[43] The increasing use of orders *nisi*—by which the court declared that the writ would issue unless *(nisi)* cause was shown to the contrary by the detaining authority—reveals the necessity to demonstrate the merits of a request before issuance. *Nisi* orders, followed by orders to send the writ when no cause to the contrary was shown, appear as early as 1601.[44] But some prisoners were not helped by *nisi* orders. John Aldworth's hope to use the writ a few months before Nicholas Lowe came to naught when his jailer, responding to such an order, showed good cause why habeas should not be issued.[45] Providing the grounds for denying the writ might as readily be done by affidavit as by oral motion in court.[46] Whether on oral motion, or on motion supported by claims in writing, the telling of stories moved the court.

The Return

Once a story had prompted one or more justices to send the writ, what did that writ command? That a body should be brought into court, and with it, information. The body was the object on which the court acted: that which would "undergo and receive" what the justices commanded. But what the court needed more than a body was the explanation of its detention. This explanation was called the return. Nicholas Lowe's writ asked London's leaders to return the cause of his detention.

But detention is not the same as arrest. The difference mattered. Any person could make an arrest. As the leading early modern law dictionary put it, "arrest is when one is taken and restrained from his liberty . . . [F]or treason, felony, or breaking of the peace, every man hath authority to arrest without warrant or precept."[47] Michael Dalton's *Country Justice* put this in slightly different terms: an arrest "may be called the beginning of an imprisonment."[48] Though Dalton conflates them here, arrest and imprisonment were distinct legal acts: by arrest, a body was taken; by detention, it was kept. Generally, a person arrested on suspicion of felony or misdemeanor was to be brought before a justice of the peace, who exercised wide discretion to decide whether to dismiss or bail the accused, impose sureties to keep the peace, or detain the accused to await trial.[49] Detention, then, was the business of jailers acting on the orders of properly constituted authorities—such as JPs—after those authorities had evaluated the reasons that had prompted an arrest.

The absence or presence in a writ of one of these terms—arrest or detention—tells us what King's Bench needed to learn from the writ's recipient. Writs of habeas corpus *ad subjiciendum* before 1628 generally asked only that the writ be returned with an explanation of the detention, not the "taking" or arrest. In this regard, the *ad subjiciendum* writ probably drew from the earlier writ of habeas corpus *ad standum rectum*, which likewise asked only for the cause of detention.[50] The *ad standum* writ typically contained within the writ itself (not in the return) a statement of the alleged wrong for which one had been taken —usually a felony—and commanded that a person should "stand to right," that is, be subjected to appropriate legal process. Upon inspecting the cause of detention, King's Bench could decide whether to dismiss or bail the prisoner, or more likely, bring the prisoner to trial. Perhaps because the clerks were imitating the *ad standum* writs, a handful of sixteenth-century writs in the *ad subjiciendum* form also contained within them statements about the legal reason for the arrest. But such statements all but disappeared in the 1590s, a timing that may not be accidental given this decade's importance in the writ's development.[51] As terse statements about the cause of arrest disappeared from the writ, the court began instead to demand ever more full information in the writ's return.

Through the first quarter of the seventeenth century, then, writs of habeas corpus *ad subjiciendum* asked only for the cause of detention. A jailer might answer this question in rather vague language: "because some legal officer with powers to order detention told me to detain this person." Explaining the cause of arrest required more information: "the prisoner was alleged to have committed a particular legal wrong."

By adding to the writ's text a demand for the cause of arrest as well as the cause of detention, habeas corpus would require more information from those who made the return. Dating the addition of a few words to the writ's formula is important. A close look at the archive makes this surprisingly easy to do.

The difference between arrest and detention was one of the central issues under discussion in one of the most politically charged habeas corpus cases of any age, the November 1627 case of the Five Knights, jailed by the Privy Council on a warrant that named no specific charge against them. William Noy, counsel for one of the knights, opened with a discourse on the language of habeas corpus. He distinguished between the "primary cause" of imprisonment—arrest—and the "subsequent cause"—detention. Noy argued that the returns stating that the knights had been detained simply "by his majesty's special commandment" had explained the reason for detention—by the king's command—but not the arrest, which everyone knew was for refusing to pay the king's loan. Noy's co-counsel, John Selden, hammered this point home: "[T]he caption [taking] is to be answered as well as the detention."[52]

A quick reading of the writ in court, however, showed plainly that Noy and Selden were wrong about the writ's actual words. Like virtually all *ad subjiciendum* writs issued before that time, those for the Five Knights required only a return of the cause of detention, not the cause of the taking. Undeterred, Selden argued that the writ implied the need for the cause of the arrest, saying that he had "seen many writs of this nature" whose returns included explanations of the arrest.[53] While he may have seen returns that answered more questions than the writ asked, he had apparently not studied the writs themselves. Almost none in the decades immediately prior to that time contained a request for information about both the arrest and the detention.[54] That Selden did not know the writs as well as he might may surprise us, but for all his eminence, no evidence survives showing that he ever argued another case on habeas corpus, before or after 1627.

While the decision to remand the knights rested principally on other issues—precedents of Privy Council habeas cases—Attorney General Heath opened the hole in Noy's and Selden's argument: the writ did not ask about the arrest. Everyone in Westminster Hall knew that while there may be a logical connection between detention and arrest, there was a critical legal distinction between them. As Heath explained, "[N]o man is bound to answer more than that which is the contents of the writ." Chief Justice Sir Nicholas Hyde agreed: "[T]here is not one word in the writ that demands the cause why they were taken." Heath helpfully suggested that if the judges liked, they could send another writ "to show the cause both of his caption and detention."[55] As a judicial writ, habeas corpus was certainly the judges' to write in any form that served their needs. No novel writs issued that November, though new language appeared in habeas corpus soon enough.

We cannot draw a neat causal line, but surviving dots point powerfully to a connection between these courtroom arguments of 1627 and a crucial change in clerical practice the following summer. Suddenly, "arrest" *(captionis)* began to appear next to "detention" *(detentionis)* in some of the writs filed in Trinity term 1628, the first term after the parliamentary debates that produced the Petition of Right, which required that no one should be imprisoned "contrary to the laws and franchise of the land."[56] The meaning of that requirement remained to be determined, but from Michaelmas 1628, *ad subjiciendum* writs uniformly contained the demand that the recipient return the cause of arrest along with the cause of detention. In addition, all writs henceforth would request the day of arrest. Arrests, especially those defined by statute, were controlled by processes that limited the amount of time a person might be held. By demanding the day of the arrest as well as the cause, the justices reading the return would know more precisely whether all limitations on powers of arrest and detention had been observed.

A close reading of writs may seem a tedious business, but by locating seemingly minor changes, we can glimpse transformative moments as they occurred. Court clerks' insertion of new language in habeas corpus beginning in the summer of 1628 marks just such a moment. That the clerks were not oblivious to the debates that rocked Parliament that spring is signaled by the unique appearance of a parliamentary text—the Petition of Right—in the middle of the bundle in which these new writs were filed, as well as the addition thereafter of a few words to every writ they wrote.[57]

The phrase they added, "the day and cause of the arrest and detention" *(die et causa captionis et detentionis),* may be found in two important places before 1628. One is Chancery's *corpus cum causa,* a writ used overwhelmingly in cases concerned with debt. The other, perhaps more significant, influence may have been the writ of habeas corpus *ad faciendum,* an instrument in aid of civil process on the Plea Side of King's Bench. But throughout the sixteenth century and the first half of the seventeenth, the occasional habeas corpus *ad faciendum* found its way into the Crown Side, typically for wrongs that resist easy categorization. After all, was it a criminal or civil trespass when Anne Harling "railed against" Anthony Willand in 1610, calling him a "foresworn knave and perjured rogue"?[58] In a similar vein, people imprisoned for refusing to pay a bastard maintenance order or for disobeying plague regulations used habeas corpus in the *ad faciendum* form, which demanded the return of the day and cause of their arrest and detention into King's Bench.[59] In 1628, the *ad subjiciendum* writ was recast to make it more useful—more aggressive—in just such borderline cases.[60] We might speculate that the *ad faciendum* form of habeas corpus contributed to the clerks' thinking as they added new language to its *ad subjiciendum* cousin.

With the addition of "the day and cause of the arrest" in 1628, the *ad subjiciendum* writ assumed its final form. In the same period, the difference between the use of the *ad faciendum* writ for pleas strictly between party and party, and the *ad subjiciendum* writ for criminal matters, became more fixed. By the 1660s, Sir Thomas Twisden could state without dissent that habeas corpus *ad subjiciendum* "is of the Crown Side."[61] A hardening distinction between one writ for private complaints and another for crimes, however, fanned doubts about the propriety of Common Pleas issuing *ad subjiciendum* writs when asked to do so in the 1660s.[62] As Chief Justice Vaughan of Common Pleas observed then, it was "more natural" that habeas corpus *ad subjiciendum* should issue from King's Bench since it was there that final determinations might be made on criminal wrongs, including misdemeanors.[63]

As Chief Justice Sir John Holt put it at century's end, "[T]he writ requires *causam captionis et detentionis . . .* and where the liberty of the subject is concerned, we must be certified of the causes."[64] The dramatic fattening of the files where writs and returns were stored in the century after 1628 suggests that demanding the time and cause of both the arrest and the detention had a substantial impact on practice. Less frequently could returns simply be written on the back of a writ, the practice in most cases up to that time. Another way to put this is that factual demands made by the writ increased in order to answer the greater legal demands the writ now expressed. The legality of imprisonment came to be concerned increasingly with the precise factual circumstances of the arrest and the factual matter that established the jurisdiction of the tribunal that ordered the detention. As we shall see in Chapter 4, demanding and receiving more facts, and better articulated facts, would encourage greater creativity by the justices of King's Bench in the decades ahead as they read deeply into the returns they received, and far beyond them too.

Hearing the Return

Lowe's writ required that the cause of his commitment be returned on October 12, 1605, the day after his writ issued. The court showed it meant business by moving quickly, and by indicating that simply sending the return was not enough—his body had to be brought as well.[65] Though not always. Variations in time and place of return, detailed in the writ, indicate judicial innovation and flexibility, especially during the last years of the sixteenth century and the first years of the seventeenth, when Sir John Popham presided.

Writs might require that the return be made on a particular date, "immediately after receipt," or "promptly"; in term or during vacation; and in court or to a particular justice's chambers, home, or somewhere else altogether. Before 1592, when Popham became chief justice, 93 percent of writs whose return dates may be ascertained were ordered returned on a specific date that was usually some days, even weeks, in the future. During Popham's and Fleming's tenure as chief justices (1592–1613), by contrast, the number of writs issuing with the demand that they be returned "immediately after receipt"—typically taken to mean the day of issuance or the next—jumped from 8 percent to one half. This rate continued until the passage of the Habeas Corpus Act of 1679, after which nine out of ten writs contained this requirement.[66] This is one of the few areas in which the Habeas Corpus Act had a clear influence on practice, though a vigorous chief justice like Popham could have as great an influence without statutory help.

We can chart a similar increase in orders requiring that returns be made to individual justices in chambers. Prior to 1592, only one in ten writs contained directions to send the return to a justice in chambers, while more than half contained this requirement when Popham and Fleming were in charge.[67] This shift should not surprise us, since writs issued for return in chambers—which were often issued during court vacations, but might also be sent during term—usually issued with a demand for immediate return.[68] The command to return to chambers in term might have been used to underline judicial anger in cases when the justices had to send multiple writs (alias and pluries) to get a return, especially when the receiving jurisdiction claimed to be exempt from Queen's Bench oversight.[69] Orders to return to a single justice—usually the chief justice—might also issue when a return had already been delayed, or on the last day of term, when there would be no time to put the return before the whole court without waiting until the next term.[70] Chambers usage would continue after Fleming's death, though not at the same rate.[71] In a similar vein, during Popham's tenure and afterward there are signs of even more creative return locations, for instance to a justice in the country, often as a matter of convenience while justices rode their assize circuits.[72]

Some objected to making returns to habeas corpus to justices in chambers. During parliamentary debates in 1674 on a proposed bill to amend habeas usage, one speaker complained that the review of returns had always been done in "public . . . but now 'tis done in private chambers; in the Court there is consideration and debate, and Counsel heard on all sides."[73] Who knew what went on when a justice was at home or in his rooms in Serjeants' Inn? A survey of chambers returns in the 1670s indicates that something different did happen when justices worked behind closed doors. From 1500 to 1800, just over one-fifth of cases were ordered returned in chambers.[74] Whereas during this period the average rate of bail or discharge for all prisoners using habeas corpus was 53 percent, the rate rose to 79 percent for those whose writs were returned in chambers. One explanation might be that writs returnable to chambers tended to issue in cases that may have concerned more dubious imprisonment orders: perhaps it was just this that inspired justices to act during vacation. But part, or all, the explanation for this release rate may have arisen from the capacity of judges to act independently when out of view.

That high release rates on chambers writs may have resulted from individual judicial temperament is suggested by Chief Justice Mansfield's decisions in private. Admiralty solicitor's papers regarding naval impressment underscore what we know from other sources: that the period when Mansfield presided, from 1756 to 1788, was one of the great ages of habeas corpus. The letters and notes of Samuel Seddon, the Admiralty board's solicitor, have almost a wistful tone at times, exasperated at others. Over and over he conceded that he and the Admiralty would have to capitulate to Mansfield's demands.[75] One clear sign of Mansfield's vigor was how much of this impressment and other habeas work he took back to his chambers: 22 percent of all writs issued during the years he led the court were returnable to him or to one of the other justices privately.[76] Mansfield likewise heard affidavits sworn, met lawyers, and issued writs from his house in Bloomsbury Square.[77] But Mansfield's appetite for working at home was not limited to impressment cases. In another area where he used the writ creatively—to examine family custody problems—he showed a similar readiness to hear affidavits, grant writs, or hear returns at home or in chambers.[78] Such energy and innovation in doing his work in private helps to explain the high rate of release on all writs of habeas corpus (80 percent) while Mansfield was in charge.

Habeas corpus *ad subjiciendum,* as a judicial writ rather than a writ of course, issued at the justices' discretion: it could be denied as well as granted. But this discretion typically erred on the side of issuance. Mansfield and other justices used this discretion broadly, and almost always let the writ go so that more might be known on its return. All the court's practices point to generosity in allowing writ use. One practice in particular underscores this tendency: grant of the writ during the long vacations between the four law terms.[79]

There is a longstanding misapprehension that before the Habeas Corpus Act of 1679, King's Bench could not and did not issue writs of habeas corpus *ad subjiciendum* during the courts' vacations.[80] This understanding is part of a story in which a weak common law writ was made strong only by statute. This story is incorrect. That we have missed vacation use of habeas corpus arises less from confusion in the early modern period than from the limited sources we typically consult in writing the period's legal history. We look to the words of famous judges, often in a few treatises or reports. In the case of vacation writs, these statements are certainly contradictory. When we study court rolls, files, and rulebooks, we see what judges did. If their dicta confuse, their deeds clarify: vacation writs were everywhere.

There is a clear point of departure for confusion about vacation usage: Sir Edward Coke's *Institutes*. Writing of Chancery, Coke proclaimed:

> [T]his court is the rather always open, for that if a man be wrongfully imprisoned in the vacation, the Lord Chancellor may grant a habeas corpus and do him justice according to law, where neither the King's Bench nor Common Pleas can grant that writ but in the term time.[81]

Yet voluminous evidence of vacation writs survives from the period during which Coke himself practiced before, then presided in, King's Bench.

Vacation writs were granted in two ways. The first was simply to grant the writ, noting the actual *teste* date on it, even when that date was during vacation. The other was to fictionalize the *teste* of the writ by dating it to the last day of the previous term. Let us consider each.

Scores of writs, from the fifteenth century through the eighteenth, have *teste* dates outside of term. Fewer such writs issued in the years from the publication of the final volume of Coke's *Institutes* in 1644 to the 1679 passage of the Habeas Corpus Act, which stated explicitly that habeas corpus should be available during court vacations. But even from 1644 to 1679, the practice did not die.[82] Before and during this period, lawyers and judges knew that King's Bench justices consistently issued vacation writs, even if the numbers declined.[83] King's Bench attorneys normally received one shilling more for writs of habeas corpus issued during the court's vacation than for those issued in term.[84] At least one Restoration-era chief justice, Sir John Kelyng, said that he would send habeas corpus during vacation. And one non-lawyer MP, in debates on a bill to extend habeas corpus in 1674, took it for granted that judges might issue the writ from chambers when the court was not in session.[85]

The Habeas Corpus Act of 1679 directed the issuance of vacation writs from any of the courts of Westminster Hall, but because the rest of that statute concerned habeas use in cases of treason or felony only, doubt persisted whether writs might be issued during vacations in non-criminal matters.[86] Such doubts were one reason for a proposed bill amending habeas corpus in 1758. During parliamentary debates on that bill, Justice Sir John Eardley Wilmot explained that Coke had been wrong. Wilmot knew well of what he spoke, having studied King's Bench records, where he found plenty of vacation writs, before and after Coke's time. Likewise, Wilmot noted that Hale said that vacation writs should come from Chancery "regularly," a word suggesting doubt in Hale's view about whether they might not issue from King's Bench at all. Again, practice spoke more loudly than words: Wilmot found dozens of vacation writs issued while Hale led King's Bench.[87] Despite the evidence, other judges in 1758 disagreed, and debate persisted about whether or not vacation writs might issue by common law, without having to rely on the Habeas Corpus Act of 1679.[88] Yet once the 1758 bill failed, Chief Justice Mansfield routinely issued vacation writs on no statutory authority, relying instead on a common law authority to do so, Coke's words notwithstanding. Actions trumped words.

That doubt about vacation writs persisted before and after 1758 is suggested by the practice of issuing writs in vacation but dating the *teste* to the last day of the previous term. How do we know a fictional *teste* was used? First, the large number of writs with *teste* on the last day of term; second, that such *teste* dates usually antedated the order by which a prisoner was imprisoned; and third, that virtually all such writs were ordered returned before a single justice in chambers on a date outside of term. An eighteenth-century clerk, noting precedents out of the files, dutifully cited Coke's dictum against vacation writs. He then explained their practice to the contrary: "[A]ll writs of habeas corpus issuing under the seal of the court of King's Bench and granted by any of the judges of that court are *tested* in term time . . . although they may in fact issue in the vacation."[89] Like all legal fictions, imagined *teste* dates permitted justices to air their doubts about vacation writs while they continued to use them.

Why haven't we seen this usage before? Because when we write legal history, we typically listen to what judges said—especially a famed one like Coke—rather than watch what they did. We also take at face value the claims of statute. This tendency is reinforced by our retrospective gaze, by which we know that Parliament, especially after 1688, would become supreme in the polity. If the parliamentary writers of statute suggested in their statutory texts that they were solving a problem, we take it for granted that the problem existed and that they solved it: we permit the makers of statute to be the heroes of a script they wrote. In the case of the Habeas Corpus Act of 1679, Parliament thus claimed to solve a problem that the judges could not. To accept this is to say that the writ itself was made by statute, not by common law.

By recovering the persistence of a common law writ—which permitted vacation use, among other things—we can correct the statutory bias that inhibits our approach to law's past. Looking at practice, revealed in court records, we see that King's Bench never stopped using vacation writs. Judges solved problems. In the use of vacation writs, there never was one.

Judicial Decision-Making

What would be done with a body once the reasons for its arrest and detention had been returned, in court or out, during term or after? The body would "undergo and receive whatever our court should then and there happen to order concerning him [or her or them] in this behalf." In this section of the writ, the *ad faciendum* ("to do") form differs from *ad subjiciendum* ("to undergo") in this one word only. The difference looks slight, but we should note two important consequences.

First, the difference between "doing" and "undergoing" is the difference between subject and object. In the *ad faciendum* writ, the body, when brought into court, would act—often by answering pleadings in a civil matter. Likewise, other forms of habeas corpus asked that the body concerned come to court to do something. Habeas corpus *ad testificandum* required one to provide evidence. Other forms asked people to respond to charges or to serve as jurors. In the *ad subjiciendum* form, however, the body became the object of the court's acting. This passivity is underscored by what we have seen concerning the writ's issuance: words of others often proved more important than words of the prisoner, which were normally absent from the rest of the record. In their returns, jailers returned their own words in which they included a transcription of the warrant of detention made by a magistrate. Lawyers then spoke about the possible meanings of those words. The justices—in the king's name—then ordered the jailer to do as they commanded. The person who spoke least on the record or in the reports was the prisoner.

That one must "undergo" points to the second crucial aspect of this formulation: only after missing information had been provided could any determination be made. Legal doubt distinguished the *ad subjiciendum* writ from its closest kin in the fifteenth and sixteenth centuries, habeas corpus *ad standum*. The *ad standum* writ issued with a wrong stated in the body of the writ; the *ad subjiciendum* writ did not. The return to the *ad subjiciendum* writ, not the writ, provided the critical factual matter. This difference between foreknowledge of the alleged wrong and doubt about it explains why the *ad standum* writ would die and the *ad subjiciendum* writ would thrive. The central purpose of the *ad subjiciendum* writ was not simply to move a body from one jurisdiction to another. It was to allow the judges to conduct the test implied by the words *ad subjiciendum*—by looking at the return, then well beyond it to determine what the prisoner's body should receive.

What did the body receive? Generally, an order to be remanded, bailed, or discharged altogether. But to see the matter clearly, we must complicate it. The justices first had to decide whether to remand the prisoner to the custody of the jailer who made the return, or to commit the prisoner to their own marshal of the Marshalsea. By committing to the marshal of King's Bench, the court took custody of both the return—which was "filed"—and the body.[90] The work of the original jailer was now finished as the king's greatest court took possession of both the prisoner and the problem.[91] In most cases, the order to commit to the marshal of the Marshalsea of King's Bench was a formality only and entailed an infinitesimally brief detention, signaling formal custody, before bail was ordered.[92] In other cases, most often those involving violent felonies or treason, commitment to the marshal of King's Bench was the prelude to arraignment and trial of the prisoner in King's Bench itself.[93] Even with the prisoner formally in King's Bench custody, further discussion might lead to the prisoner's remand to her original prison and to the process of the original tribunal that had jailed her.[94]

Strings might be attached to bail, and even to discharge. Bail might be granted pending the amendment of the return or while awaiting further discussions of legal questions whose answers remained obscure. After further hearings, the bailed prisoner might be returned to confinement or dismissed altogether. Frequently, bail was granted on the condition that one appear for further proceedings, perhaps in King's Bench, but more often in the original jurisdiction in which the matter arose. In some cases, bail or even discharge might be allowed only when the prisoner also gave sureties to keep the peace or to meet other conditions.[95] In others, discharge occurred only after a settlement had been negotiated, at the court's behest, among the parties involved in the original controversy. This variety of outcomes—much more various than simply remand, bail, or discharge—demonstrates the equitable flexibility that the justices of King's Bench enjoyed when using habeas corpus.

Compelling Obedience

A warning phrase—"and this in no wise omit, upon the peril that may befall"—began to appear in writs of habeas corpus *ad subjiciendum* in the sixteenth century. Why? To inspire obedience.

The theoretical reach of habeas corpus was vast: it extended to any person claiming to hold another by the king's law, wherever that officer might be and regardless of the prisoner's nationality. By this phrase in the writ, the court attempted to make real the writ's vast theoretical reach across all the king's dominions. This clause, and the subpoenas and attachments supporting it, served as the means by which jurisdictional claims were made manifest in the world by imposing on others to recognize them.[96] In an age of sail and animal locomotion, distance was the only barrier that would permit some jailers to disregard the writ. King's Bench would send the writ to the Caribbean. The trick was getting it to come back.[97] This phrase, and the enforcement procedures lying behind it, worked to make this happen, as Francis Hunnyngs and Captains Barber and Falkingham well knew.

Writs of many kinds were often ignored by their recipients. In response, the court issued alias (another) or pluries (further) writs, repeating the commands of the first. Warning clauses were usually inserted in these, conveying the court's indignation that it should need to repeat itself. To give more bite to this otherwise vague peril, alias writs tended to conclude with a subpoena clause spelling out the exact peril one faced for disobedience. Thus the earliest *ad subjiciendum* writ to contain the phrase "and this in no wise omit," issued in 1506, was an alias ending with a subpoena clause containing a £100 penalty for noncompliance, an amount that would certainly have impressed Dorset's sheriff.[98] Alias writs with the peril clause and a subpoena continued to appear intermittently over the next four decades. In 1546, the peril phrase suddenly began to appear more often, even in first writs and in those without subpoena clauses: two-thirds of *ad subjiciendum* writs that year contained the phrase.[99] Insertion of this general warning continued to increase, whether or not the writ issued as an alias or contained a subpoena. Its use became uniform in the mid-1590s, when, as we have seen, so many other innovations occurred, including the increased use of the kind of attachment process that had changed Francis Hunnyngs's mind about whether to honor the court's commands. By 1600, King's Bench consistently announced that habeas corpus *ad subjiciendum* was special. Its recipients should understand this at their peril.

Where did the clerks or justices get the inspiration for this language? Perhaps from Chancery. Chancery writs containing subpoena and the "in no wise omit" clauses were peculiarly associated with the king's interests. Two Chancery writs leap to mind as potential sources of influence, especially given the timing of these developments: *corpus cum causa* and subpoena. Chancery's writ of subpoena served as a general summons to the recipient, used not only to require appearance in Chancery, but also in other equity jurisdictions, such as the king's Council. Its early use was as much an aid to administrative as to judicial business.[100] One means by which King's Bench may have learned to use the same language for similar purposes—to call forth bodies and causes from inferior courts—was that writs of *corpus cum causa* out of Chancery were sometimes returned into King's Bench, especially in the fifteenth century. Taking a handful of examples from 1450–1451 of writs issuing out of Chancery but filed in King's Bench, we can see a flexibility of practice parallel with, if not derived from, Chancery. Chancery practices echoed in King's Bench during the same period that Chancery clerical practice itself became more elaborate in reply to increased usage.[101] Thus we find on King's Bench files *corpus cum causas* under the *teste* of the Chancellor, with and without subpoena clauses, but concluding with a warning to the recipient that noncompliance would be costly.[102]

A look at other writs of the same vintage but issuing from King's Bench suggests how the language of Chancery may have been transposed into King's Bench. One such writ, issued from King's Bench to the sheriff of Herefordshire, asked him to bring the body of Geoffrey

Sawyer to King's Bench so that he might stand to right to whatever should be objected against him and warned the sheriff not to omit performance, on pain of £40.[103] We might see such a writ as a general summons, not terribly different from Chancery's subpoena, by which a named person was brought into Chancery to answer an unnamed wrong, with a penalty for failure to do as bidden. The number of writs issuing from Chancery but returned into King's Bench declined sharply by 1500, just as some of the language that was once peculiar to Chancery writs began to appear more often in judicial writs from King's Bench, especially in habeas corpus *ad subjiciendum*.[104] Given what we know about the close proximity of Chancery and King's Bench personnel in Westminster Hall and beyond, we might imagine a conversation between Chancery and King's Bench practice.[105] It may even be significant that the disappearance of Chancery *corpus cum causas* from King's Bench files coincided roughly with the appearance in King's Bench writs of habeas corpus *ad subjiciendum* of the phrases "in no wise omit" and "subpoena," which may have made the Chancery's version unnecessary. It also occurred simultaneously with the increasing use of subpoena writs generally issuing under the judicial seals of both Common Pleas and King's Bench, a development some viewed with alarm, worried that by imitating Chancery, King's Bench might poach Chancery's jurisdiction.[106]

One oft-noted reason for recourse to Chancery for writs of subpoena, *corpus cum causa,* or others by which process in other courts might be moved or stopped arose from the availability of Chancery writs out of term. Many of those writs that issued on the *teste* of the chancellor yet were decided in King's Bench during the fifteenth century had been granted in vacation, returned in vacation, or both.[107] As we have seen, Chancery did not have a monopoly on vacation business in the fifteenth century. It had even less of one in the sixteenth.[108]

King's Bench might have imitated Chancery not only in order to assert new demands for compliance, but also to expand its jurisdiction. Yet although we typically discuss jurisdictional relations using metaphors of contest, the relationship between Chancery and King's Bench might be seen more clearly as one of cooptation. Well might we imagine the personnel of one court talking with those of another in the tight confines of Westminster Hall or in their inns. Attorneys, clerks, and barristers, many with practices in courts of equity as well as common law, saw one another daily. Though we cannot trace neat lines of influence, we may certainly envision a single legal culture of many intertwined parts made manifest in a legal device like this one.

"Witness, Sir John Popham"

At the end of Nicholas Lowe's writ was the *teste:* the date of issuance, with the name of the chief justice who bore witness to the authority on which it issued. Beneath the *teste* were the names of David Waterhouse and John Hare, who served as masters of the Crown Office. As the leading clerks on that side of the court, they oversaw some unknown clerk who wrote Lowe's writ. On the back was not just the chief justice's name, but also his signature: a large, scrawled, "J. Popham."[109]

What then did Lowe's writ declare? Its text demanded that any recipient send to the court, or to one of its justices, the body of a named person along with a proper return: a full account of why, as a matter of law, that person was a prisoner. As the writ explained, failure to do so would be at the recipient's peril.

In the years around the time when Lowe's writ issued, King's Bench used all the tools at its disposal to teach all who might receive these commands just what was required. The court's success in teaching that lesson would provide the force that would send the writ forth into the empire, to cover places and people well beyond England and the English. To see how Popham and other justices did this, we must now go to the conceptual core of habeas corpus: the royal prerogative. From words we turn to the very image of the monarch.

CHAPTER 3

Writ of the Prerogative

"Non sine sole iris"—no rainbow without the sun—declares the legend on the left side of the queen's portrait. A crewelwork serpent twists up Elizabeth's left sleeve, a heart-shaped device held firmly in its mouth, a celestial sphere above its head: wisdom commands Elizabeth's heart, and thus the heavens. On the lining of her cloak are eyes and ears: her sharp senses and those of her servants who had kept her informed of perils and possibilities, foreign and domestic, for the four decades during which she had ensured the protection of her subjects. The low-cut bodice of her dress is embroidered with spring flowers. Untrussed ringlets of red hair frame Gloriana's face, declaring her virginity. In her right hand, she holds a rainbow, lit by her brilliance.[1]

Perhaps the solicitor general had recently seen the Rainbow Portrait, painted for the queen's principal secretary, Sir Robert Cecil. Or perhaps Thomas Fleming was simply thinking of another of the many portraits of his queen, that "prince [*sic*] of light, the sun by whom thin[gs] of heaven the glory, and of earth the grace, hath no such glory."[2] As he entered Westminster Hall one autumn day in 1600, Thomas Fleming decided to flatter the justices of Queen's Bench as surely as the queen's portraits flattered her. But like a painting of a youthful sexagenarian queen, Fleming would show that flattery and the depiction of true greatness could be the same thing. "The jurisdiction of this court is not derived from the king [*sic*], as all the other jurisdictions in the realm are, but is the jurisdiction of the queen herself, because in this court, she is always said to be present." Fleming continued, his language becoming even more grand: "Because the jurisdiction of this court is above all other jurisdictions . . . there is no imperfection or defect in this court, but the jurisdiction of this court is supreme and absolute." Concluding, he compared all lesser courts to stars that "receive all their light from the sun, and still by this the sun loses none of its original light. Thus the jurisdiction of this court is so high above all other jurisdictions."[3]

Fleming was no astronomer, nor much of a poet. As he described the queen and the court bearing her name, he slipped from simile to reality, losing sight of the difference between them. By the time he finished, the Queen's Bench was not like the queen, it was the queen, the sun that lit the juridical heavens. *Non sine sole iris.*

The Prerogative: Miracles for the Common Weal

Chief Justice Sir Henry Montagu, writing in 1619, put it quite simply: habeas corpus is a "writ of the prerogative by which the king demands account for his subject who is restrained of his liberty."[4] Habeas corpus was a writ of the prerogative in order to be a writ of liberty. In the first two decades of the seventeenth century, the judges of King's Bench attached habeas corpus to the prerogative, taking it for their own use, thereby making themselves the sun that lit the heavens.

From different vantages, the prerogative is either within the law or outside it. In many ways, it was always both. By the end of the sixteenth century, the nature of the prerogative had become a matter of Trinitarian complexity, elusive owing to the inherent mystery of the concept and the greatness of the being who made it manifest. It had not always been so. In the later Middle Ages, commentators on the prerogative focused on those rights in land peculiar to the king. By this feudal view, the prerogative was largely a list of uniquely royal possibilities for control over property rather than a theory of power. Lawyers disagreed about which items belonged on the list: various forms of escheat, wardship, and so on. While some might have thought the list longer than others, all were more interested in the king as landlord than in the king as lord.[5] As late as 1567, William Stanford could publish a fundamentally medieval account of the prerogative that focused almost entirely on interests in land as the forms of "privilege or preeminence" that marked the prerogative.[6]

But by the time Stanford wrote, interests in the nature of the prerogative had changed in response to the king's increasing political potency. In his 1578 reading in the Middle Temple, one of the Inns of Court, where students lived and studied beside leading lawyers, James Morice focused on power, not property. The king's prerogatives were mighty things: "his lawful authorities, preheminencies, dignities, and royal privileges whereby he ruleth, excelleth, [and] is preferred and magnified over and above all other persons within his kingdom." Then Morice pulled back. "It is a common saying among many that the king by his prerogative is above his laws, which rightly understood is not amiss spoken." The key here was "rightly." Morice continued:

> But to say that the king is so superior over his laws and acts of parliament (because he hath power to make them) as that he is not bound to govern by the same but at his will and pleasure, is an opinion altogether repugnant to the wise and politic state of government established within this realm, which placeth the royal majesty of the king as the lieutenant of almighty God in the reverent throne of justice and true judgment. . . . [W]hat can be more meet or seeming to equity than [that] the prince [should] be bound by his own law?[7]

Morice identified the problem—the relationship of the king to law—but failed to resolve it. As God's lieutenant, the king was above "his laws." But Morice retreated from the implications of this claim. Dropping the assumption that law and king were distinct—in which case Morice would have to decide which was superior—he reattached them to one another in an endless circle of creation and command: the king is above his laws, his laws that place him on the "reverent throne of justice," and by which he is "bound." Was the king the Father, the Son, or the Holy Ghost? All of the above. As Sir John Dodderidge put it: "The heavens in height, the earth in deepness, and the king's heart none can search. The royal prerogative[s] of princes are sacred mysteries not to be touched."[8]

Like others, Morice brushed up against the thought of the prerogative's containment by law, then recoiled. He also emphasized that the king's laws were made with a Parliament, a native institution. This made the prerogative safe for English use, though many of the ideas by which the prerogative was expounded and expanded in the late sixteenth century drew heavily on foreign as well as native sources. The list of authorities that Dodderidge provided for his planned treatise on the prerogative included not only the obvious English ones—Fortescue, the reporters, records in the Tower of London—but also a slew of foreign ones, from the Greeks, through Aquinas, to Machiavelli and Bodin. Dodderidge planned to drink from "the fountains of divinity, philosophy, the laws of nations, and records out of which all laws, but especially the laws of this realm, are evidently deduced." When English law provided no guide, he declared that he would do "as the Sorbonists and Civilians [do and] resort to the law of nature, which is the ground of all laws."[9] It was a short step from nature to God, a step made as easily by common lawyers like Morice or Dodderidge as by Sorbonists and civilians. Common lawyers working in this cosmopolitan mode followed a tradition staked out especially well in Christopher St. German's *Doctor and Student*, where English law was not simply compatible with natural and divine law, but arose from them.[10] Once we see this, we can begin to see how the relationship between God and king, and thus between prerogative and law, worked in the early modern mind.

Early modern language assumed that the king, like God, usually operated according to known rules. The king's rules were called law; God's were called nature. But God might act outside the rules by performing miracles. The question then was whether the prerogative was to be contained within nature—within law—or whether the prerogative allowed the king to perform law's equivalent of miracles. Most answered "yes." As late as the eighteenth century, a King's Bench justice like Sir John Fortescue Aland found this a useful way to conceive the prerogative when he noted that Sir John Davies, a century earlier, had likened "the prerogative to the government of God himself, who suffers things generally to go in their usual course, but reserves to himself to go out of that by a miracle when he pleases."[11] Fortescue Aland worked hastily as he jotted down this thought. There was nothing in Davies about acting "when he pleases," as if by whim. But there was acting by miracles, "above nature."[12] If not by whim, then how?

Crucially, a miracle was not contrary to nature, nor was the prerogative contrary to law. They were complements. In the great parliamentary debate on the liberty of the subject in April 1628, Sir Benjamin Rudyard argued that

> God himself has constituted a general law of nature to govern the ordinary course of things. He has made no law for miracles. . . . So the king's prerogatives are rather besides the law than against it, and when

they are directly to their ends for the public good, they are not only concurring laws, but even laws in singularity and excellency.[13]

As God performed miracles within and upon the natural world, so too did kings wield the prerogative within and upon a world that normally revolved according to law. On both sides of the nature-miracle/law-prerogative analogy, extraordinary, rule-transcending power existed to complement ordinary possibilities traced by the rules. Juxtaposing nature and miracle, law and prerogative—a modern habit of mind—is to miss the point.

Though God was the author of nature, few would have argued that the king had the same exclusive authorship of law. That said, he, too, could perform miracles, by his absolute prerogative. The prerogative took two forms: ordinary and absolute.[14] The ordinary prerogative included those royal interests in land or customs revenues that had always been the concern of observers like Stanford. It also included all those other authorities and modes of judgment that the king exercised through law by his voluntary desire to act according to law. As Sir John Davies put it, "By the positive law the king himself was pleased to limit and stint his absolute power, and to tie himself to the ordinary rules of the law, in common and ordinary cases."[15]

While the king normally acted according to rules, he could rise above them when necessary. Davies explained that the king thus retained

> that absolute and unlimited power which was given unto him by the Law of Nations, and in these cases or points, the King's Prerogatives do consist; so as the king's prerogatives were not granted unto him by the people, but reserved by himself to himself.[16]

Sir Thomas Fleming used similar language:

> The king's power is double, ordinary and absolute, and they have several laws and ends. That of the ordinary is for the profit of particular subjects, for the execution of civil justice . . . and these laws cannot be changed without parliament. . . . The absolute power of the king is not that which is converted or executed to private use, to the benefit of any particular person, but is only that which is applied to the general benefit of the people and is *salus populi*.[17]

In this commonly asserted view, the counterpart to "ordinary" is "absolute," not "extraordinary." It is a power justified not only by unusual circumstances—war, perhaps—but also for an end: *salus populi.*[18] Claims that powers peculiar to the king were for the general benefit of the people, though not from the people, had a long pedigree. Chief Justice Sir John Fyneux reportedly said that the "prince's prerogative and the subject's privilege are solid felicities together and but empty notions asunder."[19] Stanford worked with the same idea, joining it to the corporeal trope so common in political rhetoric: the king "is the most excellent and worthiest part or member of the body of the commonwealth, so is he also (through his good governance) the preserver, nourisher, and defender of the people, [they] being the rest of the same body."[20] *Salus populi* and commonweal: this was the point of the body politic, and thus the point of absolute powers for maintaining it.

Linking king to God, and the good of the people to the need for miracles, Edward Forsett too noted that the sovereign held "certain prerogative rights of most ample extensions and most free exemptions." These he used not by whim, but moderately, "as God in the world, and the soul in the body; not to the impeach, but to the support of justice; not to the hurt, but to the good of subjects."[21] Miracles performed by the prerogative were a kind of equitable intervention into law's normal operation made legal by their being directed "for the public good," as Benjamin Rudyard put it.[22] This would be a durable idea. In the eighteenth century, it would explain what was due to prisoners of war and would underline arguments to undo slavery by bringing slaves into subjecthood, through which their bodies would be protected by the operation of the king's prerogative. In the nineteenth century, one could still hear the prerogative invoked to justify using habeas corpus in places as far away as Trois-Rivières, Quebec, and Sydney. By giving allegiance to the person of the king, the person of the free subject was protected and his birthright secured by law. In turn, the protected subject protected the king. The circularity of this thinking did nothing to diminish its force.

The King's Body, the Subject's Body, and the Use of Miracles

The protection of subjects required that their bodies were the king's to command: "The reason why the common law has such great respect for the body of a man is so that he may be ready to preserve the king."[23] Little surprise, then, that Chief Justice Popham connected the prerogative to the common law this way when discussing habeas corpus. A writ fundamentally concerned with moving, holding, and releasing subjects' bodies touched directly on this most fundamental aspect of the king's authority: his authority to control his subjects' bodies so that they might protect his body, and so in turn, that he might protect theirs. Protection was a perfectly reciprocal act.[24]

To explore this notion more fully, we return to Sir Thomas Fleming, who recorded his views about the relationship of subject to king in Calvin's case—the 1608 case regarding whether the English king's Scottish subjects might enjoy the benefits of English law. The king, he said,

> is above the laws, but not to abrogate them, which he cannot do. His absolute power hath no law to direct him. He is absolute in war and peace, and may command the subject to go whither he pleaseth.[25]

In exchange for the subject's protection by the king, it followed that the subject's body should go "whither he [the king] pleaseth." Thus Fleming emphasized that the subject's allegiance was owed to the actual person of the king, not to his political person or to some other disembodied abstraction. "They will make fearful conclusions if they lay the allegiance upon the kingdom, upon the crown, or upon the laws," rather than on the person of the king, Fleming argued.

Fleming, like the other judges in Calvin's case, emphasized the role of actual bodies in allegiance. "The derivation of *ligencia* is from *liga,* a bond." This natural bond, "begun by birth and ended by death, as between the father and son," rested on an implied oath, an act of faith.

> This oath is only to the king and to no other natural liege lord . . . and they are subjects only that have taken this oath. And this oath is reciprocal as well on the king's as on the subject's behalf. And this allegiance begins with every man's birth and is by the law of nature.[26]

By connecting Popham's formulation about the link between habeas corpus and the subject's obligation to serve with his body to Fleming's formulation concerning allegiance, we find that common law buttressed requirements already imposed on both king and subject by the law of nature. This followed James Morice's similar analysis of a generation earlier: "[E]very man, by the laws of nature and the dutiful allegiance of a subject, is bound to defend his sovereign lord and native country."[27] Coke, too, emphasized the natural origin of subjecthood, allegiance, and protection. The subject's birthright—like his or her liberties—entailed duty as well as privilege. Every natural subject, when born, "oweth by birth-right ligeance and obedience to his sovereign."[28] The powers attendant on the king's crown, by which he provided protection, likewise came to him by birthright.

Though subject and king performed allegiance and protection with and through their natural bodies, allegiance itself was a spiritual matter: a mystical force tying physical bodies together. As Coke explained, "[L]igeance is a quality of the mind." Crucially—as we shall see in the writ's imperial movement—this meant allegiance was "not confined within any place." Coke reached this insight, critical to the conception and use of habeas corpus, by developing the idea that birth within England did not, on its own, produce that birthright to which the king's protection attached. Place is epiphenomenal in the creation of this relationship, a sign of subjecthood rather than the generator of it. Given the absence of spatial constraint on allegiance, the power of the king to command his subjects' bodies extended to calling them out of the realm in order to protect the realm. This was only possible because allegiance was a matter of obedience and spiritual connection, not of place.[29] Hale carried this point further:

> [S]ubjection is not only confined to those that are born in England only, not to those only that are born within the territories and dominions of the crown of England, but [extends] to those that are born under the same king, though in separate and independent territories.[30]

This common law principle would later be proclaimed by statute, too.[31] Place might mark some who had come into the relationship of allegiance, but it did not constitute allegiance: only the mystical connection of ligeance did this.

That birthrights, like ligeance, were spiritually, not spatially, bounded will help to explain how the law concerned with the subject's body and with habeas corpus might go wherever the king's subjects went, even when other parts of English law did not. These spiritual bonds were very real: failure to appreciate this can arise only from a modern condescension to the reality in early modern minds of the "ligamen" imported by an oath, even an implied one. From the mutual oaths of the natural subject and sovereign came law and the liberties derived from and defined by law.

While the natural subject performed the bond of allegiance only with his body, the king could do more. We return then to miracles. For that is what the royal power to create sanctuary or to grant pardon was: a miracle by which the normal rules of law, which might inflict the ultimate pains on the subject's body, were suspended.[32] This same power, analogized outward and taken up by the justices of King's Bench, gave habeas corpus its unusual force. An examination of sanctuary and pardon suggests how this worked.

Sanctuary was the privilege, usually granted to a monastery, to provide refuge even from the king's justice. Sanctuary was not for providing justice. It was for extending mercy.

> For the prince of this land is sworn to do mercy as well as justice. The prince of the Romans, who was called Romulus, before the Incarnation, set up by his command a place of protection, which place he caused to be called *asylus* (that is, *locus sine tactu*). That was in the age of justice. *A fortiori*, therefore, now in the age of mercy, the prince must be more moved to mercy and pity; for the king is called *pater patriae,* and it belongs to his office sometimes to do justice and at other times mercy.[33]

By a royal charter, the king granted the franchise of sanctuary, a place marked out for mercy. But resort to sanctuary required a penalty: permanent exile, either by remaining for the rest of one's life within the sanctuary, or by abjuring the realm.[34] Either way, resort to sanctuary—extralegal mercy—broke the ties of allegiance between subject and king. Such a break could only arise from the power of the king, for these ties concerned the control of bodies, as Henry VIII's justices made clear in 1513:

> Having a sanctuary is the highest thing against the crown that may be; for the highest things the king has are governance and power over the bodies of his subjects, and this sanctuary discharges them from the law and the execution thereof.[35]

The Reformation destroyed monastic sanctuaries, so it may be more than coincidental that the period of the greatest use of royal pardons—the first two decades of Elizabeth's reign—occurred between the end of English monasticism and the onset of the writ's greatest period of development at century's end.[36] Matthew Hale called pardon "dispensation with laws" or "an exemption from government," allowable because the king thereby excused offenders "against his own suit": in other words, felons, who were prosecuted in the king's name.[37] Commentators viewed this use of the prerogative in miraculous terms. True, only God could pardon the ultimate penalties of sin. But from God "derived to princes [the power] to remit the penalty of the laws temporal." Or as James Morice asked, "[W]hat is more agreeing unto the high majesty of a king than with loving mercy to temper the severity of justice"? When the king pardoned those attainted of treason, the king simultaneously restored the inheritance of the traitor's heir. Morice explained:

> [T]he king hath again restored the father to life, being a dead person in law . . . for as the king by his prerogative may incorporate among his subjects an alien or stranger born, and make him inheritable to the laws of the realm, so may his majesty restore again him that was a lawful subject and incorrupt member of the commonwealth.[38]

Like any good simile, each side here explains the other. The king's unique capacity to pardon—to breathe life again into the "dead person in law"—was the same power by which anyone, even an alien, might become a subject, and thereby brought under the protection of the king's laws. The extension of subjecthood beyond those who were natural subjects would be one of the many marvelous attributes of habeas corpus. By protecting his subjects—natural and otherwise—where law warranted, and by granting mercy where law did not warrant, the king exercised his prerogative. In both cases, his body commanded theirs.

There was an important connection between pardons and habeas corpus in practice as well as in conception. In the sixteenth century, the writ was one of the means by which a pardon recipient might be brought into court to plead the pardon.[39] Most of these pardons pleaded on habeas corpus arose prior to conviction, which may explain why only a small portion of total pardons—most of which were granted after conviction—were pleaded by using habeas corpus: habeas may have provided the best means for being brought into court to use a pardon prior to trial.[40]

This was Bartholomew Brooksby's experience. Brooksby was an accused plotter brought before the Privy Council in September 1603. Attainted of treason, the king ordered Attorney General Sir Edward Coke to prepare a pardon for him the following March; the pardon passed the great seal in May. In June, habeas corpus issued to Brooksby's jailer. When Brooksby was brought into court, the return stated simply that he had been committed by the Privy Council—no mention was made of why he was charged. Apparently referring to matter outside the return, the court asked why the attaint for treason should not be carried out. In reply, he "pleaded letters patent of the king of pardon."[41] But in most preconviction circumstances, use of the writ preceded the pardon. Habeas corpus provided the means by which an accused felon might be committed to the Marshalsea, where he could then procure a pardon. Such practices suggest that accused traitors and felons understood that the connection between pardon and habeas corpus was more than an abstraction. The king's nearly divine power to pardon touched his nearly divine power to command the bodies of his subjects either on his own, or through his judges using habeas corpus.

Prerogative Writs

Whether the king imposed justice or granted mercy, he imposed his will on bodies, and never more clearly than when he imprisoned and released those bodies. The connection between the jailer's franchise and the subject's body was the king, as Hale explained: "The jails regularly are all in the king's disposal . . . for the law hath originally trusted none with the custody of the bodies of the king's subjects . . . but the king or such to whom he deputed it."[42] Whether a sheriff or common jailer, a tipstaff or messenger, whoever held the custody of one of the king's subjects did so by the prerogative. From the power to command bodies came the power to free them.

All magistrates acted in the king's name since all justice arose from the king. Little wonder that John Spelman should make this point so clearly when discussing quo warranto, the means by which the use of franchises more broadly was inspected by the king's judges:

> The governance of justice resides solely in the king's person, as head of
> the commonwealth, just as the five senses reside in the head of every
> man as the principal part of the body. And because its preservation is

so great a task that his own person does not suffice, it is requisite that he should commit the administration of justice to some persons beneath him.[43]

While such powers were royal ones delegated to others, not all delegates were equal. The prerogative was taken up by one group of delegates—the justices of King's Bench—who through habeas corpus gave themselves a power to inspect the work of all other such delegates. As English law and habeas corpus spread across the globe, this ultimate judicial authority would travel too, carried by the prerogative and placed in the hands of Supreme Courts, created in distant lands by royal charters, with powers analogized to their source in King's Bench. Soon after his arrival in Calcutta, Justice John Hyde of the Supreme Court there explained that "the king's prerogative extends as fully over his subjects here as in any part of his dominions."[44]

Returning to Sir Thomas Fleming, we can hear him underscore the greatness of Queen's Bench. "This court is the jurisdiction of the queen herself. It is so high that in its presence other jurisdictions cease."[45] In its medieval origins, the King's Bench was distinguished from the Common Bench—the court of Common Pleas—by the fact that the king sat there with his justices. Long after he stopped sitting with them, the King's Bench continued to move around the country with the king while his justices of Common Pleas remained behind in Westminster. Such mobility kept the court in close proximity to the king, legally as well as literally.[46]

If the king had a unique interest in his subjects' bodies, it stood to reason that enacting that interest when he no longer sat in court himself should become the function of the court claiming to be so close to his person that it was the king himself. Or so many thought, especially the justices of that court. Justice Sir Christopher Yelverton made this connection explicit:

[B]y the jurisdiction of this court it is intended that the king sits here in his own person, and he is to have an account why any of his subjects are imprisoned. And for this reason, the judges of this court may send for any prisoner to any prison in England.

Other courts issued writs of habeas corpus of many kinds. Common Pleas even issued the *ad subjiciendum* writ. Even so, as Yelverton explained in the same 1605 case, Common Pleas was limited to those instances in which the prisoner could show a privilege as an attorney or litigant in that court.[47] This explains why use of the writ by Common Pleas all but disappeared from the middle of Elizabeth's reign until the late 1660s, when there was a minor revival by an expansion of claims of privilege.[48] Acting on the claim of privilege of one court, as opposed to acting on the claim of the privilege of any subject, was a very different—and lesser—thing.

We can see better how distinctive the powers of King's Bench were at the opening of the seventeenth century by locating the conjunction between developments on the writ of habeas corpus and developments in other judicial writs from King's Bench, especially the new writ of mandamus. By January of 1608, Sir Thomas Fleming had served only one term as chief justice. On the nineteenth of that month, London's leaders imprisoned Edward Farndon, a shopkeeper, for the tongue-lashing he had given to William Bedwell, rector of St. Ethelburga. Four days later, Fleming's *teste* appeared on Farndon's habeas corpus and he was soon discharged from his confinement.[49]

But Farndon was not finished. London's leaders had not only taken Farndon's bodily freedom; they had also taken his freedom of the City. To win back the valuable privileges he had lost, Farndon employed a novel procedure, suing from King's Bench a "writ of restitution": what would later be known as mandamus. This ordered the mayor and aldermen of London to "restore the said Edward to his former liberties and franchises in the said city without delay." The long enrolled entry of the outcome of Farndon's case told the story of his troubles. Apparently after Farndon's release from Newgate prison, the City's leaders, angered by the finding by King's Bench that their explanation for his imprisonment had been "wholly defective, frivolous, and uncertain," had disfranchised him and ordered his shop and home boarded up.[50]

More was now at stake than Farndon's loss of "his liberties and franchises." Treating him this way, after King's Bench had released him, was a contempt of the king and his court. Fleming and his brethren on the bench pronounced the king's displeasure—the court's displeasure. Still speaking in the king's name, they ordered Farndon restored to the City's freedom unless London's leaders could show why he should not be restored. The justices did so because they did not wish "that Our subjects should be burdened, vexed, or hindered in any way because they seek justice in Our court of King's Bench (as all Our lieges may do freely and with impunity)."[51] When this order to the City went unanswered, the court then sent a writ of restitution. The City failed to comply, so the justices sent an alias writ—on pain of £40 for nonreturn—and then a pluries writ. At last, the City responded. After considering that response, the court ordered Farndon restored to his freedom, but with a twist. As a condition for recovering the freedom of London, the court commanded Farndon to make a speech of humble submission in the guildhall.[52]

Two things stand out about Farndon's troubles. First was the creativity shown by the participants. We cannot know who thought to craft this one-of-a-kind writ by which he was restored to the City's freedom as a follow-up to his release from jail; nor can we know who proposed the compromise conclusion. A claim of privilege—that Farndon was already a litigant in King's Bench—placed a fig leaf over what was otherwise a bare novelty: hence the mention in Farndon's special writ that he had been "vexed" by the City as he was in the process of "seek[ing] justice in our court." Having inspired the court to justify new practices on old grounds, the justices used further proceedings to mediate the dispute rather than choose a winner and a loser. Second, it was no accident that habeas corpus and the nascent writ of mandamus should be joined together; they were similar enough that later they would be lumped together in the single category of "prerogative writs." In 1759, Chief Justice Mansfield would link mandamus and habeas corpus with certiorari and prohibitions under this heading as part of a sweeping history of the writs that demonstrated their vast jurisdictional and geographical range.[53] But long before there was one label for them, there was one conception. How were these writs alike? Answering this question will help us see better the nature of habeas corpus *ad subjiciendum*.

Certiorari was the means by which the record of another court might be brought into King's Bench for further proceedings. Like most of these other writs, certiorari first arose in Chancery. Well before the end of the sixteenth century, King's Bench had begun issuing certiorari as a judicial writ to help its own process along.[54] Certiorari was used to review recognizances imposed by justices of the peace or to bring indictments into King's Bench for trial. During the seventeenth century, certiorari took on new functions, becoming an instrument for quashing the decisions of statutory authorities, such as sewer commissioners, as well as the summary judgments that an increasing number of statutes permitted JPs to make.[55] By the end of the seventeenth century and throughout the eighteenth, Crown Side recorda files bulge with certioraris for reviewing decisions of JPs, especially in their management of the poor laws.[56]

The writ of prohibition, issued by Common Pleas as well as King's Bench, was used to stop proceedings in other courts, especially church courts. This process ensured that litigation flowed through the proper channels and defended the king's interest in the delivery of justice by requiring that any tribunal should examine only those issues appropriate to its jurisdiction.[57] As Justice Sir John Croke described it, the writ of prohibition "is *breve regium* and *jus coronae*"—to deny the writ where due would be in "derogation of the crown."[58] Hale, like others before and after, saw the writ of prohibition as arising from the fact that all jurisdictions—even church courts—derived from the crown and should thus be policed by writs peculiarly associated with that same originating authority. As with habeas corpus, disobedience to a prohibition would prompt a display of the court's anger in the form of an attachment for contempt.[59]

Mandamus was in many ways the opposite of prohibition; it commanded performance of a legally mandated deed by a judicial or administrative officer rather than stopping such an officer from doing something he should not.[60] Prohibition and mandamus might thus be used together, with prohibition preventing one deed from being carried out while mandamus compelled performance of its opposite.[61] Used initially to regain offices from which one had been removed, writs of mandamus were first known as writs of "restitution," suggesting how offices were viewed as much as private property as public obligations. Thus the appearance of a prototype mandamus—in late 1605— concerned not an urban office, but a rectory, just the kind of situation that most readily conflated public functions with property interests.[62] More such writs for disputed rectories issued in the winter and spring of 1606, momentarily reversing some of the deprivations from church livings that had occurred as a result of the enforcement of the new church canons of 1604.[63]

During these same months of early 1606, King's Bench issued the first writ of restitution for an urban office. Like the writ for Edward Farndon, that for Thomas Tompson was full of unique features. Tompson's writ provided a lengthy recital of the wrongs against him.

After naming Tompson a bailiff of Cambridge in Michaelmas 1605, the mayor and others soon removed him from office after "frivolous and private quarrels."[64] But when town leaders imprisoned Tompson, he had been on his way to Westminster to consult with counsel about a matter pending in King's Bench. Again, privilege as a litigant of the court helped smooth the way to novelty. The court's unusual writ declared that preventing Tompson from exercising his office, enjoying its profits, and pursuing his action in King's Bench were "in contempt of Us and to the damage, prejudice, scandal, and pauperization of the said Thomas." As in Farndon's case, Tompson's concerned both the well-being of the subject and the dignity of the king in his bench. Because Tompson "asked Us to provide him with an appropriate remedy," and in order "to preserve inviolate the liberties and privileges of Our said court and of Our lieges," Popham's court, in the king's name, simultaneously commanded Tompson's release from prison and his restoration as bailiff.[65]

Tompson's writ, which combined habeas corpus and mandamus, shows that at this time when mandamus was just coming into being and habeas corpus was being put to new uses, the two writs were so closely linked in conception and practice that they could be fused. But these writs would soon be separated in order that their distinctive functions might be realized most effectively: recall the issuance of two separate writs for Edward Farndon two years later. In both the Tompson and Farndon cases, claims of privilege—perhaps fictional—were employed to help justify new forms in their first use. Writs for both men suggested that they corrected not only wrongs against Tompson and Farndon, but against the king, too, because the dismissal and imprisonment of each man was taken to be an affront to King's Bench. Both writs thus issued so that "justice should be done."[66]

This broad need to do justice for the subject while protecting the honor of king and court provides the key to habeas corpus, mandamus, and all the prerogative writs. Sir Edward Coke made this point forcefully in the *Institutes*. "This court," he declared,

hath not only jurisdiction to correct errors in judicial proceeding[s], but other errors and misdemeanors extrajudicial tending to the breach of the peace, or oppression of the subjects, or raising of faction . . . or any other manner of misgovernment, so that no wrong or injury, either public or private, can be done, but that this shall be reformed or punished.[67]

This was virtually the same language Coke would use in the 1615 mandamus case of James Bagge, though here in the *Institutes* he used it to describe all the prerogative writs, which were linked by the peculiar power they gave King's Bench to correct all wrongs.[68]

Beyond their grounding on the king's prerogative and on the need to compel justice, what other qualities marked the prerogative writs? First, all were judicial writs. They were created by the justices of King's Bench to aid their own process and to correct all "misdemeanors extra-judicial" or judicial where no other court instrument existed to provide relief. As judicial writs, they issued at the discretion of the justices of King's Bench.

Nor did statute create these writs. Common law judges did. Sir John Holt reminded his listeners in 1699 of this distinction when he considered certiorari to inspect the work of sewer commissioners: "[S]tatute does not give authority to this court to grant a certiorari, but it is by the common law that this court will examine if other courts exceed their jurisdictions."[69] The same was true of habeas corpus: its strength was due to its roots in common law, whatever glorious attributes later generations would ascribe to the writ as it was used according to the Habeas Corpus Act of 1679.

This issue of origins points to the next salient feature of the prerogative writs: their concern with jurisdiction. Who, or what tribunal, should manage this concern on the king's behalf? The Privy Council—on which the chief justice and other law officers usually sat—might have claimed to play this role, given its proximity to the king. So, too, the Privy Council's judicial offshoot, the Court of Star Chamber. But Coke declared that King's Bench "hath the survey of all other courts," reflecting how the justices had gained command of the language and use of the prerogative during the first two decades of the seventeenth century.[70] Thus certiorari might quash orders wrongly made in a matter of which justices of the peace otherwise had purview. And mandamus issued from King's Bench to restore urban officials not because urban corporations did not have the right to elect, and in some cases dismiss, their members. The court sent mandamus because they had acted wrongly in how they did so, even if they acted within the territorial limits of their jurisdiction and according to their own bylaws.[71]

Lord Chancellor Ellesmere perhaps understood better than anyone that by using the prerogative writs, King's Bench tried to capture the same jurisdictional ground once held exclusively by the Council. He offered an incisive critique of Coke's claims in Bagge's case. By "giving excess of authority to the King's Bench," Ellesmere wrote, Coke

> insinuate[d] that this court is all sufficient in itself to manage the state. For if the King's Bench may reform any manner of misgovernment (as the words are), it seemeth that there is little or no use either of the King's royal care and authority exercised in his person and by his proclamations, ordinances, and immediate directions, nor of the Council Table, which under the king is the chief watch tower for all points of misgovernment, nor of the Star Chamber, which hath ever been esteemed the highest court for extinguishment [of] all riots and public disorders and enormities. And besides, the words do import as if the King's Bench had a super-interdependency [*sic*] over the government itself, and to judge wherein any of them do misgovern.[72]

Precisely. By the time Ellesmere wrote this, in 1615, the development of the prerogative writs had charted a clear movement away from the Privy Council and toward King's Bench of "the survey of all other courts." Popham, Fleming, and then Coke—perhaps even with the help of the Council, in cases like Walter Witherley's—had relocated the "chief watch tower for all points of misgovernment" to King's Bench. The humiliation of Francis Hunnyngs, the jailer for the Council of the Marches of Wales—a court born of the Privy Council—simply put a human face on a movement of jurisdictional oversight that for all the trenchancy of his observation, Ellesmere could do little to prevent.

Nothing shows the peculiar nature of a prerogative writ better than the way in which the justices of King's Bench insisted that it would go anywhere in the king's dominions, including to liberties and franchises normally immune from process out of the courts of Westminster Hall. This power to intrude in such jurisdictions had been an authority once used by the Council and its courts. Star Chamber, one person argued, had jurisdiction "in all private jurisdictions, in Ireland, in the isles of Jersey and Guernsey, which have their own laws, and all other places within the King's Dominions."[73] Using the prerogative writs, King's Bench increasingly offered the same geographically and jurisdictionally broad coverage. As Hale put it when writing of Wales, "[B]*revia mandatoria,* [such] as habeas corpus and certiorari and prohibitions, did run there."[74] They also went to the palatinates, to Ireland, and beyond. When France was still held by English kings, they went there too. Not even the writ of error had such an extraordinary reach.[75] In later centuries, the king's prerogative would drive the writ everywhere that the king had created courts modeled after King's Bench. This explains how Sir Francis Forbes, a world away in New South Wales, used habeas corpus in 1829, calling it "a high prerogative writ and so much the right of the subject as to render it compulsory on the judges . . . to grant it."[76]

Witherley's case had demonstrated the power of the prerogative writs to the people who governed in the Welsh marches. But it was in a 1619 case concerning the admiralty court in the Cinque Ports, a group of coastal towns in Kent and Sussex, that Chief Justice Montagu drove this point home. Richard Bourne had taken an anchor and cable from the sea as salvage from a wreck. The Ports' admiralty court ordered that he return them to their owner or pay £40 in compensation. Bourne was jailed when he disobeyed. He then sued habeas corpus to the lord warden of the Cinque Ports. Who was the lord warden? None other than Edward Lord Zouche, the same man who had been upbraided by King's Bench when he had served as Lord President of the Council in Wales during the blowup in Witherley's case fourteen years earlier. Zouche played again to script, refusing to return the writ, claiming "that this writ was not awardable to the Cinque Ports, nor returnable by him." Montagu acknowledged that this was true enough of "writs between party and party." But, he explained, habeas corpus was "a prerogative writ, which concerns the king's justice to be administered to his subjects; for the king ought to have an account why any of his subjects are imprisoned." Montagu brushed aside claims to be exempt from King's Bench oversight with the most imperious language: "[T]o dispute [the writ] is not to dispute the jurisdiction, but the power of the king and his court, which is not to be disputed."[77] Justice Dodderidge went further: "[T]his writ is not at the suit of any subject, but of the king, and [it] is a point of distributive justice to defend the persons of subjects from wrong and restraint, and no liberty is exempt of the prerogative of the king."[78] The other judges agreed: "[T]his court is [the] Supreme Court, in which the king sits, that may demand [an] account of the imprisonment of any of his subjects."[79]

Once again, the court forced Zouche to yield.[80] But the point of forcing him to submit his judgments to King's Bench review was not necessarily to undo them. Once the court heard arguments on Zouche's return, they decided he had indeed acted appropriately when he jailed Bourne for not surrendering the anchor he had seized. The lesson Thomas Twisden took away from the case was simple: "[W]hen it appears that they have jurisdiction . . . the court takes [a] difference where they commit without cause"—as Zouche arguably did when he would make no return—"and when they commit according to maritime laws."[81] The point of bearing down on the Cinque Ports, which governed the major points of entry along the south coast, was not to destroy a distinct authority, but to supervise its use.

In teaching lessons to lesser magistrates like Zouche, King's Bench showed the last and most important of the characteristics common to these writs: demands for action. As we saw in the previous chapter, the court had three ways to compel obedience. One was to issue the writ multiple times. Later writs tended to go forth with subpoena clauses in them, typically threatening to charge the writ's recipient £40 for nonreturn of an alias, or £80 for a pluries. But amounts could vary, and it was probably a mark of the court's anger when the subpoena clause amounts rose above these norms. The £100 subpoena attached to the alias writ that Zouche received was a powerful statement owing to its rarity. Yet it appears that such subpoenas were never enforced. No sign survives in Exchequer files that a subpoena was ever collected in the seventeenth century. Commentators as early as the fifteenth century suggested that subpoenas, in Chancery and beyond, were not collectable but were included in writs only to provoke fear in the recipient.[82]

If so, King's Bench had other means for inspiring obedience. Foremost was attachment for contempt when successive writs, including those with subpoena clauses, went unanswered. Contempt process typically required someone to swear that one or more writs had been served.[83] A King's Bench attorney explained the procedure. It was the custom, he said, for the court to grant an alias "with a pain" on affidavit of service of the first writ. But if the court preferred, they might even skip the alias and pluries writs and move straight to process of attachment for contempt.[84] Another approach was to impose amercements on offenders, with or without contempt process. These often began as *nisi* orders and, where the recalcitrant remained so, concluded with peremptory orders imposing fines running from 40s. to 200 marks.[85] Threats of this kind usually worked where other threats failed: return of writs quickly followed.[86] The court might even fine those who made a return that was egregiously bad, such as when the respondent claimed immunity from the court's process.[87]

Whether one made a contemptuously bad return or made none at all, King's Bench developed technologies of jurisdiction that showed what obedience to its demands entailed and what disobedience might mean to those who dared.[88] Having captured the prerogative for their own use, the justices had made themselves supreme, making all others so many lesser jurisdictions.

A Prerogative Writ's Ambit: Social and Geographical Range

Where might habeas corpus be sent, and to whom might it apply? Habeas corpus could be used by any subject of the king. As we consider how and why habeas corpus went out across the empire to be used by Englishmen and non-Englishmen alike, we shall understand just how broad the category of "subject" could be. For now, let us consider the most basic elements of the writ's ambit: its social and geographical range.

Costs of any litigation could be high, and might curb access to judicial process for those of modest means. Figuring out just how high costs were for using habeas corpus *ad subjiciendum* is not easy given the paucity of discussion about its use in practice manuals and the difficulty of finding attorneys' or barristers' papers with information on the subject. One attorney in 1628 reported his fees for habeas process running at nearly £1 7s.[89] Perhaps because he was an especially eminent member of the bar, Heneage Finch's fee book shows a charge of £5 for six appearances in the Upper Bench in Michaelmas 1656 on behalf of Robert Green.[90] By the time he represented William Cole in early 1671, when Finch was attorney general and thus one of the most sought-after lawyers in the land, his fees came to £11.[91]

Good legal advice has never been cheap, but the cost of counsel was only the beginning. Prisoners might have faced clerical costs, for instance, to pay clerks in the Crown Office for writing the writ, entering orders for issuance and return in the rulebooks, enrolling the return when it came back into the court's offices, and filing it and recording the result. For one who was bailed, these clerical costs might run from 4s. to more than 10s. in all.[92] If habeas corpus was used to bring one into court to plead a royal pardon, a prisoner might need 13s. or more to pay the clerks.[93] Even with lawyers and clerks paid, the bill was still not settled. Given that habeas corpus moved bodies around, there might be fees for carriage, too. In 1622, Francis Oliver paid over £3 to be brought from the porter's lodge of the Council of Wales, at Ludlow, in Shropshire.[94] Even carriage from nearby Hertfordshire for two prisoners cost 30s. in 1638, though it appears that the prisoners did not have to pay the bill.[95]

The court could and did moderate fees, or even waive them altogether.[96] There is some indication, for example, that fees were charged in full for the writ only when used in the *ad faciendum* form, since it was for private pleadings, while for the *ad subjiciendum* writ, which was at the suit of the king, fees were not charged.[97] This was the position taken by Justice Sir Thomas Twisden in the 1660s, who said the sheriff of Norwich should bring up his prisoners on an *ad subjiciendum* writ "at his peril," whether or not his fees had been paid, because that writ was "of the Crown Side."[98] Other fees might be waived, too, especially for those admitted to use the writ *in forma pauperis.* Even an accused traitor might be allowed to proceed without fees, as Cecilia and Richard. Hames did in 1706.[99]

Did waiving carriage or clerical fees mean that there was full access to the benefits of habeas corpus, even for the poorest?[100] Probably not. But the fact that arrow makers, bodice makers, porters, pinners, plasterers, prostitutes, apprentices, fishermen, common sailors, and those simply called "laborers" used the writ by the hundreds suggests that cost was not a high barrier to its use.[101] That Elizabeth Whitten used habeas corpus in 1714, after she was jailed by Middlesex JPs for leaving three children chargeable to the parish and for refusing to wear the special badge that all who received poor relief were supposed to wear, suggests that costs were low, or even nonexistent.[102]

Habeas corpus was socially diffuse. Its geographical diffusion arose from the success King's Bench achieved in using attachments for contempt and other means to get jailers everywhere to return the writ. Such practices were particularly important when confronting special jurisdictions that were not normally required to return writs from the courts in Westminster Hall. A story like Francis Hunnyngs's—in which the court jailed a jailer to inspire obedience—indicates how England, though a single kingdom, was covered by a patchwork of jurisdictional peculiarities marked out by special privileges that sometimes posed problems. For instance, the Cinque Ports possessed distinctive institutions with particular privileges that had been granted in order that places so exposed to potential danger might largely govern themselves.[103] But the greatest of these privileged places, created by charters granting them a semi-autonomous status, were the counties palatine: Durham, Lancaster, and Chester.[104]

As palatine lords, successive bishops of Durham had their own courts, which obviated any need for litigants there to resort to Westminster Hall. Or so the bishops thought. The bishop, like the lord warden of the Cinque Ports, chafed under any attempts to impose on him from without. Only King's Bench—using attachments and writs with subpoena clauses—would make him yield. In 1626, habeas corpus was sent to Durham on behalf of Richard Harrison. The bishop's first gambit was to ignore it, so the court sent an alias containing the usual £40 subpoena. William Noy, arguing for the prisoner, explained why: "[W]here the king grants liberties"—the bishop's palatine powers— "he does not exclude himself." The law of franchises required that the use of any privileges granted by the king, even palatine privileges, remained the king's to supervise through his justices in King's Bench. While counsel for the bishop accepted the inevitable, he asked that a special form of the writ be sent containing language that recognized Durham's unique liberties. Justice Sir John Dodderidge brushed aside such nonsense: King's Bench would not change its "ancient forms and usages" to soothe Durham's wounded jurisdictional pride. Buttressing his argument with an analogy, Dodderidge referred to the sending of habeas corpus to Bordeaux and Calais when they were among the king's dominions.[105]

Using its instruments of enforcement, the justices had explained to the bishop of Durham that habeas corpus went everywhere, to any dominion of the king. The same ideas and practices would promote the writ's movement as these dominions multiplied to become a global empire. The writ's imperial ambit grew from the logic of its English ambit and covered all these distinctive places as if nothing distinguished them, at least where supervision of detention was concerned. In this way, habeas corpus threatened to make an empire—a unified legal zone—out of so many dominions. It failed to do so in the end only because of the realities of geography that contemporary technologies of communication could not overcome; the reluctance of officers who knew that distance might support their obstruction; and statutes made in Westminster and in assemblies around that empire that generated new definitions of what constituted legal detention. But even if distance or legislation limited the writ, the judges' understanding of their sweeping authority when using it never did.

The Equity of the Writ

As Coke's grand statement about the prerogative writs proclaimed, King's Bench could plug any existing gaps in law to right all wrongs. Ensuring that errors were corrected and "justice should be done"—to quote Tompson's unique writ—even where law had not previously provided the means to do so, was the point of the prerogative writs. Montagu's court accepted just this argument on Bourne's behalf, when it agreed with his counsel that if they did not impose on Lord Zouche, Bourne would "have no other remedy."[106]

There was and is another word for this vast authority to do justice, even in the absence of previously existing rules or remedies: equity.[107] To say that the most revered common law writ, which grew up in the chief common law court, was equitable in character might grate against our assumptions about the nature of equity and common law and about the contests between institutions in which each was practiced. No one called habeas corpus an equitable writ. But this should not keep us from considering the ways in which its use was equitable in everything but name. After all, what did the justices mean when they followed "the equity of the cause" to release three Thames fishermen jailed by the High Court of Admiralty for their alleged violation of fishing regulations?[108] King's Bench, led by Chief Justice Fleming, concluded that the Admiralty court had committed sufficiently serious violations of its jurisdiction to justify their release. But Fleming's court went further: the fishermen should be released according to "the equity of the cause."

In 1609, the year before the Thames fishermen's arrest, Thomas Ashe, in a treatise on equity dedicated to Coke, called equity

> an exception of the law of God, or of the law of Reason, from the general rules of the law of man. . . . Equity is a certain proportion or allay,

> upon good occasions, setting aside the common rules of the law, and
> [which] dispenseth with many points of the law: so that it may be called
> a ruled kind of justice, allayed with the sweetness of mercy.

Ashe, like so many of his generation, read Christopher St. German's
Doctor and Student with care. "Equity is a righteousness that considereth
all the particular circumstances of the deed, the which also is tem-
pered with the sweetness of mercy," St. German had written eight decades earlier.[109] Given the other grounds of the decision in the Thames
fishermen's case, common law could have provided all the justification
needed to discharge the prisoners. But in finishing off the matter by
asserting the "equity of the cause," Fleming's court made a broader
claim about habeas corpus, a claim that sat comfortably within Ashe's
definition of equity. The miraculous making of "an exception of the
law of God . . . from the general rules of the law of man" was the key to
the prerogative as well as the heart of equity. Both were held together
in the hands of the justices of King's Bench.

Equity, in the sense that infused the prerogative writs, brings us back
to the king. As Coke explained in Calvin's case, the words "the crown"
signified the doing of justice to maintain peace: "to separate right
from wrong, and the good from the ill." Doing this, he said, arose from
"that capacity of the king . . . endued with endowments as well of the
soul as of the body, and thereby able to do justice and judgment according to right and equity."[110] The tangency between regality and equity marked the unique capacity of the king to be merciful, his power
to except those who did wrong from the rigors of the law. Hale called
this "a dispensation" from law.[111] Coke, Hale, and others followed the
most august of authorities: Sir John Fortescue, chief justice of King's
Bench in the fifteenth century, called equity that "indulgence above
what is just, for human nature always craves for pardon." Such indulgence was required because "often written law lies dead under a covering of words and the prince by equity arouses its vital spirit."[112] What
court could have better claim to exercise this royal capacity to ensure
that law lived than King's Bench, the court that was not only closest
to the king, but as Fleming, Popham, Montagu, and their peers frequently explained, was the king himself?

We traditionally see Coke as the foe of non–common law jurisdictions, especially of the equity used in Chancery. Certainly, there was a

great flare-up between Chancery and his court when he presided in King's Bench, a flare-up fueled by writs of habeas corpus. But there was also personal rancor and institutional jealousy at work in that dispute.[113] Coke had actually worked closely with Lord Chancellor Ellesmere for years, defining and executing royal policy and overseeing the operation of English law. For his part, Ellesmere, like most of his contemporaries, found in common law a fundamentally equitable impulse. This was appropriate, as Ellesmere noted:

> [C]ommon right standeth not only in the strict right and extremity of law . . . but rather is doing right according to conscience. And the judges of the common law themselves do almost every day extend their discretion to stay and mitigate the right and strictness of the common law, and in so doing they do well.[114]

Edward Hake, writing in the last years of Elizabeth's reign, put the same point more bluntly: "[T]he common law might seem to consist most upon equity." There was no shame in saying this. To the contrary: "I would ask any man what discredit it can be unto our common law that the rules and maxims thereof are to be guided, expounded, and directed by equity?"[115]

According to Hake, this expounding by equity applied not only to the oft-discussed need to plumb the equity of a statute, but to all aspects of the common law's use.

> In all cases where the law hath not provided an express or special writ or action according to the material circumstance of a man's case, but hath a general writ or action whereunto the wrong or cause of suit touching the substance or generality thereof may be referred: I say, in all such cases, it is allowed unto a man to take his remedy by the general writ.[116]

Hake's language seems to presage Coke's later words in Bagge's case that "no wrong or injury, either public or private, can be done but that it shall be (here) reformed or punished by due course of law."[117] Allowing the kind of remedy that Coke identified was just what the justices of King's Bench did in creating and extending the prerogative writs, especially habeas corpus and mandamus.

Ideas like these constitute equity's conceptual aspect: ideas associated with the provision of mercy, attention to the specifics of every case, and the imperative that all judgments fulfill the laws of God and nature. Pursuing such ideas in practice was to open "the hidden righteousness" of the grounds of law.[118] But there was another aspect of equity: the institutions and processes through which such ideas worked. We often map the courts of early modern England into two provinces—equity and common law—that occupy two continents separated by seas of jealousy and suspicion. But as we have seen, equity, as a way of thinking about the nature and provision of justice, infused common law. The more we try to find a distinction between equity and common law in practice, the more that distinction eludes us.[119]

Chancery, the Privy Council and the conciliar courts, and the Court of Exchequer on its English side: all followed equity.[120] But in an age when the chief justices of the common law generally sat in the Privy Council and in the Court of Star Chamber; when leading barristers argued as much before the chancellor as before either common law bench; and when the personnel of these courts lived and worked cheek-by-jowl, we should not be surprised to learn that they talked to one another and even unobtrusively acquired an idea here or co-opted a usage there across a divide more apparent in our minds than in theirs. As we saw in Chapter 2, this very tendency toward silent borrowing probably explains much of the salient language in the writ of habeas corpus itself. This is not to say that conflict did not occur between institutions of equity and of common law: early modern institutions were led by ambitious people, keen to extend their authority. But we should not mistake personal conflicts for ideological ones.

The most famous institutional conflict between equity and common law was less a clash between law and equity than a clash between Coke and Ellesmere. This concerned Richard Glanvill, who had won a judgment in King's Bench in a dispute over a jewel sale. But the chancellor, in his own court, made a decree against Glanvill in the same contest; he then jailed Glanvill in the Fleet when he disobeyed Chancery's decree. King's Bench released Glanvill on habeas corpus, leading to further imprisonment orders by Lord Chancellor Ellesmere. Coke's court sent four further writs, but Glanvill was remanded after the return of each as discussions of the validity of these returns wore on.[121] What Coke insisted on, and Ellesmere resented, was that his court should have the last word. Nothing was said during this spat about the propri-

ety of equity as a body of principles nor as a particular institutional setting.[122]

If we pull back from this dispute to take in the whole of Coke's tenure in King's Bench from 1613 to 1616, we can see quite clearly in his
actions, if not always in his words, the respect Coke maintained for the
chancellor's jurisdiction, even while he objected to the chancellor's efforts to impose Chancery decrees against common law judgments in
specific instances. Of nineteen writs of habeas corpus *ad subjiciendum*
and one *ad faciendum* sent for prisoners held by the chancellor's orders
during the years Coke led King's Bench, one resulted in discharge, two
resulted in orders to bail, and the remainder ended in orders to remand the prisoners concerned.[123] It is hard to see in such results a general attack on the chancellor's imprisonment powers.

Nonetheless, Ellesmere felt threatened, and for good reason. In
another context, Ellesmere had praised the common law judges for
"extend[ing] their discretion to stay and mitigate the right and strictness of the common law" in some cases. But he saw danger, too:

> The judges of the King's Bench and Common Pleas have of late years
> taken upon them as chancellors to make orders in equity, according to
> their own discretions, not regarding nor standing upon the strict rules
> of law . . . ; and if any such orders so made by them be disobeyed, they
> award writs of attachment and imprison the parties for disobeying and
> contempt of their orders, and so confound the distinct jurisdictions
> of common law and of equity, challenging and taking both to them-
> selves.[124]

Perhaps Ellesmere was thinking again of Coke's grand gesture in his
report of Bagge's case. Whether or not those precise claims motivated
this reflection, Ellesmere appreciated how King's Bench had recast its
sphere of competence over the previous two decades by using the prerogative writs. He understood that King's Bench now exercised equity
in the conceptual sense by using the tools of equity in the institutional
sense: judicial action on the prerogative writs was enforced by borrowing practices of attachment and imprisonment for contempt that
were used in courts of equity. The problem was not that common law
thought ill of equity. If anything, common law loved equity so well that
it threatened to smother it in its embrace.

In what ways might we say that habeas corpus *ad subjiciendum,* as used by Popham, then by Fleming, was equitable? Let us begin with process before returning to ideas.

Two aspects of process running in parallel with, if not derived from, equity—as we saw in Chapter 2—relate to two expressions in the writ: *"ut dicitur"* (as it is said) and *"hoc nullatenus omittatis periculo"* (this in no wise omit upon the peril that may befall). The first concerned the telling of stories to gain the writ, and the second, the insistence of King's Bench that recipients of the writ should do as commanded. Habeas corpus is a judicial writ, issued when the justices had been convinced by a story that they should examine more closely the circumstances of a person's imprisonment. The telling of tales, and the discretion of the judges in deciding to heed the moral of such tales, was quite like the process used in most courts of equity. The Privy Council's interest was normally sparked by a petition from a subject complaining of a wrong that required the king's attention. The other conciliar courts also operated by bill procedure, as it was known. Such bills, like King's Bench affidavits, conformed to a dramatic narrative structure meant to win the court's agreement that the petitioner should be an object of its power to provide relief.[125] The stories in these bills were punctuated by forceful adjectives and adverbs, small details meant to evoke a feeling of the complainant's pain, all constructed on a narrative arc that could lead to only one conclusion: a wrong had been done that only the court could right. The "prayer" for habeas corpus, made on motion justified by such a story, whether or not told in an affidavit, was nothing if not like bill process used in equity.

Once a good tale inspired one or more of the justices in King's Bench to launch the writ, the justices demanded that the writ come back with a body and an account of that body's arrest and detention. By the mid-1590s, the court had begun consistently adding a warning phrase that its recipient should do as demanded, at his peril. One form of peril had a clear connection to practice in equity: the insertion in alias and pluries writs of the kind of subpoena clauses found in Chancery writs of the same name.[126] While rarely if ever collected, the subpoena clause set up the next stage in the process whereby the court imposed compliance: the issuance of attachments for contempt that might lead to fines and even the imprisonment of offenders. As Ellesmere understood, and as Francis Hunnyngs knew so well, such practices were no longer exclusive to courts of equity by the early seventeenth century. But they were sufficiently imitative that King's Bench's use of them, according to Ellesmere, "confound[ed] the distinct jurisdictions of common law and of equity."[127] In King's Bench as in Chancery, attachments would issue on an affidavit that the writ had been served and had not been answered. Crown Side rulebooks show that King's Bench began to make particularly vigorous use of this procedure in late 1604 and continuing through 1605–1606 and beyond: just when some of the most interesting developments on mandamus and habeas corpus were afoot.[128] By 1632, one could claim that such process was "the custom of the court."[129] Through the prerogative writs and procedural innovations connected to their development at the opening of the seventeenth century, equity had been domesticated for use at common law. This made it possible for King's Bench to manifest the king's prerogative concern for the liberty of his subjects, thereby extending both the protection and mercy peculiar to his semi-divine office. *Non sine sole iris.*

The Prerogative against Itself?

Imperious, yet a refined aesthete, Thomas Howard, Earl of Arundel, privy councilor and earl marshal, was the sort of nobleman we might say was more royalist than the king. We might expect the head of the court of the earl marshal to be an ardent defender of the prerogative.[130] Except when he was not. After all, Arundel and those who served him affronted "the monarchical prerogative and regality" of the king when they affronted the justices of King's Bench.[131]

The trouble began in September 1630, when Robert Jones sued articles of the peace against Thomas Thompson, one of Arundel's servants, without the earl's permission. Arundel took this attack on Thompson as an attack on his honor and that of his court. So he ordered Jones imprisoned "until you shall receive further order from me to the contrary." In November, King's Bench issued habeas corpus on Jones's behalf. Thomas More—who, as the marshal of the king's household, held Jones—ultimately returned the writ, explaining that he had already discharged Jones from custody. King's Bench then fined More 100 marks for making a return that did not answer the writ's central demand: that he present a body. Worse, this return was false. Jones had never been released, but had instead been transferred into the care of John Coxe, a royal messenger.[132]

Late the following January, another writ issued, this time to Coxe. Again, Thomas More made the return, now offering the marginally better explanation that Jones had been imprisoned for his contempt of the court of the earl marshal. Upon this second return, the justices of King's Bench quickly discharged Jones. Then, to the astonishment of the justices, Coxe attempted to arrest Jones again in full view of the court. Coxe now learned the lesson Francis Hunnyngs had learned a generation earlier. The angry justices jailed Coxe for contempt.

Edward Littleton, a prominent lawyer who made notes on this spat between that part of the king's authority wielded by his earl marshal and that part employed by his justices in King's Bench, identified three offenses against the prerogative by Arundel's minions. First was the arrest of Jones by Coxe after he had been "delivered by the king"— speaking through the justices of King's Bench—on his habeas corpus. Second was the apparent release of Coxe from his commitment for contempt: how, and by whom, we do not know. The last were Arundel's orders to arrest "the king's ministers"—the lawyers and clerks who had prepared and presented Jones's case and served the writs— "for doing the command of the king."[133] Littleton contended that all three deeds demeaned the prerogative. In language that could have come straight from Coke's report of Bagge's case, Littleton suggested that "[i]n all monarchies, there must be a power to examine all other[s] [and] to assume the hearing of any cause, to correct all errors, and to redress wrongs."[134] For Littleton, as for so many others, this power belonged to King's Bench, the proper seat from which to pronounce the prerogative.

Or so he thought. With the court's Hilary term over, Arundel brought the matter before the Privy Council, where Sir William Jones, the justice of King's Bench who had apparently been the principal actor in jailing Arundel's servants, was chastised "for speaking somewhat too plainly" of Arundel's court. But Sir William Jones and his fellow judges held firm, declaring that if Arundel should imprison Robert Jones again, they would release the man once more. In arguments that echoed Thomas Fleming's a generation earlier, they explained that their court was the place where "all the kings were wont to sit . . .

[and] where the judges do in so high a degree represent his majesty's person." They readily admitted Arundel's social superiority. But they would never concede the superiority of his tribunal. Arundel's servants were released from their imprisonment, and though he proposed that commissioners should be appointed to settle remaining differences, nothing more seems to have come of that idea.[135]

In the contest between the court of the earl marshal and the court of King's Bench, one claim to wield the prerogative confronted another. When challenged, the justices responded as they had for three decades: by jailing the jailer who had shown his contempt. Arundel pushed back, summoning the justices of King's Bench before king and Council. But the justices stood their ground, insisting that it was they who spoke in the king's voice; that it was their honor, and the king's prerogative, that were threatened by Arundel's behavior, not the other way around. It is unclear who prevailed.[136] But the dispute suggests how, for all the justices' capture of the prerogative, and for all their success in channeling this power into habeas corpus, their control could never be complete. By invoking the prerogative, the justices had claimed to occupy the preeminent position in the state so that they might determine who was or was not imprisoned according to law. In doing so, the justices determined what counted as law, even when great nobles chafed against their commands. To appreciate what this meant when they succeeded and when they did not, we must consider more closely how they used habeas corpus: how they used the prerogative for the subject's liberty.

PART II

Using Habeas Corpus

We turn here to how judges used the writ. How did they make judgments? How did their judgments make a jurisdiction for King's Bench, thereby making the jurisdiction of all other courts? How did their judgments make what counted as liberties?

Habeas jurisprudence was characterized by principles rather than rules, making it an all-but-equitable instrument in the judges' hands. They demanded all kinds of evidence, from far beyond the writ's return, to satisfy their demand for information about any subject's detention. In the early seventeenth century, the court's judgments trumped those of virtually all other magistrates. The writ's vigor persisted during the Civil War of the 1640s, and would live on through the eighteenth century as the justices monitored detentions made by military authorities, violent husbands, and officers of empire.

Judgments on habeas corpus also set the bounds of liberties. Many notions of liberty flowed in and around the writ. Christian liberty—as much concerned with obligation as with unimpeded will—echoed through ideas about liberties possessed by individuals or by corporate bodies. By the mid-seventeenth century and beyond, new languages of liberty appeared, expressing aspirations that the law could never entirely realize, as law's critics showed. Nonetheless, legal liberties were available to all subjects, "natural" and "alien." Ideas about subjecthood made the writ and the liberties it protected available to all sorts of people, in all sorts of places.

CHAPTER 4

Making Judgments

Laughing in church has long been frowned on. Nobody doubted that Margaret Symonds disrupted divine service one summer's Sunday in her small Suffolk parish with her "loud laughing and talking." But could she be imprisoned for it?

Yes, concluded the two justices of the peace who jailed Symonds in 1629. The statute seemed clear enough, and they followed it closely. The act of 1 Mary, session 2, c. 3 defined an "offender of preachers" as anyone who by "word, fact, act, or deed, maliciously or contemptuously," disturbed anyone authorized to preach. Though the act required only two people to testify to the deed, four gave evidence of Symonds's rudeness. This satisfied the JPs that, according to the act's terms, they should imprison her for three months.

All this happened during the long vacation after Trinity term, but getting a writ of habeas corpus was easy enough. No justices were then sitting in Westminster Hall, so the writ commanded that the return should be made to Justice Sir James Whitelocke at his home in Buckinghamshire. It was probably there that Whitelocke ordered Margaret bailed, pending further discussion before all the justices once they reconvened in October.

When Margaret appeared in King's Bench on the second day of Michaelmas, Chief Justice Sir Nicholas Hyde wondered whether the statute, made during the Marian restoration of Catholicism, had been repealed by the Act of Uniformity's restoration of Protestantism in 1559. Certainly those parts of the statute outlawing disruptions of the now illegal Roman mass had been erased. But its other provisions remained alive in law, though as the justices now used the act, they might not be for much longer. Having already freed Margaret on bail, the justices now discharged her entirely.[1] Why?

All agreed that Margaret had laughed in church. But her case remained surrounded by factual, and thus legal, doubts. What made Margaret laugh? Was the sermon so bad that she could not help herself? Or was laughter a sign of her contempt for what she considered dubious doctrine? The return to her writ did not say. What of the actions and the justifications for those actions of the JPs who jailed her? They seem to have obeyed all statutory commands—about the nature of the wrongs covered, the number of witnesses needed to convict, and the length of imprisonment—but had they properly explained their adherence to these requirements? Without answers to these questions in the return, the justices of King's Bench could not know whether the JPs had "observed the statute of the first of Mary."

There was no mention of precedents, no analogizing to ostensibly similar cases. Instead, the justices worked from what they knew about Margaret's actions as reported in the return to the writ, and from what they declared were Parliament's intentions in making a statute to punish the disturbance of preachers. The act's preamble explained its passage to preserve "tranquility and peace." Some thought Margaret's laughter had damaged the peace. Not Justice Whitelocke, who declared that "laughing is no such disturbance as intended by the statute." True enough: for all the words in the act, nothing there mentioned laughter. Whitelocke then went further, adding that the statute "intended" only "opposing of doctrine" as its target.[2] Nothing in the statute spoke of doctrine. It simply addressed "disturbances." Whitelocke read so far into the act's intentions that he had left the text behind. No one seemed to mind as they sent Margaret home.

To what, if any, theory of jurisprudence might we ascribe Whitelocke's claims and the court's judgment? The justices of King's Bench appreciated that Margaret's case turned both on facts about her alleged wrong and on facts by which the legal meaning of her wrong might be judged: in this case, facts staking out the jurisdictional bounds around JPs acting under a particular statute. To police those bounds, the justices ranged across a vast jurisprudential space, larger than any rules about facts admissible on habeas corpus and how they were to be obtained and weighed. But this is not to say that the justices did not honor certain legal principles: that all lesser magistrates must answer to them and that those answers must contain plenty of details. Based on their reading of those details, the justices then made the judgments that mattered, perhaps by following ideas of the sort applied here, by which the terms of penal statutes were narrowly construed.[3] Margaret was free, two Suffolk JPs had been corrected, a chastened Suffolk clergyman may have been angered, and a parliamentary statute had been left in tatters. And Margaret's release was no aberration, as other judgments in imprisonments ordered on the same statute show: clearly, the justices did not care much for imprisonment orders made to punish trouble in church, whatever the statute's stated intentions to pursue "peace and tranquility."[4] Even if the justices never said as much, their deeds spoke loudly enough.

Judgments like this did not just happen; they were made. Judges, not rules, made them. From the beginning of the seventeenth century to the end of the eighteenth, the principles on which judges made such decisions generated increasing judicial confidence. The writ's equity prompted a search for facts well beyond the return, and encouraged the justices to do much more than declare a prisoner remanded, bailed, or discharged when they made their judgments. By negotiating settlements, by constraining—sometimes undermining—the statutes or customs on which other magistrates acted, and by chastising those who wrongfully detained others, the justices defined what counted as jurisdiction and what counted as liberties.

The judges' flexibility, creativity, and widening purview were apparent in decisions about all types of detention. Through their deeds more than their words, successive chief justices—Hale, Holt, and Mansfield—broadened the principles that legitimated a widening oversight of detention in all forms. In the 1670s, the writ would begin to manage troubled families by correcting abusive husbands. After 1689, habeas corpus would be used aggressively to monitor detentions ordered in the name of the state's safety. In the mid-eighteenth century, the writ would oversee other forms of detention that involved no wrongdoing: apprenticeship, slavery, and naval impressment. The judges would continually allow anyone wrongly held by another to use the writ. Until the 1790s. The capacity of judges to make judgments thus traces a clear narrative arc, rising across the seventeenth century, peaking in the third quarter of the eighteenth century, and falling steeply from the 1780s. A change in court personnel, sharpening anxieties in a nation at war with a revolutionary regime in France, and problems managing an expanding empire constrained the judges' power from that time forward.

The Writ's Equity: The Return

The key to making judgments about infinitely variable circumstances was the consideration of details about why, when, how, and by whom people were imprisoned. Habeas corpus was an equitable device in all but name, enabling action in response to the particulars of a given circumstance rather than imposing obedience to a set of rules inscribed in precedents.[5] As Thomas Ashe put it,

> [E]quity is to be practiced in particular facts, which daily fall out, and have not certain line and square for them in the laws already made, so that we must be forced to deliver our judgments in them according to certain circumstances applied as nearly as we can to the principles of our law.[6]

There were two places to obtain the "particular facts" that made such work possible: in the return to the writ, which we will examine here, and from beyond the return, which we will explore shortly.

In the decades around 1600, returns to habeas corpus lengthened as greater detail was required. We can trace this in the declining number of returns that did not name the jailing authority, the cause of imprisonment, or both.[7] Why did this increase in detail occur? Part of the answer concerns the behavior of lesser magistrates, especially JPs, who were better guided in the writing of their commitment orders by books like William Lambarde's *Eirenarcha,* of 1581. It also arose from the justices' attitudes as a growing number of people were imprisoned on statutes covering an array of misdemeanors. King's Bench demanded details in order to ascertain whether the statute involved had been followed.

What did greater or lesser specificity mean for the likelihood of release? It depended on which information was included or omitted. Including or omitting the name of the jailing authority seemed to matter very little. Charting release rates across Elizabeth's reign, we find that the likelihood of release on returns that did not specify the jailing authority matched that on those returns that did name the magistrate.[8] Given that most writs in this period concerned felony, and given that felony tended to produce the shortest returns, that most of these prisoners had been committed by justices of the peace, and that these writs were more about sending prisoners to trial than about reviewing earlier proceedings, the absence of information identifying the officer ordering imprisonment was largely irrelevant to decision-making.

Vagueness about the alleged wrong, however, did make a difference: release rates on returns that did not name the cause of commitment were always higher than on returns that did. But the disparity in results between those that did and did not include a cause narrowed as the number of writs omitting it declined.[9] Three points follow from this. First, fewer returns in the decades around 1600 omitted what was increasingly seen as the most important information the return should contain. Second, as the number of writs returned without a cause fell, the disparity in release rates between those with and without that information decreased, signaling a growing understanding about the occasions when such information might be omitted. Finally, this explains why many prisoners whose returns omitted one or both of these pieces of information were remanded, whereas others with seemingly identical returns were not: details gained from beyond the return clearly continued to shape judicial decisions.

Nonetheless, the justices increasingly demanded "sufficiency" and "certainty" in the statement of wrongs in the returns sent to them. Sufficiency generally concerned statements about the wrong committed by the accused and the substance of a magistrate's claims to act as he did. Certainty concerned the clarity with which this was explained. Let us consider each.

Insufficiency in a return might arise in a number of ways. The most egregious derived from insolence, a jailer's claims to be beyond the purview of King's Bench.[10] A variation was to offer a poor excuse for not bringing a body into court: perhaps a prisoner's alleged sickness or previous release.[11] The most important form of insufficiency, however, concerned returns with no cause at all. This has traditionally been framed as a problem of "executive" imprisonment. But the matter was considerably more complex than this anachronistic language suggests. An imprisonment warrant without a cause in it made by an individual, no matter how powerful, was almost always reversed, as when Queen's Bench bailed Thomas Manock, jailed by the warrant of Attorney General Sir Edward Coke.[12] But King's Bench generally permitted both the Privy Council and Parliament to make such returns, though the power of the Privy Council to do so would be contested by the 1620s, and all but ended by 1660, even as Parliament's tendency to act without supervision by habeas corpus would grow.

Ignorance and inattention explain more insufficient returns than insolence, especially given the earlier allowance of vagueness.[13] Until the late sixteenth century, a prisoner might be remanded or committed to the Marshalsea after a return stating only that he had been imprisoned by a JP "for certain causes."[14] Even as late as 1631, King's Bench would remand prisoners on return of a JP's warrant that gave no cause.[15] In general, such results dwindled over the seventeenth century. Thus King's Bench asked the Earl of Denbigh in 1640 to amend the return made of his order to put William Brice in Oxford's jail, which had contained no cause. When he failed to do so, Brice was discharged.[16] Men less grand than Denbigh also thought themselves above having to explain their actions, as when a Middlesex JP returned that Thomas Kedway had been jailed "by command," without further explanation. Saying that William Sparrow had been imprisoned for "notorious misdemeanors" was little better. Both were bailed.[17] Jailing someone for refusing to give security for good behavior without explaining the reason why sureties had been demanded—or saying nothing more than "for especial cause of examination"—was just as dubious.[18] By the mid-seventeenth century, most magistrates seem to have learned better than to make such returns. But even in the decades after 1660, insufficiencies of this most basic kind continued to appear on occasion, and almost always led to bail or discharge.[19]

More often, a judgment of insufficiency arose not from the absence of an alleged wrong, but from powers to commit that had been omitted from the return or that simply did not exist. Most often, this arose from a failure to heed the demands of statute. As the court put it in 1730, paraphrasing Holt a generation earlier, "[I]t is very dangerous to let people depart from the words of the act, where these special authorities are given."[20] Thus while Charles Hamand could be imprisoned for refusing to pay for the maintenance of his illegitimate child, the relevant statute required two JPs to make the order rather than the one who did so in Hamand's case.[21] Yorkshire commissioners of sewers may have felt that the "disgraceful speeches" against their clerk by Matthew Brunge constituted an affront to the "authority committed to them by their commission." But nothing in their statutory powers permitted them to imprison him for this reason and Brunge was discharged.[22] Commissioners of bankrupts were especially high-handed, as when they imprisoned John Ayres, in 1634, until he should "conform himself unto our said authority." Ayres, too, was bailed, then discharged.[23]

In returns like that to Ayres's writ, we hear how insufficiency and uncertainty often ran together. Uncertainty arose less from a failure to possess power to imprison than from a lack of clarity in describing the use of that power. To make judgments, the justices needed facts: a cause of imprisonment "certainly returned."[24] But what was certainty? One struggles to find a definition in justices' words. Often, the judges said that less of it was required in a return to habeas corpus than in other legal process. "A return differs from other judicial acts . . . and such certainty is not required in returns, but suffices if the court may by the return be apprised of the substance of the matter," explained Chief Justice Montagu.[25] But the problem remained: how much was enough? Answers varied. Within the wide bounds of that variation, the justices made an equitable habeas jurisprudence that followed the facts of cases rather than rules.[26]

Certainty, like sufficiency, often turned on statute. Thomas Crompton, committed by an Essex JP in 1602 for violating a Henrician firearms statute, was bailed when his return failed to speak to all the requirements of that act: to the location of his offence or to whether he held lands of less than £100 annual value, which would bar firearms use.[27] The College of Physicians imprisoned Elizabeth Clark in 1604 for her "ill practice of physic," a matter they were empowered to decide according to the charter and statute that gave them their being. But their warrant did not describe the variety of her malpractice—statute limited the College's oversight to certain matters only—nor did it mention the place where it occurred: their purview extended only within seven miles of London. Clark was discharged.[28]

King's Bench released Richard Clarke from Stafford jail in 1694 after his conviction on a recent statute for poaching deer in Needwood forest. The warrant ordered him jailed for one year and until he should be set in the pillory. His careful lawyer noted that this warrant might permit a perpetual imprisonment: the jailer could wait until any time after the appointed year to give him his time in the pillory, before which he could not be released. Well might we guess that the committing magistrate had meant to follow the act precisely: jailing him for one year, during which he would be pilloried. The return was sufficient, expressing the correct authority in the circumstances, but as a logical matter, it was imprecise in a way that left open the possibility of a perpetual punishment. Clarke was discharged.[29]

Authority for imprisonment orders did not rest only on statute. Failure to quote words of contempt was a common form of uncertainty. All courts of record might imprison for contempt, but King's Bench insisted on being the final judge of what constituted contempt, for which it needed the words concerned. Samuel Codd, jailed by the High Commission in 1615 for refusing to pay an alimony order and "for speaking *diversa opprobriosa verba*," was bailed on a return that did not quote his opprobrious words.[30] The Privy Council, too, could be corrected in such cases. In late 1628, London merchant Richard Chambers was imprisoned "for having used insolent and contemptuous words" before the Council. But because Chambers's words were not detailed in the return, King's Bench asked that the return be amended. When the request was ignored, the justices ordered him bailed, and later discharged from bail. One year later, when Chambers was again jailed for more insolence in Star Chamber, his return came back full of the words he had spoken, and King's Bench agreed that he deserved punishment.[31]

Typically, a finding of insufficiency or uncertainty meant immediate bail or discharge. But in cases like Chambers's, the court might allow the returning officer to try again. The earliest orders to amend returns appear in 1595, but they remained rare until the 1610s.[32] An order to amend clearly expressed sympathy for, and perhaps aided, other jurisdictions and their imprisonment orders. This may have been the point. When distinctive jurisdictions, such as Berwick-upon-Tweed, returned claims of exemption from all writs from Westminster Hall, an amendment order became the means for teaching them otherwise. With some arm-twisting—fines and attachment orders—officers in places like Berwick soon learned to provide better answers.[33]

Amendment orders also allowed King's Bench to become better acquainted with other courts' practices.[34] Non–common law courts, places claiming exemption from orders emanating out of Westminster Hall, or novelties, like commissioners of accounts in the 1640s, raised the greatest possibilities for mutual incomprehension between King's Bench and the jurisdictions it supervised.[35] Amendment orders enabled a conversation by which better understanding might be achieved. Jurisdictional pride prevented some tribunals from entering into that conversation, and refusal to comply could only be met with an order to release the prisoner.[36] But compliance sometimes ended with orders to remand, that is, with the original commitment confirmed. When Robert Melvyn was jailed in May 1628, the keeper of the Gatehouse initially returned that he had been ordered by Lord Conway, the king's principal secretary, to keep Melvyn "close prisoner . . . until you shall receive further order." Perhaps because the return was made less than two months after the controversy about royal imprisonment orders that had occasioned the Petition of Right, King's Bench found that return "insufficient" and fined the keeper £10 for making it. At the same time, the justices ordered the return amended. The new return presented a new warrant of commitment explaining that Melvyn had been detained on suspicion of treason. Melvyn was now remanded on that brief, yet sufficient and certain, return.[37]

Since amend orders amounted to a second chance to justify imprisonment, prisoners usually opposed them. Typically, when a return arrived, prisoner's counsel moved to file it, especially if it appeared insufficient. Filing made the return a matter of record, which typically prevented further modification.[38] Counsel for John Beaumont, who had been imprisoned by Bedfordshire quarter sessions for refusing to pay a £20 fine and for his reproachful words to a JP, moved to file the return containing this information, perhaps expecting that the absence of Beaumont's words would be fatal to the return. The court ordered the return filed, but this did not stop counsel on the other side from proposing that it be amended. The court refused because an amendment "could not be admitted after the filing," and Beaumont was discharged.[39] Crown Side rulebooks are filled with prisoners' motions to file—they were eager to freeze a return's language, then have their counsel pick it apart—as well as counter motions to stay filing. Many contests over the quality of the return were won or lost before its content was even considered.[40] But there were also many ways the court might include matter beyond the return in its deliberations.

The Writ's Equity: Beyond the Return

Perhaps the best known "rule" concerning habeas corpus was that against controverting the return: that one could not challenge the return's factual accuracy.[41] As with the apparent rule against vacation writs, the first statement of this alleged rule appeared in Cokean dicta. While Coke was chief justice in Common Pleas, he opined that a cause of imprisonment stated in a return to habeas corpus "is not traversable": that its truth could not be challenged directly. Why? "[B]ecause there is no person in court to take issue upon that": only the jailer was in court on the return, not the officer who had made the imprisonment order and who would thus be in a position to answer a traverse. What then might a prisoner do if he believed a return was not simply uncertain or insufficient, but untruthful? Coke answered: "[T]he party is put to his action upon the case if the return of the cause be false, or may have a false imprisonment."[42] In other words, the prisoner would have to sue, by a form of trespass, a private action by which the prisoner might have the return voided and receive damages if successful. But no one appears to have pursued such a convoluted process. Let us consider why.

Whether or not this was indeed the rule matters. In the hands of some, a rule forbidding one to question facts in the return except by a separate action became a rule by which judges might be restricted to information in the return. In the words of Justice Sir John Eardley Wilmot in 1758,

> [T]he judges are so bound by the facts set forth in the return . . . that they cannot discharge the person brought up before them, if it shall most manifestly appear to the judges, by the clearest and most undoubted proof, that such return is false in fact, and that the person so brought up is restrained of his liberty by the most unwarrantable means, and in direct violation of law and justice.[43]

Was this so? For all Wilmot's confidence, the judges in 1758 expressed a wide range of views on this point.[44] Their confusion has persisted. Could the judges not discharge prisoners, even when the facts returned appeared untrue? Might they do anything for prisoners by working outside the return? The writ's possibilities hinged on the answers.

Coke's thinking may have arisen in part from the conceptual proximity of habeas corpus and mandamus. In 1615, Coke's court decided what would become the leading case in mandamus, concerning a Plymouth burgess ejected from his office. Coke made two things clear in Bagge's case. First, returns to mandamus had to be "certain" so that the justices might assess the legality of the actions described in them. Second, the only way to impugn the truth of such returns was by an action on the case for false return, of the same kind his dictum on challenging returns to habeas corpus prescribed. Scores, perhaps hundreds, of returns to mandamus were adjudicated this way during the century following. But it was an unwieldy process. Where an urban office lasted only one year—a mayoralty, for instance—the year in question might conclude before the court resolved a contested election.[45]

While the justices tolerated slow process by actions for false return in disputes about custody of office, the stakes were greater in disputes about custody of a body. This probably explains why no evidence has surfaced of actions on the case for false return or false imprisonment to challenge a return to habeas corpus. Evidence survives of a few instances of suits for false imprisonment initiated by former prisoners hoping to win damages after their release by habeas corpus.[46] This might happen years after the fact.[47] But Henry Wilkins, discharged from military custody in 1717, waited only a few days before suing false imprisonment against the grenadiers who had detained him.[48] Either way, using false imprisonment after release had nothing to do with using actions for false imprisonment to impugn a return to habeas corpus before release. Though judges repeatedly said that challenging the "facts" in a return required a separate action, no one seems to have taken that step.[49] It was too slow, and there was no need: the court had better ways to bring before them facts of all kinds, even those contradicting a return.

The apparent rule against controverting the return, like many rules, inspired new modes of proceeding. Judges followed the principles behind the rule—a commitment to decision-making based on well-grounded facts, and to seeing those facts expressed in reliable form—as they generated myriad ways to elicit evidence. Doing so did not entail "breaking" or "bending" the rule, at least not in the way in which we normally discuss rule-bound process and "violations" of it. Rather, it involved reasoning from a central principle—in this case, the principle that valued certainty of the facts that would be used to decide the matter—to new ways of doing things that honored the motivations that generated the rule.[50]

The simplest way to find facts from beyond the return was to ask people in court for information, perhaps in imitation of examination procedures used in civil law, procedures that common law courts increasingly adopted after 1600.[51] In 1611, one Stainforth and two others were jailed by JPs for disturbing a preacher at Sheffield. Once in court, two further facts were offered orally: that Stainforth and his fellows were churchwardens, and that the minister they disturbed was not licensed to preach. They were bailed.[52] This amounted to a confession and avoidance rather than an outright rejection of returned facts: counsel presented new facts in the hope of negating the legal meaning of facts in the return.[53] Confession and avoidance also led to the release of a man named Gardiner, jailed in 1601 for illegal use of a firearm. When brought in by habeas corpus, Gardiner showed that he was acting as a special bailiff at the time of his arrest for illegal weapons possession. Queen's Bench "commanded a plea to be drawn, comprising all this matter." Once done, he confessed these facts, and was released.[54]

Just as counsel might provide useful evidence not mentioned in the return, so too might the court's own officers. In 1682, the justices asked Samuel Astry, the master in the Crown Office and thus the head clerk in King's Bench, to examine the disputed churchwarden's accounts that had been the reason for imprisoning Stephen Burke. Burke was later discharged.[55]

Matter outside the return was also presented in writing, most often by affidavits. Use of written testimony was common in courts of equity and in courts that followed civil law. The usages of such courts influenced, often silently, emerging practices in common law concerning evidence, especially those procedures connected to the prerogative writs.[56] Two prisoners brought into King's Bench in 1648, for instance, were bailed on an insufficient return and on presentation of two "certificates" showing that two others had already confessed to the murder of which they were accused.[57] When the return for one Strudwick stated that he was too ill to bring in from the Fleet prison, affidavits testified to his health. The court, finding assertions in the affidavits more believable than those in the return, ordered him brought in.[58] A few years later, affidavits showed that one Crisp had not committed the highway robbery mentioned in the return to his writ, and he was released.[59]

Affidavits might also be used to argue against bail.[60] And affidavits or oral testimony might provide the means for gaining expert views about whether a person brought in by habeas corpus was indeed a "lunatic." Information of these many kinds, presented orally or in writing, arose in reply to—even in contradiction of—returns. In 1675, referring back to Gardiner's case, Justice Twisden declared that a plaintiff in habeas corpus might be allowed to plead against a return. His court thus decided to accept three affidavits showing the falsehood of a return, thereby making it "traversable . . . though there be no plaintiff and defendant."[61] Twisden had defied Coke's dictum.

How did the justices justify these practices? Because they did not usually attack the rule head on—"breaking" it—but instead redirected its force by generating novel forms of legal process as need dictated. In Gardiner's case, this was done after the return, in the manner of a confession and avoidance. A similar approach was taken after Thomas Swallow's imprisonment by London's corporation for his refusal to serve as an alderman. After filing the return, Swallow's counsel asked to plead to it by introducing the new fact that Swallow had been excused from office by virtue of his royal service as an officer of the mint. The usual objections were made: that this would amount to falsifying the return, which should be done only by a separate action. This prompted a series of new moves by which the justices worked within the rule against controverting the return. The court remanded Swallow, then followed the practice used on writs of prohibition, by which factual claims introduced in writing might be answered in kind.[62] By a writ of privilege, which the court bolstered by sending a writ of mandamus to the City ordering it to excuse Swallow from office, this new factual matter was again presented in court. Then, by issuing a new writ, a new return recognizing these facts was made, and Swallow was discharged.[63]

Another approach to bringing in new, even contrary, factual matter was possible because the return was not on record until filed. As Twisden put it, "[T]here is nothing before us judicially until the return is filed."[64] The return had to be honored only after it had become a matter of record. Until then, and even before the writ issued, anything might be done to adduce facts: witness the amendment of returns prior to filing. The simplest way to explore all available facts without resorting to collateral actions against the return was to do so earlier in the process.

As we saw in Chapter 2, habeas corpus was a writ of right, though not a writ of course: one had to make a case for issuance.[65] This was often done orally, but by at least the 1620s, one might "pray" the writ based on an affidavit. Affidavits, even those filled with heart-wrenching details, might fail to inspire the justices to issue the writ, as Elizabeth Mercer learned in 1722. Her affidavit on behalf of her nephew, Thomas Lauder, failed, despite her thorough account of his conscription into a cavalry unit when he was under fourteen.[66] Thickening affidavit files after 1689 testify to the court's reliance on facts presented by those seeking the writ and by those who made their own affidavits to defeat the writ's issuance. Richard Mitchell used an affidavit to have the writ issued to Solomon Daine, so Daine answered with his own affidavit, which put an end to their battle over Mitchell's wife, Hannah.[67] Process by affidavit prior to and after issuance of habeas corpus thus created an open space over which the justices might range in finding facts and making judgments without any concern about the supposed inviolability of the return.

As reliance on affidavits grew in the eighteenth century, the decision to issue the writ, rather than the determination of what to do upon its return, became the occasion for the most important discussions about facts and their legal meaning. If the justices had any concern about issuing the writ, they might ask to hear further arguments, usually by turning to the jailer or the magistrate who made the detention. This was sometimes done on orders *nisi,* also known as rules to show cause, which took the form that some action would be ordered "unless [*nisi*] cause is shown to the contrary." As mentioned in Chapter 2, orders *nisi* had long been used to perform many kinds of work in habeas corpus.[68] For instance, an order *nisi* might be granted to amend a return.[69] Orders *nisi* might also be used after the return, demanding that unless the jailer showed cause to the contrary, the prisoner would be discharged.[70] In either case, the order *nisi* functioned as a call for facts from beyond the return.

It was a natural extension of such practices to use orders *nisi* to issue the writ. Such orders first appeared in 1601, and perhaps, like orders to amend, reflected the court's respect of other jurisdictions because they allowed the prospective recipient to answer before a writ issued. This may explain why the first surviving order *nisi* to issue the writ concerned a Privy Council imprisonment. Only when there was a failure to show cause did the justices send the writ to the Council's jailer.[71] Other early orders *nisi* likewise involved respect for potential claims of jurisdictional integrity by those who might receive the writ. In 1619, the Duchy of Lancaster—a palatinate, and thus immune to most process from Westminster Hall—received a *nisi* order accompanied with a command that an attorney of the duchy should be notified of the order so that he might make a reply. Apparently he did: no writ issued.[72] Another instance that probably involved this kind of jurisdictional deference concerned Philip Chetwynd, who had been committed to prison by command of Parliament in late 1649. The court sent an order *nisi* to the attorney general, and only issued the writ after he left it unanswered.[73] Orders *nisi* proved important as the writ went out into the empire. The new Supreme Court in Calcutta made explicit its respect for the East India Company when it used an order *nisi* to begin its work on the case of a tax farmer jailed by the Company. Only after the Company ignored the order did the Supreme Court issue its writ for Seroop Chund.[74]

During the eighteenth century, a fundamental shift occurred in what counted as a habeas hearing, with more exploration of facts occurring before the writ issued than after the return. As affidavit use became common after 1689, orders *nisi* to issue the writ and orders to amend returns—two principal methods for seeking additional information from beyond the return—appeared less often. By the 1730s, rulebooks increasingly noted the issuance of writs based on affidavits, signaling that the discussion of facts had moved to the beginning of the process. Many prisoners now had a full review of their imprisonment without the writ ever issuing: habeas corpus without the writ. In such cases, judges were entirely unconstrained by any rule against controverting the return.[75]

These procedural innovations would become ever more important in 1756 as overlapping factors brought new urgency to the court's oversight of detention: the outbreak that May of a vast war fought on multiple seas and continents; the passage of a statute for finding men to fill regiments; the revival of Admiralty authority to find men to fill ships; and the seating that November of Mansfield as chief justice of King's Bench. Five days after his appointment, and acting on information presented in the affidavit of Mary Backas, Mansfield issued his first writ for an impressed sailor, John Backas, who was then discharged from the navy.[76] Similar affidavits were soon sworn for John Dunn, who was then held in the Savoy prison, having been taken up as a prospective soldier. Affidavits for more than a dozen other soldiers soon followed. In Dunn's case and others, King's Bench did not issue habeas corpus, but instead issued a *nisi* order to the keeper of the Savoy and the recruiting commissioners, requiring them to show cause why Dunn should not be discharged. With the agreement of the treasury solicitor—the army's principal lawyer—Dunn was indeed discharged; others soon followed.[77]

Why proceed in this manner, going so far beyond the return that the writ itself had been left behind? The recruiting act, on which these men had been conscripted, had permitted JPs and commissioners of the land tax to serve as commissioners to identify appropriate men for the army: those over seventeen and under forty-five with no known employment nor sufficient property to vote for MPs. The recruiting commissioners would turn such men over to army recruiting officers.[78] It made sense that habeas corpus might be used to test claims that one did not meet these qualifications. So why proceed by order rather than by writ?

One reason concerned the need to discharge conscripts not only from custody, but also from the army. The judge might order release from the Savoy, but this did not constitute a discharge from service. The consequences might be dire. As the recruitment act explained, new conscripts immediately became "subject to the discipline of war and in case of desertion, shall be proceeded against as a deserter."[79] It was conceivable that one could be released from the Savoy, then shot for desertion. Another problem concerned what by the 1750s was the increasing tendency to take seriously the rule against controverting returns, the seriousness of which, as we have seen, was as much the occasion for innovation—doing most work before a return—as for rule obedience. In this case, the innovation was to work by a habeas-like process that allowed an unconstrained discussion of facts as presented by affidavits. This was especially important since nothing in the statute required the recruiting commissioners to keep a record of their reasons for finding a person eligible to serve: there were simply no facts to put in a return. But facts could be adduced through evidence given orally and recorded in writing.[80]

Proceeding by orders *nisi* produced a political backlash, led by William Pitt, the new secretary of state, and Attorney General Sir Charles Pratt. They argued that the use of rules to discharge instead of habeas corpus constituted an assault on the subject's liberties, and produced a bill to address what they considered to be limitations inherent in the common law writ: that it could not issue in vacation, and that one could not controvert the return. But as Mansfield and Lord Chancellor Hardwicke showed during debates, these limitations did not actually exist, and the bill was defeated.[81] As if to prove there were no limits on the common law writ, Mansfield's court then issued them by the score in cases of naval impressment.

Unlike the recruiting of soldiers, naval impressment rested on custom and the prerogative rather than on statute.[82] This meant there was no statutory threat of desertion charges against sailors dismissed by habeas corpus. Statute did not establish legal authority for impressment. But it did influence impressment by defining exempt groups: foreigners and certain fishermen, among others, who might receive a "protection" from the Admiralty that they could show to press gangs when they came looking for sailors.[83]

How might one prove that he was indeed exempt when a press gang refused to believe it? The answers to this question show how naval impressment became the area in which King's Bench worked most energetically to gather and assess the facts of people's detention. Even as doubt about how to proceed with soldiers persisted, Mansfield began sending writs for sailors from late 1756. In all, well over a thousand sailors would use habeas corpus in the next half century. Owing to the creative ways in which habeas was—and was not—used in this work, this is probably a dramatic underestimate of the writ's impact.[84] So it is hardly surprising that the Admiralty soon expressed concern to Mansfield, through their solicitor, Samuel Seddon, that allowing habeas for sailors would create serious difficulties in manning the king's ships.[85] Rather than desist, Mansfield appears to have worked out a different mode of proceeding. Despite the usual insistence on the return of all writs, King's Bench permitted the Admiralty to discharge a sailor without bringing him into court, if the court concluded simply from affidavits that he was wrongly impressed. This meant that in many cases the writ never issued; the fact-finding work already performed on the affidavits precluded any need for it. Seddon's frequent suggestion that a sailor be discharged "to save a great expense" fills his papers.[86] This explains why most impressment writs do not have returns on file. Due to the Admiralty's routine surrender of sailors, habeas corpus had become an instrument for summary dismissal from detention.[87]

Mansfield pursued other innovations, such as a warrant of his own design by which he simply commanded a sailor discharged, without habeas. Such warrants were frequently used for apprentices who could thereby be returned to their masters on shore.[88] Mansfield expected the Admiralty's ready obedience to these warrants, as their solicitor noted: "[W]hen he issues his warrant, he expects that the pressed man be immediately discharged." Importantly, Mansfield only used warrants when there was absolutely no doubt about the circumstances. Otherwise, habeas corpus remained the key instrument for answering questions about the propriety of imprisonment or detention that it had always been.[89]

While Mansfield remained in charge through the late 1780s, King's Bench would continue to use these practices in habeas corpus and beyond to supervise impressment, probably because such practices gave it the widest possible latitude in the way it gathered evidence and made judgments. Only in the 1790s, when Lord Kenyon was in charge, did the court retreat as it disallowed arguments against the return that did not proceed by separate action, limited the writ for apprentices, refused to settle cases, and even quashed writs after they issued.[90] To appreciate how much the availability and utility of the writ declined from around 1790, we must consider further the kinds of judgments the justices of King's Bench had made in previous generations.

Varieties of Judgment

Given the broad consideration of facts from the return and beyond, we should not be surprised to find that bail, discharge, or remand represented only the elemental possibilities for habeas corpus judgments. Prisoners bailed were often required to appear elsewhere for further process.[91] Discharge too might be ordered on any number of conditions. John Harper had been put in Westminster's house of correction in 1733 as "a common player of interludes." But the return did not make clear whether the JP who jailed him had followed the statute that defined actors as "vagabonds." After all, Harper had a "great reputation" as a fat man who danced well. The meaning of "common players of interludes," as part of the statute's definition of "vagabond," remained to be considered. So the court discharged Harper on condition that he return for further debate of the act's "intention."[92] A rather different kind of condition was attached to release in an early naval impressment case. In 1694, the court discharged James Lock and two others from Colchester jail while they awaited entry into the navy. Since they had committed no wrong, the court objected to their treatment—"it is a very ill practice to put them into jail"—but not to their impressment. The justices ordered discharge on their promise to report for service three weeks later.[93]

Conditional release was similar to the settlements produced in King's Bench that ended many detentions. Through negotiations, the justices did not simply police jurisdictional bounds. They vigorously entered other jurisdictions and redefined them as they worked out solutions to the problems that had led to imprisonment in the first place.[94] From the early seventeenth century, this was common in local government cases. Use of habeas in 1600, for instance, allowed Queen's Bench to settle a ruckus in Berwick-upon-Tweed when the justices ordered Henry Brearley, a fractious local leader, released from prison and restored to the town's freedom on condition that he apologize.[95] Sometimes the court appointed arbitrators. Edward Thredder was released from Northampton jail after he had failed to present his churchwarden's accounts. At the same time, the court ordered his accounts reviewed by one of the justices at the next assizes there.[96]

Most habeas work concerned prisoners held prior to trial. But the justices also made judgments about the legality of imprisonment premised on convictions of many kinds, thus creating an opportunity to review those convictions. Given that until the late sixteenth century the majority of writs worked in aid of felony process, the use of habeas corpus after a felony conviction was more often for sending prisoners on to the end of the process rather than for raising questions about the conviction itself.[97] One purpose for the writ after felony conviction was to allow a prisoner to plead extenuating circumstances prior to entry of judgment. Agnes Walker, convicted of a felony, pleaded pregnancy, and on habeas corpus was bailed rather than executed.[98] More common were convicts pleading benefit of clergy.[99] Sometimes benefit of clergy operated as a prelude to a pardon, which one then pleaded using habeas corpus.[100] Using habeas to plead pardons gave the court a chance to attach a few strings to release, as when a convicted burglar obtained his pardon only after giving sureties to behave.[101]

Cases like these show how habeas corpus might aid felony process after conviction. But what about habeas corpus as an instrument for reviewing felony convictions? Using the writ of certiorari to summon an indictment from the assize where conviction occurred, along with habeas corpus to summon the body, was one way to do this. According to Lord Chancellor Ellesmere, this practice was on the rise in the early seventeenth century.[102] Employing the writ in this way made it possible to bail Edward Tooker after his conviction for burglary.[103] Such review was especially important in homicide, in which any number of arguments might be made to justify an otherwise wrongful death.[104] A similar practice pertained in cases of special verdicts, as when John Maddy was indicted for murder. At the suggestion of Justice Twisden, then presiding at Southwark assizes, the jury returned a guilty verdict. Certiorari and habeas corpus were then used to bring Maddy's indictment—thus the record of conviction—along with Maddy's body into King's Bench. The justices then considered the fact that Maddy had struck his victim when found *in flagrante* with his wife. The court concluded that this was manslaughter, "the provocation being exceeding great."[105]

But King's Bench might also police the murder/homicide boundary without certiorari, using habeas alone in a manner that amounted to a review of conviction before entry of judgment. Hopkins Huggett was convicted of murder on a special verdict. When he came into King's Bench on habeas corpus, the justices committed him to the Marshalsea. This enabled him to plead his clergy, on which he was sentenced to eleven months in Newgate, followed by release on giving sureties for good behavior. The dramatic reduction of his sentence was made possible by the review initiated by habeas corpus.[106]

In the sixteenth century, using habeas to review convictions might entail declaring the indictment "insufficient," even though on a return to the writ, the indictment was not before the court.[107] In the seventeenth century, commentators increasingly observed that while habeas corpus removed the "cause" along with a body into King's Bench, certiorari was required to remove the record.[108] But as we have seen, the return itself became a matter of record once filed in King's Bench. This permitted the judges to proceed on the underlying matter in order "to have the cause examined and justice done."[109] As the court noted in 1677, "a certiorari might be in nature of error to reverse [an indictment], yet this court may discharge on habeas corpus."[110] Either way—by certiorari or by habeas corpus—proceedings in the inferior tribunal halted as King's Bench took over the matter.[111] By using habeas corpus alone, King's Bench might not undo the indictment, but they could undo its most important consequence: imprisonment.[112] Using habeas corpus, King's Bench reviewed judgments and attached increasingly creative demands to offers to reduce sentences, just as they did when offering bail prior to conviction. Richard Alborough used habeas corpus to escape the hanging at Tyburn ordered for him and his partners after they robbed the Dutch post in 1686, but only on condition of transportation. By the same condition, Alexander Knightley used habeas to avoid the more awful sentence pronounced on him as a convicted traitor.[113]

For all the importance of habeas review after convictions for felony, reviews of summary convictions for misdemeanor or contempt show more signs of assertive judicial decision-making.[114] Most seventeenth-century prisoners had been jailed by summary process, not by indictment or presentment (in which a grand jury declares a crime): this, despite the politically charged claims of 1627–1628, examined in Chapter 5, that indictment and presentment were the only means to imprison by the "law of the land." Statutes that defined these misdemeanors outlined processes by which JPs might convict at their discretion. Some people were summarily convicted by "view" of the JPs who made the order: for instance, according to statutes concerned with forcible entry, which prompted the earliest Queen's Bench reviews of summary convictions.[115] Most, however, were committed on the basis of other statutes regulating particular wrongs—illegal cottages, alehouses, fishing, gambling, poaching—by which one, two, or three JPs might imprison an accused after examining him and other witnesses. In summary process, there were no indictments, no presentments, no pleadings, no juries: JPs' orders, by themselves, produced legal convictions. Habeas corpus was the chief means for reviewing such sum-

mary convictions. Summary conviction cases demonstrated how far
the justices of King's Bench would go in entering and monitoring another jurisdiction, especially the jurisdiction of these amateur judges.
This mattered because JPs imprisoned more people—and imprisoned
more people contrary to law, if we take release rates on JPs' imprisonment orders as our guide—than any other officers of the monarchical
state.[116]

Summary convictions for operating illegal alehouses, a perennial
concern of local leaders, were often reversed after review on habeas
corpus. Release orders typically resulted from insufficiency, such as
when returns mentioned little more than that an alehouse violated the
statute without saying how it did so, or from uncertainty, such as when
the duration of custody was not made clear.[117] In cases like these,
King's Bench considered both facts about the specific alehouse and
those that established the JPs' jurisdiction over the problem. John
Cole, arrested in 1627 for illegal firearm use, likewise won release owing to the poorly crafted warrant for detention made out by a JP.[118]
Sometimes, the minutest slip in the form of words would upend a summary conviction. Andrew Cater, a Presbyterian cleric, violated the Five
Mile Act—which prohibited dissenting clergymen from preaching in
towns—when he refused to swear the oath that the act required of offenders. Upon reviewing his commitment, King's Bench made the
finest of distinctions: the return to his writ mentioned only Cater's refusal, not his conviction for refusing, as the statute required. The failure to add a few words to the return meant the difference between
freedom and prison.[119] Commitments for contempt—another form of
summary conviction—ended in reversal on habeas corpus even more
frequently than did those on statutory misdemeanors. Contempt imprisonment orders were often found insufficient owing to the absence
of the words spoken or the gesture given that constituted the contempt.

So far, we have concentrated on decision-making about prisoners
confined for allegedly committing wrongs. Beginning in the late seventeenth century, the writ's focus shifted to detentions that involved
no allegations of wrong: it was used to monitor impressment, slavery
and apprenticeship, and spousal or child custody. As King's Bench began to consider these issues, the justices broadened their definition of

detention in a way that expanded their oversight to all aspects of life that might generate one person's constraint of another. By looking at such cases, we can see how the various aspects of writ use examined in this chapter might be combined in creative ways. In family disputes, the justices simultaneously demanded carefully worded returns full of information; looked far beyond returns for information; made judgments that did not just end detention, but also addressed the problem that had produced detention; and made such judgments through negotiation. As King's Bench innovated in the late seventeenth and eighteenth centuries, the writ reached its apogee.

Troubled Families: The Writ's Equity at Work

Writs used by troubled families constitute fewer than 3 percent of all writs before 1800. They make up for their small number by their significance, since they reveal more about process and the writ's possibilities than any other category of cases. These show the equity of a common law writ constrained by little more than the justices' creativity. Changes in habeas practice concerning families began in 1671, only weeks after Sir Matthew Hale became chief justice. For more than a century after Hale, habeas corpus would be one of the chief means by which King's Bench would intervene in family troubles. The court's retreat from this practice at the end of the eighteenth century was a manifestation of a broader retreat from all that the court had once done.

Family disputes bring out four aspects of habeas jurisprudence. First, they show how King's Bench could use the writ to establish new zones of competence, and how doing so had profound jurisdictional consequences, moving marital problems from ecclesiastical courts to King's Bench. Extending the writ's work depended on two other factors we have just reviewed: creativity in finding and using evidence, and creativity in using habeas to resolve conflicts beyond simply declaring someone remanded or released. Finally, as a matter of cultural as well as legal change, family cases mark a transposition in the use of the protection made available through habeas corpus: from protecting husbands from the overreach of church courts when they intervened in difficult marriages, to protecting wives and children from the overreach of husbands and parents. In using the writ this way, King's Bench would ask and answer fundamental questions about obligations and relationships within the family itself.

We begin in the years around 1605. The first family writs concerned husbands jailed by order of ecclesiastical courts, which enforced decisions in adultery and marital separations. Church courts traditionally adjudicated all disputes about marriage. Divorce was virtually impossible in 1605, but orders for separation of bed and board might be made, usually in cases of cruelty. Such separations, which did not permit remarriage, typically included orders that husbands pay alimony to support wives and children.[120] Habeas corpus was used to raise a crucial jurisdictional question: might church courts enforce orders in adultery or separation cases using imprisonment?

We can find no judicial hostility to church courts' use of *excommunicato capiendo* to imprison offenders in cases of defamation or marital trouble: King's Bench remanded on some writs, and released on others.[121] But imprisonment ordered by courts of the High Commission proved more controversial. The High Commissions were ecclesiastical tribunals created by royal letters patent in compliance with the Act of Supremacy of 1559, which charged Queen Elizabeth and her successors to create commissions "for [the] reformation . . . of all manner of errors, heresies, [and] schisms." Commissioners were to have "full power" to punish "by fine, imprisonment, or otherwise."[122] Most Protestants applauded the work of these courts, which had been created as an instrument to crush Catholicism, though some "puritans" would later object to the High Commission once its powers were turned on them. Some lawyers, while accepting imprisonment for heresy, questioned its use in other areas, including to enforce orders for the payment of alimony to wives separated from their husbands, an area in which the High Commission innovated.[123]

Between 1605 and 1611, numerous writs issued from King's Bench to inspect High Commission imprisonment orders in marriage disputes, and many of these ended in release. The commissioners imprisoned Thomas Hyett in Westminster's Gatehouse for refusing to sign a bond to provide maintenance for his wife. Other magistrates, especially JPs, routinely used such bonds to secure compliance with their commands, and King's Bench often remanded those jailed for refusing to give sureties for performance of a bond's terms.[124] Nonetheless, King's Bench ordered Hyett bailed, probably owing to the insufficiency of his return.[125] Whether in response to uncertainty or insufficiency in the return, habeas corpus in such cases actually protected the marital irresponsibility and sexual violence that the High Commission had tried to correct by using imprisonment.[126] But it was a reasonable question whether adultery or refusal to obey spousal maintenance orders counted as offences for which the High Commission might imprison. To resolve this question, the king convened a conference of the judges in 1611, which concluded with a Council order that the king should "reform the High Commission in divers points." New letters patent soon issued for the High Commission, granting greater authority to punish "by reasonable fine or imprisonment."[127]

After this, remand orders when habeas was used to inspect imprisonment in marriage cases suggest a greater deference for the High Commission. Ironically, this is most evident in the period 1613 to 1616, when Coke—who had expressed reservations about the High Commission's power to imprison—presided in King's Bench. Peter Wilcox, for example, was remanded twice to the Fleet after he refused to perform a penance assigned by the High Commission for his "infamous adultery."[128] We can also see a new habit of King's Bench: intervening directly in disordered marriages. As the court gave with one hand—remanding on the High Commission's jail orders—it took away with the other, invading the law of marriage, which once had been the sole province of ecclesiastical courts. Such an invasion was apparent even when bailing prisoners, as in the case of Robert Bradston, who had been jailed for contempt of alimony orders and for committing "infamous adulteries with several women." Coke repeated his view that the High Commission could not imprison someone for refusing to pay alimony. But he disliked Bradston's behavior as much as the High Commission did, and told him to obey their orders and to "use your wife better."[129]

Even before 1611, the justices had begun to correct spousal misconduct. Like Bradston, Hugh Edwards had been jailed after he left his wife "destitute of all manner of maintenance." So King's Bench's 1609 order for his bail came with a catch: a command that he behave well toward his wife and provide her with support.[130] The court had begun to assume the function of imposing settlements in marriage separations.[131] This support of the High Commission's marital jurisdiction, even as King's Bench invaded it, continued until the High Commission was abolished by statute in 1641.[132]

King's Bench took a crucial turn after the Restoration: it began to use habeas corpus to release wives from abusive husbands. In fact, we can date this transition: 5 June 1671, when King's Bench sent habeas corpus for Lady Elizabeth Howard to her husband, Sir Philip. A letter from Lady Elizabeth to her daughter provided the basis for the affidavit on which the court took up the issue. Francis Winnington, on her behalf, admitted the novel questions they faced, then suggested how they might be answered:

> [I]n cases of maintenance to be allowed by the husband to the wife, the ecclesiastical courts hath properly jurisdiction, yet . . . if the husband use[s] any violence to his wife, in regard the ecclesiastical courts cannot prevent a force or redress it . . . the secular courts ought to interpose and may bind the party to his good behavior.[133]

Winnington's idea was not to remove Lady Elizabeth from Sir Philip's custody, but to use habeas corpus to bring her into court so that she might swear articles of the peace against him, a practice for protecting wives from spousal violence long used by JPs, and one that in the late seventeenth century was increasingly being used by justices in King's Bench. Fearful that this might "widen the difference between husband and wife," the court first ordered that "persons indifferently chose[n]" should "compose all differences." Only after Sir Philip held out against this did the justices send habeas corpus, ordering its return to Serjeants' Inn, probably so that they could handle such a delicate matter quietly.[134] From before the writ issued until after it was returned, the court worked in an experimental mode to address the Howards' troubles.

During Hale's tenure in King's Bench, at least three families followed suit in fighting about child and spousal custody using habeas corpus.[135] As quickly as some learned to use habeas to aid troubled women, others figured out how to use it to trouble them. But Bridget Hyde, barely a teen, hardly counted as a woman in 1675. Her case suggests how readily issues of spousal and parental authority intersected, thus requiring the writ to serve as an instrument for investigating the full range of family problems. The daughter of the late Sir Thomas Hyde and a wealthy heiress, Bridget's mother had married Sir Robert Viner when Bridget was three. So it was to Viner, when he was lord mayor of London, that habeas corpus issued—multiple times—to bring Bridget into King's Bench. These were sent at the insistence of John Emerton, who claimed Bridget as his wife. Since Viner hoped that Bridget would marry the son of the Earl of Danby, the king's adviser, he balked. When Viner finally returned the pluries writ, his return said only that Bridget was not in his custody.[136]

Hale would have none of that. He not only looked beyond the return for information; he also used that information to controvert the return, "it appearing plainly"—how, we do not know—"that she had been in his house since the habeas corpus [had been] granted." Hale then set a striking scene after he finally forced Viner to bring Bridget into court:

> [M]y lord [mayor] standing on one side, and Mr. Emerton, her husband, on the other, [and] my lord chief justice placing her in the middle, my lord bad[e] her take her choice who she would go to.[137]

Bridget returned with Viner. Concluding that she "had been under some restraint" at home, the court ordered that her godmother and other relatives—though not John Emerton—have free access to her. Viner had won the first round in a long process that only ended in 1682, when Bridget finally married Danby's son, Viscount Dunblane. He played the violin well. Nonetheless, it would be an unhappy union.[138]

Bridget's case was the first in which the justices asked someone brought in by habeas corpus what she wanted. But this was only one of a string of firsts from the 1670s that suggests the influence a chief justice might have. During Hale's five years overseeing King's Bench, we find the first writs used by wives against abusive husbands, as well as the first writs employed to bring in women to swear articles of the peace; to resolve a child custody dispute; and to explore the detention of an alleged "lunatic." When we appreciate that Hale's court used the writ to pierce the cultural wall surrounding families, as well as to send judicial commands across the Atlantic, we must conclude that the early 1670s was a period of striking innovation. In extending the reach of the writ, Hale elaborated ideas we can trace back to the early years of the century about the king's prerogative, the liberty of his subjects, and the court's unique powers when using habeas corpus.[139]

The point of habeas corpus was to end custody, not to assign it. This would create conundrums when it was used for children, but it made the writ useful to wives who wanted nothing more to do with actual or alleged husbands. In general, church courts answered most questions about marriages. But with habeas corpus, King's Bench opened a space where a woman might determine the disposition of her body, if not end her marriage. As Chief Justice Sir John Pratt put it in 1720, "We have nothing to do . . . but only to see that she is under no illegal restraint; all we can do is to declare that she is at her liberty to go where she pleases." He then went one step further. Fearing that Mrs. Turberville's supposed husband had used habeas corpus to get her into the open, where he might seize her, Pratt ordered his tipstaff to accompany her home from court.[140]

Returns to spousal custody writs often said little more than that made by Anne Gregory's mother and uncle in reply to a writ sent to them at the insistence of Anne's husband:

> We do most humbly certify and return to our sovereign lord the King at Westminster that we have the body of the within named Anne Gregory, wife of Abraham Gregory, at the time and place within mentioned as by the within writ we are commanded.[141]

Because Anne had committed no legal wrong, her mother and uncle had nothing else to say in the return. Judicial decisions thus relied on information gained elsewhere: from affidavits, discussion in court, judicial observation, and especially, the preferences of the women concerned. Gregory "appeared to have been very ill used by her husband." So they declared her "at liberty to go where she thought proper." Once again, the court sent her off with a tipstaff "to secure her from any insult in her return to her friends."[142]

By bringing wives into court so they might swear the peace against their husbands, and by offering escorts so they might be "at liberty," the justices extended the meaning of the king's protection that habeas corpus had always provided. From the time of Bridget Hyde's case, the court did not decide these cases so much as create a neutral space where women decided for themselves, as Maria Stallwood did in 1793. When asked by the court, Stallwood chose her father's home over her husband's, which she had left "in a very ill and dangerous state" owing to "the venereal disease and the itch" he had given her.[143]

By leaving women "at liberty," King's Bench ended custody rather than assign it. But what of children; what of "lunatics"? What might their stories teach us about judicial creativity in finding facts, making judgments, and shaping the bounds of self-determination and of jurisdiction within and around families?

Like other firsts, the first case of a supposed "lunatic" arose in the 1670s, when habeas issued after "a certain lady, esteeming her husband to be mad, put him out to a doctor to be cured."[144] More than forty years later, Robert Norris took Joanna Green's son into his care because he was "a lunatic."[145] Many cases involved wives confined by their husbands: declaring wives "lunatics," then consigning them to a doctor, was a variation on the theme of spousal constraint, but a matter of even greater concern given conditions in "madhouses."

How to distinguish between an alleged and an actual "lunatic"? There was no talk of permitting self-determination of the kind accorded to other adults brought before the court. Initially, the justices relied on their own observations of those brought before them. Mansfield's court then tried a new approach: relying on expertise. In response to a motion for the writ, King's Bench asked Dr. John Monro to visit Deborah D'Vebre in the madhouse where her husband had put her. The following day, Monro's affidavit, concluding that he saw no ground to confine her, was read in court. Monro then offered further assurances that she was "very sensible, and very cool." On the basis of this evidence, King's Bench sent the writ, having already done all the important fact-finding needed to consider the legality of her confinement. Monro's expertise could also work to the opposite end, as it did when he testified that Ann Hunt was so "disordered . . . that she is not fit to be brought into this court." The writ to Dr. William Clarke on Hunt's behalf was thus withdrawn: no other evidence—even that provided by a return—seemed necessary.[146] Cases like these prompted parliamentary investigation, culminating in the 1774 Act for Regulating Madhouses, which established other instruments for overseeing madhouses. The need for habeas corpus in cases of alleged insanity largely disappeared.[147]

Child custody questions also first arose in the 1670s: Bridget Hyde's case, for example, raised a paternal as well as a spousal custody question. No evidence survives of any discussion then about Hyde's capacity for discretion. Hale simply asked her preferences and allowed her to act accordingly. Otherwise, King's Bench moved cautiously, denying habeas corpus in 1676 because the justices "smelled that the design was to take a child out of the hands of her guardian."[148] In cases of alleged abduction involving "outrage, violence, and force," the court might "grant a habeas corpus to correct the force," but not to decide the custody, which remained a "matter of title" that should not be decided in this manner.[149] As in spousal disputes, King's Bench wanted to find a way to end a custody they did not like, without assigning custody elsewhere. Nonetheless, this is what the court did when it negotiated custody arrangements for children brought into court on habeas corpus. In 1690, Chief Justice Sir John Holt settled arrangements for the education and care of Francis Vaughan with his guardian, Sir William Turner. Perhaps owing to the unusual terms, the writ and return were not filed: the settlement was too complex to be embodied in the kind of brief note that could be scratched onto the margin of a writ or return, so clerks entered it in full in the rulebook.[150]

The court decided what should be done for Francis, or to him, as the case may have been. But might they permit a minor to determine custody according to her own wishes, as they did in spousal conflicts? Bridget Hyde had been allowed to do so, despite her youth. Similarly, though only eighteen, counsel argued in 1701 that Eleanor Archer might choose between her separated parents. Holt's court agreed. After "examination of the daughter by the court secretly"—to allow her to speak freely, to prevent public scandal, or both—she decided to return to her father.[151] And the court's 1710 order for Lady Catherine Annesley, which simply "excused" her from the custody of Baroness Haversham, implicitly allowed the same self-determination that Bridget and Eleanor, as well as adult women, were granted in custody disputes.[152]

In cases like these, the justices allowed minors to choose their custody, leery as they were to make habeas more than a means to end confinement. Frances Howland's case changed that. A church court decree had assigned Mary Johnson as Frances's guardian. But in 1724, the girl's uncle, Matthew Howland, used habeas to command Johnson to bring the ten-year-old to King's Bench. He claimed that his brother's will had made him her guardian. Tellingly, the uncle's claim about the will constituted a claim about facts that contradicted those returned by Mary Johnson: that she was the girl's guardian. This did not trouble the justices. What did trouble them was how to decide between competing claims, and whether doing so was appropriate since it would mean assigning custody. The justices considered whether they could turn Frances over to her uncle, "or only set her at liberty," as they had Lady Catherine. But with the girl and both claimants in court—a scene reminiscent of Bridget Hyde's—they resolved that Frances was too young to choose. Though she proved "very unwilling" to leave Mrs. Johnson, "her near relation," the court assigned her to Uncle Matthew.[153] Their decision discarded the practice used in adult custody cases and in cases of other minors to date of heeding the preferences of the person concerned. The decision also marked a step in a new direction: using the writ to assign to custody, not simply to release from it. In this case, doing so also had jurisdictional effects: reversing a judgment in probate, a matter squarely within ecclesiastical courts' traditional zone of competence.[154]

Perhaps because they had overridden Frances Howland's preferences, the justices later regretted that decision.[155] Ten years later, conflicts in the Smith family created an opportunity to change course again. John Smith, soon after the birth of his son James in 1720 or 1721, delivered the infant to his brother Richard. Until his death in 1728, Richard funded the child's care, despite constant conflict with John. By his will, Richard transferred the boy's care to their sister, Penelope. He also established a trust to cover the costs of James's upbringing. All this was explained in the affidavit that Penelope Smith gave in 1734 in reply to the affidavit of John Smith, who had asked that habeas be sent to compel her to return his adolescent son to him. Like Richard, Penelope had long suffered their brother's indignities, even after she had paid debts to secure John's release from prison. Penelope concluded that his new interest in his son was simply another bid to hurt her.[156] In a singular result, the court explicitly repudiated the judgment it had given in an earlier case: Frances Howland's. King's Bench justices returned to the principle they had used previously, deciding that "they could only deliver him out of the custody of the aunt, and inform him he was at liberty to go where he pleased." James pleased to return to his Aunt Penelope.

The court had refused to assign custody by reference either to the

father's wishes—despite the common law norm of paternal custody—
or to the uncle's will. Did the decision to allow a minor to name his
guardian result from a desire to ensure that John Smith's behavior
would not be rewarded? Perhaps. But it also had precedents. Relying
on Lady Catherine Annesley's case, Chief Justice Hardwicke reasoned
that "[t]he only intent of an habeas corpus is to provide against any restraint of the party's liberty."[157] Hardwicke thus made an adult of the
child, leaving him "to his liberty" to decide. Hardwicke's reference
to Lady Catherine's case suggests powerfully his preference for self-
determination in such circumstances, even for a minor. But the relationship between paternal authority and a minor's self-determination
remained fluid.

When the issues involved a marriageable daughter—within or beyond the age of majority—stakes and tempers rose. Fathers often used
habeas corpus in the hope of winning young daughters back from
their seducers. Ann Catley's case, in 1763, explored the shadowy area
between paternal authority and a young woman's self-determination.
At sixteen, Ann had been apprenticed to a music master. At nineteen,
she left her master and ran off with Sir Francis Blake Delaval, who fur-
nished lodgings for her and her mother while she appeared onstage
at Covent Garden. Her father—who may initially have been party to
these arrangements—sued habeas corpus to retrieve her. Mansfield
and the other justices reviewed the precedents, as well as the parents'
behavior, and pointedly rejected Mr. Catley's common law claim to paternal custody. Referring to Howland's and Smith's cases, Mansfield
declared that "the true rule to be collected from all these cases is that
if the circumstances require a change of the custody, it must be delivered in court." Here was a startling claim: that the court might assign
custody, even against the father. Nonetheless, the court simply discharged Catley from Delaval's custody, thus allowing her to decide
whether to return to her father.[158] She declared, with "an unblushing
countenance . . . her attachment to Sir Francis." The court thus left
Nan, as everyone called her, "at perfect liberty."

> [N]o sooner had the chief justice concluded, than she put her hand
> under the arm of Sir Francis, and they left the court together, re-
> turning home in his chariot, which waited for them at Westminster
> Hall gate, to laugh at all parties, particularly the judges and barristers,

whom this facetious female frequently after turned into the highest ridicule.[159]

Ann Catley was a woman of sexual if not legal maturity, whose circumstances, like those of other women, blurred any lines the court might draw around self-determination.[160] The lives of children like James Smith or Lady Catherine Annesley blurred them further. This obscurity was all the more significant given common law norms that venerated paternal authority, and the use throughout the period when Mansfield led King's Bench of quasi-equitable practices that hemmed in those norms. Habeas corpus often held up a mirror to the violence by which women were constrained by a husband, lover, or father.[161] If a detained female was of age, and sometimes when she was not, the court deferred to her preferences. The justices underscored their support of those preferences by sending her off in the protection of a court officer. Thus women and minors were put "at perfect liberty," at least as a matter of law. It is less clear whether such women would be able to remain "at liberty" in a world policed by anxious fathers and by the cultural norms that made Ann Catley's life a parable, "a cautionary example to warn others of her sex from vice."[162] We shall consider further the language of the body "at liberty" in Chapter 6.

The court routinely negotiated education and maintenance arrangements for children whose parents fought. Anne Bissell's case, in 1774, resulted in a detailed settlement order. Anne's father had sued habeas corpus to force her mother to bring their six-year-old into court. Upon examination, it seemed that Mrs. Bissell had fled owing to her husband's mistreatment. Mansfield, proceeding privately in chambers, conceded that "the natural right is with the father." But the father's conduct, as well as his bankruptcy, pointed the other way, so "the court will do what shall appear best for the child." With Mansfield's help, the Bissells reached a settlement placing Anne in neutral territory: a school where both parents could visit.[163] Mansfield had done more than provide relief from wrongful custody. He had assigned custody in defiance of the father's expectation, supported by common law, that custody should be his. As in all its habeas decisions, the court declared the bounds of jurisdiction, even the jurisdiction of fathers.

In other cases, Mansfield would fail. Like the Bissells, Richard and Elizabeth Lytton ended their marriage with a formal separation, but disputes over their daughter continued. For all Mansfield's efforts to negotiate a compromise for the girl's schooling, Richard declared he would "acknowledge no jurisdiction whatever of the Court of King's Bench over my child." Mansfield tried to create an anomalous zone between a common law recognition of a father's right and a child's welfare. This time common law prevailed, and Richard won custody. Nonetheless, Mansfield insisted that by contract—the original separation agreement—Richard had to allow his wife access to their daughter.[164]

Mansfield's extralegal sentiments were equally clear in the fight between Captain John Inglefield and his estranged wife. Mansfield admitted that fathers should have custody, by law. But he also argued that "it is considerably for the benefit of the child that the father should not exert that right." Again, he tried to mediate a solution. He even considered allowing the Inglefield children to decide for themselves, but in the end, he could not go that far. Mrs. Inglefield would get no compromise. The captain prevailed.[165]

For all Mansfield's application of an equitable sensibility to common law process, paternal control rebounded in the late 1780s as Lord Kenyon took charge of King's Bench.[166] Dorothy Lintot learned just how much a change in judicial leadership might mean in 1789. After she fled with her children, her husband sued habeas corpus to get them back. When she pleaded to keep them, Kenyon answered bluntly that she stood at her husband's "mercy."[167] In 1794, despite the "exceedingly reasonable" proposal for a settlement made by Lady Augusta Murray to Sir William concerning their five-month-old boy, her husband held out for exclusive custody. And Kenyon gave it to him. All Kenyon would do to ease horrified maternal feeling was to order the babe's nurse to accompany him to his father's Scottish home.[168]

By the early nineteenth century, expectations of paternal custody that Mansfield had modified in practice had reasserted themselves, defensible in nearly all circumstances, even when husbands had initially made separation agreements relinquishing custody.[169] In the hands of justices like Kenyon, habeas corpus could do little to produce mediated solutions to family problems.[170] The writ, and judgments on it, had been and always would be only what individual justices made it.

Between the 1670s and the late 1780s, that had been quite a lot. Family custody cases, in many ways, reveal in one area all the aspects of habeas jurisprudence that we have identified as equitable. Building on the work the writ had done prior to the Civil War in invading the church courts' once exclusive competence of marriage disputes, Hale took habeas corpus in new directions in the 1670s. The important opportunities for creativity in using the writ were apparent in Hale's judgments: to protect women from violent husbands; to permit women, even minors, to determine custody disputes for themselves; and even to investigate allegations of lunacy that had led to confinement. In the family custody cases, we see the court's energy in finding and using evidence, usually far beyond the return. We see the court using the writ to negotiate solutions to problems on a case-by-case basis. In short, we see a court using habeas corpus to respond to old forms of confinement as well as to new forms generated by cultural change. At least until the 1790s.

Fear and the Individual Justice

Change in the handling of domestic custody questions in the 1790s and the generation following accompanied more general changes in habeas usage. Just as justices had made the writ, so too might they close it down. Mansfield's departure from the bench mattered; so did revolution in France, followed by a generation of war.

Sir Lloyd Kenyon presided in King's Bench, beginning in 1788, and was succeeded by Lord Ellenborough in 1802. Kenyon, a happily uxorious Christian moralist, was a sharp critic of adultery. He feared that the use of separation agreements—which threatened to make equals of husbands and wives as they made contracts with one another—encouraged a wifely self-indulgence that produced infidelity.[171] Little wonder that he saw wives separated from their husbands as unworthy of parental custody, especially given traditional legal norms favoring fathers.

His court's handling of family disputes was just one sign of a withdrawal from all that habeas corpus had become over the previous two centuries. Kenyon explicitly rejected the equitable common law jurisprudence that had made Mansfield an object of scorn and praise and that had been so important to innovations in its use.[172] Even more important was the political environment, as revolution in France, risings in Ireland, threats of invasion, and domestic political rumblings provoked fear across Britain and its empire. Kenyon's fear for the family and the polity were two faces of the same problem: fear for Britain's stability. His was a broadly shared anxiety, one that redefined the province of government—the power of the state—in the 1790s and the decades following. In response to resurgent demands for political reform from some quarters and to the outbreak of war with France in 1793, Parliament passed a string of statutes that suspended habeas corpus, broadened definitions of treason and seditious libel, and outlawed many kinds of public assembly and political association. Prosecutions for political wrongs increased until the end of war in 1815, and then beyond, as agitation for reform continued.[173]

Despite the numbers jailed for seditious libel and treason, use of habeas corpus to inspect these imprisonment orders collapsed. For the most part, the writ retreated to the purposes it had served in the sixteenth century: simply bringing people for trial or entry of judgment rather than providing a searching review of the circumstances by which they got there.[174] The writ continued to do its work supervising impressment, but this was the only front on which it operated as it once had to oversee the full range of different forms of detention.[175] Perhaps it should not surprise us to see habeas corpus so shackled during an era when revolution ran amok across the Channel and nearly constant warfare and reformist demands shook John Bull with fear.

But consider the work done exactly a century earlier, when a very different chief justice, Sir John Holt, presided in King's Bench. This too was a period of rampant fear, as England recovered from a domestic revolution. In late 1688, James II had been chased from England, and replaced by his daughter and son-in-law. Parliament declared William and Mary king and queen, and many thought the result glorious: Protestantism had been protected, and with it, England's liberty. Many benefited, including all the lawyers whom William and Mary soon appointed as justices in Westminster Hall, especially Sir John Holt. Like so many before him, Holt sat on the Privy Council as well as on King's Bench. But James II continued to fight in Ireland for his throne. Invasion from France loomed. And there were plenty of Jacobites in England who could not forswear their allegiance to the man they considered their divinely anointed king. Rebellion seemed imminent, especially when so many were arrested for printing seditious libels, for conspiring against the king and queen, or for being priests—or worse, Jesuits. Parliament fought fear with fear in the spring of 1689, passing the first suspensions of bail and mainprise in cases of alleged treason: what we usually call the suspension of habeas corpus. Suspension persisted until October.[176]

The chief justice and his court, however, responded energetically to the fear that had motivated suspension. Between the start of Michaelmas term 1689 and the end of 1690, Holt's court reviewed the fate of 251 prisoners: more than in any other period of equal length. Most (147) had been jailed for wrongs against the state: treason, seditious libel, or the more vague charge, treasonable practices. Of these, King's Bench bailed or discharged 80 percent.[177] Was Holt's court soft on treason? Hardly. Holt was never shy about using the law's full ferocity as needed. Nor was he shy about defending the government on whose success his own prosperity depended. King's Bench was quite ready to consign serious suspects to all the horrors of the law of treason; and after a review on habeas, many others were convicted on lesser charges than those for which they had first been jailed.[178]

Holt possessed a lofty sense of his court's purposes.[179] Among those purposes, the greatest was the superintendence of all other jurisdictions made possible by using habeas corpus. On the surface, those imprisoned for "endeavoring to levy war against our sovereign lord and lady," or "for publishing and dispersing false and seditious news," might have seemed unlikely candidates for bail. Others heading to France or Ireland in 1689 might on first glance have appeared to be up to no good.[180] Habeas corpus provided a second glance, allowing the court to hold the alleged facts behind each imprisonment against the relevant law. During years of war—years of fear—a second glance revealed that many men and women had been jailed on the thinnest evidence or caught in indiscriminate trawls for suspects.[181] Results across the whole of Holt's leadership of King's Bench (1689–1710) show a justice and a court ready to use habeas corpus, confident that they could distinguish the alleged traitor from the actual one, those who needed to be feared from those who did not.[182]

Judgments like these did not simply happen. Justices like Holt—and Mansfield, Hale, Montagu, Fleming, and Popham—made them. They could do so because the prerogative sent this writ forth across all the king's dominions, making all the king's officers answerable to the king's authority, an authority pronounced by the justices on his bench every time they supervised the confinement of one subject by another. In doing so, the justices defined what counted as law, even if, in cases like Margaret Symonds's, their judgments counteracted the dictates of statute. Their decisions did not simply free those wrongly held. They defined the jurisdiction of all other magistrates and tribunals. At least until the 1790s.

CHAPTER 5

Making Jurisdiction

Peter Ball, MP, made it sound simple: "The question is only for explanation of two words . . . *lex terrae.*" Ball's "only" notwithstanding, these words—the heart of Magna Carta—proved remarkably difficult to explain. Hours of discussion in King's Bench during the case of the Five Knights in November 1627 failed to settle their meaning. Further weeks of talking in Parliament, where Ball posed his question the following spring, still left "*lex terrae* yet an unfolded riddle," as Sir Roger North put it.[1]

What made "the law of the land" so elusive? Breadth and number. How many were the laws of the land: common law, statute, local customs, equity? How many were its institutional forms: assizes and quarter sessions, common law courts in Westminster Hall; Chancery and Exchequer on their equity sides; courts of admiralty and the earl marshal; church courts, too? How far did "the land" stretch? Did the Channel Isles, Ireland, or the king's American "plantations" count as "the land" over which "the law" reached?

Everyone agreed that the subject's liberties depended on the answers. After all, by what law might one person properly hold another in custody? This was the central question posed by the Five Knights.[2] The knights, imprisoned for their refusal to pay the king's loan in 1627, had sued writs of habeas corpus, which received only the briefest return: that they had been imprisoned "by his majesty's special commandment."[3] Such a return was certain. Was it also sufficient?

John Bramston, arguing for the prisoners, admitted that precedent pointed against them. So he turned instead to "the fundamental laws" of the realm. The question, he argued, concerned not what judges had decided before, but what they should have decided: that imprisonment by the king's command, without any other cause given, was against "the law of the land." But invoking Magna Carta's chapter 29 did not explain its meaning. John Selden, the most eminent of the knights' counsel, conceded, "these words '*legem terrae*' do leave . . . the matter very uncertain." The law of the land, Selden concluded, required proceeding "either by presentment or by indictment."[4] In short, Bramston and Selden hoped to win release for their clients by placing the law defining justifiable imprisonment on the narrowest possible grounds: not simply on common law, but on a thin slice of common law process, presentment and indictment. But was this all the law that had been and could be used to imprison the king's subjects?

Attorney General Sir Robert Heath answered with a more inclusive view. Would Selden have him believe, Heath asked, "that no man should be committed, but first he shall be indicted or presented?" Nonsense, he seemed to say: "[C]ertainly there is no justice of peace in a county, nor constable within a town, but he doth otherwise." Heath knew well of what he spoke. By 1600, the majority of imprisonment orders tested by habeas corpus, including most of those ending with judgments to remand, concerned prisoners jailed by process other than presentment or indictment, most by summary powers granted by statute to JPs and other special commissioners. So Heath repeated the question: "What then is meant by these words, '*per legem terrae*'?"[5] His answer relied on the very thing Bramston and Selden had avoided: precedent. As Heath showed from precedents of Privy Council imprisonment orders reviewed on writs of habeas corpus, the law of the land was many things, not just a set of practices known by Selden's narrow construction of the common law. The court could only agree, and ordered the knights remanded to their prisons.

Justice Sir John Dodderidge declared the Five Knights' case "the greatest cause that I ever knew in this court."[6] It remains a great cause still, if little understood. To the modern liberal legal imagination, it is the perfect example of a case wrongly decided. To the legal imagination of 1627, it was not. Yet for all the contemporary legal justification for the decision, it left behind a deep reservoir of political disappointment that would inspire a profound shift in the center of law-making gravity in England. Selden and others—most famously, Sir Edward

Coke—would take the issue of Privy Council imprisonment orders without a stated cause into Parliament in the spring of 1628. There they would produce the Petition of Right's declaration that none should be "imprisoned without any cause shown."[7]

The Five Knights' case and the Petition of Right have long been taken to form a point on which political history, and habeas corpus, pivoted: judges erred, Parliament corrected. But by examining legal practice before 1627, it is hard to see the court's judgment as mistaken. By examining practice after 1628, it is almost equally difficult to see how the Petition of Right fixed any apparent problem. In the end, judges, not parliamentary pronouncements, would end conciliar imprisonment orders returned without cause. Ironically, having accomplished this in the second half of the seventeenth century, Parliament would return that same power to the Privy Council with every suspension statute passed after 1689 (see Chapter 7).

There is another way to look at the contests of 1627–1628: as a struggle over the nature of jurisdiction—what it is, how it manifests itself, and where ultimate authority lies for defining it. Bramston, Selden, and Coke placed the power to imprison on impossibly narrow grounds. But Heath was right. Many more people were imprisoned by means other than presentment or indictment, before 1627 and long after. What mattered was less the definition of "the law of the land" as one kind of process, than the control that King's Bench could impose on other forms of law when they were used to imprison. With every judgment of remand or release—whether for those jailed by privy councilors or by any other magistrate—King's Bench declared what counted as jurisdiction. Thus the common law was not superior; King's Bench was.

Over the previous three decades, King's Bench had always had the last word, no matter when, how, or by whom one had been imprisoned. More important than keeping imprisonment within the narrow forms insisted on by Coke and his colleagues was the persistent capacity of King's Bench to use habeas corpus to monitor the work of all other jurisdictions. As the justices monitored the many imprisonment orders of justices of the peace and the few imprisonment orders of the Privy Council, they developed a jurisprudence of normalcy. This steady yet demanding supervisory jurisprudence then provided the ideas and instruments that King's Bench used to constrain, and sometimes kill off, novel jurisdictions as they appeared in later generations.[8] This was crucial, because the most significant threats to the subject's liberty came not from the king and his Privy Council, but from new forms of authority that a burgeoning state generated, especially in times of crisis and as the king's officers spread to new dominions across the planet. The laws of these lands were many. Using habeas corpus, the justices recognized—and made—the multipolar jurisdictional world over which they had dominion in the seventeenth and eighteenth centuries.

Jurisdiction: The Laws of the Lands

"The law of the land" was more than common law. It was a trope for talking about jurisdictional relationships. "Jurisdiction" means "law speaking."[9] Debates over the meaning of the "law of the land" concerned who should speak, how, and by what authority.

Hale gave jurisdiction a characteristically pithy definition: "the power of judicature." As always, his approach was historical: "all jurisdiction was originally translated into the crown." Who should speak, and by what authority, was thus clear. In a moment of delegation in an unspecified past, the king had "distributed the exercise of his jurisdiction to several courts according to the diversity of the matters proper for each." By invoking diversity, Hale explained how the law speaks: through many mouths, or "several courts." The practice of those courts had been "settled by usage," binding all who exercised jurisdiction so delegated, and also binding the king: "the king cannot erect any new judicatory to proceed in any matter by any other process, trial, or rule than that which by the common law is settled or allowed in the judicatory settled by law."[10]

Apparent fixity in a course of proceeding was achieved not by any jurisdiction's actions, but by the recognition of those actions by a greater jurisdiction, one whose jurisdiction was to determine—by allowance, rebuke, or alteration—the jurisdiction of others. This was the function of King's Bench, "the court wherein the king ordinarily dispenseth his supreme temporal jurisdiction." This was a power to regulate all other courts, explained Hale's contemporary, William Style, so "that they [do] not exceed their jurisdictions nor alter their forms."[11] The fiction of fixity thus became the basis for the court's exercise of supreme authority: the power to determine what counted as "settled," and in so doing, to change constantly the nature of that settlement while maintaining the pretense that no such thing happened. Thus at the center of this exercise of supreme authority was the silence by which that authority was sustained once it had been accepted, because King's Bench was the court in which the king, metaphorically, always sat.[12]

Hale's thinking shows five aspects of jurisdiction. First, inferior jurisdictions are differentiated by the status of the officer presiding in each, by the subject matter over which that officer presides, and by the processes customarily used. The second aspect concerns hierarchy: given the "diversity" of jurisdictions, one had to be "supreme." Third, jurisdictions and the differences among them are presumed to be fixed, even if in fact they are in constant motion as a result of judgments made by the supreme judicature. Fourth, a presumed fixity requires a language of boundary. Such language is everywhere in Hale and in other writers concerned with jurisdiction. Spatial metaphors by which a court's purview is conceived are more than that, and relate to the final aspect of jurisdiction, its territorial quality. Whether one jurisdiction was more notable for its distinctive purview, its special processes, its earthly bounds, or some combination of these, the triumph of King's Bench in the early seventeenth century was that it alone pronounced what did or did not count as "settled." By recognizing jurisdiction—by releasing or remanding the prisoners held by the commands of all other magistrates—King's Bench made and ordered jurisdiction. In doing so, the justices put themselves at the heart of the state.

We might boil down Hale's five aspects of jurisdiction to two suggested by "the law of the land": subject matter and territory. Some jurisdictions differed from one another largely according to the persons or problems over which they watched. But subject matter distinctions often contained a territorial element. Trade companies in London exercised jurisdictions defined by the particular types of tradesmen over whom they presided as well as by place markers: for instance, the seven-mile radius around London covered by the College of Physicians' oversight of medical practitioners.[13] Church courts differed by their powers to discipline clergy as a part of the population distinct from the laity, and by the wrongs—clerical or lay—over which no other court could preside: for instance, heresy or marital misbehavior. But territorial bounds also featured prominently in the work of church courts, distinguished as they were by diocese, archdeaconry, and so on. The norms used might even vary from one territorial unit to the next: witness the distinctive visitation articles prepared for inquiries made of parish clergy in each diocese.[14]

King's Bench tended to respect the procedures used by jurisdictions with distinctive subject matter or territorial mandates. The High Court of Admiralty was one of these. Admiralty courts addressed crimes or other deeds performed at sea; they also enforced judgments of foreign courts. In 1607, King's Bench remanded Emanuel Wyer, imprisoned by the Admiralty court in support of a judgment against him given in the court of the Count of Nassau. As Popham noted,

> [I]t is the law of nations that the justice of one nation will aid the justice in another . . . and of this law, the law of England will take notice in such cases . . . and the judge of Admiralty is the proper magistrate for this purpose, because he solely has the execution of the civil law in this land.[15]

King's Bench remanded Richard Scadding the following year after his imprisonment by the Admiralty court for assisting in the escape of a jailed pirate. Even though the rescue occurred on land—where that court's authority did not normally extend—the deed for which the suspect was held fell within its ambit by statutes defining piracy.[16] As Holt noted in a 1702 case, "Though the proceeding of the Admiralty is by the civil law, yet it is supported by the custom of the realm, and this court must not elude their process."[17] King's Bench viewed in a similar way the earl marshal's "court of Chivalry," which heard cases concerning the misappropriation of heraldic arms. "The law of chivalry is part of the law of England . . . they may proceed therein summarily and imprison before conviction," King's Bench explained in 1668.[18] The key to this power was that the court of the earl marshal was "ancient," yet subject to the ultimate supervision of King's Bench. Summary imprisonment by novel authorities would be seen quite differently from courts like these, whose practices had been fixed by time.

Jurisdiction's territorial aspects worked to unify space within and across jurisdictions, and to distinguish among them. No jurisdiction was comprehensible without some idea of the literal ground that it covered. But one did not need to know where on that ground actual boundaries might run for ideas of territorial boundedness to provide one of the principal elements defining a jurisdiction.[19] Consider, for instance, those jurisdictions that unified space within England, even as they depended on divisions across it. Justices of the peace provide the most important example. Each JP in each county had the same authority over the early stages of felony process or summary powers to correct regulatory wrongs and misdemeanors that all others had. Every county was a distinct territorial unit, but all were homogenized by the way in which the functions of all JPs remained the same from one to the next. This meant that all JPs, however various the topographies and cultures of their counties—even JPs in counties palatine—could be supervised in the same manner by King's Bench.

A county palatine was different from others. The powers used in Durham by concession of the king, signaled in successive charters to the bishops of Durham, set that county apart in some ways. Most matters in private litigation could not be taken from Durham to the courts in Westminster: in private law, a territorial principle, arising from the bishop's unique status, differentiated Durham as a jurisdiction. But in regard to other parts of law, such as those addressed by habeas corpus, the territorial principle disappeared. As far as the supervisory power of King's Bench using the prerogative writs was concerned, Durham was like all other places in the king's dominions. As Justice Heath put it in 1641, a county palatine "is corrigible by this court." He continued, explaining the significance of this oversight: "[T]he King's Bench has jurisdiction to send habeas corpus . . . because otherwise there will be a failure of justice."[20]

Starting with jurisdictional variation within England—where territory was unified for some legal purposes, and divided for other purposes—we can reason outward to understand how law did and did not make *the* empire out of what was otherwise a loose collection of legally peculiar dominions of a single king. As in Durham, the terms in every dominion differed owing to the historical circumstances of its acquisition by the king as well as to the environmental, commercial, social, or political possibilities and liabilities peculiar to each. This was most apparent in the ways property law varied from place to place, generating distinctive modes for holding land, even making certain kinds of human beings, in certain places, chattel. Property law demonstrates better than any other how law made many dominions, not a single empire.

But as practice in places from Durham in the seventeenth century to Sidney in the nineteenth shows, the jurisdictional logic of habeas corpus pointed the other way, making territorial distinctions disappear, "because otherwise there would be a failure of justice." Only technologies of communication and technologies of jurisdiction—the means by which courts enforce obedience to their commands—not ideas about territorial differentiation in the range of habeas corpus, would limit the writ's work as the king's dominions proliferated.[21] To some extent, the problem of enforcement across great distances would be answered by creating new superior courts that would issue habeas corpus in the king's faraway dominions. Thus the same principles and practices applied in Berwick, Barbados, Bengal, and both Bostons. It would remain to be seen whether, given the myriad personalities, local political circumstances, and legislative interventions involved, this usage would have the same vigor in new colonial courts that it had at its point of origin: the court of King's Bench. We shall return to this problem in Chapter 8. For now, let us explore the many laws operating in the king's lands within his kingdom.

Readings—lectures at the Inns of Court in which a senior barrister expounded a statute—give us another view into jurisdiction. Surprisingly, few readers in the sixteenth century chose to lecture on Magna Carta. When they did, they often focused on the first chapter, which addressed church privileges—perhaps because of concerns to protect the royal supremacy over the English church against the recently rejected claims of the papacy.[22] In this way, Magna Carta was used less to curb royal authority than to expand it by building a legal bulwark against foreign dogma. When readers considered Magna Carta's chapter 29, they concentrated on the meaning of "unless by legal judgment of his peers," a phrase they construed narrowly.[23]

Not everyone avoided our central question: what did "the law of the land" mean? Many responded with a list. "[T]here are divers laws used in this land," declared one reader circa 1500. One party might sue another in any of the royal courts in Westminster Hall. But there were "special courts, special jurisdictions, that are also the law of the land." The Cinque Ports—"where the writ of the king does not run"—counties palatine, and other special courts "are the law of the land, but they have special jurisdiction. Thus Ireland is the law of the land, and the laws that are there are the law of the land." More remarkable than this inclusiveness as to law and land was how little exclusion from "the law of the land" ultimately mattered for determining the legality of imprisonment orders. The courts of the admiralty, the earl marshal, and the Chancery were "used in this realm," though "not the law of the land." If so, what about their imprisonment orders? The answer depended on whether imprisonment was ordered in a matter over which the court had purview. Obedience to the forms and bounds associated with particular jurisdictions—more than "the law of the land" in the singular—determined the varieties of legal imprisonment.[24]

One of the most influential treatises of the sixteenth century took a similarly ecumenical approach to "the law of England." While Christopher St. German's purpose was to promote the common law relative to equity and ecclesiastical law, he did so by finding and promoting their points of contact: common law was not against equity, but supported by it. This was possible because all forms of law derived from custom, itself compatible with the laws of God and nature.[25] Robert Snagg's 1581 Middle Temple reading on *lex terrae*—what he called "the sum of all the charter"—followed St. German's approach. Snagg focused on one problem: whether the equity used in Chancery was within or outside the law of the land. His emphatic answer: within. To show this, Snagg provided a mythohistorical account of law's genesis. *Lex terrae* is "the ancient custom of the country." All varieties of law—statutes, the prerogative, local and general customs—were "all but species of" the law of the land, which had been made by "kings, nobles, and commons, whosever and whensoever they were, that instituted the law of the land."[26] The land's laws, for all their variety, were all legitimated by origins in which the king and all subjects participated.

We must wait until August 1616 for the most important interpretation of chapter 29: Francis Ashley's.[27] Ashley was an active JP in his native Dorset, and thus knew well the complexity of questions about jurisdiction raised in the everyday use of the land's laws.[28] Perhaps reflecting on his own experience of JPs who used their discretion to imprison too liberally, Ashley was especially concerned with the orders of JPs as he ran through a list of jurisdictions to consider what each might or might not do by law.

Ashley's view reflected the eclecticism of his predecessors. All imprisonment orders made according to common law, statute, or custom were legal. So were others, because there are "divers other laws exercised within this realm which are also authorized, and the proceedings by them are legal so long as they do not exceed their limits."[29] Where the king's charter made a corporation with a court of record, it might imprison since that power was incident to such courts. But the king could not grant power by charter to imprison any tradesman who set up a shop without the corporation's permission, because it was against the law of the land "to restrain any Englishman" from pursuing his livelihood, "except in London."[30] This was an important exception, demonstrating as it did that London had liberties others did not have, including liberties to imprison that might override the liberties that subjects generally enjoyed against imprisonment.

Throughout, Ashley used recent cases to make his point. The preceding winter, Edmund Spencer had been imprisoned in London for violating a City custom concerning orphans. Spencer's barrister argued that the custom was contrary to law. Perhaps his argument would have won Spencer's release in most jurisdictions, but London's "legal and special custom," in part sanctified by Magna Carta's chapter 9, held him fast.[31] Even law that was common varied across space, across jurisdictions.

Ashley's law of the land embraced the common law used in the courts at Westminster and "particular customs, which are legal (because general customs are common law, as Dr. and Student says), and statute law." Like previous readers, Ashley listed tribunals and the processes appropriate to each according to their subject matter and territorial bounds. The punishment of blasphemy, incest, and nonpayment of tithes by ecclesiastical courts was the law of the land. Admiralty court usage was the law of the land for things done upon the sea; the law of the marshal was the law of the land within the verge of the royal household. Martial law became part of the law of the land according to time, not place: during invasions a county's lord lieutenant might imprison "without ordinary course of trial, and that is [by] *jus gentium.*" Equity used in Chancery and elsewhere was also the law of the land. This included the Court of Requests, the conciliar court legitimated by its obligation to answer pleadings of the poor. The law of the land was vast, taking in all forms and processes "warranted by custom." And like

St. German, Ashley saw statute as a capacity to modify or elaborate the law of the land, as his treatment of ecclesiastical courts shows. "Imprisonment by any ecclesiastical judge is against [Magna Carta]," Ashley declared, except when statutes made imprisonment by church courts legal, as the 1559 Act of Supremacy did in cases of heresy or schism.[32]

If all these things counted as the law of the land, what counted as lawful imprisonment? "Courts that proceed by discretion, without limited rules of law, may imprison one until he performs the order of the court," answered Ashley. Star Chamber might do so, "because it is no other but in effect the ancient court of the king and his counsel for criminal causes." "But," explained Ashley, "in all these courts it is to be intended that none may exceed their proper jurisdiction because then . . . [the] judgment given is not by the law of the land."[33] The argument was tautological, but it conveys the legal ecumenism that Ashley shared with his forebears: the law of the land was that law performed by a tribunal within its "proper jurisdiction." Ashley understood that the making and unmaking of "proper jurisdiction" was the ongoing work of the supreme judicature, King's Bench. King's Bench would control the relationship among varieties of law—common law and equity; the church courts and the admiralty; felony and misdemeanor—all of which used imprisonment for different ends and by different processes. In doing so, King's Bench continually made and modified all other jurisdictions by determining what counted as "proper jurisdiction" with every judgment on habeas corpus. All magistrates learned this lesson as the court's decisions allowed some imprisonment practices while killing off others, especially novel ones.

A Jurisprudence of Normalcy: JPs and Other Commissioned Authorities

Most accounts of habeas corpus focus on imprisonment orders made by the Privy Council. But before 1627, these occasioned relatively little controversy. For most people, the potential for oppression did not come from Whitehall. It came from the tyrant next door: the local justice of the peace.

JPs and other local officers made four times as many imprisonment orders as did the Privy Council.[34] No jurisdiction covered all of England so thoroughly, none had purview of so many wrongs, and none was staffed by literally hundreds of men of such varying ability. Thus no jurisdiction required supervision more than JPs. The potential for abuse of magisterial discretion was Francis Ashley's greatest worry. "[T]he law of necessity must refer many particulars to the discretion of the [JP]," he wrote, but that did not justify "unlimited discretion."[35] The function of King's Bench was to limit discretion. In the process of this work, it created a jurisprudence of normalcy, a habeas practice that was predictable if not rule-bound.[36]

Until the late sixteenth century, the majority of habeas work aided felony process, more often by moving prisoners forward to trial than by reviewing circumstances preceding imprisonment. JPs made most orders on suspicion of felony. The process they followed arose from the common law, but statute had modified it, most notably through two statutes of the 1550s. The first of these required that bail could only be taken for accused felons in quarter sessions or by two JPs acting together after having taken an examination, in writing, of the prisoner and witnesses. The second statute broadened the written examination requirement, imposing it not only for those bailed, but also for those jailed to await trial. Parliament thereby increased the role of written matter from the outset of felony process, building in part on examination procedures required of JPs in dozens of nonfelony wrongs defined by statutes passed during the previous two centuries. The new statutory requirements were also influenced by the examination process used in the conciliar courts, especially in Star Chamber.[37] As St. German and Ashley noted, statute was nothing if not the means to transform custom.

The influence of these requirements may be inferred from results on writs sent for those imprisoned by JPs for suspicion of felony. In the first half of the sixteenth century—before these statutes—King's Bench released accused felons jailed by JPs less often than others who used habeas corpus. But during the half-century following, release rates for those charged before JPs outstripped general release rates.[38] Heeding the Marian statutes' higher standard for the form of committal orders, King's Bench drew in the bounds of JPs' felony jurisdiction.[39] The court's concern moved from bringing felons to trial to reviewing the initial grounds of commitment. This review was made possible by the examinations required by the Marian committal statutes, even if this information was not part of the record returned with the writ. As time went by, the number of jail orders on suspicion of felony requiring habeas review declined, perhaps because the results of earlier reviews had encouraged JPs to do their work with greater care.

How did this closer review of JPs' work vary according to whether they jailed felons or lesser criminals? From 1500 to 1800, 50 percent of those jailed by JPs on suspicion of felony were released after habeas corpus hearings, compared to 59 percent of those jailed for nonfelony wrongs. There was also a clear temporal pattern in habeas oversight of lesser offences. As the use of habeas corpus to monitor JPs' imprisonment orders for misdemeanor increased in the latter part of the sixteenth century, so too did release rates. From the end of the sixteenth through the seventeenth century, orders made by JPs to jail people for misdemeanors were reversed roughly two-thirds of the time. As numbers like these suggest, this kind of magisterial business was the target of King's Bench's most energetic supervisory work.

Attorney General Heath was right when he asked John Selden in 1627 whether it was possible to believe that one might not be imprisoned by means other than indictment or presentment. Probably thousands of people were convicted and imprisoned, every year, by other means: by JPs using summary process, not in advance of jury trial, but instead of it. JPs and other commissioned authorities enjoyed extensive summary powers, in part by statutes that extended traditional authority to commit for wrongs done within the magistrate's own view. One of the best examples of this concerned a statute of the 1390s permitting one or more JPs, upon complaint of a forcible entry, to take "sufficient power of the county" to the place in dispute. If the justices observed that an illegal entry had been made, they were to commit the wrongdoers to "the next gaol, there to abide convict by the record of the same justices."[40] William Lambarde's manual for JPs provided in such cases a standard form of the mittimus (an order to send someone to jail), in which JPs were to write that those committed had been "convicted of the said forcible holding by mine own view, testimony, and record."[41]

The key to such a statutory power was that it be used with care, a care that habeas corpus ensured. Thus Richard and George Blackwell were discharged in 1660 for the "insufficiency" of the return to their habeas corpus, which showed only their conviction without the other language of limitation that Lambarde had recommended for the mittimus, namely words that explained that prisoners should be held only until they paid their fines and then were to be released by "due order of law."[42] Even close obedience to forms might not prevent the reversal of JPs' orders, as two of them learned in 1610 after John Lant, whose warrant for commitment was a near copy of that in Lambarde's book, was bailed.[43] We can only imagine, given the obedience to form, that other issues brought out in courtroom discussion had made it apparent that the JPs had been remiss in sending Lant to jail.

While some prisoners were summarily convicted when a JP personally viewed the wrong, many more were summarily convicted using the examination procedures like those in Star Chamber and like those appointed by the Marian bail statutes that were to precede indictment and trial in felony.[44] Let us consider just a few of the many statutes granting this authority, and see how and why habeas was needed to curb magisterial enthusiasm in the use of that authority. JPs in some parts of the country, motivated by religious zeal to reform the manners of their neighbors, led an assault on illegal alehouses. The alehouse statute of Edward VI's reign permitted only a three-day imprisonment for violators, though it was also vague about the sureties required of them to behave henceforth. Questions thus arose as to whether JPs might jail longer those who did not provide sufficient sureties.[45] The potential for a perpetual imprisonment arising from a warrant of commitment that was uncertain as to the sureties demanded for release explains why William Patching, jailed for an illegal alehouse, was bailed on his habeas corpus.[46]

Other statutes—for instance, those concerned with poor relief, plague, and poaching—fared little better as King's Bench decisions on habeas corpus trimmed the jurisdictional overreach of JPs.[47] Individual prisoners must have rejoiced, but it is less clear that the public joined them. After all, statutes appointing summary process had been created to promote general welfare. The preamble to the Edwardian alehouse statute, like others, declared its concern to correct "intolerable hurts and troubles to the commonwealth." Many must have been disappointed when those imprisoned for illegal alehouses were released. Similarly, mothers of illegitimate children whose fathers had been imprisoned by JPs to enforce maintenance orders must have been disappointed to see those imprisonment orders reversed by King's

Bench. It is hard to imagine that the people of Broadstreet ward, London, or "Maria, a Blackamore woman born in India" and mother of John Edwards's child, cheered when Edwards was discharged from custody by habeas corpus after he had refused to support the infant.[48]

Statutes also created other specially commissioned authorities with summary powers to imprison, powers that were similarly curtailed by habeas corpus. Commissioners of sewers managed the creation and maintenance of sewers and drains. These ranged from humble works removing urban waste to huge projects by which fens were transformed into pasture and cropland. To enforce their commands, a statute of 1532 granted broad powers to them to proceed by fines "or by other punishments . . . according to your wisdoms and discretions."[49] But when sewer commissioners committed William Hetley to Peterborough jail in 1613 for refusing to end his suit brought to prevent the commissioners' seizure of his cattle, they overstepped their jurisdiction on two counts: by putting pressure on someone proceeding at common law, and by ordering what amounted to a perpetual imprisonment—"without bail and mainprise, until you shall receive sufficient order for his delivery." King's Bench ordered Hetley's discharge and sent attachments against the commissioners. Though the court recognized that the statute accorded "discretion," its orders made clear that this meant sound discretion, unmotivated by the "apparent malice" at work against Hetley.[50]

Similar powers were given to special authorities created by charters whose terms had been outlined in statutes.[51] The College of Physicians, like many companies and corporations, received powers to imprison in their charters. In the Physicians' case, such powers arose from their 1518 charter of incorporation, confirmed by a statute four years later, by which the college had purview of all physicians in London and for seven miles around the City.[52] It also granted powers to punish "by fines, amercements, and imprisonments" any physicians who violated their ordinances. These powers were clarified by a 1553 statute that permitted the president of the college to send all offenders "to any ward, gaol, or prison."[53]

The statute's language conveyed the broadest possible authority: that the college might imprison, "without bail or mainprise, until such time as such offendor or offenders, or disobedient, be discharged of the said imprisonment, by the said lord President." Nothing in this language suggested a limitation of time or defined the processes or modes of judgment that the college should follow. Nonetheless, Elizabeth Clark, jailed for her "ill practice of physic," was discharged by King's Bench in 1604. The problem was uncertainty in the return, which made it impossible to determine whether the college had acted "according to their authority or not," because the warrant did not state how her practice was ill nor whether her physic had been applied within seven miles of London.[54] Greater certainty did not help the physicians justify other imprisonment orders. The warrant by which Thomas Tenant had been jailed, unlike Clark's, laid out the college's powers by statute and charter and named the persons on whom he used "evil practice." To no avail: Tenant, a Paris educated physician, was discharged.[55]

King's Bench clipped powers to imprison as it released those whom the college had imprisoned, despite the scrupulous attention the physicians paid to the use of the authority granted by statute and by charter. In doing so, the court effectively redefined the college's jurisdiction. But because justices made the judgments, judgments might change with the justices. This explains the very different outcome in the case of William Blanck, who had been jailed on terms nearly identical to those for Tenant. Blanck's writ was returned in the transformed judicial environment of the 1630s. John Bramston—who had argued so energetically for the Five Knights ten years earlier—was chief justice when Blanck's writ was discussed in 1637. Bramston supported the college's statutory "power to punish evil practicing," even though Blanck's counsel had raised precisely the same objections about uncertainty in the return that had led to the release of the college's prisoners a generation earlier. Blanck was remanded.[56]

Powers to imprison granted to JPs, statutory commissioners, and other chartered authorities were essentially inquisitorial: powers to examine witnesses, to convict summarily, and to imprison on conviction or for failure to follow their peremptory procedures. In this way, statute brought into common law practices used in Star Chamber and other conciliar courts. Though such tribunals were targets of common law criticism, their summary procedures and evidentiary practices— imposing prison on those who refused to answer interrogatories under oath—were no different from those used by JPs and others empowered by Parliament.[57] Little wonder that King's Bench, using habeas corpus, watched what JPs or the College of Physicians did as carefully as they watched the work of Admiralty or conciliar courts. Higher release rates for those jailed by JPs than for those jailed by these other tribunals suggest where the court's greatest concerns about the possibility of injustice lay.[58] Appreciating this, we can now make sense of the use of habeas corpus to monitor imprisonment orders made by king and Council.

A Jurisprudence of Normalcy: King and Council

Discretion in the use of summary powers to commit without indictment or presentment generated the need for King's Bench supervision, whether the Council or a JP used those powers. The likeness in the issues in supervising each is hardly surprising: council members were routinely named in the commission of the peace for each county and they routinely dealt with the same issues as JPs.[59] Rather than see the Council as an "executive," standing over and against the benches in Westminster Hall, we should see it as contemporaries did: as one of many instruments of authority derived from the king in a world in which no one authority existed over and against—"checking"—any other.[60] Such authorities often worked together. Conciliar support was probably the key to the success of King's Bench in supervising jurisdictions like the Council in the Marches of Wales, as we saw in Chapter 1. Once we appreciate the involvement in the Council's work of common lawyers—including sitting or future judges, like Popham and Coke—we can make sense of simultaneous judicial deference to and oversight of Privy Council orders, at least until 1627.

We begin with a critical distinction among writs to the Council: between those returned with a cause of detention and those without. Conciliar returns made with a cause were like returns with a cause made by JPs, and were generally treated in the same way.[61] Those returned without a cause, by contrast, raised different issues and were treated quite differently. Whereas jail orders made by JPs or others without a cause were almost always rejected by King's Bench, those without a cause by the Council were not. Given what we have seen of the justices' readiness to look beyond the return, the court was never lacking for ways to make serious judgments about those imprisoned by the Council, even when the Council returned writs without a cause of imprisonment.

From the start of Elizabeth's reign to the Revolution of 1688, only a tiny fraction of imprisonment orders inspected on habeas corpus had been made by the monarch, the Privy Council, or the principal secretary or secretary of state.[62] Of these, 30 percent were returned without a cause of imprisonment. Just over half of writs returned in this way issued before the 1628 passage of the Petition of Right, with the remainder issued thereafter.[63]

Release rates suggest that King's Bench showed greater deference to conciliar returns than to those of other magistrates. As Coke himself put it in 1615, the Council might return writs "without expressing any cause, because there are *arcana imperii*, and great inconvenience may ensue if they are revealed."[64] For this reason, the court showed greater deference to Council writs returned without a cause than to those with one. This changed after 1627–1628: while release rates on conciliar imprisonment orders returned without a cause before 1628 ran at under one-third, for the period 1628 to 1689, they reached 55 percent, on par with average release rates for all other writs in that period. Results on both sides of this moment should catch our eye, but for opposite reasons: because before 1627–1628, King's Bench did in fact dismiss some Privy Council prisoners whose writs were returned without cause; and because it did not dismiss some of these prisoners thereafter, despite the requirements of the Petition of Right and the 1641 Star Chamber statute.[65]

These numbers matter, for two reasons. First, they show the court's willingness to explore the legality of Council imprisonment orders returned without a cause stated, even before 1627 and despite the court's posture of respect toward the Council. That respect had limits, explicable in part by the ease of communication between a Council and a court that shared membership. Information flowed easily between court and Council, whether or not it was in a return. Second, as we saw in Chapter 4, these results show that the court must have considered evidence from beyond the return. There is no other way to explain divergent results on returns that said nothing about the facts of detention. There was no simple rule about Privy Council imprisonment orders returned without a cause, requiring either remand or release, before or after 1628. Instead, the court handled these on a case-by-case basis. Judges, not rules, made the decisions. Even so, the judges' approach to making those decisions changed after 1628, and especially after 1641.

During the early sixteenth century, King's Bench sorted felony suspects jailed by the Council in the same way they sorted those jailed by JPs: freeing some, while sending others on for trial.[66] The justices sorted traitors too. In 1558, habeas corpus brought six traitors accused before Queen Mary's Council before Queen's Bench, which released two while sending the others on to trial and execution.[67] The same process might be used whether the accused was committed by order of the king, the entire council, or one councilor alone.[68] In such cases, writs returned without cause functioned as part of otherwise routine criminal process. For instance, no concern about the absence of a cause from the return to the writ for Peter Leper and John Stevens appears in the court's arraignment of them for murder in 1542.[69] Some cases of conciliar commitment without a cause were more politically charged. Sir Robert Sheffield, fresh from a conflict with Lord Chancellor and Cardinal Thomas Wolsey, was arrested by the king's command in 1518. Even so, habeas served a procedural rather than a review function; it brought Sheffield to King's Bench, where he was remanded to the Tower.[70]

By the middle of the sixteenth century, we can make two observations about habeas use to supervise imprisonment orders made by the king, his council, or a single councilor. First, most such writs and their returns looked rather ordinary, especially when compared to JPs' jail orders. The majority concerned allegations of felony or treason, with the writs being used to send the accused to trial. Second, in cases for which the Council returned no cause, the court showed great, though not complete, deference. Clearly, it considered such returns on a case-by-case basis, working beyond the return in doing so. Given that the court ordered remand in the majority of imprisonment orders made by JPs before 1558—whether or not their returns noted the charge— the court's similar response to conciliar orders should not surprise us.[71]

How did the justices understand the work of king and council when ordering imprisonment? In a 1532 discussion of royal imprisonment orders, they concluded:

[I]f any man is imprisoned by the king's command, he is not replevi-
sable [bailable], from which it appears that the king can send a man to
prison. And his discretion is not to be argued about, any more than
[that] of any other justice. But whether the cause for which he sent him
to prison is lawful or not may be determined by the law; [for] the statute of Magna Carta is *nullus liber homo capiatur, etc* . . . from which it appears that the king cannot treat his subject contrary to the law.[72]

The key here is "contrary to the law." By the Statute of Westminster I,
the king's imprisonment orders were legal, so long as he acted within
law.[73] Despite the apparent tautology, this analysis reveals the contra-
puntal relationship between court and council, in which the "discretion" of each raised questions for the discretion of the other. The parallel drawn between the king and "any other justice" was important.
The king's discretion—and, by extension, conciliar discretion—might
be "determined by the law," just like the discretion of any JP. The court
showed its respect for royal and conciliar decision-making at the same
time that it bounded such decision-making, just as it did when watching the work of JPs.

James Morice developed this view of the king as "the supreme judge
of the realm" in his 1578 reading on the prerogative. The king, "by his
prerogative, may command any subject to be arrested and imprisoned." Nonetheless, royal orders might be reviewed and should only
have temporary effect:

[Y]et is his majesty by justice bound to publish and declare in time convenient the cause of such imprisonment and the party so committed is
to be arraigned, tried, and judged for his offence according to the laws
and customs of the realm, for this is the liberty of the subject confirmed by the great charter of England.[74]

Some arrested at the command of the king or one of his councilors, upon being brought into court by habeas corpus, were released.
Whether or not a cause was returned, and whether the prisoner had
been committed by command of the king, the council, or a single
councilor mattered little to the outcome, which was determined by the
justices' response to individual cases as they came before them.

We can detect signs of this emphasis on judicial discretion rather
than on rules in 1562, as Chief Justice of Common Pleas Sir James

Dyer made notes of two earlier writs. The return for Thomas Apryse, in 1518, indicated nothing more than that he had been imprisoned by command of Cardinal Wolsey; no cause was named. King's Bench bailed, then discharged him. The other, for John Hodges and Thomas Heyth in 1546, concerned their commitment by conciliar order without any cause named. Both were committed to the Marshalsea and later ordered to hang. Dyer concluded that these cases showed

> that the court of King's Bench has authority to send for any prisoner in the realm, to examine the cause of committal, and to bail him or commit him to the Marshalsea or enlarge him if it seems expedient.[75]

Dyer emphasized judicial discretion rather than working to rule—"if it seems expedient"—an approach that jibed with the view expressed in the 1532 discussion and in Morice's reading.

It is difficult to know what, if anything, to make of the difference between Dyer's two cases: that Apryse was committed by an individual, while Hodges and Heyth had been committed by the entire Council.[76] In the mid-sixteenth century, the court increasingly focused on this distinction. Nonetheless, as late as the spring of 1538, King's Bench had remanded a prisoner whose imprisonment had been ordered, without a cause stated, by a single councilor: Thomas Cromwell, lord privy seal and the king's secretary.[77] Perhaps owing to Cromwell's own execution in 1540, the court adopted a more critical view of imprisonment orders made by a lone councilor.[78] But prison orders made by the king alone or the entire Council continued to end either in remand or release, whether or not the returns contained a cause. The principle asserted by Morice in 1578—that those imprisoned without a cause in the warrant should soon be proceeded against according to law for a known cause—persisted as the justices continued to take a case-by-case approach to royal imprisonment orders.[79] Whether or not the cause was named in the return mattered little in such an approach.

These issues were discussed by all the justices in 1592. The report of that discussion, made by Sir Edmund Anderson, chief justice of Common Pleas, underscored the distinction between imprisonment orders by individual councilors and those by the queen or the whole Council. A manuscript report suggests that the discussion was prompted by the imprisonment of John Agmondesham, ordered by the lord chamberlain after Agmondesham brought suit against one of the queen's servants, thus violating royal privilege.[80] The judges' resolution in the printed reports noted vaguely that "divers persons" had been imprisoned "for suing ordinary actions and suits at the common law." Habeas corpus had been issued for them, "upon which writs no good or lawful cause of imprisonment hath been returned or certified." The court had then discharged such prisoners, "according to the laws." The justices thus recommended that in the future, the queen's "subjects may not be committed nor detained in prison by commandment of any nobleman or councilor against the laws of the realm."[81]

The 1592 resolution, made in response to the Council's request for advice, outlined three ways that prisoners might be committed: "by her Majesty's commandment from her person"; by order of the whole Council; or by any one or two councilors, if their warrant specified high treason as the cause.[82] In any case, the court could still send writs to ensure that one of these reasons was the cause of detention. If upon review the justices found the commitment "certified to the judges as it ought to be," then the prisoner would be remanded. The "ought" has generated confusion in understanding this resolution.[83] "As it ought to be" meant any order by the queen or the entire Council, with or without a cause, or an order by a single councilor that had to state a cause. Either way, Queen's Bench might always issue habeas to explore the matter and do as it saw fit by "the laws of the realm." The justices had mapped out zones of deference to royal authority, zones that look very much like those charted in the discussion of 1532 and in Morice's reading. But as both those commentaries had emphasized, deference was not a bar to supervision. The court would continue to monitor Privy Council imprisonment orders. In doing so, Queen's Bench declared what counted as jurisdiction, whether it released prisoners or remanded them.

Many writs returning an imprisonment order made by the whole Council, without a cause stated, continued to end in orders to remand after 1592.[84] When such returns produced the prisoner's release, we can only conclude that the judges had made their decisions based on information off the return. In the autumn of 1597, Edward Harcourt was taken into custody on suspicion of having uttered "traitorous words." An order was then given to the attorney general, Sir Edward Coke, to examine him. The following winter, habeas corpus issued on Harcourt's behalf. He was bailed on a return showing his imprisonment by the Council that made no mention of traitorous words or of any other cause.[85] Given that five months later a similar return on behalf of Robert Barnes ended with a remand order, we must conclude that what mattered was not the absence of a cause in the return when committed by the entire Council, but the particular circumstances of each case, as revealed orally in court.[86]

This usage persisted through the early decades of the next century. Nothing appeared in the return to the writ for Edward Lord Vaux, except the Council's command that he be held "until further order be taken from us." Evidence beyond the return shows that, like other Catholics, Vaux had refused to swear the oath of allegiance, by which he would have to foreswear the Pope's authority. In Vaux's case, the writ may have been used not to test the legality of an imprisonment warrant made without cause, but to bring him into court to ask again if he might swear the oath. Reports show that there was no shortage of discussion of facts from beyond the return as the justices quizzed Vaux. Like others in his predicament, Vaux refused the oath, but proclaimed his readiness to swear his "allegiance to the king in temporal matters." His effort to separate spiritual and secular loyalty was of little avail. King's Bench returned him to prison at the king's pleasure, the terseness of the return to his writ notwithstanding.[87]

A string of cases of 1615, while Coke was chief justice, underscored what by then were two widely accepted notions: that the king or full Council might commit a subject to prison on a warrant that did not express a cause; and that King's Bench might send habeas corpus for any such prisoner, review the return, and then remand. Citing the statute of Westminster I, the foundation for this view since at least 1532, Coke declared that a prisoner "committed by the Council is not bailable . . . because the Council is incorporated in the king." Coke invoked the analogy used in 1532, likening the Council to other courts or justices. Similarly, he noted, if he, as chief justice, or his court ordered imprisonment, no other court could grant bail.[88] This explains why Privy Council orders received the respect they did: not out of deference to the Council's "executive" quality, but because the Council, like King's Bench, was one of the king's courts, using a jurisdiction simultaneously honored and bounded by the judgments of King's Bench.

Given all this, the judgment in the Five Knights' case in November 1627 must have made perfect sense to the judges.[89] The court acted on that occasion within two consistent and well-articulated understandings: that King's Bench might send habeas corpus to any prison to investigate any imprisonment order; and that upon learning that one had been imprisoned by order of the king or full council without a cause returned, the justices would remand or release the prisoner as they saw fit. Since the court had reached just this conclusion on another writ earlier in 1627, their judgment to do the same in November should not surprise us.[90]

The law did not change in 1627, but its political meaning did. Appreciating the legal ground of the decision in the Five Knights' case heightens rather than diminishes the importance of the parliamentary debates of 1628 and the resulting Petition of Right's new requirement that none should be imprisoned "without any cause showed." But for all the seeming clarity of the phrase "without any cause showed," there was little immediate change in the court's decisions, in part because the justices of King's Bench in the 1630s showed such a different temperament from their predecessors. Release rates on habeas corpus plunged during the reign of Charles I until the start of the Civil War in 1642.[91] Little wonder that in 1641, as political tensions grew and as members of Parliament pursued their complaints against many who served the king, refusals by the justices to grant habeas corpus in some cases, or to order release in others, figured prominently in public debate.[92]

Novelties: Civil War and Revolution

By exploring hundreds of cases across many decades, we can gain a sense of practices and principles, if not rules, that constituted a jurisprudence of normalcy. At the center of this jurisprudence stood the idea that the court might inspect imprisonment orders made at any time, anywhere, by any authority. This simple idea, grounded in the prerogative, marked the point from which the justices' use of the writ expanded. Rather than analogize among cases—follow precedents—their thinking radiated in every direction from this core principle.[93] The court's work thus covered novelties as soon as they appeared, restraining new practices or jurisdictions that posed greater threats to law and liberty than did older ones. The jurisprudence of normalcy that the court had developed in order to watch the work of JPs or the

Privy Council would be critical as novelties proliferated during civil war in the 1640s and thereafter. Remarkably, judicial authority would persist, with the prerogative living on in the judges' hands even after the king himself was destroyed.

In the summer of 1642, armies in Parliament's pay began to fire on armies in the king's pay. Few had wished that the controversies that had begun to gather in the late 1630s should burst into the full flood of war. But after an invasion from Scotland, then a rebellion in Ireland, Charles I's three kingdoms were at war, and none more disastrously than England, at war with itself.[94] Civil war presents the ultimate jurisdictional nightmare. Who was in charge, and by what right? How, during war, might the potential for peace be sustained by those who traditionally answered these questions? These were the problems faced by the judges who remained in Westminster Hall in the 1640s. Crisis generated new jurisdictions that used new powers to imprison. King's Bench would exercise its superior jurisdiction and contain such novelties, even kill them off, as it remained energized by the activating principle behind habeas corpus, the prerogative.[95]

Parliament held London as military fortunes favored one side, then the other. Courts remained open, but the judiciary was in disarray.[96] In King's Bench, Justices Sir Thomas Malet and Sir Robert Berkeley were impeached and imprisoned by Parliament. In June 1642, after the king commanded his justices to come to him at York, Justice Sir Robert Heath left London. Chief Justice Bramston dithered, so the king named Heath to replace him. But Heath would remain in Oxford, the heart of royalism, and would never sit in Westminster Hall. In October 1642, as the first season of military campaigning drew to a close, Charles—at Bridgnorth, in Shropshire—knighted Francis Bacon and made him a justice of King's Bench. Bacon then went to London, where, for the next three years, he would work alone. As litigation in general collapsed, habeas use persisted.[97] Though appointed by the king, Bacon's legitimacy and integrity would never be challenged by Parliament, even as his judgments on habeas corpus offered a running critique of the jurisdictional novelties Parliament generated to prosecute a war against their king.[98]

Bacon made his judicial temperament immediately clear. Though he could not open the court for Michaelmas term until November 21—just one week before the term's traditional end—he quickly issued habeas corpus for nine prisoners.[99] In deference to tradition and to the king's new chief justice, all these writs went forth with Chief Justice Heath's name in the *teste* clause at the end. All further writs granted until Heath's removal by Parliament in November 1645 would issue in the same form. But Bacon's decisions were what mattered, indicating as they did his independence in the face of political turmoil.

Isaac Pennington, eager parliamentarian and London's mayor, learned repeatedly that his overactive use of imprisonment in support of his cause was illegal. He should not have jailed William Hayward, a clergyman Pennington called "an ill affected person to the state" after Hayward's refusal to read a parliamentary ordinance in his parish. Nor should Pennington have put John Davys in the Poultry Counter "until you shall have order for his discharge"—a potentially indefinite order for imprisonment—for "publishing a scandalous paper against the Parliament." Pennington sent John Cooke to the same lockup, but did not even bother with a reason. He simply commanded—in a manner once used by the Privy Council of the king he now fought—that Cooke should be kept "until further order from me."[100] Bacon released them all.

More remarkable was the help Bacon extended to those imprisoned by Parliament. House of Commons journals show imprisonment orders for dozens in the months leading up to and opening the war in 1642. Some were jailed for seditious words, others for failing to support the military effort. Among these, a handful thought to test their imprisonment. Only days after he had reopened King's Bench, Bacon sent writs on behalf of Samuel Mason and two others jailed by parliamentary command after their refusal to serve in the militia and because they were "notoriously known to be malignant and refractory." Some of Parliament's most prominent leaders had signed the warrants for their commitment, including John Pym and Henry Vane. Even so, upon considering the returns, Bacon ordered these political prisoners bailed. The House of Commons reacted angrily, giving orders the following February that the court should stay its proceedings. The Crown Side rulebook shows Bacon's persistence as Mason and the others remained on bail. Only after Hilary term ended did the Commons approve an order to jail Mason and the others once again.[101]

A contest between court and Parliament had now begun. A writ sent in the summer of 1643 for Edward Bower, imprisoned by various MPs "for the safety of the kingdom," was returned, and the return was read in court, but nothing more came of it.[102] Perhaps the precedent had now been set that no imprisonment order of either House might be reversed by writs from King's Bench. If so, the opening months of civil war could not have been the best time for MPs to take to themselves the same power to imprison without review that so many had opposed when claimed by the Privy Council fifteen years earlier. In the generations before the Five Knights' case and the parliamentary debates of 1628, a balance had persisted between the Privy Council and King's Bench about which authority would determine jurisdiction in cases involving the imprisonment of subjects. Beginning in 1628, Parliament's increasing insertion of itself into the life of habeas corpus produced a struggle, culminating in the 1640s and 1650s, between court and Parliament. Modern democratic assumptions about a partnership between legislative and judicial action mean that we do not normally approach the history of habeas corpus from this perspective. As we shall see more fully in Chapter 7, however, action in Parliament and colonial legislatures would impose the most serious limits on the writ's work from this period onward.

The pattern Bacon established in late 1642 would persist throughout the war in answer to the novel jurisdictions Parliament created. Without a king to approve their legislation, Parliament produced "ordinances": statutes by another name. Ordinances generated the bewildering array of committees created to manage the war by building militias, procuring supplies, and collecting funds. Their work shows up in the writ files as imprisonment orders—made to enforce the committees' will—that were challenged by habeas corpus. These usually ended with the release of prisoners. Committees for accounts were especially aggressive in 1646, as the costs of war came to a head. Soldiers arrested soldiers when they refused to present their accounts for review. Habeas corpus released them.[103]

Among the other authorities that Parliament created were those concerned with imposing a new religious settlement. The Book of Common Prayer was abolished and Parliament tried to establish a national presbyterian church to replace the now outlawed episcopal one. Clergy who refused to go along lost their parishes. Among the ordinances passed to effect these changes was one "for keeping in godly ministers." Other ordinances outlawed unlicensed preaching. Clergymen imprisoned by those who enforced these ordinances, though arguably committed according to a strict reading of their terms, were released on habeas corpus.[104] So too were others imprisoned by army and militia committees.[105] Given the court's assertive monitoring of JPs and all other commissioned authorities in the generations before 1642, prison orders made by novel authorities during civil war must have seemed even more dubious in King's Bench.

Some of this judicial work came close to reversing Parliament's own prison orders. Thomas Payne was released from the Gatehouse by habeas corpus after he was confined there by order of the House of Commons' "Committee for Dispersers of Scandalous Pamphlets."[106] John Albany, jailed by the same committee, was initially remanded, but later bailed.[107] Christopher Hudson, who refused to pay his tithes, was taken into custody by Parliament's serjeant-at-arms, yet he too was discharged.[108] Although to some it may have seemed by 1642–1643 that parliamentary imprisonment orders were above question, these later cases show that the issue remained unsettled. One jurisdictional novelty after another saw its work undone by habeas corpus even though, since the autumn of 1645, Bacon had been joined in King's Bench by a new justice, Henry Rolle, who had been appointed by the same Parliament whose committees and ordinances these writs challenged.

Much changed after the execution of Charles I in January 1649. Law itself appeared threatened after the law of treason—once defined as compassing the death of the king—had been used to put the king himself to death for his treason against the people. Lawyers, including many who had vigorously supported Parliament, were aghast when a nonmonarchical commonwealth was proclaimed. Bacon, like other judges, resigned. But Rolle stayed on, accepting appointment as chief justice of what was now called the Upper Bench.

What would become of a writ whose greatness had arisen from the king's prerogative when there was no king? Habeas use declined markedly during the 1650s.[109] But in Rolle's hands, there were glimmers of its old power to prevent the worst excesses of novel authority. The writ blunted the force of draconian ordinances concerned with blasphemy.[110] It also checked the work of the committee of indemnity.[111] William Gotely, jailed by the militia committee, used habeas as late as April 1651 to gain his freedom.[112] The writ's persistence testifies to the autonomy from its source—the prerogative—that it had achieved in practice. The language of sovereignty would continue to operate through habeas corpus as a justification for its work. But there was only so much the writ and the justices could do in circumstances as strange to the English legal imagination as these, when England was led by parliaments of dubious legitimacy and by a great military leader turned Lord Protector, Oliver Cromwell.[113] Yet even military commanders, if not the Lord Protector, might be made into so many lesser jurisdictions by King's Bench.

Novelties: Military Jurisdictions

King's Bench made a new jurisdiction for itself out of the wreckage of the Civil War as it supervised imprisonment orders by military officers for the first time. Early in the war, it bailed prisoners committed on the warrant of the Earl of Essex, commander of Parliament's armies, when the returns to their writs made no mention of why he imprisoned them.[114] Shortly before the Restoration, the justices of the Upper Bench bailed Francis Lord Willoughby, former governor of Barbados and royalist conspirator, from military custody at Hull.[115] But the most serious assertions of judicial oversight of military detentions occurred after 1689, when Chief Justice Holt's court monitored the Privy Council's orders to commit prisoners suspected of crimes against the state.

In the late seventeenth and eighteenth centuries, King's Bench reviewed detentions concerning insubordination and soldiers' other crimes, as well as desertion, conscription and impressment, and prisoners of war. The court would show that commitments made by a military officer's oral command and returned without naming a charge were no better than orders in the same form made by a single privy councilor or JP.[116] King's Bench might also become involved when there was a charge written into the warrant committing a soldier to custody, whether for felony or for wrongs peculiar to military life. Thus Holt's court discharged Conrad Greven from his confinement by the Duke of Schomberg, commander of the king's forces, for forgetting "the respect due to me and other superior officers."[117]

This supervision of detention for wrongs known only to military law persisted across the eighteenth century and into the nineteenth. Lt. Richard Blake sued habeas corpus in 1814 in order to avoid being sent

to court martial in the Netherlands after his regiment had shipped
there from Windsor, where his alleged acts of insubordination had occurred. Upon considering the extensive affidavits made out for his
writ, King's Bench ordered that he remain in England for trial.[118] In
1799, William Merrin and two of his shipmates aboard HMS *Ulysses*
were confined by order of their captain on allegations that they had
pilfered a chest owned by a Spanish POW they had been transporting
from Minorca to Barcelona, probably for a prisoner exchange. Despite
their repeated requests, Merrin and his companions were never tried
according to Admiralty law. It took habeas corpus to move things
along.[119]

King's Bench might even review judgments and sentences of courts
martial. After John Suddis, an artilleryman, was convicted in 1801 by
court martial at Gibraltar for receiving stolen goods, he was sentenced
to transportation and then returned to England to await shipment to
Australia. While there, Suddis used habeas corpus. After making its review, King's Bench concluded that Suddis had been properly tried,
and he was sent on to Botany Bay. Once again, the court had underscored the principle that had formed the writ's core for two centuries:
that the court might use the writ to explore the circumstances of
detentions of any kind, including those made by the military. As Chief
Justice Kenyon put it, "[W]e may examine into this question on a return to a habeas corpus."[120]

Desertion—a wrong assigned by statute to the jurisdiction of courts
martial—might be monitored by King's Bench in the same way.[121]
James Alexander, for example, was discharged by the court from the
Savoy, the principal military prison, after his 1706 confinement for desertion.[122] Desertion was closely connected to claims of dubious impressment or conscription. William Smith, imprisoned in 1692 as a de-
serting sailor, was bailed on what must have been a determination that
the impressment that had put him in the navy was legally incorrect.[123]
Mordecai Elias's circumstances were more pitiful, he being "uncured
of his lunacy" when, in 1761, he broke free from the chains that held
him at home. He managed to make it out into the street, where he was
met by Captain David Parkhill's recruiting party. Parkhill immediately
enlisted him, then tried unsuccessfully to extort twenty guineas from
Mordecai's father for his release. Elias was apparently released by a negotiated settlement in reply to the writ his father had sued for his dis-

missal from service. Parkhill's return claimed that Elias was a soldier, properly enlisted, though affidavits from keepers of Bedlam and St. Luke's hospitals testified to his insanity. Regardless of the outcome, issuance of the writ again signaled the court's readiness to supervise the behavior of military officers pursuing charges of desertion.[124] One of the first writs of habeas corpus issued in Australia in 1824 likewise concerned desertion, with the chief justice clearly feeling free to examine military detentions of this kind.[125]

Impressment was the most frequent occasion of a King's Bench review of military detention. In 1694, habeas corpus had been used to ensure that those forced into naval service did not also have to suffer the indignity of imprisonment along the way.[126] Further need for the writ arose in the wake of successive statutes authorizing JPs to take men without employment and turn them over to recruiting officers, "to be entertained as soldiers in her majesty's service." Once conscripted, the receiving officer would read the articles of war, which explained the punishment for desertion: death.[127] Because these recruiting statutes excepted certain kinds of persons—namely those with visible means of support or those able to participate in electing MPs—they provided the basis on which a handful would test their recruitment using habeas in the years following.[128] A single ostensible soldier, Thomas Reynolds, would be released by habeas corpus in the 1740s.[129] But doubts persisted about the propriety of using the writ this way, especially since ordering the discharge of soldiers might not indemnify them from punishment for desertion. This explains the more common practice of King's Bench in the 1750s of releasing wrongly conscripted soldiers by making rules for discharge, though habeas corpus would continue to be used on occasion in the decades ahead for the same purpose.[130]

Habeas corpus, as an instrument by which complex settlements were negotiated, would remain useful in a situation like John Parkin's. Parkin may initially have signed up with an artillery regiment to avoid finishing his apprenticeship to a Sheffield cutler in 1757. When his master complained to his company's commanders, Parkin was restored to the cutler's service on the understanding that he would return to his regiment when his apprenticeship concluded that December. When the time came, however, life as a journeyman cutler apparently began to look better to Parkin, so he remained at his forge in Sheffield until he was seized by members of his regiment as a deserter and put in the house of correction at Wakefield. Parkin's master now sued habeas corpus, and he was soon discharged.[131]

In the same way that King's Bench supervised custody of felonious soldiers, deserters, and impressed sailors, it also inspected the custody of "prisoners at war." To understand how, we must first examine ideas and practices concerning POWs. Throughout the seventeenth century, there was little in the way of doctrine about how, in law, to think about or handle such prisoners. This is not terribly surprising, for two reasons. First, when prisoners were taken during war, no one intended that they should be held very long. Second, and related to this, the chief value of POWs was not as adversaries removed indefinitely from combat, but as objects for exchange, either for ransom or for England's own POWs held by an adversary.

Medieval POW practice focused on ransom, "the price of [the prisoner's] life." As Sir Matthew Hale explained, those taken in battle were negotiable commodities, wherein various parties have an "interest whereof the common law takes notice," since king and captor shared the ransom.[132] By the 1620s, when England was battling France and Spain, most captives were taken at sea by privateers who kept them in England until ransomed. Doing so raised concerns about the safety of the state. In response, the king proclaimed that privateers' captives should be kept in confinement so that they could not "confer with our ill affected subjects." But the intention remained the same as always: to hold them as briefly as possible until they might be offered in "exchange for our subjects, which shall happen to be prisoners."[133]

This focus on the exchange value of prisoners of war persisted throughout the seventeenth and eighteenth centuries. There was little need to develop a law for managing POWs, or even for investigating their status, since the point was to be rid of them quickly.[134] The Admiralty's Commissioners for Sick, Wounded, and Prisoners of War, first established during the Dutch wars of the 1660s, oversaw POWs, both soldiers and sailors. Reestablished when war resumed in 1689, the commissioners managed the care of POWs and maintained contacts with opposing powers to arrange exchanges.[135] Private vessels plied the Channel, carrying human cargoes for exchange, for which their owners were paid by the head. The profit motive continued to shape the handling of POWs. Even so, "private capture is a part of public justice," as one author writing in the midst of the Seven Years' War put it, and had to be monitored to curb opportunities for embezzlement.[136]

Of increasing interest as the scale of war grew after the 1690s, and especially after 1756, was the value of enemy prisoners as the means by which captive Britons might be returned home. To those who opposed the return of POWs out of fear that they might bolster enemy forces, one author argued that exchanges, by increasing faith between belligerents, would shorten war because foes would care better for each other's prisoners. The emphasis on brief confinement of POWs persisted as exchanges became the means by which Britain's sovereign extended to his own subjects the protection owed to them for their allegiance: "[T]he state is under an obligation to procure, as soon as possible, the release of its subjects from those evils to which they become subjected in its defense." Every POW had a cash value, according to rank, in order to simplify the accounting required for swapping them and bringing them home as quickly as possible.[137]

A paucity of reported cases has left confusion about the role of habeas corpus in monitoring the keeping of POWs.[138] The issue has typically been approached by asking whether a POW could be released by habeas corpus. Even in the 1690s, the answer to this question was no: a person properly categorized as a "prisoner at war" could only be dismissed by exchange. But this is the wrong question. Instead, we must ask whether the writ could be used to investigate whether a person was correctly labeled a POW.

Given the intensity of war on multiple fronts in the 1690s, and given what we have seen of Holt's energy in overseeing the related imprisonment orders for alleged traitors, we can readily understand how this would be the critical period for the monitoring of POWs by habeas corpus. The court's interest in all forms of confinement arising from political anxiety explains how King's Bench responded to Abraham Fuller's situation in early 1690. Fuller's writ was returned with no information about any charges against him. It noted only that he had been committed by order of three commissioners of the Court of Admiralty and by a subsequent order in the Privy Council that he be held "as a prisoner at war." King's Bench discharged him, perhaps because the Council warrant for his arrest, made the previous November, alleged "treasonable practices." Fuller had landed in Chester, the usual point of entry from Ireland, when much of Ireland was in arms for James II and thus those arriving from there provoked suspicion. But none of this was explained in the return, which simply indicated that he should be held as a POW.[139] We might speculate that habeas corpus had permitted the kind of broad investigation of his status—by examining facts from beyond the return—that made clear the absurdity of his assignment to the category of POW.

Other cases point to the same conclusion. The return to Garrett Cumberford's 1697 writ claimed only that he had been put in Newgate in February 1693, and that two years later, he, with thirty-one others, was transferred to the Savoy as a POW. The return to his writ mentioned no other charge. He too was bailed.[140] John Golding's story ended less happily, though as a matter of law, it expressed exactly the same principle: that King's Bench should supervise the detention of POWs. Golding had been captured at sea off the Lizard Peninsula in 1692 by an English galley ironically called the *James*. A Dublin native, Golding was "second captain" of the *Sun,* a Jacobite vessel flying French colors. All this was recounted in the return to his writ, which then concluded that he was detained as a "prisoner at war." Golding was bailed on giving surety to appear at the next Admiralty sessions. It was there that he was tried for treason, found guilty, and later executed at Rotherhithe Stairs between the low and high tide marks.[141]

The goal in these cases was not to dismiss actual POWs, but to assess whether they had been properly categorized as POWs. Judging from the names of those involved, we might guess that each was actually a subject of one of the British crowns. This was true of Golding, an Irishman in the employ of an enemy prince, turned over to trial for treason after an enquiry into his status was performed by habeas corpus. We might surmise that Fuller and Cumberford, too, were shown to be subjects, and thus wrongly labeled as POWs. War in the 1690s was a messy business, especially in regard to the subjecthood of the combatants, many of whom, by their loyalty to James II, had renounced any allegiance to William and Mary. Many Britons fought as privateers against the new monarchs, some in the pay of James II, others commissioned by Louis XIV. Distinguishing aliens from subjects became a delicate business, on which much hinged. When ships filled with sailors speaking multiple languages were captured, we can imagine that the first impulse would be to declare all the captives POWs. But it would take more work to figure out just who those people were and what, by law, should become of them.[142] Some captives discovered to be English, Scottish, or Irish subjects were summarily dismissed after swearing oaths of loyalty. Others were kept for trial as traitors. In a few instances, distinguishing foreign POWs from subjects potentially guilty of treason was only possible by using habeas corpus to make a review.

The contrasting treatment of French captives shows more clearly the sorting function performed by habeas corpus. French captives, combatants and noncombatants alike, were ordered held, sometimes in private houses or other places offering loose confinement "according to their quality," in other words, their social station. On petition, some might be freed until they could be exchanged.[143] A few, like Peter Depremont and three fellow French merchants trapped in England when the war began, sued habeas corpus and were brought into King's Bench. The return to their writs explained that they were Frenchmen, to be held *"durante bello"* (during the war) and that a dozen English merchants were in similar circumstances at Morlaix. On this, they were remanded, to await an exchange for their English counterparts.[144] John Dupuis, a Frenchman captured at Exeter "on suspicion of being a spy," was likewise remanded to await exchange after his imprisonment order was inspected by King's Bench.[145] Daniel DuCastre and Francis LaPierre were also labeled "alien enemies and spies" in the return to the habeas corpus, but they were bailed, and later discharged.[146]

What shall we make of these Frenchmen? First, King's Bench used the writ as it had been used since the beginning of the seventeenth century: as a means to review the circumstances behind the confinement of any person, held anywhere, by anyone. Second, upon receiving a return stating that a prisoner was a POW, the court explored the evidence supporting the captive's assignment to that category. The court never released a person it concluded had been properly designated as a POW. But the justices did release those who were discovered to be something else. The court did the work it always performed with habeas, supervising the jurisdiction of others to ensure that it was rightly used. In the case of John Golding, incorrect labeling as a POW was corrected by relabeling him a suspected traitor and then proceeding according to law. In the case of Abraham Fuller, incorrect labeling as a POW was corrected by releasing him.

After 1697, POWs disappear from the writ files and reported cases until 1759. Why? That the papers of the Admiralty's Commissioners for Sick, Wounded, and Prisoners of War survive only from 1698 points to important changes in the organization of Britain's military prisoner establishment during these years.[147] As we have seen, the commissioners' work concentrated on exchanges, the means by which virtually all POWs would be freed. The emphasis on speed remained, with one treaty requiring exchange within four weeks of capture.[148] This commitment to exchange was underscored by what exchange meant for one's own prisoners: it was a patriotic imperative to recover for captive British soldiers that "perfect right"—their freedom—arising from "allegiance and protection."[149]

Protecting British subjects was accomplished not only by exchanging for them, but also by caring for foreign soldiers as if they were British subjects, because they were. POWs were consistently understood as being within the protection of a subjecthood that arose from surrender, by which "hostility ceases."[150] Thus a POW might be tried for felony, or even treason; he might sue or be sued. British courts congratulated themselves on the impact of civilization, which had "soften[ed] the rigors of war," in part by granting POWs access to courts.[151]

If a POW, like other aliens, was in law's protection, what might he do with habeas corpus? Since the Admiralty commissioners worked to exchange them quickly, we need not be surprised to find few POWs questioning their detention in court. Furthermore, since no one thought a person properly designated as a POW could be released, few would have been inspired to proceed by this means. In accounts of the legal expenses incurred in keeping POWs, no sign survives of costs in habeas cases.[152] But a few captives called POWs did employ the writ to review their cases. What happened to them?

Bernard Schiever was an unfortunate Swede. His 1759 affidavit showed that he had left home hoping to find work in the English merchant marine. Along the way, his ship was taken by a French privateer. Later, he was captured by the British and carried to Liverpool, where he was detained as a POW. On his affidavit, and that of another sailor who confirmed his story, motion was made for habeas corpus. Full arguments on the motion were held, after which King's Bench denied him the writ. The key to the decision lay in Schiever's affidavit: that "upon his own showing" he was "clearly a prisoner of war."[153] No further investigation was required since the fundamental fact that he was a POW was conceded by his own testimony.

Three Spanish sailors captured twenty years later ended up in the same situation, for much the same reason. All gave affidavits in Spanish, which were then translated. These narrated their capture from a Spanish privateer. Though their king was an American ally then at war with Britain, the Spaniards agreed to help crew an English merchant ship from Jamaica on condition that they would be exchanged at voyage's end. But when they reached England, their captain not only refused their promised wages, he also turned them over as POWs. Despite what the judges thought was the captain's deceit, the Spaniards were refused release since in their own affidavits they called themselves "prisoners of war."[154]

To understand these cases, we must recall the discussion (in Chapter 4) of orders *nisi* and the increasing tendency to gather and sort facts about detention prior to the issuance of the writ rather than after its return. By the 1750s, many prisoners—POWs and others alike— would receive what amounted to full investigations of their confinement by habeas process before the writ issued. This is what happened in these two cases, in which the justices had a full discussion of the relevant facts. All these sailors remained in custody because, upon considering the evidence provided by their own affidavits, they were found to be properly within the jurisdiction bounded by the words "prisoner of war." Anyone correctly within the category of POW—like anyone correctly within the categories of suspected murderer awaiting trial, or prisoner convicted by properly used summary process—could not be released on habeas corpus.[155] But habeas corpus could still be used to answer the crucial question: had these prisoners been assigned correctly to those categories given the circumstances lying behind their detention?[156]

Prisoners of war, like others in military custody, remained, like all novelties, subject to the supervision of the king's "supreme judicature." As the POW cases show especially well, and as we shall see further in Chapter 6, "subject" was a highly elastic status, one that included any person held by another who acted by the king's authority. From the Civil War on, the justices of King's Bench had continued to apply the basic lesson that the prerogative, running through habeas corpus, always taught: that no jurisdiction, whether normal or novel, was beyond their oversight.

Novelties: Slaves

The story of James Somerset is well known, yet worth telling again. Born in Africa, he became one of those who, "by the laws of Virginia," could be "sold as goods and chattels." By the laws of Virginia, Charles Steuart made Somerset his chattel in 1749, when the violently displaced African was probably in his early teens. Twenty years later, Somerset accompanied Steuart to England, where he waited two years, until October 1771, to flee his master. In response, Steuart had Somerset seized and put aboard a ship bound for Jamaica, where he ordered him to be sold in the slave markets. It was then that Granville Sharp and other abolitionists obtained habeas corpus requiring the ship's captain to bring Somerset, along with the cause of his detention, into King's Bench. After lengthy arguments, Mansfield's court determined that a return stating that Somerset was Steuart's slave was insufficient, and ordered that he be discharged. It was a narrowly cast, and briefly explained, judgment, one that comported with the ways in which habeas decisions had been made and explained for centuries.[157]

Slavery was hardly novel in Virginia or Jamaica, though using habeas to question it in 1772 was. Recent dicta suggested that the writ might release individual slaves.[158] And in 1732, Ann Cartor—alleged to be a slave—had used the writ after being jailed "as a loose, idle, [and] disorderly person." On that occasion, the court disregarded claims that she was a slave, and simply released her from Bridewell, thus avoiding the problem of slavery as a legal practice.[159] In 1770, Sharp and others apparently used habeas to retrieve a slave called Thomas Lewis from a ship as it was about to sail for Jamaica.[160] In later proceedings on the indictment for assault and imprisonment brought by Lewis against his master, Mansfield mentioned that he had previously issued habeas on the affidavits of masters whose slaves had been impressed. The purpose of such writs, however, was not to free slaves, but to move them from one form of involuntary labor to another: to retrieve them from the navy's service so they could return to their masters' service, in the same manner that habeas was used to retrieve runaway apprentices from impressment.[161] Only in Somerset's case was habeas put to work directly on the question of whether one might be a slave in England.

The result was immediately and widely celebrated, though the decision freed just one slave, not all slaves. In fact, the Somerset judgment did not free a slave so much as it protected him from deportation, his counsel having relied, in part, on the 1679 Habeas Corpus Act's prohibition of the transportation of any person outside the realm without his or her agreement.[162] Though there were then thousands of people living in England who might be considered slaves, no rush for writs to release them followed. This resulted in part from Mansfield's terse judgment, which simply found the return to Somerset's writ insufficient. Habeas corpus, by its nature, could not enable a judge to declare illegal an entire system of bondage created by colonial legislatures.[163] The following year, habeas corpus won freedom for two African brothers, but by settlement rather than judgment.[164] In other cases, masters parried the writ by claiming that a slave was actually an apprentice. Thus Kenyon's King's Bench refused to send habeas corpus for John Hamlet in 1799.[165] In such closeted forms, slavery would persist.[166]

Somerset presents us with the Janus-faced quality of habeas corpus: that it could do so much, and so little, at once. As the language of liberty became ever more insistent in the late eighteenth century, the demands on habeas corpus grew. These demands expressed ideas about liberty that arose outside law and were now brought to law for protection. Such aspirations would sometimes be realized, as the crowd that cheered James Somerset's release learned. But they would also be disappointed.

To some extent, disappointment was only natural as the demands grew. And disappointment would become more apparent as the writ retreated from its work with political prisoners and troubled marriages beginning around 1790. Habeas corpus had released one slave, and perhaps a few others. But slavery's foes would be disappointed that habeas corpus had not, with one fell swoop, ended an infamous regime of oppression.[167] Across the Atlantic, slaves remained chattel. And all over the growing empire, as the eighteenth century became the nineteenth, the varieties of servitude proliferated, made possible by statutes passed at Westminster and in colonial assemblies around the globe. Nonetheless, the result in Somerset would live on, less as a precedent than as a way of articulating a demand that would not cease until slavery as a legal institution was brought down.[168] Habeas corpus would sometimes serve as a symbol of that demand, but would never serve as its ultimate instrument.

The most significant aspect of Somerset's case, as in POW cases, was not the result, but that it was a case at all. In Schiever's case, the court had maintained its jurisdiction over POWs by deciding whether that Swede truly counted as a POW. Similarly, for James Somerset, the fact of the writ's issuance was of the first importance. King's Bench issued the writ by reasoning not from precedents, but from the writ's central premise: that it exists to empower the justices to examine detention in all forms.[169] If the justices had any doubts about the propriety of doing so for a slave, they could look back on more than a century of novel uses found for the writ by the same process of reasoning that radiated from this core proposition. This way of conceiving and using habeas corpus had enabled the court repeatedly to explore detention situations in which there were no alleged wrongs: to confront violence in families or to handle detentions aboard his majesty's ships. There were no real precedents, but there was nothing any more surprising about using the writ for a slave trapped on a ship in the Downs than there was for a sailor trapped on a ship in the same waters. By issuing the writ, King's Bench fitfully made a new jurisdiction for itself; by its judgment, it began—very slightly—to kill off the jurisdiction of slaveholders over their slaves, just as it had always contained the jurisdiction of all others who held the bodies of the king's subjects. It now remains to consider what liberties this constraint of others' jurisdiction made for the king's subjects, and just who those subjects might be, African-born slaves among them.

CHAPTER 6

Making Liberties, Making Subjects

Mary Lady Rawlinson decided to marry again. We can only guess about any misgivings the widow may have had about her groom, Michael Lister. But before she married, she made a common enough arrangement, putting "her estate in her own power and out of his control." Perhaps Mr. Lister came to resent this arrangement, or maybe something else came between them; in any case, the marriage collapsed. Like other estranged couples in an age that did not countenance divorce, the Listers made a deed of separation, then went their separate ways, still married in law, but with a contract between them to fund their lives apart. This worked for a time, until Mr. Lister tried to reconcile. His wife refused: all he wanted was more money. So one Sunday, as she left church, Mr. Lister and an accomplice dashed up in a coach, grabbed Mrs. Lister, and "hurried her away to a remote place." Somehow, friends or family learned of her plight and gained a writ of habeas corpus on November 13, 1721. Four days later, Mr. Lister brought his wife before the justices of King's Bench.

Lister admitted abducting his wife, honestly explaining that he did so to encourage her to renegotiate their separation agreement. His counsel asked the justices not to "interpose between husband and wife." After all, "by law, the husband has a coercive power over the wife." The court could only agree, but added that this was "not a power to confine her; for by the law of England she is entitled to all reasonable liberty, if her behavior is not very bad." As long as the mutually informing statuses of husband and wife provided the frame for viewing the issue, the justices had a vague, culturally informed notion of "reasonable liberty" to apply in deciding what to do. Such a liberty was limited by the "coercive power" a husband might use to allay his and society's worry that a wife might "make an undue use of her liberty." A husband, "to preserve his honor and estate," would be justified "to lay such a wife under a restraint." But there was more here than a contest between a husband's lawful "coercive power" and a wife's "reasonable liberty." By contract—a separation agreement—the status of husband and its attendant liberties had been recast. For this reason, Mrs. Lister was "discharged from his custody."[1] The judges sent Mr. and Mrs. Lister their separate ways again.

The modern imagination smiles upon hearing such a story. Habeas corpus had answered its great purpose. The writ had humbled an oppressive and greedy husband, and a woman of independent means and mind had regained her liberty. But what did this mean?

We might feel tempted to answer by turning to the history of political thought. Few early modern ideas have received more treatment than "liberty," whether one emphasizes its republican or liberal character, its origins in the natural law notions of Hugo Grotius and John Selden, or its roots in the ostensibly ancient constitution of Sir Edward Coke.[2] Given that Mrs. Lister's troubles concerned the authority of husbands and the obedience of wives, we might try to read the case in terms of the contest between the divine-right patriarchal theories of Sir Robert Filmer and the natural rights that John Locke advanced to demolish them. But we should resist the temptation.

Mrs. Lister's barrister, Sir Thomas Reeve, had a case to win. The justices of King's Bench had a domestic conflict to resolve. Neither saw philosophy providing the right path through the issues. But if we listen carefully, we can hear all the actors speaking a vernacular liberty. "Reasonable liberty," allowable to those not "very bad," is hardly the stuff of great political thought. But it was just such language—incisively vague—that appears again and again in the use of habeas corpus and that proved so useful as lawyers argued and judges judged the cases of those who claimed to be wrongly denied their liberties.

Three aspects of liberty stood out in solving Mrs. Lister's problem. First, liberty was not an aspect of individuals; it was a quality in their relationships. Second, such liberties did not arise from an abstract cause—God or nature—from which flowed a host of qualities that defined liberty and humanity as ideas that held each other in a mutual embrace. Instead, the liberties at issue stood on commonsense norms and English law. Third, one could adjudicate among competing liberties in part by referring to the status of the parties involved. Such status might be understood in general social terms: in this case, the statuses of husband and wife. But general status conditions might be modified by other terms of law. In the Listers' case, contract did this work: first a premarital property agreement, and later, a deed of separation.

These ideas about liberties running through the writ of habeas corpus arose from and marked out an astonishingly vast subjecthood. Subjects varied—wives were not husbands, "natural-born" subjects were not "local" subjects—but all were subjects. As subjects, many were their liberties, all rapidly in motion as English law covered more people across the globe. Liberties came from subject status and thus from those parts of law that defined who were subjects. If liberties came from law, they were also subservient to law. At law's boundaries we shall find liberty's, as the Listers did, for liberty was law's subject.

Some would try to transpose law and liberty, to make law into liberty's subject. Because they worked through a critique of English law, they would fail. Even as they did, such critics, from John Lilburne to Granville Sharp and beyond, would call upon law to serve higher purposes: to protect liberties they thought were greater than law. In their hands, habeas corpus would become more than a legal device by which judges supervised jailers. It would become a synecdoche for liberty itself, a marker of what law ought to be or do, even when it wasn't or couldn't. They would make of habeas corpus a "bulwark," a "palladium" of liberty, using it to protect liberty for individuals when it could be made to work effectively, or as a rhetorical weapon against the powers that be when it did not.

To see how this worked, let us begin by considering vernacular conceptions of liberties before exploring their use in habeas litigation. For it was through use of this writ that law would trace the shifting bounds of liberties and of subjecthood. We will proceed in a roughly chronological way through a succession of ideas about liberties. In doing so, we do not chart a misleadingly neat, progressive line toward modern liberty. Rather we will observe a sedimentary process, in which new ideas layered on old ones, never entirely obscuring them from view.

Liberties in One Body Corporate

To open vernacular understandings of the liberties that arose from subjecthood, we must begin in theology, for the typical early modern Englishman was more likely to hear a discussion of liberty from a pulpit than at the bar. Christian moralists invoked St. Paul:

> Stand fast therefore in the liberty wherewith Christ hath made us free, and be not entangled again with the yoke of bondage. . . . For, brethren, ye have been called unto liberty; only use not liberty for an occasion to the flesh, but by love serve one another.[3]

The Apostle James used even stronger language: "So speak ye, and so do, as they that shall be judged by the law of liberty. For he shall have judgment without mercy, that hath showed no mercy."[4] Preachers doing exegetical work on texts like these often referred to a Christian liberty in which liberty and right action constituted one another.

George Downham, bishop of Derry, appreciated that Christian liberty displayed qualities both "positive" and "privative," or as we might say, negative.

> Neither is Christian liberty only privative, as being a freedom and immunity from bondage . . . it is also positive, as being a liberty, power, right, and interest to the privileges of God's children.[5]

Downham told readers of his 1635 book *The Christian's Freedom* that this right and interest entails obligation, transforming "slaves of Satan, subject to the curse of the law, and to eternal damnation," into "servants of righteousness. . . . [H]e that is called, being free, is the servant of Christ."[6] The language of slavery was certainly pervasive in republican discussions of liberty.[7] But in the sixteenth and seventeenth centuries, one was more likely to read the Bible than Livy to find that common trope at work. Traditional theology taught that the servitude of faith would defeat the slavery of sin. How? Liberty is the gift of Christ's sacrifice, to which Christians are called. By justification, they receive liberty. Through sanctification, they live according to liberty's dictates: to love God and one's neighbor, or, in St. James's formulation, to show mercy. Justification liberates; sanctification obligates.[8]

By this formulation, liberty was a spiritual and eternal condition, manifested physically and temporally by the body's servitude. Thus

Downham took Christian liberty beyond negative and positive, portraying it as both and more: as freedom from, as freedom to, and as a host of duties performed by the properly self-constrained body. From the pulpit in 1606, Alexander Chapman developed the same idea: "No, no, this Christian liberty, it is not an immunity from mercies, compassions, and charity's good works, but it is a servitude unto them . . . that by love we serve one another." He concluded with a prayer:

> The God of might and mercy, give us all the spirit . . . of liberty, not licentiousness; of freedom, not looseness . . . that all combined in the one and single divine inspiration of it, we may understand our liberty rightly; practice it unabusively; in religious liberality to the poor charitably; . . . in obedience to the magistrate and his laws most dutifully . . . and thus in love serving all one another most christianly.[9]

Liberty declares itself in servitude, rightly placed and practiced, as Chapman's dualities suggest. Failure to recognize the centrality of servitude might lead one into antinomian heresy, in which one mistakes redemption as a full and perfect liberation from sin, and thus from the dictates of divine laws that properly direct behavior. Those who emphasized the role of Hebraic law in controlling human actions were derisively called "legalists" by their antinomian foes, who thought that only through full liberation could they live out their salvation here on earth. On the other side, "legalists" condemned the lawless freedom proclaimed by antinomians as licentiousness: not liberty at all, but its evil twin.[10] Liberty could be wrongly as well as rightly conceived and practiced, especially where it was not practiced through servitude: through mercy and charity. While there were actual antinomians in the late sixteenth and seventeenth centuries, fear of them was always greater than their numbers warranted. Most people embraced the belief that by martyring the body through servitude to God's laws and others' needs, the soul achieved or declared—depending on one's soteriology—its liberty. Christians were Christ's subjects as surely as the English were their king's. From subjecthood came liberty.

Sin is natural to humans, Christian liberty is not. It is a gift from without, given to those

> who are also heirs of God, and coheirs with Christ . . . and citizens of heaven. Even as they who are made freemen of London, or any other

terrestrial city, are not only exempted from being servants or apprentices, but also are endowed with the liberties and privileges of free burgesses and citizens.[11]

Downham's figuration of Christian liberty as inheritance and as citizenship was no accident. Corporate liberties enjoyed by grant and inheritance, not by nature, constituted one of the other pervasive vernacular expressions of liberty. Collective persons, created by the king's charter, enjoyed liberties denied to others: for instance, rights to trade in a given commodity or to restrict the trade of others, or rights to make bylaws for self-government. Just as Christians, by their liberty, were incorporated into the body of Christ, so people in corporations— trade companies, colleges, urban governments—were joined together into "one body corporate." It was no accident that this expression appeared both in royal charters that granted corporate liberties and in the Book of Common Prayer's thanksgiving after receipt of the Eucharist, a ritual that made English women and men "very members incorporate in the mystical body, which is the blessed company of all faithful people." Incorporation subsumed individuals, generating liberty by bringing people into communion with each other, whether in the legal being that governed a city or in the body of Christ.[12]

As Downham's simile suggests, Christian and corporate liberties share a number of characteristics. First, they entail individual servitude to something greater than the self: to righteousness or the corporate will. Second, the individual's capacities and incapacities arise from a greater authority that grants liberties and marks their bounds: God, or the king. One is not born with such liberties by virtue of being human or English. Rather, liberties pass by descent, by inheritance in various forms, or by election, forms established in the first instance by the grace of the original donor, be it God or the king. Far from being natural and universal, such forms of liberty are exclusive to certain kinds of people: to Christians or corporation members. Both the possibilities and the prohibitions that constitute such liberties are entailed on succeeding generations in restricted lineages. Regardless of one's beliefs about the operation of salvation—whether it is achieved by human deeds or God's predestinating choices—all the many different views concerned with grace arrived in the same place: the liberation they called "redemption." Getting there required passing through servitude.

Languages of liberty connected to corporate or Christian ideals not only enabled action; they required action by defining the good toward which one should act. This is how liberty arose from servitude. We might conclude that this put one in the Rousseauian position of being "forced to be free."[13] But in an early modern vernacular of liberty made of servitude, one was not forced into freedom, one was called to it, by election: of Christians by God and of corporate freemen by corporate leaders. The distinction between force and calling was crucial. It meant not only that one must act in a certain way—for instance, according to the republican's *virtu*—but also that one must do so toward certain ends: salvation and the collective good.[14]

Related to this, a commitment to the "common weal" suffused colloquial political ideas. As John Barston, Tewkesbury's town clerk, proclaimed in 1576, "[E]very society of people is established for commonweal." We must all have "care of [the] common weal, [and] a well-disposed mind to prefer the universal of all as willingly as any private cause or singular intent."[15] Modern students of commonweal ideology stress the classical humanist roots of republican ideas.[16] But if we look beyond the limited cast of classically educated theorists that populate most scholarship on the history of political ideas, we find commonweal ideals typically tied to Christian ones in a vernacular discourse spoken in the "unacknowledged republic" of the parish.[17] This vernacular was lived as well as spoken, linking a broadly understood Christian piety to what the educated few might also have heard as the language of classical virtue. Sir Thomas Smith, in his *Discourse of the Commonweal*, slid easily between classical and Christian idioms, between civic virtue and the redemptive power of those forms of charity by which one sublimates, then liberates, the self.

> We be not born only to ourselves but partly to the use of our country, of our parents, of our kinfolk, and partly of our friends and neighbors. And therefore all good virtues are grafted in us naturally, whose effects be to do good to others, wherein shows forth the image of God in man whose property is ever to do good to others and to distribute his goodness abroad . . . let us study to do good to others, not preferring the

ease of this carcass, which is like the brute beast's, but rather the virtues of the mind, wherein we be like God himself.[18]

Thus Smith distinguished between an ennobling servitude that liberates and the slavery that destroys: the brute beast's carcass.

Liberties, social and spiritual, constrained as they empowered. They were also capacities: privileges granted and revocable from without, arising from subjecthood to God and king.[19] These vernacular liberties have little to do with modern liberal ideas exalting the autonomous moral subject. Rather, they permitted a more complete obedience to the divine as part of the believer's participation in the work of redemption, and required full engagement in the community.[20] Christian and corporate liberties would be joined by new languages of liberty across the seventeenth and eighteenth centuries. But they would never disappear, vital as they were in conceiving liberty as a possession—enjoyed in the plural or the singular—when people talked about habeas corpus and what it might do.

Possessive, Plural: The Liberty to Imprison

The principal language of liberties running through arguments on habeas corpus took the possessive form. There was nothing remotely Lockean about this.[21] To possess something is not the same as having a property in it by virtue of that which ostensibly inheres in all humans by nature. Rather, the liberties possessed by parties in habeas litigation show the same qualities we have observed in Christian and corporate liberties: given from without; to some, not to all; and only enjoyed in conjunction with obligations. All the limits and possibilities of such liberties sprang from the fundamental fact of subjecthood. This was true whether liberties belonged to a living being or to a corporate one.

In early modern habeas cases, "liberty" almost never referred to the attributes of an individual; rather it described a franchise: a power of the king's delegated to others.[22] "Liberty" referred both to a physical place—a jurisdiction with distinct privileges, including immunities from the interference of other jurisdictions—and to any one of the many powers, enumerated in a charter that might be exercised in such a place. One such franchise was the liberty to imprison. Before the dissolution of the monasteries in the 1530s, abbeys were some of the most common holders of specific liberties: for instance, powers to keep prisons, to provide sanctuary, or to punish their own inhabitants.[23] Episcopal authorities continued to possess such liberties within their cathedral precincts long after the Reformation.[24] Other such liberties had always been secular. Some were ancient, held by prescription—presumably granted by a royal charter long since lost—while other places still possessed the charters that laid out their franchises in detail.

Liberties to imprison, not individual liberty claims, thus occupied the center of habeas jurisprudence and were invoked to stop habeas corpus rather than to support the writ on a prisoner's behalf.[25] In keeping with a franchise view of the writ, habeas operated to ensure that the liberty to imprison was properly used. This meant that the writ went anywhere someone claimed to hold the body of another. This franchise theory—not natural rights claims—explains the writ's sweeping ambit as to persons and places. Within England, we can watch as the writ humbled some of the proudest, most independent jurisdictions in the land: not to assert individual liberties, but to assert the primacy of King's Bench over all other jurisdictions. In Chapter 8, we will see how this oversight by King's Bench worked to extend habeas corpus around a global empire. For now, let us consider how the writ humbled liberties within England.

Among the most important chartered liberties were palatinates like Chester. When Chester's leaders received a habeas corpus for John Lloyd in 1641, they argued that because Chester was a county palatine "time out of mind," writs from King's Bench did not run there. As in Bourne's case, this was true enough for those writs used to initiate suits between private parties.[26] But writs in which the king was the suitor, owing to his interest in the subject's liberty, were different. A clerk's note at the foot of Chester's arrogant return shows how little it amused King's Bench. The justices declared the return "insufficient" and ordered another writ to Chester with "a great pain"—a subpoena of £80—to encourage a more respectful reply.[27] The liberty claims of Chester had been rejected. Liberty claims of John Lloyd—if there were any—were absent from the discussion.

The franchise focus of habeas corpus jurisprudence is even more apparent in the many cases involving the greatest holders of liberties: the City of London and its trading companies. Consider the case of Robert Fisher, who sold pins. So did the members of the Pinners'

Company of London, which did not like Fisher selling pins improperly. On October 7, 1637, Fisher was committed to the custody of a royal messenger on the Pinners' complaint. The return to the writ issued on Fisher's behalf recited at length the company's liberties, granted by a royal charter made only the year before "for the well ordering and government of the art or mystery of pin making." The justices probed the return to understand what Fisher had done and whether the Pinners' Company possessed the liberty to do with Fisher as they had. The issues were worthy of the best scholastic debates: How many pins had Fisher sold? The counting of pins was the key to bigger questions: had he violated the company's ordinances? Most important, were those ordinances properly made according to powers granted to the company by royal charter? Could the Pinners ask for one's imprisonment for violation of those ordinances?[28] No. The court released Fisher from bail. The individual's singular liberty had trumped the company's multiple liberties. Or had it? Upon closer inspection, we find that the company had not violated Fisher's liberty at all; they had violated their own. Among their powers was one to seize pins made contrary to the charter, but there was no mention of a power to imprison someone in defense of the company's control of the pin trade.[29]

The case of Richard Edwards ended with the opposite result, though it was decided on similarly franchisal grounds. Edwards was imprisoned in 1615 for refusing to pay a £10 fine for using a hot press contrary to City ordinances. His counsel requested his release, making the novel claim that preventing his use of a hot press—which "is profitable for stuffs and fustians"—would "suppress trading." The City responded that such presses posed a fire hazard. But neither claims for free trade nor the need to control dangers to the public in a half-timbered city were relevant. As Chief Justice Coke noted, the return was good on its face. All that mattered was that the City possessed the liberty to imprison to enforce its ordinances. Edwards was remanded.[30]

Both of these cases demonstrate a central aspect of habeas corpus jurisprudence: that the judges were less concerned with the liberty claims of jailed individuals than with the liberty claims of jailers. The court remanded Edwards because a liberty to imprison, granted by charter and custom and confirmed by Magna Carta, had been rightly used. Fisher's release, too, was won not by claims to individual freedom premised on humanness or on his status as an English subject. It was won by showing that the Pinners had exceeded the liberties—the franchise—given to them as a royally chartered company. The court thus emphasized liberties in the possessive plural. But it also recognized liberty in the possessive singular.

Possessive, Singular: The Liberty of the Subject

"Liberty of the subject" was the most common way to refer to liberties in the singular possessive form. As in Christian liberty, subjecthood imported a conception of liberty that relied on relationships beyond the self. There was nothing paradoxical in the idea that liberty should arise from subjecthood: the ties of allegiance bound the bodies of king and subject to one another in a relationship of mutual protection, a relationship arising from and managed through law. Law preceded liberties, and thus determined both the limits and possibilities of habeas corpus. Law would drive habeas corpus into places where other parts of English law did not go, thereby expanding subject status beyond England and the English. Law would also determine the things habeas could not do, cutting off attempts to reshape English law by reference to claims about transcendent rights, whether of divine, natural, or national origin, even as popular political rhetoric made ever louder claims for rights of these kinds.

Nonetheless, a pronounced national streak—a vain streak—runs through discussions of liberty in the singular possessive. "The liberty of the subject of England is greater than that of all other nations," wrote Sir Henry Finch. He continued: "[T]his liberty was purchased for the subjects of England with the blood of many people, noble and ignoble."[31] Like the king who granted his franchises by letters patent, the nation's history granted its own franchises. These were held by all English people and by all who owed allegiance to the king. This was not a gift of nature; it was a gift of law, which was the product of history.

The same law that gave these liberties policed their bounds. If all subjects shared the same liberties, then each had as much need as the others to ensure that these liberties were rightly held relative to one another. This was precisely the issue addressed by King's Bench when dealing with the Listers' broken marriage. Maintaining clarity of boundaries among the liberties of the king's many subjects was the point of habeas corpus. King's Bench justices appreciated the delicacy of the work they performed, thus the phrase they used repeatedly was that "the law is tender in restraint of liberty."[32] Justice Dodderidge said this only a few years after he had observed that habeas corpus was a prerogative writ. Liberties' vulnerability required law's "tenderness," its protection by the ultimate power available to judges when using habeas corpus.[33]

For all law's tender touch, liberty was unmistakably law's object. An imprisonment order made according to law was an "abridgement of the liberty of the subject," not a seizure or elimination of it.[34] Seizure—the language of quo warranto—was an either/or matter; abridgment, by contrast, was a matter of degree. A return to a writ of habeas corpus was an "account of the restraint of the liberty of the subject."[35] Having read such an account, judges then decided whether the amount of restraint reported in the return had been calculated correctly relative to the facts of the situation and the appropriate law. Thus the Privy Council ordered that Richard Beckwith and Miles Reynard "be restrained of their liberty" by being committed to the Gatehouse in 1615.[36] One might need to be imprisoned—as William Brigham was, by the Court of Requests—because otherwise "he hath more liberty than is fit to be allowed."[37] Given the contempt that Brigham had shown to the judges in Requests, the judges in King's Bench could only agree that not being in prison would accord him too much liberty; Brigham was remanded. Habeas corpus jurisprudence, where it considered tenderly the liberty of the subject as well as of the liberties of jailers, was a delicate business of balancing competing liberties.

Judges, like preachers, knew that unrestrained liberties could turn into licentiousness. For this reason, they returned Sir Edward Plowden to prison in 1640. Plowden had been brought before the High Commission "for cruelties to his wife," Mabel. The High Commission made a separation order and commanded Sir Edward to pay Lady Mabel an annual alimony of £200. They also required that he give a bond that he would perform as ordered. He refused, and "went abroad at his pleasure, whereby he was animated to persist in his contempts." So the High Commission ordered him kept "close prisoner" until he obeyed. Nonetheless, two weeks later, Mabel complained that he was still at large, which put her "in daily fear" of him "by reason of his said liberty." His liberty impinged on hers. Despairing for her safety and her alimony unless the court took bolder measures, she pleaded that Sir

Edward be "wholly barred of his liberty." And so he was. Having made "undue use" of his liberty, he was remanded to the Gatehouse. By closing the bounds of Sir Edward's liberty, the justices opened the bounds of Lady Mabel's.[38]

The contest between Sir Edward and Lady Mabel demonstrates that habeas corpus did not concern liberty in a pure form, for there was no such thing. Theirs was a contest between liberty claims in the singular possessive form. Resolving that contest required law's tenderness. Even more tenderness was needed where liberty claims in the singular possessive confronted liberty claims in the plural. But in a contest between mine and yours, liberties to imprison were easily confirmed or refuted by reference to charters, statutes, or custom. Liberty claims of individuals in the possessive form were only rarely articulated, even as liberties of the subject. How then to balance between or among competing claims of liberties?

Adjudicating Liberties: Reasonableness and the Public Good

Ordinarily, anyone chosen an alderman of London jumped at the chance to serve. Not John Langham and Thomas Andrews. Of course, January 1642 was no ordinary time. The night before their election, Charles I had fled London as his struggles with Parliament sharpened. Perhaps they refused to take up office owing to the burdens it imposed. Perhaps it seemed to be the worst of times to raise their public profile. Regardless of their motives, and in accordance with custom, the City jailed them. The next day, Langham and Andrews sued writs of habeas corpus.[39] The City's returns to their writs explained these circumstances, though only after laying out London's ancient liberties and customs. One custom concerned the oath every freeman took, by which he swore to serve in office if called to do so. By refusing the alderman's oath, Langham and Andrews had violated their oaths as freemen. Enforcing the obligation to serve meant invoking one more custom: the liberty to imprison.

Four prominent lawyers attacked the City's imprisonment order on multiple fronts. But at the center of the case was a contest between liberty claims: those of the City against those of individuals. An imprisonment order based on City customs was "a thing of great concernment in law," explained John Maynard, one of England's greatest lawyers.[40]

Maynard then threw down his trump card: Magna Carta and its famed chapter 29, which stated that no one should be imprisoned except by "the law of the land." But Recorder Sir Thomas Gardiner—the City's leading lawyer—could play Magna Carta too: chapter 9 guaranteed London's "ancient liberties." Like religious controversialists, Maynard and Gardiner hurled chapter and verse from the same scripture at one another. The justices had to decide which to apply: *"legem loci"* or *"legem terrae."* Law against law, liberty against liberty, Magna Carta against itself.

London's collective liberties, confirmed by Magna Carta, bounded individuals' liberties. Gardiner conceded that the City had some "unreasonable" customs, but they were supported by law, even if they "trencheth . . . upon the liberty of the subject." If unreasonable customs were the "law of the land," then so much the more were its reasonable ones. The reasonableness of the custom to imprison those who refused office was apparent by its "necessity." Gardiner explained: if all who were elected were permitted to refuse, none would serve. Without officers, the City's charter would be forfeit, its corporation destroyed, and the people of London left ungoverned. No practice could be more "fit for attaining of its end"—the encouragement of those elected to serve, and thus the City's well-being—than the threat of prison. This made imprisonment the "most reasonable custom." Chief Justice Sir John Bramston agreed, finding London's custom to imprison "good and reasonable" because it was in "support of government." This, he explained, was "for the public good." Here was the key to the judgment: collective liberties that outweighed individual ones in the interest of the public good. Compelling freemen to serve in office, as they had promised when sworn as freemen, was for the common weal. After all, liberties carried obligations as well as opportunities. Remanded by the court's order, both men soon thought better of their choices.[41] Three days later, they swore their oaths. As Gardiner had predicted, imprisonment gained its end: compliance.

Like any analytic standard, "public good" could operate as forcefully by its absence as by its presence. This explains the result, three years later, for John Chambers and John Wood. As freemen of the Weavers' Company, they had appeared at the election of new company wardens. Company leaders denied their demands to vote, telling them that only those who wore the company's livery could do so. Referred to the

Court of Aldermen after their refusal to leave, both were imprisoned as "factious disturbers of the peace." Habeas then brought them before King's Bench, where London's recorder showed the same City customs that had been used to imprison Langham and Andrews. But this time, the court ordered bail. While Langham and Andrews had to be corrected for "the public good . . . [and] for the peace and quiet of the city," disturbing a livery company by contesting election rights was just an "inconvenience."[42] Ends—"necessity," to use the language of Langham's case—still provided the test of custom's reasonableness, though here with the opposite result.

Public good and reasonableness, collective liberties and individual liberties, continued to dance around one another in the later seventeenth century. Samuel Grafton, chosen in 1669 as an officer of the London Drapers' Company, also refused to take office. So the company fined him, then imprisoned him when he refused to pay. London rolled out the usual arguments from Langham's case: as an ancient City, with powers to imprison by custom and charter, the jail order was good. But the court resorted to the case of Chambers and Wood, invoking public interest negatively: there was no public interest in jailing Grafton since this concerned a company office rather than the aldermancy. Where there was no threat to the public good, as in Grafton's case, there could be no liberty to imprison. Grafton was thus discharged by reading the meaning of Langham's case in a mirror.[43]

The language of reasonableness was also spoken in the case of Ralph Harwood, jailed in 1671 for not paying a fine imposed by London's court of orphans after he married one of their wards without permission. Harwood's counsel opened by declaring "unreasonable" the custom by which the City claimed a liberty to imprison in such cases. The court was not ready to go this far, and accepted the legality of the custom and of the imprisonment order. Harwood was remanded, but the liberty of the City, used in this way, made the court nervous. In what amounted to a negotiated settlement, the court recommended that because "there was no disparagement by the marriage"—a judgment about reasonableness—"upon the submission of Harwood to the Court of Orphans . . . they should do well to remit the fine."[44]

Reasonableness arose again the following term. This concerned one Broadney or Broadnox, jailed for refusing to pay a 40s. fine for bringing wood into the City in violation of a bylaw limiting carts there. The court distinguished between the City's control of "foreign" carriers conveying goods out of the City, which they thought might be regulated, and the control of carriers bringing wares into the City in their own carts. Chief Justice Sir Matthew Hale relied on the same principles that produced the negotiated result in Harwood's case, declaring "unreasonable" the custom to control all "foreign" carts entering the City. "No bylaw," the justices said, "can restrain a man from exercising his lawful calling." Worse, requiring a foreign wood monger to unpack every load at the City's gates was "extremely inconvenient."[45]

In cases like these, and in cases like Mrs. Lister's, liberty existed within bounds drawn by law with the help of other ideas: status, reasonableness, the public good, convenience. Vague as such ideas were, they stood at the center of the justices' work of balancing the many claims about liberties that came before them. In their work, we hear echoes of ideas that ran through Christian liberty: that liberty is relational, imposing obligations as well as providing opportunities, and that the use of one's liberty must be considered against the need for quietness, charity, or mercy toward one's neighbors. Reference to concepts like reasonableness or public good began to move the discussion away from a husband's or the City's liberty—the power to constrain or imprison—and toward liberties, still only implied, possessed by individuals. This was an analytically serious business, though one that employed philosophically simple tools of the kind that lay audiences would have understood well.

We might be tempted to begin drawing from the remand of Langham and Andrews to the discharge of Mrs. Lister a progressive line pointing toward the triumph of individual liberty over liberties to detain. But note the negative formulation of these results: release occurred because there was no public good to justify customary liberties—the City's or a husband's—to detain others. Mrs. Lister's liberty was nothing more than what was "reasonable." This was a long way from saying that she or others had individual liberties arising from within themselves. Far more impressive than an imagined progressive liberal line we might try to draw across the seventeenth century was the persistence of a jurisprudence that focused on franchisal liberties: a jurisprudence in which liberties derived from a law of the judges' making rather than one in which liberty preceded law. Some, such as John Lilburne, would try to reverse this ordering of law and liberty.

John Lilburne: Birthrights, Liberty, and English Law

Birthright was Christian liberty's corollary. Preachers loved to tell their parishioners the story of Esau, son of the biblical prophet Isaac. Having come from the hunt faint with hunger, Esau asked, "[W]hat profit shall this birthright do to me?" Lacking faith in its value, Esau "sold his birthright unto Jacob," his younger twin brother, for "a mess of potage." "Thus Esau despised his birthright."[46] Esau did not violate human law when he alienated his birthright. He violated the laws of God and nature. Like Adam and Eve, Esau made the wrong choice, satisfying his carnal appetites, succumbing to the slavery that is damnation rather than embracing the self-restraining liberty that redeems. Once his birthright was sold "for a mess of red broth," Esau lost "all title to heaven."[47]

Inheritance and birthright are not synonyms. Inheritance operates simply by human law. A birthright precedes human law, logically and temporally, as an aspect of human nature reflecting the human creation's likeness to its creator. Rejecting this "birthright, the dignity of his nature, the high prerogative of [the human's] state," was inconceivable.[48] In the language of inheritance, the priority of law over liberty was clear. In birthright, these poles threatened to flip.

Legal and liberal rhetoric came closest to this reversal during the Civil War and its aftermath.[49] No one spoke more powerfully to this end than the period's most energetic pamphleteer, John Lilburne.[50] Lilburne was also the most public and persistent habeas corpus litigant of any age. In Lilburne's hands, habeas corpus would nearly break out of the bounds of national law to answer transcendent demands—based on nature and divine will—on behalf of the individual's liberty. His failure revealed the limits of habeas corpus, of English law, and of claims of liberty to impose on law.

Having fought for Parliament in the Civil War, Lilburne spent the years following increasingly disappointed that the cause for which he had bled failed to produce the godly commonwealth of which he and other Levellers dreamed. He began to scold every authority in the land, hoping to inspire them to liberate the people of England following the victories they had won over the king. Were battlefield triumphs not signs of God's will, he reasoned? Rather than inspire, Lilburne offended. The House of Lords, the House of Commons, and the Lord Protector: each imprisoned him in their turn.[51] Finally, on the morning of May 8, 1648, Lilburne stood before Justices Bacon and Rolle in King's Bench to argue for release by habeas corpus. Asked by Justice Bacon where his counsel was, Lilburne replied—in "a shrill voice"— that he demanded "the same benefit and privilege that Paul always enjoyed from the hands of the Pagan and Heathen Roman judges." To plead his own cause was his "undoubted natural right by the light and law of nature, yes and by the ancient common law of England." Such a right was due to "every man upon the face of the earth in what country soever."[52]

Lilburne was at the top of his form, having already spent most of the previous three years imprisoned by the House of Lords for libels against the Earl of Manchester and by the House of Commons for treasonable practices. For much of that time, he had been joined in the Tower by the Welsh royalist judge David Jenkins, and by Sir John Maynard, who had argued on behalf of Langham and Andrews. Lilburne was drawn to these supporters of monarchy who shared his concern about arbitrary Parliaments and who gave him a thorough tutorial in law.[53] Lilburne also read plenty of Coke: his Pauline references came from a lawyer, not a theologian. By the time he appeared in King's Bench, Lilburne had published more than a dozen pamphlets in which his literal prison became the metaphorical prison in which all England suffered. If Lilburne stood for an England in chains, then habeas corpus was not just another legal device. It was the key that would unshackle the nation as it unshackled him.

Lilburne put on his spectacles to read from his lengthy brief. Consistency not being the hallmark of his style, he began by saying that he depended on the wisdom of the justices before him—the same justices he had just hectored about his "natural right" to argue his own cause. Having signaled his reliance on judges, Lilburne then turned the other way, and dismissed the many judicial precedents against him as "worth nothing." Why? Statutes: chapter 29 of Magna Carta, the Petition of Right, and the Star Chamber Act of 1641 ensured to him and all England the privilege of habeas corpus. He thus disposed of the work of judges and lawyers by referring to the products of Parliament, the legitimacy of whose imprisonment orders he now challenged. Parliament's statutes, he argued, showed that Parliament's orders to imprison him were "impoisoned arrows shot through the principal vitals of England's liberty."[54]

Enough: the judges "would not let me go on with my rhetoric," he reported.[55] Hardly surprising, since Lilburne had given them a long harangue already. It took only a few minutes before Justice Bacon ordered Lilburne remanded to the Tower on the view that the House of Lords was a court higher than King's Bench. But Lilburne always had the last word:

> [God] punisheth judges with the law of like for like, unto whom I mournfully commit my cause, and now as my last legal hopes, if from your hands I can get no justice, but must be exposed by your hard heartedness to ruin and destruction, then a desperate disease must have a desperate cure, and the will of God be done.[56]

Virtually all the elements of Lilburne's arguments in more than two dozen pamphlets written between 1645 and 1656 may be found in his 1648 brief, published as *England's Birthright Justified*. We can hear Lilburne invoke statutes, then damn the same Parliament that made them. We hear him demand what he considered his procedural rights by English law and then attack the judges of that same national law.[57] We hear him proclaim his freedoms as an Englishman in one breath, and in the next, resort to the laws of God and nature to show the inadequacy of the laws and liberties of England. Lilburne could invoke a statute or praise the occasional English legal usage—he could build a pragmatic argument—but in the end, he depended on transcendent sources of authority: "the will of God be done."

Lilburne conflated in "birthright" English and natural law, both subject to God's law. Parliament had, in Lilburne's view, disposed of this birthright by imprisoning him. This was "a prophaneness like Esau's," by which posterity would be subjected "to vassalage and slavery." Acquiescing in such an imprisonment was suicide, itself prohibited by natural law. It was thus lawful, "by the light of nature and the law of God . . . by all means possible to preserve myself."[58] How? By habeas corpus, the use of which was justified by "a righteous God in heaven that judgeth righteously and hears the sighs and groans of his poor oppressed and distressed prisoners."[59] At a stroke, Lilburne had transformed habeas corpus from a mundane legal device used to adjudicate among liberty claims in the plural that arise from human law, into an instrument of divine will safeguarding a transcendent, universal liberty in the absolute singular.

Lilburne erected a platform from which he fired down on English law, whether made in Parliament or by judges.[60] In the words of William Ball, Lilburne's Leveller compatriot, people

> do not disinvest themselves of their right natural. . . . [T]hey may defend their liberties and proprieties even by the law of nature, which no special or national laws can nullify, unless men will become, or be made slaves, and lose the right of nature.[61]

Ball and Lilburne answered Paul's Epistle to the Romans, chapter 13.[62] Yes, "all power is of God": a stock claim justifying obedience to kings. Everyone was certainly subject to a higher power. But only "so far forth as that power doth lawfully extend (for God commandeth no unlawful thing) either by divine law, or by law of nature, or by law of nations." Parliament, as a legislative power, might address those things "disputable," but not things "indisputable, such as is the general and fundamental liberty and propriety of the subject grounded upon the law of nature."[63] Any abuse of this authority "is odious to God and man," contrary not only to the Petition of Right, but to "the direct rule alleged in scripture."[64] Divine reason bars unjust imprisonments: no statute, no judicial precedent, could make it otherwise. How did Lilburne know? Because God, the only "absolute sovereign," made humans in his image and gave them that divine spark, reason.[65] Lilburne thus told the story of Adam and Eve to different ends than most contemporaries. Omitting any claims of Adam's superiority—from which patriarchal government flowed—he focused instead on the equality that, "by nature," all humans derived from their creation. Though made of scriptural matter, Lilburne's vast, universalizing conception of human liberty departed dramatically from older ideas about Christian liberty.[66]

We have come full circle, which is hardly surprising given the circularity of Lilburne's thinking, in which he praised here that which he damned there. Lilburne made a critique of English law from a position based on fundamental law. Having done so, he returned to English law to demand, via habeas corpus, that it obtain for him that which he said was his due by fundamental law. Through a critique of English law, Lilburne tried to push habeas corpus beyond the limitations inherent in common law, limitations that always made liberty law's subject rather than the reverse.

Sir John Maynard, Lilburne's friend while in the Tower, was released not long after Lilburne's appearance in King's Bench. In July 1648, Maynard defended him in the Commons: "[I]t is not in the power of parliaments to make a law *against the law of God, Nature, or Necessary Reason.*"[67] This sounds like Lilburne himself. But Maynard's requirement of English law was a bare nonrepugnancy principle: that English practice should not be against the reason of God or nature. Maynard, and most of his generation, believed that what to them was English law's internal coherence signaled its consonance with divine law. Such a view marked a great tradition in English legal thought, stretching back to Christopher St. German and earlier.[68] Lilburne, by contrast, had looked outside English law for the standards by which he might assess it. In doing so, he had threatened that tradition, aspiring to eradicate those practices in English law that, in his view, violated divine demands. "The will of God be done."

John Lilburne would be disappointed. English law would continue to take priority over liberties: coming before them, determining their existence, balancing among them. The most triumphant whigs of later years would accept this, satisfied as they were by a blinding national pride that encouraged their belief that English law could only manifest divine will. Henry Care, one of the most effusive whig writers of the next generation, proclaimed that "in England, the law is both the measure and the bond of every subject's duty and allegiance."[69] The title of Care's paean to English law tells us all we need to know about Lilburne's failure: *English Liberties: or, The Free-Born Subject's Inheritance.* Birthrights had been stripped of the scriptural electricity with which the likes of Lilburne had charged them, reduced to nothing more than the inheritance of national law. In this, we find the limits of habeas corpus. But as we shall soon see, this national law would show a paradoxical openness in its embrace of subjects of many kinds. And during the later seventeenth and eighteenth centuries, a new language of liberty would increasingly be heard in court.

Liberty as a Place

A new idiom appeared, one that helped redirect law's attention from liberties to imprison, to liberties of individuals not to be imprisoned. This was a move from the language of liberties as a possession to one of liberty as a place. This place operated both as metaphorical situation where one might choose without constraint, and as the literal situation that one's body occupied as a result of that choosing. In conflating the metaphorical and the literal, the language of place in habeas litigation—"at liberty"—gave new impetus to the claims of individuals and to the ways in which those claims might be imagined and lived.[70] In doing so, the language of place also constrained customary and collective liberties. But there was more in this language than a simple absence of—liberty from—physical constraint. And despite the development of this idiom, the court continued to balance among this and other liberty claims expressed in the philosophically cramped language of English law: of liberties, like Mrs. Lister's, that were "reasonable" or "not bad."

A 1695 case highlights this movement from liberties as plural possessions to liberty as a singular place. A man named Grascot taught dancing without joining London's Musicians' Company. When he refused to pay the fine the company imposed for doing so, the City jailed him. The mayor and aldermen of London returned his habeas corpus with the usual recital of their ancient liberties and the custom that they could make bylaws regulating the trade of those not free of City companies. Grascot's counsel contended that a bylaw permitting fines in such cases was void because "at common law any man was at liberty to use any trade in any place, provided he had skill and ability." The court agreed, finding such a bylaw void. "Besides," they added, "this act is bad, for it would set a price upon dancing."[71]

There was an important public good to protect here: dancing should not be too expensive. There was also an implicit claim about the nature of the imprisoned individual. We can hear it in the phrase used by his counsel: "at liberty." Liberty was a place where a person might do something. Putting Grascot "at liberty" relied on a positive assertion about the individual's liberty vying with the positive assertion about the City's liberties. But we must be careful in what we make of this. Even dancing was a liberty known only to law, not to nature, found in that part of common law that permitted "any man" to use a trade so long as he had "skill and ability." Grascot was to be "at liberty" not because he was a person, nor even an Englishman. Rather, a status distinction generated Grascot's liberty: his dancing skills. And the liberties involved were not only his. They were liberties of all who wanted to dance. There was a public good at stake, and an assumption about the reasonableness of the price of dancing. Sadly, we do not get any sign of how the court assessed Grascot's ability, which had been the key to disallowing his imprisonment: surely a missed moment for the history of the law of evidence.

Two things are noteworthy about liberty as a place: its increasing invocation over time, and its use in family custody cases. We might conclude that there was a growing tendency to break out of legal norms that confined thinking about liberties in habeas jurisprudence. We might also suggest that we are more likely to find signs of this happening when a detention relied on no allegations of wrong. This quality made family custody cases enormously important because such cases exploded one of the central premises behind the writ's earlier use: that they were to test the legality of imprisonment orders made in cases in which there was at least the suspicion of some wrong committed by the person detained. There were no wrongs in custody cases, only claims about rights: those of a husband and a wife, so long as she was not "very bad."

We should note a third aspect of these cases: judges were just as likely as barristers to use a language of place. Thus we hear over and over in the eighteenth century of women set or left "at liberty" by court orders. This happened in the case of Mary Wilkes, wife of John Wilkes, heroic libertarian and libertine, loving father and lousy husband. In 1756, the Wilkeses negotiated a deed of separation, just as the Listers had a generation earlier. Then, like Michael Lister, Wilkes hoped to renegotiate his separation agreement by pressuring his wife. Unlike the Listers, it was John, not Mary, who sued habeas from King's Bench to Mary's mother, Mary Mead, to produce his wife in court in the hope that King's Bench would return the younger Mary into his care. The mother's return recounted at length the separation agreement, and explained that by its terms, Mary was "to be at liberty" to live with her mother according to "her free will and choice." As the return explained, the daughter lived with the mother "of her own accord and under no restraint." Thus the court ordered John to leave Mary alone.[72] Liberty was not Mary's possession. It was the place where she was free of her husband's company, free by virtue of their separation agreement and by her own choosing. As in the Listers' case, status, modified by contract, defined that place where she could choose.

"At liberty" was a zone of opportunity in which someone like Mary

Wilkes acted with "free will" to determine the literal place where her body belonged. The job of King's Bench was to ensure that the place claimed by the individual—in Mary Wilkes's case, against a writ of habeas corpus—might be occupied legally. In the same year, Lord Mansfield's court set Lydia Henrietta Clarke "at liberty to go wheresoever she pleases" after she was brought into King's Bench on a writ brought by her father.[73] As in Mary Wilkes's case, free will—"at liberty"—was invoked as often by those returning writs of habeas corpus as by the court. This parity underscores the way in which all parties to habeas proceedings saw liberty as a place signifying a capacity of the individual will to express itself through physical action. When Cecil Bishop received a habeas corpus on behalf of Anne Mose in 1770, he replied that he did not have her and that she was "at large and at full and perfect liberty and under no restraint or control whatsoever from me . . . against her will."[74] The writ for Catherine Maria Bearcroft came back with a similar return four years later: that she was "now at liberty and free from all restraint," and that for the whole time she had lived with John Berkeley—who made the return—she had "done so with her own free will and consent and singular choice." Despite Berkeley's claims, the court ordered that she "be at liberty to go where she pleases."[75] We do not know whether she was pleased to go back to Berkeley or elsewhere. But the court had made clear that it was for her to decide what place her body would occupy.

Why was Bearcroft given the liberty to go where she pleased? Because in cases of private custody like these, there was no law or other norm—even reasonableness or public good—that could suggest anything to the contrary. As we saw in the Listers' case, law and cultural norms together defined certain obligations and capacities for both husbands and wives. Neither could exercise much restrictive power, by law, over the free movement of the other. And the "reasonable" powers that husbands might exercise over wives according to eighteenth-century legal and social norms might be modified by contract. Such cases, in which liberty was a place, not a possession, bring us close to the possibility that English law might later recognize some abstract conception of humanness that required enjoyment of a condition called "liberty" that existed beyond the confines of law.

During this era, however, even as courtroom arguments gave less countenance to liberties to imprison, and more to the demands of individuals to be "at liberty," that place remained bounded by law. The judges would always define, impose, and sometimes move the boundaries. The significance of boundaries appears all the greater as we think back over cases like the Listers', for there the boundaries were not between a liberty to imprison and a liberty from imprisonment; they were boundaries between the mutually constituting liberties of husband and wife, each of whom expected things from the other according to legal and lay norms. Deciding the boundaries meant making a legal determination that then rippled back into the practices of husbands and wives.[76]

Whether conceived as a possession or as a place, liberty remained law's subject. In the language of reasonableness and convenience, we can hear extralegal norms shaping legal thinking, but by no means controlling it. And even in family custody disputes, where there was no allegation of wrong at issue, law continued to control liberty. English law proved remarkably resistant to a reversal of this priority, for all the efforts of a John Lilburne. Nonetheless, many kinds of people would come into that place called liberty, a place bounded by law where one might act according to one's will. Many were the subjects of English law.

Subjects: English and Otherwise

The matter looks straightforward in Blackstone's *Commentaries:* "The first and most obvious division of the people is into aliens and natural-born subjects." This neat pairing arose out of a centuries-long process by which assumptions concerning fundamental status distinctions in English law moved from those separating free from servile to those dividing subjects from aliens.[77] Blackstone's conclusion marked the logical end to this process:

> Natural-born subjects are such as are born within the dominions of the crown of England, that is, within the ligeance, or as it is generally called, the allegiance of the king; and aliens, such as are born out of it. Allegiance is the tie, or *ligamen,* which binds the subject to the king in return for that protection which the king affords the subject.[78]

Here we have a simple dichotomy, at least until we ask why Blackstone modifies "subjects." Might there be more than one kind? Interest quickens when we turn to the heading of Blackstone's chapter: "Of the People, whether Aliens, Denizens, or Natives." Many were the kinds of "people." Might they all be subjects?

There were certainly different kinds of aliens, including some who might be subjects by various means. English law had long recognized a variety of foreigners in England. Medieval foreign merchants, like Englishmen, received "liberties" from the king to trade.[79] This did not make a subject of an alien. Instead the alien occupied one of many gray areas in between: a capacity given to certain aliens to enjoy the perquisites of subjects in particular circumstances. In his *Law-Dictionary*, Thomas Blount followed most by going beyond a simple dichotomy between subject and alien, joining the "natural subject" with the "denizen" as kinds of persons who were not "aliens." A denizen was made when "an alien born becomes the king's subject, and obtains the king's letters patents to enjoy all privileges as an Englishman." While naturalization was performed by statute, denization arose from a power "annexed to [the king's] royal person, for the law esteems it an high prerogative, to make aliens subjects of the realm and capable of lands and inheritances, as natural born subjects are."[80] As we saw in Chapter 3, one way to view the prerogative was as the king's capacity to perform miracles upon a world otherwise governed by nature. By such miracles, aliens might be made "natural born subjects." In the sixteenth century, James Morice connected this aspect of the prerogative to the power of pardon. In both cases, the king possessed a peculiar capacity to make those dead in law alive and thus capable of enjoying law's benefits.[81] The notion had long been available that foreigners might be brought into the benefits of subjecthood.

The most important discussion of the nature and variety of subjects occurred in Calvin's case of 1608, during which England's judges decided that the *post-nati*—those born in Scotland after the Scots' King James VI ascended the English throne as James I in 1603—were subjects not only of the Scottish king, but of the English king, too. This meant that Scots could hold property in England, a legal capacity closed to aliens. While there were differences in their approach to the issues, the judges in 1608 agreed that allegiance arose by natural law, by which the natural person of the subject owed his allegiance to the natural person of the king.[82] This reciprocal relationship explains how the prerogative activated habeas corpus on the subject's behalf. The case, then, considered just how far allegiance and protection might extend.

Sir Edward Coke's approach to these problems was complex. Allegiance was owed by nature, what Coke called "birthright." But there was more than parentage or place of birth involved here. Birth "within the king's dominions . . . without obedience, can never produce a natural subject," Coke explained. Something more was required, a spiritual something. "[N]either the climate nor the soil, but *'ligeantia'* and *'obedientia'* . . . make the subject born." Allegiance, "and faith and truth, which are her members and parts, are qualities of the mind and soul of man, and cannot be circumscribed within the predicament of *ubi*." That "faith and truth," not place, was the marker of subjecthood explains how those born at Calais, when it was still under the "actual obedience and commandment of the king," or those born at Berwick-upon-Tweed, were subjects of the English king though neither place had ever been part of England.[83] This primacy of "qualities of mind" over place in constituting allegiance explains how habeas corpus would move across the empire.

Such an approach to allegiance did not leave behind just two categories, subjects and aliens. There were shades of inclusion and exclusion, different kinds of subjects. Sir Matthew Hale followed Coke's lead by identifying four kinds of allegiance: natural born; acquired subjects, "by purchase or acquest"; feudal subjects; and the most important one for this discussion, "local subjects."[84]

To understand this multifaceted approach to allegiance, we must return to the law concerned with protection, the king's prerogative, and the role of law in ensuring the safety of bodies, both the king's and his subjects'. Coke's formulation here was elegantly simple: protection draws subjection, and subjection draws protection.[85] The force of this inclusive reciprocity was widely accepted. "Protection," according to Thomas Blount, is "that benefit and safety, which every subject, denizen, or alien, specially secured, hath by the king's laws." Immediately, our distinct categories of people begin to open to one another, joined under the king's protection. How? The answer lies in the last of Hale's categories of subjects, those by "local allegiance": "every person that comes within the king's dominions owes a local subjection and allegiance to the king, for he hath here the privilege of protection." Hale followed Coke, who saw in local subjecthood the same reciprocity that operated in natural subjecthood, even if it arose by different means. As Coke put it, "[A]s there is a local protection on the king's part, so there is a local ligeance on the subject's part."[86]

Such protection was a form of mercy that "flow[s] from the fountain of grace," covering all kinds of subjects—including local ones—within the bounds of possibility traced by the prerogative.[87] This protection applied not only to the "alien friend."

> [I]f an alien enemy reside or come into the kingdom, and not in open hostility, he owes an allegiance to the king *ratione loci,* and if he attempt any treason, he shall be indicted as doing it *contra ligeantiae suae debitum.*[88]

Aliens, even enemy aliens, were understood as owing the allegiance of a subject, even if this allegiance was given only locally, or temporarily, as a result of being within the queen's dominions and thus under her protection. Place marked, but did not constitute, this reciprocal condition of allegiance and protection. "Faith," not the "predicament of *ubi,*" raised those aspects of subjecthood that even an alien might enjoy as a local subject.

Thus aliens might enter into some of the perquisites of subjecthood, even the status of freeman. Sir Francis Ashley, in his 1616 reading on Magna Carta, began simply enough, noting that "none may be freemen except those who are subjects." But he continued: "or born or resident within the fee of the king and within his protection." An alien, then, was a freeman according to Magna Carta, but this status pertained only while an alien was in the king's dominions, "because his allegiance and protection is only local." Other non-English Britons—the Irish, Welsh, Manx, and residents of the Channel Isles or Berwick-upon-Tweed—partook of the same local allegiance just as other aliens did. Even an alien enemy, who came by safe conduct, was a "freeman because he has the protection of the king and thus by the law of nations (which is only the law of nature) must have the privilege of the laws of the realm."[89]

To be in the king's protection did not mean that an alien could enjoy the benefits of all English law. Most notably, an alien could not hold landed property. This had been the issue in Calvin's case: could a Scot, born since the king of Scotland had become a king of England, hold property by English law? While the answer was an emphatic yes, no one would have argued that Coke was incorrect when he declared that an alien "can have no real or personal action for or concerning land."[90] But the law concerned with property was not the same as that part of law concerned with the subject's body.[91] To be an alien in the condition of local subjecthood was to enjoy the capacity to use, and be subject to, other parts of the king's laws, even if one could not hold real property. No part of the king's law was more important than that at the heart of the reciprocal relationship between king and subject, formed by that obedience that made allegiance. As a local subject, an alien might use habeas corpus. When and how did aliens do so? In virtually all the same ways, in the same instances, and with the same results as the king's other subjects.

Judging from the inconclusive evidence of the names of those who used habeas corpus, scores, perhaps hundreds, of foreigners sued the writ from the sixteenth century to the nineteenth. The absence of further evidence of alien status in cases of litigants whose names have a French or Spanish sound to them suggests how little such status concerned the clerks who made the writs, the lawyers who argued about them, and the judges who determined the outcome.

Our suspicion here is confirmed when we find the same lack of discussion about nationality in those instances known to have involved aliens. Habeas corpus was used for aliens just as it was for subjects charged as traitors or felons: to bring them into King's Bench for arraignment and trial. A spectacular example occurred when the Spaniard Roger Lopez and two other aliens, who served as the queen's physicians, were accused of a conspiracy to poison her in 1594. No one seemed to think it odd that habeas corpus might be used to bring them to a traitor's death. What mattered was not their alien status, but that they had violated their obedience as local subjects.[92] In 1662, the Marquis de Brabant and his companion, a knight of Malta, fared better; they were bailed after their conviction at Maidstone for shooting three watermen "with whom they had difference."[93] In cases of treason or felony, local subjects—aliens—were treated just like natural subjects when it came to using habeas corpus to review the circumstances of imprisonment.[94]

In fact, claims of alien status were sometimes the most effective way to get a writ issued. In the second half of the eighteenth century, scores of foreigners used habeas corpus to escape impressment in the

Royal Navy. Joseph Silvy and Peter Fretus, two Portuguese sailors, had been impressed "against their wills" onto HMS *Ambuscade* while the *Clarendon,* the merchant ship on which they sailed, was berthed in Port Royal, Jamaica, in 1798. It took an affidavit from a London interpreter to tell their story, but this was enough to gain a writ on their behalf. As so often happened, the Admiralty ordered their discharge without putting up a fight.[95] Far from assuming that their alien status should prevent use of habeas corpus, everyone knew it was the very thing that had enabled their discharge from the navy.

In nearly all cases of alien use of the writ, we can only infer from silence in the reports and court records that nationality status was irrelevant to determining who might use habeas corpus. In only one surviving report do we encounter an explicit claim that foreigners might not enjoy the same privilege to use habeas corpus as other subjects. Counsel against Daniel DuCastre and Francis LaPierre—Frenchmen whose king was then at war with England's king—contended that aliens were not included in the terms of the Habeas Corpus Act. Sir Bartholomew Shower, counsel for many who used habeas corpus in this period, argued successfully to the contrary. Having spent eighteen months in prison on allegations that they were "alien enemies and spies," DuCastre and LaPierre were bailed and later discharged.[96] As we saw in Chapter 5, other enemy aliens were both released and remanded on habeas hearings. But no one argued that Anthony Didier, John Dupuis, or others could not use habeas corpus to ask judges to monitor the legality of their detention.

This approach to enemy aliens manifested a traditional view of the protection of the king's laws for all people in the custody of his officers: holders of the king's franchise whose behavior must be supervised. Such protection often operated in the prosecution of aliens and prisoners of war who became subject to the law of felony—by admiralty or common law—for their crimes, including those committed aboard ships far from English waters.[97] From the late seventeenth century, this view of law's protection was underscored by a broader sense that English law generally could and should serve a broader human dignity that looked beyond national belonging. As one lawyer put it in 1697, "commerce has taught the world more humanity." The judges agreed, declaring that an enemy alien living peaceably in the kingdom was "in protection" of the king, and as such might sue his bond.[98]

Judges scorned pleas in bar of "alien enemy" as ethically dubious. Citing Grotius, one lawyer a century later dismissed the legal utility of the category of "alien enemy" altogether as being "founded on an idea of a right in the conqueror to reduce his prisoners to slavery, which is contrary to the law of nations." And Sir Robert Eyre, chief justice of Common Pleas, called the idea that "alien enemy" status might bar access to the courts "one of the harshest, one of the most impolitic, nay immoral defenses that ever was."[99]

The 1810 case of the so-called Hottentot Venus raised the same issues about the nationality of an applicant for habeas corpus by everyone's silence about national status. The report of the proceedings on behalf of the woman more properly known as Saartjie Baartman described her variously as "a helpless and ignorant foreigner" and as "a female native of South Africa" who had been "clandestinely inveigled" from her homeland, brought to England, and "exhibited against her consent" because she was "remarkable for the formation of her person."[100] Zachary Macaulay, one of Baartman's abolitionist champions who hoped to make of her case an antislavery cause célèbre, enthusiastically declared that "no English judge would refuse a habeas corpus, which should assert the right of humanity."[101] True enough: no English judge would deny habeas corpus, though Baartman had not been born a subject of the English king.[102] But he was wrong that "the right of humanity," as he understood it, would decide the matter. English law would. As in other cases involving foreigners, Baartman was interviewed with the help of translators. After examining the affidavits, including her own, the judges concluded that Baartman had acted by her own consent when she left her home. And so Baartman returned to the podium on which she was displayed to gawking Englishmen. As in the Listers' case, contract—even if a dubious one—settled the matter.

What interests us is not the outcome or its justice according to "the right of humanity," but the events leading up to it. As in Somerset's case, no one thought it worth arguing that Baartman could not use habeas corpus since she had been born out of the king's dominions. Cases like these suggest powerfully that neither free nor slave status, nor apparent place of birth, precluded using habeas corpus. By their presence in England, or by living under the control of other of the king's subjects, such people were accepted as subjects for the purpose of investigating the legality of one person's detention by another. Paradoxically, a specifically English law defined a subjecthood that stretched beyond the bounds of nationhood, then beyond England's shores. This was the power of the prerogative at work. From allegiance, actual or implied, came liberties. Put more anachronistically, what modern law would call "standing" was simply not an issue. Subject status, or the lack of it, points more vividly than any other factor to the absence of concern about the legal nature of the detainee using habeas corpus.

Granville Sharp: Slavery, Liberty, and Imperial Law

> *This was the charter, the charter of the land,*
> *And guardian angels sang this strain:*

> *Rule, Britannia!*
> *Britannia rule the waves.*
> *Britons never, never, never shall be slaves.*

Early modern political rhetoric, like "Rule Britannia," tells us repeatedly that Englishmen could not be slaves.[103] But could slaves be Englishmen; could they be subjects? Yes. Even the lawyers who argued against James Somerset's release from his master did not contend that his status as slave or his birth in Africa made him an alien or barred his use of habeas corpus. Perhaps no one figured more prominently in the public debate around questions concerned with humanness, the claims of liberty, and the moral necessity that law should recognize those claims through the use of habeas corpus than Granville Sharp, who had also been the driving force behind using the writ to free Somerset.

Sharp, a clergyman's son who lacked the wealth to attend university, became an extraordinary autodidact. After teaching himself Greek and Hebrew to further his studies in theology, his mastery of languages allowed him to write important works on the English language and on Greek scriptures. But it was his concern with the many threats he saw to human liberty that inspired his most sustained work. His writings across the 1770s and 1780s formed a comprehensive indictment of the interconnected ways in which imperial legal practices restricted liberty for people of all kinds. He combined antislavery zeal with support for the American rebels, condemnation of naval impressment, and the need to reform parliamentary representation: all these problems were made of the others, each manifesting a servitude born of the moral and spiritual corruption generated by empire. Sharp melded Lilburne's zeal and command of the Bible with broader learning in philosophy, law, and history. Unlike Lilburne, who never became much more than a barb in the side of the body politic, Sharp generated a force to be reckoned with, even if his efforts only rarely produced victory.[104]

At the center of Sharp's thinking about liberty stood God the creator, a generative force in which spiritual necessity and natural law operated together. Juxtaposing public good with private greed, his critique of slavery was part of a broader assault on unfreedom in all forms. He thus damned

> *the illegality* of reducing or subjecting mankind to *involuntary servitude,* either under political or private dominion, as all pretensions to an *unlimited authority* of any man or men over others, are contrary to *Natural Equity* and the *Laws of God,* as well as baneful to mankind in general; which effect is unhappily demonstrated by the numberless instances of *unnatural* oppression now prevailing to the destruction of mankind, in almost every part of the world.[105]

Here, in his 1777 treatise on natural law, Sharp showed his facility with Samuel von Pufendorf and Roman law, but the epigraphs from Galatians and St. Matthew, along with the ten index pages devoted to the scriptural references peppering the book, reveal the most important source of his ideas. Sharp developed themes reminiscent of Lilburne's, playing variations on the same passage from St. James long used by preachers concerned with Christian liberty, in which "the law of liberty" became the "Royal law, by which mankind will certainly be judged!" Like his predecessors, Sharp invoked liberty's redemptive possibilities, though he pursued redemption not only within himself and for eternity, but also in the world here and now: across an empire where slavery was "the work and service of the *Grand Enemy of Mankind,* and consequently ought to be esteemed highly offensive to Almighty God."[106]

Though there was much in English law that he admired, Sharp, like Lilburne, remained suspicious of it, especially in contemporary practices arising from imperial exigencies. In considering the limits and possibilities of common law, "universal benevolence," he argued, "should always regulate and limit . . . patriotism," and the blindness it might create. Natural and divine law established the means by which eyes might be opened, by which English law might be perfected and restored to its better self. Sharp thus recalled the universalizing "natural equity" that St. German had identified in English law more than two centuries earlier. All that was needed was to recover this equity by renewed practice. By the Gospel, he argued, Britons must consider themselves "*Citizens of the World.*" "[E]very Man," he continued, "without any *partial distinction* of Nation, Distance, or Complexion, must necessarily be esteemed *our Neighbour,* and *our Brother.*"[107]

Sharp's critique of English law's blinders increasingly became a critique of legislation and the legislatures that made it. Like Hale, Sharp argued that Britons took to the king's colonial dominions "all the rights, liberties, and privileges of the British constitution." Yet displaced Africans were brought into those same places as slaves, a circumstance made possible by statutes "repugnant" to the laws of England, by which novel forms of property and contract had been generated.[108] The greed that empire encouraged was abetted by the actions of corrupt colonial assemblies. Sharp condemned Caribbean legislators as "miserably degenerate," promulgating laws whose "natural *unlawfulness* and wickedness" could not be made lawful by their statutory origin: no positive law could stand against God's law. Though disgusted by Caribbean legislators, Sharp saved his full contempt for Americans whose slave regime belied their "theatrical bombast and ranting expressions in praise of liberty."[109]

Sharp was deeply concerned to answer what he thought were spurious scriptural justifications of slavery. But he worked in another mode too: a monarchical one, in which subjecthood operated as the source of legally defensible privileges and the prerogative served as the means of their protection.

> The king is invested, by his office, with a kind of *limited property,* in the persons of all his *free subjects,* by which he is enabled, and, indeed, bound in duty to claim, and *free* them whenever their persons are unlawfully seized, imprisoned, or otherwise detained at home or abroad,

under pretence of right of service, whereby their *persons* are claimed as *private property*, acquired by purchase, custom, or any other mode of acquisition whatsoever.[110]

This traditional conception of allegiance defied any idea of one subject's having property in another. And anyone—by virtue of "his *human nature*"—who came into the king's dominions enjoyed a "just right to the king's protection." This pertained "wheresoever the bounds of the British empire are extended," making slaves everywhere "as much the king's natural born subjects as the free natives of England." Even if colonial statutes permitted the slave, or the slave's master, to make contracts for possession or transfer of a human being, "no contract whatsoever, can untie [the slave's] indispensable obligation and allegiance to the king and the laws." No person could bargain away the liberty that arises from subjecthood. All the arrangements in imperial private law that erected and sustained slavery violated the king's protection of his subjects, and amounted to "the grossest infringement on the king's prerogative."[111] In Sharp's vision, transcendent laws of God and nature converged with traditional notions of subjecthood whence came liberty and the king's protection of liberty.

Habeas corpus fit into Sharp's thinking in two ways: as a part of English law from which to make an attack on slavery; and as a way of addressing other forms of unfreedom currently allowable by law. As we saw when examining Somerset's case, that attack had been relatively straightforward and successful in the early 1770s, even if it had only a limited effect. Decisions in the cases of Lewis and Somerset could not end slavery in Britain or in the Caribbean, but they had prevented the unwilling deportation of individuals who would have suffered the consequences of slavery if transported to Jamaica. If no contract for property in a person was good because it violated the king's protection, then transporting people against their will was also illegal. This is where Sharp invoked the Habeas Corpus Act, which precluded transportation out of the realm of any person without his or her agreement. Sharp made this into an imperial principle, thereby opening to question the entire system of slavery, premised as it was on transporting people against their will. It made no matter, by Sharp's reading, that those transported were Africans, and thus not subjects at the start of the process: "the Laws of the Land, and especially the Habeas Corpus

Act, are expressly and clearly *on One Side of the Question,* without the least exception whatever concerning any difference or distinction of Persons."[112]

In 1778, Sharp applied similar reasoning to the suspension of habeas corpus approved the year before by Parliament, and also to naval impressment, which he argued was simply suspension by another name. Both practices, like slavery, arose from imperial realities, and both amounted to a suspension of God's law: "*no human authority* upon *earth* can *suspend* or *annul* any part of the *eternal law,* without grievous sin!" Sharp mocked the common justification of such measures: "No plea *of necessity* could render such a parliamentary exertion even excusable." Impressment, like slavery, did nothing but provide "warrant to take a man *by force,* to drag him away, like a thief, to a *floating prison.*" Like slavery, impressment and the suspension of habeas corpus—though a direct attack on the liberty of some—was indirectly an attack on the liberty of all.[113] Few of his contemporaries were convinced, however, as Britannia's empire grew.

Britannia ruled the waves by impressing sailors, whose conscripted labor secured the profits extracted from the labor of slaves on the other side of the Atlantic. While habeas corpus answered the needs of some, it could never serve as an instrument for voiding the larger legal apparatus on which empire rested. From Lilburne to Sharp and beyond, many asked the writ to serve as the means by which some "eternal law"—God's or nature's—might be used not just to release individual prisoners, but also to undo the statutes or customs that left countless more in the custody of others. They would be disappointed. At its greatest, habeas had been an instrument used by judges to watch other magistrates and officers. In individual cases, judges prevailed when there was no other authority greater, and as long as they could rely on the kinds of prerogative arguments that Sharp made in order to bolster judicial authority. But there was a greater authority: Parliament. Liberty would remain law's subject. And no law was greater than that which was made when legislators acted as judges, whether they ordered detention directly, or indirectly by making statutes. Legislation would bind judges, and bind the writ, even as it spread farther across law's empire.

PART III

Habeas Corpus,
Bound and Unbound

Both statute and empire constrained habeas corpus as its geographic reach grew. We tend to think of legislative action in benign terms. But the Star Chamber Act of 1641 and the Habeas Corpus Act of 1679 did little to improve the writ's utility that judges had not already accomplished. Worse, statutory changes encouraged a legislative impulse that took more insidious forms. Only Parliament would imprison without judicial supervision. Parliamentary supremacy over judicial action would expand dramatically in 1689, as statutes suspended the writ's work for the first time.

By then, the writ had begun to move about the empire, following lines traced by common law. This movement arose from the writ's capacity to enter all jurisdictions of the king, even those from which other forms of legal process were normally barred. Nonetheless, the writ would be hemmed in by statutory pronouncements from Westminster, and then from assemblies from Quebec to New Zealand, as imperial Britons responded to anxieties generated by colonial rule.

Some judges resisted these constraints, but others hesitated to use the writ as vigorously as their predecessors. By the nineteenth and twentieth centuries, for all that the palladium of liberty was worshipped, habeas corpus was more often invoked as an aspiration for what law might do than used by judges in the vigorous manner of their forebears: as the means to control all other jurisdictions, wherever, however, and whomever they imprisoned.

CHAPTER 7

Legislators as Judges

William Williams, Welsh barrister and political gadfly, followed the traditional line as he asked King's Bench to order the Earl of Shaftesbury released from the Tower in June 1677:

> You have a case before you wherein the King, the subject, and this court are highly interested: the king in his prerogative, the subject in his liberty, this court in its jurisdiction. . . . It is the prerogative of the King to deliver all prisoners upon habeas corpus or to be satisfied that there [is] just cause for their imprisonment. It is the right of the subject to be so delivered and it is the right of the court to deliver them.

Williams channeled Sir Edward Coke's ghost, reprising arguments made in Witherley's case seven decades earlier. But whereas Coke had successfully deployed the prerogative against a conciliar court, Williams now failed because he aimed at a greater target: Parliament.

The return to Shaftesbury's habeas corpus was nearly as curt as that made for the Five Knights five decades earlier, saying only that he had been imprisoned by the House of Lords, at their "pleasure . . . for high contempts committed against this House." Williams conceded that Parliament was a superior court, even to King's Bench. But it could not be superior to law itself, law of which only the justices might judge.

> The commitment by the Lords in Parliament cannot alter the law. If the cause of the commitment be not legal, their commitment cannot make it so, otherwise the Lords may commit without law; nay, they may commit against law. Is not this to set the House of Lords above the law and above the King's prerogative?

It was the most powerful of arguments, in which the king's prerogative, the subject's liberty, and the supreme jurisdiction of King's Bench
intertwined. But Williams faced the simplest contention in reply.
King's Bench might be "superior to all courts of ordinary jurisdiction,"
according to the aging but still vigorous Sir John Maynard, but the
House of Lords "is the supreme court of the realm." The justices
agreed, and back to the Tower the earl returned.[1]

In many ways, the history of habeas corpus turns more on a contest
between King's Bench and King-in-Parliament than on one between
King's Bench and the king's Council. The lawyers arguing Shaftesbury's case had been major players in this contest since the 1650s and
would be into the 1690s. The contest was fought on multiple fronts:
over Parliament's power to imprison without review, the propriety of
statute to amend a common law writ, and the use of statute to suspend
the writ. Shaftesbury's own life suggests the complexity of countervail-
ing claims to superiority among King's Bench, Council, and Parliament from the 1640s onward. When the king—law's center of gravity—disappeared in the 1650s, English lawyers largely pretended that
nothing had happened, substituting one personification of sovereignty for another: a Lord Protector, Oliver Cromwell, became king in
all but name. King's Bench lived on as the Upper Bench; the Privy
Council became the Council of State. Parliament was reduced—the
Lords' House was abolished in 1649—and was frequently reconsti-
tuted as political crises came and went. In this environment, Shaftesbury—then plain Anthony Ashley Cooper—served on the Council as it
began the first experiments with sending prisoners to insular places in
hopes of keeping them beyond the writ's reach. By the end of the
1650s—after Cromwell's death, but shortly before monarchy's restoration—Cooper had joined others in criticizing such practices and in
launching an effort to address them through statute.

Shaftesbury's work in Parliament, and his treatment by Parliament,
points to a central irony in the writ's history: that Parliament was the
only institution that could imprison without judicial review, while at
the same time, it was thought to be the one place where work might be
done to improve the writ's operation. Shaftesbury would play a central role in that work when the Habeas Corpus Act was passed in
1679. That act accomplished less than is commonly believed, because
it merely prescribed practices that King's Bench, using the common

law writ, had already developed. But the 1679 statute did generate a
new insistence that statute was required to make the writ effective. This
statutory expectation would threaten to undermine the writ's work as
well as support it, a threat that became most pronounced in statutory
suspensions of habeas corpus in England and all over the empire. Further adding to the irony of Shaftesbury's long experience with habeas
corpus, the statute of 1679 would leave one issue unaddressed: parliamentary imprisonment.

By 1689, suspension statutes would take from the justices their authority to supervise certain imprisonment orders, while returning that
power to the same Council from which Parliament had worked so hard
to take it in the generations preceding. By bringing to light the relationship between court and Parliament in the seventeenth century, we
will be in a better position to understand both why transcendent conceptions of liberty could never impose on law (see Chapter 6), and
why the writ could go to all the king's dominions, yet be easily constrained. The writ would move across the empire along lines of common law, traced in and through royal charters that made and modified
superior courts in new dominions from Jamaica to Ceylon. But the
common law writ would always be dogged by statutory expectations as
colonials demanded a Habeas Corpus Act of their own. Because of
their insistence, the common law writ was denatured. The logic of suspension followed in the wake of statutory extensions of the writ, con-
suming the judge's autonomy along the way.

Throughout this chapter, we shall be as concerned with Parliament's imprisonment orders as with its statutes, because prison orders
and legislation both asserted Parliament's sovereignty. From the end
of the sixteenth century, legislative interventions in the writ's work
were always shadowed by legislative imprisonment orders that no court
could monitor. The power to imprison and the power to change the
judges' use of habeas corpus were so intertwined because Parliament,
too, was a court, the highest court. The Earl of Shaftesbury understood this as well as anyone.

The High Court of Parliament and Control of Imprisonment

Parliament's character as a "court" was a commonplace.[2] But what
kind of court was it? How did it use imprisonment? Could King's

Bench supervise its imprisonment orders? Answers to these questions changed as Parliament fought a war in the 1640s against one king, and then deposed another king and declared his successors in the late 1680s. By such dramatic deeds, Parliament showed that it could declare judgment and control it.

Parliament's supremacy had long been accepted, though the nature of that supremacy remained in doubt, and turned on the question of what were Parliament's component parts. Sir Matthew Hale gave the usual tripartite answer: "The Parliament [is] the high and supreme court of this kingdom, being a convention of the commons by their proxies, [and] the lords or peers, together with the king."[3] Only the whole—of three parts, not two—was supreme.[4] Statute required the concurrence of king, Lords, and Commons; other forms of parliamentary judgment did not. Parliament thus possessed a double jurisdiction: "supreme, consisting in the whole parliament, and a subordinate, ordinarily exercised in the House of Peers."[5] To them "belongs a peculiar jurisdiction, though not the supreme, yet superior to any other courts."[6] The Lords had a broader jurisdiction than the Commons: they were charged with putting peers on trial for felony or treason, and with hearing writs of error from the courts in Westminster Hall. What did the Commons' judicature include? Answering that question will show how far the Commons might go in imprisoning the queen's subjects, and illuminate the mutually respectful interaction between Parliament and Privy Council.

No one doubted that the Commons, like the Lords, might imprison for any contempt committed by one of its members or for nonmembers' violations of members' privileges. In 1576, MP Peter Wentworth spoke for freedom of speech in Parliament, even if that meant addressing religion or the royal succession, normally taboo topics. A horrified Commons sent him to the Tower.[7] A zealous Protestant, Wentworth feared a Catholic takeover when the childless queen should die, so he decided to raise these issues again in 1593. Before he could do so, news of his intentions leaked; now the Privy Council sent him to the Tower.[8] The inverse corollary to the Commons' power to imprison members was that no one else could do so. Even so, the House made no complaint on Wentworth's behalf, because it shared with the Council the same notions of what amounted to contempt. Otherwise, Parliament defended members' privilege of freedom from arrest: for instance, reacting in fury when MP Sir Thomas Shirley was jailed in a private suit in 1604. The Commons simultaneously put Shirley's foe in the Tower for breach of privilege, and sent its own writ of habeas corpus to the Fleet on his behalf. When the Fleet's warden refused to make a return, the Commons jailed him too. In the end, Shirley won his release.[9]

Cases like these demonstrate, first, that by imprisoning and releasing from prison, the Commons asserted an authority distinct from the superior authority that the three parts of Parliament held jointly. Second, the Commons was aided rather than obstructed by the Council—which was hardly surprising, since many councilors were also MPs.[10] But there were limits to the power of the Commons to imprison, limits found at the boundary of the definition of "contempt."

Edward Floyd was the kind of Catholic that Jacobean Protestants feared most: vocal. By the spring of 1621, religious war had been waged for three years to control the heart of Europe. The previous November, a Catholic army had routed forces of the Protestant king of Bohemia, Frederick, whose wife, Elizabeth, was James I's daughter. The Privy Council first imprisoned Floyd after hearing reports that he had celebrated the defeat of the king's daughter.[11] But this did not prevent proceedings against him in the Commons, where MPs competed to devise the most creative punishments possible. When the king learned of their zeal, he sent his thanks, but asked "whether the house's power extend[s] to punish one who is no member of the House." It was a good question. While the Lords had a traditional criminal jurisdiction, the Commons did not. The upper House thus condemned the Commons' judgment of Floyd as an attack on the Lords' privileges.[12]

Members of the Commons now believed that their honor depended on whether their judgment to fine, pillory, and imprison Floyd was carried out. The Commons justified this through a neat syllogism by which Floyd's words became a contempt of the Commons: Floyd's attack on the king's daughter was an attack on the king, and by attacking the king, Floyd had attacked Parliament and thus impugned the Commons. But in the end, under pressure, the Commons retreated from the case, leaving the Lords to judge Floyd's wrongs on their own.[13]

The debate over Floyd coincided with the Lords' revival of their authority as a superior court, an authority that they had not used since the fifteenth century.[14] The Commons first raised the prospect of impeachment by its attacks that spring on holders of royal monopolies. When a search of records turned up no precedents of the Commons' having passed judgment for anything but contempt of its own House, the members referred the despised monopolists to the Lords. In the impeachment of Lord Chancellor Sir Francis Bacon, which followed in May, the Lords carried the burden of investigation and judgment. As punishment for corruption in the granting of monopolies, the Lords removed Bacon from office and imprisoned him during the king's pleasure. In 1641, Parliament extended impeachment to the justices themselves, most spectacularly when Sir Robert Berkeley was arrested while presiding in King's Bench. His trial in the Lords, in September 1643, concluded with a judgment that he remain in prison "during the pleasure of this House."[15] There was no better indication of where ultimate control over imprisonment now resided.

Amending Habeas Corpus, to 1641

As we have seen, Parliament made a number of experiments with its powers to imprison in the early seventeenth century. Crucially, at each of these moments—1593, 1604, 1621, 1641—Parliament simultaneously discussed amending habeas corpus. When read alongside concurrent debates about Parliament's own prisoners, debates about amending habeas corpus take on a somewhat sinister cast. The power to imprison, and the power to modify judicial supervision of imprisonment using habeas corpus, revealed the same impulse toward parliamentary dominion.

In February 1593, two days after his friend Peter Wentworth went to the Tower, James Morice initiated the first important effort to intervene in the work of habeas corpus by statutory means. Morice had steered clear of Wentworth and his plans to speak of the queen's succession, applying himself to other work instead. When he introduced his bill "confirming a branch of Magna Carta," Morice aimed not at the Privy Council—whose leader William Cecil, the Baron Burghley, had long supported him—but at the High Commission and its use of oaths *ex officio,* by which one answered questions under oath without first knowing the charges.[16] Far from criticizing that practice as arising from the prerogative, Morice saw it as an affront to the prerogative. As he put it in his treatise of oaths, the High Commission's practice injured "the prince [*sic*] in her regality and her people in their lawful liberty."[17] Morice's bill condemned oaths *ex officio* and the use of imprisonment to enforce them by appointing treble damages for any imprisonment against "the great charter and ancient good laws and statutes." It also provided that any of the common law courts might award habeas corpus for such prisoners, and would fine jailers £10 for neglecting to return the writ.[18] Despite his resort to the prerogative to justify his bill, Morice offended the queen by touching her ecclesiastical authority, so the speaker of the House of Commons, Solicitor General Sir Edward Coke, set the bill aside.[19]

In 1604, shortly before the Commons examined Shirley's imprisonment, a new "bill to confirm unto the subjects of England their ancient liberties" appeared.[20] Again, the principal target was probably the High Commission, not the Privy Council. This likelihood is underscored by the fact that throughout Elizabeth's and James's reigns, every general pardon passed by Parliament released all prisoners except those committed "by express commandment from the Queen's Majesty, or by the commandment or direction of any of her majesty's Privy Council."[21] MPs, like King's Bench justices of the same period, continued to believe that the Council's prisoners merited different treatment from others. But this bill, too, failed.

The most serious effort to pass "An Act for the better Securing of the Subjects from wrongful Imprisonment" arose in the spring of 1621 at the same moment that the Commons asserted its imprisonment powers against Floyd. According to Coke, the text of Sir William Fleetwood's bill followed Morice's bill.[22] It included penalties for imprisonment orders contrary to Magna Carta, and required that warrants should contain "the cause of the commitment." It also ordered judges to issue habeas corpus, though it excepted from this requirement "commitments by six privy councilors . . . for matter of state not fit to be revealed."[23] As Coke explained, prisoners jailed by the Privy Council, including those whose warrants gave no cause of imprisonment, could not be bailed.[24] Though no one yet knew it, the six-signature standard was telling: a warrant by six councilors would be required in every statute that suspended habeas corpus after 1689. The amendment and suspension of habeas corpus would soon be revealed as the Janus-faced consequences of parliamentary control of imprisonment.

The 1621 bill targeted justices of the peace, not the Privy Council. Two problems sank the proposal. First, some MPs worried that stiff penalties for illegal imprisonment orders might undermine the local peace that JPs had tried to preserve through summary convictions. They thus asked "that corporations and justices of peace might be excepted."[25] But that would defeat the bill's purpose, as Serjeant Francis Ashley explained. Ashley had given his reading on Magna Carta just five years earlier, and still saw the chief threats to the subject's liberty coming from JPs. Ashley argued that JPs would face no danger from the bill so long as they did not imprison contrary to law. This did not satisfy critics, many of whom were JPs themselves, and worried about their liability for wrongful imprisonment by the bill's terms. The bill failed not because it did too little to control jailers by encouraging habeas corpus, but because it did too much. Second, many saw the six-councilor requirement as an undue restriction on legitimate authority. Upon reviewing precedents, including the judges' resolution of 1592, many MPs could not support a bill that now required so many to sign a warrant, a view confirmed by the most august of authorities: former Chief Justice Coke. Others worried about the damages imposed for noncompliance with the bill's demands for granting the writ, which might be "dangerous to the judges."[26] The bill failed. When Fleetwood introduced it again in 1624, the result was no better.[27]

Considered in the context of these discussions and of views of Privy Council imprisonment powers—discussed in Chapter 5—the events of 1627 and 1628 mark a dramatic turn rather than just another moment on a progressive march begun long before. In November 1627, during courtroom arguments on the Five Knights' writs, John Bramston made the most effective arguments. Admitting that precedent did not favor the knights, he suggested that something beside precedent—some greater source of law—required that any prisoner's writ be returned with a full explanation of the cause of imprisonment. For Bramston, that greater source was statute, from Magna Carta through the Edwardian due process statutes.[28] Although this view did not convince the justices of King's Bench, it did set up the issues for discussion in Parliament the following spring. There Coke, John Selden, and others succeeded in upending widely held understandings of this aspect of law by arguing that the innovations they proposed marked a resort to tradition.[29] Against the demands of statute as they now interpreted them, precedents—the decisions of fallible judges—became irrelevant. Ironically, no judge's pronouncements were more dramatically reversed than Coke's, who now repudiated the favor he had once shown to conciliar imprisonment orders as attorney general and as chief justice.

For all Coke's embarrassment—he spoke at length about why his view had changed since 1621—another principle that he had long promoted provided the core of the language concerning habeas corpus that made it into the Petition of Right.[30] "By the law of God, none ought to be imprisoned, but with the cause expressed in the return of his imprisonment, as appeareth in the Acts of the Apostles," was how he once put it.[31] In the laws of God and of nature, as well as in the statutes that Selden and others labored over, were the transcendent requirements of law that demolished judicial precedents of remand orders for those imprisoned by the Privy Council without a cause expressed. In the Petition of Right, Parliament made the most profound assertion yet of a parliamentary power to direct the writ's work.

In June 1628, Charles I replied to the Petition: "The king willeth that right be done according to the laws and customs of the realm."[32] This was a grand yet innocuous answer to a petition whose language was equally grand yet vague. The Petition complained that "divers of your subjects have of late been imprisoned without any cause shown" yet had been denied release on habeas corpus. Thus it demanded "that no freeman . . . be imprisoned or detained . . . contrary to the laws and franchises of the land."[33] For all the seeming power of this language, the Petition did little to change judicial work in the years immediately following. Charles I's judges—who released prisoners at a much lower rate than their predecessors—understood "the law of the land" to accommodate conciliar imprisonment without cause, just as the resolution of 1592, Coke's old pronouncements, and decades of precedent had taught them.[34] Writs returned between 1628 and 1642 containing conciliar imprisonment orders without a cause stated in them continued to end in remand or bail as the bench continued to go behind the return to make decisions on a case-by-case basis.[35]

The most spectacular remand orders occurred after the spectacle in the Commons in March 1629, when a group of members held the speaker in his chair to prevent the dissolution the king had just ordered. Among the leading actors then were John Selden and Denzil Holles, a young MP married to the daughter of the same Sir Francis Ashley who had figured so prominently in discussions of the subject's liberty in recent decades.[36] They and the other leaders of the ruckus were imprisoned. When habeas corpus issued on their behalf, the Council did return a cause, though in the vaguest possible terms: "by our special command . . . for notable contempts . . . committed against ourself and our government." The return was silent about the prisoners' behavior in Parliament, this being the last issue that privy councilors wanted discussed in court. A troupe of leading lawyers defended the prisoners—Ashley argued for his son-in-law—but all were remanded.[37] As we shall see, the episode made an impression on Holles.

The Petition of Right is one of those legislative utterances—it was not a statute, though it was put on the statute roll—that would have greater influence as later generations turned it into an icon. But its text was too flimsy to direct judicial action. During debates, the Commons had produced a more robust statement about legal imprisonment when it resolved that no one should be imprisoned by royal or conciliar commands "unless some cause . . . be expressed"; that habeas corpus "ought to be granted" in all such cases; and that where the writ was returned without a cause, the prisoner "ought to be delivered or bailed."[38] These requirements mirrored those inserted in the bills considered in 1593, 1604, and 1621. Though the Petition of Right had none of this precision, these requirements would form the foundation on which Parliament would work again.

The result, in July 1641, was the "Act for the Regulating of the Privy Council and for taking away the Court Commonly called the Star-Chamber." As the title suggests, its principal concern was to slay the Star Chamber, which during the 1630s had become a target of discontent among people of widely varying political persuasions. The next entry in the statute book abolished the High Commission, suggesting how Parliament, in the summer of 1641, reconstructed the judicial system, by which effort moderates hoped to avert a more serious crisis.[39] While efforts to reform religion in 1641 remained hotly contested, most agreed on these and other reforms of law. The Star Chamber Act was opposed by some, such as the Earl of Manchester, who would become supporters of Parliament when war began one year later. It was promoted by others—including Edward Hyde, a long-time critic of the king—who would soon become supporters of the monarch. These efforts at law reform provided some final moments of consensus before more contentious matters brought the nation to a boil.[40]

As before, parliamentary discussions of habeas corpus in 1641 occurred as Parliament flexed its muscles in other areas concerned with imprisonment. Denzil Holles, Edward Hyde, and prominent lawyers such as John Maynard led an effort to redefine jurisdictions—destroying some, transforming others—while bearing down on King's Bench itself. They reported on work to reform or abolish the earl marshal's court, Star Chamber, and the Council of the North—which had obstructed the use of habeas corpus—and on the misdoings of Chief Justice Sir John Bramston.[41] Bramston, who had represented the Five Knights, was now chastised for his refusal to release various Privy Council prisoners on returns to habeas corpus that showed no cause of imprisonment. More ironically, a Parliament now focused on undue use of imprisonment powers soon jailed King's Bench Justices Sir Robert Berkeley and Sir Thomas Malet.[42] Once again, debates about amending habeas corpus occurred as Parliament extended its own use of imprisonment.

The 1641 Star Chamber Act opened with a reference to Magna Carta and a condemnation of imprisonment without "due process of law."[43] After abolishing Star Chamber, the Council in the North, and the Welsh Council, the act declared that anyone imprisoned by order of the king, the Privy Council, or any councilor might use habeas corpus. It required that the returning officer "certify the true cause" of imprisonment, on pain of large fines. The 1641 act thus employed some of the devices proposed in earlier parliamentary discussions about amending habeas. But the act marked an important shift, in two ways. First, unlike the bills before 1628, the 1641 statute aimed squarely at the Privy Council and other conciliar courts rather than at church courts or justices of the peace. Second, the 1641 statute marked a greater accomplishment in law than the Petition of Right, whatever the Petition's inchoate rhetorical force may have been. A transformation had occurred in what counted as lawful imprisonment for reasons of state. The most vigorous use of imprisonment orders beyond judicial review would henceforth come not from king and Council, but from Parliament itself. Justices Berkeley and Malet understood this. To appreciate how this transformation happened, we must consider again the legal effects of civil war and life without a king.

Rebuffing Habeas Corpus, 1642–1660

The work of King's Bench continued through the 1640s and 1650s. The name of the court changed—it became the Upper Bench in 1649—but little about its habeas jurisprudence did. As we saw in Chapter 5, the court would often face down Parliament by using the writ, especially against imprisonment orders by the Commons. But the Commons would strike back, as Samuel Mason and others learned when they were jailed for refusing to be listed with the militia in 1643. After their release by habeas corpus, the Commons simply made new orders for their imprisonment "during the pleasure of the House," language echoing that used in Privy Council orders targeted by the Star Chamber Act. The House also commanded the justices to stay further proceedings and ordered the prisoners jailed in Portsmouth, where jailers were instructed to make no returns to any writs they might receive. The Commons tried to put their prisoners on a legal island, cutting them off from judicial review.

King's Bench responded, ordering that the prisoners should remain on bail. That worked until the court's vacation, during which the Commons made new orders reprimanding the jailers for obeying King's Bench and ordering that Mason and the others be taken into custody by the House's serjeant.[44] If court vacations had become a problem for the liberty of the subject, Parliament's actions had shown just how serious the problem might be. King's Bench would win other contests of this kind in the 1640s, but in general, Parliament prevailed.[45] Sir John Stawell's troubles reveal this as well as anyone's. He was captured in 1646 after the fall of Exeter, one of the last royalist strongholds, and the Commons then ordered his commitment to Newgate for treason. Stawell failed to win release by habeas corpus in 1648. In 1650, he was tried in the Upper Bench, but no judgment was entered. He would languish in prison until the Restoration, trapped on a legal island.[46]

The increasing likeness between conciliar and parliamentary commands was driven home in a string of imprisonment orders made in Parliament and confirmed by Oliver Cromwell's Council of State, or vice versa. The two bodies worked hand in glove, often through the efforts of individuals who were members of both, just as Councils and Parliaments had done earlier in the century. In the mid-1650s, the most significant of these figures was Anthony Ashley Cooper, the future Earl of Shaftesbury. Though he had spent a brief spell in Lincoln's Inn, he never practiced law. But he was a close observer of law's work, having served as sheriff of Dorset, then Wiltshire. In 1652, he served on a law reform commission, headed by Hale. Though nothing came of their work, it must have furthered Cooper's sense of law's possibilities and limits, and the idea that since nothing in law was sacred, it might be changed.[47] After Cooper joined Cromwell's Council in July 1653, he was put on the committee for law. Cooper remained on the Council until the end of 1654. Until then, and long after, many of the signal developments in habeas corpus would pass through his hands.

Two habeas cases of 1653–1654 were especially important: those of John Streater and John Lilburne (also discussed in Chapter 6). Using its assumed judicial authority, the Commons banished Lilburne in 1652 for his ostensibly treasonous libels against a prominent MP. Lilburne nonetheless returned from the Netherlands in 1653 and was then tried for breaking his banishment. A London jury acquitted him, so the Council of State quizzed the judge and jurors.[48] It was Anthony Ashley Cooper who reported these proceedings to Parliament, which responded by permitting the Council to take further action on its behalf. On this authority, the Council sent Lilburne to the Tower and instructed his keeper to disregard any habeas corpus that might be sent for him, both of which orders Parliament repeated.

Of course, Lilburne immediately sued the writ, to which the Tower's lieutenant returned the Council's command. Nonetheless, Chief Justice Rolle demanded a proper return. Only silence followed.[49] Fearing that Lilburne would press on, the Council sent him to the Isle of Jersey the following March. Though there was some confusion, nothing in law prevented sending habeas corpus to the Channel Isles. But Cromwell and his councilors clearly expected that geography, and the obedience of the castle's governor, if not law itself, had put Lilburne beyond court oversight. Never one to quit, Lilburne again sued habeas corpus, and Justice Richard Aske agreed to send it. But before he could, Cromwell ordered the court adjourned. Power, not law, had won.[50] Whether in Jersey or the Tower, whether on a literal island or a metaphorical one, the effect was the same: as a matter of practice if not of law, Council and Parliament continued to put prisoners beyond judicial oversight more effectively than Charles I ever had. Lilburne now suffered not simply from imprisonment beyond court supervision, but also from what we might call a policy for transporting prisoners, even those not yet convicted.[51]

Lilburne's troubles overlapped in part with those of John Streater, a London printer and parliamentary officer who was imprisoned in September 1653 by the Council of State for publishing "seditious pamphlets."[52] He sued habeas corpus, but before a return could be made, Parliament—perhaps sensing the legal weakness of a commitment made in such nonspecific terms by the Council—made an additional imprisonment order. The keeper of the Gatehouse returned both warrants.[53] Slight attention was paid to the conciliar order in court, perhaps because few considered it legally sound. The serious question concerned the parliamentary order: was it beyond review on habeas corpus?

Though he had three first-rate lawyers, Streater did most of the talking, boiling his argument down to one that may have been borrowed from the pamphlets Lilburne had written during his own habeas case five years earlier: "God himself bindeth himself by his laws." Like God, Parliament could make no statute, much less an order to imprison, contrary to that supreme law. Streater hammered on the link between imprisonment orders without cause made by Charles I's Privy Council and those made by Parliament. Turning to the Petition of Right and the Star Chamber Act, he declared his imprisonment "perfectly repugnant" to Parliament's "honor." But Commonwealth justices thought like royal ones, and remanded Streater. The court seemed a bit embarrassed, even resigned: "If it had been a cause we could have meddled in, something might have been done."[54]

If no court had ever done so before, the court now made plain the principle of parliamentary superiority, even to the point that Parliament need not imprison according to statutes of its own making. Soon thereafter, Cromwell dissolved Parliament, at that time a radical body nominated by Cromwell's Council and known ever since as Barebone's Parliament. So Streater sued the writ again in early 1654. Dissolution changed the issue from whether the justices might review a parliamentary imprisonment to whether an order to imprison lapsed with the Parliament that made it. The simple answer was yes. As Chief Justice Henry Rolle put it, while his was "a standing court," each Parliament was "a new court."[55] Its superiority ended when any Parliament did.

The tales of Streater and Lilburne suggest that imprisonment orders by Parliament or Council represented two manifestations of the same claim: that commitment orders made for reasons of state were beyond judicial review. Streater had been held on a legal island, Lilburne on an actual one. Both had been put beyond reach by a claim that parliamentary and conciliar prison orders were beyond judicial review.

Increasingly, Cromwell's Council used real islands to obstruct habeas corpus. Royalist John Ashburnham was sent to Guernsey three times in the 1650s. Robert Overton, first put in the Tower in early 1655, was sent by the Lord Protector's warrant in early 1658 to the Isle of Jersey, where he remained without trial or charge. John Biddle, too, would end up in a place surrounded by waves to keep him beyond law's gaze. As in Lilburne's case, it was a parliamentary order that first put Biddle in the Gatehouse in late 1654 for writing books declared blasphemous for their anti-Trinitarian views. He was released when Parliament was dissolved in January 1655, but was soon imprisoned again for blasphemy, a capital crime in the 1650s. In part to protect him from trial and danger of execution, Cromwell ordered Biddle sent to the Isles of Scilly.[56] Twice habeas corpus issued for Biddle, with the first returning nothing more than the Lord Protector's command to the islands' governor to hold him "until you shall receive orders." The Council later ordered Biddle moved to a London prison, from which he was dismissed on his second writ, clearly by the Council's allowance.[57] Throughout, the Council, not the court, controlled Biddle's body.

Much changed between late 1654, when Anthony Ashley Cooper left the Council of State, and 1659. In 1655, Chief Justice Rolle resigned, at least in part owing to the tussles he had had with Council and Parliament in cases like Streater's. Criticism of insular imprisonment mounted, notably from William Prynne, who had once suffered confinement in Jersey. Unlike insular imprisonment orders of the 1650s—made when prisoners had not been charged, much less tried—Prynne had been sent there in the 1630s after conviction in Star Chamber for seditious libel. Prynne now laid bare the likeness between Caroline and Cromwellian practices: they both put prisoners in "foreign isles . . . without any legal sentence."[58] With Oliver Cromwell's death soon after Prynne's *Demophilos* appeared, the floodgates of criticism opened wide. In March 1659, Robert Overton was brought from Jersey before the House of Commons, where the vague warrant for his incarceration was read. The House then voted to declare that warrant, and those of others then held in the Channel Isles, "illegal and unjust."[59]

During the ensuing discussion about the Channel Isles, everyone recognized that Cromwell's Council had sent prisoners there in hopes of avoiding judicial review. But disagreement arose as to whether, as a matter of law, habeas corpus might be sent there. It could certainly go to Scilly: those islands, as part of the county of Cornwall, were within the realm of England. But what of the Channel Isles, outside the realm but one of the king's dominions by his Norman inheritance? Perhaps thinking back to his own complicity in sending Lilburne there in 1654, Anthony Ashley Cooper thought habeas could not go there. Others disagreed. Hale, writing around this time, explained why the writ could go to the Channel Isles.[60] Either way, the House resolved that the issue could be answered by statute, and ordered the formation of a committee to prepare a bill "concerning persons committed to prison in any the islands belonging to this Commonwealth, out of the reach of an habeas corpus."[61] At the top of the committee list was John Maynard, along with Cooper and others, though nothing came of their work before the rapid sequence of events leading to the restoration of monarchy began to unfold.

Cromwell's protectoral regime had hoped that water and military control of island castles would put prisoners beyond the court's supervision. After Cromwell's death, insular detentions continued, with no protest from Parliament in the early 1660s, perhaps because its victims were as reviled by members of the "Cavalier Parliament" as by anyone. Of twelve people known to have been imprisoned in the Channel Isles in the 1660s, five were convicted regicides whose execution had been commuted: a very different kind of prisoner from those sent without charge or trial. A sixth, John Lambert, though not a regicide, had been excepted by Parliament from the general indemnity granted at the Restoration.[62] Of the six others arrested on suspicion of involvement in plots and sent to various insular places, one—Sir Henry

Vane—would be brought back from the Isles of Scilly, tried, and executed at Parliament's insistence.[63] Two others would be released without using habeas corpus after various periods of imprisonment.[64]

That leaves three prisoners of the 1660s whose stories sent more worrying signals about how the restored monarchical regime used islands to circumvent habeas corpus. Edward Salmon and Robert Overton—imprisoned again in late 1660—were sent to Jersey.[65] Political theorist James Harrington, first imprisoned in the Tower, was sent to St. Nicholas Island (Drake's Island), off Plymouth, to avoid a habeas corpus on his behalf in 1662.[66] That the writ had just as much trouble going to an island within the county of Devon as it did to Jersey suggests that the problem in getting a return was not the jurisdictional distinctiveness of the Channel Isles in the justices' minds, but geographical reality and the still limited technologies of jurisdiction used to enforce the court's commands.[67]

Prisoners in the Tower, whether sent by the Privy Council or by Parliament, encountered similar obstacles in using habeas corpus in the 1660s. The most spectacular example concerned John Fenner, who had been put in the Tower by conciliar order before the Restoration. When Fenner finally sued habeas corpus in 1667, Chief Justice Sir John Kelyng, assuming that he must be a "dangerous person," dismissed his petition. His court would "not strain the rule of law to enlarge those persons which will use their liberty to set the kingdom in a flame." But by the autumn of 1667, King's Bench had begun taking a more aggressive stance toward such imprisonment orders. Many imprisoned for alleged plotting, including William Careswell, who had spent the previous five years in prison on a conciliar order, used habeas corpus to win bail.[68] The timing of these writs and the favorable response they met was no accident given renewed agitation in Parliament.

Amending Habeas Corpus, 1660–1678

After the Restoration, the pre-1642 pattern repeated itself. Parliament considered amendments to habeas process at the same time that disputes arose over specific imprisonment orders. In 1667 and 1668, a number of issues concerning control of imprisonment converged: renewed conflict between Lords and Commons over their respective imprisonment powers; an attack on the chief justice of King's Bench concerning his use of habeas corpus; a growing critique of insular imprisonment orders; and the first parliamentary efforts since 1660 to reform habeas corpus. These contests came to a head in late 1667, as the House of Commons demanded that the Lords imprison the Earl of Clarendon while impeachment proceedings against the king's great minister moved forward.[69]

The attack on Clarendon was packed with ironies. When he was still plain Edward Hyde, he had been a lawyer and, in 1640–1641, a prominent critic of Charles I who had helped to pass the Star Chamber Act. Like other lawyers concerned that Parliament was beginning to go too far against the king, Hyde left London in 1642 and became one of Charles I's principal advisers. When the king's military cause collapsed in 1646, Hyde was one of a number of royalists who went—of all places—to the Isle of Jersey for safety. He remained in exile with Charles II through the 1650s, becoming his lord chancellor. For his loyalty, he was rewarded after the Restoration with ennoblement. His enemies blamed him for everything that went wrong in the 1660s, and in November 1667, Clarendon's service was repaid with impeachment proceedings. Among the charges was that he had "procured divers of his majesty's subjects to be imprisoned against law, in remote islands, garrisons, and other places, thereby to prevent them from the benefit of the law."[70]

More ironies followed when the Commons demanded Clarendon's imprisonment, which the Lords rejected as legally dubious because the Commons' charges were so vague. Left free, Clarendon fled again into exile. Intense but ineffective recriminations followed from the Commons. In conference with them, the Lords explained their reasons for not jailing Clarendon in language echoing Coke, Lilburne, and the Book of Acts: because it "seem[ed] contrary to natural justice and reason that a person accused should be punished before he knows his crime." The Commons responded by carrying claims for the Commons' judicature to their logical extreme, with one member arguing that they might imprison without cause shown "and yet it is not against Magna Carta."[71] Why? Because "Parliaments are confined to no rules or precedents." Whatever it declared in the imprisonment of the king's subjects was good law—or so the Commons contended. Thus in the same days that the attack on Clarendon was launched, the

Commons attacked Chief Justice Sir John Kelyng for, among other things, deriding "Magna Farta" and refusing habeas corpus where appropriate.[72] In 1667 as in 1628, parliamentary control of imprisonment, whether at the expense of the king's minister or of the King's Bench, had become a major site of conflict.

Throughout the contest over Clarendon's impeachment, MPs asserted an independent judicature greater than that rejected in the Edward Floyd dispute in 1621. Conflict between the two Houses about the imprisonment powers of each flared again the following spring when the Lords jailed MP Sir Samuel Barnardiston for his contempt of the Lords' judgment on a writ of error. Proceedings on error had long been used by the Lords, but did Commons' privileges prevent the Lords from using such proceedings against a Member of the Commons? Just as this battle between the Houses intensified, the Commons took up the first post-Restoration effort to pass a bill "to prevent the refusal of habeas corpuses." Once again, a struggle over an actual imprisonment converged with discussions about how judicial oversight of imprisonment should be amended.[73]

Nothing came of that 1668 bill, but the effort was revived in early 1674, in a bill "to prevent imprisonment beyond [the] sea." It addressed two new issues: commitments to the Tower, especially by the Privy Council, and the practice—for which little evidence survives—of sending prisoners to Ireland or Scotland or to other dominions outside England, such as Tangier.[74] During debates, speakers emphasized that water or distance posed only physical problems, not legal ones. The issue concerned technologies of jurisdiction: the means by which judges might enforce legal commands against those who hoped to evade them by sending prisoners to remote places. The bill thus appointed penalties for those who would send prisoners to such places.

Some argued that the bill should also address confinement in military garrisons, which presented a similar problem since sheriffs could not enter them to serve writs.[75] But most speakers sought to strike a balance between ending those practices that many feared were dangerous to the liberty of subjects and retaining certain kinds of authority to deal with suspicious persons. We can detect a broad consensus at work during debates about what constituted proper forms of imprisonment and sufficient allowance for its oversight in a political environment that, in the 1670s, was otherwise becoming increasingly divided by partisan differences. A critic of royal ministers such as Sir Thomas Clarges, who worried about the numerous royal imprisonment warrants issued since 1660, echoed the judges who had said that "many things were unlawful"—including such warrants—"yet justified by the necessity." Henry Powle, who usually promoted curbs on royal power, likewise expressed concern that the bill appointed penalties for judges who refused the writ without punishing those who issued the writ too liberally. On the other side, those who tended to promote royal authority, like Attorney General Sir Francis North, conceded that the king could not imprison without cause.[76] Given such broad agreement among those who disagreed with one another about many other things, the bill survived amendment and three readings before Parliament was prorogued in late February 1674. Persistent support made it easy to revive the same bill at the opening of the next session, in April 1675, when concern again focused on the danger of sending prisoners outside England.[77]

The 1675 bill failed, too, owing to yet another controversy between the Houses concerning their respective imprisonment orders. This happened when the Commons imprisoned a group of lawyers it felt had violated the House's privileges by providing counsel to a suitor who had brought an MP, Thomas Dalmahoy, before the House of Lords on a writ of error. The Lords shot back by sending habeas corpus to the Tower for the lawyers put there by the lower House. The Commons ordered the Tower's lieutenant to disobey the writs: a fine example to other jailers given the bill they were then debating. Indeed, some of the most important proponents of the bill to prevent illegal imprisonment were among the most vociferous in bridling the Lords and preventing their use of habeas corpus to release Commons' prisoners in the Tower. An exasperated Charles II could do nothing but send the Commons home.[78]

For all the irony of disputes between the Houses about their respective powers of imprisonment, broad agreement persisted across the 1670s about the content to be included in any bill to amend habeas corpus. In the winter of 1677—shortly after the Lords ordered Shaftesbury to the Tower—the Commons completed a new bill and sent it to the Lords.[79] Once again, Parliament's adjournment meant that another bill disappeared without passage that spring. But defining by statute new or fuller powers for supervising Privy Council imprisonment orders seemed more pressing than ever, given that the Commons was investigating the imprisonment by the Council of John Harrington during the same period. For all Parliament's concern about conciliar imprisonment, when King's Bench examined Harrington's imprisonment by habeas corpus, the justices ordered him bailed.[80] The failure of another bill to amend habeas corpus seems to have mattered little to the court's actual work.

Our sense of the court's continuing effectiveness is bolstered when we observe what the writ by common law accomplished across the 1660s and 1670s. For instance, the writ was revived in Common Pleas, as part of the sharpening contest over the enforcement of Restoration statutes that permitted imprisonment of Protestant dissenters.[81] Thus Common Pleas discharged the famed dissenting cleric Richard Baxter, who had been jailed for preaching in a conventicle.[82] The Quaker Thomas Rudyard made use of the traditional claim of privilege as an attorney of Common Pleas in 1670 to persuade that court to issue the writ on his behalf after his imprisonment for attending conventicles. In Rudyard's case, Chief Justice Sir John Vaughan applied a simple balancing test:

> There is on the one side a concern of persons disaffected with the government that they should have no countenance from courts of justice. The other is that the legal liberty that does belong to persons should not at all be impaired by those laws that are made for the conservation of peace.[83]

In this case, the court achieved that balance by releasing Rudyard for an insufficient return from his jailer.

Rudyard's case was connected to the struggles of other Quakers. The most important Common Pleas habeas case arose from the Old Bailey trial of Rudyard's coreligionists William Penn and William Meade, who had been indicted for a "tumultuous assembly" for worship. When they were acquitted, the angry City JPs who conducted the trial jailed the jury for what they said was a verdict against the evidence. One of the jurors, Edward Bushel, followed Rudyard's example and sued habeas corpus from Common Pleas. Chief Justice Vaughan initially opposed granting the writ, saying the justices could only issue it on a claim of privilege of the court, as they had done for Rudyard. But the other justices sent the writ, and in the end, it was Vaughan who delivered the famous judgment declaring illegal the punishment of jurors for their verdicts.[84] These cases notwithstanding, doubts persisted among the justices of Common Pleas about the propriety of their court's use of habeas corpus.[85]

These were also the years in which King's Bench, led by Kelyng and then Hale, first sent the writ to the Channel Isles and first used it in cases of spousal violence. MPs recognized the importance of such judicial innovation, which occurred without parliamentary intervention. Even the supporters of a habeas bill, like Serjeant Richard Croke, pointed out that much of what the 1675 bill proposed was already law, and noted that the writ went to the Channel Isles without statutory help.[86] If one of the motivations behind a habeas statute was to prevent sending prisoners outside England, the common law writ had shown its success by releasing Robert Murray, a Scot twice imprisoned in 1677, first for "defamation of his majesty and his government," and then more vaguely "in order to his being sent into Scotland to be tried there according to law for several crimes." In both cases, King's Bench bailed Murray rather than allow his deportation.[87]

Though there was a broadly shared view of what the law was, and though the justices had shown this consensus at work in their judgments, many still favored a statutory intervention. Whatever the common law was, there were reasons for doubt. Hale had issued habeas corpus to the Channel Isles and to Jamaica, but could not compel a return.[88] A more common problem remained: the use of the writ during court vacations. Once common, vacation use had dwindled since 1660. The need for such vacation writs, however, grew as England's political life became more fractious owing to the growth of anti-Catholic bigotry and of fears about what it meant that Charles II's heir—his brother, James Duke of York—was an avowed Catholic. These concerns grew as the so-called Cavalier Parliament, first elected in 1661, wore on, its legitimacy ever more dubious in the minds of those concerned about Charles's policies. The increasing use of habeas corpus by minor figures like Harrington and Murray, and by greater ones like the Earl of Shaftesbury, indicated the sharpening of political conflict.[89]

Francis Jenks learned especially well how tricky it could be to obtain habeas corpus between terms. A London merchant with old Leveller ties, Jenks roused listeners at City elections in June 1676 with a speech demanding parliamentary elections. The Privy Council summoned Jenks for stirring a tumult, and after he spoke too rudely to the king, sent him to the Gatehouse. It was then the vacation between Trinity and Michaelmas terms. Making arguments echoing Lilburne's, Jenks failed to convince Chief Justice Rainsford or anyone else to issue the writ. He would only be released when the king commanded it.[90] In February, when Parliament reconvened, Jenks's noble allies, the Duke of Buckingham and the Earl of Shaftesbury, made arguments quite like Jenks's for a dissolution. They too were jailed, for what their peers believed was their contempt of Parliament. Buckingham apologized and was released, but Shaftesbury followed Jenks's lead and tried to use habeas corpus.

When Parliament finally finished work on a habeas corpus bill two years later, it would go a long way toward solving the problem that had caused Jenks such suffering—the difficulty of getting the writ between terms—but it would leave entirely unaddressed the problem that Shaftesbury confronted: Parliament's own prison orders.

The Habeas Corpus Act, 1679

The spring of 1679 was among the most remarkable in the annals of English politics.[91] During the previous autumn—what turned out to be the last months of the Cavalier Parliament—a long-chinned serial liar named Titus Oates whipped up fears of illusory Catholic conspiracies in an episode known ever since as the "Popish Plot." Worries about Charles II's relations with France's Louis XIV and about Charles's Catholic brother only made matters worse. Many saw the seating of the first new Parliament in eighteen years as the perfect moment to transform their anxieties—fomented by a flood of pamphlets coming from London presses and by debates in City coffeehouses—into a comprehensive attack on the king and his brother. Among proposed policies were those for limiting the authority of any Catholic king in England, or more extreme, excluding the king's brother altogether from the succession.

Vigorous use of imprisonment formed the backdrop against which political maneuvering occurred. Five Catholic noblemen, caught in Oates's wild accusations, were sent to the Tower. The Earl of Danby, the king's leading minister, joined them in mid-April, impeached after letters surfaced showing his questionable contacts with the French.

As one sensational claim after another ended with someone else in prison, habeas corpus did the work it had always done, sending some to arraignment, trial, and execution, while sending others home.[92] Despite an atmosphere in which earnest Protestants thought Jesuits lurked in every dark alley, there was no shortage of imprisonment orders shown to be wrongful during habeas hearings. Of thirty Catholic plotters accused in the first half of 1679 who used habeas corpus and for whom results are known, thirteen were bailed or discharged, including quite a few priests. Some had even been imprisoned on orders of the House of Lords, though their release on habeas corpus came only after Parliament was dissolved in late January.[93]

With scores in prison and dozens using habeas corpus, the Parliament seated in March 1679 soon took up a bill "for the better securing the liberty of the subject." The bill went quickly through the obligatory three readings in the Commons, then on to the Lords. Throughout, parliamentary imprisonment orders intruded on the debate, souring relations between the Houses. Speakers reprised arguments made since 1621 about the imprisonment powers appropriate to each House as many in the Commons pursued the impeachment of the Earl of Danby. Though Charles pardoned Danby, many demanded that he and the five "popish Lords" remain in the Tower. Some MPs noted with embarrassment that while the Catholic Lords remained untried in the Tower, the Commons had "asserted the habeas corpus, &c, 'that the subject shall not be without trial.'" Sir William Coventry asked, "[S]hall we assume that [power to imprison without trial] to ourselves?" Sharpening the rancor, the habeas bill became entangled with the pursuit, by some, of the exclusion of James Duke of York from the succession. Many feared that attacking traditional norms controlling the succession would undermine other work Parliament might achieve, like amending habeas corpus. Nonetheless, the effort succeeded—barely—as a series of conferences produced a bill to which both Houses agreed in time for it to receive the king's assent before he prorogued Parliament in late May.[94]

Who was responsible for writing and passing the "Act for Better Securing the Liberty of the Subject and for Prevention of Imprisonments beyond the Seas"?[95] Many were, reflecting the broad consensus about the writ evident in debates during the previous half-dozen years. Attorney General Sir William Jones may have drafted the bill, though if he did, he apparently worked from a template made by earlier measures.[96] Sir Francis Winnington—recently dismissed as solicitor general—was another critical supporter. Sir John Maynard, one of the oldest and greatest lawyers, played his part, just as he had in the disputes of the 1640s and 1650s. And others helped, such as Sir Thomas Clarges, an opponent of the Duke of York's exclusion, and Sir Thomas Meres, a lukewarm supporter of exclusion. Both Clarges and Meres had figured prominently in debates on earlier habeas bills. Those who favored excluding the Duke of York from the succession—like Jones and Meres—as well as those who did not—such as Winnington and Clarges—supported the Habeas Corpus Act.

Many hands helped in the House of Lords. Shaftesbury has often been credited with playing a major role in the bill's passage. More important may have been Baron Holles, who as Denzil Holles had been imprisoned without a stated cause in 1629 by the Privy Council and had played a central role in crafting the Star Chamber Act in 1641.[97] When it came time to amend the Commons' bill in the Lords, Baron Finch, the lord keeper, had the most prominent voice. Like others, he was uncertain the bill was necessary: he reminded everyone that the common law writ was strong, having long extended its reach beyond England. Nonetheless, notes he prepared for debates show his influence in increasing the penalties for obstruction or disobedience in the use of habeas corpus, terms that would give the act its potency.[98] In an age of rising partisan anger, the Habeas Corpus Act represented a rare moment of consensus around a measure that did nothing to change law, but did give law greater force to protect subjects from wrongful imprisonment. Or so many hoped.

What problems did the act address? Three stand out: obstacles to issuing the writ; "great delays" in making returns; and imprisonment in "privileged places." Let us consider each in turn.

How difficult had it been to get the writ before 1679, and how hard was it to do so thereafter? Habeas was a judicial writ, issuing at judicial discretion. Only rarely was the writ denied. It had once been as easy to use the writ during court vacations as during term, at least until the publication of Coke's *Institutes* in the 1640s sowed doubts about doing so.[99] Even so, dozens of writs issued during vacations through the 1660s, though the practice declined in the 1670s.[100] During debates on the 1674 bill, some criticized vacation use, hoping to limit rather than expand it since it involved justices working out of public view.[101] But the act promoted vacation writs by requiring justices to issue them. After 1679 the majority of vacation writs issued according to the statute, rather than by common law.[102] Nonetheless, the act's support of vacation writs marked a revival, not an innovation.

More important was the provision permitting the writ's issuance by the justices or barons of the other courts in Westminster Hall. Though most prisoners still sought the writ from King's Bench, one might now get it from the Exchequer or Common Pleas. During vacations, this meant that there were effectively three times as many judges who might be able to send it. Owing to these two provisions, the most important accomplishment of the act was to make it easier to obtain the writ in the first place.

It is less clear that the act mattered as much for ensuring that a writ, once sent, would be returned. The court had always used contempt process vigorously to enforce returns. The act did specify the speed required of returning officers based on their distance from London, and it prompted a significant increase in the number of writs marked simply "return immediately upon reception." But within London and Middlesex, this had long meant the day of issuance or the next: that is, faster than actually required by the act. Writs issued after 1679 that specified a return date required return speeds that were no faster, on average, than before. In this regard, the act made little difference.

The act declared as well that habeas might be sent to all "privileged places within the kingdom of England, dominion of Wales, or town of Berwick-upon-Tweed and the islands of Jersey or Guernsey." Again, this was no innovation. King's Bench had long sent the writ to the palatinates, Wales, and Berwick, and most agreed that the common law writ could go to the Channel Isles, even if enforcing its return had been a problem. Now such problems ceased. The clearest beneficiary was Richard Creed, imprisoned in Guernsey by the Council in 1670 "until our further pleasure." In June 1679, days after the act took effect, Creed sued the writ and was soon bailed.[103] The Privy Council continued to imprison, but never again in distant isles in the hopes that prisoners would be beyond law's reach. This was fitting; after all, the act was "for prevention of imprisonments beyond the seas," according to the second half of its title. The act made it illegal to transport any prisoner out of the realm, a feature that would prove important in slave cases.

But the practice of sending prisoners out of the realm did not end entirely, as a group of Scots, accused of committing treason in England, would learn in 1683 when they were sent north of the border in order to be investigated by torture. Avoiding the act's terms on that occasion turned on taking a narrow, novel reading of what constituted an English subject. All within the realm were normally considered subjects for the purposes of using habeas corpus, by which subjects received the king's protection. Such usage should have been underscored here by the situation of the Scots, who had been considered natural subjects of the English Crown since Calvin's case. Nonetheless, on a strained plea denying they could be subjects of English law in this regard, the Scotsmen were transported from England.[104] Like the common law writ, even the statutory writ would only be as strong as those with ultimate political authority would permit. Allowing deportation amounted to a suspension of the writ by conciliar fiat: a deed Parliament had worked since 1628 to curtail. Soon Parliament itself would begin to suspend habeas corpus by returning to the Council authority to make decisions of just this kind. This move carried ominous portents of later imperial practices, which often involved transporting political prisoners far from their homelands after summary convictions, courts martial, or no trial at all.

No evidence has appeared that any judge was ever fined £500 for wrongfully refusing the writ, as the act required. But this provision may help explain the rapid growth in the use of affidavits as part of the process for gaining habeas corpus. As we saw in Chapter 2, affidavits had been used before this time, and a statute of 1677, which appointed process for taking affidavits, had encouraged the practice. But it was only after 1679, and especially after 1689, that the procedure became more common. One can readily imagine the appeal of affidavits to the justices: sworn statements about the evidence on which a writ was granted or denied might later indemnify any judge sued for denial. But the more frequent use of affidavits also encouraged a shift in focus in habeas process from the stage after the return to the stage prior to granting the writ. This allowed the judges to rely on evidence from well beyond the return when making judgments.

The act's apparent impact diminishes if we look at the notations made on the writs in the century after 1679 to distinguish whether they issued by statute or common law.[105] Especially in term, but during vacations too, judges performed their most innovative work using the common law writ, in part because the statute applied only to imprisonment for felony or treason. Ironically, the Earl of Danby—reviled by those who made the act—used the writ by statute, though he was remanded.[106] Daniel DuCastre's writ, returning that he was an "enemy alien and spy," also issued according to the statute, but all the other POW writs examined in Chapter 5 issued by common law.[107] Likewise, major cases involving even treason, as well as key innovations involving family custody or impressment, show that use of the common law writ was as vigorous as ever.

But the courtroom is the wrong place to look for the act's significance. We should look instead in streets and coffeehouses, at political pamphlets, and in Parliament. The act would always be greater as a rhetorical club for beating alleged ministerial tyrants than as a legal shield held up in the courtroom. To explore the rhetorical uses of the act is to examine a host of ironies about who argued what liberties were threatened by whom. Political pamphlets poured from the press in this period, but the act received surprisingly little notice during the years right after its passage.[108] The act has traditionally been associated with whig political rhetoric, in which the subject's liberty was set against ostensibly arbitrary kingship. But tories referred to the act more often in the early 1680s, invoking it as an example of the king's concern for his subjects and their liberties.[109] The act even figured in tory songs then popular on London streets:

> The Habeas Corpus Act is past,
> And so far we are safe;
> He can't Imprison us so fast,
> But strait we have Relief.[110]

The song's publisher, Nathaniel Thompson, published more than his share of tory books, and had more than his share of prison experience. In 1682, he would use habeas corpus, issued according to the act's terms, to win bail from Newgate, where he had been committed for seditious libel.[111] The complex partisan effects of the act are all the more apparent when we consider that most of the writ's beneficiaries in 1679–1680—a time of Popish Plot hysteria—and again in 1689–

1690, would be Jesuits and other Catholics: those who were most oppressed by earnest Protestants who celebrated their own English liberties.

The key moment in the act's early history came when it was used to
challenge imprisonment orders made by the Commons. In December
1680, the House considered the alleged role of Thomas Sheridan
in the Popish Plot and then committed him to the Commons' serjeant-
at-arms "during the pleasure of this house"—that is, for as long as
the House wished. The Commons' speaker—none other than William
Williams, who had spoken so eloquently against the Lords' imprisonment of Shaftesbury—argued that the act did not apply to parliamentary imprisonment. Other whig lawyers, all prominent in the act's passage, agreed. These included Sir John Maynard, and most important,
the former attorney general who perhaps penned much of the act, Sir
William Jones. Sir Francis Winnington suggested that the central purpose of the act had been to prevent prisoners from being sent out of
the realm to other dominions. It "was never intended against commitments of the House of Commons . . . it was never intended that injustice should flow from this House."[112] Here was the central claim that
would not only keep Sheridan in prison, but also allow the suspension
of habeas corpus: Parliament could do no wrong.

This claim embarrassed some. Henry Powle accepted the traditional
view that king, Lords, and Commons jointly exercised a judicial power,
as did each House in cases of privilege. But imprisoning Sheridan
"goes beyond your ancient Privilege." Sir Thomas Clarges, crucial to
the act's success, likewise contended that Sheridan might use habeas
corpus.[113] While the debate continued, Sheridan took Clarges's advice
and asked every judge he could find to grant the writ according to the
act's provision allowing individual justices to do so during the court's
vacation. One judge after another hedged, "unwilling to deny, and not
daring to grant" the writ. Chief Justice Sir Richard Rainsford, of King's
Bench, went so far as to ask advice from the Commons, a kind of judicial cowardice for which he was roundly shamed. Finally, Sir Richard
Weston, baron of the Exchequer, "to his immortal honor," ordered the
writ.[114] It took some effort just to serve it on the Commons' serjeant,
but once he returned the writ, Weston ordered Sheridan bailed, followed by a full discharge when Parliament was prorogued soon thereafter. The act had been successfully used against Parliament itself.

Tory critics mocked parliamentary whigs for forgetting Magna Carta and the Petition of Right as they imitated Charles I's orders to imprison by "special command." Sheridan and Weston, one wrote, had vindicated the right of the subject against a greater threat to liberty than any king posed.[115] No one beat the Commons harder with its own stick than the tory controversialist Sir Roger L'Estrange. L'Estrange, who spent his early years in Gray's Inn, argued that claims of an independent Commons power of judicature was "never heard before Sir Edward Coke's fancy." Like others before him, L'Estrange saw that the Commons expanded its judicature by broadening what counted as privilege. By claiming a power rebuffed in Floyd's case six decades earlier, and by imprisoning Sheridan and obstructing his use of habeas corpus, the Commons had effectively suspended its own Habeas Corpus Act.

L'Estrange drove home the likeness of these deeds to those of the Caroline Privy Council:

> [T]he words of the statute were so full, as admitted of no comment, and so plain for the Liberty of the Subject, as made it undeniable, that prisoners, unless for treason or felony, were still bailable, by what person or persons soever committed, not excepting the King and Council, much less the House of Commons, who had no legal power to commit any criminal.[116]

A Parliament that had been so concerned "that the *Prince* should not use *arbitrary power,* took all possible care to keep it in their possession."[117] As if to underscore the apparent hypocrisy, a report circulated that Sheridan would pursue the Habeas Corpus Act to the letter by suing Chief Justice Raymond for refusing the writ.[118]

Sheridan and tory argument prevailed—for the first time in decades, a parliamentary imprisonment order had been reversed on habeas corpus—though not for long. For the most part, Parliament would win future battles for precedence in the use of imprisonment, but it would not go unopposed. Sir John Holt challenged Parliament, working in part from a set of natural law principles by which the propriety of parliamentary claims might be judged. He relied on the conventional view, expressed by Hale and others, that Parliament was only supreme as a whole, and that neither House, any more than any other court, could be the judge of its own privileges. In the great habeas case of the Aylesbury voters, in 1705, he explained:

> When the House of Commons exceed their legal bounds and author-
> ity, their acts are wrongful and cannot be justified more than the acts of
> private men: that there was no question but their authority is from the
> law, and as it is circumscribed, so it may be exceeded. . . . If there be a
> wrongful imprisonment by the House of Commons, what Court shall
> deliver the party?[119]

Holt thought his own court should. He did not win, but the idea of Parliament's fallibility and potential for tyranny would persist.

Beyond this vexing issue, the 1679 Act left unaddressed two others that many observers increasingly thought important: the writ's avail-ability in cases of detention that did not involve accusations of felony or treason, and the ability of judges to consider factual matter contra-dicting the return. As we saw in Chapters 4 and 5, neither of these was a significant problem in practice. Many kinds of innovation had been made possible by the common law writ. Its use had been pushed fur-thest beyond felony in the generations immediately preceding 1679. During the same period, it had also allowed a vigorous pursuit of fac-tual matter off the return.

Nonetheless, many thought that these apparent limits should be ad-dressed by an additional statute. Spurred by what appeared to some to be wrongful denials of the writ to conscripted soldiers, a bill was in-troduced in Parliament in early 1758. One reason for doing so was what the bill's proponents suggested had been the paradoxical conse-quence of the 1679 Act: that by speaking only to felony and treason, the act seemed to deny the writ in other cases of detention. The new bill's proponents admitted that the writ by common law was indeed available in such cases, but they argued that its use had been under-mined by the act.[120] Then, having argued that statute had damaged the writ, proponents proposed addressing the issue by another stat-ute, without considering that more statutory words, and the silences around them, might do further damage.

The bill was defeated, fearful as opponents were that "passing it into a law will rather weaken than add strength to public freedom."[121] Mansfield was especially condescending toward those who promoted

it out of ignorance of what law already availed.[122] Lord Chancellor
Hardwicke agreed that there was no need for it "since all the advan-
tages proposed by [the bill] were already secured by the common
law."[123] Mansfield demonstrated just this point by his work over the
next thirty years, during which he routinely considered evidence from
beyond the return—even contrary to it—and released impressed sailors by the score.[124] His practice showed clearly that the common law
writ continued to do what it had always done.

In 1816, Parliament did pass a statute that addressed many of the
concerns of 1758: it declared the writ's availability in noncriminal matters, permitted the prisoner to controvert the return, and allowed process by affidavit "in a summary way."[125] But all these usages had been
available at common law, and there is reason to question the praise
this statute has traditionally received. A new Aliens Act, essentially
suspending the writ for foreigners, passed in the same year.[126] More
striking, in March 1817, Parliament voted to suspend habeas corpus in
response to domestic political unrest.[127] Political caricaturist George
Cruickshank, reflecting protests in Parliament and beyond, condemned the suspension with the most powerful visual language: liberty, bound and gagged, hanging from a noose, with Magna Carta, the
1689 Bill of Rights, and habeas corpus in her dying fingers.[128]

Though the 1679 Habeas Corpus Act had been passed on the assumption that it would cut only one way, subsequent practice showed
that it worked as a double-edged sword, cutting down the common law
writ by promoting the assumption that the writ could be effective only
when supported by statute. Warnings that the writ's force by common
law was being damaged in this way began at least as early as 1689, during the first debates on suspending the writ.[129] In his 1729 law dictionary, Giles Jacob took pains to remind readers that

> [t]he Writ of *Habeas Corpus* was originally ordained by the Common
> Law of the Land, as a remedy for such as were unjustly imprisoned, to
> procure their Liberty; and it is a mistaken notion that this Writ is of a
> modern date, and introduced with the reign of King Charles 2.[130]

A mistaken notion, with surprising effects. What Parliament made it
could unmake, too.

Suspending Habeas Corpus, 1689 and Beyond

Ten years after passing the Habeas Corpus Act, Parliament suspended it for the first time. Much had changed, even though many MPs of 1679 were still there ten years later. Once inchoate fears of a Catholic king had been realized, leading in the closing days of 1688 to an invasion of England, a palace coup, and a revolution, by which the Catholic James II had been chased from England. In February 1689, Parliament declared that James had abdicated his throne and that his daughter, Mary, and her husband, William Prince of Orange, were his lawful successors. But worry persisted: from all over England arrived news of counterrevolutionary plotting, real and imagined; from across the Irish Sea came reports of James's preparations to recapture his throne; and from south of the Channel rumbled noises of a potential invasion. The threats were real, at least until James's cause was destroyed in battle at the River Boyne, in Ireland, in July 1690. Thereafter England, then the United Kingdom following the Treaty of Union in 1707, would be in a near constant state of war with France until 1713.[131] What would such a climate of persistent fear do to habeas corpus?

It was a sign of how much political circumstances had changed that Richard Hampden, an active supporter of exclusion and the Habeas Corpus Act, came into the Commons on March 1, 1689 to ask, on the new king's behalf, to suspend the writ by statute. Though suspension passed both Houses in under a week, that speed belied the controversy it occasioned. Many went along because it was set to last just one month, so each time the request arrived to extend suspension, opposition intensified. Extended twice, this first suspension persisted, with only several days' break in April, until October 23, 1689. An attempt to pass a new suspension in the spring of 1690 would fail, despite anxieties then about the military situation in Ireland.[132] Each time the idea came before the Commons, proponents pounded on "necessity": it was "the last necessity," for "the security of the public." Two features helped soothe those worried about suspension: it would be limited in duration, and it could only be enacted by Parliament. "If dispensed with by the executive power," Hugh Boscawen remarked, "'tis fatal always; by the legislative power, there is no danger."[133] A creative corollary to this argument was that parliamentary action, even suspension, confirmed earlier parliamentary action: the Habeas Corpus Act.[134]

Suspension's foes answered cries of "necessity" with cries of "liberty." Care in the use of imprisonment was no abstraction for Sir Christopher Musgrave: "I speak by experience. I have lain in prison." Parliamentary action, far from comforting opponents, made matters worse. "Content yourselves with the laws you already have," pleaded the tory Sir Joseph Tredenham. Critics identified two awkward aspects of parliamentary suspension. First, Parliament now took to itself the same power to suspend statute that it had criticized when Charles II and James II had suspended the Test Acts, by which Catholics were barred from office. Second, Parliament gave to the Privy Council powers to imprison without judicial oversight that two generations of parliamentary rhetoric and action had condemned. Sir Thomas Clarges, a central figure in passing the Habeas Corpus Act, exclaimed: "We have had a struggle for it . . . and now, upon suggested necessities, to dispense with this Law!"[135]

The Habeas Corpus Act articulated a fundamentally consensual view of the writ's purposes. For all the criticisms, repeated suspension acts likewise articulated a consensus about when and how the writ's work might be constrained. From 1689 to 1747, Parliament followed a formula, whether the "necessity" occasioning suspension was a "detestable conspiracy . . . by papists and other rebellious persons for invading the realm from France to the utter subversion of the protestant religion and the laws and liberties of this kingdom" (1708), or "a wicked and unnatural rebellion" in Scotland (1745).[136] Let us examine that formula closely so we can see the significance of changes to it in 1777, and again in the 1790s.

Crucially, no statute known as a suspension of habeas corpus ever "suspended" the writ of "habeas corpus." The words "habeas corpus" do not appear in them, nor does "suspend," except after the 1707 Treaty of Union, after which they "suspended" the 1701 Scottish act "for preventing wrongous imprisonment." The absence of the language of suspension explains why these were officially acts "empowering his majesty to apprehend and detain such persons as he shall find cause to suspect." These empowered six or more privy councilors, or one of the two secretaries of state, to make an order to detain someone "without bail or mainprise" on suspicion of treason or "treasonable practices."[137] All the suspension statutes named a date of expiration. Until 1777, the average duration was five months. And each included a proviso near the end declaring that upon expiration, those imprisoned by the act's terms would have the benefit "of all laws and statutes any way relating to or providing for the liberty of the subjects." In this way, the suspension statutes did confirm the Habeas Corpus Act, with the writ's full ambit serving as the norm to which law returned at the appointed time.

Suspension operated not by suspending habeas corpus, but by expanding detention powers. Over time, imprisonment for "suspicion" —on evidence not given under oath—would be the most controversial aspect of suspension, leery as many were of the possibility that vindictiveness posing as loyalty might end in the imprisonment of innocents.[138] In 1715, Lord Harcourt unsuccessfully proposed a clause for the bill debated during the Jacobite rebellion of that year that would have imposed a penalty for malicious informers.[139] His failure meant that the power to assess information about an accused traitor remained with the Privy Council, without judicial oversight. Sir William Whitlock had been especially sharp on this count in 1690: "If an angel came from heaven that was a privy councilor, I would not trust my liberty with him one moment."[140]

Nonetheless, even some accused traitors could use habeas corpus during suspension. Often, this meant testing imprisonment orders made by JPs, proceeding by the writ at common law. James Hunt, jailed in March 1696 by a JP for "holding correspondence with France," was bailed, though a suspension was then in effect.[141] In other cases, use of the writ during suspension served a traditional procedural purpose, bringing an alleged traitor to trial and execution.[142] But John Purser fared better; he was bailed on a common law writ after his imprisonment "for treasonable practices" by the secretary of state in the wake of the 1745 rebellion.[143] Judicial practice and statutory language show that the suspension statutes did not in fact prevent supervision of detention by judges. Rather, they constrained judges' authority to release prisoners who had been jailed in specified ways. Until 1777, suspensions made no distinction among law's subjects by nationality or by place of capture or detention.

More important than the common law writ's persistence during suspensions was the writ's revival when they ended. Some had feared that suspension would establish a new norm by which judges might restrain themselves, even after suspension.[144] As we saw at the end of Chapter 4, evidence from the period beginning with the start of Michaelmas 1689—when the first suspension lapsed—suggests the opposite: Chief Justice Sir John Holt's court released four out of five state prisoners who came before it.[145] Who presided in King's Bench mattered: though Holt was a crucial supporter of the new regime, he showed astonishing independence by releasing prisoners jailed by that very regime. In the year following the end of the next suspension, in September 1696, Holt's court released all twenty-three brought before it by habeas corpus who had been imprisoned by the Privy Council or by other royal officers. Some were released sooner. Edward Ridley had been jailed for suspected treason on a conciliar warrant. Ridley's writ issued according to traditional vacation practice—that is, by antedating it to the last day of the previous term, even though that date was within the suspension. He was then bailed.[146]

While many objected to any suspension, four factors consistently informed suspension practice until 1777. First, suspension could only be ordered by Parliament. Given the disrepute attaching to royal suspensions of statutes before 1688, no one argued thereafter that statute could be suspended by any but statutory means. Second, parliamentary suspensions were always for a fixed, brief period. Third, the common law writ persisted throughout, ready for use, at least on the king's behalf, even during suspensions. Finally, when suspension ended, the writ sprang immediately back to life, as usage on the first day of term after each suspension shows.

The civil war that broke out within the British empire in North America in the 1770s led to changes in this practice, changes that would make Americans acutely aware of how they were targeted not only by new statutory practices, but also by practices that cut them out of the benefits that had always arisen from subjecthood. Soon after the war began, cases arose that suggested to authorities in London that something had to be done to modify habeas use. In October 1775, Stephen Sayre, an American-born banker who had long resided in London and supported the American cause, was ordered arrested by Secretary of State Lord Rochford on bizarre charges that he planned to seize the king. Sayre was brought before Mansfield by habeas corpus and bailed, a result triumphantly reported in American newspapers. The following summer, Sayre sued Rochford for false imprisonment and won a verdict for £1,000 in damages from a London jury, though the result was reversed following post-trial motions in Common Pleas.[147]

Sayre's case was straightforward, involving a wrong allegedly committed in England. But what of wrongs done outside England? The imprisonment of Ebeneezer Smith Platt raised this question. Platt was arrested in Savannah on accusations of transferring royal munitions to the rebels, then tried for treason in Jamaica, where he was acquitted. Nonetheless, he remained a captive, and was put in irons aboard the *Pallas*—a meaningful name—and carried to England. Though kept aboard one ship after another, probably to prevent attempts to sue habeas corpus, someone obtained the writ for him in early January 1777. Before it could be served, he was moved again on order of the Treasury solicitor. After gaining another writ, Platt was at last taken to Newgate to await further proceedings.[148] Americans followed Platt's story closely: "He is the first American that [the British] government has meddled with, and much depends on his fate."[149]

Could Platt be tried in England for a wrong committed in another dominion, and could he be tried again if already acquitted for that wrong? Normally, no. If he could not be tried, could he be detained indefinitely? The answer to this question would affect the lives of hundreds of American sailors in captivity by early 1777. Though some were held on land at places like Pendennis Castle, most were kept aboard hulks at Plymouth and Portsmouth, not as POWs, but as traitors or pirates. Since they might use habeas corpus, Mansfield recommended that they be kept aboard ships to obstruct their access to courts and judges. But conditions on ever more cramped vessels made this impractical.[150] One way to bring them ashore while limiting their chance for release using habeas corpus would be to label them prisoners of war. But doing so would implicitly recognize American claims of independence. So another approach was taken: suspension.

The king's chief minister, Lord North, introduced a bill in February 1777 to create a power to confine captive Americans "like other prisoners of war," while keeping them in the legal category of rebellion and treason, to which laws they might be subjected at a later date.[151] North's suspension quickly became law, and was renewed each year until 1783. It addressed the rebellion "traitorously levied . . . in certain of his majesty's colonies and plantations in America" by permitting the imprisonment, "without bail or mainprise," of those taken for high treason or piracy in America, or on the high seas, on the order of "any magistrate of competent authority." The act included a telling proviso: that it would not apply to any prisoner, except those "as shall have been out of the realm" when committing their alleged offence.[152] The ministry and its supporters celebrated this aspect of the law, arguing that it retained the widest liberty possible in a time of danger by distinguishing among varieties of subjects based on the location of their arrest. Critics saw the same provision as the thin edge of a tyrannical wedge that would divide the empire by distinguishing among subjects. Some suggested it would be better to suspend the writ for all rather than for some. Edmund Burke, in Parliament and in a pamphlet widely read on both sides of the Atlantic, argued that a full suspension of the kind always used since 1689 would invigorate the entire nation to restore and maintain liberty. "Liberty, if I understand it at all, is a *general* principle," Burke argued. "Other laws may injure the community; this tends to dissolve it. It destroys *equality*, which is the essence of community."[153]

The suspension of habeas corpus from 1777 to 1783 marked a number of innovations. First, it occurred when no one argued that there was a rebellion on British soil or an imminent invasion. This was less about "necessity"—protecting state and nation from physical danger— than about ensuring that large numbers of people could be held without judicial review of their detention. To critics, parliamentary suspension was no better than royal suspensions from before 1689. Granville Sharp argued that no "necessity" could justify overriding "God's indispensable laws," and condemned "the haughty omnipotence of parliament, the Pope of England!"[154] Second, though no one knew it in 1777, Parliament had begun what would be the longest period of suspension yet, one that would last six years. Third, and alarming in a manner suggested by Burke, the suspension made invidious distinctions among subjects. Until 1777, there had always been a unitary subjecthood honored by habeas corpus: it had been equally available or denied to all. The suspensions of 1777 and after, by contrast, distinguished among people in a way that would increasingly be mimicked in imperial practice: in India, Quebec, New Zealand, and beyond.

By distinguishing among subjects by place of capture, suspension confirmed just how far habeas reached. By declaring the writ unavailable for those taken in America or at sea, the act recognized the common law principles by which the writ had extended to precisely those places: not only to all dominions of the king outside England, but beyond, to the sovereignless sea. Hundreds of American sailors captured at sea were barred from using habeas corpus even after they were moved to prisons on land. When Ebeneezer Platt again sued the writ in May 1777, he was remanded. In Quebec, Governor Sir Frederick Haldimand would proclaim the suspension and then imprison dozens, some for years.[155] Throughout, American newspapers covered debates in Westminster and beyond. Suffering the denial of habeas corpus became a marker of liberty and independence, a point of honor by which Americans would sustain rebellion.[156]

Newly independent American states would provide for the writ in their constitutions.[157] And the experience of suspension informed the insertion of the Suspension Clause in the U.S. Constitution. The clause was negative in construction, presuming the writ rather than importing it: "The privilege of the writ of habeas corpus shall not be suspended, unless when in cases of rebellion or invasion the public safety may require it."[158] These terms reflected suspension usage in England between 1689 and 1747, while rejecting the novel terms of suspension that Americans endured starting in 1777.

Just as the writ had spread readily across Britain's empire, by the time the U.S. Constitution's Suspension Clause was penned in the summer of 1787, the writ was already moving across a North American empire in the making. The Northwest Ordinance, proclaimed earlier that summer to annex the vast territories between the Ohio River and the Great Lakes, declared that "the inhabitants of the said territory shall always be entitled to the benefits of the writ of habeas corpus."[159] Nonetheless, by this time, one American state—Massachusetts—had suspended the writ.[160] Habeas corpus had traveled the globe, becoming part of Americans' collective sense of self at the moment they launched their national project. But as habeas corpus spread, suspension followed, like a shadow.

Renewed war with France led to another round of British suspensions between May 1794 and July 1795, and again from 1798 until 1801. In the first instance, Parliament responded to fears of domestic rebellion that could introduce "the system of anarchy and confusion which has so fatally prevailed in France," and in the second, to what seemed like an imminent French invasion. The first round of suspensions reverted to the forms used between 1689 and 1747, as did the second, at least at the outset.[161] But with the act extending suspension in May 1799, a new provision was added, one permitting more strict confinement of some prisoners. It also gave greater latitude to the secretaries of state to move prisoners around among prisons and made provisions for holding prisoners who were involved in the rebellion then afoot in Ireland.[162]

One jailer in particular seems to have used vigorously the oppressive practices made possible by the 1799 suspension. Thomas Aris, governor of the new Cold Bath Fields prison in London, was brutal, according to many of his prisoners. MP Sir Francis Burdett took up their cause, becoming a thorn in the side of a parliamentary majority happy to concur in ministerial measures for "public safety." Burdett forced the creation of a Commons committee to investigate conditions in the prison, and Aris was forced to admit some of his brutishness, but no correction of the jailer followed. So prisoners took up the matter themselves, in court. In May 1801, John Heron sued a criminal information against Aris in King's Bench. Chief Justice Kenyon and the others ruled against Heron for his failure to sue by such special process within the appropriate time.[163] But the effort made an impression.

Because the suspension of habeas corpus was then drawing to a close, and because Heron or others might sue for damages by false imprisonment—which would put Aris's abuses before a sympathetic London jury—the ministry began working to pass a statute to indemnify jailers for their actions. Parliamentary debates suggest that the chief concern of the bill's supporters was to protect Aris. To counter this effort, Burdett mustered petitions to the Commons from Heron and other prisoners who condemned Aris and the proposed indemnity.[164]

Attorney General Edward Law tried valiantly to cover the measure with a fig leaf of precedent, but his critics easily pulled this aside, showing just how novel was this proposed indemnity for jailer abuse. The attorney general pointed to indemnity acts of 1746 and 1780. True, three acts had passed in 1780 to indemnify jailers, but these had nothing to do with indemnifying official acts under the suspension of habeas corpus then in effect, which concerned American rebels and explicitly did not apply to people arrested in England. In fact, the 1780 indemnity did not address the treatment of prisoners at all, but their escape: those who had fled from Newgate and other prisons as they burned during the anti-Catholic Gordon riots that summer.[165] Likewise, the indemnity of 1746, like the few others granted since 1689, principally concerned the behavior of soldiers acting during a rebellion, and thus focused on illegal provisioning and quartering more than on imprisonment. The 1746 indemnity, like many of the others, also indemnified jailers for escapes, not for wrongful custody.[166]

Despite the attorney general's gestures toward illusory precedents, there had been no practice of indemnifying jailers for actions connected to suspension. In fact, most suspensions had not been followed by an indemnity of any kind. The focus of the Indemnity Act of 1801 was not the fact of imprisonment, but its quality: it concerned not incarceration, with or without access to habeas corpus, but jailer abuse. This is clear from the fact that the 1801 indemnity covered all official actions dating back to France's declaration of war in February 1793. Since then, there had been long periods without a suspension.[167] The 1801 indemnity thus marked an innovative, even ominous, turn in the ministry's approach to the detention of state prisoners, not a resort to old practices.[168] It was another sign of just how much had changed in habeas jurisprudence and practice since the late 1780s.

Beginning in the 1790s, suspension became just one part of wider statutory campaigns against political dissent in all forms. These included tougher measures against sedition, a broadened law of treason, and an act outlawing meetings of more than fifty people, targeted especially at societies that had sprung up to promote political reform. During 1799 there were stepped up arrests of United Irishmen in Manchester and London, as well as United Englishmen, arrests made possible by the interaction of these laws with the new suspension of habeas corpus.[169] New domestic practices would soon become imperial ones, repeated in various forms during the nineteenth and twentieth centuries wherever instability threatened.

A related measure was the Aliens Act of 1793, which imposed new burdens on aliens, including the many Frenchmen then streaming across the Channel in search of refuge. The act permitted JPs to imprison those who violated its provisions "without bail or mainprise," in some cases as a prelude to deportation, in others, as punishment.[170] When Viscount Fielding first announced that he would introduce such a measure, he called it "a bill for suspending the Habeas Corpus Act, as far as it should relate to the persons of foreigners." Proponents took the usual line, justifying it as "necessary" for "the safety of the state." But Lord Landsdowne condemned the act precisely because it would serve as "a suspension of the Habeas Corpus Act." Baron Grenville claimed that law "had always made a marked distinction between natural born subjects and aliens," with aliens owing only a "local and transitory allegiance." Foes, like the Earl of Guilford, countered that it was the "boast of our constitution, that, to every man living under it, it extended the equal protection of the law." This was certainly a traditional understanding of the work of habeas corpus and its equal coverage of local subjects and natural ones.

Like the suspension used during the American war, the Aliens Act appeared to many as a threat to liberty because it targeted some within British law's protection instead of all. But by the end of the eighteenth century, universalizing conceptions of subjecthood had lost influence, and failed to carry the vote. The Aliens Act passed, perhaps because Edmund Burke—the oratorical powerhouse opposing suspension in 1777—supported it as "necessary," that is, as "calculated to keep out of England those murderous atheists who would pull down church and state, religion and God, morality and happiness."[171]

Suspension by many names, in many forms, proliferated, in England and beyond, now in combination with other measures: "coercion acts" in Ireland; "sedition acts" at home; and acts for "preserving the peace" across the empire. The logic of suspension went forth with the writ into the empire. Even individuals might be targeted by what amounted to unreviewable parliamentary imprisonment orders made by statute. Napoléon Bonaparte was declared a POW and exiled by statutes that also indemnified his keepers.[172] This practice would go all the way to New Zealand, where a local statute suspended the writ for two Maori who caused too much trouble in the 1880s.[173] Across the globe, there would be no end of ways that statute might undo habeas corpus.

Extending Habeas Corpus?

Habeas corpus went to new imperial dominions by common law. But colonial subjects in such dominions generally clamored for a habeas corpus act of their own. One of the 1679 act's most important consequences was to inspire the idea that only a statute would make the writ effective. In the Caribbean and North America, one colonial legislature after another passed an act in imitation, though in each case, it required approval of the Privy Council, through the Board of Trade and Plantations, to take effect. In the late seventeenth century, such approval was not always forthcoming; sometimes it came decades after the effort began. In such cases, or where approval was denied altogether, the penalties and other operative terms in the act were often brought into a dominion's laws by special instructions to the governor.[174]

But as the Habeas Corpus Act passed into the law of new dominions in various forms, so too did suspension and other statutory practices that constrained the writ by restraining the judges who used it. In Ireland, the suspension power was placed in the kingdom's Habeas Corpus Act. Many had long sought such an act for Ireland, though as in England, many also realized it was unnecessary: the writ by common law had long operated there as it did in England. Seventeen times, from the 1690s forward, Ireland's House of Commons had passed a bill, and seventeen times, either the Privy Council in Dublin or in London had rejected it. Across the generations, the problem of how to make legal distinctions between Protestants and Catholics in the operation of habeas corpus loomed large. Many argued that any bill providing safeguards for using the writ in the manner of the English act also had to include clear procedures for enacting suspensions whenever Catholic-inspired political danger should rear its head. The act passed in Dublin in late 1781, and approved early the next year in London, did just that. It included a virtual transcription of the 1679 English act, with an added provision permitting the Irish Council to suspend the writ "during such time only as there shall be an actual invasion or rebellion in this kingdom [of Ireland] or Great Britain."[175] In America, many celebrated the Irish act, focusing only on those portions of it that enacted the terms of the English statute. But those who read all the way to the end knew better, and condemned the power reserved to the Council:

> [T]his suspending power will be a *sword of Damocles* in their hands, to be dreaded most by those who are most distinguished by the brilliancy of their parts, the soundness of their principles, and the integrity of their minds.

This critic, like others who opposed statutory amendment of the writ, admitted that the common law writ was at times a "slow remedy," but it was also a sure one.[176]

A similar story would unfold in the 1790s in Canada, where most of the elements of the 1679 English act were introduced by an ordinance of the Legislative Council, only to be followed in short order by a string of suspensions lasting until 1812. Ironically, councils in Dublin and Montreal possessed a greater power than the English Council, which still required parliamentary permission before it could imprison without judicial review. This greater power appeared virtually everywhere that imperial governors and their councils and assemblies worked in new dominions over the following century. Suspensions, indemnity acts, and increasingly, martial law reduced habeas corpus into nothing but a rallying cry: a central element in a critique of colonial governance rather than an effective instrument by which judges might supervise the use of the jailer's franchise to ensure that the king's subjects were not held by his jailers to the deprivation of their liberty or the king's honor. Colonial subjects often quoted Blackstone, praising the Habeas Corpus Act as "that second Magna Carta, and stable bulwark of our liberties."[177] This sounded marvelous rolling off the tongue, but had little to do with practice, except perhaps to hide the once vigorous common law writ behind its chimerical statutory twin. It was remarkable how many places the writ would go. And it was remarkable how constraints would always follow.

CHAPTER 8

Writ Imperial

The justices of Queen's Bench faced two questions in the autumn of 1600, one of theory, the other of practice. As a matter of law, might they send the writ of habeas corpus to Berwick-upon-Tweed? Certainly. Then how should they convince the burghers of Berwick to send it back, along with the prisoner's body? This was a question of power, a question about the judicial tools and extrajudicial support required to convince others to do as ordered. To enact the theoretical claim that the writ might go to one of the English queen's dominions outside her realm, the justices would need help.

These questions had been raised by the imprisonment of Henry Brearley, a local leader who had been a bother more than once before to his neighbors in Berwick. In early 1600, he violated his freeman's oath by some of his business dealings. When the corporation fined him £100 "as a light and gentle admonition," Brearley refused to pay, for which he was jailed.[1] He remained in prison until autumn, when he sued habeas corpus. The writ went north, but only silence came in reply. The clerks of the Crown Office in Queen's Bench sent further writs, to no effect. Now the court showed its steel—a £200 fine on the mayor and bailiffs for their disobedience—and then issued one writ more, with a subpoena clause imposing a 500 mark penalty should local leaders fail to return it. To ensure that Berwick understood that further contempts would not be tolerated, the justices sent a command to Lord Willoughby, governor of Berwick castle, to attach the bodies of the mayor and bailiffs and bring them to Westminster.[2]

Behind Berwick's disobedience stood the town's peculiar jurisdictional situation. Located on the north bank of the river that formed the boundary between Scotland and England, Berwick had been taken, lost, and retaken by Edward I and Edward III.[3] As the burgesses explained in their answer to Brearley's writ, their town was a dominion of the queen, though outside her English realm and governed by Scottish law. All true enough. As a result, they concluded, no writs from courts in Westminster Hall could take effect there.[4] It was here that they erred.

Berwick had long asserted its unusual jurisdictional situation to fend off intrusions by other magistrates. In another dispute just months before Brearley's case, Berwick had rebuffed both the Council of the North and the Privy Council. The Privy Council, annoyed by this previous insult, may have been especially ready to support Queen's Bench in order to bring Berwick to heel.[5] This may also explain the court's decision to enlist Lord Willoughby to serve the attachment against Berwick's leaders. His action, on the court's behalf, made practical the theoretical assertion that the writ could go to any of the queen's dominions.[6] To reinforce this point, Queen's Bench ordered the mayor and two bailiffs jailed for contempt. In the meantime, Brearley was bailed.[7] Not long thereafter, the original controversy was ended in a settlement by which the corporation agreed to reduce Brearley's fine and restore him to the town's freedom once he made a humble submission for his wrongs.[8] Neither side had won. The only victor was Queen's Bench, which had showed Berwick that there were indeed some writs it must return, the town's unusual status notwithstanding.

The Brearley case highlighted the problem that in English law, there was no empire in the singular; there were only dominions in the plural. How, then, might the Queen's principal court in England supervise the work of lesser magistrates and officers in dominions outside of England? Her justices offered a clear answer: by what they would soon call prerogative writs, those judicial writs that they issued in cases in which the queen had an interest, for instance, when her subjects' liberty was at stake.

This was true enough, in theory. Few doubted that habeas corpus might be sent to any of the queen's dominions to inspect legally dubious detentions. But how would theory be practiced? Lord Willoughby helped Queen's Bench establish the force of its contempt process against Berwick, a process the court turned against others on those

rare instances when they faced disobedience. But what of places farther afield: Jersey, Barbados, Calcutta? It was easy to send writs from
Westminster, but harder to get them to come back. The solution would
be to create new courts to issue the writ in such places. Some of these
would be made by Englishmen turned colonists on the west side of
the Atlantic, who established courts in the seventeenth century after
having been granted only the sketchiest authority to do so by royal
charters. Charters of the later eighteenth century would create such
courts more explicitly, in places much farther away.

New courts issuing an old writ manifested long-held notions about
how some aspects of English law traveled with Britons as they moved
about. Making such notions effective required that instruments of
power—for instance, attachments for contempt—should be available
to judges using the common law writ in new dominions. And they
were. But the utility of such instruments would be curbed in practice
by legislative dictates from Westminster and from colonial assemblies.
Such directives gave colonial governors the confidence, if not always
the authority, to defy courts in their midst. Their desire to obstruct the
use of habeas corpus arose in large part from the political crises confronted as the queen's dominions proliferated. As more people who
were ethnically and culturally distinct from the English came under
English law, that law was increasingly fragmented. What had once
been a singular subjecthood increasingly manifested itself in distinct
kinds of subjects of greater and lesser kinds. A common law writ that
knew no theoretical bounds would be hemmed in by political and statutory constraints the farther it went forth.

Singular Writ, Plural Dominions

Everyone who encountered Brearley's case recognized its importance,
even though no report of it survives. Looking back from a century's
distance, Henry Walrond certainly did. As a King's Bench clerk, one of
his jobs was "to make out all special writs . . . on the Crown Side."[9] He
was thus a successor to the clerks who wrote the writs and orders
for Henry Brearley. In the mid-1710s, Walrond studied the court's
rulebooks, noting the interesting entries he found there. He transcribed in full the order fining Berwick's leaders, literally underscor-
ing its significance by underlining those portions concerning non-

return, the resulting fine, and the command that another writ issue.[10] Walrond appreciated that what made this writ great enough to enter an otherwise distinct dominion was the power that judges used to make sure it was returned.

Walrond's book of precedents provided a guide to later clerks and the justices they served. In 1759, Chief Justice Mansfield referred to the same order as he considered yet another dispute about whether Berwick must answer the prerogative writs. Though the famed report of Cowle's case focuses on Mansfield's discussion of the writ of certiorari, Cowle had earlier used habeas corpus, too. In an echo of Brearley's case, Mansfield's court threatened an attachment for contempt to ensure its return. Mansfield worked carefully through his answer to the question: just what, as a legal matter, was Berwick-upon-Tweed?[11] His conclusion was predictable for all who knew what had happened to Berwick's leaders in 1601. Even "if Berwick was to be deemed a dominion of the Crown, and no part of the realm of England," Mansfield remarked, "it may be under the control and superintendence of the king in this Court." How? By the prerogative writs, which "may issue to every dominion of the Crown of England." "This court alone can judge of their franchises," he declared. "There can be no redress but here."[12]

Where did Mansfield get such notions? By reading cases like Brearley's, Coke's report of Calvin's case, and Sir Matthew Hale's *History of the Common Law*.[13] As Hale explained, even in places like Berwick, "where the suit is immediately for the king"—as on the prerogative writs—"the king may make his suit in any of the courts here, especially in the court of King's Bench."[14] In Chapter 3, reading Hale helped us understand the law of franchises and their place in a comprehensive view of how all jurisdictions arose out of the king. In Hale's work as chief justice in the 1670s, his theory explaining the vastness of King's Bench's supervisory authority met practice, making this a period of innovation. Now we turn again to Hale to see the consequences of his franchisal theory and his judicial practice as shown in his account of the king's laws in the king's ever more numerous dominions.

When we write of empire, we often slip into language of "*the* empire," reducing to the singular what Hale and his contemporaries understood in the plural: the "places or territories to which the government of the king of England extends."[15] By highlighting the legal plurality of the king's dominions, Hale helps us see how French property law would persist alongside English criminal law in Quebec after 1763; how Dutch law would operate in Ceylon after it was ceded to the British in 1796; and how slavery, unrecognized in England, would flourish in Barbados, just as other novel forms of bondage would shape society in New South Wales. But for all the legal variety in so many places, Hale also shows us how one part of law would pertain in all of them. Habeas corpus promised to make a singular empire from a multitude of dominions.

Hale's approach to jurisdictional geography was temporal rather than spatial. In *The Prerogatives of the King*, subjects' presence within, or far from, England tells us nothing. What mattered for explaining variations in law across space were the peculiar circumstances when the king acquired a territory or assigned to it certain legal characteristics. Different aspects of law, including those called "common," moved from one place to another by different means, at different times, and to different degrees.[16] Even within England, the relationship of certain places to the king varied, despite the apparent unity created by William's conquest in 1066. The palatinates of Durham, Chester, and Lancaster were within the realm of England, yet distinct. They, like the Cinque Ports, possessed certain powers not used elsewhere, franchises granted by the king's letters patent. Chief among these was their exemption from writs issuing from courts in Westminster Hall in suits between private parties. But no palatine privilege could block entry of the prerogative writs, for no franchise could "bar the king of his suit."[17]

Though outside the realm, Berwick had a similar character. Scottish law determined disputes about property and debt there. In the Channel Isles, Norman rather than English law performed this role since Jersey, Guernsey, Alderney, and Sark remained the king's as part of his otherwise defunct Norman patrimony. Berwick and the Channel Isles had been "annexed unto the crown of England": Berwick by charter, the Isles "by long usage."[18] But ancient laws, distinct from English laws, remained in use in both.

Because they were dominions of the king, even if outside his realm of England, such places "were rendered in some kind of subordination to the English jurisdiction." This subordination operated by the power of King's Bench to supervise franchisal authorities using *brevia mandatoria* such as habeas corpus. In his *History of the Common Law,* Hale drove this point home:

> [A] writ of habeas corpus lies into [the Channel] islands for one imprisoned there, for the king may demand, and must have an account of, the cause of any of his subjects' loss of liberty; and therefore a return must be made of this writ to give the court an account of the cause of imprisonment; for no liberty, whether of a county palatine, or other, holds place against those *brevia mandatoria.*

Edward I conquered Wales, just as he conquered Berwick. Unlike Berwick, however, Wales became English in law: annexed to the crown, and in the reign of Henry VIII, fully incorporated into England by statute. Until then, Wales remained a distinct jurisdiction to which ordinary writs did not run. But long before statute drew Wales into England, the king's *brevia mandatoria* went there, just as to Berwick or Guernsey.[19]

Ireland occupied yet another historical, thus legal, situation. Henry II and his son John "made a perfect conquest of Ireland, and in token thereof introduced the English laws." How? Ireland was "not only a conquest *in regem,*" like Wales, "but a conquest *in populum.*" Irish people as well as the Irish realm were taken; English people entered with an English king.

> [T]hough the victor gets by right of conquest upon the conquered, yet these English planters and colonies [*sic*] were free Englishmen and carried with them their rights and liberties of Englishmen, though into a country acquired not only in point of superintendency but in point of propriety by the conquering king.

Like Berwick and the Channel Isles, Ireland was "a distinct kingdom still, though not a distinct dominion." Thus *brevia mandatoria* ran from King's Bench in England into Ireland, even though that kingdom had its own court of King's Bench that might issue such writs too. All these places across the British archipelago were the king's *"terrae,"* distinct in law because distinct in their mode and moment of acquisition, yet they were uniformly dependencies of the same king.[20]

Hale's survey of dominions concluded in America and the Caribbean. At first, his treatment of these areas seems different:

If the king issue a commission under the great seal of England to take possession of a continent . . . he is seised [*sic*] thereof in the capacity of England, and I conceive hath the sole power of making laws &c. and it is not subject to the laws of England till the king proclaim them.

Hale then argued from analogy to Ireland and the Channel Isles, where "time and usage . . . may by custom annex it."[21] Like Berwick, transatlantic possessions were "parcel of the dominions though not of the realm of England." As in Ireland, English laws might be introduced in America "by the king without the concurrence of an act of parliament." And as to Ireland, the English carried with them "those English liberties that are incident to their persons," even if "other laws that concern the lands, and propriety, and disposal of them, are settled according to the king's pleasure."[22]

Hale makes a critical point here: the law of the land, as it moved into new dominions, was not one. For our purposes, we can reduce the kinds of law in motion to two: those concerned with land and those related to persons. Property law was spatially bounded; witness the distinct laws of property in Berwick and Jersey. But law concerning the subject was bounded only in the relationship of allegiance. As we saw in Chapter 3, it was by the protection that the king gives in return for allegiance that the prerogative ensures the subject's liberty. The king's *brevia mandatoria*, like habeas corpus, entered a territory prior to any other formal accession of that territory to the crown. As in Berwick or Jersey, so too in America: the king's subjects might hold lands by tenures unknown to English law. But they would still hold those liberties "incident" to their subjecthood, because the bonds of allegiance stretched as the king's subjects moved. The law concerned with habeas corpus thus marked a huge zone of inclusion, the farthest reaches of a singular subject status, even while other aspects of English law remained immobile.

We can see two analytic perspectives at work here. Both rely on the prerogative. First, Hale puts the relationship between king and subject at the center of his analysis. The same concepts of allegiance and the need for the king to command his subjects' bodies that explained the writ's operation in England show us how that authority moved beyond England.[23] By the grant of liberties in colonial charters, English subjects—native born and those born within the new territory—possessed "all the privileges of free denizens and persons native of England, and within our allegiance, in such like ample manner and form, as if they were born and personally resident within our said realm of England."[24] As if they were born: subjecthood, bounded only in the relationship of subject and king, could never be bounded by place. Subjecthood arose by birthright, that which could never be alienated. Esau had learned this, and John Lilburne hammered on this point in the 1650s. A more circumspect lawyer like Hale appreciated it as well. And it made all the difference in how some parts of law followed subjects as they moved.

Second, seeing how this worked in practice brings us back to Hale's view of franchises. All charters—like the East India Company's of 1726 —declared that the king granted authority "of our special grace, certain knowledge, and mere motion."[25] Such language echoes the metaphors of miracle that ran through ideas about the prerogative. Hale's discussion of extraterritorial dominion arose as a logical consequence from his understanding of the use of the prerogative to make corporations and commissions, extending beyond England an idea of how law organized jurisdictions within England. There was a conceptual and practical interchange among the charters by which the corporations that governed English towns and trades were made and the charters by which law framed colonial enterprises.[26] All were subject to the same law of franchises and to the same judicial oversight.

We might call Hale's account of the king's dominions an antitheory: an approach so historically grounded that it defied rather than generated typologies by which imperial acquisitions were to be consigned to one or another category. Other jurists, including Coke, but especially Blackstone, created typologies by which to differentiate places acquired by discovery from those gained by conquest, and in so doing, ran over distinctions among dominions in a way that obscures rather than illuminates our understanding of the legal differences— and points of connection—among them.[27] By providing a historical account of territorial acquisition, Hale rejected such categories and focused on contingencies. Likeness did not hold legally distinct dominions together; principles did. Hale's historical sensibility helped him see the persistence of the prerogative as a generative force in law, even as it showed itself differently from one moment to the next. This makes for a messy account of law's past, but one that gets us closer to law as lived and used.[28] Yet Hale's account of the law of franchises, the prerogative writs, and of habeas corpus also made a theoretical unity of all those different places deriving authority from a single source. How, if at all, would the justices realize that unity in practice?

Insularity: Theory Meets Practice

Beginning with Brearley's case, King's Bench reminded one ostensibly exempt jurisdiction after another that they were not exempt. As William Noy pointed out in 1626, when arguing that the justices should send habeas corpus to the otherwise autonomous Bishop of Durham, "wherever the king grants liberties, there he does not exclude himself." Under pressure, the bishop admitted as much, but asked that the new writ sent to him might confirm his privileges by reciting them in the writ. The court rejected that idea out of hand.[29] After all, reasoned Justice Sir John Dodderidge, habeas had issued to Berwick.[30] Three years later, while justifying a mandamus to the Cinque Port of Winchelsea, Justice Sir William Jones again pointed out that habeas corpus had long been sent to Berwick, and "in ancient times" to Gascony, "which are not any part of the realm."[31] Cases like these represented the imperial problem writ small. New measures and new courts would be required to maintain a unity of practice across the king's dominions as distances grew. And even new supreme courts in distant lands that issued habeas corpus would depend on the support or compliance of royal governors and colonial regimes to ensure the writ's return. This would determine the extent to which the writ's vast theoretical ambit might be realized in practice.

The Channel Isles presented the same legal situation as Berwick or Winchelsea, but a more difficult geographical one. By examining the circumstances there, we can see how distance and weak technologies of jurisdiction, rather than law, might limit habeas corpus.[32] Could King's Bench contempt process on its own accomplish in Jersey or Guernsey what it had in Berwick?

Imprisonments in faraway places became an issue during the 1650s, when Parliament and Oliver Cromwell's council imprisoned enemies in Jersey, Guernsey, and other islands. In the 1660s, Edward Salmon, Robert Overton, and Richard Creed were detained after their involvement in unsuccessful plots against the restored monarchy of Charles II. All ended up imprisoned in Jersey or Guernsey; all used habeas in hopes of release; and all failed. Salmon and Overton first sued the writ in late 1668 and early 1669. Multiple additional writs issued, to no avail.[33]

Richard Creed had a worse time of it. He had been imprisoned after John Lambert's rising in the spring of 1660, as the Restoration was still unfolding, and was later moved to Pendennis Castle, in Cornwall. Habeas corpus was sent there on his behalf in October 1669, but never returned. Perhaps to avoid service of an alias writ, Creed was moved to Guernsey in September 1670 on a warrant that named no charge. The warrant simply instructed Governor Lord Hatton "to keep [him] close prisoner within that our island until our further pleasure." Only in Trinity term 1679, immediately after the Habeas Corpus Act became effective, did Creed's writ issue again; when it was returned with no other cause than the warrant of 1670, Creed was finally bailed.[34]

These insular cases return us to Brearley's case, which concerned what was claimed to be a legal, if not an actual, island. The justices saw no legal problem in sending habeas corpus to real islands. The only issue concerned practice: how to compel performance? At Berwick, the military governor aided the process. His obedience to judicial commands made real the writ's legal range. In the insular cases, the disobedience of military governors explained the writ's failure. If in cases of disobedience military governors served writs of attachment, then to whom might attachments issue when such governors refused? All the legal theory supporting the writ's use meant nothing in the face of jailers defended by distance, waves, and the commands of the Lord Protector or king's Council.

Hale seemed frustrated when considering the Channel Isles. In his *History of the Common Law*, he declared that "a writ of habeas corpus lies into those islands."[35] Here Hale did not simply describe law; he entered an argument, advocating a view that arose logically from his vision of the king's authority over all jurisdictions as expressed through King's Bench. There had been debates in Parliament in the 1650s and beyond about the authority of judges to send habeas corpus to the Channel Isles, and this was one of the issues that MPs addressed as they tried to craft a habeas statute in the 1660s and 1670s. But as we saw in Chapter 4, Hale's use of habeas corpus for new purposes in the 1670s shows how he believed that he needed no parliamentary permission to innovate, a point made plain by his issuance of the writ to Jamaica in

1672.[36] Hale actively applied in his practice his broad conception of franchises and the need for King's Bench to police the power to imprison in all dominions. But the practical problem remained.

Compelling returns from insular places was the most significant rationale for the passage of the Habeas Corpus Act, which, as explained in Chapter 7, was officially known as "An Act for the Better Securing the Liberty of the Subject and for Prevention of Imprisonments beyond the Seas."[37] Sea, not the common law writ, was the problem. The act thus created new powers—by new procedures and by threats of steep fines against the recalcitrant—to supply the place of a Lord Willoughby when no one might otherwise be found to serve process. In this way, the act tried to make real the theoretical claim that the writ might go anywhere.[38]

These new powers helped to overcome limits on the writ's work around the British Isles, but other islands presented other problems. Solving those would require creating new courts empowered to act in ways modeled after King's Bench. Their authority to use habeas corpus was clear. So too were persistent problems in practice. Some thought that colonial officers, like officials in Berwick, should and would obey the writ issued by common law. Others believed that only enforcement mechanisms like those in the Habeas Corpus Act would ensure compliance. The insistence on extending the 1679 statute to other dominions would generate both the writ's greatest potential beyond the British archipelago, and the most important limitations on it.

Barbados: Jurisgenesis in a Tropical Paradise?

Richard Ligon fled England's instability for Barbados in 1647. Upon his arrival, he pondered the possibility of a tropical commonwealth:

> Being now come in sight of this happy island, the nearer we came, the more beautiful it appeared. . . . There we saw the high, large, and lofty trees, with their spreading branches and flourishing tops, [which] seemed to be beholding to the earth and roots that gave them such plenty of sap for their nourishment . . . [w]hilst they, in gratitude, return their cool shade, to secure and shelter them from the sun's heat, which, without it, would scorch and dry away. So that bounty and goodness in the one, and gratefulness in the other, serve to make up this

beauty, which otherwise would lie empty and waste. And truly these vegetatives may teach both the sensible and reasonable creatures what it is that makes up wealth, beauty, and all harmony in that *Leviathan,* a well-governed commonwealth, where the mighty men and rulers of the earth, by their prudent and careful protection, secure them from harms, whilst they retribute their pains and faithful obedience to serve them in all just commands.[39]

Three years later, back in a London without a king and confined in prison for debt, Ligon wrote of his Caribbean journey and developed this rich metaphor for the traditional idea of subjection exchanged for protection. Ligon's Barbados was a place of astonishing fecundity, of huge trees. It was also rife with rot and disease. It remained to be seen whether Barbados would be an island of "all harmony," in which rulers were "retributed" with the obedience of the ruled.

In 1625, Captain John Powell first carved "James, King of England" on a tree, thereby completing the island's conquest.[40] Barbados was now the king's, though by the time Powell reached home, that king was James's son, Charles. All that remained was for Charles to provide the means to make law in his new dominion so that it might become a "well-governed commonwealth." The language of the letter patent that Charles gave to the Earl of Carlisle was like most others that passed the great seal whenever English monarchs made an urban corporation, a hospital or college, or an enterprise sent forth to plant in one of the king's dominions beyond the seas. In June 1627, Charles granted to Carlisle authority to act in his name in Barbados "for the good and happy government of the said province." To promote this end, Carlisle was to make laws "with the consent, assent, and approbation of the free inhabitants of the said Province." What Robert Cover called the "jurisgenerative" impulse had been thrown forth, by the king's command, into an insular world.[41] But the king restrained jurisgenesis, too. He declared that Englishmen in Barbados should only make laws "agreeable and not repugnant unto reason nor against it, but as convenient and agreeable as may be to the laws, statutes, customs, and rights of our kingdom of England." In Barbados, "every subject" was to "be as free as they that were born in England."[42]

A previously uninhabited tropical island might seem as good a setting as any in which a people might generate new law. Instead, they regenerated old law so that the inhabitants would "possess all the liberties, franchises, and privileges" of Englishmen.[43] Even so, new growths sprang up: laws that made humans into property or that made novel courts in which the island's governor might be a judge in his own cause, even when he imprisoned someone.[44] Barbadians wanted their old law protected by a jurispathic judge who might prune such dangerous growths using old tools like habeas corpus.[45] But try as they might to curtail them, novelties flourished.

As early as 1628, Charles Wolverston, whom Carlisle had appointed governor, acted with others to make law, beginning with the appointment of justices of the peace. By 1630, quarter sessions were hearing misdemeanor accusations; in 1631, courts of common pleas began to hear civil complaints; and in the 1650s, a "grand sessions" convened twice yearly to handle felonies. Barbados now had a jail and the justices and other officers needed to put people in them. But although Barbadian JPs expressed a commitment to English law, and their charter said they must not violate that law, they had no more legal training than their counterparts in England, and probably a good deal less. We thus see evidence from the seventeenth century of complaints about casual attention to procedure.

But had the writ of habeas corpus crossed the Atlantic to supervise the work of Barbadian JPs? Was there a judge who might kill off dangerous novelties in the use of imprisonment? Yes, in Westminster. In 1692, Samuel Eyre asked King's Bench to send habeas corpus to the governor of Barbados on behalf of William Moore. "We cannot deny the writ," Justice Sir William Dolben replied, and all the justices agreed.[46] No further proceedings on the writ survive, perhaps because Moore had already been released. Or perhaps distance defeated the justices' intentions.[47] Given that water and distance, not to mention detention by military governors, had blunted the writ's force in Jersey and Jamaica in the 1660s and 1670s, we can hardly be surprised if a writ to Barbados fared no better.

If using the writ from Westminster failed as a matter of physical if not legal reality, how else might Barbadian jailers be monitored? One or both of two practices might be used. The first was suggested by King John's conquest of Ireland, the second by more recent work in Parliament. In 1210, King John "ordered the laws of England to be observed in Ireland."[48] English judicial institutions followed. By the seventeenth century, the courts of Common Pleas and King's Bench in Dublin had a practice for using habeas corpus like that in England.[49] By law, the writ might go anywhere from Westminster, even to Ireland, though it had its own King's Bench. But as a practical matter, it might work better in far-flung dominions to imitate Irish usage by establishing new courts closer to the magistrates they would supervise.

Barbados adopted this practice in the 1640s, when a local statute that made the island's provost marshal keeper of "the cage" in St. Michael's presumed the presence of habeas corpus by common law in the fees it set for court officers. Of course, the governor appointed the provost marshal. Who was to watch the governor and the marshal? Who or what court might issue habeas corpus? One possibility was for one of the courts of Common Pleas, created by a 1661 Barbadian statute, to issue the writ. But as in other island courts, the governor appointed the justices of Common Pleas.[50] They could hardly be expected to judge impartially either his orders or those of any jailer who answered to him. Another possibility might be to resort to the "Court of Grievance," a practice in use by the 1650s in which the governor and his council heard "petitions of grievance."[51] Given this tribunal's interest in "equitable matters," it might have been a good venue in which to hear complaints in the nature of habeas corpus. But the governor and his council sat as justices of the peace in quarter sessions and in grand sessions, and they constituted this court of review: thus the governor might sit in review of his own orders or of those of the officers he had appointed.[52] The problem in Barbados was not that there was no court from which habeas might issue. The problem was that there was no court whose authority did not rely, in the end, on the governor.

The second approach would be to bolster the writ's availability with a Barbadian version of the Habeas Corpus Act. And indeed, just six months after the English Habeas Corpus Act passed, the Barbados assembly set to work on "a bill for habeas corpus as near as may be to the law of England." Though passed unanimously, the governor refused to approve it. The assembly produced another bill in 1681, with the same result.[53] Why did Governor Sir Richard Dutton object? Perhaps because such an act would mean that he or some other authority he appointed would be granting the writs and hearing their returns on imprisonments ordered by himself or by his appointees. The fundamental problem would remain: Barbados had no judge or jailer whose authority did not come from the governor's own.[54] Nonetheless, demands for an act persisted, and in 1683, the assembly produced another bill. The need seemed greater than ever: by the autumn of that year, articles had been exhibited in London against Dutton complaining of his oppressive imprisonment orders.[55]

Dutton prepared to sail to England, in part to answer criticisms against him. He appointed John Witham to serve as deputy governor in his absence. When Dutton returned in the autumn of 1684, he accused Witham of maladministration and jailed him pending trial in Barbados, where he was heavily fined and removed from office.[56] But Witham would have his revenge for this illegal imprisonment when he and Dutton returned to London. There, before the Privy Council's Lords for Trade and Plantations, Dutton was severely reprimanded for proceeding on matters for which Witham "was accountable to your majesty and to no other person whatever." The Council ordered that Witham be restored to all his dignities, that his fines be remitted, "and that he may have leave to take his remedy at law against Sir Richard Dutton." This was what Witham did, winning a judgment in an action for false imprisonment.[57] Witham prevailed, but it had taken months of work on the other side of the ocean: hardly an expeditious way to handle arbitrary imprisonment orders by a determined island governor.

In 1697, the Barbados Assembly again produced a habeas corpus bill, which the governor ultimately accepted, but only in 1702 did the colonial statute appear before the Privy Council and the Board of Trade, where it had to be confirmed. The Board of Trade detected significant differences between the Barbadian statute and the English act it imitated. What had been so hard won in Barbados was thus rejected in London. Rather than rely on a local statute, the Privy Council ordered that instructions should be sent to the island's governor to protect subjects from "long and unreasonable imprisonment."[58] Noting delays in Barbadian courts, the instructions recommended the governor's "constant care and watchfulness over the conduct of the inferior courts." To promote his care, the royal instructions commanded that any prisoner should "have free liberty to petition" the chief baron of the Court of Exchequer or any justice of Common Pleas in the island for habeas corpus. Any judge who refused the writ was to be removed. Any jailer who waited more than six hours to return it might also be removed.[59]

These were serious measures, and given the form of the instructions, they assumed the existence of habeas corpus by common law in the island. But they did not answer the central question of how to make the writ effective in a place where the governor appointed not only the judges who issued the writ, but also the provost marshal who received it. Complaints persisted of prisoners who had been "refused and delayed the benefit of their habeas corpus."[60] If Barbadians were to restrain unlawful imprisonments, they would need an independent judiciary: a jurispathic court that could kill off the legal novelties generated by a governor who made both law and the judges of that law.

The same problem operated in other colonies along North America's Atlantic coast and across the Caribbean, where charters permitted the creation of new courts using new laws, so long as they were "not repugnant" to English law. This nonrepugnancy principle became the means by which many common law practices, including habeas corpus, appeared in new colonial courts. Jamaicans, like colonists elsewhere, assumed "that writs of habeas corpus were always granted by the common law," simply by the presence of such courts. A Jamaican statute created a "Supreme Court of Judicature," possessed of all powers "as the Courts of King's Bench, Common Pleas, and Exchequer, within his Majesty's kingdom of England."[61] Such colonial courts could issue habeas corpus, but lacking the enforcement mechanisms that made the writ from King's Bench effective in and around England, the Jamaican writ would not have the same force. In Barbados, Jamaica, and the mainland colonies, English subjects passed statutes to undergird the writ's use, protecting it from the power of their governors. But because colonial statutes generally required approval of the Privy Council, this returned to the Council the same authority to control the writ's use that, during the seventeenth century, so much political and legal effort had sought to contain. And while white Barbadians, Jamaicans, and Americans celebrated the "sweets of *English* liberty," which they held by birthright as "natural born subjects," habeas corpus would never be available to their slaves.[62]

Quebec: "O ciel! où est donc cette fameuse loi d'habeas corpus?"

Royal governors sometimes proved to be an obstacle to using habeas corpus in the colonies, even though all understood that the writ was present by common law: theoretically, by the power of King's Bench to send it to them, as it did to Berwick or Jersey, and more practically, by the presence of new courts that could do so, too.[63] To correct for the problem posed by gubernatorial independence, royal instructions to bolster habeas corpus went to governors in many dominions besides Barbados: among others, to Nova Scotia in 1749, Prince Edward Island in 1769, and New Brunswick in 1784.

The situation in Quebec was more complex. The Treaty of Paris of 1763 transformed the role that Britain's law would play in a dramatically enlarged empire. In India, French military power was largely broken. Frenchmen in Grenada, and many more in Quebec, became British subjects. But what of their law? Had English law been introduced? An immediate if vague answer was given by a royal proclamation of October 1763, which enacted English law in Quebec. One year later, a governor's ordinance established courts using English law, including "one superior court of judicature, called the King's Bench." By this means, Quebec's attorney general believed, "the laws of England are generally supposed to be in force."[64]

Puzzles remained, however, and as the 1760s wore into the 1770s, further reforms were debated, largely with an eye to accommodating the province's French population. As in colonies to Quebec's south, some thought reform should include an explicit statement

> to introduce the substance of the English law relating to the writ of *habeas corpus*, by declaring that no person in the province should be committed to prison, or detained in prison, by the order of any magistrate without a warrant in writing under the hand of the magistrate, expressing particularly the cause of his commitment or detention.[65]

The Quebec Act of 1774, which made allowance for the French majority's Catholicism, said nothing about habeas corpus, though it did confirm English criminal law. Critics condemned this omission, asserting that only by statutory statement would the writ operate there.[66] But government apologists took the opposite view, arguing that by the presence of English criminal law, "the writ of habeas corpus in criminal matters is *ipso facto* carried with it, and equally issuable in the courts [in Quebec], as in England."[67] Ironically, libertarian critics of the Quebec Act—exaggerating the negative effects of its silence about habeas corpus to win points in political debate—emphasized the writ's weakness without a statutory statement, while the government's friends saw the writ at work by common law.[68]

If habeas was not available by common law, then it is hard to explain the fuss that occurred a few years later. Soon after his arrival in Quebec in 1778, the new Swiss-born governor, Sir Frederick Haldimand, proclaimed the current parliamentary suspension of the writ there. He then ordered the arrest of more than two dozen suspected subversives. Many would be held until the suspension ended in 1783. But this did not stop some from trying to use habeas corpus. The stories of two such men stand out: Pierre du Calvet and Charles Hay.[69]

Pierre du Calvet came to Quebec from France in 1758, only to see the province ceded to the British five years later. He decided to remain, however, in order to "enjoy the benefits of the British government." The American war interrupted those benefits. Du Calvet was arrested for seditious libel in 1780, acquitted, then seized again for corresponding with the rebels. No formal charge was entered, so he petitioned twice for habeas corpus, and twice King's Bench in Quebec declared the writ unavailable "with respect to such persons as were imprisoned by the order of the governor." Whether this was because the writ had not been received into the law of the province, or because of the suspension, the justices did not say.[70]

Charles Hay likewise sued habeas corpus. The counsel assigned by the court to assist him, perhaps fearing trouble, refused to help. So Mary Hay was left to prepare a petition on her husband's behalf, in which she argued that the writ was available by common law, if not by the act of 1679. This she demonstrated through an incisive critique of the parliamentary suspension then in effect as "totally repugnant to the spirit of the British constitution."[71] Though she laid out the most comprehensive case imaginable, Hay—like du Calvet—would have to wait until war's end for release.

The court of King's Bench in Quebec—which was then jointly led by a commission of three men, only one of whom was a lawyer—had declared habeas corpus unavailable. But had they done so according to law? After the war, Hay and du Calvet went to London to pose this question in the form of actions for false imprisonment against Haldimand. Their efforts garnered much public notice, but it was du Calvet's that took on the trappings of a Lilburnesque campaign. As an erstwhile Frenchman made into his Britannic majesty's subject by the

Treaty of Paris, du Calvet's critique of Haldimand—foreign born him-self—amounted to a call to defend British liberty. He worked with a group of emigré Canadiens in London, and with former attorney general of Quebec Francis Masères, to reform the Quebec Act by making an explicit incorporation of habeas corpus into Quebec's law.

Du Calvet exhausted his fortune in a multipronged assault on Haldimand and by publishing two books, each widely read on both sides of the Atlantic. The first, in English, focused on the injustices he suffered. The second, in French, provided a more comprehensive critique of Haldimand's governance, thereby laying the ground for reforms he and his compatriots sought. Like Granville Sharp, du Calvet praised Englishmen for the greatness of their law's aspirations and damned them for the ignominy of its failures. He invoked natural law and the law of nations, and rattled through a list of ancient or foreign authorities—Gratian, Pufendorf, Grotius—before arriving in the perfection of laws found in England, "a nation celebrated across the world for the spirit of wisdom and constitutional rectitude." The problem, he argued, lay not in the constitution, but in "false interpretations" of it. Like Lilburne more than a century earlier, correcting the wrong against du Calvet was only part of a larger project to restore English law's "intrinsic spirit" of "humanity, justice, unity . . . and the glory of liberty" for all.[72]

Haldimand fought Hay and du Calvet with all the delaying tactics available. Most important, he won from Chancery special commissions that were appointed to travel to Quebec to take evidence in both cases. So du Calvet returned to America to monitor the process, his efforts followed by admiring newspapers in the United States. Then, having succeeded in his work, he traveled from Quebec to New York, from which he sailed in May 1786 into a storm from which none aboard his ship emerged alive.[73] Although du Calvet had perished, Hay's case against Haldimand continued, ending in King's Bench in June 1787 with a verdict for Hay.

The result highlighted two points. First, no one questioned that Haldimand had acted in an official capacity. But doing so beyond the bounds of what had now been determined to be his legal authority made him personally liable for the wrongs that Hay had suffered. After all, the warrant for Hay's detention gave no cause, which was illegal even during a statutory suspension that applied only to charges of treason or piracy. Second, the verdict and judgment, especially given Justice Francis Buller's charge to the jury that "there was no law which could justify such a commitment," relied on the assumption that habeas corpus had been available in Quebec by common law all along.[74] This amounted to a vindication of Mary Hay's arguments for the writ on her husband's behalf six years earlier.

In the meantime, actions taken in Canada had cleared much of the confusion about the writ's status there. Ironically, it was Governor Haldimand who had recommended to the Legislative Council to make an "An Ordinance for Securing the Liberty of the Subject, and for prevention of Imprisonments out of this Province," the terms of which included most of those in the Habeas Corpus Act.[75] Promulgated in French as well as English in 1784, the Quebec Habeas Corpus Ordinance predated by only a few years the first French translation of Richard Burn's *Justice of the Peace,* the most widely used manual for JPs of the eighteenth century and one that included an extensive discussion of habeas corpus.[76] In the 1790s, habeas corpus would be available in cases of slavery and illegal military conscription, as well as for criminal matters.[77]

But as in England, statutory intervention in judicial work could cut both ways. In Quebec, the Legislative Council passed its own Aliens Act in 1794.[78] This act adopted the terms of its British model and more, allowing deportation on the governor's warrant, and giving him detention powers that effectively permitted him to suspend habeas corpus. Quebec's attorney general ordered the arrest of as many as a hundred foreigners immediately after its passage. When the Quebec Aliens Act lapsed, another was passed that more explicitly suspended habeas corpus. Unlike British suspensions, Quebec's permitted imprisonment without review upon the signature of only three members of its Council. And unlike its British counterpart, which lasted until only 1802, Quebec's suspension would persist with little interruption until the beginning of 1812.[79]

From the 1790s forward, Canada, like other dominions around the globe, would experience moments of political unrest during which suspension was usually the least dramatic means by which prisoners were detained outside the bounds of law.

Some of these detainees would be moved to other dominions without judicial review. The most notable example in Canada occurred in the wake of rebellions there in the late 1830s. The first round of trouble blew up in the autumn of 1837 as the provincial Assembly, dominated by Canadiens, called for political reform. Mass meetings soon became armed rebellion. By early November, as volunteer forces mustered to put down the *patriotes,* Governor Lord Gosford feared the worst "unless some extraordinary powers be immediately placed in the hands of the local executive, such as that of suspending the habeas corpus and declaring martial law."[80]

In early December, Gosford, with the concurrence of his Special Council and the province's law officers, declared martial law. He received legal cover after the fact in the form of a parliamentary statute permitting the governor of Lower Canada to institute emergency measures.[81] His own Council followed with an ordinance indemnifying all who had acted according to the governor's declaration of martial law. But imprisoned rebels remained a problem, especially since at least one King's Bench justice in Montreal had been willing to use habeas corpus. The solution was an ordinance to suspend habeas corpus, with the blessing of the Colonial Office, even as martial law came to an end.[82]

Conflict soon erupted again, and on November 4, 1838, Sir John Colborne—former lieutenant governor of Guernsey and now commander of forces in Canada—again declared martial law.[83] The Special Council he appointed quickly confirmed his decision by making "An Ordinance for the Suppression of the Rebellion." This allowed any officer who received habeas corpus to return it by noting a prisoner's detention according to the ordinance. Though martial law by its nature imported a suspension, a further ordinance was made to allow the detention of those charged with treason and treasonable practices. Its language borrowed from the now 150-year-old tradition of suspension statutes, granting the governor authority to order such suspects held "without bail or mainprize."[84] Scores, then hundreds, were arrested, filling Montreal's new prison and requiring the reopening of its old one.

Though legislation made at Westminster and at Montreal seemingly cut off all opportunity for judicial review of imprisonment, some of the province's judges were not so easily cowed. In December, Philippe Panet and Elzéar Bédard, justices in Quebec, issued habeas corpus for John Teed, arguing that the governor's Special Council had exceeded the authority granted by Parliament's 1837 statute for "Temporary Provision for the Government of Lower Canada" by essentially amending the Habeas Corpus Act of 1679. Following a common law practice that looked back to the cases of Witherley and Brearley more than two centuries earlier, these Francophone judges attached the jailer for contempt when he disobeyed their commands. Colborne responded like a confident soldier, and simply suspended the judges from the bench without consequence to himself.

Little worried by that example, Justice Joseph-Rémi Vallières de Saint-Réal, at Trois-Rivières, took the same view as Panet and Bédard, and sent habeas corpus for Célestin Houde.[85] In a powerful opinion published soon thereafter, Vallières de Saint-Réal went to the writ's source: the judge's authority by common law. His words were reminiscent of William Williams or Sir Thomas Fleming: he declared habeas corpus a thing of "high prerogative, for it must ever be the right of the sovereign to have the reasons explained to him, why any one of his subjects is deprived of his liberty, wheresoever it may be." That prerogative had "the same legal ubiquity as the sovereign himself." But he went further: "Personal liberty is a natural right," he explained, and "a British subject carries this natural right, adhering to his person, into every part of the empire. It is the same at Quebec and in London."[86] The twinned ubiquity of the prerogative and liberty was all the more important given that his and other courts had continued to operate across the province, signaling the absence of the kind of "necessity" typically invoked to justify martial law and other emergency measures.[87] It was a rhetorically powerful, and remarkably traditional, legal argument.

But Vallières de Saint-Réal was suspended, too. The power of a royal governor, a power made by charters and expanded by statutes, was greater than the judge's. In the colonies, authority to suspend—taken after much struggle from royal councils in England by legislative action in 1641—had been returned to the colonial governors and their councils by the same means. Imperial anxieties generated by the demands of Canadiens and others who were legally but not culturally British turned the history of habeas corpus back on itself. Statutes of suspension made within Britain since 1689 had provided the template on which the same was accomplished across the empire, as colonial assemblies gave to colonial governors and councils powers that a seventeenth-century Privy Council might only dream of.

In Quebec, culture distinguished Canadiens from Anglophone subjects, but law did not: they were all subjects. People of both cultures used habeas corpus when available, and people of both suffered when it was not; indeed, people of both cultures were convicted by courts martial in 1839, and fifty-eight of them were then transported to New South Wales. Their deportation mapped a process by which legal practices generated in the face of political crisis moved about the empire, carrying special gubernatorial and legislative powers that would constrain habeas corpus even as it appeared on the other side of the globe.[88] Whereas habeas corpus had always worked on a notion of the unified subject status of all in the king's protection, subjecthood would fracture as empire grew.

The Calcutta Supreme Court and the Common Law Writ

In 1601, at about the time that habeas corpus broke into Berwick-upon-Tweed, Queen Elizabeth granted a charter by which she made scores of men into "one body corporate" for "trading into the East Indies." The East India Company was empowered to make all ordinances for its governance, and to use imprisonment and other punishments to enforce those ordinances, so long as they did nothing "contrary or repugnant to the laws . . . of this our realm."[89] As in Barbados, so in Bengal: chartered powers operating in a new environment provoked a fertile jurisgenesis. But in India, English law encountered a complex legal culture that had been in place long before its arrival. As in Quebec, habeas would go to India via common law, though it would do so in more independent courts constituted by different means. The writ would cover Britons and other Europeans there, and Indians, too. But that coverage would fluctuate as statutes were created at Westminster and pronouncements were made by governors in India. Such fluctuations would distinguish among the kinds of people living under the king's protection.

Over the seventeenth and eighteenth centuries, a succession of charters gave Britons in India an increasing authority to adjudicate disputes and punish wrongs committed among themselves. Acting on this authority, Company governors made judicial institutions and gave Company officers powers to imprison. By the end of the seventeenth century, these powers were in use against Indians as well as Britons.[90] A charter of 1726 further defined judicial authority in the presidency towns of Bombay, Madras, and Calcutta, while another, enacted in 1753, empowered JPs to hold jail delivery sessions where they were to proceed, "as in England," by indictment and jury trial.[91] But until 1774, there was no superior tribunal in India that might supervise the work of an amateur magistracy.

The impetus for creating new supervisory powers arose from transformed political circumstances after the success of Company arms at Plassey, in 1757.[92] By the 1765 Treaty of Allahabad, Shah Alam, the Mughal emperor, granted to the Company the *diwani:* the civil administration and power to collect revenues in Bengal, Bihar, and Orissa. The Treaty of Allahabad was not a cession of territory, but a "union" of "contracting powers."[93] The Company—created by Great Britain's sovereign but acting only indirectly on his behalf—arranged with the sovereign of that part of South Asia to exercise authority within his territories as *diwan.* The *diwani* did not entail a unitary sovereignty. How could it in a place where multiple cultures interacted in a diverse collection of territories nominally ruled by the Mughal emperor, but governed by lesser princes, and intruded on by a corporation chartered by a British monarch? Rather than think in modern terms of sovereignty, we might do better if we consider the treaty as a charter itself: as a grant of authority by an Asian sovereign to a commercial and political entity empowered to act in the name of a sovereign thousands of miles away. The result? A distinct, historically contingent political form: a sovereign company.[94]

The presence in Bengal of multiple forms of law highlighted the multivalent quality of sovereignty there. Shah Alam granted the *diwani* on the understanding that the Company should govern "agreeably to the rules of Mahomed and the law of the [Mughal] Empire."[95] Muslim and Hindu courts remained. Further complicating this jurisdictional picture, in 1772, Governor Warren Hastings approved new judicial structures that expressed, as he put it, "the ancient constitution" of Bengal.[96] An ostensibly traditional civil and criminal law would persist under the gaze of Company power operating within the realm of the Mughal sovereign. Into this environment came more judges, and the writ of habeas corpus. With them came questions. From what authority did judicial powers arise where there were multiple sovereigns? Who was subject to what monarch in Bengal? By what means, in legal theory and judicial practice, might that subjecthood be expressed and protected?

In 1774, Britain's king offered an answer to these questions when he created a court in Bengal by granting a new charter to the East India Company. That charter passed the great seal after Parliament passed a statute that, among other things, recommended the making of that charter—as always, even when a statute outlined the terms, it was the charter that made the new court and extended the law that the court would carry to India. Throughout the eighteenth century, and in the nineteenth too, only the monarch could create a new jurisdiction.[97]

The 1773 Regulating Act expressed the need for such a new court "to prevent various abuses which have prevailed in the government and administration" of the East India Company.[98] The king's charter thus created a "Supreme Court" in Calcutta and appointed justices. Operating by simile in a manner that would be used to create other superior courts across the empire, those justices were granted "the like jurisdiction and authority as may be executed by the chief justice and other justices of the court of King's Bench in England." All other courts, magistrates, and officers made by earlier charters would henceforth be "subject to the order and control of the Supreme Court, in the like manner as inferior courts and magistrates in England are subject to the order and control of the court of King's Bench."[99] The problem of Barbados—which had habeas corpus by common law but not a judiciary that could use it effectively—had been solved for Bengal by creating a facsimile of the court that had humbled Berwick nearly two centuries earlier.

The Regulating Act also spoke to the complex issue of peoples and places covered, declaring that the Calcutta court covered "all British subjects who shall reside in the kingdoms or provinces of Bengal, Bihar, and Orissa." Just who were these "subjects . . . under the protection of the said United Company"?[100] What about native Indians in Calcutta or in the rest of the *diwani* territories? Were they subjects? Were they under the "protection" of the Company? If so, were they subjects of the king who made that Company? The charter itself gave few solid answers. Only its implementation would do so.

What about habeas corpus? The charter authorized the Supreme Court to "award writs of mandamus, certiorari, procedendo, and error, directed to the said inferior courts."[101] Nothing here about habeas corpus. But the charter also declared that the justices of that court should have the same authority as justices of the court of King's Bench in England. This was not the same as declaring that the Calcutta court would have the powers of King's Bench. A discussion of mandamus soon after the new justices arrived in India in 1775 went right to this issue. Justice John Hyde mistakenly believed that the charter had made no mention of mandamus. Though incorrect, he went on to say that this was beside the point. Mandamus was, he noted, "a prerogative writ." It could go anywhere, "because the king's prerogative extends as fully over his subjects here as in any part of his dominions." Where the charter said nothing to the contrary, Hyde explained, their new court should use any instrument "as would be issued in the like cases in England."[102] Justice Stephen Lemaistre agreed, noting that their charter granted them all powers necessary for administering justice. Ability to issue the prerogative writs was inherent to the authority of any superior court and to its justices, as made apparent by the simile between Calcutta's justices and Westminster's.

Justice Sir Robert Chambers approached the issues a bit differently, connecting mandamus directly to habeas corpus. The "power of granting prerogative writs," he argued, "can only be given by express words." He concluded that there was no power of the court to grant mandamus or habeas corpus, though a justice could do just that: "[W]e are empowered to grant the writ of habeas corpus by the power given to us severally."[103] He developed this same point in a case six years later. The court could not issue habeas,

> but the power of justices of the court of King's Bench at common law are given severally and respectively to the judges of this court; and as (according to Blackstone) the judges of the King's Bench used to issue writs of habeas corpus severally, we have agreed that we have severally authority to issue the writ, but not jointly as a court.[104]

Elsewhere, Chambers explained how this authority arose directly from the charter that created his court and had assigned to the justices all powers possessed by King's Bench, which included a power to use habeas corpus that existed "by the common law, before the Habeas Corpus Act."[105] Whether by Hyde's more expansive form or Chambers's narrower one, this common law theory became the foundation of habeas corpus in India, as it had elsewhere. "The power of granting" such writs, Chief Justice Sir Elijah Impey explained, "has been founded on Mr. Blackstone's opinion that the judges of the King's Bench have a right by common law to allow them."[106] But for whom?

"The natives," Impey declared, were under the protection of the Company, and thus of English law. We return then to the question of subjects. Who were subjects, at least for the purpose of using habeas corpus? Following Impey's lead, the answer takes us back to the prerogative and to the protection provided by the king, through his law, to his subjects, "natural" and "local." Impey considered this issue in a letter to Hastings and the rest of the Council in Calcutta in May 1775. Only eight months since their arrival, court and Council had already butted heads over the jurisdiction proper to each. Hastings claimed an authority for the Company's Council to hear petitions of prisoners, which might prevent use of habeas corpus. Impey replied: "You assert that the government being vested in you, the natives are the immediate objects of your care and protection." Perhaps, but only so far:

> Though the natives without question are under your general protection, they are more immediately so under that of the laws[. O]ne great end of the institution of our court is their protection, particularly against British subjects vested with real or pretended authority. I have no doubt but the laws will be found to be in practice what they are universally esteemed in theory, a better security to the people than the discretionary power of any council of state.[107]

Impey picked up the traditional notion of protection arising from the prerogative, then ran it through the reality called "our court." But from what or whom would his court provide protection? "Particularly against British subjects." Here we learn not only who was to be protected, but why they needed protecting. The issue was not the prisoner's status—British, Indian, or otherwise—but the jailer's. Where that jailer was a franchisee of the British king, justices of the Supreme Court of Calcutta, by virtue of their common law authority to use the king's most sacred judicial instruments, might send the writ, regardless of who that prisoner was.

Impey, and especially Lemaistre, sometimes expressed grander ideas to justify their use of habeas corpus. No country, Lemaistre proclaimed, was "so arbitrary and despotic that a conscientious judge is bound to admit as lawful a ministerial power to imprison without bail or mainprise."[108] Impey explained his use of habeas corpus to help Indians who "feel themselves entitled to the rights of humanity in common with the Europeans."[109] To think in this manner—what we might read as a concern with natural justice or human rights—was to focus on prisoners. But the justices in Calcutta understood that the writ's strength derived from its concern with jailers. They built their authority on a franchise theory like Hale's. As Chambers noted, the prerogative writs

> are not like other writs directed in the ordinary course of justice to sheriffs or other ministerial officers, but are addressed to the person himself who is complained of, and who is bound by his allegiance to obey that command which the king by his prerogative has authority to give.[110]

Chambers made clear that any servant of the Company was just such a "ministerial officer."

> I conceive every man in these provinces, whether subject to our jurisdiction or no, to be entitled to a habeas corpus, upon an affidavit which gives the judge to whom application is made, reason to believe he is imprisoned without any just cause, *by a person employed by the East India Company.*[111]

Hastings admitted as much: "[T]he court cannot avoid issuing such writs, if the complainants swear that the defendants are employed in the service of British subjects."[112] As Impey explained to the Company's London directors, the justices would prevent Company officers "under the color of legal proceeding, from being guilty of the most aggravated injustice."[113] The Company was like Berwick, and subject to the same kind of judicial supervision, regardless of its distinctive legal status. In this way, the Supreme Court made all prisoners—Britons and Frenchmen, Indians too—into subjects of the king and his law.

Impey and Hyde thus issued the first habeas corpus in India in July 1775, for Kemaluddin Khan, who had been jailed by the Company's Council at Calcutta for his debts as a revenue farmer. The Company complained that Kemaluddin's release would destroy the "active coercive authority" that the Company had to exercise in order to safeguard revenue collection.[114] Impey professed his court's concern for the Company's exercise of authority, but when the court released Kemaluddin, Impey reiterated his understanding that the justices must oversee the use of the Company's powers.

The following spring, the justices seemed ready to act again on this understanding of their jurisdiction. Justice Hyde issued a writ for one Sanson, "a low Frenchman" imprisoned in the jail of the *faujdari adalat* at Midnapoor. But on hearing the return, Chambers and Impey ordered remand, "because it appeared clearly that he was not personally subject to our jurisdiction and because that court, and only *that* [court] can try offenses committed in Midnapoor." Though the return, written in Persian, was not correct in its form, they decided "it was our duty to support, not to weaken, the authority of criminal courts actually existing in the country by whatever authority constituted." By now Chambers had come to regret his part in releasing Kemaluddin. From Sanson's case onward, a division appeared in the court—between Impey and Chambers on one side, and Lemaistre and Hyde on the other—over the range of their jurisdiction.[115] Chambers complained that Lemaistre

> showed . . . on this occasion more than any other, a disposition to extend the jurisdiction of our court beyond all bounds . . . Mr. Lemaistre declared that, in his judgment, for which however he gave no reason, Mr. Sanson might be tried in our court for the offence of which he was accused and said that it was contrary to natural justice to remand him, "because the foujdarry courts were only pretended courts of justice held by the instruments of power."[116]

Here the doctrine of protection, through habeas corpus, collided with culturally delicate questions about sovereignty, subjecthood, and the relationship of Indian and English legal norms. The Company, especially Hastings, thus developed a line of argument that would restrict the Supreme Court and habeas corpus by honoring the integrity of Indian legal practices.[117] One consequence would be that Indians, even as they became subject to various aspects of English law in the generations ahead, would increasingly be differentiated as subjects from Britons. The unitary subjecthood arising from protection, on which habeas corpus had developed, and which had even embraced Quebecois, began to break apart into many kinds of imperial subjects.

In January 1779, the Supreme Court threatened to attach—imprison—Suder al Haq Kahn, the nawab's deputy at Murshidabad, for contempt for not returning its habeas corpus. The Company complained just as bitterly as Berwick once had about such treatment. Why, they asked, did the judge of a traditional Indian court have to answer the writ at all when the matter concerned Bengali natives accused of forgery? The accused did not owe allegiance to George III, they argued, "having been born and educated and now living and having always lived out of his protection." Surely the nawab's deputy might claim "as thorough an exemption from the control of our laws, as nature has given him an alienage from us in blood, temper, and complexion." To force him to answer an attachment—which the court withdrew—would be a

> usurpation . . . extending the powers of the court beyond the bounds prescribed to them by the act of Parliament and Charter of Justice, and of imperceptibly drawing every class and character of the people of these provinces within the sphere of its attraction.[118]

Increasingly, the Company attacked the Supreme Court for what it said were violations of an idea of natural justice in which law arises within culturally particular settings. Claims about natural justice in defense of native practice now answered claims about natural justice that Lemaistre, and even Impey, had relied on to extend the range of habeas corpus. A Mughal common law was increasingly juxtaposed to an invasive English common law.

By 1779, arguments like these had been heard in London. One author conceded that the 1773 Regulating Act had caused "the English laws [to be] introduced in their full extent" in Bengal, "without any regard to religious institutions or local habits." Damage to the Company's revenues, the oppression of natives of India, and the introduction of "an arbitrary" regime were all "evils" arising from "the introduction of English laws and customs."[119] English critics appreciated "the great wisdom of the municipal law of England . . . founded in the true and universal principles of abstract justice." But the universal must manifest itself through the particular. English law, "though highly beneficial to ourselves, would be intolerable to any other people." Mughal India, like Britain, had its "ancient constitution" that had to be respected. Native Indian interest and Company interest became one as the Company's assault on the Supreme Court quickened.[120]

Critics like these argued that the only way to ensure the successful interaction of multiple legal cultures would be to use the sovereignty of Parliament to restrain the judicial monster that its statute of 1773 had helped to create. Doing so meant adjusting, with a new statute, those terms of 1773 that the justices of the Supreme Court had clearly misconstrued. At least, this was the hope of the Company's council in Calcutta as they wrote to the Company's directors in London in 1780. After all, the court had originated in Parliament, they reasoned, and now might be repaired by Parliament, which was "best qualified to judge of its own intentions in framing the law."[121]

The resulting 1781 Judicature Act granted the Company much of what it wanted. It limited the ambit of habeas corpus, though in terms that did not prevent the justices from continuing to use the writ to re-shape the bounds of imperial subjecthood. The act's second section permitted anyone sued in the Supreme Court for a deed performed on order of the Company's council—for instance, imprisonment—to show such an order as legal justification.[122] The third section stated that when detention orders concerned "any British subject or subjects, the said court shall have and retain as full and competent jurisdiction as if this act had never been made." Thus, as regarded Company imprisonment orders, habeas corpus had been protected for use by Britons, though not by natives. This amounted to a suspension of the writ for Indians, and, as had happened to Americans under the suspensions of 1777 to 1783, put Indians beyond the bounds of subjecthood. But the act also permitted the Supreme Court to make judgments against natives of Bengal "as may accommodate the same to the religion and manners of such natives, so far as the same may consist with the due execution of the laws and attainment of justice."[123] Here would be the position from which the justices might still use habeas corpus for natives of Bengal.

The writ would persist, though it was now restrained. In 1787, the *India Gazette* could praise Chambers's court for issuing habeas on behalf of an Indian. Doing so, the paper commented, showed "the benefits arising to the natives of this country from [the court's] jurisdiction . . . as it marked in a high degree their participation of *British Liberty*—an

Englishman would have conceived himself in *Westminster Hall.*"[124] But these benefits had already been curtailed as distinctions among subjects proliferated. In a 1782 case, one of the lawyers noted that the "use of the term 'European British subjects' in the [Judicature] Act shows that it contemplated the existence of other British subjects in India, who were *not European* British subjects." Impey thus decided the case based on his determination that the defendant "was not that sort of British subject" concerned in the act.[125] The writ, and with it the benefits of subjecthood, now began to narrow in response to legislation and a more limited judicial temperament. This process multiplied the varieties of subjects, each of which had different legal attributes. Indians were not fully "English" or "British" subjects; they were "subjects of his majesty."[126]

To see how this happened, we must turn to section 23 of the 1781 Judicature Act, which declared "that the governor general and council shall have power and authority, from time to time, to frame regulations for the provincial courts and councils." The Council in Calcutta thus received the same power to legislate as assemblies and councils in Barbados and Quebec enjoyed. Pitt's India Act of 1784 confirmed this result. Lord Cornwallis, a failure in North America, resurrected his imperial career as the new governor in Bengal in 1786, and made extensive use of this power to legislate by gubernatorial decree. His Regulation XLI of 1793 recast much of British Indian law. These actions were then confirmed by parliamentary statute in 1797, which extended the power of governor and council to legislate by making regulations.[127] The most significant use of this power to curb habeas corpus appeared in Regulation III of 1818, "A Regulation for the Confinement of State Prisoners." The preamble declared that "reasons of state" might sometimes "render it necessary" to hold prisoners "otherwise than in pursuance of some judicial proceeding." Like the first suspensions of 1689, the Irish habeas statute of 1781–1782, and the locally authorized Quebec suspensions of the 1790s and 1800s, Bengal's 1818 Regulation III gave to the governor-in-Council authority to order detention "without having recourse to any judicial proceeding."[128] The writ had arrived in India by common law; so too had its suspension, in the broadest forms, by powers granted to governors by statute.[129] In India, as in Quebec and in England, the writ and the judges who had made it were pushed into retreat from the last years of the eighteenth century onward.

From the Indian Ocean to the South Pacific

The writ continued to appear, and to be clipped, as British dominions proliferated. Charters would create courts with common law authority to use the writ by analogizing to King's Bench. Colonial legislators would then curb that power in order to control ethnically various subjects during periods of political disquiet created by cultural conflict and by Britons' seizure of lands once occupied only by indigenous peoples.

Ceylon became Britain's by a 1796 treaty with the Dutch. As in Quebec, where French civil law in property matters blended with England's common law of crime, Dutch private law persisted in Ceylon as new courts were made, first by the governor's proclamation in 1799, then by a royal charter of 1801. The charter erected a Supreme Court of Judicature at Colombo like that which had been sitting at Calcutta for a generation. It was given "a general superintendance" over all officers and magistrates "in such manner and form as the inferior magistrates of . . . England are by law subject to the order and control of our court of King's Bench."[130] Neither this charter nor subsequent ones of 1810 and 1811 mentioned habeas corpus, and they expressly limited the Colombo Supreme Court's jurisdiction over native Sinhalese in most aspects of private law. Only in 1815 was "the dominion of the Kandyan provinces," which occupied the island's core, "vested in the sovereign of the British empire." Following a rebellion, a gubernatorial proclamation of 1818 transferred into British hands most forms of traditional judicial authority that had once been derived from the king of Kandy. Both the manner and the result of this process marked a sharp departure from the judicial reforms of Hastings, who had tried to incorporate local legal practices loosely into British ones.[131] All Ceylon now seemed subject to a British governor and a British Supreme Court.

For all the greater gubernatorial power in Ceylon, justices in Colombo saw themselves as having a broad supervisory jurisdiction, just as justices in Calcutta once had. When granting habeas corpus in 1826 for Siva Poonian—who had been jailed in a debt dispute between two Sinhalese—the Supreme Court declared that if it did not have power to use the writ, "the king's subjects in Ceylon would have been without a shadow of remedy against any oppression which might be exercised."

To clarify, they followed the 1801 charter's language back "to the practice of the Court from which it has been adopted": King's Bench.[132]

But for all the judicial power implied by that origin, habeas use was sharply curtailed by the governor-in-Council's authority to legislate by making regulations. As elsewhere in the empire, habeas corpus in Ceylon would participate in the writ's general decline in the early nineteenth century, just as the writ arrived in that island. Regulation I of 1824, for instance, granted a sweeping power to suspend habeas corpus by allowing the governor to sign warrants of imprisonment that could not be reviewed by any court.[133]

Successive chief justices of the Supreme Court protested these changes. Charles Cameron, one of the royal commissioners appointed to propose legal reforms for Ceylon, reported almost immediately after his arrival in March 1830

> on the dangerous uncertainty in which the right of the Supreme Court
> to issue writs of habeas corpus was involved, and on the encroachment
> which had been made on that right, supposing it legally vested in the
> Court, by a Regulation of Government.[134]

Later that year, the governor's Council repealed Regulation I. As in Quebec, Cameron and others recognized that the writ had arrived by the common law, as signaled by the court's use of the writ, by the justices' explanation for that use, and by the Council's enactment of a provision permitting suspension whenever the governor saw fit. Though the writ was present in his reform proposals, Cameron advised that an explicit statement about habeas corpus should be made. This was done in a new charter to Ceylon in 1833, which provided that the Supreme Court, "or any judge thereof," might grant habeas corpus "to bring up the body of any person who shall be imprisoned within any part of the said island or its dependencies."[135]

But the same power that gives may take away. Local ordinances, reinforced by another charter of 1843 and by further ordinances made by the Legislative Council in Colombo, continued to enlarge the governor's capacity for unilateral action.[136] Indeed, the 1843 charter explained that greater gubernatorial authority, including even authority to amend that charter, was necessary for responding "to the exigencies of society within the said island."[137] Such exigencies arose just a few years later, as Sinhalese rioted against new taxes and religious policies. In reply, Governor Viscount Torrington proclaimed martial law. Though the uprising was quickly put down, and though throughout civilian courts using common law remained open, martial law persisted. While it did, those detained had no recourse to judicial review of their detention, much to the consternation of some in Westminster. They were concerned that the governor, having been given greater autonomy by the Colonial Office, had used his new powers to constrain justice in Ceylon.[138] But of course martial law—which always contained in it an implied suspension of habeas corpus—was by the 1840s a long-established imperial practice, from Ireland to Quebec to New Zealand.

Following the same process of extension through which new courts used habeas corpus by common law, the writ continued to travel farther to the southeast, to New South Wales and Van Diemen's Land (Tasmania), then to New Zealand. The writ's arrival in Australia was occasioned by its status as a place initially settled by convicts transported there by virtue of statutes made in Westminster. The 1679 Habeas Corpus Act had declared that "no subject of this realm" could be sent as a prisoner to any "places beyond the seas . . . within or without the dominions of his majesty."[139] The transportation act of 1779, refined by another in 1784 after the loss of America, overrode that prohibition by permitting the transportation of prisoners, "any law, statute, or usage to the contrary notwithstanding."[140] Australia thus became a nexus for the imperial work of imprisonment and detention, not only for felons convicted in England and Scotland, but also for those rounded up during periods of political crisis when the writ was suspended in Ireland, Quebec, or New Zealand.[141]

In Australia as elsewhere, the creative energy behind the making of charters continued to emanate from the monarch and operate by the prerogative. A charter of 1787, which passed the great seal pursuant to a statute of the same year, extended criminal jurisdiction into New South Wales and provided for magistrates with administrative and judicial powers like JPs in England.[142] A second charter established a Supreme Court in 1814, but its purview covered only civil matters. Its charter made no mention of the authority of that court's single judge to supervise the work of other courts. The new chief justice reported that the first matter he heard was an application for habeas corpus, but he refused the writ because "no such power has been granted to any of the courts or to the judges thereof to issue" it. He did recommend, though, that the problem be addressed in what had become the usual manner: by creating a new Supreme Court explicitly modeled on King's Bench.[143] This is what a third charter accomplished, twice over. As in the creation of Calcutta's Supreme Court, an 1823 statute appointed that the new charter create two new Supreme Courts for New South Wales and Van Diemen's Land. The statute declared that the power granted in that charter would give to these Australian superior courts all jurisdiction "as His Majesty's courts of King's Bench, Common Pleas, and Exchequer at Westminster."[144]

Sir Francis Forbes, New South Wales's first chief justice, was the quintessential imperial legal figure: he was born in Bermuda, educated in law in London, and served as chief justice in Newfoundland before returning to London, where he helped to write the 1823 statute. He set to work acting as a supreme judge almost immediately after his arrival in Sydney in 1824, issuing a writ of mandamus to require justices of the peace to proceed by jury trial.[145] He granted habeas corpus before year's end, the first on behalf of a runaway from HMS *Tamar*, William King. Though Forbes recognized the statutory ground for the punishment of deserters, he also asserted his authority to "look to the whole range of matter before him, and [to] see if the party had actually committed a felony; if he had not, certainly the court would order his discharge." Given King's confession and the other evidence against him, the court could not discharge him, but the chief justice had made clear that any evidence for imprisonment was his to review, as judges had done since the time of Popham and Fleming.[146] Chief Justice John Lewes Pedder of Van Diemen's Land was even more energetic in using habeas corpus. In October 1824, Pedder went to Thomas William Warton's prison cell to take the deposition on which the petition for this first Tasmanian writ depended. The local newspaper praised "the excellent magisterial example he has set by visiting the captive, and affording him a legal opportunity to move for his deliverance."[147]

Forbes used language that could easily have come from Impey or Chambers fifty years earlier to explain why he could use habeas corpus in a place so far from its origins. The writ was, as he put it, "a high prerogative writ, and so much the right of the subject, as to render it compulsory on the judges." He admitted his reluctance to send it for prisoners of the Crown, especially in such an unusual colony as his.

Prisoners of the Crown in this colony are placed in a very different situation from the mass of the King's subjects in the Mother Country. I have been fearful to let it go abroad in a community where so many persons are under legal disability and restraints by reason of sentences passed upon them at home that they had a right to be brought up for the purpose of seeing why and wherefore they were kept in confinement.

But this hesitation did not keep him from using habeas corpus where there might be any question about legality. Thus his court sent the writ for Jane New to the Female Factory at Parramatta, even though she was there on a conviction.[148]

Habeas corpus performed work in Australia familiar to any English judge of the previous two centuries: it inspected summary convictions. In Australia, no summary convictions were more common than those arising from the enforcement of master-servant laws.[149] Statutes from the Legislative Councils in Australia sharpened statutory powers to imprison servants—powers that JPs in England had possessed since the sixteenth century.[150] Upon its appearance in Australia, habeas immediately went to work supervising this magisterial authority. Results varied. Unlike in England in earlier centuries, Forbes's court often decided that if jurisdiction granted by statute had been used in a given case, they would look no further into how it had been used. Forbes's approach marked a kind of jurisdictional self-limiting principle that had become more apparent in English jurisprudence as well, but only since the 1790s.[151]

In other cases, the court might look more closely: for instance, in those involving extensions of a servant's period of servitude on conviction of minor wrongs. As in England, the court might proceed by an order *nisi,* thus giving the master concerned a chance to make the case for his servant's extended service. This process might curtail, though not preclude, the writ's utility against summary convictions.[152] Again, Pedder's court, in Hobart, may have used habeas more aggressively to look within the jurisdiction that local magistrates exercised. Harriet Morgan thus used habeas corpus after two JPs ordered her imprisoned for six months "for neglect of work." Unlike Forbes, Pedder went well beyond the fact of jurisdiction, raising incisive questions about its use. In Morgan's case, such questions led to her release.[153]

More often, especially in Sydney, the Supreme Court recognized the admittedly enormous discretion that local statutes accorded magistrates to imprison, even when they did so with a vague warrant. In a problem that echoed hundreds of seventeenth-century cases when JPs made insufficient warrants, Alexander Lookaye had been consigned to the *Phonix,* a prison hulk in Sydney Cove, on an "informal commitment" that he was "a runaway from Bathurst." Forbes's court found this warrant wanting for precision, but in what amounted to an order to amend the return, the justices commanded the magistrates to make a new warrant so as to "make their sentence complete." Forbes concluded that his court "had no jurisdiction to enquire into the merits of the proceedings of the justices below, in as much as the offence attributed to the prisoner was within the scope of their jurisdiction." Back to the hulk he returned.[154] A narrow view of jurisdiction, joined to provincial legislation whose strictness peaked in the mid-nineteenth century, meant that during the fifty years after the Supreme Courts were established in Sydney and Hobart, only the tiniest fraction of the tens of thousands of servants imprisoned by summary convictions on master-servant laws received a review.[155]

In New Zealand, local legislation rather than statutes made at Westminster would open a Supreme Court in Auckland in early 1842.[156] As elsewhere, any individual justice as well as the entire court might issue the writ, typically on evidence presented by affidavit and after an order *nisi.* Habeas corpus thus performed functions in New Zealand like those it performed elsewhere: for instance, it protected mothers' custody of their illegitimate children. But as was increasingly the case in Australia and other dominions in the nineteenth century, the Auckland court followed a self-limiting principle, narrowing its inquiry to questions of jurisdiction only. The result was leniency toward summary convictions and poorly made warrants of commitment.[157] And cases like these concerned only European inhabitants. More evident in New Zealand was the difficulty the writ had in doing any work in the politically fraught struggles with the Maori over land.

These struggles arose, in part, from the confusing circumstances by which British law came to New Zealand. In 1835, the British resident there signed a Declaration of Independence recognizing a Maori assertion of "all sovereign power and authority."[158] In part because of growing French threats, and in part because of increasing British settlement, the Treaty of Waitangi, by which the Maori ceded all "rights and powers of sovereignty," was signed by hundreds of Maori chiefs in 1840. In return, the queen gave "to the natives of New Zealand Her royal protection and impart[ed] to them all the Rights and Privileges of British Subjects."[159] Upon that sovereignty, the Legislative Council there, by ordinances of 1841 and 1844, established a Supreme Court with "jurisdiction in all cases, as fully as her majesty's courts of Queen's Bench, Common Pleas, and Exchequer at Westminster, have in England."[160] As in Canada, in times of political turmoil, that jurisdiction would be more notable for its absence than for its presence. The absence of oversight would affect the queen's new Maori subjects more than others.

During repeated spells of violence in the decades following, the work of habeas corpus was interrupted often in New Zealand, usually by means other than suspension. The violence arose from conflicting understandings of the Treaty of Waitangi and increasing British settler encroachment on Maori lands. Martial law was proclaimed six times between 1845 and 1847, and again in 1860–1861. Despite the terms of the 1679 Habeas Corpus Act against transportation, hundreds were sent into exile in Tasmania or the Chatham Islands after little if any trial. Further Maori risings prompted the Legislative Council to pass the 1863 Suppression of Rebellion Act, which permitted summary trial in certain areas and detention without trial aboard hulks. The act's third section, which declared that no deed performed under its terms "shall be questioned in Her Majesty's Supreme Court of New Zealand or in any other court," constituted a sweeping suspension of habeas corpus. The Disturbed Districts Act of 1869 likewise cut off habeas corpus for anyone detained by gubernatorial warrant.[161]

More difficulties arose against the claims of colonial government in the late 1870s and 1880s, due to nonviolent acts of civil disobedience led by two charismatic Maoris. Te Whiti o Rongomai and Tohu Kakahi established at Parihaka what amounted to a legally autonomous community that drew adherents from across New Zealand. Claims of self-governance, in large part predicated on straightforward readings of the 1835 Declaration, the Treaty of Waitangi, and later enactments, provoked a showdown in which a nervous colonial regime decided to assert fully its pretensions to sovereignty.[162] This assertion of one view of British law was made possible only by dropping what many Antipo-

dean Britons considered a central marker of English legal ideals—
habeas corpus—notwithstanding the third article of the Treaty of
Waitangi's recognition that the Maori would possess "all the rights and
privileges of British subjects." Hundreds were detained. The passage of
the Maori Prisoners Act of 1880 then cut off any hope of a proper trial
by preventing any judge from reviewing their detention. The Prisoners' Detention Act, which followed, erected even stronger legal defenses around the government's actions. Hundreds of Maori were sent
into internal exile as a result.[163] As we shall see in Chapter 9, forced resettlement of this kind would be a precursor of more dramatic policies
of the same kind in the twentieth century.

All this was made possible by a legislative sovereignty carried into colonial law to a triumphalist extreme, then fully effected by the Colonial
Laws Validity Act of 1865, by which colonial legislatures were unloosed
from parliamentary constraints and from traditional nonrepugnancy
principles. The act's fifth section gave every colonial legislature "full
power within its jurisdiction to establish courts of judicature, and to
abolish and reconstitute the same, and to alter the constitution thereof,
and to make provision for the administration of justice therein."[164]
Using this authority, New Zealand's Legislative Council passed the Act
for Preservation of the Peace in the West in 1882, a statute whose title,
if not its terms, echoed similar statutes made for Ireland in times of
trouble. The work of empire always involved a global conversation
about how to design the legal boxes used to contain political dangers,
wherever they appeared.[165] In a manner reminiscent of Napoléon's
statutory exile to St. Helena, the Preservation of the Peace Act placed
Te Whiti and Tohu, by name, into a legal limbo without trial or judicial
review of their imprisonment. The Council then passed an Indemnity
Act imitative of the 1801 Indemnity in Britain, thereby removing any
danger of legal liability for those who had made the mass arrests at
Parihaka.

Some were embarrassed using a power almost entirely detached
from common law norms and contravening revered statutes, even if
the Habeas Corpus Act had not been formally imported into New Zealand's law. Two members of the Council entered protests that the Preservation of the Peace Act was "repugnant to the English statute law,
and deprives British subjects of the privileges granted them by the Habeas Corpus Acts."[166] But as so often happened since 1689, and more

so since the 1790s, fears of "a constant menace to the peace of the colony"—as one member of the Council described the Maori at Parihaka—trumped concerns about a liberty that might be protected by habeas corpus.[167] A once great common law writ had crossed the empire from Berwick to Auckland, carried by traditional ideas of the prerogative. Forbes in Australia, and Vallières de Saint-Réal in Canada, still remembered these ideas. But that prerogative interest in the subject's liberty, which once flowed through the judge's hands, had been cut off by statute and by the governors now made great by legislation. Who would watch the jailer now?

John Anderson and the End of the Writ Imperial

John Anderson's life was filled with the kinds of details from which great stories are made. But it was in the legislative conclusion, in a terse statutory pronouncement after his release from custody, that the most astonishing deed was done.

The story began when Anderson killed a man.[168] Neither he nor anyone else denied that awful fact. But the circumstances mattered. Anderson, a Missouri slave separated from his wife and child, had come increasingly into conflict with his master over visits with his family. After his master sold him in order to be rid of the problem, Anderson escaped, and headed for Canada in 1853. He had traveled only three days, and was still in Missouri, when he encountered Seneca Digges. Suspecting Anderson was a runaway, Digges told Anderson to come with him and his own slaves. Anderson complied at first, but then made a breakaway. After a chase and a scuffle, Digges lay on the ground, with knife wounds from which he died two weeks later. Meanwhile, Anderson made it across the border to Windsor. Though now an international fugitive, he managed to blend into his new Canadian community as a successful mason. Only in March 1860 was he recognized as Missouri's fugitive murderer and taken into custody. Extradition proceedings began immediately. The first habeas corpus issued soon thereafter.

The story was followed as closely in British papers as by American and Canadian ones, in part because it energized debates about Britain's deference to American slavery after Britain had abolished the practice, and in part because Anderson's story unfolded as the United

States itself was coming apart over slavery. A first writ, demanding Anderson's release to prevent his extradition, issued from the Queen's Bench of Upper Canada. Upon hearing the case in mid-December, Justice Archibald McLean agreed. One Dublin newspaper celebrated how McClean enunciated "principles with which every Englishman will cordially sympathize" when he found the warrant for Anderson's commitment and the evidence against him insubstantial. McLean then went quite a bit further, declaring that murder committed while fleeing slavery amounted to justifiable homicide by natural law, a doctrine he said accorded with the "British constitution."[169] But two of the justices, arguing from current treaty relationships, ordered that Anderson remain in jail to await extradition to Missouri.

Some talked of appealing to the Privy Council. Instead, Anderson's abolitionist supporters set to work on another front: Queen's Bench in Westminster.[170] It seemed as if the logic of two centuries of imperial judicial development—during which new superior courts modeled on Queen's Bench had been created around the empire to supervise magisterial authority—would be reversed. One month after the decision in Toronto, the original Queen's Bench heard motions for habeas corpus in Westminster. Though widely understood to be an alien, Anderson was described in the affidavit for his writ as "a British subject." Edwin James, one of Anderson's lawyers hired by the British and Foreign Anti-Slavery Society, argued simply that "the writ of habeas corpus may issue to Canada" from England. To support his point, he made all the expected references, beginning with medieval writs to Calais. Like Justice McLean, James then attached British law to natural law, explaining that the ancient practice of sending writs from King's Bench to dominions outside England was "in accordance with the general law of nations."[171]

In the end, James's argument came to rest in Berwick-upon-Tweed. He quoted Mansfield's judgment in Cowle's case, in which Mansfield had explained that the prerogative writs ran to any dominion "under the subjection of the Crown of England." James conceded that getting the writ returned from distant places might be difficult—which explained why new courts had been made in such places—but that was no reason not to do what law allowed, even required, where there might be a failure of justice in a colonial court. Though admitting the complexities of the case, the justices in Westminster Hall now reclaimed an authority their court had never lost, an authority that Hale had articulated so well two centuries earlier. They ordered a writ that "in the absence of any prohibitive enactment, goes to all parts of the queen's dominions." Noting more recent writs from Westminster to the Isles of Man, Jersey, and St. Helena, one more went beyond the seas. Anderson was soon freed.[172]

In their judgment, the justices of Queen's Bench repeatedly observed that only a legislative statement might prevent using habeas corpus, which had always been theirs to send by common law to any dominion. Parliament took the hint. In May 1862, it passed a statute declaring that

> no writ of habeas corpus shall issue out of England, by authority of any judge or court of justice therein, into any colony or foreign dominion of the Crown where Her Majesty has a lawfully established court or courts of justice having authority to grant and issue the said writ.[173]

Parliament thus made exactly the pronouncement that Queen's Bench, the year before, had indicated was the only thing that might prevent their sending habeas corpus to other dominions. What had momentarily been an empire, with one law concerning judicial supervision of anyone holding any of the queen's subjects anywhere by any authority, was split again into so many dominions. Subjecthood fractured along with it.

A writ that had been made by judicial capture of the king's prerogative, a writ that in turn had made judges great so that they might inspect the behavior by all who acted in the sovereign's name: this writ had been gradually denatured over the course of its imperial journey. The problems it faced did not arise from its origin in common law. As Berwick's leaders learned, the common law writ might go to any of the queen's dominions, regardless of the other kinds of law that pertained in each. This had always been an imperial writ.

The key to the writ's success in Berwick was a powerful court. In that instance, the court had needed a powerful friend to make judicial theory operate in practice. The success of Queen's Bench against Berwick meant that other jurisdictions claiming autonomy would ultimately yield without the need to summon the help of a friend like Lord Willoughby. But as the writ went "beyond the seas," it faced ever more difficult realities. At Barbados, the absence of such a powerful judge meant that habeas corpus operated as only a shadow of its theoretical self. In Bengal, a court made by new means had momentarily threatened to be great enough to realize the writ's potential because that court's powers were modeled on those of the greatest court of all. Justices in Calcutta in 1775, and in Sydney in 1825, saw themselves working in precisely the same mode used by justices in Queen's Bench in 1601. Their charters said that they did, a point they often repeated. But imperial realities and parliamentary sovereignty would strip those attributes by which such courts tried to make real the writ's authority to monitor all who acted in the king's name.

Whether by direct statutory grant of powers to imprison or by grant of authority to colonial governors to widen imprisonment powers; whether by explicitly limiting the work of habeas corpus by suspension, or by implicitly doing so by declaring martial law; and whether any of these acts were made by an imperial Parliament in Westminster or a colonial assembly in a far-flung dominion; the effect was the same: the neutering of the judicial discretion that had made habeas corpus effective in places like Berwick. Even in the fledgling American Republic, which placed in its Constitution a clause forbidding the suspension of habeas corpus "unless when in cases of rebellion or invasion the public safety may require it," the federal writ would survive largely in statutory form.

John Marshall, chief justice of the Supreme Court, declared in 1807 "that for the meaning of the term habeas corpus, resort may unquestionably be had to the common law." Then he continued: "but the power to award the writ by any of the courts of the United States, must be given by written law."[174] Yes, Marshall reasoned, the Constitution recognized a writ knowable by common law. But it seemed to be present in federal law largely by grace of the legislature, with some of the same potentially limiting consequences that had dogged the writ as it followed its shambling imperial course. Though independent and differently constituted, the United States continued to participate in law's empire in many of the same ways as did the queen's dominions. Wherever they worked, the kind of judges who had made and used habeas corpus in the seventeenth and eighteenth centuries were increasingly bound in the nineteenth, even as the writ covered ever more of the globe.

CHAPTER 9

The Palladium of Liberty
in Law's Empire

"The great palladium of the liberties of the subject" was what Charles
James Fox called habeas corpus during Commons debates to suspend
the writ in 1777. Fox damned "the insolence and temerity" of those
"who could thus dare to snatch it from the people." John Wilkes,
who spoke too, must have savored the irony that Ebeneezer Smith
Platt—the American captive whose cause he and Fox championed—
had been brought to London aboard the *Pallas*.[1] Everyone in the
House knew Fox and Wilkes as promoters of liberal reform, lovers of
wine and women, and masters of Greek and Latin. Even those who had
been dullards at school understood their classical allusion. They all
knew the story of the palladium.

In Greek mythology, Odysseus and Diomedes literally crawled
through the filth to steal the palladium, the statue of the goddess
Pallas, better known as Minerva or Athena. The palladium had fallen
from the heavens, right into the temple the Trojans built to honor her.
The oracle of Apollo had told them that as long as they kept their icon
of Pallas safe, Troy would be safe too. So to conquer the city, the
heroes slunk through Troy's sewers, then carried away the image of
the virgin goddess. Troy fell.[2]

The story of the palladium was the perfect metaphor for the theft
the ministry now attempted by proposing to suspend habeas corpus.
Fox's "snatch" was hardly an idle word choice. Many were the palladi-
ums of liberty sculpted in the rhetoric of eighteenth- and nineteenth-
century parliamentary debate and political writing: jury trials, free-

dom of the press, the Bill of Rights, as well as habeas corpus. The image was a telling one: liberty was fragile, in need of a protectress at once pure, wise, and strong. Just how fragile was liberty; how powerful was its protector? Was the palladium easily stolen?

Albert Venn Dicey, a century later, felt sure that the palladium of liberty was safe. In his 1885 *Law of the Constitution,* Dicey celebrated England's "judge-made law," a pragmatist's body of practices. One did not need airy declarations in the French manner—and he made this comparison explicit—to protect "rights." One needed only "remedies": habeas corpus, made strong by the statutes of 1679 and 1816.

> [T]he securities for personal freedom are in England as complete as laws can make them . . . any person, whether charged with crime or not, who is even suspected to be wrongfully imprisoned, has . . . the certainty of having his case duly investigated, and, if he has been wronged, of recovering his freedom.[3]

The key to the writ's effectiveness was the independence it gave judges relative to "the executive," by investing them "with the means of hampering or supervising the whole administrative action of government."[4] But Dicey didn't stop there. With no apparent sheepishness, he considered next those parliamentary suspension acts and even more draconian measures that had neutered habeas corpus in the interest of controlling other lands, most recently Ireland and New Zealand. Dicey could not bring himself to see just how tightly statute bound his law-making judge: that Parliament might be the palladium's thief. Like many a confident Victorian, he comforted himself with the idea that suspension, coercion acts, and acts for preserving peace were, by their statutory nature, safe: "no doubt an exercise of arbitrary sovereign power," he admitted, but because parliamentary, maintaining "in no small degree the real no less than the apparent supremacy of law."[5] The palladium seemed pure and strong, if one did not inquire too carefully about her.

Others were more skeptical. Dicey was a legal positivist, Frederic Harrison a Comtean positivist. He had a much harder time celebrating English law's Englishness. "I should be the last person to attach a sacramental efficacy to the British constitution," Harrison observed in a public address just a few years after Dicey wrote. He continued, archly:

But though Frenchmen and Germans may, I do not doubt it, exist happily under their own civil law, even without a jury, or the Habeas Corpus Act, and the other safeguards which English men think their birthright and their palladium, still the fact remains that the birthright, or
palladium (whatever it be) is abrogated to the people of Ireland.[6]

For all the casualness of his "whatever it be," the once lauded student
of literature certainly knew what a palladium was and how it worked as
legal metaphor. He was simply less certain that habeas corpus was such
a thing or that the palladium was still there, at least in the empire. But
one could find pieces of it everywhere.

Habeas Corpus, Writ Global

Edwin James, victor in Queen's Bench on John Anderson's behalf in
1861, wrote only weeks before his triumph to the Count of Cavour, recommending that Italy assign a place for habeas corpus in its new law
code, telling him that it was "the palladium of all British liberties."[7] A
nice gesture, perhaps, but a presumptuous one, too?

Casting our eyes about the globe in the 1860s, it is hard not to be
astonished by the number of places that the writ had appeared. Colonial dominions everywhere had adopted it, often attempting to bolster
it by statute. In the years right around the American Anderson's victory in an English court over his Toronto jailer, one Canadian province after another imported the 1679 Habeas Corpus Act into its own
law.[8] The writ, long available there by common law, had become a part
of each province's statute book by 1867, when Parliament created
the Dominion of Canada "with a constitution similar in principle to
that of the United Kingdom."[9] But given Canada's federal structure—
within which each province had its own superior court—it would be
in the provincial, rather than federal, courts that the writ would be
used.[10]

Statutory practices, in addition to common law, helped to make a
global writ. But if we keep our gaze on the 1860s, we will find many colonial realities, abetted by statute, that would cut down habeas in the
years to come. The statute of 1862 restricting Queen's Bench from
sending the writ to the colonies, and the 1865 Colonial Laws Validity
Act, gave new powers to colonial assemblies. Colonial legislators often

put these powers into the hands of governors, who sidestepped bare suspension and pursued tougher measures in times of crisis.

The most important of these special powers was the declaration of martial law. In St. Vincent, in 1862, the governor quieted a political storm by what he called "the wise and salutary exercise of Her Majesty's undoubted prerogative in executing martial law." He ended martial law in mid-October "so as to permit the common law to resume its functions." By a wave of his hand, the governor stopped common law in its tracks, and with another wave, signaled it into motion again. In imitation of the 1801 British Indemnity Act and others used after similar episodes of political violence elsewhere, a local indemnity act was quickly passed to protect those who had done the ugly work required. The same act also suspended habeas corpus to allow more time to prepare charges against those detained.[11] Combination measures like these—martial law, indemnity, suspension, and perhaps local ordinances for "preserving the peace"—built on well-established colonial practices used to squelch trouble in Canada in the 1830s, the Cape Colony in 1835, and Ceylon in 1848. This last episode had turned especially nasty, leading to a lengthy parliamentary inquiry and a struggle for the soul of imperial law. At stake was what might count as the rule of law where raw colonial power was used to contain rebellion.[12] In the Caribbean, repeated bouts of emergency law made habeas corpus all but irrelevant without resort to suspension, a practice that now seemed quaint by comparison. Barbados twice endured martial law, in 1805 and 1816. And on Demerara, under martial law in 1823, more than two hundred people were executed after summary trials.[13]

The worst troubles arose in Jamaica. The central fact of Caribbean life for two centuries had been that a nonwhite slave population dwarfed a white planter population. Little surprise then that a small legislative assembly representing a tiny group of landholders lived in fear. This fear persisted long after the island's slaves were emancipated in 1838, and led to floggings and imprisonments used so routinely as to inure the white populace to the repression they wrought.[14] But for all the racist loathing that generated such policy, law structured its making, giving it moral legitimacy in the eyes of those who made it by the simple fact of its being "law" of the kind Dicey celebrated. A statute passed by the Jamaican assembly in 1681—and never disallowed by the Privy Council, though the Council was charged with voiding any colonial enactments "repugnant" to English law—empowered the governor and his council there to declare martial law in times of rebellion.

Just such a rebellion erupted in 1865. When the governor proclaimed martial law in order to contain it, the island's attorney general declared that legality had been honored: "[F]rom the time of the actual settlement of [Jamaica] as a British possession, there never has been a day during which martial law, or the power of declaring martial law, has not been a normal provision of the statute book."[15] Statutes that maintained exceptional powers ready for use whenever colonial governors saw fit always proved greater than a writ that one could no longer find when buried under claims of "necessity" and "emergency." "When martial law is declared," as Benjamin Disraeli put it, "all other laws are suspended."[16]

Long after the trouble in Jamaica ended, martial law persisted as Jamaican courts martial set to work, cutting off civilian legal process. Sydney Leivens, a white newspaper editor convicted of seditious libel by a special commission, learned this when his attempt to use habeas corpus to overturn his conviction came to nothing.[17] Meanwhile, MPs debated the Jamaican debacle in Westminster, just as they had debated earlier uses of extraordinary measures after other troubles, like those in Ceylon. The usual criticisms of illiberal measures were met by invoking "necessity." Ever since 1689, when MPs first resorted to "necessity" to justify suspension, it had made suspension and martial law into legal norms as pervasive as the writ itself.[18] These norms would endure, reproducing themselves in Ireland, where habeas corpus was suspended between 1866 and 1869. This had the "magical" effect, as one officer put it, of permitting the arrest of hundreds without requiring a declaration of martial law.[19]

The 1860s brought change in habeas usage to India, notably the writ's expansion in scope with the creation in 1861 of High Courts.[20] If one did not know what had happened in so many other dominions, it might seem ironic that only days before the statute creating these courts took effect, another had been passed that gave the governor-general in council greater power to regulate courts in India. But there was no irony, only the playing of a variation on a persistent theme. A significant clause in the Indian Councils Act inverted the traditional nonrepugnancy principle. Rather than preventing the governor from making laws repugnant to English law, the statute declared that his regulations should "not affect . . . any part of the unwritten laws or constitutions of the United Kingdom of Great Britain and Ireland."[21] It was not Indian law that needed protection by ensuring its likeness to English law; instead English law needed protection from Indian law. Everyone understood that colonial law generated measures repugnant to the vaunted liberties of the English; now they feared that such usages might come home to roost in the heart of empire.

Although the United States was no longer a part of Britain's empire, its law continued to run in channels in part carved by previous English experience. As elsewhere around the globe, the 1860s would prove critical to the American writ's work. Habeas corpus was suspended by President Abraham Lincoln during the Civil War, with Congress later approving his actions. Just like those of British colonial governors in the same period, Lincoln's suspension was justified by "necessity."

Due to the distinctiveness of the Constitution in the United States, the major questions surrounding habeas corpus since 1789 were quite novel when viewed against the backdrop of practice across Britain's imperial dominions. In the United States, such questions centered on the relationship of federal to state courts in the handling of state convictions for felony. As we have seen, in English law, there had been little postconviction use of the writ in felony. But the writ had always been at its most effective when judges used it to address new problems. Following the Civil War, the 1867 Habeas Corpus Act seemed ready to extend the federal writ to prisoners in the states.

Just as in similar situations during the seventeenth century, the concern in making this statute was not with "executive" authority, but with clarifying the supervision of inferior courts by superior ones. In the socially and politically fraught circumstances of Reconstruction in the U.S. South, the most serious threats to liberty seemed to arise within the states. Nonetheless, federal courts soon retreated into a deference of a kind that would have made great judges like Hale, Holt, and Mansfield blanch. Federal courts imposed on themselves self-limiting practices in their habeas jurisprudence by defining "jurisdiction" in the narrowest terms possible, and then acting on the assumption that the writ was only to be used to inspect whether another magistrate had jurisdiction over the matter and prisoner in question. Unlike their English forebears, U.S. judges often refused to go inside that jurisdiction to supervise its use, as King's Bench had done when monitoring church or admiralty courts, the imprisonment orders of JPs, the detentions of military officers and husbands, and even the work of the Privy Council on most occasions.[22]

The purpose of examining uses of habeas corpus in the 1860s around the world is not to seek analogies, either among places or across time. The purpose is to see how, as the writ went to work in distinct cultural environments and legal regimes, conflict between two principles persisted. One was the principle of public safety. This generated a persistent logic of detention, a logic by which people, regardless of the many factual circumstances that distinguished them, were gathered together in the same broad category in order to contain them, legally and literally. The other was the most traditional principle of all, the one on which the writ had been made: a principle of judicial supremacy, by which the sighs of individual prisoners might be heard and their prayers answered by an equitable majesty.

Habeas Corpus Bound: The Persistent Logic of Detention

People might be detained by law in many places, for many reasons, in many ways. In the end, a polyglot collection of dominions could not be subjected to one law, however grand were ideas about the prerogative and the sovereign's interest in the subject's liberty that had carried habeas corpus so far. Even in dominions with courts that possessed powers "as fully and amply . . . as the Courts of King's Bench, Common Pleas, and Exchequer, within his majesty's kingdom of England," the logic of detention would grow. Powers given to governors by imperial and local legislation overwhelmed those the once-great English judge had used.[23]

We can trace this logic back to 1689, when members of Parliament first comforted themselves that the use of the language of necessity was appropriate because it was now they, rather than the king's councilors, who spoke it. By passing the first suspension statute, Parliament returned to the Council that which Parliament had denied it by the Star Chamber Act of 1641. This happened as law's imperial movement began in earnest. The holding and transporting of bodies, often overseas, thus became the inverse corollary to habeas corpus: powers given to colonial leaders to imprison by summary conviction or by no conviction at all; powers to detain those suspected on "reasonable" grounds

—or on none at all—based on one's apparent membership in an officially worrisome category.[24] We have already seen how this idea of lumping people together by their outward characteristics had shaped the response to troubles in Canada in the 1790s and the 1830s, and in New Zealand in the 1860s and 1880s. Scores, then hundreds, were sent into exile.

The logic of detention expanded as more people, regardless of their having performed any wrong previously known to law, became subject to forms of detention that barred judicial supervision. By the Westmeath Act of 1871, for instance, the Lord Lieutenant of Ireland was empowered to detain, without trial, anyone suspected of being a member of the Ribbon Society, a group of activists for agrarian reform known as "Ribband men." It directed that "no writ of habeas corpus shall issue" for those detained.[25] A decade later, further detentions without trial or judicial review were made possible by a similar statute; nearly a thousand people were taken.[26]

The application of a classificatory approach to detention was even more expansive in response to thuggee and other allegedly criminal groups in India. Indian legislation in the 1830s had first made apparent membership in such a group, regardless of an individual's actions, the basis on which one might be imprisoned for life or transported to Burma. This approach reached its zenith in the Bengal Criminal Tribes Act of 1871, which empowered local governors to declare as a "criminal tribe" any "gang" or "tribe" "addicted to the systematic commission of nonbailable offences." The governor's declaration alone would be taken as "conclusive proof" of collective guilt, the validity of which "no court of justice shall question." Those deemed to be members of such a "criminal tribe" could then be relocated into "reformatory settlement[s]," their members often having "thug" permanently tattooed on their foreheads.[27] The Andaman Islands, already established as a penal settlement in the wake of the 1857 Uprising, soon gained thousands of exiled settlers or prisoners by this means.[28]

The logic of detention operated repeatedly across the empire's dominions. In New Zealand during the 1860s, hundreds were cast into exile; thousands more joined them during the 1880s. During the Boer War, tens of thousands were herded into camps.[29] In Kenya in the 1950s, the numbers defied imagination, with the logic of detention utterly silencing habeas corpus in response to the popular rising known as Mau Mau. As in New Zealand a century earlier, this was a "land and freedom" movement, concerned with retrieving for Africans lands taken from them by colonial settlers. It was shaped by a prominent ethnic component—most of its adherents were Kikuyu—and driven by a spiritual force, as evidenced in the oath-taking rituals in which huge swathes of the population secretly participated.[30] Rather than resort to martial law, Sir Evelyn Baring's government responded with regulations of a kind that would have been immediately recognizable to governors of the last two centuries, from Canada to Ireland to New Zealand. In Kenya, however, these measures were implemented on a scale that would have left them breathless.

In October 1952, Governor Baring promulgated the first of a string of emergency regulations that operated even beyond the formal end of the emergency in 1960. Finding that "for the purpose of maintaining public order, it is necessary to exercise control over any person," he would henceforth have powers to detain any and all as he deemed fit. Many were the kinds of detainees and forms of their detention, most held according to what would not have satisfied even the summary conviction process that JPs had used so commonly three centuries earlier. Most were detained after "screening," which involved little more than a hooded informer identifying someone as having sworn the Mau Mau oath. Some knew that they could appeal their detention to a special advisory committee, modeled after the British wartime Regulation 18B and staffed by someone with a bit of judicial experience. But these were perfunctory reviews, tainted by fabricated evidence. Of hundreds of thousands held, only a tiny proportion received even these reviews, and no more than 250 were released.[31]

Though habeas corpus was absent during the onslaught, one potential counterweight to these emergency regulations was the European Convention for the Protection of Human Rights, which Britain had signed in 1950. Forced removals of huge portions of the population and detention without trial—even after acquittal—should have been barred according to that agreement. But the Convention's Article 15 contained a suspensive power of the sort that parliamentary and colonial statutes of the nineteenth century had long conveyed to imperial governors. This permitted governments during war or any "public emergency threatening the life of the nation" to "take measures derogating from its obligations" under the Convention, "to the extent strictly required by the exigencies of the situation." Debates among lawyers in the Colonial Office ultimately resolved the potential embarrassment of mass detentions by making further ordinances that seemed to keep the Kenyan policy within the loose bounds set by the Convention's derogation provision. But criticism in Parliament, in the newspapers, and beyond pressed on these practices. The spirit of Granville Sharp lived on in such critics, who railed at mass detentions and invoked habeas corpus to remind those in power what was due to the powerless. Their efforts had little effect. Depending on how one defined detention—whether or not, for instance, one counted forced removals into desolate areas, as well as those put in barbed-wire compounds—the numbers held in Kenya ranged anywhere from 80,000—the official toll—to as many as 1.5 million.[32]

In Kenya in the 1950s, New Zealand in the 1880s, and India in the 1870s, classificatory schemes generated by legislation made by Parliament, colonial assemblies, or governors replaced judgment. Even if the scale of later episodes was much greater, the suspensive logic since 1689 had been the same: to define classes of people—alleged traitors, those taken in North America, Maori squatting at Parihaka, thuggees, Mau Mau—as those who could be treated as dangerous simply by their apparent membership in a group. Crucially, practices by which legislatures empowered governors and other colonial officers to suspend the writ and to generate regulations by which they detained large numbers of people without judicial supervision circled back from the colonies into law at the empire's heart. By passing the Defense of the Realm Acts of 1914, Parliament handed to the king's Council power to "issue regulations for securing the public safety and defense of the realm." The result was an order of Council made the following year, Regulation 14B, by which those deemed to be of "hostile origin or associations" might be interned without further inquiry.[33]

The use of legislation to delegate law-generating authority to the king's Council in Britain had plenty of colonial precedents. We might trace this back at least as far as Pitt's India Act of 1784, by which Lord Cornwallis and his successors began making regulations to cut off the work of India's Supreme Courts starting in the 1790s. During the nineteenth century, this practice was repeated in Quebec, New Zealand, and beyond.[34] That it should ultimately find its way to Britain should have surprised no one. After all, it had started there. Law—its concepts, usages, and personnel—had always moved easily from Westminster, across the empire, and back again. Habeas corpus certainly had; so had the means of its containment.

It was no accident that the most important courtroom test of Regulation 14B should involve a detainee held in an Islington detention center commanded by Sir Frederick Loch Halliday. Halliday was the grandson of a mid-nineteenth-century lieutenant governor of Bengal notable for his vigor during the 1857 Uprising. Sir Frederick himself had served for decades in Bengal, ultimately becoming commissioner of police in Calcutta.[35] Arthur Zadig, a German-born naturalized subject, would use habeas corpus against Halliday to test his detention under 14B during the Great War. The test failed. Zadig remained in detention. Brian Simpson has suggested that his case represented a "watershed between the world of Victorian liberalism and the world of the vigilant state."[36] Perhaps. Or perhaps it simply represented how the vigilant state, perfected in the empire of Victoria and before, had come home, just as Sir Frederick had.

Whether in Quebec in the 1830s, England in the 1910s and 1920s, or Kenya in the 1950s, the purpose of legislation that enabled largely unfettered gubernatorial action was to prevent judges from supervising the use of policies that detained people according to their apparent membership in a labeled group. Officers of the domestic and colonial state pleaded that they would be overburdened if judges required that they look carefully at the circumstances of individuals in order to determine whether each was held according to law. Of course, that was precisely what judges—like Holt—had once done so well, sometimes even with large numbers of prisoners. But now the work of detention had been put into the hands of bureaucrats: keepers of registers who enrolled the names and shipped their bearers off. Habeas corpus, bound by the logic of detention, could do little to slow their work.

Habeas Corpus Unbound: The Persistent Judge

Sometimes judges tried to stop them, even when governors and statutes told them not to. Justice Vallières de Saint-Réal had not flinched in the 1830s, insisting that broad categories of illegality designed by legislation be replaced by judicial review of imprisonment that only he and other judges could provide.

[A] British subject could not otherwise lose his liberty than by the commission of some great crime, and according to the precise dispositions of the law, and one of the most beautiful features of the law of England is that clearness and precision with which it has defined the time, causes, and extent of a legal imprisonment.[37]

Using judicial review with precision required that every individual be jailed on a warrant full of specifics, as English judges had required since the early seventeenth century, "in order that the court, upon a habeas corpus, may judge of their validity, and may, according to circumstances, either discharge or bail or remand the prisoner." He continued: "The greatest public good, the most pressing necessity, in my opinion, is that we should respect the laws."[38] For all the vigor of his words, and for all his efforts to use traditional means to distinguish alleged from actual wrongs, Vallières de Saint-Réal lost, overwhelmed by Quebec's governor and the rule of imperial law. Was the judge, who had made the writ circa 1605, gone?

In 2001, the U.S. Supreme Court suggested that it should interpret the U.S. Constitution's Suspension Clause, and thus the use of habeas corpus, "at the absolute minimum . . . 'as it existed in 1789.'"[39] As a matter of American jurisprudence, this might make sense, so long as this requirement is not taken to rest on a claim about history. But it does. Underlying the proposed standard is condescension: a belief that during later epochs, including our own, habeas corpus has more nearly reached its ideal form. That presumption relies on the oldest of Anglo-American narratives, one so deeply engrained—as the thinking of an often and easily cited figure like Dicey reveals—that we are unaware of how it obscures our view of the past and of how it guides our thoughts and actions in the present. It is a story in which the life of habeas corpus—thus the life of liberty, we insist—is assumed to have followed a nearly consistent upward path.

But the writ's vigor may have peaked in the 1780s. As we have seen, many factors point to the 1790s as years when a major turning in law's relationship to liberty began. If we value the subject's liberty—as did Edward Coke, Matthew Hale, John Lilburne, Granville Sharp, and Joseph-Rémi Vallières de Saint-Réal—and if we hope that habeas corpus might be its palladium, we may find that 1789 was no minimum at all.

At Westminster, Mansfield retired in late 1786, to be replaced by Kenyon, whose jurisprudence in family law suggested his more circumscribed sense of judicial self. War with France, rebellion in Ireland, and threatened dislocations across the empire in the 1790s and beyond would be the greatest forces altering the legal environment in which judges worked, or perhaps did not work. The 1790s would mark the start of a legislative onslaught on liberties of every kind, a unified assault against which the writ proved almost powerless. Statutes passed then, including the Indemnity Act of 1801 and the various measures targeting Ireland in the same years, would serve as models for the many practices used to maintain quiet, if not liberty, across law's empire during the nineteenth century and beyond.

Statute bound the hands of judges. Some struggled. Vallières de Saint-Réal failed. Others arguably did better. In Australia, Pedder and Forbes celebrated the prerogative that empowered them to do all that their predecessors had done. Yet even Forbes, in his practice, moved away from the ideas that once energized the writ, seeing himself as little more than a policeman of self-evidently fixed jurisdictional boundaries, rather than as the judge of behavior within those bounds. Forbes's and Pedder's voices were faint echoes of the booming voices of their predecessors. Perhaps the writ had never been greater than when Mansfield, Holt, Hale, Bacon, or Fleming used it, keenly aware as each was that when he did so, he used his king's or queen's prerogative and spoke in his or her voice.

In India, initially confident judges who proclaimed their use of habeas corpus by common law and by the prerogative in the 1770s were reined in during the 1780s and after by the demands of the East India Company. Parliament was the Company's partner in this work. In Quebec, the Habeas Corpus Act would be proclaimed by the governor, only to be suspended in the 1790s in terms more severe than those used in England. Americans, struggling as they created a new nation, began to suspend the writ almost immediately. When they wrote their Constitution, Americans introduced habeas corpus by negative implication, then compounded confusion with the 1789 Judiciary Act's awkward language conferring powers on federal judges to use the writ.[40] Chief Justice John Marshall would make bold pronouncements in 1807—in the case of accused conspirator Dr. Justus Erich Bollman—about the meaning of the act and of a persistent common law writ in the United States. But confusion about what U.S. law took from English and imperial ideas and practices would persist.[41] Looking across the whole of law's empire, the narrative we ought to tell is perhaps neither as comforting nor as inspiring as we might like it to be.

The king's power may not be where we expected to begin the story of what we have always liked to call "the Great Writ of Liberty." And we may have ended in a place that we like little better. Beginning with royal power, and ending with a power whose logic is the detention of people on a scale that defies judiciousness, is discomfiting. But this is not to say that habeas corpus has not been a great writ. The writ did its most effective work in the supervision of other jurisdictions during the seventeenth and eighteenth centuries. Even after that, habeas corpus has had its moments of vigor. John Anderson learned what it could do, just as James Somerset, Mrs. Lister, Margaret Symonds, and so many others did in the centuries before him.

For all the writ's triumphs on behalf of such prisoners, perhaps the original idea of habeas corpus—*that* the judge may judge of all prisoners, held by anyone, anywhere—has been more powerful outside of courtrooms than inside them. John Lilburne, Granville Sharp, and others were often disappointed in the liberating ambitions they pursued at law. In cases like theirs, and so often since, the idea of habeas corpus has continued to influence public debate, where it has been invoked almost poetically as those who have been disappointed have encouraged others to honor the palladium again.

The history of habeas corpus traces an ongoing tension between the logic of detention and the persistent judge: between what is in our law and what we would like to be in it. In law's empire, that tension has tightened and relaxed, again and again. The exigencies of colonial rule, the technologies of detention, and the instabilities of postcolonial societies have long conspired together to generate the "necessities" by which even those who have trumpeted the writ's virtues have comforted themselves as they bound the judge and muffled the prisoner's sighs. Perhaps, by understanding this history better, we will be able to hear those sighs again.

Appendix: A Survey of Habeas Corpus Use 1500–1800

Supporting much of the analysis in this book is a survey of all uses of the writ of habeas corpus *ad subjiciendum* issuing from the court of King's Bench, every fourth year from 1502 to 1798, inclusive. This survey yielded information on 2,757 individual prisoners that was then gathered into a database for analysis.[1] Doing this helps us detect large-scale patterns of use, and permits correlating outcomes to different kinds of variables, especially the wrongs for which prisoners were held and the jurisdictions that ordered confinement. Here we examine the basic findings from this survey after a brief examination of the archives explored and the methods used in making it.

Survey Methods and the King's Bench Archive

Files, rolls, and rulebooks were examined fully for every fourth year, beginning with 1502 and continuing to 1798. In addition, the Michaelmas term before and the Hilary term following each survey year were studied to ensure that no writs actually issued in the survey year would be missed. For purposes of inclusion, the writ's *teste* date, not its return date, has been used to determine whether a writ falls within the survey year. Thus a writ *teste* in November 1601 but returned in Hilary 1602 would not be included in the survey, whereas a writ issued in November 1602 but returned in Hilary 1603 would be included. In cases where the *teste* date is unknown, the term of return has been used to determine inclusion or exclusion from the survey. Owing to problems in record quality or survival, the following years in the quadrennial series almost certainly contain incomplete information: 1510, 1518, 1534, 1654, 1658, 1674, 1678, and 1686.

Three classes of records from the Crown Side of King's Bench, held in the National Archives in London (Kew), have been studied to generate most of the information aggregated in the survey.

Recorda Files (KB145 [to 1689] and KB16 [post 1689], with strays in KB11 and KB32). These are bundles, often quite large, of individual parchment documents held together by a thong, a long leather cord strung through a hole punched in each item as it arrived in the Crown Office of King's Bench. These bundles—one for each regnal year—contain writs and other instruments of process on the Crown Side, including writs of *excommunicato capiendo,* informations in the nature of quo warranto, and writs of mandamus and certiorari, as well as habeas corpus and returns to them. In the sixteenth century, such returns tended to be brief and could usually be written on the reverse of the writ. As returns lengthened, however, especially beginning in the early seventeenth century, they were increasingly written on a separate parchment leaf attached to the writ. After 1679, the verso of the writ also contains a note about whether the writ issued by common law or according to the terms of the Habeas Corpus Act. Results of the judges' decisions were usually written in the left margin of the return, or in earlier periods, in the left margin or top of the writ. The recorda files are the only source for writs issuing or returned during vacation and for those returned to a justice in chambers, since the rulebooks and controlment rolls were not maintained out of term or in chambers.

Controlment Rolls (KB29). The controlment rolls are rolls of parchment organized by regnal year and term. The recorda portion of the roll, in which were enrolled many writs of habeas corpus and their returns, may usually be found at the end of each term's entries. During most of the sixteenth century, the text of most writs and their returns were enrolled in full. The judgment on the writ was usually entered in the left margin. By the end of the sixteenth century, the texts of the writs were entered less often. During the seventeenth century, the reliability of the controlment rolls as guides to what may be found in the recorda files declined. Often, only a précis of the return, rather than a full transcript, was enrolled. Increasingly, they also omitted the judgment. While the quality of the rolls improved in the early Restoration, by 1680 they only listed the names of those using habeas corpus, with no other information. By the mid-1690s, even these lists disappeared from the controlment rolls.

Crown Side Rule and Order Books (KB21). The Crown Side rule and order books, which commence in 1589, were organized by regnal year and term, then by day of sitting, using festal rather than modern calendar dates. These contain entries of rules and orders made from the bench in all matters heard on the Crown Side. They reveal how and when writs issued. They often include information about outcomes absent from the recorda files or controlment rolls, especially when the outcome involved a settlement: for instance, when the writ concerned a child's custody. In cases of prisoners bailed on habeas corpus—as noted on the filed writ or in the controlment roll—we often find in the rulebooks further orders concerning the bailed prisoner's appearance(s) on a recognizance, and in many cases, of discharge from bail. Most important, the rulebooks allow us to watch the court's use of affidavits and of attachments and other court process to enforce the return of writs. They also show how habeas was sometimes used with other devices: for instance, with writs of certiorari to bring up a record of indictment along with the body of a prisoner. The rulebooks are thus critical for understanding most aspects of court process that are not otherwise observable in the writ files, rolls, or case reports.

Most information about the writs in the survey has been obtained by triangulating information from these three series of records. In some periods, full information is available in the controlment rolls while the quality of the notes made in the rulebooks was low; in other periods, the reverse was true. Where necessary—because information is missing owing to clerical omission or damage—use has been made of information found elsewhere. Such information can sometimes be found minuted on the outside of an affidavit, in the reports, or in letters or diaries: for instance, the diary of Narcisus Luttrell is full of details on proceedings in King's Bench during the late seventeenth century.[2] Admiralty archives (TNA, ADM) provide information in impressment cases.

The following information was gathered into the database: dates of issuance, return, and other orders; the clerks writing and the justices *testing* the writs; the jurisdiction making an imprisonment order; the cause of imprisonment; and results. This information was further linked to information found in manuscript and printed reports of cases, affidavits, and other sources. Information found in reports must be used with care: the records themselves often reveal the reports to be inaccurate or incomplete in critical ways. For instance, since most reports cover only one court hearing, reports of cases heard on multiple occasions are usually incomplete, especially regarding the case's final disposition.

The unit of measure is the prisoner, not the writ. Some prisoners used multiple writs. And many writs contained multiple prisoners, especially in the sixteenth and early seventeenth centuries, when dozens might be named in a single writ, though their review on habeas corpus often produced different results. Over time, fewer writs issued for multiple prisoners, though the practice continued, especially for impressed sailors.

In total, information was compiled for 4,869 distinct users of the writ, including the 2,757 in the survey years.

Total Usage and Rates of Release for Prisoners Using Habeas Corpus

More than 11,000 prisoners or detainees of other kinds used habeas corpus between 1500 and 1800. Across three centuries, 53 percent of all those who used the writ were released. Given variable record quality, and because most writs used by impressed sailors in the eighteenth century were not returned—most such sailors were simply dismissed from service without contest—the actual numbers of users and of those released may have been much greater. The table on page 323 shows the numbers using the writ—in the quadrennial survey years only—grouped in twenty-year bands. When discussing numbers in any given period, one can generally multiply the table numbers by four to get not only a rough sense of total activity in that period, but also a general idea of how the writ was used more or less intensively over time.

Four periods deserve comment, because large swings from average annual numbers of writs issued (37 per year, 1500–1800) also mark

Total number of prisoners using habeas corpus, in quadrennial survey years, 1500–1800, grouped into two-decade periods

Period	Number
1500–1520	205
1520–1540	107
1540–1560	265
1560–1580	155
1580–1600	129
1600–1620	149
1620–1640	249
1640–1660	118
1660–1680	174
1680–1700	453
1700–1720	160
1720–1740	106
1740–1760	72
1760–1780	105
1780–1800	310

large swings in release rates and in the objects of judicial oversight according to the wrongs alleged or the officer ordering imprisonment. These coterminous swings suggest causation as well as correlation, causation that usually takes us to who led the court during any given period.

The first of these periods is the mid-sixteenth century, where the large bump in usage is explained entirely by two writs used to bring 97 accused rebels to trial in 1554. Here the writ did nothing more than serve its traditional purpose as an aid to criminal process. The second period, 1620–1640, is more interesting. This peak is explained in large part by the 81 people imprisoned in 1622, half of whom (40) were imprisoned for religious offences, especially Catholic recusants: those who refused to attend their parish churches or to receive the Eucharist according to the rites of the official church. The release rate for 1622 was roughly three-quarters for all users as well as for those imprisoned for reasons of religion (70% and 76%, respectively). The years 1634 and 1638 also had higher than average activity, reflecting more intensive use of habeas corpus to review imprisonment for regulatory wrongs defined by statute and for other misdemeanors (53 prisoners, of 109 total, were jailed for such wrongs in those two years). Only one-third of these 53 prisoners were discharged or bailed from imprisonment for such wrongs, a sharply lower rate of dismissal, on average, than for those imprisoned for the same wrongs in other periods. This reflects the much more restrictive view of the writ taken by King's Bench between the accession of Charles I and the outbreak of the Civil War (1625–1642). This restrictive view is also evident in the decline in release rates between the survey years 1622 and 1626 (70% and 7%, respectively). Sir Ranulph Crewe was appointed to replace Sir James Ley as chief justice in 1625, a change reflected in these numbers. After Crewe was himself removed at the end of 1626, release rates under the next chief justice, Sir Nicholas Hyde, returned to the three-century average of 53%. But in general, release rates across Charles I's reign remained below average until the Civil War began.

The third spike, 1680–1700, indicates the work of Sir John Holt after 1689, when the cases of hundreds arrested on political charges were reviewed. In the 1690s, the court dismissed 79–83% of all prisoners, and roughly similar proportions even of those the government considered most dangerous. Perhaps more interesting is the fact that the survey years 1682 and 1686 also saw higher than average total usage (71 and 83 prisoners, respectively) and higher than average release rates (63% and 69%, respectively), despite the common view in the centuries since that the judiciary then were toadies of Charles II and James II. Because the recorda files are in poor condition for 1682 and 1686, it is difficult to learn more about the circumstances of imprisonment in many of these cases. Such information that does exist—often only the result—comes from bare lists of names of prisoners in the controlment rolls and from orders in the rulebooks.

The final increase considered here appears at the end of the eighteenth century. The spike is composed entirely of impressed sailors, and is especially dramatic in the survey year near the end of the American war (1782) and the survey year early in the French wars (1794). Again, change in use correlates with change in outcomes and court leadership. This increased resort of sailors to the writ contributed to high rates of release in 1782 and 1786 (81% and 88%, respectively), rates that might be found to be even higher if we had full information on all impressment writs. In the survey year 1778, all 41 detainees or prisoners using habeas corpus were released. After Mansfield's departure from the bench, in 1788, the results once again changed dramatically, with release rates in the 1790s ranging from 31% to 38%.

Figure 1 shows the rates of bail or discharge of prisoners or other detainees using habeas corpus in the same twenty-year bands used in the earlier table. These release rates show a correlation, though not a perfect one, with periods of greater total habeas usage. As the previous discussion suggests, only by looking carefully into the wrongs and jurisdictions monitored in periods of higher-than-average release rates can we make sense of what was happening. Having done that, we can then return to release rates to sharpen our explanation of fluctuations in them.

Wrongs Monitored

Figure 2 shows the varying proportions of different kinds of wrongs alleged against all prisoners who used habeas corpus from 1500 to 1800. Of the 2,757 total, information about the alleged wrong is missing for

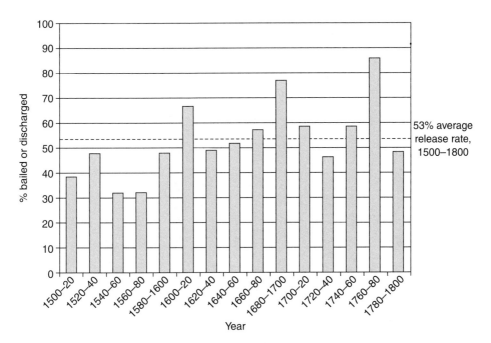

Figure 1. Release rates for those using habeas corpus. Proportion released in survey years of all prisoners with a known result.

436 owing to gaps in the record. Significantly, this number does not include those returns that were clearly complete but which did not specify a wrong: for instance, those that returned that the accused had been imprisoned "by special command," or "until further order," without naming any legal wrong. For the purposes of aggregating the types of wrongs reported in returns to writs of habeas corpus, the following categories were created for use in the database.

Unspecified. There were 158 prisoners that had writs returned with no information about the allegation of wrong that was normally reported to justify imprisonment. A plurality of such orders (70) were made by justices of the peace or by unnamed officers who were most likely JPs, judging from other information in those orders. The release rate for prisoners whose returns specified no wrong, from 1500 to 1800,

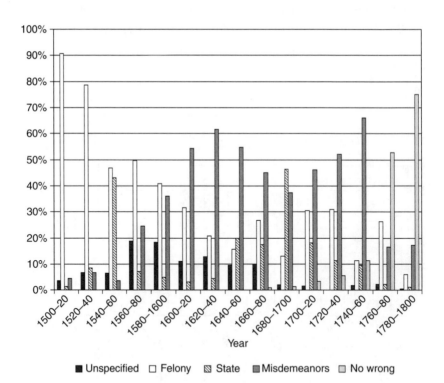

Figure 2. Changing varieties of wrong monitored by habeas corpus. Proportion of prisoners using habeas corpus in survey years, by type of alleged wrong.

was 60%. This rate rose consistently, from 50% in the sixteenth century—when the largest number of returns not specifying a wrong were made—to three-quarters by the late seventeenth century, and to 100% in the eighteenth century. Thus as the number of such returns declined, the court tended to judge ever more strictly those that continued to appear without specifying a wrong to justify imprisonment.

Felony. A total of 798 accused felons used the writ. Most such returns concerned murder and other wrongful deaths, as well as theft, robbery, and burglary. Rape, arson, piracy, witchcraft, and accessory to felony appear only rarely. Of these 798 prisoners, 689 had been committed by justices of the peace or another unnamed officer, presumably a JP, judging from the local contexts of the order. Another 75 were committed by a justice of King's Bench or Common Pleas, usually at assizes. The remainder were imprisoned by privy councilors or specially commissioned authorities. From 1500 to 1800, release rates for accused felons averaged 47%. Here, too, release rates gradually climbed as the number of accused felons reviewed by habeas corpus fell; release rates reached 60% by 1660, and 70% by the opening of the eighteenth century. As the number of cases reviewed declined—in cases of unspecified wrongs, because fewer such orders were made, and in cases of felony, because fewer were tested—the rate of release for those who did use the writ increased.

State Wrongs. There were 374 prisoners ordered held for wrongs against the state, including high treason, coining, misprision of treason (countenancing a treasonous act, without direct involvement), treasonable practices, and seditious libel. Release rates for those accused of crimes against the state averaged 48% across three centuries. Few were released prior to 1640. For the remainder of the seventeenth century, however, the release rate for such prisoners climbed above 60%, peaking at over 80% in the years immediately after the Revolution of 1688 and throughout the 1690s.

Misdemeanors. A total of 712 prisoners had been jailed for misdemeanors, including sexual wrongs (adultery, fornication, bigamy, incest, and bawdry); wrongs against justice (for example, perjury, contempt of court); religious offences (recusancy, or refusing to attend services of the Church of England; attending conventicles, that is, religious gatherings outside of the Church of England; violation of the Five Mile and Test Acts, which restricted the movement and preaching of dissenting ministers and set a religious test to hold public office, respectively; and refusal to pay tithes); as well as other wrongs defined by statute (bastardy, vagrancy, poaching, forcible entry, and violations of statutes of sewers, ale, firearms, and so on). Release for these minor wrongs averaged 57% between 1500 and 1800. Release rates were more generous between 1580 and 1620, as the number of such cases rose (peaking at 72% released in 1600–1620), after which release rates for misdemeanor generally fell. As the number of such cases declined in the eighteenth century, so did release rates. By the second half of the eighteenth century, the proportion of those bailed or discharged on misdemeanor charges had fallen to one-third.

No Wrong. There were 279 detainees' writs returned with no allegation of wrong. Instead they contained other explanations of detention, including "lunacy," family custody disputes, and impressment. Of these detainees for whom results are known, 96% were released. The few who were not released were sailors found to have been impressed according to law.

One final issue concerns the stage in the legal process during which the writ was used for both felony and misdemeanors: namely, whether the writ was employed before or after conviction. When summary convictions are included in this analysis—the means by which most misdemeanants were convicted—postconviction writs peaked in the early to middle part of the seventeenth century, as overall use of habeas corpus for misdemeanors peaked. For the period 1600 to 1650, nearly one-third (31%) of writs issued after conviction. In general, the postconviction release rate was 46%.

Jurisdictions Monitored

Of 2,757 prisoners, information about the magistrate who ordered imprisonment is missing for 624, owing to writ damage or other record loss. Another 20 were known to have been jailed by order of Parliament and 260 were jailed by judges of the central courts, usually in felony process at assizes. Release rates were consistently below average in both instances. Information on the remaining 1,853 prisoners has been organized into five groups to facilitate further analysis; see Figure 3.

Unspecified.   Fully legible returns for 346 prisoners did not specify who ordered imprisonment. Such vagueness in returns about the tribunal or officer who detained someone decreased in the early seventeenth century, in a manner similar to, but slightly in advance of, the increase in detail in returns concerning the charge against prisoners. The vast majority of returns that did not name the jailing authority reported felony, and in all likelihood concerned imprisonment orders by JPs who neglected to identify themselves as such. In the sixteenth century, there was little indication that lack of specificity on this score was seen as a problem by the justices in King's Bench, because such writs were often used simply to move accused criminals into King's Bench for trial.

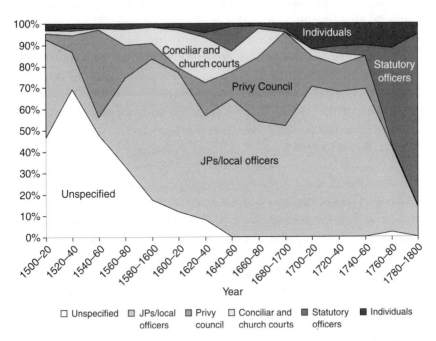

Figure 3. Varying jurisdictional oversight by habeas corpus. Proportional usage, in survey years, according to type of authority ordering imprisonment or detention.

Justices of the Peace and Other Local Officers.   Of 778 prisoners in this category, 561 had been jailed by order of one or more JPs outside of sessions, and another 94 by JPs in quarter sessions. The remainder were
jailed by sheriffs, bailiffs, and constables. Most were held for felony or
misdemeanor, including statutory wrongs such as those concerned
with regulating economic or religious life. Rates of release from 1500
to 1800 for those jailed by JPs ran slightly ahead of average, at 59%.
Rates of release for those jailed by JPs first peaked in the period 1592
to 1613 (67%), and again from 1660 to 1710 (ranging from 64%, in
1660–1680, to 81% over the next three decades). After Sir John Holt's
death in 1710, the numbers of those imprisoned by JPs whose cases
were examined on habeas corpus fell sharply. So did release rates (the
rate for 1710–1756 was 57%). This trend marked a decline in interest
in inspecting the work of JPs, as the total number of writs issued fell in
the mid eighteenth century.

Privy Council.   A total of 301 people were imprisoned by royal officers
in the survey years, including 192 jailed by Privy Council order, and another 79 by order of one of the secretaries of state. The remainder
were imprisoned by order of other major royal officers, for instance,
the chamberlain of the household or the lord treasurer. Considering
only those imprisoned by the Council or by one or more of its members, release rates were always low (averaging below 20%) until the
Civil Wars of the 1640s. Release rates for such prisoners then rose
steadily from the period 1640–1660 (60% released) to a peak in the
1680–1700 period (85%).

Conciliar and Church Courts.   Ninety-two prisoners are found here, including 45 committed by church courts. Of these, 25 were jailed by di-
ocesan and archidiaconal courts, and 20 by the High Commission before its abolition in 1641. Twelve more were committed by courts of
Admiralty, and the remaining 35 by conciliar courts: six by a palatine
or duchy court; five by the Council of the North and nine by the Council in the Marches of Wales; ten by Requests; four by Star Chamber;
and one by the Court of Wards.

Others Commissioned by Statute.   No fewer than 256 prisoners were
jailed by commissioners of sewers or bankrupts or by other statutory

commissioners, including special commissions created in the 1640s: for instance, those concerned with the militia, military accounts, or reforming the ministry. By far the largest group of detainees held according to special statutes was that of impressed sailors, which explains the bulge in this category beginning in the 1740–1760 period.

Individuals. Eighty people detained by a named individual, but without any office or other authority indicated, are grouped here. In the period before the mid-seventeenth century, most of these were probably people acting in an official capacity, which the return failed to specify. After 1670, these cases overwhelmingly involve family custody issues or other detentions made by individuals acting in a nonofficial capacity.

Scanning patterns of varying intensity of supervision of these different jurisdictions, some important general patterns appear. Most evident is the overwhelming importance of habeas as an instrument for monitoring the work of local justice, especially in the period from 1600 to the mid eighteenth century. Second, imprisonment orders by the Privy Council or other royal officers comprise much less activity than most accounts of the writ imply by their focus on conciliar orders. Supervision of conciliar orders peaked not in the early seventeenth century, but at century's end, especially in the decade following the Revolution of 1688. This usage by Chief Justice Sir John Holt was also marked by very high rates of release. Finally, the majority of uses of habeas corpus concerned impressment or family custody matters by the second half of the eighteenth century, suggesting that the writ's use as an instrument in felony process—or even as the means for supervising imprisonment for regulatory offences or other misdemeanors—had faded. This may be accounted for, in part, by the increased use of certiorari in the eighteenth century to monitor work performed by JPs.

The Difference a Justice Makes

By dividing the three centuries of the survey into units bounded by the careers of particular chief justices rather than into arbitrary units of twenty years, we can identify correlations between the leadership of certain justices and variations in the intensity of oversight according to wrong or jurisdiction. Figure 4 plots release rates grouped into the careers of chief justices. This shows peaks during the careers of five of them: Popham and Fleming; Bacon; Holt; and Mansfield. Bacon, though a puisne justice (a justice other than the chief justice), is included here since then Chief Justice Sir Robert Heath remained with the king during the Civil War, while Bacon presided alone in King's Bench in Westminster Hall.

The figure suggests the high degree of variation in release rates among the different justices, and shows just how much individual judicial temperament mattered not only to the purposes the writ served—changes in the wrongs and jurisdictions supervised—but also to outcomes. This correlation is made obvious by the sharp change immediately after the departure from the bench of each of these justices. Thus while Sir Thomas Fleming still presided in 1610, 95% of those who

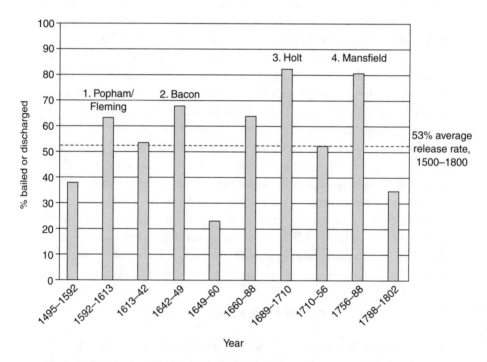

Figure 4. Four ages of habeas corpus. Release rates, in survey years, grouped by chief justices.

used the writ were released, but in 1614, when Sir Edward Coke led the court, only 36% were so fortunate.[3] Likewise, release rates between 1646 and 1650, after Bacon left the court upon the king's execution in early 1649, fell by half: from two-thirds to one-third.[4] Sir John Holt died in March 1710. If we take the survey year before that (1706) and compare it to the survey year following (1714), we find a decline from 78% to 40% in release orders among those using the writ once his successor, Sir Thomas Parker, took the helm. Finally, between 1786—the last survey year in which Lord Mansfield led King's Bench—and 1790, by which time Sir Lloyd Kenyon had taken charge, release rates fell from 88% to 31%, and persisted near that rate for the remainder of the 1790s.

Notes

Abbreviations

Baker, *Introduction*	J. H. Baker, *An Introduction to English Legal History,* 4th ed. (London, 2002)
Baker, *Laws*	J. H. Baker, *The Oxford History of the Laws of England,* vol. 6: *1483–1558* (Oxford, 2003)
BL	British Library, London
Bod.	Bodleian Library, Oxford
CD 1621	Wallace Notestein et al., eds. *Commons Debates, 1621* (New Haven, 1935)
CD 1628	Robert C. Johnson et al., eds., *Commons Debates, 1628* (New Haven, 1977–1983)
CSPC	*Calendar of State Papers, Colonial Series* (London)
CSPD	*Calendar of State Papers, Domestic Series* (London)
CUL	Cambridge University Library
Dyer Reports	J. H. Baker, ed., *Reports from the Lost Notebooks of Sir James Dyer,* Selden Society, 109–110 (1994–1995)
ER	*The English Reports* (1907–1909; Abingdon, 1979–1986): references are by reporter's name and page number, according to traditional usage, and by volume and page number in the modern series of reports
GI	Gray's Inn
Grey, *Debates*	Anchitell Grey, *Debates of the House of Commons, from the Year 1667 to the Year 1694* (London, 1763)

Hale's Prerogatives	D. E. C. Yale, ed., *Sir Matthew Hale's The Prerogatives of the King*, Selden Society, 92 (London, 1976)
HLS	Harvard Law School
LI	Lincoln's Inn
ODNB	*Oxford Dictionary of National Biography* (Oxford, 2004)
Parl. Hist.	*The Parliamentary History of England* (London, 1811–1816)
Spelman Reports	J. H. Baker, ed., *The Reports of Sir John Spelman*, Selden Society, 93–94 (1976–1977)
ST	T. B. Howell, *A Complete Collection of State Trials* (London, 1809–1816)
TNA	The National Archives, London (formerly the Public Record Office)
YLS	Yale Law School

Introduction

1. See 3 Bulstrode 109, 81 *ER* 94 (Codd, 1615). Festus's words were sometimes invoked directly in court, for instance, in 1607, by Nicholas Fuller, in his arguments on behalf of the habeas corpus for Thomas Ladd et al.: *The Argument of Master Nicholas Fuller, in the Case of Thomas Lad . . .* (1607), 12. Here, Fuller attributes this idea to Felix, Festus's predecessor (at Acts 23:35). See also YLS, GR29.18, f. 220.

2. John Lilburne, *The Prisoners Mournfull Cry, against the Iudges of the Kings Bench; or, An Epistle Writ by Lievt. Col. John Lilburne, Prisoner in the Tower of London* (1648), 3. Lilburne's subtitle—"an epistle"—was no accidental Pauline reference.

3. The earliest reference to the "great writ of English Liberty" I have found is in Giles Jacob, *A New Law-Dictionary* (1729), s.v. habeas corpus.

4. For a thoughtful critique of this "mythology," see David Clark and Gerard McCoy, *The Most Fundamental Legal Right: Habeas Corpus in the Commonwealth* (Oxford, 2000), chapter 2, especially 35–36. For more on earlier writing on the writ's history, see Chapter 1.

5. Legal history, like the history of political thought, might do well to heed Quentin Skinner's reminder that "one of the present values of the past is as a repository of values we no longer endorse, of questions we no longer ask." See *Liberty before Liberalism* (Cambridge, 1998), 112. As Skinner eloquently puts it, we must reject the "depressingly philistine failure to appreciate what we can hope to learn about ourselves from a serious study of unfamiliar modes of thought. . . . [T]he 'relevance' of such studies lies in their capacity to help us stand back

from our own assumptions and systems of belief, and thereby to situate ourselves in relation to other and very different forms of life." Skinner, *Regarding Method,* vol. 1 of *Visions of Politics* (Cambridge, 2002), 125.

6. This is not the place for a full discussion of the many forms of "originalism." But many people across the jurisprudential-political spectrum contend that claims about the past, in one form or another, should shape how we understand many problems before U.S. courts, especially those that concern how we read language in the Constitution. This debate has focused on methodological problems—for instance, how to open past linguistic uses to critical understanding—and less concerned with the quality and range of sources consulted, especially of English ones. Insofar as American law turns to English law prior to 1789, it has generally done so by resorting to some of the sources that historians of the period find most dubious. For a thoughtful discussion of how to expand American law's attempts to recover a useable English legal past, see Bernadette Meyler, "Towards a Common Law Originalism," *Stanford Law Review* 59 (2006–2007): 551–600. For a brief discussion of source problems, see Paul D. Halliday and G. Edward White, "The Suspension Clause: English Text, Imperial Contexts, and American Implications," *Virginia Law Review* 94 (2008): 588–593.

7. While "texts are acts," Quentin Skinner helpfully adds that "acts are in turn texts: they embody intersubjective meanings that we can hope to read off." Skinner, *Regarding Method,* 120.

8. For discussion of problems inherent in English reports, especially printed ones, see J. H. Baker, "Why the History of English Law Has Not Been Finished," *Cambridge Law Journal* 59 (2000): 62–84, and A. W. Brian Simpson, *Leading Cases in the Common Law* (Oxford, 1995), especially 10–12.

9. Though written nearly eighty years ago, Herbert Butterfield's elegant critique of this approach to the Anglo-American past remains as trenchant now as then: see his *The Whig Interpretation of History* (New York, 1931).

1. The Jailer Jailed

1. Witherley's story has been constructed from reports in HLS, 118, ff. 57–58 and HLS, 1180, ff. 68v.–70, and from the record in TNA, KB21/2/166v.; KB21/3/24–32v., passim; and KB29/246/22–23. Hunnyngs was deputy porter of the Porter's Lodge in Ludlow. At the same time, habeas issued to Rowland Scudamore, the porter, perhaps owing to doubt as to who had legal custody. Sometime during the vacation after

Michaelmas term, the court sent an alias writ, requiring a return early in Hilary term, which started in January, with a subpoena of £20. No record survives of when or on what terms Witherley was released, though orders of 12 February 1605 suggest that he was then free: TNA, KB21/3/32v.

2. *CSPD* 1603–1610, 181; Historical Manuscripts Commission, *Report on the Salisbury (Cecil) Manuscripts* (London, 1976), vol. 24, p. 51.

3. That the king participated in resolving the dispute in favor of King's Bench is suggested by a later report, in Henry Rolle, *Un Abridgment des Plusieurs Cases et Resolutions del Common Ley* . . . (1668), s.v. "habeas corpus," 2d pagination, 69. One of the Welsh Council's main supporters was Solicitor General Sir Francis Bacon. Bacon and Coke disliked each other, having competed for advancement. On Coke, Bacon, Ellesmere, and the ways in which jurisdictional disputes were entangled in factional politics, see Louis A. Knafla, *Law and Politics in Jacobean England: The Tracts of Lord Chancellor Ellesmere* (Cambridge, Eng., 1977), 145–148; Allen D. Boyer, *Sir Edward Coke and the Elizabethan Age* (Stanford, 2003), 243–254; and James Spedding et al., eds., *The Works of Francis Bacon* (London, 1879), vol. 7, pp. 569–611. More generally, see Penry Williams, *The Council in the Marches of Wales under Elizabeth I* (Cardiff, 1958), 298–306. On the Council in the Marches in this period, see Christopher W. Brooks, *Law, Politics, and Society in Early Modern England* (Cambridge, Eng., 2008), 126–128.

4. The report uses passive language, noting simply that Coke "was present in the court when the case was moved": HLS, 118, f. 57.

5. HLS, 1180, f. 69-v. Witherley's case ran simultaneously with two others from the Welsh Council. These resulted in commands to the Council's jailer to return writs, all of which commands were initially ignored, but later obeyed. These are the cases of John Farley and Nicholas Rowles: TNA, KB21/2/166 and KB/21/3/21–63v., passim. Hunnyngs had been released by Trinity term of 1605. The experience apparently humbled him, since he made returns in these subsequent cases.

6. TNA, KB29/246/23.

7. On declining litigation in the Council of Wales, see Penry Williams, "The Activity of the Council in the Marches under the Early Stuarts," *Welsh History Review* 1 (1960–1963): 133–160.

8. J. C. Holt, *Magna Carta* (Cambridge, Eng., 1965), chapters 5 and 6, and Ralph V. Turner, *Magna Carta through the Ages* (Harlow, 2003), chapters 2 and 3.

9. Turner, *Magna Carta*, 226–228.

10. Faith Thompson, *Magna Carta: Its Role in the Making of the English Constitution, 1300–1629* (Minneapolis, 1948), chapter 4.

11. Turner, *Magna Carta,* 231.

12. On the numbering of clauses, see ibid., 86–88. On being the first in the "notional canon of statutes," see Baker, *Introduction,* 205.

13. Daniel Meador, *Habeas Corpus and Magna Carta* (Charlottesville, 1966), 13–24. William McKechnie long ago noted that the "unthinking adulation [of Magna Carta] has not been entirely confined to popular writers; judges and institutional authors, even Sir Edward Coke himself, have too often lost the faculty of critical and exact scholarship when confronted with the virtues of the Great Charter." See McKechnie, *Magna Carta: A Commentary on the Great Charter of King John* (Glasgow, 1905), 156. William F. Duker rightly omits Magna Carta from his discussion of medieval antecedents, first mentioning it when considering the controversies of 1627–1628: see his *A Constitutional History of Habeas Corpus* (Westport, 1980), 45. So, too, does R. J. Sharpe in his *The Law of Habeas Corpus,* 2d ed. (Oxford, 1989), 10–11.

14. The writ's origin "is lost in obscurity," concluded Joshua Scholefield and Gerard R. Hill in their *Appeals from Justices, Including Appeals to Sessions* (London, 1902), 267.

15. For example, see Rollin C. Hurd, *A Treatise on the Right of Personal Liberty and on the Writ of Habeas Corpus,* 2d ed. (Albany, 1876), 66–74; and William S. Church, *A Treatise on the Writ of Habeas Corpus,* 2d ed. (San Francisco, 1893), 3–4.

16. Duker, *Habeas Corpus,* 12, 62, and 63.

17. Herbert Butterfield, *The Whig Interpretation of History* (New York, 1965), 12. He dismissed such work as a "short cut" through complexity (22).

18. John Kenyon, *The History Men: The Historical Profession in England since the Renaissance* (Pittsburgh, 1984), 68–114. Looking back on the generation before him, Edward Jenks lambasted those who thought "vague flourishes about ancient liberties are supposed to account for [the writ's] existence. It would almost seem as though it were indiscreet to inquire too closely into the origin of this sacred instrument." Jenks, "The Story of the Habeas Corpus," *Law Quarterly Review* 18 (1902): 64.

19. Examples of such devices are given by Maxwell Cohen in "Some Considerations on the Origins of Habeas Corpus," *Canadian Bar Review* 16 (1938): 117.

20. Elsa de Haas, *Antiquities of Bail: Origin and Historical Development in Criminal Cases to the Year 1275* (New York, 1940), chapters 3 and 4. For more on problems of abuse, or confusion, in using shrieval powers, see Wil-

liam F. Duker, "The Right to Bail: A Historical Inquiry," *Albany Law Review* 42 (1977): 43–58. See also Jenks, "Story of Habeas Corpus," 66–67; and Cohen, "Origins of Habeas Corpus," 96–102. For a brief review, see Sharpe, *Habeas Corpus,* 1–4.

21. F. Solly-Flood, "My Abridged History of the Writ of Habeas Corpus" (manuscript treatise of 1886–1887 in the Royal Historical Society's library, London), 96.

22. Patricia M. Barnes, "The Chancery *Corpus Cum Causa* File, 10–11 Edward IV," in R. F. Hunnisett and J. B. Post, eds., *Medieval Legal Records* (London, 1978), 429–746; Baker, *Laws,* 188–189 and 278–279; Duker, *Habeas Corpus,* 24–27.

23. By at least 1429–1430, Chancery *cum causa* writs may be found in the rolls and files on the Crown Side of King's Bench. See TNA, KB29/62/3, 10d., 27d., and KB145/6/8: writs for Richard Rose and Thomas Stale, 1429, and for John White, Edward Barton, Nicholas Clerk, and others, 1430. These concerned unspecified felonies.

24. On this usage in the early sixteenth century, see Baker, *Laws,* 91–94, and Baker, "Personal Liberty under the Common Law, 1200–1600," in *The Common Law Tradition: Lawyers, Books, and the Law* (London, 2000), 341–343.

25. This usage was often invoked in the seventeenth century. See Cro. Jac. 543, 79 *ER* 465–66 (Bourne, 1619–1620); and HLS, 5016 f. 80 and CUL, Ll.3.13, f. 170v. (Harrison, 1626).

26. On poverty, see Paul Slack, *From Reformation to Improvement: Public Welfare in Early Modern England* (Oxford, 1999), chapters 1–2. On internal migration, see Peter Clark and David Souden, eds., *Migration and Society in Early Modern England* (Totowa, 1987), chapters 1–2. For demographic contexts and London's impact, see E. A. Wrigley and R. S. Schofield, *The Population History of England, 1541–1871* (Cambridge, Eng., 1981), chapter 6.

27. Christopher Haigh, *English Reformations: Religion, Politics, and Society under the Tudors* (Oxford, 1993), chapters 14–16.

28. On litigation rates, see Christopher W. Brooks, "Litigation and Society in England, 1200–1996," in *Lawyers, Litigation, and English Society since 1450* (London, 1998), 63–128, especially 68–71.

29. Ronald A. Marchant, *The Church under the Law* (Cambridge, Eng., 1969). On sexuality and marriage, see Martin Ingram, *Church Courts, Sex, and Marriage in England, 1570–1640* (Cambridge, Eng., 1987). On defamation, see Laura Gowing, *Domestic Dangers: Women, Words, and Sex in Early Modern London* (Oxford, 1996).

30. Brian Levack, *The Civil Lawyers in England, 1603–1641: A Political Study* (Oxford, 1973).

31. On the popularity of Star Chamber, see Steve Hindle, *The State and Social Change in Early Modern England, c. 1550–1640* (Basingstoke, 2000), chapter 3. On Requests, see Tim Stretton, *Women Waging Law in Elizabethan England* (Cambridge, Eng., 1998).

32. For a marvelous treatment of legal institutions and ideas within the political and cultural contexts of this period, see Brooks, *Law, Politics, and Society,* passim, especially chapter 5.

33. J. J. Scarisbrick, *Henry VIII* (Berkeley, 1968), 507.

34. This is the pithy formulation of Conrad Russell in *Parliaments and English Politics, 1621–1629* (Oxford, 1979), 3n.

35. See 1 James I, c. 31: An Act for the Charitable Relief of Persons Infected with the Plague.

36. For all aspects of legislation, see David Dean, *Law-Making and Society in Late Elizabethan England: The Parliament of England, 1584–1601* (Cambridge, Eng., 1996).

37. On JPs, see J. H. Gleason, *The Justices of the Peace in England, 1558–1640* (Oxford, 1969), and Anthony Fletcher, *Reform of the Provinces: The Government of Stuart England* (New Haven, 1986).

38. William Lambarde's *Eirenarcha; or, Of the Office of the Iustices of Peace* first appeared in 1581, going through further editions as the statute book grew. Michael Dalton's *The Covntrey Ivstice: Conteyning the Practise of the Ivstices of the Peace out of their Sessions* appeared in 1618.

39. On the state's institutions and their functions and boundaries, see Michael J. Braddick, *State Formation in Early Modern England, c. 1550–1700* (Cambridge, Eng., 2000), especially parts 1 and 2.

40. Popham was the first chief justice to have served previously as solicitor or attorney general since Richard Lyster's death in 1553. Popham served as solicitor from 1579 and was promoted to attorney in 1581, where he remained until he became chief justice in 1592. Coke became solicitor in 1592, advancing to attorney in 1594, where he served until 1606, when he became chief justice of Common Pleas. Fleming was solicitor from 1595 until 1604, when he became chief baron of the Exchequer. See Sir John Sainty, *A List of English Law Officers* (London, 1987), 45 and 61. See also *ODNB;* Boyer, *Coke;* and Douglas Walthew Rice, *The Life and Achievements of Sir John Popham, 1531–1607* (Madison, 2005).

41. Catherine F. Patterson, *Urban Patronage in Early Modern England: Corporate Boroughs, the Landed Elite, and the Crown, 1580–1640* (Stanford,

1999), chapters 1 and 5. On recorders, see especially 60–61 and 70. On the revival of the information of quo warranto in the early seventeenth century to police these franchises, see Patterson, "Quo Warranto and Borough Corporations in Early Stuart England: Royal Prerogative and Local Privileges in the Central Courts," *English Historical Review* 120 (2005): 879–906.

42. Catherine F. Patterson, "Corporations, Cathedrals, and the Crown: Local Dispute and Royal Interest in Early Stuart England," *History* 85 (2000): 546–571.

43. Hindle, *State and Social Change*, 71–74.

44. Lacey Baldwin Smith, *Treason in Tudor England: Politics and Paranoia* (Princeton, 1986), chapters 7–9; and Boyer, *Coke*, 280–290.

45. All three men, while serving as attorney or solicitor general, were appointed in commissions to use torture; see John Langbein, *Torture and the Law of Proof: Europe and England in the Ancien Régime* (Chicago, 1977), 73–74, 81–87, and 104–121. On Coke's participation in the interrogation of the Jesuit John Gerard, see Boyer, *Coke*, 266–271.

46. TNA, KB145/13/40 (4 November 1597), and KB29/235/37d; *CSPD* 1595–97, 236, 240–243, 245, and 249–252.

47. On Chancellor Ellesmere's endorsement of the propriety of discussions about jurisdictional relations among judges in the Privy Council, see HLS, 1023, f. 1. Accounts of the Council as an "executive" are often premised on fallacies concerning "the Stuarts' drive toward absolutism," and other shibboleths about early seventeenth-century politics. See Alan Clarke, "Habeas Corpus: The Historical Debate," *New York Law School Journal of Human Rights* 14 (1998): 380. See also Duker, *Habeas Corpus*, 40–48, and Sharpe, *Habeas Corpus*, 7–9. Much writing by historians of the last generation has corrected the traditional whig account from which such shibboleths come, but this scholarship has not made its way very far beyond professional historians, and into legal scholarship that looks back on the period. For a succinct introduction to this historiography, see Ronald Hutton, *Debates in Stuart History* (Basingstoke, 2004). For a powerful analysis of this as an era of ideological consensus, see Glenn Burgess, *Absolute Monarchy and the Stuart Constitution* (New Haven, 1996).

48. YLS, GR29.18, f. 222v. (Ladd et al., 1607: jailed by High Commission for contempt, result unknown).

49. Duker thus heads the sections in his discussion of this period as the common law "versus" each of the other bodies he examines. The process of conflict he envisions thus helped in "delineating the executive power." See Duker, *Habeas Corpus*, 33–44.

50. Two important works have studied the controlment rolls: Baker, "Personal Liberty under the Common Law"; and the manuscript treatise written by Frederick Solly-Flood in the 1880s and now in the library of the Royal Historical Society, London. The principal modern accounts rely almost exclusively on printed reports: ibid. and Sharpe, *Law of Habeas Corpus*. As John Baker has noted of early modern printed reports, "Some of them were so bad that judges forbade their citation, or resorted to manuscripts to supply their deficiencies: a discipline which the student of legal history must necessarily emulate." Baker, *Introduction*, 183–184.

51. TNA, KB16/1/6 (23 Jan. 1697) and KB21/25/149 and 210. For more, see Chapter 5.

52. For more on the survey's methods, sources, and findings, please see the Appendix.

53. This was done by general precepts in the form of habeas corpus to major abbeys, such as Westminster, Bury, or St. Albans. These required the return of all imprisoned there (unnamed in the precept), with the cause of their "arrest and detention." Prisoners would then "undergo and receive" what the court ordered: typically arraignment and trial in King's Bench. Some were bailed, but usually only after receiving some indication of the prisoner's good character or the absence of any indictment. These precepts issued throughout the fifteenth century. For a late example, see TNA, KB145/9/21 (Michaelmas 1506, returning Reginald Taylor et al., for felony, committed to the marshal).

54. TNA, KB29/187/20d. and KB145/12/1 (Walter Rydwyn et al., 7 February 1554, 65 jailed by the Council; and Philip Robynson et al., 32 jailed by two judges.).

55. Thus in the survey years during Popham's time on the bench (1594, 1598, 1602, and 1606), the proportion of wrongs not connected to felony or treason investigated on habeas corpus jumped from 23% in 1594 to 48–50% in the period 1598 to 1606.

56. On summary process, see Robert B. Shoemaker, *Prosecution and Punishment: Petty Crime and the Law in London and Rural Middlesex, c. 1660–1725* (Cambridge, Eng., 1991), 35–40, and Peter King, *Crime, Justice, and Discretion in England, 1740–1820* (Oxford, 2000), chapter 4.

57. From 1590 to 1610, 60% were released. Though the three-century survey of writs is quadrennial, I have examined all writs surviving for this period. Looking beyond 1610—the only survey year within Fleming's period on the court—at all habeas users from Michaelmas 1607 through Trinity 1613 (95) for whom we have results (77), we find that 78% (60) were discharged or bailed. During Coke's tenure, Mi-

chaelmas 1613 to Trinity 1616, a total of 119 writs issued, with outcome information surviving for 76 of these, of whom 36% (27) were discharged or bailed. One possible explanation for the lower rate of release under Coke might be that Coke was more ready to grant the writ in the first place. Getting the writ, however, was in some ways more difficult under Coke than under his predecessor and successor, as indicated by the dramatically lower use of writs returned to an individual justice in chambers, a proxy for writs granted during vacations. During Coke's time in King's Bench, the court granted such writs returnable to chambers twice per year, on average. Return to chambers was ordered with this frequency: 1606: 18; 1610: 14; 1614: 2; 1618: 7; and 1622: 14. For more on vacation and chambers practice, see Chapter 2.

58. To be exact, 73% were released. Only five terms from the quadrennial survey fall within the war and postwar period. To ensure that the small sample size would not obscure results, this number is based on information for all writs from the period. From Michaelmas 1642 to the end of 1648, 202 prisoners used the writ. Of the 131 for whom we have results, 67 were bailed, 29 were discharged outright, and 35 were remanded.

59. Ridyard was discharged: see TNA, KB29/292/8 and KB21/13/27.

60. We should not overstate this decline, since the rate of release in the 1650s was actually slightly greater than the average for the period 1500–1800. From Michaelmas 1648 through the end of 1659 (for all years, not only those in the quadrennial survey), at least 201 writs issued, for which we have results on only 101. Of these, 43 were bailed, 16 discharged, and 42 remanded: a release rate of 58% in the Interregnum, compared to the three-century average of 53%. Even so, as shown in Chapter 7, the Lord Protector's Council played some of the same games with its prisoners that Charles I's Council had played in the 1620s and 1630s. Our understanding of those results is hampered by the absence of Crown Side rulebooks, and by other kinds of clerical negligence, during the years 1652 to 1660.

61. Enforcement of religious penal laws, especially the Conventicle and Five Mile Acts of the 1660s, was patchy, since it was usually only undertaken by zealots. See Anthony Fletcher, "The Enforcement of the Conventicle Acts, 1664–1679," in W. S. Shiels, ed., *Persecution and Toleration* (Oxford, 1984), 235–246.

62. For instance, see the case of Robert Sedden, who was committed by three JPs for violating both the Act of Uniformity and the Five Mile Act. He was bailed, though by all appearances the JPs followed those statutes carefully: see TNA, KB145/17/27 (23 October 1675), and KB21/18/101v., 102, and 103; 3 Keble 531, 84 *ER* 862.

63. From 1500 to 1660, 66 prisoners jailed for religious wrongs used ha-
    beas corpus in the survey years. Of the 56 for whom results are known,
    29 (52%) were released. Between 1660 and 1689, as numerous statutes
    were passed that permitted imprisonment of Protestant dissenters, re-
    lease rates rose. Of those jailed for religious wrongs, 17 used habeas
    corpus in the survey years in this period, and for the 16 of these for
    whom results are known, 10 (63%) were released. For the period after
    the so-called Toleration Act of 1689 (1 William and Mary, c. 18), 15 im-
    prisoned for religious wrongs used habeas corpus in the survey years,
    the last in 1734. Of the 14 for whom results are known, 13 (93%) were
    released. This included a number of alleged Catholic priests or Jesuits
    imprisoned during the invasion scares of 1690.

64. Restoration justices tended to impose strict readings on the so-called
    Five Mile Act of 1665: see 17 Charles II, c. 2. Robert Franklyn, jailed for
    preaching at a 1670 conventicle, was bailed as a result of his habeas
    corpus when the justices decided that the return was uncertain, in part
    because it was unclear how his actions were seditious, though the stan-
    dard of sedition was not expressed in that statute; see LI, Misc. 500, f.
    108, and TNA, KB145/17/22 (16 June 1670). Franklyn was initially re-
    manded, but later bailed, then discharged of his recognizance: see
    TNA, KB21/17/45v., 47, 48v., 49, 56, and 56v. Justice Twisden seems to
    have taken an especially demanding view of what a good arrest warrant
    in such situations required, saying that it must state that the jailing JP
    was one of the quorum, that is, one of those specially charged JPs
    whose presence was required to hold sessions: see GI, 35, p. 683.

65. Looking just at 1690, 95 (56%) of the 171 prisoners who used the writ
    that year had been jailed for wrongs against the state. Of the 85 prison-
    ers accused of wrongs against the state in 1690 for whom results are
    known, 19 were remanded, 27 bailed, and 39 discharged outright, for
    an overall release rate of 78%.

66. Release rates for the whole of Holt's chief justiceship ran at 82%.

67. For more on POWs, see Chapter 5. There were 381 cases in the qua-
    drennial survey years for Holt's period in King's Bench (1690, 1694,
    1698, 1702, 1706, and Hilary term 1710: Holt died in March of that
    year). Multiplying by four, we reach a projected total of approximately
    1,524 habeas cases for 1689–1710. In both printed and manuscript re-
    ports, we find reports for 48 distinct users of habeas corpus during this
    period. We thus might conclude that we have reports for just over 3%
    of the total in these years.

68. The supervision of summary process that did remain was increasingly
    done by certiorari, which permitted review of other jurisdictions with-
    out their first having to have imprisoned a body; see Norma Landau,

The Justices of the Peace, 1679–1760 (Berkeley, 1984), 345–355. One can see this shift in the recorda files (TNA, KB16), which from the late seventeenth century onward become literally thicker with certioraris.

69. See the case of Peter Fretus and Joseph Silvy, both Portuguese subjects impressed at Port Royal in Jamaica. The Admiralty solicitor recommended that they be discharged in reply to their writ of habeas corpus: see TNA, ADM1/3686 (unfol.), 29 May 1798.

70. I have found 236 sailors' writs in the court files for the quadrennial survey years after 1750. Given the state of the evidence and habeas practice in impressment (see Chapter 4), this is almost certainly an undercount. See also Kevin Costello, "Habeas Corpus and Military and Naval Impressment, 1756–1816," *Journal of Legal History* 29 (2008): 239–240.

71. TNA, KB16/15/1 (13 November 1756), and KB21/37/556, 567, 576, and 605.

72. See 16 Charles I, c. 10: the Star Chamber Act; 31 Charles II, c. 2: Habeas Corpus Act.

73. Paul D. Halliday and G. Edward White, "The Suspension Clause: English Text, Imperial Contexts, and American Implications," *Virginia Law Review* 94 (2008): 644–651.

74. This from the affidavit of service by Frederick and Mary Franks, sworn before Mansfield on 19 April 1758: see TNA, KB1/13/3. Frederick Franks may have been the owner or captain of the merchant ship *Martha* on which the two Danes had served, hence his interest in their release: see his affidavit of 11 April 1758 in the same bundle. Orders for the writs are in KB21/38/110.

75. TNA, ADM1/3677/262: Seddon to John Clevland, secretary to the Lords of the Admiralty, 4 July 1758.

76. TNA, ADM1/3678/105–07: Interrogatories on charge of contempt in King's Bench, against John Falkingham, with his answers.

77. TNA, ADM1/1787, unfol., Falkingham to John Clevland, 26 and 29 November 1760. Perhaps worn out by the ordeal, Falkingham requested shore leave at this time.

78. TNA, ADM1/1787, unfol., note on verso of Falkingham's letter of 4 February 1761 to Clevland; and ADM1/3678/102 and 111.

79. For Falkingham's better attitude, see TNA, ADM1/3678/123, 137, 169, and 199; and ADM1/1787, passim.

80. Seddon's letters are filled with advice to the Lords of the Admiralty that they not contest particular writs: TNA, ADM1/3677 and 3678, passim.

81. The statute of 4 George II, c. 26 (1731) made English the language of legal record keeping. This took effect in 1733. On the change in 1628, see Chapter 2.

2. Writing Habeas Corpus

1. Thomas Blount, *NOMO-ΛΕΞΙΚΟΝ: A Law Dictionary* (1670), s.v. *"teste."*
2. TNA, KB145/14/3; KB29/246/110; and KB21/3/44, 54, and 56; HLS, 118, f. 113.
3. For a sampling, see *Thesaurus Brevium, Or a Collection of Approved Forms of Writs* (1687), under the headings for writs of attachments, various forms of *capias, non omittas,* and others.
4. These appear only rarely on the Crown Side of King's Bench, signed by clerks of the Plea Side: e.g., KB145/13/9 (Thomas Lawrence, 9 November 1566, to prosecute an information on the statute of laborers; jailed by the Privy Council, unspecified charge; bailed, then discharged by pardon); and KB145/13/16 (Thomas Miller, 22 May 1574, to prosecute a trespass; jailed by the Privy Council, unspecified charge, remanded).
5. Ridg. t. H. 151, 27 *ER* 787 (Smith, [1734]).
6. TNA, E215/868, f. 1 (1628). This was for use by those held in execution on debt or trespass. Some complained these were abused by the forging of judges' or clerks' signatures: see E215/883/2.
7. There are rare instances of habeas *ad respondendum* being used in criminal matters. In 1558, William Bennett, arrested at Hertford for a felony committed at Islington, was brought to King's Bench, tried, and hanged in 1558 on such a writ to respond to felony, issued from the Crown Side: see TNA, KB145/12/5 (7 May 1558), and KB29/191/45d.
8. TNA, KB164, contains rolls with brief entries of habeas corpus *ad faciendum* on the Plea Side of King's Bench. These writs issued during vacation as well as during the court's term. KB155 is the Plea Side habeas file. On distinguishing the Plea and Crown Sides, see Baker, *Introduction,* 38.
9. In 1666, one lawyer opposed the return of a writ, it "being only *ad faciendum & recipiendum,* this being against the course of the Court, and per curiam, there ought not to be any habeas corpus [on the Crown Side], but only *ad subjiciendum.*" See 2 Keble 134, 84 *ER* 85. I have seen no *ad faciendum* writs on the Crown Side after that for Francis Creed and his wife, jailed for contempt in 1650; no result: TNA, KB29/298/146d. A sharpening distinction between Crown and Plea Sides, and between civil and criminal process, seems to be one source of doubt about whether the *ad subjiciendum* form could be used in Common Pleas across much of the seventeenth century: see 1 Mod. 235, 86 *ER* 852 (Jones, 1677).
10. Louis A. Knafla, "The Writ of Habeas Corpus in Early Modern En-

gland: A View from Within," in William Kaplan and Donald McRae, eds., *Law, Policy, and International Justice* (Montreal, 1993), 365–384.

11. One exception is William Style's *The Practical Register, Or the Accomplish'd Attorney*, 2d ed. (1670), 232–235. He discusses habeas *ad subjiciendum* as well as *ad respondendum*, noting the sharp divide between Crown and Plea Sides that had become commonplace. But most manuals gave little notice to the *ad subjiciendum* writ: e.g., Richard Antrobus and Thomas Impey, *Brevia Selecta: Or, Choice Writs* (1663), 3, and *Praxis Utriusque Banci: The Ancient and Modern Practice of the Two Superior Courts at Westminster* (1674), 1–4. The definition of "habeas corpus" in the oft-cited *Les Termes de la Ley* (1667), 400, made only passing reference to the writ's use for "a man indicted of any trespass before justices of the peace," concentrating instead on these other forms.

12. BL, Egerton 3376, ff. 34–35.

13. BL, Add. 32,520, ff. 66–67. North distinguished between private franchises—such as parks and warrens—and public ones, though quo warranto might be used to inspect and seize both. Hale made a similar distinction, though he termed what North called private franchises "liberties," and reserved "franchise" for those things North labeled public. See *Hale's Prerogatives*, 227–240.

14. BL, Add. 32,518, f. 182. North's thinking throughout his discussion of franchises, like Hale's, mirrors John Spelman's in 1519: "Abuse is where someone uses his liberty otherwise than as the law wills, in derogation of the common weal or of the king." See J. H. Baker, ed., *John Spelman's Reading on Quo Warranto*, Selden Society, 113 (London, 1997), 101.

15. Catherine Patterson, "Quo Warranto and Borough Corporations in Early Stuart England: Royal Prerogative and Local Privileges in the Central Courts," *English Historical Review* 120 (2005): 879–906. For orders in quo warranto cases during this period concerning Salisbury, Yarmouth, Wigan, and other towns, as well as private liberties, see TNA, KB21/6, passim. Some of these cases are reported in CUL, Ii.5.32, ff. 46v., 50, 79v., 115, and 131v.

16. This was the usual locution in such orders: see CUL, Ii.5.32, f. 79v. (Wigan, 1619).

17. Godbolt 44, 78 *ER* 27 (Anon., 1586).

18. YLS, GR29.14, f. 224v (Winch, 1601).

19. Holt, KB 334, 90 *ER* 1085; Fortescue 243, 92 *ER* 836; and LI Misc. 713, p. 142 (Fowler, 1700). The Lincoln's Inn report shows Fowler's discharge.

20. On public/private claims in mandamus, see Paul D. Halliday, *Dismem-*

bering the Body Politic: Partisan Politics in England's Towns, 1650–1730 (Cambridge, Eng., 1998), 139–143.

21. John Seymour, "*Parens Patriae* and Wardship Powers: Their Nature and Origin," *Oxford Journal of Legal Studies* 14 (1994): 162–173.

22. Rachel Weil, *Political Passions: Gender, the Family, and Political Argument in England, 1680–1714* (Manchester, 1999), especially 67–79 and 125–126.

23. BL, Add. 32,527, f. 61; LI, Misc. 500, f. 174; and TNA, KB21/17/71 and 72.

24. TNA, KB1/12/6: affidavits sworn in early 1757 by Sir William, Theophilus, and Anne Meredith, Mary's siblings, and their lawyer, Henry Dewhurst.

25. TNA, KB21/37/582, 600, and 607, and KB21/38/2 and 107. See Jonathan Andrews and Andrew Scull, *Undertaker of the Mind: John Monro and Mad-Doctoring in Eighteenth-Century England* (Berkeley, 2001), 193–215. Lady Ferrers was not the only noblewoman to use habeas in order to swear articles against her husband. Mary Eleanor Bowes, Countess Dowager of Strathmore, did so in 1786. Her husband and others were ultimately attached for contempt of the writ, and later, for violating his recognizance to keep the peace to his wife. See TNA, KB21/44/225, 233, 253, 260, 262, 276, and 279, and KB21/45/312 and 314; as well as *The Times* (London), 27 April, 3; 9 May 1785, 3; 17 November 1786, 2; and 28 November 1786, 2.

26. TNA, KB16/14/1 (20 May 1751, no result).

27. "*Ut dicitur*" appears also in the writs *de homine replegiando*—used for obtaining bail from certain kinds of custody, though by the seventeenth century it was only rarely employed—and *pone,* by which pleas might be moved from the country into King's Bench or Common Pleas. Anthony Fitzherbert, *La Novel Natura Brevium. . .* (1635), ff. 66v.–67 and 70.

28. The report of Lowe's case states simply that "he came into the King's Bench and prayed habeas corpus." See HLS, 118, f. 113. Neither here nor in the rulebook entry of the grant of Lowe's writ is there any mention of a barrister, and the possibility exists that he could have prayed the writ in person. Usually, an entry in the rulebooks noted that the writ was granted "at the motion of" a named barrister. But names were also omitted in many cases. No names of barristers making motions were recorded in the rulebooks for 1605, so the absence of a name here means little about whether a lawyer helped Lowe.

29. TNA, KB21/19/158–63v.

30. See the writ sued by Richard Hughes, a London slater, for his appren-

tice, Henry Beddon, in April 1762: TNA, ADM1/3678/233. Beddon had joined the navy against Hughes's wishes. The Admiralty ordered that Beddon be released from naval service after Hughes showed proof of apprenticeship in the form of Beddon's indentures.

31. Justice Sir John Wilmot declared in 1758 that both before and after the Habeas Corpus Act of 1679, writs issued by a single justice in vacation required that a copy of the commitment be submitted to make out the case for the writ: see Wilm. 89, 97 *ER* 36. I have seen only one possible reference to such a practice, when in 1649, Henry Rolle, chief justice of the Upper Bench, refused to grant a writ until he had seen the mittimus of the prisoner in question. See Style 182, 82 *ER* 629 (Anon.).

32. For a sample of such a fiat, see a precedent book of procedure made by a King's Bench clerk in the later eighteenth century: TNA, KB15/50/48. Examples of writs specifying an hour as well as a day of return abound, e.g., that for Henry Nelson et al., to be returned to Justice Sir Francis Gawdy, in Serjeants' Inn, at 7:00 A.M. on 24 June 1594: see TNA, KB29/232/30. This writ issued on 19 June, on the expectation that it should travel to Ross, in Herefordshire, and back in five days. The writ was returned unperformed, with the explanation that it had arrived late and thus could not be performed according to the terms stated therein.

33. For example, see the order that a return to habeas corpus for Hugh ap [illegible] be made to the justices of assize in Shropshire in the summer of 1629: TNA, KB21/10/21v.

34. See 29 Charles II, c. 5: An Act for taking of Affidavits in the Country.

35. Thus Justice Wilmot could declare in 1758 that "in cases not within the Act of the 31 Car. II, writs of habeas corpus *ad subjiciendum,* by the law as it now stands, ought not to issue of course, but upon probable cause verified by affidavit." Wilm. 82, 97 *ER* 32.

36. TNA, KB1/2/1, affidavit of Thomas Cooke, Dorothy Cooke, and Andrew Parnell (7 April 1722, enclosing Marsden's letter of 13 March); and KB21/31/543. No result on her writ survives.

37. TNA, KB21/8/28; Style 182 (Anon., 1649) and 432 (1655); 82 *ER* 629 and 838.

38. LI, Misc. 500, f. 174. Lady Leigh told a similar story: see TNA, KB21/18/67, 68v., and 72v.

39. Crown Side rulebooks (TNA, KB21) contain references to affidavits showing service of unreturned writs. These provided grounds for alias or pluries writs or for issuing an attachment for contempt against the nonreturning officer: see LI, Misc. 499, p. 200. See also KB21/3/24v. for the 1604 issuance of an attachment for contempt, and KB21/3/

102v. for issuance of an alias writ in 1607 (alias issued to the Court of Admiralty on oath of Nicholas Manning for others). In arguments in 1632, the court corrected Attorney General Noy, who claimed affidavits were not used to get attachments, by saying that this had been done since at least Chief Justice Popham's time (1592–1607): CUL, Gg.2.19, f. 252v. The same process was used in 1604 against Francis Hunnyngs, and consistently thereafter: see KB21/3/24v.

40. Making a petition or bill to the Chancellor may once have been done orally, but by the fifteenth century, one increasingly did so in writing. For discussion of the process and for examples of surviving records, see Patricia M. Barnes, "The Chancery *Corpus Cum Causa* file, 10–11 Edward IV," in R. F. Hunnisett and J. B. Post, eds., *Medieval Legal Records* (London, 1978), 431–433 and 446–476. On this likeness between Chancery and King's Bench practice, see Chapter 3.

41. It is no accident that the majority of surviving King's Bench affidavits concern habeas corpus and other prerogative writs: mandamus, certiorari, and quo warranto. Affidavits are in TNA, KB1 and KB2; indexes to the affidavits, which survive from 1738, are in KB39. For more on bill process, see W. J. Jones, *The Elizabethan Court of Chancery* (Oxford, 1967), 190–199, and Henry Horowitz, *Chancery Equity Records and Proceedings, 1600–1800* (London, 1998), 12–18.

42. On judicial versus original writs, see Baker, *Introduction,* 53–67.

43. Grey, *Debates,* vol. 3, p. 280.

44. TNA, KB21/2/113v. and 115v.–117 (James Robson et al., 1601; jailed by the Privy Council, for riot, and bailed). For examples of *nisi* rules followed by issuance on failure to show cause, see KB29/296/38, and KB21/13/90, 93, 94, and 94v. (William Brouncker, jailed by JPs for barratry, 1647, and bailed); and KB21/16/48 and 50v.: rule for the attorney general to show cause why habeas corpus should not issue (John Fenner, 1667).

45. TNA, KB21/3/34, 34v., 35, and 37.

46. TNA, KB21/7/37 (Gyres, 1621).

47. *Termes de la Ley* (1671), 56. On private arrests, see Cynthia B. Herrup, *The Common Peace: Participation and the Criminal Law in Seventeenth-Century England* (Cambridge, Eng., 1987), chapter 4.

48. Michael Dalton, *The Covntrey Ivstice* (1618), 294. Blount, *Law Dictionary,* s.v. "arrest," took a similar view that conflated the distinction between arrest and detention: "Arrest is taken for the execution of the command of some court or officer of justice, and a man stopped, staid, or apprehended for debt, etc., is said to be arrested; which may be called the beginning of imprisonment."

49. On examination and bail or detention of criminal suspects, see John H. Langbein, *Prosecuting Crime in the Renaissance: England, Germany, France* (Cambridge, 1974), part 1. On binding over to keep the peace, see Steve Hindle, *The State and Social Change in Early Modern England, c. 1550–1640* (Basingstoke, 2000), 97–113.

50. Use of habeas in the *ad standum* form dwindled from the 1550s and all but ceased by 1600. Such writs were filed (in TNA, KB145) and enrolled (in KB29) with writs of habeas corpus *ad subjiciendum*. Their use to bring bodies in for arraignment on known wrongs makes them virtually indistinguishable from habeas in the *ad subjiciendum* form when used in the same way: as an aid to criminal process.

51. Thus, rarely, writs of habeas *ad subjiciendum* stated that the person in question was arrested for suspicion of felony or murder, as *ad standum* writs did. Late examples, from 1594, may be found for John Markendall (bailed after imprisonment by a JP for treason), William Robicut (remanded after imprisonment for murder), and others, in TNA, KB29/232/30 and 57, and KB145/13/37. I have seen on the files only one *ad subjiciendum* after 1595 stating a cause of arrest in the writ: that for Rowland DeBoys, who was bailed after arrest at Colchester on suspicion of theft. See KB145/14/15 (9 July 1617).

52. *ST*, vol. 3, pp. 13 and 17.

53. Ibid., 17.

54. I have seen one *ad subjiciendum* writ in the fifty years before 1627 that contains the words *"una cum causa captionis et detentionis"*: for Merse or Marsa Jerman, committed for murder by a JP (result unknown). Nothing else about the writ or process on it was unusual, suggesting this was simply a clerical oddity. See TNA, KB29/218/18d. and KB145/13/25 (26 November 1582).

55. *ST*, vol. 3, pp. 31 and 52.

56. Charles I signaled his acceptance of the Petition of Right on 7 June 1628 and prorogued Parliament on 26 June: see ibid., 230–232. Trinity term began on 13 June. The writ for Henry Billingsley is the first on file in this form: see TNA, KB145/15/4 (29 June 1628; jailed by the chamberlain of the king's household, for a violation of privilege; bailed). Most of the writs of Michaelmas 1628 contain this language. Virtually all those following include the full phrase *"die et causa captionis et detentionis."* For the Petition's text, see J. P. Kenyon, *The Stuart Constitution: Documents and Commentary* (Cambridge, Eng., 1969), 82–85.

57. A full copy of the Petition of Right is on file in the recorda at the beginning of Michaelmas term, 1628: see TNA, KB145/15/4. For more on the Five Knights' Case and the making of the Petition, see Chapter 5.

58. Harling said these things while before a London justice of the peace. If she had said them to the justice while he was serving in an official capacity, they would have amounted to a contempt for which he might jail her. As it was, the JP ordered her to find sureties for good behavior. Upon refusing to give sureties, she was imprisoned until she did so. Harling's writ was returned to Justice David Williams in his chambers in Serjeants' Inn. Upon hearing this return, Williams bailed her: see TNA, KB29/252/33.

59. TNA, KB29/240/95: writ of Edmund Leaver, 1602, who was jailed by JPs for not maintaining an illegitimate child of whom he was the reputed father. See also KB145/14/5 (28 November 1607): writ of Roger Osborne, 1607, who was jailed because "he did put out certain persons then dwelling therein [in a house in Drury Lane] being sick of the plague, whereby he did endanger many of his neighbors." Both were bailed.

60. The overlap between criminal and civil wrong and between writ forms was so persistent that the clerks themselves might be confused, thus enrolling a writ of one type by the name of the other. Writs *ad faciendum* for John Bykkeley in 1514 and for Samuel Wheeler in 1594 were entered in the controlment roll as writs *ad subjiciendum*. In Wheeler's case, confusion may have arisen because the wrong for which he was committed was felony, and the *ad faciendum* writ was not normally used in felony cases. Compare the enrolled note of these writs to the writs themselves, in TNA, KB29/146/9 and KB145/10/6 (Bykkeley, 13 February 1514; committed by an individual, no office named, for an unspecified wrong, and bailed); as well as KB29/231/83d. and KB145/13/36 (Wheeler, 14 June 1594; committed by a JP for felony, and remanded).

61. Bod., North.f.16, f. 66. In this case, the court found in contempt a sheriff who had refused to return an *ad subjiciendum* writ until the habeas plaintiff paid his costs.

62. Thus in a 1668 Common Pleas discussion of habeas corpus, Justice Archer quoted Chief Justice Richardson's remarks forty years earlier that "you must move in B[anco] R[egis] for habeas corpus." See LI, Hill 83, p. 293. By the following summer, Common Pleas had indeed issued habeas, the form of which is unknown, for the famed dissenting minister Richard Baxter, who was discharged. The following year, the court used habeas again in another conventicle case, this time concerning Thomas Rudyard. As an attorney of Common Pleas, he could have used the writ on a claim of privilege. See Bod., Rawl.C.719, pp. 37–44 and 69–88; LI, Misc. 500, ff. 42 and 100; and TNA, CP45/466/24d.

63. Carter 221, 124 *ER* 928 (Anon., CP, 1671?). Until the passage of the Habeas Corpus Act in 1679, use of the *ad subjiciendum* writ from Common Pleas or the Court of Exchequer depended on a claim of privilege: that one was a servant of or suitor in the issuing court. For more on privilege, see Chapter 3.

64. See 5 Modern 21, 87 *ER* 495 (Bethel, 1695).

65. Apparently there had been problems with recipients of habeas corpus thinking that it was a command to free someone, rather than to return the body. See Essex Record Office, D/Y/2/7, f. 305: a 1609 order of the justices commanding jailers, on receipt of the writ, to be sure they returned the body to King's Bench, and did not release it.

66. The language used in most such writs was simply "immediately" or "promptly." In survey years to 1592, only 39 of 498 writs with known return dates (8%) demanded return immediately. During Popham's and Fleming's tenure, 58 of 113 did so (51%). From 1613 to 1678, 174 of 367 (47%) writs with known return dates issued with the command to return "immediately." After 1679, 547 of 603 (91%) did so.

67. In the survey years before 1592, 70 out of 688 writs (10%) had this requirement; from 1592 to 1613, 88 of 161 (55%) had them.

68. TNA, KB29/209/109d. and KB145/13/6 (29 May 1574, for John Grange). A return to chambers during term was unusual, and in this case, may be explained by the return's being made to Justice John Southcote. The return showed Grange's commitment by Chief Justice Sir Robert Catlin, without demonstrating cause. Grange was bailed and later pardoned.

69. See orders to the Court of Admiralty, in 1599, and to Berwick, the year following: TNA, KB21/2/58 and 84v. On Berwick and other jurisdictions claiming exemption from these writs, see Chapters 3 and 8. Term-time return to chambers was sufficiently unusual that an eighteenth-century King's Bench clerk, Henry Walrond, thought it worth notice—"note, it is term time," he wrote—as he copied these orders into a precedent book: see TNA, KB21/124, unfoliated, but in chronological order.

70. Thus see TNA, KB21/3/54 (to the Court of Admiralty, for Thomas Redwood, Michaelmas, 1605) and 59 (to the Clink, for Isaac Newman, Hilary, 1606). Newman had been jailed by the High Commission when he refused to pay a fine for contempt against that court. He was bailed. See KB29/246/139 and KB145/14/3 (12 February 1606: last day of the term).

71. During the survey years 1613–1678, 80 writs were issued with a require-

ment of return before a named justice, of 402 writs in the same period for which we have information (20%).

72. See writs returnable before Justice John Clench, at King Hall, at Colchester, in 1594. These were for Peter Smyth and John Taylor. Both were bailed, Taylor after allegedly gilding copper coins to make them look like double pistolets, and Smyth for an accidental death: see TNA, KB145/13/36 (Smyth, 4 May 1594) and KB29/231/84 (Taylor).

73. Grey, *Debates,* vol. 2, p. 433.

74. Of the 2,757 cases in the quadrennial survey, we know of 1,898 cases where the return was ordered to be made. Of these, 412 (22%) were ordered returned in chambers.

75. Seddon's letters, coupled with a large survival of captains' letters, offer an unparalleled chance to watch court and clerical business: see TNA, ADM1 and ADM7.

76. Mansfield routinely ordered writs from his chambers and ordered their return there as well, e.g. TNA, KB21/41, Friday after the octave of Hilary, 18 George III (1778, to John Prince, commander of the *Latham,* East India vessel, for Richard Smith, impressed sailor, result unknown); KB21/43, Wednesday next after the octave of Hilary, 22 George III (1782, to Capt. Sir Hyde Parker, of the *Golial,* for impressed sailors Johanne Hamlen et al., result unknown) and Wednesday next after the morrow of All Souls, 23 George III (1782, to Admiral Robert Roddam, for impressed sailors Theakston Harrison et al., result unknown).

77. For Mansfield taking affidavits at home, see TNA, ADM1/3678/232 (affidavit of Christopher Huddy, 7 April 1762), and ADM1/3680/124 (letter of Seddon, 28 December 1776).

78. TNA, KB1/13/3 and KB21/38/133. The affidavit of James Mervin, on which the writ for Lydia Henrietta Clarke issued, was sworn before Mansfield in chambers, 23 May 1758.

79. Vacations, that is, times when the common law courts were not in session, spanned nearly three-quarters of the year. See Baker, *Introduction,* 65. For the dates of terms and vacations, see C. R. Cheney, ed., *A Handbook of Dates for Students of British History,* rev. ed. by Michael Jones (Cambridge, Eng., 2000), 98–105 and 112–143.

80. Maxwell Cohen, "Habeas Corpus Cum Causa—The Emergence of the Modern Writ—II," *Canadian Bar Review* 18 (1940): 188 and 195; R. J. Sharpe, *The Law of Habeas Corpus,* 2d ed. (Oxford, 1989), 17–19.

81. Sir Edward Coke, *The Fourth Part of the Institutes of the Laws of England* (1644), 81.

82. For example TNA, KB29/318/14 and KB145/17/18 (12 February 1666, antedated to last day of term, for Ambrose Whitamore, remanded after being jailed at Norfolk sessions, for poaching), and KB145/17/19 (28 November 1667, antedated to last day of term, for Lawrence Brown, bailed as a barrator committed at sessions in Yorkshire). That the use of vacation writs was a matter of keen interest is suggested by the fact that Justice Twisden noted a number of vacation writs in his commonplace book, as if organizing evidence for arguments on the question. See HLS, 5016, f. 83v.

83. The only pre-1644 report I have seen discussing vacation writs concerns Howkyn's case, 1573: see *Dyer Reports*, vol. 2, p. 287. There was some discussion here of the propriety of a writ *teste* by the chief justice during vacation. The return to his writ shows that Howkyns had been convicted of robbery; on this return, he was committed to the marshal and later pardoned. See TNA, KB29/209/36.

84. This according to an attorney, Richard Longe, describing his fees to the commission of fees in 1628: see TNA, E215/821. A one-shilling difference between term and vacation writs is also noted in an anonymous attorney's notes, circa 1660: see CUL, Gg.2.29, f. 39v.

85. See 2 Keble 256, 84 *ER* 159 (Daberon, 1667); Grey, *Debates*, vol. 2, pp. 433–434.

86. See 31 Charles II, c. 2, §9.

87. Wilm. 94–101, 97 *ER* 38–40. A look at Kings Bench recorda files confirms Wilmot's assertion about vacation writs issued by Hale's court. See, for instance, writs for John Evans and William Richardson: TNA, KB145/17/27 (23 May 1675 and 23 January 1676, respectively). Evans was imprisoned by one JP, on an unspecified charge. Richardson had been jailed at Middlesex sessions, for seditious words. Both were bailed.

88. See Hardwicke's notes in BL, Add. 38,161, ff. 103v.–104v. After 1679, most writs had a note on them showing whether they issued according to the statute, or by the court's order by common law.

89. TNA, KB33/22/1, unfol. The Admiralty board was thus confused about a writ received by Capt. John Falkingham that seemed to issue impossibly early, given that the sailors named in it had been impressed at Jamaica at around the date of the writ's *teste*. Samuel Seddon, the Admiralty solicitor, explained "that all writs of habeas corpus granted out of term are dated the last day of the term." See TNA, ADM1/1787, Falkingham to John Clevland, 10 October 1760, with notes.

90. Upon filing the return, the court became "seized of the record." See Style 397, 82 *ER* 808–809.

91. Entries of writs and returns in the controlment rolls (TNA, KB29) generally state that the prisoner was committed to the marshal before noting whether the prisoner was bailed.

92. On one's not being able to be bailed or discharged until formally in the custody of King's Bench, see Bod., North.f.16, f. 20 (Smith, 1662); and BL, Add. 32,527, f. 28v. (Walcott, 1673).

93. In some cases, this might entail bringing earlier proceedings from another jurisdiction into King's Bench along with the bodies of the defendants. John Gibson et al. were brought into King's Bench from Bristol by habeas and arraigned for robbery on the indictment, which was brought up by certiorari. They were then convicted and sentenced to hang: see TNA, KB21/12/64v., 67, 74, and 76v. (1637).

94. Typically when the court decided to remand, it did so without first committing to the marshal, but not always. See Twisden's remarks: GI, 34, p. 457 and 1 Sid. 78, 82 ER 981 (Crofton, 1662). For more on commitment versus remand, and on the relationship of commitment and filing of the return, see 1 Keble 146 (Baily, 1661) and 1 Ventris 330, 83 ER 865 and 86 ER 213. The record shows that Baily was later discharged: TNA, KB21/14/75v.

95. Evan Owen was discharged from Newgate in 1637 after giving security for good behavior: see TNA, KB21/12/55v., 56, and 62v. William Curslowe, jailed at Bridgnorth, Shropshire, was excused from custody in 1686, though he was required to give a bond for good behavior for one year: see TNA, KB21/23/47.

96. These means are good examples of what Shaunnagh Dorsett has helpfully identified as "technologies of jurisdiction." See her "'Since Time Immemorial': A Story of Common Law Jurisdiction, Native Title, and the Case of Tanistry," *Melbourne University Law Review* 26 (2002): 33–35.

97. TNA, KB21/17/103 (Thomas Meade, to Jamaica, 1672) and KB21/24/151 (William Moore, to Barbados, 1692).

98. Judges or clerks of the early sixteenth century found these clauses sufficiently novel that they entered the writ's complete text on the controlment roll (writs were normally calendared rather than transcribed in full). See TNA, KB29/135/41 (John Hymmerford and Alice Jermyn). The following term, the bailiff of the liberty of Westminster Abbey likewise received a precept with the same phrase and a £20 subpoena.

99. TNA, KB29/178 and 179, and KB145/10/37 and 38. A comparison of hands in writs with and without the phrase does not suggest any pattern of clerical control over this. The best we might do is to speculate that this new usage had something to do with the appointment of Sir Richard Lyster as chief justice of King's Bench at the end of 1545.

100. Such phrases appear as standard components of a number of Chancery writs: e.g., *de heretico comburendo,* by which a heretic was turned over to royal authority for execution. See Fitzherbert, *Novel Natura Brevium,* f. 269. On subpoena and *corpus cum causa,* see Barnes, "Chancery *Corpus Cum Causa*"; Jones, *Elizabethan Chancery,* 177–181; and Baker, *Laws,* 188–189 and 278–279. On subpoenas, see W. M. Ormrod, "The Origins of the *Sub Pena* Writ," *Historical Research* 61 (1988): 11–20.

101. This is indicated by the creation, by the early 1460s, of separate files in Chancery of subpoenas, writs of *corpus cum causa,* and petitions for *cum causa.* See Barnes, "Chancery *Corpus Cum Causa,*" 430 and 433.

102. See the writ for John Joly and John Reynolds (6 November 1450), containing a subpoena, or that for Geoffrey Rygby (25 August 1450), which contained no subpoena: TNA, KB29/82/5 and 6d.; KB145/6/ 29. These writs, like others issuing from Chancery that ended up in King's Bench, specified that they should be returned to Chancery. It is unclear why they were returned to King's Bench.

103. TNA, KB29/82/4; KB145/6/29 (10 November 1450).

104. A few more Chancery writs may be found returned to King's Bench during the early sixteenth century. The latest I have seen was in 1539: *corpus cum causa* for Thomas Becher, noted as issuing from Chancery, TNA, KB29/171/42d.

105. By 1450, Inns of Chancery served an educational role for the attorneys and other clerks of King's Bench. Contacts between the Inns of Court and Chancery were more numerous before the sixteenth century, a period when clerks generally played a greater role in developing and promulgating the learning of the law than they would later. See C. W. Brooks, *Pettyfoggers and Vipers of the Commonwealth* (Cambridge, Eng., 1986), 159–164. For further discussion, and specific examples, see *Spelman Reports* ii, introduction, 54–57, and 123–135.

106. Lord Chancellor Ellesmere criticized the increasing use of subpoenas in both Common Pleas and King's Bench during the early seventeenth century. By issuing subpoenas under their own judicial seals, the common law courts circumvented any need to resort to Chancery for process; as a result, "his majesty is defrauded of the profit of his great seal." See Ellesmere, "Memorialles for Iudicature," printed in Louis A. Knafla, *Law and Politics in Jacobean England: The Tracts of Lord Chancellor Ellesmere* (Cambridge, Eng., 1977), 278.

107. See the writs of 1450 for Thomas Blak (19 March) and Nicholas Brugeys (23 September). These issued from Chancery and stated that they should be returned there, but the controlment rolls show that final disposition of these cases was made in King's Bench. Blak and Brugeys were bailed. See TNA, KB145/6/29 and KB29/82/5.

108. Two writs of habeas corpus *ad standum* that were issued during a vacation were those in 1430 for Walter Grace (2 May) and Thomas Holt (14 February) in TNA, KB145/6/8 and KB29/62/23 (Holt's writ was enrolled as an *ad respondendum*). Nonetheless, vacation business was more active in Chancery than in King's Bench in the fifteenth century: see Barnes, "Chancery *Corpus Cum Causa*," 431–432.

109. Such signatures were important, guaranteeing that the writ did not issue as a result of fraud, a common complaint, though one that probably came up more often for forms of the writ associated with civil process than with the *ad subjiciendum* writ. The statute of 1 and 2 Philip and Mary c. 13, An Act Appointing an Order to Justices of Peace for the Bailment of Prisoners, declared that no habeas corpus or certiorari should be used for a prisoner unless "the same writs be signed with the proper hands of the chief justice." That this statute did not solve the problem entirely is suggested by the letter the justices sent to local leaders in 1609, a copy of which survives as sent to the mayor and bailiffs of Colchester. This warned such officials to be wary of counterfeit writs gained on the suggestion that "the prisoner hath found sureties in the King's Bench or before any judge of that court for his appearance there or elsewhere." See Essex Record Office, D/Y2/7, f. 305.

3. Writ of the Prerogative

1. On the Rainbow Portrait, painted circa 1600, perhaps by Marcus Gheeraerts the Younger, see Roy Strong, *Gloriana: The Portraits of Queen Elizabeth I* (London, 1987), 156–161. For the appearance of armillary or celestial spheres in Elizabethan portraits, see Strong's discussion of the Ditchley Portrait, more certainly by Gheeraerts, of 1592, at 134–141. Such iconography had a powerful connection to law. John Davies, who would become one of the most important lawyers in England and a judge in Ireland, was a leading poet and was employed by Cecil to prepare major entertainments at court. See Roy Strong, *The Cult of Elizabeth: Elizabethan Portraiture and Pageantry* (London, 1977), 46–54.

2. From the legend on the Ditchley Portrait, see Strong, *Portraits*, 137.

3. LI, Misc. 492, f. 27 and HLS, 2076, f. 17.

4. Palmer 54, 81 *ER* 975 (Bourne, 1619).

5. On fifteenth- and sixteenth-century readings at the Inns of Court on *Prerogativa Regis*, see Margaret McGlynn, *The Royal Prerogative and the Learning of the Inns of Court* (Cambridge, Eng., 2003).

6. William Stanford, *An Exposition of the Kings Prerogatiue. . .* (1607 ed.), f. 5.

7. BL, Egerton 3376, ff. 8 and 13v. A variant text is BL, Add. 36,081, ff. 243v–244v, quoted in Christopher W. Brooks, *Lawyers, Litigation and English Society since 1450* (London, 1998), 213. For discussion of the reading, see Brooks, *Law, Politics, and Society in Early Modern England* (Cambridge, Eng., 2008), 79–81 and 96.

8. BL, Harleian 5220, f. 3.

9. Ibid., f. 4v.

10. For the idea more generally that English law was deeply informed by European thought, see Brooks, *Law, Politics, and Society,* chapter 4, especially 81–83.

11. BL, Stowe 1011, f. 88. For the persistence of miracles in eighteenth-century thought, see Jane Shaw, *Miracles in Enlightenment England* (New Haven, 2006).

12. Davies wrote that the king "doth imitate the Divine Majesty, which in the government of the world doth suffer things for the most part to pass according to the order and course of nature, yet many times doth show his extraordinary power in working of miracles above nature." Quoted in J. W. Tubbs, *The Common Law Mind: Medieval and Early Modern Conceptions* (Baltimore, 2000), 139.

13. *CD* 1628, vol. 3, p. 128.

14. Glenn Burgess, *The Politics of the Ancient Constitution: An Introduction to English Political Thought* (University Park, Pa., 1992), chapter 6, especially 139–140.

15. Quoted in Tubbs, *Common Law Mind,* 135–136.

16. Ibid.

17. Quoting Fleming in Bate's case, 1606, in ibid., 136–137. For more on the ordinary/absolute distinction, see ibid., 133–140, and Burgess, *Ancient Constitution,* 139–149.

18. On the prerogative, especially as connected to commonweal, see Brooks, *Law, Politics, and Society,* 76–77 and 135–142.

19. Quoted in Baker, *Laws,* 56.

20. Stanford, *Prerogatiue* (1607), f. 5.

21. Edward Forset [Forsett], *A Comparative Discovrse of the Bodies Natvral and Politiqve. Wherein out of the principles of Nature, is set forth the true forme of a Commonweale, with the dutie of Subiects, and the right of the Soueraigne* (1606), 21.

22. *CD* 1628, vol. 3, p. 128.

23. HLS, 105, f. 85v. (Ladd, 1607).

24. For the durability of this idea of reciprocity, see the argument in *Considerations on the Exchange of Seamen, Prisoners of War* (London, 1758), 9, concerned with what was owed to POWs.

25. William Paley Baildon, ed., *Les Reportes del Cases in Camera Stellata, 1593 to 1609* (N.p., 1894), 363.

26. Ibid., 361–362. For more on allegiance, see Chapter 8.

27. BL, Egerton 3376, f. 21. These ideas about the necessity to serve in return for protection persisted through the seventeenth century and beyond. For Sir Francis North's views on protection and service, probably from the 1670s, see BL, Add. 32,520, f. 26v.

28. *ST,* ii, 614 (Calvin's case, 1608).

29. *ST,* ii, 619–624 and 640. On Calvin's case as it relates to access of aliens to use of habeas corpus, see Chapters 6 and 8. Morice noted that, by his prerogative, the king could make a proclamation preventing all subjects from leaving the realm in order to ensure its defense: BL, 3376, f. 21v.

30. *Hale's Prerogatives,* 54.

31. See 7 Anne, c. 5, An Act for Naturalizing Foreign Protestants: "[T]he children of all natural born subjects, born out of the ligeance of her majesty . . . shall be deemed, adjudged, and taken to be natural-born subjects." This was confirmed by 4 George II, c. 21.

32. Paul D. Halliday and G. Edward White, "The Suspension Clause: English Text, Imperial Contexts, and American Implications," *Virginia Law Review* 94 (2008): 614–616.

33. J. H. Baker, ed., *Reports of Cases by John Caryll,* part 1: 1485–1499, Selden Society, 115 (London, 1999), 285.

34. Peter Iver Kaufman, "Henry VII and Sanctuary," *Church History* 53 (1984): 465–476; Krista Kesselring, "Abjuration and Its Demise: The Changing Face of Royal Justice in the Tudor Period," *Canadian Journal of History* 34 (1999): 345–358.

35. J. H. Baker, ed., *The Notebook of Sir John Port,* Selden Society, 102 (London, 1986), 38.

36. K. J. Kesselring, *Mercy and Authority in the Tudor State* (Cambridge, Eng., 2003).

37. *Hale's Prerogatives,* 177 and 225–260. For similar notions of pardon as an extension of the king's miraculous power to protect by granting mercy, see the discussion by Heneage Finch, the Earl of Nottingham, ca. 1679, in HLS, 5093, especially pp. 1–2 and 25.

38. BL, Egerton 3376, ff. 11, 16v., and 20.

39. Pardon use of habeas corpus occurred regularly, if not frequently, in the early sixteenth century. The practice peaked between 1558 and 1574, when 78 of 162 (48%) of all *ad subjiciendum* writs from Queen's Bench found in the quadrennial survey years (1558, 1562, 1566, 1570, and 1574) ended with the pleading of a pardon. This peak in pleading

of pardons by habeas corpus coincides with a peak in the total of special pardons in the same period: see Kesselring, *Mercy and Authority*, 74. The practice then declined rapidly, though it continued to appear infrequently throughout the seventeenth century. This may have been connected to increasing use of transportation. See Cynthia Herrup, "Punishing Pardon: Some Thoughts on the Origins of Penal Transportation," in Simon Devereaux and Paul Griffiths, eds., *Penal Practice and Culture, 1500–1900: Punishing the English* (Basingstoke, 2004), 121–137. The last known use of habeas to plead a pardon was in 1730, for Dirk Wonters, arrested at Plymouth after a coroner's inquest for the mortal stabbing of Thomas Jeffs. Wonters was convicted and sentenced to hang, but his name was added to a general pardon. Wonters then used habeas corpus to be brought into King's Bench, where he was discharged on his pardon. We might speculate that his conviction, though for murder, may have involved what jury and judge considered to be justifiable homicide, on which grounds he had obtained his pardon. See TNA, KB16/10/1 (23 October 1730) and KB21/33/313.

40. In the quadrennial survey of writs, of 108 writs ending in pardon, for which the stage of proceedings is known, only 18 concerned prisoners after conviction. This may explain how habeas was being used in pardon process, distinguishing, as it apparently did, between those who received and used pardons before conviction from those who pleaded pardons by other means after conviction. The majority of prisoners pleading pardons by habeas corpus were detained on suspicion of felony and had not yet been arraigned. Krista Kesselring notes that 16% of pardons enrolled in Chancery were for unnamed offences: see her *Mercy and Authority*, 76. These may represent the group of those pardoned prior to conviction: having not yet been convicted, there would have been only an allegation, not a known wrong, to name on the pardon roll. A report of Henry VIII's reign noted the following about process on pretrial pardons: "[I]f someone has the king's pardon for felony and when he is arraigned he does not plead his pardon, but [pleads] Not guilty, and it is found against him, and then he pleads the king's pardon, he shall not there have the benefit of his pardon after the trial, for he has passed his opportunity." The pretrial pardon was apparently to be introduced as one's plea during arraignment; habeas would bring one in for that arraignment. See J. H. Baker, ed., *Reports of Cases from the Time of King Henry VIII*, vol. 1, Selden Society, 120 (London, 2003), 92.

41. TNA, KB29/244/61d. and KB145/14/2 (25 June 1604). For proceedings in Council, see *CSPD* 1603–1610, 38, 53, 87, 115, and 116.

42. *Hale's Prerogatives,* 228–229.

43. J. H. Baker, *John Spelman's Reading on Quo Warranto,* Selden Society, 113 (London, 1997), 119.

44. T. C. Morton, *Decisions of the Supreme Court of Judicature at Fort William in Bengal* (Calcutta, 1841), 207.

45. LI, Misc. 492, f. 27v. When the justices of King's Bench entered a county with the king, the eyre of that county was automatically superseded, as Fleming pointed out.

46. *Hale's Prerogatives,* 182. Richard Crompton, *L'Avthoritie et Ivrisdiction des Covrts de la Maiestie de La Roygne* (1594), 68.

47. Yelverton continued: it was "otherwise in the Common Bench because there must be cause of privilege," meaning the writ would issue only for servants of the court or its litigants. See HLS, 105, f. 86 (Ladd, 1605). Dyer's notes emphasize privilege as the basis for granting habeas corpus from Common Pleas for Alexander Scroggs in 1560; see 2 Dyer 175b; 73 *ER* 386–387; *Dyer Reports,* vol. 1, pp. 54–57, and for discussion, lxxvii–lxxix. See also Baker, "Personal Liberty under the Common Law, 1200–1600," in *The Common Law Tradition* (London, 2000), 343–344. Most of the reported cases of the writ's use from Common Pleas during the rest of the sixteenth century involve privilege claims of attorneys or litigants in that court. For examples see *Dyer Reports,* vol. 1, p. 143 (Lee, 1567) and vol. 2, pp. 355–356 (Hinde, 1576); 1 Leonard 70, 74 *ER* 65–66 (Searche, 1587); and 12 Co. Rep. 104, 77 *ER* 1379–1380 (Thomlinson, 1605). Not all reported Elizabethan Common Pleas writs contain apparent privilege elements, though this may be a result of the reports' brevity: see 2 Leonard 175, 74 *ER* 455 (Hellyard, 1587); 1 Leonard 70, 74 *ER* 66 (Howel, 1587); HLS, 5016, f. 82 and HLS, 105, f. 22v. (Deane, 1599).

48. Thus see Common Pleas cases in the 1660s: Richard Baxter and Richard Crompton, 1668–1669: TNA, CP45/466/24; LI, Hill 83, f. 293; and Bod., Rawl.C.719, pp. 37–45. While it is impossible to prove a negative, a brief survey of Common Pleas rolls has turned up no sign of the use of habeas corpus *ad subjiciendum* before this period: see TNA, CP45 and CP60.

49. TNA, KB145/14/5 (23 January 1608); KB29/248/142d.; and KB21/3/116.

50. TNA, KB29/249/16. A translation is in Edith G. Henderson, *Foundations of English Administrative Law* (Cambridge, 1963), 167–171.

51. Ibid., 169–170.

52. This last writ carried a subpoena of £100. Henderson, in ibid., says no record of a result survives. None may be found in the controlment roll

or recorda file, but orders on Farndon's restitution may be followed in TNA, KB21/3/125v.–145v., passim, the last showing the result. In the final order, the words that Farndon was ordered to use in his apology were entered in full.

53. Thus Mansfield wrote in Cowle's case: "Writs, not ministerially directed (sometimes called prerogative writs, because they are supposed to issue on the part of the king), such as writs of mandamus, prohibition, habeas corpus, [and] certiorari . . . may issue to every dominion of the Crown of England." See 2 Burr. 855–856, 97 *ER* 599.

54. Henderson, *Administrative Law,* 96–97. Evidence on controlment rolls suggests that this development probably occurred earlier than Henderson suggests. For two writs of 1573, see TNA, KB29/209/34 and 36d. That there should be an order to amerce a bailiff for non-return of certiorari on the opening folio of the earliest surviving Crown Side rule book suggests that the writ's use in Queen's Bench may have been of long standing: see TNA, KB21/1/6 (Hilary 1589).

55. For the development of certiorari, see Henderson, *Administrative Law,* chapter 3.

56. Norma Landau, *The Justices of the Peace, 1679–1760* (Berkeley, 1984), 345–354.

57. Thus "the king may sue this writ for himself, even though the plea in court Christian is between two common people, for this suit"—one wrongly pursued in a church court—"is in derogation of the crown." See Anthony Fitzherbert, *La Novel Natvra Brevivm. . .* (1635), f. 40.

58. See 3 Bulstrode 120, 81 *ER* 103.

59. *Hale's Prerogatives,* 160–161. Fitzherbert noted that "the king may sue attachment" where the prohibition was neglected. See also Fitzherbert, *Natura Brevium,* f. 40. For an example of an attachment for disobedience on prohibition, see TNA, KB21/7/35v. (1622). See as well Charles M. Gray, *The Writ of Prohibition: Jurisdiction in Early Modern English Law* (New York, 1994), vol. 1, pp. xviii–xxii.

60. As Chief Justice Montagu pointed out in 1619: "When they in the spiritual court do anything against our law, prohibition goes. . . . [T]he same law is intended when they omit something that by law they should do. There the king's court commands them to do what pertains to the law." See Palmer 50, 81 *ER* 973. Palmer misnamed this case St. Balaunce. It actually concerned Sutton Valence, Kent, and the appointment of churchwardens: see TNA, KB29/266/72d.

61. One Dorset parish learned this in 1641 when a prohibition went to an ecclesiastical court officer to prevent his swearing one person as

churchwarden while a mandamus went to command that the oath be given to another. See TNA, KB21/12/177 and 186.

62. This was a writ of restitution ordered, and later canceled, for the rectory of Shawell, Leicestershire. See TNA, KB29/246/108; KB21/3/52.

63. These writs reversed the effects of writs *vi laica removenda*, a Chancery writ issuing in response to a surmise made by one claiming a rectory that another forcibly held against him. See Fitzherbert, *Natura Brevium*, ff. 54–55. The first writs of restitution concerned a group of Sussex parishes and one in Hampshire: see TNA, KB29/246/124 and 138d.; KB29/247/32d.; and KB21/3/58 and 61v. At Steyning, Stephen Vinall was one of ten Sussex clergymen removed for alleged nonconformity. See T. P. Hudson, ed., *The Victoria County History of Sussex* (London, 1980), vol. 6, part 1, p. 243. Events in the Steyning case can be followed in a bill filed in the court of Exchequer, where a countersuit was begun later in 1606: see TNA, E112/127/166.

64. The writ gave a full account of his election according to a recently granted charter. A translation of Tompson's writ is in Henderson, *Administrative Law*, 163–167. For orders, see TNA, KB21/3/62v.–74, passim.

65. Later rules for the return to him of lost profits of office suggest that Tompson was restored: see TNA, KB21/3/72 and 74.

66. This is the language in Tompson's writ. Farndon's writ was justified by the same need to do justice. See Henderson, *Administrative Law*, 166 and 170.

67. Sir Edward Coke, *The Fourth Part of the Institutes of the Laws of England* (1644), 71. Coke thus elaborated: "[I]f any person be committed to prison, this court upon motion ought to grant an habeas corpus, and upon return of the cause do justice and relieve the party wronged. And this may be done though the party grieved hath no privilege in this court."

68. Coke's report of Bagge's case is in 11 Co. Rep. 93b, 77 *ER* 1271–1281. For discussion, see Paul D. Halliday, *Dismembering the Body Politic: Partisan Politics in England's Towns* (Cambridge, Eng., 1998), 68–69.

69. See 1 Ld. Raym. 469, 91 *ER* 1212 (Greenwell [Groenvelt], 1697).

70. See 3 Bulstrode 116, 81 *ER* 100 (Pannel, on prohibition, 1615).

71. On the breadth of the idea of jurisdiction in early modern law, see Henderson, *Administrative Law*, 126–127.

72. "Observacions upon ye Lord Cookes Reportes" in Louis A. Knafla, *Law and Politics in Jacobean England: The Tracts of Lord Chancellor Ellesmere* (Cambridge, Eng., 1977), 307–308.

73. HLS, 1128, f. 73 (1632). The report does not note who was speaking.

74. *Hale's Prerogatives,* 26.

75. Ibid., 36 and 206–210.

76. In re Jane New, in Dowling, Select Cases, v. 2, Archives Office of New South Wales, 2/3462, http://www.law.mq.edu.au/scnsw/Cases1829–30/html/in_re_jane_new__1829.html (accessed July 20, 2009).

77. Cro. Jac. 543, 79 *ER* 466 (Bourne, 1619).

78. Palmer 55, 81 *ER* 975 (Bourne, 1619).

79. Palmer 96, 81 *ER* 996 (Bourne, 1620). See also CUL, Ii.5.32, f. 116.

80. TNA, KB145/14/17 (29 November 1619: the first day of vacation after Michaelmas); KB29/266/198; and KB21/6/41v.

81. HLS, 5016, f. 81v.

82. Marjorie Blatcher, *The Court of King's Bench, 1450–1550* (London, 1978), 6. A thorough search of Exchequer files turned up no signs of collected subpoenas in records listing fines paid by sheriffs and other local officers for poor performance of their duties. See, for instance, TNA, E101/109/16; E101/110/1–5; E101/124/2; and E101/616/28.

83. For instance, TNA, KB21/3/24v. and 102v. (1604 and 1607).

84. CUL, Gg.2.19, f. 253 (Allen, 1632). For further discussion of the attachment process, see 2 Barn. KB 35, 94 *ER* 339 (Anon. 1731).

85. For example, see TNA, KB21/1/21v.–22: orders to William Uvedale, jailer of Hampshire, for William Packington and Richard Townsend. Uvedale finally did return the writ, explaining that the Marquess of Winchester, the county's lord lieutenant, had ordered them jailed for failing to give sureties on an unspecified wrong. Uvedale's return that remarkably both were too ill to be brought to Westminster is at KB29/226/93 and KB145/13/32 (both writs of 19 May 1590). There is no sign of further proceedings against Uvedale.

86. Thus a 1614 *nisi* order to a sheriff to return a writ or be fined £5 gained a quick return: see TNA, KB21/5/13v. (the writ was for Ludovic Davies to the sheriff of Worcestershire; he was remanded on his imprisonment for engrossing fish, contrary to statute). A 1622 example required a threat of £100, but then produced a return: KB21/7/23v.–28v. (writ for Humphrey Frodesham to the sheriffs of Middlesex, for felony, no result).

87. Thus see the 1643 writ for Edward Thompson. As a Cinque Port town, Rye claimed immunity from writs out of King's Bench. When the first writ went unreturned, the court fined the mayor £10, but then stayed the fine when the second writ was returned. See TNA, KB29/292/29d. and 30; KB21/13/30v. and 31v.

88. On technologies of jurisdiction, see Shaunnagh Dorsett and Shaun

McVeigh, "Questions of Jurisdiction," in McVeigh, *Jurisprudence of Jurisdiction* (New York, 2007), 11–12.

89. TNA, E215/821: fees of clerks in King's Bench, 1628.

90. Leicestershire Record Office, DG7/Box XVIII/Law 17: Heneage Finch fee book, 1656–1672, unfol. Green had been imprisoned in Norfolk as an excise subcollector who had failed to make his accounts. No result was recorded on his writ: see KB145/16/1656 (22 November 1656).

91. Cole had been committed for violating London's custom against forestalling fish coming to market. Finch successfully argued against the custom and Cole was released. See Leicestershire Record Office, DG7/Box XVIII/Law 17. A report of Finch's arguments is in LI, Misc. 500, ff. 148v.–49.

92. A note about fees from the late 1630s put the total at 4s. 10d.: see TNA, KB15/55, f. 2. But an Upper Bench fee book for the 1650s says bail on habeas would run 6s. 2d. in fees: see KB15/57, unfol. By the 1730s, fees for the writ were 4s., and another 6s. 10d. for processing bail: see KB15/64, p. 13.

93. TNA, KB15/64, p. 32.

94. TNA, KB21/7/39v. and KB21/8/9v.: committed by Council of Wales for contempt, and bailed.

95. TNA, KB21/12/86v.

96. In 1652, the court ordered the sheriff of Lincolnshire to meet with the master of the Crown Office (called the Capital Office, when there was no king), to discuss moderating his fees for carriage and maintenance of William Armstrong and Alexander Anthony, whom he had brought to town on habeas corpus. See TNA, KB21/13/207.

97. Entries of both *ad subjiciendum* and *ad standum* writs in the controlment rolls (TNA, KB29) in the sixteenth century noted that they had been sued "at the suit of the king himself," a point underscored by Justice Sir John Dodderidge in Bourne's case in 1620: see Palmer 55, 81 *ER* 975.

98. Bod., MS North f.16, f. 66.

99. They were bailed: see TNA, KB16/4/1 (23 October 1706), and KB21/27/73. Proceeding *in forma pauperis* was typically noted in the Crown Side rulebook, when the writ was granted.

100. In discussing the meager evidence we have about the range of social access to habeas corpus, and in suggesting that it may have been wider than we might imagine, I make no attempt to answer the very difficult questions about access to justice more broadly, questions that historians of crime have debated over the last generation. For a succinct account of this debate, see Peter King, *Crime, Justice, and Discretion in England, 1740–1820* (Oxford, 2000), 2–5, and the works cited there; as

well as the conclusion, especially 364–373. For the classic consideration of the issue of the social breadth of access to justice and about plebeian reliance on and commitment to a "rule of law," see E. P. Thompson, *Whigs and Hunters: The Origin of the Black Act* (Harmondsworth, 1975), 258–269.

101. Clerical practice regarding the insertion of a social or occupational descriptor in the writ varied, and generally declined beginning in the early seventeenth century. This precludes making estimates of proportional writ use according to social station, reported in writs.

102. TNA, KB16/16/3 (29 November 1714). No result survives on Whitten's writ.

103. Baker, *Laws*, 318. A bare note in Spelman's reports for 1540 states that habeas would go to the Cinque Ports; see *Spelman Reports*, vol. 1, p. 186. But the lord warden of the Cinque Ports, and the mayors and leaders of the constituent towns in the Ports, such as Dover, Sandwich, or Rye, would continue to fight service of the writ within their precincts until the middle of the seventeenth century.

104. For the counties palatine, see Baker, *Laws*, 293–298.

105. CUL, Ll.3.13, f. 170v., YLS, GR 29.23, f. 166, and HLS, 5016, f. 80. See also Latch 160, 82 *ER* 325 (Harrison [Jobson, 1626]); TNA, KB21/8/56v.–67, passim.

106. CUL, Ii.5.32, f. 116.

107. J. H. Baker has hinted at just this, referring to what he calls "Coke's common-law brand of equity." See Baker, *Introduction*, 144.

108. LI, MS Maynard 21, f. 256v. TNA, KB29/252/96 (John Vaughan, et al., 1610).

109. Thomas Ashe, *Epieikeia* (1609), sigs. Ai and Aiiii; Christopher St. German, *Doctor and Student*, T. F. T. Plucknett and J. L. Barton, eds., Selden Society, 91 (London, 1974), 95.

110. *ST,* vol. 2, p. 627.

111. *Hale's Prerogatives,* 177.

112. Quoted in Norman Doe, *Fundamental Authority in Late Medieval English Law* (Cambridge, Eng., 1990), 102.

113. John Baker, "The Common Lawyers and the Chancery: 1616," in Baker, *The Legal Profession and the Common Law: Historical Essays* (London, 1986), 205–229.

114. Knafla, *Law and Politics,* 127–128 and 320–321.

115. Edward Hake, *Epieikeia: A Dialogue on Equity in Three Parts*, D. E. C. Yale, ed. (New Haven, 1953), 56.

116. Ibid., 105. For Ellesmere's own discussion of the equity of the statute, see *A Discourse upon the Exposicion & Understandinge of Statutes,* Samuel E. Thorne, ed. (San Marino, 1942), 140–154.
117. See 11 Co. Rep. 98a, 77 *ER* 1278.
118. Hake, *Epieikeia,* 56, following St. German; see also, generally, St. German, *Doctor and Student,* 95–104. For general discussions of equity, see J. H. Baker, introduction to *Spelman Reports,* vol. 2, pp. 37–43; and Tubbs, *Common Law Mind,* chapter 4.
119. "The classification of courts into groups according to their equitable or conciliar nature, in presumed distinction to those of common law, is . . . inappropriate." See W. J. Jones, *The Elizabethan Court of Chancery* (Oxford, 1967), 18.
120. See the reading of Francis Ashley (1616): BL, Harl. 4841, ff. 52v.–53 on the Privy Council, Star Chamber, and Requests as courts of equity.
121. TNA, KB145/14/12 and 13, writs dated 24 November 1614 (*ad faciendum,* discharged); and 9 May 1615, 16 June 1615, 30 January 1616, and 3 February 1616 (all *ad subjiciendum,* remanded on each).
122. As J. H. Baker has noted, this dispute "was not about the need for equity in suitable cases, but about the finality of judgments at common law and the enlargement of Chancery jurisdiction at the expense of the law courts." See Baker, "Common Lawyers and Chancery," 207–208. See also Knafla, *Law and Politics,* chapter 7. On relations between common law and equity in the 1610s and 1620s, see Brooks, *Law, Politics, and Society,* 145–152.
123. TNA, KB145/14/12–14; KB29/257–59; and KB21/5 and 5a, passim. The following used writs and were remanded, except as noted: William Allen (three writs), Michael Apsley (two writs: remanded in Hilary, then bailed in Trinity 1615), Gilbert Beare, Henry Boughton (two), Richard Glanvill (one *ad faciendum* writ, on which he was discharged in Michaelmas 1614, then four *ad subjiciendum* writs, on which he was remanded), Barnabas Gooche, John Parrat (bailed, Hilary 1616), Richard Prideaux, Henry Rosewell (two: no result on first writ, remand on second, Trinity 1615), John Smyth, and William Smyth.
124. Knafla, *Law and Politics,* 321 and 280–281.
125. On bill process in the Court of Requests, see Tim Stretton, *Women Waging Law in Elizabethan England* (Cambridge, Eng., 1998), 79–80. On narrative strategies of those using bills, see chapter 8.
126. On Chancery subpoenas, see Jones, *Elizabethan Chancery,* especially 161–162 and 177–181. On bill and subpoena process in Star Chamber, see Thomas G. Barnes, "Due Process and Slow Process in the late Eliza-

bethan–Early Stuart Star Chamber," *American Journal of Legal History* 6 (1962): 227–230.

127. Knafla, *Law and Politics,* 281.

128. For 1604–1606 examples in King's Bench, see TNA, KB21/3/24v., 32, 37v., and passim. Use of this process continued. On Chancery attachments, see Jones, *Chancery,* 229–230.

129. CUL, Gg.2.19, f. 253.

130. Arundel, however, had been instrumental during parliamentary debates on the liberty of the subject in the spring of 1628 by producing compromise language that helped pave the way to the Petition of Right. See S. R. Gardiner, *History of England from the Accession of James I. . .* (London, 1891), vol. 6, pp. 277–279 and 288; *ODNB,* s.v. Thomas Howard, Earl of Arundel. On the court of the earl marshal, see Baker, *Introduction,* 122–123; James S. Hart Jr., *The Rule of Law, 1603–1660* (Harlow, 2003), 29–30; and Richard P. Cust and Andrew Hopper, eds., *Cases in the High Court of Chivalry, 1634–1640,* Harleian Society (London, 2006), n.s., xviii, Introduction. My thanks to Richard Cust for help in understanding this episode.

131. CUL, Mm.6.57, f. 18: Notes by Sir Edward Littleton. These include a précis of the many affidavits made in the case, which show the contempt of King's Bench by the actions of the earl marshal's servants.

132. The falsity of the return was revealed in a later affidavit. The two writs for Jones are in TNA, KB32/10, part 1 (25 November 1630, and 6 February 1631) and KB29/279/111d. and 140d. Contents of the affidavits in support of the contempt process pursued later are in notes made by Sir Edward Littleton: see CUL, Mm.6.57, f. 18-v. Further details are in the rule books: see KB21/10/109v., 114, 117v., 120v., 122, 124, and 125.

133. Arundel had imprisoned Sir John Howland, the JP who tipped off the affair by demanding surety for the peace from Thompson, on Jones's behalf; Thomas Husband, the friend who apparently sued Jones's "habeas coxcomb" for him; Richard More, who had served the writ; and both the attorney, Mr. Barrell, and the barrister, Mr. Tisdale, appointed by the court to represent Jones. See CUL, Mm.6.57, f. 18.

134. CUL, Mm.6.57, ff. 18-v. Littleton became a member of the High Commission in 1633, was made solicitor general in 1634, and was knighted in 1635. See *ODNB.*

135. All this is reported in a letter of 27 February 1631 from the Rev. Joseph Mead to Sir Martin Stuteville, in Thomas Birch, *The Court and Times of Charles the First* (London, 1848), vol. 2, pp. 97–98. Mead reported—secondhand—that the matter "was discussed . . . but not decided," given

that Arundel's jailed servants had by then been released. Apparently, Arundel was told by the Council that he might proceed again against Robert Jones. Arundel replied by citing a statute of 13 Richard II, c. 2, which he claimed required that anyone who wanted to contest the earl marshal's jurisdiction over a given suit must first obtain permission from the king's council. Others suggested this referred not to the Privy Council, but to "the king's great council of lords in parliament." This letter reports that the discussion in the Council occurred on 18 February ("Friday was sennight" before 27 February), though another letter dated 17 February suggests that the discussion may have happened on 16 February. This letter, as well, gives no conclusion, only noting that the debate was too "full of unprecedented passages too long for a letter." See *CSPD* 1629–1631, 512.

136. King's Bench may have continued the struggle. TNA, KB21/11/8 contains two orders of May 1631 on contempt process against William Davies, deputy to Thomas More, marshal of the king's household and thus one of those who had detained Robert Jones. We can only speculate that these may have been connected to this dispute, in which Davies would have been involved. But other signs show how King's Bench took a more restricted view of itself in the 1630s. In the survey years of 1630, 1634, and 1638, the release rate fell from a near average 53% in 1630, to 39% in 1634 and 1638. This change in habeas usage may be connected to the appointment of Sir Thomas Richardson as chief justice after the death of Sir Nicholas Hyde, in 1631; and of Sir Robert Berkeley as justice after the death of Sir James Whitelocke in 1632; see *ODNB*. The court's retreat is also evident in response to habeas cases involving jail orders by servants in the royal household. Edward White was committed to the marshal of the household by Arundel's warrant—though it did not refer to his office of earl marshal—for having given "an insolent abuse against Mrs. Stafford in her honor." Upon reviewing his detention on habeas corpus, White was remanded: see TNA, KB29/282/69 (Trinity, 1633), and KB21/11/115v. and 118v. Three others were committed by the treasurer of the household, and remanded on habeas corpus, in Easter 1634. John East and Richard Robyns were committed "for refusing to pay his majesty's composition" (KB29/283/44d.); and Richard Nightengale, originally detained by the coroner of Westminster, was transferred into the custody of the household by a warrant of the treasurer of the household so that he might be tried for an apparent killing within the verge (KB29/283/47d.). For orders in these cases, see generally KB21/11/145v.–50, passim, and 161.

4. Making Judgments

1. Following common vacation practice, the writ was antedated to the day after the last day of the previous term, 25 June 1629. Her laughter occurred on 12 July; imprisonment was ordered on 25 July. See TNA, KB145/15/5; KB29/278/121d.; and KB21/10/31; also CUL, Gg.2.19, f. 67.

2. In his commonplace book, Thomas Twisden found this formulation of "opposing of doctrine" sufficiently interesting that he noted White-locke's words: see HLS, 5016, f. 82v.

3. On strict construction of penal statutes, see Ellesmere's comments in Samuel E. Thorne, ed., *A Discourse upon the Exposicion & Understandinge of Statutes* (San Marino, 1942), 154–155.

4. Of thirteen others who challenged imprisonment on the statute against disturbing preachers, one was remanded: Jones, T. 159, 84 *ER* 1196 (Paul Moone, 1681). Twelve were discharged or bailed: see TNA, KB21/4/72 and HLS, 2077, f. 93 (Stainforth and two others, 1611); KB145/14/11 (Barnabas Doake and two others, 11 October 1613), KB29/255/130d., and KB21/4/130v.–31; KB29/296/114 and KB21/13/104v.–08v. (Thomas Bruce and Michael Beaver, 1647); KB145/16/1656 (Henry Blashfield, 24 January 1657); KB21/19/74v. and 3 Keble 803, 84 *ER* 1021 (John Nichols and Benjamin Robinson, 1677); and KB16/4/1 and KB21/27/64–65 (Christopher Mendel, 5 June 1706, discharged).

5. Throughout this chapter, and elsewhere, the distinction I want to make between rules and principles, and my emphasis on an equitable approach to decision-making, is influenced by Stephen L. Winter's analysis of metaphor's operation in legal thinking, in particular as he develops it in his discussion of radial categories. See Winter, *A Clearing in the Forest: Law, Life, and Mind* (Chicago, 2001), especially chapter 4. For more on equity, see Chapter 3.

6. Thomas Ashe, *Epieikeia* (1609), sig. Av.

7. Half (49%) of returns made between 1500 and 1560 lacked information about the jailing authority, the cause of imprisonment, or both. This practice fell to one-quarter by 1600; 5% by the Restoration; and all but disappeared by 1700. In the early sixteenth century, 58% came into King's Bench with no jailing authority mentioned. After 1560, this dropped: to 25% in the period 1560–1580; 15% during 1580–1600; 10% in the two decades following; and zero by 1630. Returning officers generally showed more care in naming a cause than in identifying the

type of jailing magistrate. Before 1560, well under 10% of writs were returned without a wrong named in them. From 1560 to 1600, this rose to 18%, an increase explained by the increase in writs to JPs returned without cause during these years. After 1600, that proportion fell by half and remained at around 10% until the 1680s, when vagueness about the cause all but disappeared. These numbers do not include returns on which pardons were pleaded, since these did not normally contain this information. For more, see the Appendix.

8. For the period 1560–1580, release rates on returns without the authority named and for all writs were 32% and 32%, respectively; for 1580–1600, the rates were 50% and 48%, respectively.

9. Release rates on returns that omitted the wrong compared to all returns for the same period, were, respectively: 1540–1560, 47% and 32%; 1560–1580, 50% and 32%; 1580–1600, 53% and 48%; and 1600–1620, 67% and 67%.

10. For a case at Chester, which as a palatinate claimed immunity from writs out of Westminster, see HLS, 113, p. 123; KB145/15/17 (for John Lloyd, 7 June 1641) and KB21/12/171v., 176, and 179v. The struggle to get the constable of Chester Castle to return the writ carried on until the constable made a return in late May 1642 on a writ issued in February, reporting that Lloyd had been jailed in a private suit in the Exchequer of Chester. No result survives: see KB32/20 (4 February 1642) and KB21/13/5–21, passim.

11. For fines for returns found insufficient in this way, see TNA, KB21/9/45 and 53 (1628); KB21/11/67v. (1632); and KB21/13/30v. (1643).

12. TNA, KB145/13/40 (4 November 1597) and KB29/235/37d.

13. Some returns without cause may have been the means by which prisoners could plead pardons. See TNA, KB29/209/35d. (Robert Suckerman), 37d. (James Hyckeford), and 108 (William Rochester), all in 1573–1574. That these writs were probably to bring them in to plead pardons is underscored by the fact that the returns for all three omit any information about the wrong each had committed.

14. TNA, KB145/9/21 (Cornelius Worley, 24 January 1506).

15. TNA, KB32/7 (William Gresham et al., 28 November 1631).

16. Cro. Car. 593, 79 ER 1109–1110; TNA, KB21/12/158 and 159v.

17. TNA, KB145/13/37 (Kedway, 19 June 1594) and KB29/232/29d. KB29/240/96 (Sparrow, 1602).

18. King's Bench bailed Robert Anderson: see TNA, KB145/14/7/2 (20 January 1610) and KB29/251/133d. There are many examples of releasing those jailed for failure to provide security without naming the

underlying cause: for instance, KB29/242/78 and KB145/13/45 (George Mady, 29 November 1602); and KB145/14/4 (Joanna Kiteley, 5 February 1607).

19. TNA, KB145/17/27 (John Evans, 23 May 1675: bailed); KB16/1/1 and KB21/23/407 and 416 (George Monson et al., 28 June 1690: discharged); and KB16/1/4 and KB21/24/285 and 287 (Thomas Phillips et al., 8 June 1694: discharged).

20. See 2 Strange 880, 93 *ER* 914 (Nathan).

21. HLS, 5016, f. 184 and TNA, KB21/9/23 (1627: discharged).

22. TNA, KB29/296/152d. and KB21/13/111 (1648).

23. King's Bench ordered the return amended. After the order was refused, Ayres was discharged. See TNA, KB29/283/46d., and KB21/11/156v., 159, and 160.

24. Justice Dodderidge, in CUL, Gg.2.30, f. 37v. (Jones, 1624).

25. CUL, Ii.5.32, f. 116 (Bourne, 1620).

26. Thus habeas decision-making did not fit a "rule-of-law" paradigm. An extensive literature addresses rule-of-law assumptions. For an approach through modern theories of cognition, which avoids the trap of seeing rule-following and indeterminacy as the only possibilities, see Winter, *Clearing in the Forest,* especially chapters 6 and 8.

27. See 33 Henry VIII, c. 6: An Act Concerning Crossbows and Handguns; TNA, KB29/240/95 and KB21/2/125v. YLS, GR29.14, f. 272v.

28. LI, Misc. 492, f. 539.

29. TNA, KB16/1/4 (10 November 1694) and KB21/24/309 and 313. Comberbach 305, 90 *ER* 493; LI, Hill 49, f. 223v. 3 William and Mary c. 10, §1, An Act for the . . . Punishment of Deer Stealers, required those who could not pay their fines to "suffer imprisonment by the space of one whole year" and to be pilloried for one hour. For a similar case, see Robert Green, discharged from commitment for poaching hares on a return that ordered him held until discharged by law, when it should have been for three months, according to the relevant statute: Fortescue 274, 92 *ER* 850 (1714).

30. Codd was remanded on a second writ after being jailed again. This time, the return omitted mention of contempt, thereby making the return more certain since now it focused strictly on his disobedience to the High Commission's order to cohabit with his wife. See 3 Bulstrode 109 and 146, 81 *ER* 94 and 125; and Bod., Rawl.C.382, f. 79v.; also TNA, KB145/14/13 (17 November 1615), KB29/259/138d., and KB29/261/147.

31. TNA, KB145/15/4 (12 October 1628), KB145/15/5 (24 October 1629), and KB29/278/120d; TNA, KB21/9/52–59v. and KB21/10/

36v. and 37v.; Cro. Car. 133 and 168, 79 *ER* 717 and 746–747; HLS, 1128, f. 26; and CUL, Gg.2.19, f. 91.

32. TNA, KB21/1/94: *nisi* order to amend a return to the mayor and aldermen of London, or be fined £5 (Easter 1595). Evidence of amendment orders appears in the rulebooks, but these survive only from 1589. For earlier Common Pleas orders to amend, see *Dyer Reports*, vol. 2, p. 355 (Hinde, 1576); and 1 Leonard 70, 74 *ER* 66 (Howel, 1587).

33. TNA, KB21/2/87 (Brearley, 1601). For more on this case, see Chapter 8.

34. Thomas Jones had been imprisoned by the Council in the Marches of Wales on a vague return of contempt. King's Bench ordered Jones bailed while it awaited an amended return. By amending its return, the Council explained better its use of its jurisdiction, and Jones was remanded. See CUL, Gg.2.30, f. 37v.; TNA, KB21/8/21v.–32, passim (1624).

35. Parliamentary commissioners of accounts returned that Col. Francis Hacker had been jailed "until you shall receive further order from us" after he had failed to present his account. Though uncertain owing to the return's potential for indefinite imprisonment, the court ordered Hacker remanded while the commissioners were allowed to amend. No amendments were made, so Hacker was discharged. See TNA, KB32/7 (22 October 1646); KB29/295/86; and KB21/13/78–82, passim.

36. For instance, King's Bench ordered the High Commission to amend its return for Henry Williams, who had been jailed for abusive words against the Bishop of Llandaff, the bishop's wife, and clerical marriage generally. Williams was bailed, then discharged after the commission failed to amend. See TNA, KB145/14/4 (24 May 1606), KB29/247/31d., and KB21/3/64, 65, 65v., and 88; HLS, 118, f. 126v.–27; and Noy 17, 74 *ER* 988.

37. TNA, KB145/15/4 (14 June 1628) and KB21/9/44, 45, and 46. Melvyn would be bailed the following winter on a second writ: KB145/15/4 (12 February 1629).

38. Changes after filing sometimes occurred. Sir Francis North condemned this "abuse"; see BL, Add. 32,518, f. 17v. But Justice Wilde suggested that "it might be amended if [the return] were filed." See LI, Misc. 386, f. 28 (Hyde, 1675).

39. TNA, KB145/17/31 (9 May 1679) and 1 Ventris 336, 86 *ER* 217. The report says the writ was for "J.S.," but the return suggests this must be the report on Beaumont's writ.

40. Rulebooks (TNA, KB21) show scores, if not hundreds, of rules to file

returns, to stay filing, and so on. These increased dramatically after 1640.

41. For discussion of this apparent rule and the means for avoiding it, see R. J. Sharpe, *The Law of Habeas Corpus,* 2d ed. (Oxford, 1989), chapter 3, especially 64–71. For an early awareness of the rule's porosity, see Rollin C. Hurd, *A Treatise on the Right of Personal Liberty, and on the Writ of Habeas Corpus,* 2d ed. (Albany, 1876), 257–270.

42. Noy 149, 74 *ER* 1111–1112. Noy ascribes this view to "the court." That it was Coke is confirmed by the report of his discussion in HLS 1058, f. 104 (Wharton, ca. 1608–1610: a churchwarden who refused to take the oath on the 39 Articles, remanded). Coke would repeat this view in 1615. See 1 Rolle 192 and 219, 81 *ER* 425 and 445; and Bod., Rawl. C.382, ff. 56v.–57v. (Rosewell, 1615).

43. Wilm. 106, 97 *ER* 42.

44. Kevin Costello, "Habeas Corpus and Military and Naval Impressment, 1756–1816," *Journal of Legal History* 29 (2008): 226–230.

45. See 11 Co. Rep. 93b, 77 *ER* 1271–1281. A 1711 statute (9 Anne, c. 20) would end the need to proceed by a separate action for false return to mandamus, thus permitting much shorter contests. See Paul D. Halliday, *Dismembering the Body Politic: Partisan Politics in England's Towns, 1650–1730* (Cambridge, Eng., 1998), 67–73, 131–145, 291–295, and 319–320.

46. This typically concerned brief detentions: YLS, GR.29.6, ff. 13v.–14v. (Collett v. Webbe, 1582). One might also sue after being put in the stocks: see Cro. Eliz. 204 and 287, 78 *ER* 460 and 541 (Stretton v. Browne, 1590, and Beal v. Charter, 1592).

47. John Chambers, jailed with John Woods for disturbing a London election, waited two years after release on habeas corpus before suing false imprisonment; see Style 78 and 84, 82 *ER* 544 and 549–550 (1648). For his 1645/1646 habeas corpus, see TNA, KB29/294/54, and KB21/13/59–77v., passim; HLS, 113, pp. 249–251 and 277–278; and HLS, 145, pp. 1–3 and 6–7.

48. TNA, KB16/7/1 (24 October 1717), and KB21/31/10, 19, and 24. Admiralty solicitor's letters show signs of false imprisonment used after the fact in wrongful impressment cases: see, e.g., TNA, ADM1/3677/135–36 (6 November 1756).

49. It is impossible to prove a negative conclusively. But I have read scores of printed and manuscript reports on false imprisonment, and have seen no signs of false imprisonment or false return sued by a person then in prison who sought thereby to impugn a return to habeas corpus as a means to procure release.

50. On rule making and following as a "motivated" activity, see Winter, *Clearing in the Forest*, 187–193, 206–216, and 221.

51. Michael MacNair, *The Law of Proof in Early Modern Equity* (Berlin, 1999), 167–176.

52. HLS, 2077, f. 93; TNA, KB21/4/ 72.

53. On confession and avoidance, see Baker, *Introduction*, 77.

54. Cro. Eliz. 821, 78 *ER* 1048. Gardiner's case would figure in Goldswain's case, on habeas corpus for impressment, in 1778. Justice Sir Henry Gould explained, "I do not conceive that either the court or the party are concluded by the return of a habeas corpus, but may plead to it any special matter necessary to regain his liberty." See 2 Black. W. 1209, 96 *ER* 712.

55. TNA, KB145/17/34 (3 May 1682), and KB21/21/149, 154, 159, 162, 164, and 182.

56. Barbara Shapiro notes the embarrassment of common lawyers regarding the influence of Romano-canon law on common law evidence, which "militated against explicit borrowing. When borrowing did occur, it was safely anglicized through citations to Bracton or Coke." See Shapiro, *"Beyond Reasonable Doubt" and "Probable Cause": Historical Perspectives on the Anglo-American Law of Evidence* (Berkeley, 1991), 121. Michael MacNair, in discussing the relationship among common law, civil law, and equity, argues that new evidence practices "suggest equitable influence on the law rather than the reverse." Like Shapiro, MacNair notes it was "more acceptable to borrow civilians' arguments than actually to cite them directly." See MacNair, *Law of Proof*, 277 and 293.

57. Style 96, 82 *ER* 559 (Anonymous). After being brought into King's Bench on habeas corpus from the New Prison, Elizabeth Claxton was committed to the Marshalsea on affidavits that showed her to be "a lewd woman and a frequenter of bawdy houses." See Holt KB 406, 90 *ER* 1124; and LI, Misc. 713, p. 190 (1701).

58. See 1 Barn. KB 402, 94 *ER* 271 (1730). He was then remanded on further affidavits showing that he was being sued in Common Pleas.

59. Sess. Cas. 62, 93 *ER* 63 (as "Crest"), and 2 Barn. KB 271, 94 *ER* 495 (1733).

60. A good example concerns Henry Jackson, who was jailed in Chester after allegedly leading a shipboard mutiny. Habeas corpus was used to bring him into King's Bench. Despite affidavits complaining of his crimes and the lack of substance of his proposed sureties, Jackson was bailed to await the next admiralty sessions. See TNA, KB16/7/1 (26 May 1718); KB21/31/90 and 106; and KB1/1/2, affidavits of Hockenhull Short, Thomas Bell, and James Gillaspy.

61. LI, Misc. 386, f. 27, and 3 Keble 470, 84 *ER* 829 (Emerton, née Hyde, 1675).

62. Charles M. Gray, *The Writ of Prohibition: Jurisdiction in Early Modern English Law* (New York, 1994), vol. 1, pp. xviii–xxii.

63. TNA, KB145/17/18 (26 May and 28 June 1666); KB29/317/116; KB21/16/11v.–22, passim; 1 Sid. 287, 82 *ER* 1110–1111; 2 Keble 50 and 54, 84 *ER* 32 and 34. When discussing the history of habeas corpus in parliamentary debates in 1758, Wilmot declared, incorrectly—as it appears from the record—that the method used in Swallow's case brought the factual dispute to a jury trial. He also declared, "[I]t was agreed in that case that matter contrary to the return could not be pleaded, but the party is put to his action for the false return"; Wilm. 112, 97 *ER* 45. There is no sign of such a declaration, though there was recognition of the rule, and then this method taken to circumvent it. In his report of Goldswain's case (1778), Blackstone would cite Swallow: "[I]t seems that no one can controvert the truth of the return to a habeas corpus, or plead or suggest any matter repugnant to it; yet he may confess and avoid such return, by admitting the truth of the matters contained in it, and suggesting others not repugnant, which take off the effect of them"; see 2 Black. W. 1211, 96 *ER* 713.

64. See 1 Sid. 78, 82 *ER* 980–981. This was true in the case of Zachary Crofton, who was jailed by Council order for treason, and remanded; see TNA, KB145/17/14 (30 May 1662). He was later discharged by the king's command: see GI, 34, p. 457.

65. Mansfield pointed this out in the 1758 debates on the bill to amend habeas corpus: see *Parl. Hist.,* vol. 15, p. 900n.

66. TNA, KB1/2/1, affidavit of Elizabeth Mercer, 20 April 1722.

67. TNA, KB21/34, Tuesday after the morrow, and Monday after fifteen St. Martins (1738). Daine was Hannah's father, to whom she had gone after leaving her husband. For Daine's affidavit, see Elizabeth Foyster, "Parenting Was for Life, Not Just for Childhood: The Role of Parents in the Married Lives of Their Children," *History* 86 (2001): 326.

68. I use the expression "order *nisi*" rather than "rule *nisi*"—the more common expression in the period—to prevent confusion between rules as guides followed by judges, and rules as orders or commands made by the justices. Jailers who had not made a return might receive a rule *nisi* imposing fines, or releasing a prisoner, unless they made a return. The earliest known example is a threatened £5 amercement against the mayor of Canterbury if he did not return a writ for Robert Steele and Walter Aldyce in Easter term 1589: see TNA, KB21/1/10v.

69. London's sheriffs were threatened with a £10 fine unless they

amended the return to a writ for Nicholas Hurde: see TNA, KB21/1/126 (Michaelmas, 1596).

70. This was how Nicholas Lowe was released: see TNA, KB21/3/56, and Chapter 2. See too Henry Williams, jailed by the Bishop of London's court: KB21/3/88; Alphonse St. Victoire, committed by the College of Physicians, and later discharged: KB145/14/12 (29 June 1614), KB29/257/68d., and KB21/5/29v.; and Edward Walford, committed for not making his hearth tax account, and discharged on his readiness to appear in the Court of Exchequer: KB145/14/22 (4 February 1670), and KB21/17/29v.–30v.

71. The return showed a conciliar order in support of an imprisonment order by the vice chancellor of Cambridge against James Robson and others for contempt of university privileges in a dispute over the town's markets. Robson and his fellows, then held in the Gatehouse in Westminster, were bailed. See TNA, KB29/240/42, and KB21/2/113v.–23, passim.; as well as *CSPD* 1601–1603, 54 and 123.

72. TNA, KB21/6/4. See the similar case for Francis Oliver to the Marches of Wales, to which the writ issued in 1622 after multiple *nisi* orders: KB145/14/20 (10 July 1622), KB29/271/116d., and KB21/7/5, 5v., 6, 7, and 9. Oliver was bailed from his imprisonment for contempt.

73. TNA, KB145/16/1650 (6 May 1650), and KB21/13/162, 164v, and 165. Committed "during the pleasure" of Parliament, Chetwynd was remanded.

74. *Report from the Committee to whom the Petition of John Touchet and John Irving, Agents for the British Subjects residing in the Provinces of Bengal, Bahar, and Orissa. . .* (1781), General Appendix no. 9 (unpaginated, at rear).

75. This is especially important for some prisoner of war cases: see Chapter 5.

76. TNA, KB16/15/1 (13 November 1756), and KB21/37/556, 567, 576, and 605.

77. Extensive affidavits in these cases, made initially to move for habeas corpus, are in TNA, KB1/12/6. Notes on the outside of these show the process: motions for the writ were denied, then converted into a motion for the rule, followed by more affidavits to show the service of the rule, and then the final discharge. For orders in Dunn's case, see KB21/37/583 and 593.

78. See 29 George II, c. 4; Costello, "Habeas Corpus and Impressment," especially 215–218.

79. See 29 George II, c. 4: An Act for the Speedy and Effectual Recruiting of his Majesty's Land Forces. See also Philip C. Yorke, *The Life and Cor-*

respondence of Philip Yorke, Earl of Hardwicke (Cambridge, Eng., 1913), vol. 3, pp. 1–4.

80. Wilm. 83, 97 ER 32n–34n.

81. For full accounts of parliamentary debates and the 1758 bill, see James Oldham and Michael Wishnie, "The Historical Scope of Habeas Corpus and INS v. St. Cyr," *Georgetown Immigration Law Journal* 16 (2002): 485–503, and Costello, "Habeas Corpus and Impressment," 218–234.

82. As Solicitor General Charles Yorke put it, "[T]he authority by which the warrants for impressing seamen are issued is part of the prerogative of the crown, to be executed under the orders of the Lords Commissioners of the Admiralty." See TNA, ADM7/298/548: opinion of 17 January 1757. Two 1641 statutes "for the raising of mariners" had long since expired: 16 Charles, cc. 5 and 26. The few returns made to impressment writs describe the authority of press officers arising from an impress warrant from the Admiralty, which had been issued on commands of the Privy Council: e.g., KB16/21/3 (Jacob Pennyman and Matthew Cockburn, 12 February 1794). No result for their writ survives.

83. One did not actually have to have a protection in order to be exempt. And though having one was helpful, it was no guarantee of being left alone. Many sailors using habeas corpus complained that they had been pressed even after showing a protection; see TNA, ADM1/3680/83–85, and ADM1/1788: John Falkingham to John Clevland, 2 April 1762. Among statutes defining protected classes of seamen, see 13 George II, c. 17: An Act for the Increase of Mariners (foreigners; those under 18 or over 55) and 11 George III, c. 38: An Act for Support of the Greenland Fishery (Greenland fishermen). See also J. A. Woods, "The City of London and Imprisonment, 1776–1777," *Proceedings of the Leeds Philosophical and Literary Society* (1957): 114–115.

84. In all, 239 sailors used the writ in the quadrennial survey years, suggesting a total of nearly a thousand. But because most writs were not returned, and because many issued during vacations, when there would be no record of even an order to issue the writ, this is probably a significant undercount.

85. TNA, ADM1/3678/112v., order of 5 February 1761.

86. For examples, see TNA, ADM1/3678, 4, 74, and 123, and ADM1/3680/428–429 and 456.

87. For more on habeas process in naval impressment, see Costello, "Habeas Corpus and Impressment," 234–249.

88. This may have been necessary in such cases since all habeas could do was release from custody, not reassign it, as might be required to en-

sure that an apprentice was returned to a master from whom he may have fled. For Mansfield's discussion, see 1 Leach 203, 168 *ER* 204 (Anon., 1779). Like habeas corpus, these warrants issued on the basis of an affidavit, usually from a master. For an example, see TNA, ADM1/3680/172–74: Samuel Seddon to Philip Stephens, 23 April 1777, recommending discharge of apprentice James Nicholson from HMS *Conquistador.* For an early example, see ADM1/1787, unfol.: John Falkingham to Philip Stephens, 17 October 1761, with discussion and order for discharge at ADM1/3678/169. Falkingham reported that William Walker, the sailor in question for whom Mansfield issued one of these warrants, had enlisted voluntarily, exchanging the servitude of apprenticeship as a coach painter for service at sea.

89. TNA, ADM1/3680/510: James Dyson to Philip Stephens, 30 December 1778.

90. On these practices, see Costello, "Habeas Corpus and Impressment," 241–242 and 248. It is only after 1788 that we find the court ordering remand of sailors to their ships after hearing full returns to their writs: e.g., TNA, KB16/20/5 (Jeremiah Boutcher and George Hipkins, 11 November 1790), KB21/45/328, 335, and 341.

91. Thomas Walcott was jailed in Ireland before transfer to the Tower of London. The return to his 1673 writ showed suspicion of treason. Nonetheless, he was bailed on the condition that he appear at King's Bench in Ireland to respond to the charges. See BL, Add. 32,527, f. 28v. and TNA, KB21/18/15, 16v., 17v., and 18. In Stainforth's case— see earlier and KB21/4/72—the prisoners' bail required their appearance at the next Yorkshire assizes, and that resolution of the dispute be referred to the archbishop of York.

92. TNA, KB21/34, Friday next after the Morrow of St. Martin and Tuesday after eight days from St. Martin, 7 George II (1733). 2 Barn. KB 349, 94 *ER* 546–547. The statute was 12 Anne, sess. 2, c. 23. Harper later showed he was a householder and was fully discharged. His imprisonment was part of a struggle over theater licensing in London. For a similar case of 1738, see James Lacy, who was remanded to the house of correction: KB16/11/4 (27 January 1738), and KB21/34, at Friday in fifteen Hilary, 11 George II (1738). On Harper and Lacy, see *ODNB.*

93. TNA, KB16/1/4 (25 April 1694) and KB21/24/270, 274, and 275. LI, Hill 49, f. 205, and Comberbach 245, 90 *ER* 456.

94. There is a common misconception that English habeas did nothing more than test jurisdictional competence, without looking inside the jurisdiction to consider its use. Until at least the turn of the nineteenth

century, this was far from the case. See Larry W. Yackle, *Federal Courts: Habeas Corpus* (New York, 2003), 17–19.

95. For more on Brearley's case, see Chapter 8.

96. TNA, KB16/1/1 (25 June 1690) and KB21/23/404, 410, and 412; also Carthew 152, 90 *ER* 693. For referral of another parish dispute to arbitration, see TNA, KB21/19/121v. and 126 (Stephen Weller, 1678). In 1715, an overseer of the poor was jailed by two JPs when he refused to present his accounts, as required by statute. He was released on habeas after giving his recognizance to bring his accounts to the next quarter sessions. See Fortescue 272, 92 *ER* 849 (Gibson).

97. A person convicted of felony was less likely to be released (30%) than one appearing prior to conviction (49%).

98. TNA, KB145/10/38 (22 October 1546) and KB29/179/34.

99. Henry Frank was bailed on a plea of clergy when brought before Chief Justice Catlin at his London home during the vacation after conviction for homicide; see TNA, KB145/13/8 (26 December 1565) and KB29/200/52d. On benefit of clergy, see Baker, *Introduction,* 513–515.

100. Richard Humpton pleaded clergy after his conviction at Aylesbury assizes for burglary in 1506. This bought him time to procure a pardon, which passed the great seal that September. The following month, habeas corpus issued on his behalf. Once in King's Bench, he pleaded his pardon and was discharged: TNA, KB145/9/22 (14 October 1506) and KB29/136/9. For the pardon, see *Calendar of the Patent Rolls* (London, 1916), Henry VII, vol. 2, p. 499. After John Howkyns was convicted of robbery at Warwick assizes, the justices ordered his execution stayed. This provided time for King's Bench to send habeas corpus to bring Howkyns before Chief Justice Catlin. Howkyns was ultimately pardoned; see *Dyer Reports,* vol. 2, p. 287. The report indicates that the return was ordered to be made to his home in the country, though the controlment entry shows that the return was to be made to Catlin in Serjeants' Inn: TNA, KB29/209/36.

101. TNA, KB21/11/190v. (Barfoote, 1635). On pardon process, and in particular on the increasing attachment of the condition of transportation to allowance of pardon from the middle of the seventeenth century, see Cynthia Herrup, "Punishing Pardon: Some Thoughts on the Origins of Penal Transportation," in Simon Devereaux and Paul Griffiths, eds., *Penal Practice and Culture, 1500–1900: Punishing the English* (Basingstoke, 2004), 121–137.

102. Louis A. Knafla, *Law and Politics in Jacobean England: The Tracts of Lord Chancellor Ellesmere* (Cambridge, Eng., 1977), 277.

103. TNA, KB145/14/4 (12 February 1606), KB29/247/32d., and KB21/3/54.

104. Sir Philip Lloyd was convicted of homicide, then bailed on habeas: see TNA, KB29/341/75, and KB21/21/101, 102, 107, 115, 116, and 142 (1682).

105. See 1 Ventris 158, 86 *ER* 108 (Maddy, 1671).

106. TNA, KB29/318 (9 November 1666) and KB21/16/30–31. For what was probably a similar use of pardon after conviction for homicide in extenuating circumstances, see KB32/10, part 1 (29 April 1630, John Eve).

107. John Hychborne was ultimately discharged by these means after his conviction on an insufficient indictment for felony; see TNA, KB145/10/37 (28 January 1546) and KB29/178/38d.

108. William Sheppard makes this distinction: see his *A Sure Guide for his Majesties Justices of Peace* (1663), 370. See also Holt CJ: "The record is never removed by a habeas corpus, as it is on a certiorari . . . and the return is only an account of their proceedings": Holt KB 335, 90 *ER* 1085 (Fazakerley v. Baldo, 1704).

109. William Sheppard, *A Grand Abridgment of the Common and Statute Law of England* (1675), part 2, 284. By filing the return, the court became "seised of the record": see Style 397, 82 *ER* 809 (Streater, 1653).

110. See 3 Keble 803, 84 *ER* 1021 (Nichols and Robbins, 1677: jailed for disturbing a preacher, and bailed).

111. Numerous observers commented on this effect of both writs. See Sir Francis North: BL, Add. 32,519, f. 111. For punishment of JPs proceeding after certiorari, see Bod., North.f.16, f. 45.

112. King's Bench discharged Dr. Greenwell in 1697 from imprisonment for malpractice by the College of Physicians, but explained that if he wished to sue false imprisonment, he would have to use certiorari to acquire the record of conviction on which to proceed. See LI, Misc. 9 (1), p. 29.

113. On Alborough, see TNA, KB21/22/334 and 337 and KB21/23/4, 26, 28, 54, and 62; and *CSPD* 1686–1687, 145, 179, 183, and 191. On Knightley, see KB16/2/1 (24 October 1698), KB21/25/279, and *CSPD* 1698, 367 and 410. On transportation, see J. M. Beattie, *Crime and the Courts in England, 1660–1800* (Princeton, 1986), chapter 9.

114. On summary process, see Robert B. Shoemaker, *Prosecution and Punishment: Petty Crime and the Law in London and Rural Middlesex, c. 1660–1725* (Cambridge, Eng., 1991), 35–40, and Peter King, *Crime, Justice, and Discretion in England, 1740–1820* (Oxford, 2000), chapter 4.

115. For the first, see TNA, KB145/13/8 (Thomas Baker, et al., 2 May 1566: bailed, then pardoned); KB29/200/79d.

116. For more on release rates and JPs' imprisonment orders, see the Appendix.

117. Thus Thomas Curtys was discharged: see TNA, KB145/14/2 (4 May 1604). The warrant that jailed Thomas Price put no term on his imprisonment, and he was bailed: KB145/14/3 (3 June 1605), and KB29/246/65d. On JPs' work on alehouses, see Peter Clark, *The English Alehouse: A Social History, 1200–1830* (London, 1983), chapter 8.

118. TNA, KB145/15/3 (14 November 1627); KB21/9/19v. and 25; and Jones W., 170, 82 *ER* 91.

119. See 17 Charles II, c. 2; TNA, KB145/17/34 (11 November 1682), KB29/341/80, and KB21/21/254 and 257; Skinner 80, 90 *ER* 38.

120. R. H. Helmholz, *The Canon Law*, vol. 1 of *The Oxford History of the Laws of England* (Oxford, 2004), chapter 10; and Martin Ingram, *Church Courts, Sex and Marriage in England, 1570–1640* (Cambridge, Eng., 1987), 146–150 and chapter 5.

121. *Excommunicato capiendo* was a writ issued from Chancery to make an arrest of someone in order to enforce a church court order of excommunication. On excommunication, see Helmholz, *Canon Law*, 619–622. For examples, see the 1602 writs for Helen Acres and Katherine Fludd, both of whom were jailed for defamation by church courts using excommunication process, then remanded on habeas corpus: TNA, KB29/240/117, and KB29/242/46d. and KB145/13/45 (22 October 1602). Jane Barrett's discharge on her writ apparently resulted from a finding that proper process had not been followed: see KB145/13/45 (12 October 1602) and KB29/24/46. Imprisonment in cases of contempt often ended with the prisoner's discharge: Anne Rooper (1608), for example, was discharged after imprisonment by the archdeaconry court of Leicester for not appearing in a defamation suit; see TNA, KB29/248/144.

122. See 1 Elizabeth, c. 1. There were multiple commissions, the two main ones being for the archdioceses of Canterbury and York. Commissions were also created for individual dioceses. The standard work on the subject remains Roland G. Usher, *The Rise and Fall of the High Commission* (Oxford, 1913).

123. Helmholz, *Canon Law*, 286–289 and 558–560, and R. H. Helmholz, *Roman Canon Law in Reformation England* (Cambridge, Eng., 1990), 73–79.

124. Nicholas East, jailed for refusing to obey a sessions order to give bond

to pay maintenance for his illegitimate child, was remanded: see TNA, KB145/14/10 (1 July 1612).

125. His warrant contained no clause stating when his imprisonment might end; see TNA, KB145/14/2 (9 February 1605) and KB29/244/129d. Similarly, Ralph Broughton confessed his attempt to lure a woman into a bigamous match. He too was bailed from an imprisonment for refusing to give his bond: see TNA, KB145/14/3 (1 June 1605) and KB29/246/65.

126. The writ might also bail a man like Robert Eyre, jailed by the High Commission for helping his sister avoid entering into a marriage to which she had already contracted: see TNA, KB145/14/5 (25 June 1607) and KB29/248/66.

127. Usher, *High Commission,* 343. The discussion was prompted by Chancey's case (1611) in Common Pleas, in which the justices, led by Coke, disagreed about the High Commission's powers to imprison in marital disputes: see 12 Co. Rep. 82, 77 *ER* 1360, and Sir Edward Coke, *The Fourth Part of the Institutes of the Laws of England* (1644), pp. 324–335. Given that his twelfth volume of reports (first published in 1656) and the fourth of the *Institutes* (completed in the 1630s) were completed after Coke left the bench in 1616, and after the debates of 1627–1628, one must be skeptical about how well they report earlier discussions.

128. The first of three writs for Wilcox was not filed. The court decided to consider further after hearing the return to the first, then ordered another writ to issue. This explains the absence of a judgment on the first. For the other two, see TNA, KB145/14/13 (27 April and 16 June 1615); KB29/259/47d., 48, and 68; and KB21/5a/13v., 15, 19v., 23v. and 25. See also John Cornish, imprisoned for adultery and remanded: KB145/14/13 (16 June 1615), KB29/259/68d., KB29/261/81, and KB21/5a/25, 69v., 72, and 73. Cornish apparently paid a fine of £100 before his troubles ended: see TNA, E101/616/28. John Packington, committed for refusal to pay alimony, was also remanded: see KB29/261/146 (1616).

129. See 2 Bulstrode 300, 80 *ER* 1138; TNA, KB145/14/12 (26 November 1614); KB29/257/119d.; and KB21/5/39v., 40, and 48 (the last of these is a *nisi* order to excuse).

130. TNA, KB29/251/67d. and KB21/4/13. Ralph Brooke's imprisonment for failure to maintain his wife also ended in a mediated settlement. See KB145/14/13 (5 May 1615), and KB21/5a/10v.–16v., passim; also Moore KB 840, 72 *ER* 940–941.

131. Sir Edward Plowden's violence to his wife was the occasion in 1640 for High Commission orders for separation. When he was jailed for non-compliance, the return to his habeas contained a verbatim entry of Lady Mabel's complaint against him, as well as the order for separation and alimony. King's Bench remanded him on this return, then made its own order for him to pay alimony in the same terms imposed by the High Commission. See TNA, KB32/7 (10 October 1640), and KB21/12/148, 156, 157v., 158, and 158v.

132. See 16 Charles I, c. 11: An Act for Repeal of . . . Commissioners for Causes Ecclesiastical.

133. LI, Misc. 500, f. 174.

134. This also explains why no further orders on the writ survive. See ibid., and TNA, KB21/17/71–72. William Lambarde describes the practice of swearing articles for the peace in *Eirenarcha: or of the Office of the Iustices of Peace* (1581), chapter 16, especially 87–88. On bonds to keep the peace sued by wives against their husbands at a later period, see Joanne Bailey, *Unquiet Lives: Marriage and Marriage Breakdown in England, 1660–1800* (Cambridge, Eng., 2003), 40–43.

135. In 1674, King's Bench ordered a writ for Lady Leigh so that she might swear the peace against her husband. In doing so, the court referred to Lady Howard's case, though it "was the first that ever was granted"; see BL, Add. 32,527, f. 61. Again, the justices tried mediation, apparently with success. See TNA, KB21/18/61–72v. 1 Freeman 376, 89 *ER* 280.

136. TNA, KB145/17/27 (30 January, and 11, 14, and 15 May 1675).

137. LI, Misc. 386, ff. 28, 29, and 34.

138. See 1 Freeman 389 and 401, 89 *ER* 289 and 298; TNA, KB21/18/67v.–101v., passim. Proceedings continued around other issues concerning whether Viner's returns constituted a contempt. His role as goldsmith to the king, if not as lord mayor, protected him from the court's anger: see LI, Misc. 386, f. 34; and *ODNB*, s.v., Sir Robert Viner, and Peregrine Osborne, Viscount Dunblane and second Duke of Leeds.

139. For the writ to Jamaica for Thomas Meade in 1672, see TNA, KB21/17/103.

140. See 1 Strange 444, 93 *ER* 625 (Rex v. Clarkson [Turbervillle]).

141. TNA, KB16/16/3 (6 November 1766), and KB21/39, unpag., Thursday next after the morrow of All Souls.

142. Ibid.; 4 Burr. 1991, 98 *ER* 38 (1766).

143. TNA, KB16/21/3 (26 April 1793) and KB21/46/152. For a similar resolution—the court declared "you may go where you please"—see Ridg. t. H. 152, 27 *ER* 787–788 (Edgar, 1789).

144. BL, Add. 32,527, f. 61 (Anon., n.d.). No result survives.

145. TNA, KB16/7/1 (John Green, 2 July 1718). No result survives. For a possible earlier case, involving [Frances Oldfield?] in 1691, see LI, Hill 49, f. 138.

146. The D'Vebres agreed to separate. See TNA, KB1/14/5, 27 January 1761: affidavits of Peter Bodkin and John Monro, 2 Burr. 1115, 97 *ER* 741. For Hunt, see KB21/39/17 and 20; as well as 3 Burr. 1362, 97 *ER* 875–876 (1762). See also Jonathan Andrews and Andrew Scull, *Undertaker of the Mind: John Monro and Mad-Doctoring in Eighteenth-Century England* (Berkeley, 2001), 156–157 and 172–173.

147. See 14 George III, c. 49: An Act for Regulating Madhouses. For the 1763 Commons report on madhouses, with further cases, see *Parl. Hist.*, vol. 15, pp. 1283–1290. One later occasion for habeas was for Elizabeth Airey to Dr. John Hall of Newcastle-upon-Tyne, in whose custody she had been put by her husband. The writ was ordered returned to Justice Buller, at Northumberland assizes, which explains why no result survives in King's Bench records, but see TNA, KB21/44, Saturday after fifteen Trinity, 26 George III (1786). See also Elizabeth Foyster, "At the Limits of Liberty: Married Women and Confinement in Eighteenth-Century England," *Continuity and Change* 17 (2002): 54 and 57; and Andrews and Scull, *Undertaker of the Mind*, 158–160.

148. BL, Add. 32,527, f. 93v. (Anon., 1676).

149. LI, Misc. 375, p. 7 (Selick, 1686).

150. TNA, KB21/23/431 and 441.

151. This even though the writ had issued on the basis of affidavits alleging the father's violence to her. See TNA, KB21/26/100 and 106; LI, Misc. 713, p. 164; HLS, 1124, p. 83; and Fortescue 196, 92 *ER* 816.

152. TNA, KB21/28/48 and 49. Lady Catherine Annesley was daughter of the late third Earl of Anglesey. In 1699, the earl had married Lady Katherine Darnley, illegitimate daughter of James II. Their daughter arrived in 1700; their marriage ended in 1701 with a parliamentary separation due to the earl's cruelty. The mother married the Duke of Buckingham in 1706. Baroness Haversham was the second wife of that baron, whose late first wife had been the daughter of the first Earl of Anglesey, thus constituting a distant kinship with Lady Catherine. We can only guess that she went with her mother. On child custody issues generally, see Elizabeth Foyster, *Marital Violence: An English Family History, 1660–1857* (Cambridge, Eng., 2005), chapter 3.

153. See 2 Ld. Raym 1333, 92 *ER* 370 and 1 Strange 579, 93 *ER* 711–712; see also TNA, KB21/32/143, 155, 156, and 166. There had been some trouble inducing Mary Johnson to return the writ, as attested in the affidavit of service of John Buckley, KB1/2/3/3 (5 February 1724).

154. That probate decision may have contradicted a statute that, at the least, confused the issue of where and how the terms in wills concerning guardianship might be made effective. The reports show no sign that the justices considered the 1660 Act for Taking Away the Court of Wards (12 Charles II, c. 24), which declared that a father might appoint a guardian by will for any minor. It also appointed recovery of guardianship by action of ravishment or trespass. Habeas corpus would certainly have been a more expeditious way to handle such a dispute.

155. Justice Raymond reportedly "repented of what was done." See 2 Strange 982, 93 *ER* 983.

156. TNA, KB1/4/2/1: affidavit of Penelope Smith, 15 June 1734.

157. The court noted that the father could proceed by other means to recover custody, which by common law, he should have. But they refused that it should "be determined by them in this summary way." See 2 Strange 982, 93 *ER* 983 and Ridg t. H. 149, 27 *ER* 787. These reports misdate the case. The record shows that it was 1734: see TNA, KB21/34, Friday next after fifteen Easter, Friday on the morrow of Ascension, and Monday next after the octave of Trinity.

158. See 1 Black. W. 413, 96 *ER* 235.

159. Miss E. Ambrose, *The Life and Memoirs of the Late Miss Ann Catley, the Celebrated Actress. . .* (1789), 29 and 32; *The Laws Respecting Women, as they Regard their Natural Rights. . .* (1777), 362–367.

160. For Elizabeth Vernon, whose aunt allowed her to run off with an Irish officer, see TNA, KB21/39/1, and 1 Black. W. 386, 96 *ER* 218 (1762). For Sarah Woodcock, who decided to remain with her seducer, Lord Baltimore, see 1 Black. W. 648, 96 *ER* 376–377 (1768).

161. Consider, too, the case of Lydia Clarke. The affidavit by James Mervin alleged the violence of Lydia Clarke's father as the reason she had fled. Mr. Clarke's return to the writ sent to him showed instead that she had been carried off, with Mervin's connivance, so that she might marry a former servant. Clarke retrieved her with the help of six armed men. In court, when Mansfield left her "at liberty" to go where she pleased, she chose her father. Mansfield then recommended Mervin's prosecution for perjury. See TNA, KB21/38/133. The return is excerpted at length in *Laws Respecting Women*, 360–362; Mervin's affidavit is at KB1/13/3, 23 May 1758.

162. Ambrose, *Ann Catley*, 4.

163. TNA, KB21/41, Saturday after fifteen days of St. Martins, 15 George III (1774). Loftt 748, 98 *ER* 899: this is by the name "Blissett," but all the details in the report accord with the record in Bissell's case. See Foyster, *Marital Violence*, 160. On differing standards for deciding child

custody, in habeas and beyond, during the eighteenth century, see Danaya C. Wright, *"De Manneville v. De Manneville:* Rethinking the Birth of Custody Law under Patriarchy," *Law and History Review* 17 (1999): especially 275–284.

164. Lawrence Stone, *Road to Divorce: England, 1530–1987* (Oxford, 1995), 175–176. On the rise of contract ideas in marital relations, and the reassertion of patriarchal norms against those ideas in the late eighteenth century, see Susan Staves, *Married Women's Separate Property in England, 1660–1833* (Cambridge, 1990), chapter 6.

165. TNA, KB21/44, Monday after fifteen St. Martin; *The Times* (London), 30 January 1786, 3. King's Bench considered at least three other child custody cases that year, for Robert Pledge (Monday after the octave of Hilary, 26 George III), Mary Bartlett (Monday next after the morrow of St. Martin; Tuesday next after the octave of Hilary; and Monday next after the octave of Purification, 26 George III), and Theresa Ryves (pp. 237 and 249): all in TNA, KB21/44. Writs issued for all three, but no results survive, suggesting, perhaps, some kind of negotiated resolution.

166. On Mansfield's equitable impulses, his avoidance of overly rulebound process, and his interest in settling disputes, see James Oldham, *English Common Law in the Age of Mansfield* (Chapel Hill, 2004), 27–34 and 60–76.

167. TNA, KB21/45/175; *The Times* (London), 1 December 1789, 3. No result survives; the *Times* reported that no settlement was reached.

168. TNA, KB21/46/159, 225, 233, and 264; *The Times* (London), 2 June 1794, 3, and 9 July 1794, 3.

169. The case of Caroline de Manneville, daughter of a French refugee military officer and an English mother, drove this point home. See 5 East 221, 102 *ER* 1054–55 (1804); *The Times* (London), 14 May 1804, 3; and Stone, *Road to Divorce,* 170–173. Danaya Wright marks the crucial turning in de Manneville's case, though she also suggests that this was presaged by other cases of the 1790s: see her *"De Manneville v. De Manneville,"* especially 283–299.

170. Ironically, mothers of illegitimate children retained custody of their children against their fathers in habeas disputes; see, e.g., TNA, KB21/46/750 (Harriett Keighley, 1798). This is also reported in a note to de Manneville's case, as *Rex v Mosely:* 5 East 224, 102 *ER* 1055–1056. For another instance of the mother of an illegitimate child retaining custody against the father, see *Rex v. Moses Soper:* 5 Term Rep. 278, 101 *ER* 156–157 (1793).

171. *ODNB,* s.v. Lloyd Kenyon, first Baron Kenyon. On Kenyon's rejection

of husbands and wives contracting with each other, see Staves, *Separate Property*, 179–181.

172. "Junius" attacked Mansfield's "arbitrary power of doing right" and his "natural turn to equity" when he released prisoners on bail: see *The Letters of Junius* (1775), ii, 192, and 196.

173. On political suspicion and its intrusion into private life, see John Barrell, *The Spirit of Despotism: Invasions of Privacy in the 1790s* (Oxford, 2006). On prosecutions for seditious libel in the 1790s seen against a wider temporal backdrop, see Michael Lobban, "From Seditious Libel to Unlawful Assembly: Peterloo and the Changing Face of Political Crime, c. 1770–1820," *Oxford Journal of Legal Studies* 10 (1990): 307–352. On government prosecutions generally, see Clive Emsley, "Repression, 'Terror,' and the Rule of Law in England during the Decade of the French Revolution," *English Historical Review* 100 (1985): 801–825.

174. William Holland had been convicted at Middlesex sessions in 1793 for unspecified misdemeanors. In early 1794, as his one-year sentence in Newgate was coming to an end, he was brought into King's Bench for trial on new charges of seditious libel: see TNA, KB16/21/3 (31 January 1794), and KB21/46/190 and 191. Jeremiah Samuel Jordan, also charged with seditious libel, was brought in for entry of judgment after his trial in Guildhall: see KB16/22/3 (12 November 1798), and *The Times* (London), 18 July 1798, 2, and 16 November 1798, 3.

175. For the survey years (1790, 1794, and 1798) during Kenyon's tenure, 69 prisoners used habeas in cases of alleged treason, felony, or misdemeanor. Of the 48 of these with surviving results information, 40 (83%) were remanded. Only one writ survives on which the court ordered a prisoner discharged after reviewing an order to imprison on an allegation of wrong: that of James Browne, who had been convicted summarily by a JP as a rogue. See TNA, KB16/22/3 (8 November 1798). Seven others were bailed. The remainder of those excused by the court involved either impressment or family custody disputes.

176. Three statutes established, then extended, the suspension from March to October 1689, with a brief hiatus in April between the first two acts: 1 William and Mary, sess. 1, cc. 2, 7, and 19. For their passage, see Clarence C. Crawford, "The Suspension of the Habeas Corpus Act and the Revolution of 1689," *English Historical Review* 30 (1915): 613–630. For analysis, see Paul D. Halliday and G. Edward White, "The Suspension Clause: English Text, Imperial Contexts, and American Implications," *Virginia Law Review* 94 (2008): 616–628. For more on suspension, see Chapter 7.

177. Writs for this period are in TNA, KB11/14 and KB16/1/1; the rule-

book is KB21/23. See also Halliday and White, "Suspension Clause," 626n.

178. Godfrey Cross, after being remanded on his writ, was tried, convicted, and executed for treason; see TNA, KB16/1/1 (9 July 1690), and KB21/23/427 and 443; *CSPD* 1690–1691, 56, 61, and 92. For examples of those tried on reduced charges, see Thomas Saxton, originally committed for treason by Secretary of State the Earl of Sunderland, then remanded for trial for perjury instead. He was convicted and sentenced to a fine, the pillory, and whipping; see TNA, KB11/14 (23 October 1689), and KB21/23/330. See also Joseph Guilstrop, initially taken for treason, though later charged and convicted on grand misdemeanor, for which he was fined and pilloried: KB11/14 (23 October 1689) and KB21/23/368, 377, and 392; also *CSPD* 1689–1690, 317. John Lowthorpe, initially remanded for treason upon hearing the return to his writ, was convicted for publishing *A Letter to the Bishop of Sarum*, for which he was imprisoned and fined £500. See KB16/1/1 (7 June 1690), KB21/23/413 and 416, and *CSPD* 1690–1691, 348.

179. *ODNB*, s.v. Sir John Holt.

180. John Lloyd and Charles Fitzherbert were discharged from imprisonment for alleged treason during the brief hiatus between suspensions in April 1689: see TNA, KB11/14 (17 April 1689) and KB21/23/297, 298, 303, 313, 325, and 327. William Canning was bailed, having been committed for sedition: see KB11/14 (28 October 1689), and KB21/23/333 and 336. Francis Williamson was arrested at Dover, apparently on his way to France, then discharged: TNA, KB11/14 (23 January 1690), KB21/23/361, 365, 370, and 399, and *CSPD* 1689–1690, 448.

181. See writs for Anne Kattony: TNA, KB16/1/1 (2 June 1690), and KB21/23/401 and 418; and Storer Bythwood: KB11/14 (1690), and KB21/23/399; *CSPD* 1689–1690, 542 and 552. Both were jailed for seditious words and discharged on their writs.

182. The release rate for all writs in the survey years from 1689 to 1710 was 82%.

5. Making Jurisdiction

1. *CD* 1628, iii, 280 and 292; also 269–271, 281, 288–289, and 292. The best points of entry into the literature on the Five Knights and the Petition of Right are John Guy, "The Origins of the Petition of Right Reconsidered," *Historical Journal* 25 (1982): 289–312; and Mark Kishlansky, "Tyranny Denied: Charles I, Attorney General Heath, and the Five Knights' Case," *Historical Journal* 42 (1999): 53–83. For a

thoughtful overview of the critical issues, see Christopher W. Brooks, *Law, Politics, and Society in Early Modern England* (Cambridge, Eng., 2008), 169–177.

2. Richard Cust, *The Forced Loan and English Politics, 1626–1628* (Oxford, 1987).

3. Writs and returns for four of the knights are in TNA, KB145/15/3. The case is also known as Darnell's case, though Sir Thomas Darnell had made his submission and been released before arguments in November.

4. *ST,* iii, 10 and 18. *ST* mistakenly says "42 Elizabeth." That Selden cited 42 Edward III, c. 3, is evident in manuscript reports—HLS, 105, f. 22—and by reference to the statute.

5. *ST,* iii, 38.

6. Ibid., 31.

7. J. P. Kenyon, *The Stuart Constitution: Documents and Commentary* (Cambridge, Eng., 1969), 83.

8. I refer to Robert Cover's language of courts as "jurispathic" by flipping the poles of his analysis. Cover lamented the jurispathic impulse, by which "state law shuts down the creative hermeneutic of principle that is spread throughout our communities." I want to suggest that far from killing off "the jurisgenerative principle by which legal meaning proliferates in all communities," King's Bench killed off novel jurisdictional forms generated by states run amok. As Cover later suggests, the judges "assert a regulative function that permits a life of law rather than violence." After all, "commitment to a jurispathic process that does not defer to the violence of administration is the judge's only hope of partially extricating himself from the violence of the state." See Cover, "Nomos and Narrative," *Harvard Law Review* 97 (1983–1984): 4–68, quotations at 40, 44, 53, and 59.

9. For discussion, see Shaunnagh Dorsett and Shaun McVeigh, "Questions of Jurisdiction," in McVeigh, *Jurisprudence of Jurisdiction* (New York, 2007), 3–18.

10. *Hale's Prerogatives,* 179, 180, and 183.

11. Ibid., 205. As we shall see in Chapter 7, the key here is "ordinarily," for the king exercised his "supreme extraordinary jurisdiction" through Parliament (181, 206). See also William Style, *The Practical Register, Or the Accomplish'd Attorney. . .* (1670), 83. This was the second edition of this work, the first of which (1657) does not contain this language.

12. The normalcy of arrangements by which King's Bench was considered supreme depended "for its efficacy," as Bradin Cormack puts it, "on a

continuous process of moving past questions of how it became norma-
tive." See Cormack, *A Power to Do Justice: Jurisdiction, English Literature,
and the Rise of Common Law, 1509–1625* (Chicago, 2007), 30.

13. Margaret Pelling, *Medical Conflicts in Early Modern London* (Oxford,
2003), 1.

14. R. H. Helmholz, *The Canon Law,* vol. 1 of *The Oxford History of the Laws
of England* (Oxford, 2004), 143–146, 219–221, 282–307.

15. HLS, 118, f. 183 (Wyer, 1607).

16. TNA, KB21/3/138v., 139, and 143v.; Bod., Rawl. C.382, f. 31v.; LI, Hill
122, f. 45v.; Yelverton 134, 80 *ER* 91; and Noy 131, 74 *ER* 1095.

17. Holt 335, 90 *ER* 1085: Keach, the prisoner, was remanded to the Admiralty prison, where he was held on a sentence of that court.

18. This was Parker's case, which concerned the inappropriate conduct of
Lord Gerrard's funeral. Parker was remanded, though apparently discharged soon thereafter upon his submitting to the authority of the
earl marshal in such matters. See LI, Hill 83, p. 268; also BL, Hargrave
65, f. 88, and GI, 35, p. 591. Similarly, Sir James Tilly was remanded on
his imprisonment for refusing to answer charges in that court that he
had "caused certain arms and supporters to be engraved under his picture to which he had no right"; see HLS, 1071, f. 11 (1687).

19. I thus question the deceptively neat narrative of jurisdiction moving
"from status to *locus.*" Richard Ford emphasizes the development of
cartography as the chief means by which territorial modes of jurisdiction came to the fore. See Ford, "Law's Territory (A History of Jurisdiction)," *Michigan Law Review* 97 (1999): 845. This emphasis, however,
overlooks the many ways in which ideas about territory connected
to, undergirded, and manifested status and other means for making
and distinguishing jurisdiction long before modern cartography. One
did not need to be able to make accurate maps to envision jurisdiction's spatial dimension. County lines established before 1066 and traditional practices such as the beating of parish bounds—among many
others—demonstrate the force of a geographical imagination in the
making and operation of jurisdiction without modern technologies
such as mapping. A more subtle account of cartography in the re-
conceptualization of jurisdiction may be found in Shaunnagh Dorsett,
"Mapping Territories," in McVeigh, *Jurisprudence of Jurisdiction,* 137–
158.

20. HLS, 1166, f. 273, and March 165, 82 *ER* 459: the case of William
Rickaby, a Durham murderer. Hale had argued on Rickaby's behalf, so
he knew the issues well. For his use of the case in his analysis of the pre-

rogative writs, see *Hale's Prerogatives*, 207–209. For the record, see TNA, KB145/15/17 (29 November 1641); KB29/290/119 and 152d.; and KB21/12/184–186v., and KB21/13/4–7.

21. As Hale put it, "Coercion is that whereby the judicative power is acted and without which there can be no jurisdiction" (*Hale's Prerogatives*, 191). On technologies of jurisdiction, see Dorsett and McVeigh, "Questions of Jurisdiction," 11–12.

22. Christopher W. Brooks, *Lawyers, Litigation and English Society since 1450* (London, 1998), 217–219.

23. As one put it, this meant simply "peers of the parliament." See Bod., Rawl.C.294, f. 14v. Robert Chaloner, in his 1522 Gray's Inn reading, likewise concluded that "peers" applied only to peers of the realm; see GI, 25, f. 51.

24. HLS 13, p. 441: anonymous reading on Magna Carta, tentatively dated to the years around 1500 by J. H. Baker, *Readers and Readings in the Inns of Court and Chancery*, Selden Society, suppl. ser. 13 (London, 2001), 478.

25. Alan Cromartie, *The Constitutionalist Revolution: An Essay on the History of England, 1450–1642* (Cambridge, Eng., 2006), chapter 2, especially 46–49.

26. Robert Snagg, *The Antiquity and Original of the Court of Chancery . . . Being a . . . Reading Upon the 28* [sic] *Chapter of Magna Charta* (1654), 11, 17, 19, and 36–37. On Snagg's central claims, see Cromartie, *Constitutionalist Revolution*, 112–114. Snagg, with support from the Privy Council, and over the opposition of then Solicitor General Sir John Popham, was named Middle Temple reader for February 1581, not 1571, as erroneously reported on the title page of the printed version of his reading: see Baker, *Readers and Readings*, 166, 354, and 610–611.

27. The timing may have mattered: in the summer of 1616, the battle between Sir Edward Coke and his foes was coming to a head. He would be dismissed as chief justice in November. Prior to this, in 1607, Welsh lawyer Rice Gwynn read on chapter 29. Given how much habeas corpus and the prerogative writs changed in this period, and given that Coke attended Gwynn's reading, this may have been an important occasion as well. No text survives of what someone called a "reading on the power of the crown." See Baker, *Readers and Readings*, 94 and 601.

28. Ashley's notes as JP show that he only rarely ordered imprisonment, even for some of those suspected of serious felonies, and instead took bonds from those accused. See J. H. Bettey, *The Casebook of Sir Francis Ashley, JP, Recorder of Dorcheseter, 1614–1635*, Dorset Record Society, 7 (1981).

29. BL, Harleian 4841, f. 58. For a broader look at Ashley's reading, see Brooks, *Law, Politics, and Society*, 156–157, 420–422, and 423–424. For Ashley's reflections on the ideas in his reading during the parliamentary debates of 1628, see 174–175.

30. BL, Harleian 4841, f. 9v.

31. See 1 Rolle 316, 81 *ER* 512; TNA, KB145/14/13 (24 January 1616) and KB21/5a/45v.–47v.; discussed by Ashley in BL, Harleian 4841, ff. 9v.–10.

32. BL, Harleian 4841, ff. 9v.–10, 11, and 58–59; 1 Elizabeth, c. 1. The Act of Supremacy also gave the new High Commissions that it created the power to imprison. Like others, Ashley wanted to keep the High Commissions within bounds, and explained that though they might handle canonical offenses such as simony or usury, they could not imprison to enforce their judgments "where they have [no] jurisdiction."

33. BL, MS Harleian 4841, ff. 11 and 59.

34. This came to 36% and 9%, respectively, of all imprisonment orders from 1500 to 1800. For more details, see the Appendix.

35. Ashley discussed the powers of JPs to imprison, and the importance that they accept bail where appropriate, perhaps reflecting his tendency to take bail in most cases. See BL, Harleian 4841, f. 10v., and *Ashley Casebook*, passim.

36. On predictability of outcomes, even when justices did not decide cases by following rules as we usually think of them, see Steven L. Winter, *A Clearing in the Forest: Law, Life, and Mind* (Chicago, 2001), especially 6–12.

37. See 1 and 2 Philip and Mary, c. 13: An Act Appointing an Order to JPs for the Bailment of Prisoners; and 2 and 3 Philip and Mary, c. 10: An Act to take the Examination of Prisoners. Also see John Langbein, *Prosecuting Crime in the Renaissance: England, Germany, France* (Cambridge, 1974), 5–77.

38. From 1500 to 1550, 38% of those jailed by JPs on felony accusations were released, compared to 45% of all who used the writ. For the second half of the sixteenth century, 39% of felons accused before JPs were released, compared to 29% overall.

39. Release rates rose as writs concerned with JPs' orders for suspected felons decreased as a proportion of all writs. For the period 1600 to 1650, release rates generally ran at 56%, while the release rate for accused felons committed by JPs was 63%. From 1650 to 1700, respective release rates were 71% and 63%. For more, see the Appendix.

40. See 15 Richard II, c. 2, which defined and expanded the power to imprison those convicted of forcible entry appointed in 5 Richard II c. 7,

which mentioned no summary power. By contrast, 8 Henry VI, c. 9, which laid out the process for JPs to make restitution of property forcibly entered, did not address summary convictions and commitments.

41. William Lambarde, *Eirenarcha: or of the Office of the Iustices of Peace* (1592 ed.), 154. Michael Dalton's popular manual used the same language of conviction "by mine own view, testimony, and record"; see his *The Covntrey Ivstice* (1618), 350.

42. TNA, KB29/309/7, and KB21/14/8v. and 9v.

43. The two JPs, after noting that they had seen matters for themselves, wrote that Lant had been "convicted of the said forcible holding by our record, commanding you and every of you in his majesty's name that you receive him and safely to keep in your said jail until he shall have made his fine and ransom to the king and be delivered thence by the order of law." See TNA, KB29/252/36d.

44. Langbein, *Prosecuting Crime,* 68–72.

45. See 5/6 Edward VI, c. 25: An Act for Keepers of Alehouses. On alehouse regulation, see Peter Clark, *The English Alehouse: A Social History* (London, 1983), chapter 8.

46. TNA, KB145/14/12 (12 February 1614), and KB29/257/41. See the similar circumstances of Richard Bullman in KB32/10, part 1 (16 June 1630), and KB29/279/68.

47. TNA, KB145/15/14 (13 June 1638, for Richard Stanlake, bailed after refusing to pay for plague relief), and KB21/12/97–98; KB16/1/1 (25 June 1690, for Edward Thredder, discharged after not presenting poor relief accounts), and KB21/23/404, 410, and 412; and KB16/1/4 (28 November 1694, for Aaron Darby, bailed after poaching).

48. TNA, KB145/14/4 (10 May 1606) and KB29/247/31.

49. See 23 Henry VIII, c. 5, An Act Concerning Commissions of Sewers, which expanded powers set out in 6 Henry VI, c. 5.

50. Cro. Jac. 336, 79 *ER* 287, and LI, Maynard 22, f. 69; TNA, KB145/14/11 (24 January 1614) and KB29/255/166. For others discharged in sewer cases, see Christopher Browne et al. (1647), and Matthew Brunge (1648): TNA, KB29/296/37 and 152d.; KB21/13/90–91v., 111, and 118v.; and HLS, MS 145, p. 20.

51. Statute might delineate the powers that such commissioners exercised, but only the king's letter patent—a charter or commission—created the corporate or commissioned authorities that were empowered by means other than by the common law to commit someone to prison. Appreciating this distinction explains the possibilities and limitations of statutory powers, and how habeas corpus moved about the empire

along lines of franchisal authority traced by royal charters. See Chapter 8 for this distinction in the statute and charter creating the Calcutta Supreme Court.

52. See 14 Henry VIII, c. 5: An Act Concerning Physicians.

53. See 1 Mary, sess. 2, c. 9: An Act Touching the Incorporation of Physicians in London.

54. LI, Misc. 492, f. 539 and LI, Maynard 66, f. 283v.

55. TNA, KB145/14/11, KB29/255/44, and KB21/5/6v. See also the similar case of Alphonse St. Victoire, who was discharged: TNA, KB145/14/12 (29 June 1614), KB29/257/68d., and KB21/5/29v. On Tenant, see Pelling, *Medical Conflicts*, 123n., 212, 267, and 295. For a marvelous evocation of life in London's medical community, see Deborah E. Harkness, *The Jewel House: Elizabethan London and the Scientific Revolution* (New Haven, 2007), chapter 2.

56. CUL, Gg.2.20, f. 1096v.–97; TNA, KB29/286/194d.; and KB21/12/72 and 74. Blanck had had trouble with the College for decades: see Pelling, *Medical Conflicts*, passim.

57. Such powers made of JPs what John Langbein has called "lay inquisitors." See Langbein, *Prosecuting Crime*, 25, 43–45, 72–73. On Star Chamber influence in the development of the common law of misdemeanor, see Thomas G. Barnes, "The Making of English Criminal Law: Star Chamber and the Sophistication of the Criminal Law," *Criminal Law Review* (1977): 316–326.

58. Of sixteen cases of Star Chamber and Admiralty imprisonment orders tested in the quadrennial survey years, seven (44%) were released. The release rate for those jailed by JPs was 59%.

59. Lionel K. J. Glassey, *Politics and the Appointment of Justices of the Peace, 1675–1720* (Oxford, 1979), 4.

60. The tendency to see Privy Council action as "executive" is largely an American one, and reflects a predilection to think about early modern English arrangements as analogues to constitutional arrangements in the United States. Such an anachronism leads to fundamental misapprehensions about early modern political and legal arrangements, and to a misreading of the history of habeas corpus. For an example of this tendency in habeas scholarship, see William F. Duker, *A Constitutional History of Habeas Corpus* (Westport, 1980), 40–44.

61. One's chance of release after imprisonment on a Council order returned with a cause was 41% between 1558 and 1627, and 59% from 1627 to 1689, compared to a release rate on all imprisonment orders of 54% and 54%, respectively.

62. The proportion was 86 (7.4%) of 1,155 prisoners in the survey years

for that period. If we extend the period back to 1500, this fraction rises to 10%, but the increase is entirely accounted for by one writ returning the names of 65 accused rebels in 1554, with the writ being used by the Council to bring them to Queen's Bench for trial and judgment.

63. Thus 26 of the 86 (30%) Council imprisonment warrants inspected in the quadrennial survey years between 1558 and 1689 were returned without a cause, 14 before 1627, and 12 afterward. We can thus estimate that a total of 344 prisoners were jailed by the Privy Council during this period, 104 without a cause given in their returns.

64. Bod., Rawlinson C.382, f. 57.

65. The Petition of Right and Star Chamber statute of 1641 are explored in Chapter 7.

66. John Langbein notes this likeness of Council pretrial process and that of JPs: see Langbein, *Prosecuting Crime,* 71 and 80–81. Jailed in 1522 on a conciliar order for suspicion of an unnamed felony, habeas corpus brought Thomas Dune into King's Bench, where twelve men swore to his integrity. He was bailed and later pardoned. In 1522, Thomas Banaster, an accused murderer, had sought sanctuary in a churchyard and later pleaded that he had the king's pardon, to no avail. See TNA, KB29/154/19 and 20; *Spelman Reports,* vol. 2, Introduction, 344–345.

67. TNA, KB29/191/28d.: John Pollard et al.

68. In 1518, Richard Aleyn and Arthur Gatager were jailed by Cardinal Wolsey's order for an unspecified felony, brought to King's Bench on habeas corpus, and remanded. See TNA, KB29/149/26.

69. They were later convicted and hanged: see TNA, KB29/175/33d. For further examples of this usage, see *Dyer Reports,* vol. 1, p. lxxvi, n. 36.

70. TNA, KB29/150/18; *Spelman Reports,* vol. 2, Introduction, 77; J. A. Guy, *The Cardinal's Court* (Hassock, 1977), 76–78.

71. For the survey years in the period 1500–1558, the release rate for conciliar orders returned without a cause, or stating felony without specifying the type, was 38% (6 of 16). For JPs' orders of the same kind, 44% (35 of 80) were released. For all orders (with and without cause), the release rate for JPs was 38% (43 of 112), and for the Council, 12% (12 of 98). This latter Council number includes the 65 accused traitors in essence transferred from the Council to Queen's Bench for trial by habeas corpus in 1554.

72. This from the report of Serjeant Humphrey Browne's case: *Spelman Reports,* vol. 1, p. 184. Baker dates this discussion to 1540, correcting it to 1532 in Baker, *Laws,* 91n and 681n.

73. See 3 Edward I, c. 15: Act Concerning Which Prisoners Be Mainpernable, and Which Not.

74. BL, Egerton 3376, ff. 24 and 26v; Brooks, *Law, Politics, and Society,* 96. For more on Morice's reading, see Chapter 3.

75. Apparently convicted for receiving a thief, Heyth was pardoned, while Hodges was ordered to die. See KB29/179/13; *Dyer Reports,* vol. 1, pp. 77–78, with discussion at lxxviii; and Baker, *Laws,* 93.

76. TNA, KB29/150/34 (Apryse), KB29/179/13, and KB145/10/38 (27 May 1546); see also Baker, *Laws,* 93. Another factor distinguished the two writs. Apryse was bailed on an *ad subjiciendum* writ, while Hodges and Heyth were brought in on an *ad standum* writ. The controlment roll entry notes that this was an *ad standum* writ, but only in the recorda file can we see "suspicion of felony" named in the writ's text, as was common usage with the *ad standum* writ. The cause was known, in the writ itself, if not in the return.

77. TNA, KB29/171/12d.: John Littleford was remanded, after which it became clear he had been arrested on appeal of felony. He died in prison (1538).

78. In 1541, a prisoner still in custody of the marshal of the king's household on Cromwell's order was bailed on habeas corpus. See TNA, KB29/174/38d., for Edward Foster.

79. TNA, KB29/175/33d.: writ for Peter Leper and John Stevens, committed by command of the king, without cause, and remanded in 1542. They were later executed for murder. John Gray was committed on order of Queen Mary. The return to his writ named no cause, but he was later executed for treason: see KB145/12/1 (25 May 1554), and KB29/187/41.

80. YLS, GR29.9, ff. 32v.–33. The copyist of this manuscript began to write "Edmund Anderson," then "Amerson" (Agmondesham), apparently confusing the name of the lawyer arrested by the lord chamberlain with the name of the chief justice. Because it also indicates that the prisoner was a Middle Temple reader, this almost certainly must be John Agmondesham. That a prominent barrister was involved may help explain why all the justices were concerned to resolve the issue.

81. See 1 Anderson 297; 123 *ER* 482–483.

82. Ibid.

83. Maxwell Cohen suggested that the resolution required the insertion of a cause in all returns: "Habeas Corpus Cum Causa—Emergence of Modern Writ—I," *Canadian Bar Review* 18 (1940): 34. Duker rightly notes that the resolution was "no more than an accurate restatement of the existing case law": see his *Habeas Corpus,* 43.

84. Many examples exist, e.g., the remand order by Popham CJ on return to the writ for John Kelly, jailed by the Council: TNA, KB145/13/36

(10 May 1594) and KB29/231/83. Valentine Thomas was arraigned and hanged after being brought into court on a return of a conciliar commitment: see KB145/14/1 (31 May 1603) and KB29/243/19d. Nicholas Blundesden was remanded on a similar return: see KB145/14/20 (5 July 1622) and KB29/271/64d. He was bailed on another writ later that year: see KB145/14/20 (28 November 1622).

85. TNA, KB145/13/40 (23 January 1598) and KB29/235/62; *Acts of the Privy Council* (London, 1904), n.s., vol. 28, pp. 28–29 and 35.

86. Barnes was then arraigned. See TNA, KB145/13/40 (29 June 1598) and KB29/235/118d.

87. TNA, KB145/14/10 (11 May 1612); HLS, 1180, f. 409; and YLS, GR.29.19, ff. 412–415. Vaux was later pardoned: see *ODNB*, s.v. Thomas Vaux, Edward's great-grandfather.

88. See 1 Rolle 134, 81 *ER* 382–383. This is called the Brewers' case. The writ issued for James Desmaistres et al. is at TNA, KB145/14/12 (23 January 1615), KB29/257/153d., and KB21/5/41v. Desmaistres and the others were jailed by the Council without a stated cause, and were remanded after consideration of the returns to their writs.

89. As Duker notes, arguments by the Knights' counsel "were emotionally appealing," though not "congruent with case law as it had developed by 1627": see his *Habeas Corpus*, 43.

90. The return to Thomas Rogers's writ explained his 1624 imprisonment by a Council order, with no cause. He was remanded. See TNA, KB145/15/2 (9 February 1627) and KB21/8/71v.

91. While release rates across three centuries ran at 53%, between 1625 and 1642, only 37% of prisoners were released on habeas corpus, the lowest rate for any reign after Mary's. For royal pressure on the bench and the 1641 parliamentary response, see James S. Hart Jr., *The Rule of Law, 1603–1660* (Harlow, 2003), 67–74.

92. See the charges against Chief Justice Bramston and Justice Berkeley in Maija Jansson, ed., *Proceedings in the Opening Session of the Long Parliament* (Rochester, 2003–2007), vol. 4: 658–659 and 662–663, and vol. 5: 401. Likewise, among the charges against the Earl of Strafford, for which he would be executed, was his refusal to return habeas while Lord President of the Council of the North.

93. Though Steven Winter discusses "radial categories" largely as a way by which to understand decision-making in individual cases, the same notion of judges reasoning outward from a "prototype effect" helps explain this extension of jurisdictional supervision that was unbound by rules, though not arbitrary. See Winter, *Clearing in the Forest*, chapters 4 and 6.

94. Austin Woolrych, *Britain in Revolution, 1625–1660* (Oxford, 2002). For an analysis of the war's origins, see Conrad Russell, *The Causes of the English Civil War* (Oxford, 1990).

95. As Robert Cover put it: "In a truly violent, authoritarian situation, nothing is more revolutionary than the insistence of a judge that he exercises such a 'jurisdiction'—but only if that jurisdiction implies the articulation of legal principle according to an independent hermeneutic." See Cover, "Nomos and Narrative," 59.

96. Stephen F. Black, "The Courts and Judges of Westminster Hall during the Great Rebellion, 1640–1660," *Journal of Legal History* 7 (1986): 23–52.

97. Litigation generally declined over 70% on the Crown Side of King's Bench from 1640 to 1643: see Black, "Westminster Hall," 31. Using the quadrennial survey, comparing survey years 1634 and 1638 to 1642 and 1646, we find only a 20% drop in habeas use.

98. Charles tried to adjourn his courts in Westminster Hall, and in 1644, commanded justices there to join him in Oxford, to no avail. Crown Side rulebooks show adjournment orders in Hilary and Easter 1643, but also indicate the court's continuing work: see TNA, KB21/13/24v. and following. *Teste* dates on writs suggest likewise.

99. The start of the term is clear in TNA, KB21/13/22.

100. TNA, KB32/10 (writs of 21, 23, and 24 November); KB29/291/90 and 91d; and KB21/13/23ff.

101. TNA, KB32/10 (26 November 1642); KB29/291/91, and KB21/13/22v.–26v; and CJ, ii, 954 and 981. Mason's companions were ordered released by the House later that year: see CJ, iii, 78 and 112.

102. TNA, KB29/292/30 and KB21/13/31-v.

103. See the writ for Colonels Francis Hacker and Francis Inge, committed by the committee of accounts at Leicester for failing to present accounts, and ordered held "until you shall receive further order from us." Bacon ordered the return amended, but Hacker and Inge were still released; see TNA, KB32/7 (22 October 1646), KB29/295/86, KB21/13/78–82. See also writs for Nehemiah Rawson and John Simpson, arrested by the committee of accounts for Lincolnshire. They too were bailed: KB32/7 (29 May 1646), KB29/295/41, and KB21/12/92v.–142, passim, and KB21/13/73–78v.

104. C. H. Firth and R. S. Rait, eds., *Acts and Ordinances of the Interregnum, 1642–1660* (London, 1911), 999–1000. In January 1647, John Vandowall and Thomas Dore were discharged from their imprisonment; the mayor of Harwich had ordered them held according to the ordinance against unlawful preaching (see TNA, KB29/296/37d. and

KB21/13/92v.–96). John Armiger and others were released from their 1648 imprisonment by the Committee for Plundered Ministers: see KB29/296/152 and KB21/13/111v., 113v., 114v., 116, and 117. This is probably the anonymous case reported in Style 90, 82 *ER* 554.

105. Hatton Easton and John Somerland, imprisoned in December 1646 by the Committee for the Army at Guildhall for not paying army assessments, were bailed on their writ, despite a reference to the parliamentary ordinance made in the return: see TNA, KB29/296/66d. and KB21/13/88v.–103v., passim.

106. TNA, KB29/296/66d. and KB21/13/102, 102v., and 104v. (1647).

107. TNA, KB29/296/37d. and KB21/13/95, 95v., and 101 (1647).

108. TNA, KB29/298/63 and KB21/13/145v., 147v., 148v., and 149v. (1649).

109. Record keeping clearly declined as well, and the Crown Side rulebooks for 1652 to 1660 were either lost or not kept at all. Some of what thus appears to be a decline in usage may be a result of problems with the records.

110. Thus Ralph London and Samuel Oates were discharged in the summer of 1649 after being jailed on the blasphemy ordinance: see TNA, KB29/298/63d. and KB21/13/153–156v; also Firth and Rait, *Acts and Ordinances*, 1133–1136.

111. Edward Collier was bailed from his imprisonment ordered by the committee of indemnity in late 1649: see TNA, KB29/298/109d. and KB21/13/154–155.

112. TNA, KB145/16/1651 (25 April 1651, bailed) and KB21/13/186–190, passim.

113. Given the general collapse in habeas litigation in the 1650s, and given that the Protectoral Council used insular imprisonment orders that remained beyond the writ's reach, it is difficult to see the Interregnum as a period of "great advances." But as Duker rightly notes, the regime of the 1650s in essence continued many of the imprisonment practices of the era before 1640. See Duker, *Habeas Corpus*, 52.

114. TNA, KB32/10 (John Roane, 28 November 1642, and Edward Hudson, 23 January 1643); KB29/291/109d. and 110; and KB21/13/24v., 25, and 26v.

115. Hull's governor had wanted to release him earlier, but Willoughby insisted on using habeas corpus to establish the legality of his release. See TNA, KB145/16/1659 (6 February 1660).

116. In 1717, Henry Wilkins was released after his writ was returned with an imprisonment order given by a commander of the King's Grenadier Guards, without cause. After his release, he sued for false imprison-

ment. See TNA, KB16/7/1 (24 October 1717), and KB21/31/8, 10, and 19.

117. TNA, KB16/1/4 (18 June 1694), and KB21/24/290 and 298. That same year, a soldier named Acman was also bailed for giving his general "saucy language." The court went so far as to say "they inclined to have discharged him, it if had been moved." See Comberbach 278, 90 *ER* 477. George Read, another soldier, was less fortunate, and was remanded for desertion: see TNA, KB16/1/1 (6 November 1690), and KB21/23/425 and 432; LI, Hill 49, f. 106v.

118. TNA, TS11/1054/4653. Arguments were on a rule *nisi* for the writ's issuance, rather than on a return, so that the court could proceed on the basis of information received in affidavits on both sides. Blake's court martial, conducted at Harwich, concluded with the sentence that he be cashiered: see *The Times* (London), 27 October 1814, 4.

119. For the affidavit of Merrin and his fellows, see TNA, ADM7/304, no. 425, September 1799. No note was made there of the final resolution of their case, but there was a comment, apparently expressing the opinion of the attorney or solicitor general, that recommended making a return to the writ by attaching a note of the charges against them.

120. See 1 East 306, 102 *ER* 119–123; *The Times* (London), 10 February 1801, 3. In a more prominent case, habeas corpus issued from the King's Bench in Dublin for Theobald Wolfe Tone, the Irish rebel leader convicted by court martial, but he took his life before the writ could be served. See R. B. McDowell, *Ireland in the Age of Imperialism and Revolution, 1760–1801* (Oxford, 1979), 663–664.

121. See 1 Anne, sess. 2, c. 16: An Act for Punishing Soldiers who Mutiny or Desert; renewed regularly, e.g., by 2/3 Anne, c. 20, and 3/4 Anne, c. 16.

122. TNA, KB16/3/4 (31 January 1706), and KB21/27/26. See also John Winter, released from York Castle, where he had been confined for desertion: KB16/15/1 (14 May 1757), and KB21/38/18 and 27. No result survives for an alleged naval deserter awaiting court martial in 1762: see KB16/15/6 (Robert Brownless, 12 February 1762).

123. TNA, 16/1/1 (15 July 1692).

124. TNA, KB16/5/5 (16 April 1761), and KB21/38/474. Affidavits of Jacob Elias, the father, and of Joseph Mansfield and Thomas Hodges, the hospital keepers, are in KB1/14/6 (bundle 1 Easter George III). A note on the outside says he was "to be del[ivered] up on payment of 4 g[uinea]s," which suggests that some compromise as a condition of release had been made.

125. For more on this writ, see Chapter 8.

126. James Lock et al., TNA, KB16/1/4 (25 April 1694).

127. See 2/3 Anne, c. 19: An Act for Raising Recruits; and 3/4 Anne, c. 11: An Act for Better Recruiting.

128. For two cases of Anne's reign, see Kevin Costello, "Habeas Corpus and Military and Naval Impressment, 1756–1816," *Journal of Legal History* 29 (2008): 228–229.

129. Thomas Reynolds was bailed from the Tower, where he was held while awaiting delivery to the regiment in which he was to serve, having been "duly impressed to serve as a soldier according to the Act of Parliament." He was bailed. See TNA, KB16/13/2 (22 June 1745), and KB21/36/12, 23, and 26; as well as Costello, "Habeas Corpus and Impressment," 216–217 and 229.

130. Wilm. 83, 97 *ER* 32–34n. In addition, *29* George II, c. 4, §14, reemphasized the penalties for desertion that had been laid out in the recruiting statutes during Anne's reign. For more on this issue, see Chapter 4.

131. TNA, KB1/13/3 (affidavits of John Parkin and John Cannar, 14 and 17 April 1758), and KB21/38/117 and 124.

132. *Hale's Prerogatives,* 131–132.

133. *By the King: A Proclamation Directing How Prisoners Shall bee Ordered which are Taken at Sea* (1628).

134. But many POWs captured during combat among Britons, including those taken at Colchester in 1648, and at Dunbar and Worcester in 1650–1651, were transported to Virginia or the Caribbean. This put the late king's subjects beyond judicial supervision by habeas corpus. See Cynthia Herrup, "Punishing Pardon: Some Thoughts on the Origins of Penal Transportation," in Simon Devereaux and Paul Griffiths, eds., *Penal Practice and Culture, 1500–1900: Punishing the English* (Basingstoke, 2004), 130.

135. Work on exchanges with the French began in June 1689. The Commission for Sick and Wounded was appointed in July. Prisoners were initially kept in private houses, though by September, better arrangements were in train: see TNA, PC2/73/132, 177, 188, 244, and passim. For prisoner exchanges from as early as March 1690, see Narcissus Luttrell, *A Brief Historical Relation of State Affairs from September 1678 to April 1714* (Oxford, 1857), vol. 2, pp. 19, 32, 116, and passim.

136. Richard Lee, *A Treatise of Captures in War* (1759), 217. For accounts of fraud, see Samuel Baston, *Baston's Case Vindicated: Or, A Brief Account of Some Evil Practices of the Present Commissioners for Sick and Wounded . . .* (1695).

137. *Considerations on the Exchange of Seamen, Prisoners of War* (1758), 11. For

values assigned by rank, see *Traité et Conventions pour les Malades, Blessés, et Prisonniers de Guerre . . .* (1759?), 2–14.

138. The earliest report I have seen for a person called a "prisoner at war" concerned a debt on a bond, in which case POW status was irrelevant to the discussion. See 1 Keble 883, 83 *ER* 1299 (Erington v. Hurst, 1665). The absence of serious legal thinking about the nature of POWs is indicated by the fact that Giles Jacob wrote a treatise on military law that made no mention of them: see his *The Law Military; or a Methodical Collection of all the Laws . . . Relating to the Armies and Soldiery . . .* (1719).

139. TNA, KB11/14 (23 January 1690); KB29/348/92; KB21/23/362; and PC2/73/316 and 351; and *CSPD* 1689–1690, 329.

140. TNA, KB16/1/6 (23 January 1697); KB21/25/120. In May 1695, the Privy Council gave an order for Cumberford's discharge from the Savoy on the condition that he take the oath of allegiance. Whether he refused the oath, or another cause intervened, nothing happened then: see PC2/76/65v.

141. TNA, KB16/1/3 (4 November 1693) and KB21/24/264; see also M. J. Prichard and D. E. C. Yale, eds., *Hale and Fleetwood on Admiralty Jurisdiction,* Selden Society, 108 (London, 1993), 332–341. On privateers commissioned by James in the 1690s, see J. S. Bromley, *Corsairs and Navies, 1660–1760* (London, 1987), 156–159.

142. The Privy Council ordered that when enemy ships were taken, written examinations of their crews should be made to ascertain their nationality. See TNA, PC2/76/26–27 (February 1694/1695).

143. TNA, PC2/73/305–07, and PC2/76/28v.–29 and 96. For petitions, see ADM97/119 (post 1704), and ADM97/114/2 (1740s–1750s).

144. TNA, KB11/14 (7 February 1690); KB21/23/367, 370, and 372; and PC2/73/245, 260, 279, 300, 328, 361, 366. See also Luttrell, *Brief Relation,* vol. 2, pp. 13 and 19.

145. He too was exchanged. See TNA, KB16/1/5 (12 April 1695), and PC2/76/116v.

146. TNA, KB16/1/6 (23 January 1697), and KB21/25/149 and 210; Fortescue 195, 92 *ER* 816; see also Chapter 6.

147. Correspondence for early prisoner exchanges exists in TNA, ADM97 (in-letters, from 1702), which also contains petitions from prisoners of war and related papers. ADM99 contains commissioners' minutes, from 1698. Out-letters (ADM98) survive only from the 1740s, and registers of prisoners (ADM103), from the 1750s.

148. *Traité . . . Prisonniers de Guerre,* 1–2.

149. *Considerations on . . . Prisoners of War,* 9.

150. See 1 Taunt. 26 and 33, 127 *ER* 739 and 741 (Depardo, 1807, manslaughter by POW while in custody in China; and Maria v. Hall, 1800, in assumpsit).

151. See 1 Bos. and Pul. 163, 126 *ER* 837 (Sparenburgh v. Bannatyne, 1797, in debt).

152. TNA, ADM7/185, part four, contains accounts for legal expenses for POWs, 1739–1749.

153. See 2 Burr. 765, 97 *ER* 551–552; 2 Keny. 473, 96 *ER* 1249.

154. See 2 Black. W. 1324, 96 *ER* 775–776 (1779).

155. Nor could an admitted POW be brought into court on a habeas corpus *ad testificandum:* see *The Times* (London), 9 December 1796, 4.

156. No POW cases arose during the American Revolution since captive American combatants were treated as potential traitors, not as POWs. Because habeas corpus had been suspended for suspected traitors and pirates, no writs could issue for them. Only in March 1782 were they declared prisoners of war, after which their release soon followed. See Sheldon S. Cohen, *Yankee Sailors in British Gaols* (Newark, 1995), 26–29 and 201–202; and Francis D. Cogliano, *American Maritime Prisoners in the Revolutionary War* (Annapolis, 2001), 43–47 and 130–133.

157. *ST,* xx, 1–82; Mark S. Weiner, "New Biographical Evidence on *Somerset's Case,*" *Slavery and Abolition* 23 (2002): 121–136; and James Oldham, "New Light on Mansfield and Slavery," *Journal of British Studies* 27 (1988): 45–68. For background on the law of slavery before *Somerset,* and for an imperial "conflict of laws" reading of the case, see George Van Cleve, "*Somerset's Case* and Its Antecedents in Imperial Perspective," *Law and History Review* 24 (2006): 601–645.

158. Lord Chancellor Northington had declared that a slave might use habeas corpus "if restrained of his liberty." See 2 Eden. 127, 28 *ER* 845 (Shanley v. Harvey, 1762).

159. W. Kel. 98, 25 *ER* 511. 2 Barn. 215, 94 *ER* 457–458.

160. Prince Hoare, *Memoirs of Granville Sharp,* 2d ed. (London, 1828), vol. 1, pp. 78–80. The writ may have been issued by Edward Willes JKB, or by Baron Sir Sidney Stafford Smythe, of the Exchequer. I have seen no evidence in King's Bench records of it there. For Mansfield's notes in the assault case *King v. Robert Stapylton et al.,* see James Oldham, *The Mansfield Manuscripts and the Growth of English Law* (Chapel Hill, 1992), vol. 2, pp. 1242–1243.

161. Hoare, *Sharp,* vol. 1, p. 89. For apprentices discharged to their masters, see TNA, ADM1/1787, unfol., John Falkingham to Philip Stevens, 17 October 1761, and ADM1/3678/169 (William Walker); and ADM1/3678/187 and 223 (Andrew Fisher and Henry Beddon, 1761–1762).

162. *ST,* xx, 67. For further discussion on this point, see Chapters 6 and 7.

163. On the narrowness of Mansfield's judgment, see Van Cleve, *"Somerset's Case,"* 635–637, and Oldham, "New Light," 65.

164. On the case of Little Ephraim Robin John and Ancona Robin Robin John [*sic*], see Ruth Paley, "After *Somerset:* Mansfield, Slavery, and the Law in England, 1772–1830," in Norma Landau, ed., *Law, Crime, and English Society, 1660–1830* (Cambridge, Eng., 2002), 166–174.

165. Ibid., 178–179. In another case of 1812, the writ was refused for ten African crewmen on a Portuguese vessel in Truro harbor. This refusal may well have resulted from a franchise view of the writ's work: that those held by Portuguese sailors were not within the writ's purview—that is, they did not need to answer to the king of Great Britain (175).

166. Ruth Paley, "Imperial Politics and English Law: The Many Contexts of *Somerset,*" *Law and History Review* 24 (2006): 662–664.

167. Sharp apparently had at least one other success with habeas corpus for a slave. In that case a writ issued in July 1786, during the court's vacation, for the slave Harry Demane. The writ reached the ship on which Demane was about to be transported just as it was setting its sails. See Hoare, *Sharp,* vol. 1, pp. 369–370.

168. Douglas Hay and Paul Craven, *Masters, Servants, and Magistrates in Britain and the Empire, 1562–1955* (Chapel Hill, 2004). On Somerset's mythologizing power, see Paley, "After *Somerset,*" 181–184. The case inspired imitative uses of the writ in some American colonies, where it had been widely reported. On American attention to the case, see Van Cleve, *"Somerset's Case,"* 602, 625n., and 642–644. A sampling of newspaper reports of slaves using habeas corpus includes the *Connecticut Journal,* 28 February 1782, 3; *New-Haven Gazette,* 16 December 1784; and the *Pennsylvania Packet,* 8 March 1786.

169. This then is reminiscent of Coke's pronouncement, derived from Bagge's case, that the prerogative writs gave King's Bench "not only jurisdiction to correct errors in judicial proceedings, but other errors and misdemeanors extrajudicial, tending to the breach of the peace, or oppression of the subjects." See Sir Edward Coke, *The Fourth Part of the Institutes of the Laws of England* (1644), 71.

6. Making Liberties, Making Subjects

1. See 8 Modern 22, 88 *ER* 17; 1 Strange 478, 93 *ER* 645–646; TNA, KB21/31/497 and 499. On maintenance contracts, see Susan Staves, *Married Women's Separate Property in England, 1660–1833* (Cambridge, 1990), chapter 6.

2. On republican ideas, see Quentin Skinner, *Liberty before Liberalism* (Cambridge, Eng., 1998). On natural law, see Richard Tuck, *Natural Rights Theories: Their Origin and Development* (Cambridge, Eng., 1979). On the ancient constitution, see J. G. A. Pocock, *The Ancient Constitution and the Feudal Law: A Study of English Historical Thought in the Seventeenth Century* (Cambridge, Eng., 1957). For a rebuttal to Pocock's implication of Sir Edward Coke's typicality in seventeenth-century legal and political thought, see Glenn Burgess, *The Politics of the Ancient Constitution: An Introduction to English Political Thought, 1603–1642* (University Park, 1992), especially chapter 2, and J. W. Tubbs, *The Common Law Mind: Medieval and Early Modern Conceptions* (Baltimore, 2000), 129–130 and chapter 7. For a revival of a "constitutionalist" view, if not of the ancient constitution, see Alan Cromartie, *The Constitutionalist Revolution: An Essay on the History of England, 1450–1642* (Cambridge, Eng., 2006), especially 198–200.

3. Epistle to the Galatians 5:1 and 13.

4. James 2:12–13.

5. George Downeham [*sic*], *The Christians Freedome, Wherein is fully expressed the Doctrine of Christian Libertie* (Oxford, 1635), 12.

6. Ibid., 3, 10–11.

7. For a succinct account of the classical republican view of liberty as the opposite of slavery, see Quentin Skinner, *Renaissance Virtues,* vol. 2 of *Visions of Politics* (Cambridge, Eng., 2002), chapters 11 and 12.

8. Just how salvation worked, and thus what liberation meant, was a matter of intense theological and political debate in early modern England. For conflicts within the Church of England over the role that human action could play in salvation, see Nicholas Tyacke, *Anti-Calvinists: The Rise of English Arminianism, c. 1590–1640* (Oxford, 1987). For a marvelous account of similar debates among so-called Puritans in London in the 1620s and 1630s, see Peter Lake, *The Boxmaker's Revenge* (Stanford, 2001), passim, and on the difference between sanctification and justification, 20–35 and 208–210.

9. [Alexander Chapman], *Christian Liberty Described in a Sermon Preached in the Collegiate Church at Westminster, by a Minister of Suffolk* (1606), sig. D2 and F2.

10. On antinomians, see David Como, *Blown by the Spirit: Puritanism and the Emergence of an Antinomian Underground in Pre–Civil War England* (Stanford, 2004), especially 2.

11. Downeham, *Christians Freedome,* 12–13.

12. On language in urban charters, see Paul D. Halliday, *Dismembering the Body Politic: Partisan Politics in England's Towns, 1650–1730* (Cambridge,

Eng., 1998), 1–2 and 29–34. For the thanksgiving in the Eucharist, see *The Book of Common Prayer, 1559* (Charlottesville, 1976), 265.

13. Jean-Jacques Rousseau, "The Sovereign," book 1, chapter 8 of *The Social Contract* (New York, Everyman's Library edition, 1973), 177.

14. I thus mean to mark a clear contrast to that other early modern language of liberty, the republican one, as characterized by Quentin Skinner, who notes that republican writers "never suggest that there are certain specific goals we need to realize in order to count as being fully or truly in possession of our liberty." See Skinner, "Paradoxes of Political Liberty," in David Miller, ed., *Liberty* (Oxford, 1991), 195, and generally 195–201.

15. John Barston, *Safegarde of Societie: Describing the institution of lawes and policies, to preserve euery felowship of people by degrees of ciuil gouernment* (1576), quoted in Markku Peltonen, *Classical Humanism and Republicanism in English Political Thought, 1570–1640* (Cambridge, Eng., 1995), quotation at 62, and for discussion, 59–73.

16. Peltonen, *Classical Humanism,* especially the introduction and chapters 1–2.

17. This is Mark Goldie's insightful formulation in "The Unacknowledged Republic: Officeholding in Early Modern England," in Tim Harris, ed., *The Politics of the Excluded, c. 1500–1850* (Basingstoke, 2001), especially 176–184. See also Steve Hindle, *The State and Social Change in Early Modern England, c. 1550–1640* (Basingstoke, 2000), especially 26–27, and Patrick Collinson, *De Republica Anglorum; or, History with the Politics Put Back* (Cambridge, Eng., 1990).

18. Sir Thomas Smith, *A Discourse of the Commonweal of This Realm of England,* ed. Mary Dewar (Charlottesville, 1969), 16–17.

19. The idea that liberties arose from subjecthood and were connected to Christian ideas of obligation was by no means exclusively English. For an excellent discussion of these idioms in seventeenth-century Mexico, see Brian P. Owensby, *Empire of Law and Indian Justice in Colonial Mexico* (Stanford, 2008), chapter 5.

20. For more on this important point, see J. C. Davis, "Religion and the Struggle for Freedom in the English Revolution," *Historical Journal* 35 (1992): 507–530.

21. While this is not the place to reopen the debate on so-called possessive individualism, I do mean to trace a different path for the development of ideas of liberty—as revealed in habeas corpus use—from that provided by traditional liberal narratives equating secularization with the rise of modern liberty. This line was drawn most famously in C. B. Macpherson, *The Political Theory of Possessive Individualism: Hobbes to*

Locke (Oxford, 1962). Macpherson wrote an entire chapter on the Levellers that gave virtually no consideration to the theological impetus driving Leveller aspirations, even though he quoted works such as John Lilburne's *Ionahs Cry out of the Whales Belly* (1647).

22. Liberty, John Spelman explained, "is the name given to such particular privilege given by the king as no one may have except through the king; for in the beginning all liberties and franchises were in the king." Quoted in J. H. Baker, *John Spelman's Reading on Quo Warranto,* Selden Society, 113 (London, 1997), 120.

23. In returns to habeas corpus, the abbot of Ramsey and the leaders of Norwich made sure to mention that they presided over "liberties." See TNA, KB29/145/27d. (William Warner, 1514) and KB29/142/17 (William Sage, 1510).

24. On conflicts between city corporations and cathedral chapters, see Catherine Patterson, "Corporations, Cathedrals, and the Crown: Local Dispute and Royal Interest in Early Stuart England," *History* 85 (2000): 546–571.

25. On the liberty or franchise of a jail, and its abuse, see Baker, *Spelman's Reading,* 103 and 131.

26. On Bourne's case (1619–1620), see Chapter 3.

27. TNA, KB145/15/17 (7 June 1641) and HLS, MS 113, p. 123. The second return likewise contained language emphasizing Chester's ancient liberties: see KB32/10 (4 February 1642). This prompted a battle with the mayor, who was attached for contempt. No record of the outcome on a third writ ordered to Chester survives, which might be explained by its issuance shortly before the first shots of the Civil War were fired. See TNA, KB21/12/171v., 176, and 179, and KB21/13/5, 5v., 15, 18, 18v., and 21.

28. Fisher was detained on a two-part warrant, with one part issued by a company assistant to arrest him to answer company charges, and the other under the privy seal. The reports show the court's focus on the company's warrant, out of an interest to define the bounds of the Company's authority to request imprisonment for such a wrong and on such an ordinance. See CUL, MS Gg.2.20, ff. 1097 and 1157v.–1158v. HLS, 1167, p. 151.

29. TNA, KB32/10, part 1 (16 November 1637); KB29/286/201; and KB21/12/68–74, passim.

30. See 1 Rolle 312, 81 *ER* 509; TNA, KB21/5a/20v. and 58.

31. Here, in Ladd et al. of 1607, Finch quoted the late Lord Burleigh, Queen Elizabeth's principal adviser. See HLS, 118, f. 188v. and YLS, GR29.18, f. 220.

32. CUL, MS Gg.2.30, f. 37v. (1624). This is the earliest example I have found of this kind of locution or of a mention of liberty in this high a degree of abstraction.

33. Thus Dodderidge, in Bourne's case, in Hilary 1620, opined that "no liberty is exempt of the king's prerogative." See LI, MS Maynard 22, f. 407.

34. Thus John Maynard argued against the return to the writ for John Langham and Thomas Andrews in 1642: see HLS, MS 113, p. 141.

35. LI, MS Hill 49, f. 238v. (Bethel, 1695).

36. TNA, KB145/14/12 (31 January 1615): bailed on return showing no cause. See also the order to "restrain" Giles Broadway "of his liberty": TNA, 32/7 (4 May 1631): remanded on return without cause shown, by the Privy Council.

37. TNA, KB32/7 (17 October 1631). Brigham had shown his contempt for that court's orders in 1631 by shooting at the sheriffs who served those orders on him.

38. TNA, KB32/7 (10 October 1640), and KB21/12/148–58v., passim.

39. On Langham and Andrews, see Valerie Pearl, *London and the Outbreak of the Puritan Revolution: City Government and National Politics, 1625–1643* (Oxford, 1961), 240–245, 309–311, and 321–323.

40. HLS, MS 113, p. 141.

41. Ibid., 140–150; HLS, MS 1166, ff. 296–99v.; and LI, MS Coxe 93, unfol. A brief printed report is in March 179, 82 *ER* 465. Bramston, it should be noted, had argued on behalf of the Five Knights in 1627 (see Chapter 5). Their writs are in TNA, KB145/15/17 (7 February 1642) and KB29/290/153, with orders in KB21/13/6v.–9v. Langham and Andrews would serve together as sheriffs of London in 1642–1643, in which capacity they would make returns to at least nine writs of habeas corpus, some concerning prisoners jailed in legally dubious circumstances connected to the political turmoil of that year. See TNA, KB29/291 and 292, and KB32/10/part 2 (18 Charles I), passim. Both would serve the parliamentary cause.

42. Though bailed, inconclusive discussions continued for three more terms. The court did not want to decide the underlying question about election privileges, and instead "advise[d] the recorder and the prisoners to make agreement." See HLS, 113, pp. 249–251 and 277–278, and HLS, 145, pp. 1–3 and 6–7. Chambers and Wood continued to appear in court on their bail until Michaelmas 1646, after which the case disappears from the record: see TNA, KB21/13/59–77v., passim.

43. TNA, KB21/17/19 and LI, Misc. 500, f. 55.

44. Harwood was bailed in late 1671, pending full discussion in Hilary

1672, when he was remanded on these arguments. The City claimed that by custom, the permission of the mayor and aldermen was required for any who hoped to marry its wards. See 1 Ventris 178, 86 *ER* 121–122; 2 Keble 855, 84 *ER* 541; and Misc. 500, f. 185v. TNA, KB21/ 17/86–91.

45. BL, Add. 32,527, f. 8v., and 1 Ventris 195, 86 *ER* 132–133.

46. Genesis 25:30–34.

47. John Rogers, *A Discourse of Christian Watchfulnesse* . . . (1620), 280. For the devil's influence and the likeness of Esau's action to Adam's and Eve's, see Thomas Adams, *The Deuills Banket Described in Foure Sermons* (1614), 45; and Edward Reynolds, *Three Treatises of the Vanity of the Creature* (1631), 35 and 81.

48. Godfrey Goodman, *The Fall of Man, or the Corruption of Nature, Proved by the light of our Natural Reason* (1616), 394.

49. See, for instance, William Prynne, *Demophilos, or the Assertor of the Peoples Liberty. Plainly Demonstrating by the Principles even of Nature itself.* . . (1658), 45 and 49. Even for Prynne, who fused law and liberty, their logical priority never reversed. Perhaps because he was a lawyer, not even Prynne could bring himself to subject law to liberties rather than the other way around. Doing so would require exposing common law to criticism.

50. For a thoughtful discussion of Lilburne's efforts at law in multiple courtroom moments and pamphlets in the 1640s and 1650s, see Thomas A. Green, *Verdict According to Conscience: Perspectives on the English Criminal Trial Jury, 1200–1800* (Chicago, 1985), chapter 5.

51. Pauline Gregg, *Free-Born John: A Biography of John Lilburne* (London, 1961).

52. *The Lawes Funerall. Or, An Epistle written by Lieutenant Col. John Lilburne* (1648), 3. Lilburne made the same demand to serve as his own counsel during his treason trial in October 1649, "which I now humbly crave as my right, not only by the law of God and man, but also by the law and light of nature"; see *ST,* iv, 1271. Lilburne followed Acts 26:1: "Then Agrippa said unto Paul, Thou art permitted to speak for thyself." For more on Lilburne's arguments in 1649, see Diane Parkin-Speer, "John Lilburne: A Revolutionary Interprets Statutes and Common Law Due Process," *Law and History Review* 1 (1983): 276–296.

53. Lilburne had been imprisoned in June 1646, then again in July of that same year, for libels against Parliament. He was then imprisoned the following year for his words against Manchester and also committed by the Commons in January 1648 for treasonable practices in an alleged Leveller conspiracy. See TNA, KB32/10, part 2 (6 May 1648); KB29/

297/31; and KB21/13/118–121; Gregg, *Free-Born John*, 120, 137–142, and 197–198.

54. *Lawes Funerall*, 5, 10, and 18.

55. Ibid, 18.

56. *The Prisoners mournfull cry, against the Judges of the Kings Bench. Or An Epistle writ by Lievt. Col. John Lilburne, Prisoner in the Tower of London, unto Mr. Justice Rolle: Declaring the illegall dealing of himself, and Mr. Justice Bacon with him, in reference to his Habeas Corpus* (1648), 3. The title tells us most of what we need to know.

57. *Englands Birth-right Justified Against all Arbitrary Usurpation, whether Regall or Parliamentary* (1645), 4–5. Similarly, Lilburne demanded his freedom by demanding habeas corpus as a part of the law of England. As "a sensible Englishman," he was "compelled to struggle for my portion in the laws and liberties of my native country . . . it being your petitioner's birthright and inheritance." See ibid., 1 and 6.

58. *The oppressed mans importunate and mournfull cryes to be brought to the Barre of Iustice, or An Epistle writ by Lievt. Col. John Lilburne, (without all shadow of Law and Iustice, imprisoned in the Tower of London)* (1648), 1 and 4.

59. *Prisoners mournfull cry*, 3.

60. Lilburne regularly warned his judges that they would answer to a greater judge. God "abhors those that turn judgment into wormwood and gall, and leaves of righteousness in the earth, and commits mighty sins in afflicting the just." See *Lawes Funerall*, 5; also *ST*, iv, 1377.

61. William Ball, *Tractatus de Jure Regnandi, & Regni* (1645), 13–14. On Ball, see J. T. Peacey, "John Lilburne and the Long Parliament," *Historical Journal* 43 (2000): 633–634, 639.

62. "Let every soul be subject unto the higher powers. For there is no power but of God: the powers that be are ordained of God . . . Wherefore ye must needs be subject, not only for wrath, but also for conscience sake." Epistle to the Romans, 13:1 and 5.

63. Ball, *Tractatus*, 15.

64. *England's Miserie And Remedie in a Jvdiciovs Letter from an Utter-Barrister . . . concerning Lieutenant Col. Lilburn's Imprisonment* (1645), 1–3 and 5; *The Grand Plea of Lievt. Col. John Lilburne, Prerogative Prisoner in the Tower of London, against the present tryannicall House of Lords* (1647), 5.

65. *The Free-mans Freedome Vindicated. Or A true Relation of the cause and manner of Lievt. Col. John Lilburns present imprisonment in Newgate* (1646), 11.

66. In writing this, I want to suggest that Lilburne's bibliocentric approach should not prevent us from seeing the universalizing ideas his claims generated: that rights were natural, because they arise from creation, and thus are universal and equally shared among all "men." Lilburne's

thinking raises serious questions for any history of "human rights" that sees them arising within secularizing idioms, in the eighteenth century, and largely in revolutionary France. For such an analysis, see Lynn Hunt, *Inventing Human Rights: A History* (New York, 2007).

67. Sir John Maynard, *A Speech Spoken in the Honourable House of Commons* (1648), 6, emphasis in original; Gregg, *Free-Born John*, 245.

68. Thus St. German made the relationship of English law to divine and natural law one of nonrepugnancy, "because the said customs be neither against the law of God nor the law of reason and have been alway[s] taken to be good and necessary for the common wealth of all the realm." See Christopher St. German, *Doctor and Student*, T. F. T. Plucknett and J. L. Barton, eds., Selden Society, 91 (London, 1974), 45–47.

69. Henry Care, *English Liberties: or, The Free-Born Subject's Inheritance . . .* (1680?), 2.

70. Judges and lawyers, by using the phrase "at liberty," expressed the idea that all thought is embodied, or, as Stephen L. Winter puts it, "thought originates in our sense of spatial and kinesthetic orientation in the world . . . human rationality is an embodied process that is experientially grounded and imaginatively elaborated." See Winter, *A Clearing in the Forest: Law, Life, and Mind* (Chicago, 2001), 23 and 56, and generally, chapters 2 and 3.

71. LI, Misc. 713, pp. 55–56 and 259. A case involving the Porters' Company in 1704 came to much the same end. When they imprisoned a porter for unloading boats when he was not free of their company, Queen's Bench resolved that they could not make any bylaw binding on strangers "unless founded on public convenience." See Holt 433, 90 *ER* 1138–1139 and 1 Salk. 192, 91 *ER* 174 (Estwick).

72. The writ, dated the last day of the 1758 Hilary term, was ordered returned to Justice Sir Thomas Denison in chambers, so no record of the result survives in court files. For the writ and order, see TNA, KB16/5/2 (13 February 1758). For background, see Arthur H. Cash, *John Wilkes: The Scandalous Father of Civil Liberty* (New Haven, 2006), 9–10, 17–20, 43–44, and 46–47.

73. TNA, KB21/38/133.

74. TNA, KB16/17/1 (6 November 1770). The writ had been sued by William and Anne Burnett, who were probably Ann Mose's parents: see the orders at KB21/40, Tuesday after the morrow of All Souls and Wednesday after the morrow of St. Martin's, 11 George III (1770). Because the return claimed that Mose was not in Bishop's custody, no body was returned and thus no result of judgment survives. We might

conclude that Mose was indeed "at liberty" and there was nothing for the court to do further unless she were confined again and then sued habeas corpus.

75. TNA, KB16/17/4 (1 February 1774) and KB21/40, Friday next after the octave of Purification, 14 George III (1774).

76. For a discussion of some of these issues in marriage, see Elizabeth Foyster, "At the Limits of Liberty: Married Women and Confinement in Eighteenth-Century England," *Continuity and Change* 17 (2002): 39–62.

77. Keechang Kim, *Aliens in Medieval Law: The Origins of Modern Citizenship* (Cambridge, Eng., 2000), introduction, especially 1–9.

78. William Blackstone, *Commentaries on the Laws of England* (Chicago, 1979), vol. 1, p. 354.

79. Kim, *Aliens in Medieval Law,* chapter 2, especially 29–41.

80. Thomas Blount, *ΝΟΜΟ-ΛΕΞΙΚΟΝ: A Law-Dictionary* (1670), s.v. "alien"; *Les Termes de la Ley* (1667), 246.

81. BL, Egerton 3376, f. 20.

82. For some recent analyses of Calvin's case, see Polly J. Price, "Natural Law and Birthright Citizenship in Calvin's Case," *Yale Journal of Law and the Humanities* 9 (1997): 73–146; Daniel Hulsebosch, *Constituting Empire: New York and the Transformation of Constitutionalism in the Atlantic World, 1664–1830* (Chapel Hill, 2005), 20–28; and Kim, *Aliens in Medieval Law,* chapter 8.

83. *ST,* ii, 614, 617, 619, 640, 647, and 650.

84. *Hale's Prerogatives,* 54. Coke's categories differed slightly. They were allegiance "by nature and birth-right"; acquired allegiance, in other words, denization; "local obedience or ligeance"; and legal allegiance, erected by oaths. This last then is not unlike Hale's category of feudal allegiance, which likewise arose from the swearing of actual oaths. See *ST,* ii, 615.

85. In the original, *"protectio trahit subjectionem, et subjectio protectionem."* See *ST,* ii, 614.

86. Blount, *A Law-Dictionary,* s.v. "protection"; *Hale's Prerogatives,* 56; *ST,* ii, 616.

87. BL, Harleian 5220, f. 11v.

88. *Hale's Prerogatives,* 56.

89. BL, Harl. 4841, ff. 6–7. Not all agreed with Ashley that aliens might thus be freemen within the terms of Magna Carta. See Baker, *Laws,* 611, citing BL, MS Harleian 4990, f. 161v., a reading on chapter 1 of Magna Carta from the mid-sixteenth century. Also, Ashley drew the line at non-Christians, because "the law presumes perpetual hostility . . . between infidels and Christians." See BL, Harl. 4841, f. 6.

90. *ST,* ii, 636.

91. The distinction between the incapacity of aliens to hold property, while they could enjoy other aspects of English law, came out forcefully in the Putney debates of 1647. General Henry Ireton argued that political participation required that one have a "permanent fixed interest" in the land. The *reductio ad absurdum* of the counterargument was that if landholding was not required, then an alien might participate in politics. This could appear absurd to Ireton and his listeners only because all assumed that foreigners could not hold land. But Ireton was careful to signal his recognition that aliens enjoyed the other parts of English law to which, by their presence in the kingdom, they had voluntarily made themselves subject. Thus an alien should have "air, the passage of highways, the protection of laws, and all that by nature." See A. S. P. Woodhouse, *Puritanism and Liberty: Being the Army Debates (1647–1649) from the Clarke Manuscripts* (Chicago, 1951), 54 and 66.

92. TNA, KB29/231/83d. In his report of Calvin's case, Coke noted the case of Lopez and his alleged co-conspirators as one demonstrating the allegiance owed by those in "local obedience" and what would befall them, like any natural subject, should they defy that obedience and commit treason. See *ST,* ii, 617.

93. TNA, KB145/17/14 (12 February 1662). One of the watermen had died, so the charge was murder. These aliens had two writs, one before and one after conviction. They were joined in the first of these by a third alien suspect.

94. Haagon Swanson and his co-conspirators were brought into King's Bench by habeas corpus for trial in 1702 for forcibly marrying Pleasant Rawlins, "a gentlewoman of a great fortune." Swanson was ultimately ordered hanged. See TNA, KB16/3/1 and KB21/26/220, 222, 225, and 228.

95. TNA, ADM1/3686, unfol., letter of 29 May 1798, quoting a letter from Admiral King, from Plymouth, with Admiralty order on the verso. The order for the writ is in KB21/47/8.

96. TNA, KB16/1/6 (23 January 1697). The note on the back of their writ showed clearly that it had been issued by the terms of the statute rather than at common law. The return to their writ quoted the warrant for their commitment made out by Secretary of State the Duke of Shrewsbury. They were initially bailed, and after appearing on their recognizances for two terms, were discharged altogether: see TNA, KB21/25/149 and 210. Both names appear in highly varied forms in the record, LaPierre at one point being called "Stone." There is a brief report: Fortescue 195, 92 *ER* 816, as "Du Castro's" case. This report ap-

pears to have concerned not the hearing of the return, but the hearing two terms later on the motion to discharge them from their bail. This is when counsel argued that, as foreigners, they were not entitled to bail. Though one cannot prove a negative, this is the only report, in print or manuscript, that I have seen in which there is an explicit claim that alien status should bar the writ.

97. See, for instance, the case of Jean Prevôt, a Frenchman convicted at Old Bailey Admiralty sessions for mutiny and murder aboard the *Lady Shore* of the New South Wales corps when it was off the African coast. See *The Times* (London), 5 December 1799, 3.

98. Opposing counsel argued that if that view was accepted, then even a prisoner of war might be able to use habeas corpus, though no answer was given to this surmise. See 1 Ld. Raym. 282, 91 *ER* 1086 (Wells v. Williams, Common Pleas).

99. See 1 Bos. and Pul. 163, 126 *ER* 837 (Sparenburgh v. Bannatyne, 1797).

100. See 13 East 195, 104 *ER* 344–345; Yvette Abrahams, "Disempowered to Consent: Sara Bartman and Khoisan Slavery in the Nineteenth-Century Cape Colony and Britain," *South African Historical Journal* 35 (1996): 89–114.

101. Rachel Holmes, *African Queen: The Real Life of the Hottentot Venus* (New York, 2007), retells the story of the trial in chapters 6 and 7; quotation at 58.

102. Baartman was born circa 1790, before British control of the Cape Colony began in 1806. Even then, it was not until the making of Ordinance 50 in 1828 that "Hottentots and other free persons of color" were declared to possess most of the legal privileges of "other of His Majesty's Subjects." See Eric A Walker, ed., *The Cambridge History of the British Empire* (Cambridge, Eng., 1963), vol. 8, chapter 8, especially 294–295.

103. James Thomson, setting by Thomas Arne, "Rule Britannia" (1740).

104. For an excellent treatment of Sharp's writings in the context of empire, see Christopher Leslie Brown, *Moral Capital: Foundations of British Abolitionism* (Chapel Hill, 2006), chapter 3.

105. Granville Sharp, *A Tract on the Law of Nature and Principles of Action in Man* (1777), 2. Emphasis in original.

106. Granville Sharp, *The Law of Liberty, or, Royal Law, By which all Mankind will Certainly be Judged!* (1776), 6, quoting James 2:12; and *An Appendix to the Representation, of the Injustice and Dangerous Tendency of Tolerating Slavery* (1772), 23. Emphasis in original.

107. Granville Sharp, *The Law of Retribution; or, A Serious Warning to Great Britain and Her Colonies, Founded on Unquestionable Examples of God's Tempo-*

ral Vengeance Against Tyrants, Slave-holders, and Oppressors (1776), 6, 16, and passim. Sharp frequently invoked St. German, especially to suggest how common law was subject to "law eternal," where "we find an immoveable foundation of *justice, of right, of the rights of man, of righteousness.*" See *Extract of a Letter to a Gentleman in Maryland, Wherein is demonstrated the Extreme Wickedness of Tolerating the Slave Trade* . . . (1793), 6. Emphasis in original. On "natural equity," see also *A Declaration of the People's Natural Right to a Share in the Legislature* . . , 2d ed. (1775), iv–v; *Appendix to the Representation,* 9–12; *An Essay on Slavery, Proving from Scripture its Inconsistency with Humanity and Religion* (1773), 19 and 22; and *The Just Limitation of Slavery in the Laws of God* . . . (1776).

108. *Essay on Slavery,* vii–viii. On the nonrepugnancy principle in colonial charters, see Chapter 8.

109. *Appendix to the Representation,* 25. This concern arose in part from a broader one about Parliament's lack of representativeness, a circumstance more marked in the makeup of most colonial assemblies. See, generally, *Declaration. A Representation of the Injustice and Dangerous Tendency of Tolerating Slavery* . . . (1769), 81.

110. *A Short Tract Concerning the Doctrine of "Nullum Tempus Occurrit Regi"* (1779), 3. Emphasis in original.

111. *A Representation of the Injustice and Dangerous Tendency of Tolerating Slavery,* 16, 20, 51, 71, 92, and 152–159. Sharp defended this point in part by reference to statute, namely 32 Henry VIII, c. 16, "Concerning Strangers": "every alien and stranger born . . . which now or hereafter shall come in or to this realm or elsewhere within the king's dominions, shall . . . be bounden by and unto the laws and statutes of this realm" (21).

112. *Appendix to the Representation,* 19–20; also 4. Emphasis in original. See also *Nullum Tempus Occurrit Regi,* 3–4n. For more on the Habeas Corpus Act, see Chapter 7.

113. *An Address to the People of England: Being the Protest of a Private Person Against Every Suspension of Law that is Liable to Injure or Endanger Personal Security* (1778), 23, 25, and 57n. Emphasis in original.

7. Legislators as Judges

1. Shaftesbury was released seven months later, after he begged the pardon of the House. See National Library of Wales, Coedymaen 6, f. 1, and Coedymaen 8, f. 4v; *ST* vi, 1269–1310, especially 1273, and 1290. For a full account of arguments, see Coedymaen 9 and 11; for a variant

report, see BL, Landsdowne 484, ff. 49–53. On Shaftesbury, see K. H. D. Haley, *The First Earl of Shaftesbury* (Oxford, 1968), chapters 19 and 20.

2. Thus the title of chapter 1 of the fourth volume of Coke's *Institutes:* "Of the High and most Honorable Court of Parliament."

3. *Hale's Prerogatives,* 135.

4. Sir Matthew Hale, *The Jurisdiction of the Lords House . . .*, ed. Francis Hargrave (1796), 17.

5. *Hale's Prerogatives,* 181. Hale thus distinguished between Parliament's extraordinary and other courts' ordinary jurisdictions. In the making of statute, king-in-Parliament was supreme. But in their "supreme ordinary jurisdiction," the judges of the courts of Westminster Hall were supreme (206).

6. *Hale's Prerogatives,* 136; Hale, *Lords House,* 84–86; Alan Cromartie, *Sir Matthew Hale, 1609–1676: Law, Religion, and Natural Philosophy* (Cambridge, Eng., 1995), 114–117.

7. T. E. Hartley, ed., *Proceedings in the Parliaments of Elizabeth I* (Leicester, 1981), vol. 1, pp. 425–439, 476–477, and 491.

8. Hartley, *Parliaments,* vol. 3, p. 68; J. E. Neale, *Elizabeth I and Her Parliaments, 1584–1601* (New York, 1958), 251–266; *ODNB,* s.v. Peter Wentworth.

9. CJ, i, 149–150, 167, 171, and 204–207; *ODNB,* s.v. Sir Thomas Shirley.

10. For other examples of this cooperation, see the Commons' imprisonment in 1581 of MP Arthur Hall, who had also been rebuked by the Council for a book he wrote: CJ, i, 125–127 and 136; Hartley, *Parliaments,* vol. 1, pp. 509, 532–533, and 536. See also the 1604 imprisonment ordered by the Speaker, and approved by the Commons, of Anthony Erbury, a minister who libeled the Bishop of London. The Commons referred him to the Council for examination, but the Council let the Commons order his release upon his humble petition. See CJ, i, 210 and 253; Roland Usher, *The Reconstruction of the English Church* (London, 1910), vol. 1, pp. 346–347.

11. The Commons only learned of Floyd's wrongs when making an unrelated inquiry into the mistreatment of prisoners in the Fleet; see *CD 1621,* v, 112 and 116–117; Colin G. C. Tite, *Impeachment and Parliamentary Judicature in Early Stuart England* (London, 1974), 122–131.

12. *CD* 1621, ii, 337–338, and v, 131–132; LJ, iii, 110 and 111.

13. LJ iii, 119, 122, 124, 127, 128, 133–134, and 148–149. Some MPs were outraged, insisting that they, like the Lords, constituted a court of record. Others, like William Noy, were less certain. He conceded the Commons' longstanding purview of matters "touching themselves,"

but doubted that they might judge of "foreign matter." See CJ, i, 599–600 and 607–609; *CD* 1621, ii, 335, 337–338, 361–362, and 380–381, and v, 126–136, 154–156, 161–162, 359–361, 371, and 381.

14. Tite, *Impeachment,* chapters 4 and 5; James S. Hart, *Justice upon Petition: The House of Lords and the Reformation of Justice, 1621–1675* (London, 1991), introduction and chapter 1.

15. LJ, vi, 214; Conrad Russell, *Parliaments and English Politics, 1621–1629* (Oxford, 1979), 103–114; *ODNB,* s.v. Sir Francis Bacon and Sir Robert Berkeley; W. J. Jones, *Politics and the Bench: The Judges and the Origins of the English Civil War* (London, 1971), 137–143.

16. For a full discussion of Morice's effort, see Christopher W. Brooks, *Law, Politics and Society in Early Modern England* (Cambridge, Eng., 2008), 105–111; *ODNB,* s.v. James Morice.

17. James Morice, *A Briefe Treatise of Oathes. . . ,* 52, which was probably printed at Middleburg, sometime in the 1590s: *ODNB,* and Faith Thompson, *Magna Carta: Its Role in the Making of the English Constitution, 1300–1629* (Minneapolis, 1948), 218.

18. BL, Harleian 6847, ff. 64–65, excerpted in Thompson, *Magna Carta,* 394–395. His speech, and the text of another bill he presented concerned with oaths, is in Hartley, *Parliaments,* vol. 3, pp. 30–49.

19. Morice was chastised by the Privy Council for raising the issue in Parliament rather than privately before the queen; see Thompson, *Magna Carta,* 218–221 and 224–226, as well as Christopher W. Brooks, *Lawyers, Litigation, and English Society since 1450* (London, 1998), 220. For a vivid account, see Neale, *Elizabeth and Parliaments,* 267–279. For more balance, see David Dean, *Law-Making and Society in Late Elizabethan England* (Cambridge, Eng., 1996), 116–119.

20. CJ, i, 152, 157, 169, and 176.

21. This clause was virtually the same in all the pardon statutes passed at the end of each Parliament; see, e.g., 35 Elizabeth, c. 14, §8; 39 Elizabeth, c. 28, §8; 43 Elizabeth, c. 19, §8; 3 James I, c. 27, §9; and 21 James I, c. 35, §10.

22. *CD* 1621, iv, 274, and v, 113 and 355; CJ, i, 609–610.

23. *CD* 1621, v, 226.

24. *CD* 1621, iv, 308.

25. Ibid., 307. The bill was "for the better Securing of the Subjects from wrongful Imprisonment and Deprivation of Trades and Occupations, contrary to the 29th Chapter of Magna Charta." See CJ, i, 596, 609–610, 628, 647, and 653; Russell, *Parliaments,* 57–58.

26. *CD* 1621, ii, 397; iv, 308 and 382; and v, 143–144 and 226.

27. CJ, i, 672, 673, and 680; Russell, *Parliaments,* 159 and 196.

28. *ST* iii, 6–11. On the Edwardian statutes, known as the six statutes, see Thompson, *Magna Carta*, 90–94.

29. What Quentin Skinner has noted of political argument applies as well to legal argument: that the "innovating ideologist," like all revolutionaries, is "obliged to march backwards into battle." See Skinner, *Regarding Method*, vol. 1 of *Visions of Politics* (Cambridge, Eng., 2002), 149–150.

30. *CD* 1628, ii, 191–192, 197, 213, and 218.

31. See 3 Bulstrode 109, 81 *ER* 94 (Codd, 1615).

32. Russell, *Parliaments*, 377.

33. J. P. Kenyon, *The Stuart Constitution: Documents and Commentary* (Cambridge, Eng., 1969), 83–84.

34. In the survey years during Charles I's reign before the start of the Civil War (1626, 1630, 1634, 1638), 37% of those using habeas corpus were bailed or discharged, compared to a release rate of 56% in the period from 1558 to 1625, and 53% from 1500 to 1800.

35. In the survey years between 1628 and 1640, four were jailed by the Council on warrants that did not name a cause. Two were remanded: TNA, KB29/283/46d. and 124d., and KB21/11/153v. and 167v. (Richard Leachford and Edward Courtney, 1634). And two were bailed: KB145/15/14 (Nehemiah Rawson, 28 May 1638) and KB145/15/14 (Robert Barkham, 29 May 1638); KB21/12/92v.–127v., passim. Barkham was discharged from bail the following year.

36. *ODNB*, s.v. Denzil Holles.

37. *ST* iii, 235–294.

38. CD 1628, ii, 356.

39. See 16 Charles I, cc. 10 and 11. For developments in the 1630s, especially in the Star Chamber, which had been a widely popular court before a handful of politically charged cases attracted fierce criticism, see Kevin Sharpe, *The Personal Rule of Charles I* (New Haven, 1992), chapters 11 and 12, especially 665–682 and 758–765.

40. The Star Chamber statute is often misdated to 1640. The correct date matters, both because no Parliament met in the summer of 1640, and because the political environment during its passage was so different from that of a year earlier. On Hyde and others around whom a consensus operated for reform of law in mid-1641, see David L. Smith, *Constitutional Royalism and the Search for Settlement, c. 1640–1649* (Cambridge, Eng., 1994), part 1, especially 75–77, and Conrad Russell, *The Fall of the British Monarchies, 1637–1742* (Oxford, 1991), chapter 9, especially 354–355.

41. Maija Jansson, ed., *Proceedings in the Opening Session of the Long Parlia-*

ment (Rochester, 2000–2007), especially vol. 2, p. 488; vol. 3, pp. 93, 106, and 234, and passim; vol. 4, pp. 85–86, 100–104, 657–659, and 662–663; and vol. 5, pp. 401, 410–412, 421, 423, and 425. For Hyde's attacks on the marshal's court, see G. D. Squibb, *The High Court of Chivalry* (Oxford, 1959), 62–67.

42. The most important case of refusal to release on habeas corpus concerned Alexander Jennings, who refused to pay ship money, a traditional tax for naval defense controversially extended from coastal areas to inland ones by Charles I. Jennings was remanded on a 1637 writ returning only his imprisonment "until further order." He sued further writs, and was released on a fuller return in Trinity 1638. See TNA, KB32/10, part 1 (27 June 1637), and KB145/15/14 (7 May 1638); KB21/12/60–114, especially 98; and *ODNB,* s.v. Berkeley and Malet.

43. See 16 Charles I, c. 10, §§1 and 8.

44. They would be released in the spring, but by command of the Commons rather than the court. See TNA, KB21/13/26v; CJ, ii, 953, 954, 981; and CJ, iii, 79 and 112.

45. For instance, Thomas Huxley, imprisoned by a Commons committee for his obedience to orders of the king's court of Wards, at Oxford, was released in 1647. See TNA, KB29/296/38, and KB21/13/95, 95v., and 99.

46. CJ, iv, 647–648, and CJ, v, 437; Style 104, 82 *ER* 564–565; TNA, KB29/297/33, and KB21/13/111–123, passim; *ODNB,* s.v. Sir John Stawell. See too the remand order on the habeas for Philip Chetwynd, committed without cause shown, on a parliamentary warrant ordering him held "during the pleasure of this House": CJ, v, 338; TNA, KB145/16/1650 (6 May 1650); and KB21/13/162, 164v., and 165.

47. Haley, *Shaftesbury,* 70; *ODNB,* s.v. Anthony Ashley Cooper, first Earl of Shaftesbury.

48. On Lilburne's trial and its significance in law concerned with jury process, see Thomas A. Green, *Verdict According to Conscience: Perspectives on the English Criminal Trial Jury, 1200–1800* (Chicago, 1985), chapter 5, especially 192–199.

49. Pauline Gregg, *Free-Born John: A Biography of John Lilburne* (London, 1961), 310–346. Lilburne's Old Bailey trial is in *ST* v, 407–460. See also CJ, vii, 309 and 358; Style 397, 82 *ER* 809. Crown Side rulebooks do not survive for this period, nor does the writ or return, since the writ was never filed.

50. BL, Hargrave 48, 34v. Lilburne was sent to Dover Castle in October 1655, and ultimately paroled, before dying in 1657. See *ODNB,* s.v. John Lilbunrne.

51. It may be significant that this early use of what amounted to a sentence of transportation occurred in the early 1650s, soon after the first use of transportation for prisoners of war, after the siege of Colchester, in 1648. See Cynthia Herrup, "Punishing Pardon: Some Thoughts on the Origins of Penal Transportation," in Simon Devereaux and Paul Griffiths, eds., *Penal Practice and Culture, 1500–1900: Punishing the English* (Basingstoke, 2004), 129–132.

52. The account here largely follows James S. Hart Jr., *The Rule of Law, 1603–1660* (Harlow, 2003), 265–269.

53. TNA, KB145/16/1653 (12 November 1653); CJ, vii, 353; *ST* v, 371.

54. *ST* v, 374, 380, and 387.

55. *ST* v, 400.

56. *ODNB*, s.v. John Ashburnham, Robert Overton, and John Biddle; CJ, vii, 400 and 416.

57. TNA, KB145/16/1658 (29 April and 11 June 1658).

58. William Prynne, *Demophilos, or the Assertor of the Peoples Liberty. . .* (1658), 55.

59. CJ, vii, 614.

60. John Towill Rutt, *Diary of Thomas Burton* (London, 1828), vol. 4, pp. 158–159; Hale, *History of the Common Law*, 118–121.

61. CJ, vii, 614–615.

62. *ODNB*, s.v. John Lambert, Gilbert Millington, Henry Smith, James Temple, Thomas Waite, and Sir Hardress Waller. Lambert was moved to St. Nicholas's Island, off Plymouth, where Robert Lilburne, John's brother, was also imprisoned on a commuted sentence for his part in the regicide.

63. This was accomplished by using habeas corpus: see TNA, KB145/17/14 (30 May 1662), and KB21/14/86v.–88. The return gave no cause of imprisonment; see *ODNB*, s.v. Sir Henry Vane, the younger.

64. *ODNB*, s.v. John Ireton and John Wildman. Wildman was later moved to Pendennis Castle, also within the county of Cornwall, and thus within the writ's generally accepted purview.

65. TNA, KB21/16/101v., 107, 108v., and 114v., and KB21/17/5v. and 24v. 1 Sid. 386, 82 *ER* 1173, and 2 Keble 450, 84 *ER* 282.

66. The order for his writ is in TNA, KB21/14/78v. The writ and return are not on file (KB145/17/14 or 15), suggesting it was never returned. See *ODNB*, s.v. James Harrington.

67. For more on this issue, see Chapter 8. I borrow the phrase "technologies of jurisdiction" from Shaunnagh Dorsett and Shaun McVeigh, "Questions of Jurisdiction," in McVeigh, *Jurisprudence of Jurisdiction* (New York, 2007), 11–12.

68. In addition to Careswell, Clement Ireton and three others in the Tower, who had been committed two years earlier by order of the Duke of Albemarle, were bailed. The writ also went to the Isle of Wight for Edward Bagshaw, a dissenting minister imprisoned for "treasonable practices." He was also released that November. See TNA, KB21/16/60–63v.; LI, Hill 83, pp. 243 and 246.

69. Andrew Swatland, *The House of Lords in the Reign of Charles II* (Cambridge, Eng., 1996), chapter 5 and 127–134.

70. *ST* vi, 330.

71. *ST* vi, 365 and 370.

72. The matter was dropped when Kelyng made a combination apology and defense. See CJ, ix, 35–36 and 37; Grey, *Debates*, vol. 1, pp. 53 and 63. On Kelyng's tendency to impose on juries and his other excesses, see Green, *Verdict According to Conscience*, 208–221.

73. CJ, ix, 78, 86, and 87–88. See also Caroline Robbins, ed., *The Diary of John Milward* (Cambridge, Eng., 1938), 253, 271, and 278; and Helen A. Nutting, "The Most Wholesome Law—The Habeas Corpus Act of 1679," *American Historical Review* 65 (1959–1960): 532.

74. Tangier had become a crown possession by the marriage treaty with Portugal that united Catherine of Braganza and Charles II.

75. CJ, ix, 293, 296, 298, 310–311, and 313; Grey, *Debates*, vol. 2, pp. 270, 301–303, 338, 349–350, 364–367, and 389–390.

76. Powle and others were also concerned that judges acting individually, in chambers, would be too ready to grant the writ and bail prisoners. See Grey, *Debates*, vol. 2, pp. 414, 421–425, 433–435, and 446.

77. CJ, ix, 319, 321, and 326; Grey, *Debates*, vol. 3, pp. 1 and 105–106. This concern with Scotland reflected a growing dislike of the Duke of Lauderdale's governance there. See Tim Harris, *Restoration: Charles II and His Kingdoms, 1660–1685* (London, 2005), 116–132.

78. Grey, *Debates*, vol. 3, pp. 239–255 and 260–289; CJ, ix, 338–339 and 356–357. On the row over Dalmahoy's case, and the simultaneous one involving proceedings in the Lords against another MP, John Fagg, see Hart, *Justice upon Petition*, 251–258. When Parliament reconvened in October, the Commons passed the same bill through two readings before the session ended again without a final product. See CJ, ix, 368 and 376.

79. CJ, ix, 386, 391, 403, and 405; LJ, xiii, 100.

80. Grey, *Debates*, vol. 4, pp. 261–283; TNA, KB145/17/29 (4 May 1677).

81. For instance, 16 Charles II, c. 4 (Conventicle Act), and 17 Charles II, c. 2 (Five Mile Act).

82. Conventicles were secret religious gatherings. TNA, CP45/466/24d.

Bod., Rawl.C.719, pp. 37–45 and LI, Misc. 500, f. 42. The first I have found was a Common Pleas writ to Chester in Michaelmas 1668. On its return, the court seemed uncertain about whether or not, and if so how, they might use the *ad subjiciendum* writ; see LI, Hill 83, p. 293 (Crompton). No sign of this writ survives on the roll: see CP45/463.

83. Bod, Rawl.C.719, p. 81; LI, Misc. 500, f. 100; and HLS, 5016, f. 83.

84. Jones, T. 13, 84 *ER* 1123–1125; 1 Freeman 1, 89 *ER* 2–5; and *ST* vi, 951–1026. Green, *Verdict According to Conscience,* 221–249, and especially 230–236. On Rudyard's involvement in their cause, see Gary DeKrey, *London and the Restoration, 1659–1683* (Cambridge, Eng., 2005), 112–114. More generally, see Craig W. Horle, *The Quakers and the English Legal System, 1660–1688* (Philadelphia, 1988).

85. Carter 221, 124 *ER* 928 (Anonymous, 1671?); 1 Mod. 235 and 2 Mod. 198, 86 *ER* 852 and 1023–1024 (Jones, 1677).

86. Grey, *Debates,* vol. 3, p. 105.

87. TNA, KB145/17/29 (4 May and 4 July 1677).

88. For more, see Chapter 8.

89. Tellingly, Harrington and Murray were directly linked to the earl. See Haley, *Shaftesbury,* 424–426.

90. *ST* vi, 1189–1208; DeKrey, *London,* 144–149.

91. Harris, *Restoration,* chapter 3.

92. Among those brought in by habeas corpus for trial in Michaelmas 1678 were alleged plotter William Stayley—overheard saying frightening things in French—and Edward Coleman, the Duchess of York's secretary: see TNA, KB21/19/158, 160, and 160v.; *ODNB,* s.v. Edward Coleman and William Stayley; and John Kenyon, *The Popish Plot* (London, 1972), 98–99.

93. The three jailed by order of the Lords were Capt. Francis Spalding, Charles Price, and George Milbourne. See TNA, KB145/17/31 (23, 24, and 25 January 1679, respectively); and KB21/19/165–211, passim. Price and Spalding, the governor of Chepstow Castle, had allegedly been involved in a plot in the west. Both were certainly Catholics. See Kenyon, *Popish Plot,* 94–95, 107, and 213. The others released were Roger Earl of Castlemaine, Daniel Arthur, Ralph Sheldon, Francis Curson, Francis Lord Brudnell, Mark Preston, Edward Griffin, John Crumpe, Francis Mannock, and his father, Sir Francis Mannock. See KB145/17/31, passim.

94. CJ, ix, 578, 582, 584, 590, and 617; Grey, *Debates,* vol. 7: 218, 292, and 294–295; LJ, xiii, 511, 541, 544, 548, 549, 552, 558, 561, 583–584, 589, and 594.

95. See 31 Charles II, c. 2.

96. This from a marginal note of Narcissus Luttrell in his copy of *Absalom and Achitophel:* Nutting, "Habeas Corpus Act," 540–541.

97. Haley, *Shaftesbury,* 359–360. He may have been responsible for drafting the proviso against transporting prisoners from England without consent that was first proposed in 1674: see Swatland, *House of Lords,* 223, citing House of Lords Record Office, Committee Minutes, vol. 3, p. 78. See also Mark Knights, *Politics and Opinion in Crisis, 1678–81* (Cambridge, Eng., 1994), 133–134.

98. Leicestershire Record Office, DG7/Box XI/pp60, i: Finch Papers.

99. See Chapter 2.

100. For the survey years 1662, 1666, and 1670, 17% (18 of 107) of dateable writs issued during vacation. A search of nonsurvey years in the 1660s shows a similar pattern. No vacation writs issued in the survey year of 1674; no recorda file survives for 1678. For the first half of 1679, before the Habeas Corpus Act took effect, only 2 of 42 dateable writs issued in vacation.

101. Grey, *Debates,* vol. 2, p. 433.

102. In the second half of 1679, 12% of dateable writs (6 of 51) were issued in vacation. In the next survey year, 1682, 18% (12 of 68) were.

103. TNA, KB145/13/31 (21 June 1679) and KB21/19/201. Creed had previously been in Pendennis Castle. He was apparently moved to Guernsey after habeas had been issued on his behalf to Pendennis in late 1669: see KB21/17/18.

104. W. B. Gray, "The Scottish Deportees of 1683 and the Habeas Corpus Act," *Juridical Review* 35 (1923): 353–361. The Act did permit sending prisoners for trial in other dominions for crimes committed in those other places. This reading of the Act was confirmed by the judges when discussing the case of Col. Robert Lundy. Accused of treasonable practices while governor of Derry in 1689, he was captured in Scotland after he fled, then was imprisoned in England. Though the judges resolved that the Act did not prevent his being sent back to Ireland for trial there, he was bailed, and later discharged, by habeas corpus. See TNA, KB11/14 and KB21/23/369 and 375; Holt KB 333, 90 *ER* 1084. In 1729, Daniel Kimberley was remanded to Woodstreet Compter on his habeas corpus, having been committed for forcing a woman into marriage with him in Ireland. But confusion persisted about how to accomplish such a transfer according to law. See KB21/33/234v., 236, and 237; Fitzg. 111, 94 *ER* 677.

105. See 31 Charles II, c. 2, §1, which directed that writs issuing according to the Act be inscribed *"per statutum tricesimo primo Caroli Secundi Regis,"* which was usually written on the verso of the writ, instead of the customary *"per regulam curiam."*

106. TNA, KB145/15/34 (26 May 1682).
107. TNA, KB16/1/6 (23 January 1697).
108. On political print, see Mark Knights, *Representation and Misrepresentation in Later Stuart Britain: Partisanship and Political Culture* (Oxford, 2005), especially chapters 1–2 and 5.
109. See, for instance, John Dryden, *His Majesties Declaration Defended* (1681), 9–10, and [George Savile, Marquis of Halifax], *A Seasonable Address . . . Concerning the Succession, the Fears of Popery, and Arbitrary Government, by a true Protestant* (1681), 4–5.
110. "The Whigs' Downfall," in Nathaniel Thompson, *A Choice Collection of 120 Loyal Songs* (1684), 208.
111. TNA, KB145/17/34 (13 February 1682) and KB29/341/76. Though bailed, he would be convicted on the charge that summer: see KB21/21/203. See also *ODNB*, s.v. Nathaniel Thompson. On street politics and songs, and Thompson's work as a tory publisher, see Tim Harris, *London Crowds in the Reign of Charles II* (Cambridge, Eng., 1987), chapter 6.
112. Grey, *Debates,* vol. 8, pp. 121 and 229–230.
113. Ibid., 232 and 259; CJ, ix, 702.
114. Anonymous, *A Short Account, or State of Mr. Sheridan's Case before the Late House of Commons, in a Letter to J. T.,* 2d ed. (1681), 23.
115. *Sheridan's Case,* 29.
116. Sir Roger L'Estrange, *The Lawyer Outlaw'd, or, . . . some useful remarks on the Commons proceedings in the last Parliament at Westminster* (1683) 17–18.
117. Ibid., 29 and 30. Emphasis in original.
118. Bod., Carte 222, f. 256. No sign survives that Raymond was sued.
119. See 2 Salk. 504, 91 *ER* 431 (Regina v. Paty). For an important discussion of Holt's approach to judicial review of parliamentary action, see Philip A. Hamburger, "Revolution and Judicial Review: Chief Justice Holt's Opinion in *City of London v. Wood,*" *Columbia Law Review* 94 (1994): especially 2096–2112 and 2141–2146. See also *ODNB:* s.v. Sir John Holt.
120. *Parl. Hist.,* vol. 15, pp. 881–882.
121. Ibid., 885.
122. Ibid., 900n.
123. Ibid., 897n.
124. See Chapter 4. On the debates in 1758, see James Oldham and Michael J. Wishnie, "The Historical Scope of Habeas Corpus and INS v. St. Cyr," *Georgetown Immigration Law Journal* 16 (2002): 487–496.
125. See 56 George III, c. 100.
126. Ibid., c. 86.
127. See 57 George III, c. 3, extended in May 1817 by 57 George III, c. 55.

In March 1818, this was repealed by 58 George III, c. 1. For the debates, see T. C. Hansard, *The Parliamentary Debates* (London, 1817), xxxv, 765–775 and 825–836.

128. George Cruikshank, "Liberty Suspended" (March 1817) described in M. D. George, *Catalogue of Political and Personal Satires . . . in the British Museum* (London, 1949), vol. 9, p. 741.

129. See, for instance, the comments of Sir Francis Russell and Sir Joseph Tredenham: Grey, *Debates,* vol. 9, pp. 263 and 274–275.

130. *A New Law-Dictionary* (1729), 348.

131. On this period, see Tim Harris, *Revolution: The Great Crisis of the British Monarchy, 1685–1720* (London, 2006).

132. See 1 William and Mary, sess. 1, c. 2, with extensions: cc. 7 and 19. See also Clarence C. Crawford, "The Suspension of the Habeas Corpus Act and the Revolution of 1689," *English Historical Review* 30 (1915): 613–630.

133. Grey, *Debates,* vol. 9, pp. 136 and 263.

134. Ibid., 134.

135. Ibid., 264–265, 267, and 268. For more on dispensation and suspension as transposed from royal to parliamentary hands, see Paul D. Halliday and G. Edward White, "The Suspension Clause: English Text, Imperial Contexts, and American Implications," *Virginia Law Review* 94 (2008): 613–628.

136. After the three suspension statutes of 1689, others were passed as follows, through 1747: 7/8 William III, c. 11 (effective 20 February to 1 September 1696); 6 Anne, c. 15 (10 March to 23 October 1708); 1 George I, sess. 2, c. 8 (23 July 1715 to 24 January 1716); 1 George I, sess. 2, c. 30 (renewal to 24 May 1716); 9 George I, c. 1 (10 October 1722 to 24 October 1723); 17 George II, c. 6 (29 February to 29 April 1744); 19 George II, c. 1 (18 October 1745 to 19 April 1746); 19 George II, c. 17 (renewal to 20 November 1746); 20 George II, c. 1 (renewal to 20 February 1747).

137. The first statute (1 William and Mary, sess. 1, c. 2) made no provision for imprisonment on a secretary's warrant, though the second (c. 7) did. The third (c. 19) omitted this provision, though the fourth (7/8 William and Mary, c. 11) and subsequent ones contained it.

138. See the petition to Parliament from London against the suspension of 1777: *Addresses, Remonstrances, and Petitions . . . from the Court of Common Council* (1778?), 138–139. See also Anonymous, *Serious Consequences Attending the Suspension of the Habeas Corpus Act. Exemplified in the Case of Thomas Humphreys. . .* (1794), especially 3–4.

139. *Parl. Hist.,* vol. 7, p. 275.

140. Grey, *Debates,* vol. 10, p. 141.
141. TNA, KB16/1/6 (12 June 1696). The suspension was that of 7/8 William III, c. 11. A note on his writ shows that it was sued by the attorney general.
142. TNA, KB21/31/608 and 612 (Christopher Layer, 1722); KB16/13/4 and KB21/36/157 and 158–159 (Charles Ratcliffe, 10 November 1746); and 1 Black, W. 3, 96 *ER* 2–4. This was also a common law rather than a statutory writ, sued by the attorney general to bring Ratcliffe to trial.
143. TNA, KB16/13/4 (27 November 1746), and KB21/36/164.
144. See the comments of William Ettrick in Grey, *Debates,* vol. 9, p. 266.
145. Writs for 1689–1690 are in TNA, KB16/1/1 and KB11/14, with orders in KB21/23. See also Halliday and White, "Suspension Clause," 625–628.
146. The vacation usage is conjectural, based on the fact that end of term writs were often antedated vacation writs, and because it issued by command of Justice Thomas Rokeby according to the terms of the statute, another strong indicator of vacation usage. See TNA, KB16/1/6 (1 July 1696).
147. *The Trial on the Cause of Action Brought by Stephen Sayre, Esq. against the . . . Earl of Rochford . . . for False Imprisonment* (1776) and 2 Black. W. 1165, 96 *ER* 687–690. Among dozens of American reports of each step in the proceedings, see *Pennsylvania Packet,* 8 January 1776; *Essex Journal,* 19 January 1776; *The Pennsylvania Ledger,* 2 March 1776; and *The New-York Gazette,* 28 October 1776.
148. Much of this information is from that provided by John Wilkes in the course of debates in February 1777: see *Parl. Hist.,* vol. 19, pp. 29–30.
149. *The Norwich Packet,* 5 May 1777, 2.
150. K. G. Davies, ed., *Documents of the American Revolution* (Dublin, 1976), vol. 12, pp. 176–180; Sheldon S. Cohen, *Yankee Sailors in British Gaols* (Newark, 1995), 26–29.
151. *Parl. Hist.,* vol. 19, p. 4.
152. See 17 George III, c. 9 (20 February 1777 to 1 January 1778); renewed by 18 George III, c. 1 (to 1 January 1779); 19 George III, c. 1 (to 1 January 1780); 20 George III, c. 5 (to 1 January 1781); 21 George III, c. 2 (to 1 January 1782); and 22 George III, c. 1 (to 1 January 1783).
153. *A Letter from Edmund Burke . . . to* [*the*] *Sheriffs of Bristol* (1777), 14–15 and 17. Emphasis in the original.
154. The use of "dispensation" was no accident, given how close dispensing from statutes was to suspending them. Both practices had been heavily criticized when performed by Charles II and James II to pro-

tect their Catholic subjects from penal statutes. Sharp developed this point at length, connecting these dispensations and suspensions to "popery," a connection commonly made by Protestant controversialists. See [Granville Sharp], *An Address to the People of England: Being the Protest of a Private Person Against Every Suspension of Law that is Liable to Injure or Endanger Personal Security* (1778), 13–19 and 42. For more on Sharp, see Chapter 6. For discussion of dispensing, see Halliday and White, "Suspension Clause," 613–625.

155. *An Argument in the Case of Ebenezer Smith Platt . . . [with] the Opinion . . . of King's Bench* (1777), and 1 Leach 157, 168 *ER* 181–187. See also Jean-Marie Fecteau and Douglas Hay, "Military Justice and the Legal System in Quebec, 1775–83," in F. Murray Greenwood and Barry Wright, eds., *Law, Politics, and Security Measures, 1608–1837*, vol. 1 of *Canadian State Trials* (Toronto, 1996), 150–156.

156. American newspapers thus published the text of the London Common Council petition protesting against the then pending suspension bill in February 1777: among others, see the *Continental Journal*, 29 May 1777. Lengthy excerpts of Burke's letter to Bristol also appeared in various American papers, e.g., *New-England Chronicle*, 2 October 1777. In his widely published manifesto of September of 1777, George Washington noted that among the many other offenses given to Americans was "the suspension of the Habeas Corpus Act." See *Continental Journal*, 5 March 1778. On the suspensions during the American war, and their effect on the American experience leading to the Suspension Clause, see Halliday and White, "Suspension Clause," 644–651 and 670–676.

157. Dallin H. Oaks, "Habeas Corpus in the States—1776–1865," *University of Chicago Law Review* 32 (1965): 247–251.

158. U.S. Constitution, art. I, §9, cl. 2. For discussion of its adoption in the United States, see Eric Freedman, *Habeas Corpus: Rethinking the Great Writ of Liberty* (New York, 2001), chapter 2. For a reading of the clause in English and imperial contexts, see Halliday and White, "Suspension Clause," passim.

159. Peter Onuf, *Statehood and Union: A History of the Northwest Ordinance* (Bloomington, 1987), 63, and for discussion, passim.

160. For a contemporary critique of the Massachusetts suspension in late 1786 and 1787, see *The Massachusetts Centinel*, 17 March 1787.

161. See 34 George III, c. 54, renewed by 35 George III, c. 3 (with continuance until 1 July 1795); and 38 George III, c. 36, renewed by 39 George III, cc. 15 and 44; 39/40 George III, c. 20; and 41 George III, cc. 26 and 32. For a 1794 effort by the London Corresponding Society to collect funds to support prisoners held without trial, see TNA, TS24/3/60.

162. See 39 George III, c. 44, §6.
163. *The Times* (London), 22 May 1799, and 11, 13, and 16 May 1801. Heron had been acquitted of sedition in June 1798. See Clive Emsley, "Repression, 'Terror' and the Rule of Law in England during the Decade of the French Revolution," *English Historical Review* 100 (1985): 806–810 and 816–817.
164. *The Times* (London), 6 June 1801, 1. *Parl. Hist.*, vol. 35, p. 1511.
165. By this string of three indemnity acts, jailers were protected from their traditional liability for debts lost when jailed debtors escaped. See 20 George III, c. 63 (An act to Indemnify such Persons who have acted in the Suppression of the late Riots) and c. 64 (An Act to Prevent any Mischief . . . to Jailers . . . by Prisoners having been set at Liberty during the Late Tumults); as well as 21 George III, c. 1 (renewing the latter). These statutes had no connection whatsoever to the suspension then in effect for those taken at sea or in North America.
166. See 19 George II, c. 20 (1746).
167. See 41 George III, c. 66, §1, which appointed the indemnity to cover the entire period dating back to 1 February 1793. No suspension had been in effect until May of 1794, nor between July 1795 and 1 February 1799.
168. I emphasize that the 1801 Indemnity Act marked a new practice because others have suggested that it reflected a "stable historical understanding" used in indemnifying jailers following suspensions since 1689. See, for example, Trevor W. Morrison, "Suspension and the Extrajudicial Constitution," *Columbia Law Review* 107 (2007): 1541. This assertion is incorrect, and arises in part from relying on A. V. Dicey's poorly grounded discussion of the issue: see his *Introduction to the Study of the Law of the Constitution* (1885; Indianapolis, 1982, from the 8th ed. of 1915), 142–145. It also arises from reading claims made in the nineteenth century backward onto the eighteenth. Neither the 1801 statute, nor the assertions of speakers in 1801, nor Dicey's claims constitute evidence of eighteenth-century practice. The attorney general's 1801 invocation of the 1780 indemnity statute was either uninformed or disingenuous, since that statute addressed escapes of prisoners, not actions during suspension. The 1801 indemnity was a novelty, used in a political environment that differed markedly from earlier epochs of suspension owing to the anxieties generated during the French wars. It is also explained by the new, yet unsuccessful, effort to sue Aris for his abuses, not for his actions under a suspension as such. It behooved the attorney general in 1801 to misrepresent the Indemnity Acts of 1746 and 1780 in order to create a false sense of consistent practice to ease

passage of something so novel. We should not rely on his testimony of earlier statutes' contents when the texts of those statutes are still available to us to read. No act of indemnity accompanied or followed the suspensions of 1696, 1708, 1723, 1744, 1747, or those of 1777 to 1783. The indemnity acts that were passed in 1690, 1716, and 1746 addressed illegal imprisonment not in the context of suspension—during which warrants were made out by the secretaries of state according to statutory terms—but in the context of the more general problem of overzealous action by people on the ground during periods of political unrest. Thus these indemnity acts dwelt on illegal requisitioning of supplies and quartering of soldiers more than on imprisonment: see 1 William and Mary, sess. 2, c. 8 (1690); 1 George I, sess. 2, c. 39 (1716); and 19 George II, c. 20 (1746). This last statute applied to wrongs by officers committed before 30 April 1746. The suspension then active lasted until November and was then renewed until February 1747. Thus no indemnity covered the period after April 1746. This signals that suspension itself was not the problem addressed by the offer of a statutory indemnity.

169. Albert Goodwin, *The Friends of Liberty* (London, 1979), chapters 8–12, especially 333–334 and 365–368; Emsley, "Repression, 'Terror' and the Rule of Law," 806–810 and 816–817.

170. See 33 George III, c. 4. §§23–24, which did permit review of such imprisonments by justices of the courts in Westminster Hall or other justices by appointment of the secretary of state, but from the language of these sections, it is not clear this would carry the same procedural safeguards that a hearing of imprisonment on habeas corpus would provide. See J. R. Dinwiddy, "The Use of the Crown's Power of Deportation under the Alien Acts, 1793–1826," *Bulletin of the Institute of Historical Research* 41 (1968): 193–211.

171. *Parl. Hist.*, vol. 30, pp. 10, 156, 157, 159, 161, and 188.

172. See 56 George III, cc. 22 and 23; H. H. Bellot, "The Detention of Napoleon Buonaparte," *Law Quarterly Review* 39 (1923): 170–192.

173. See 46 Victoria no. 5, 1882 (NZ): Act for Preservation of the Peace in the West.

174. Oaks, "Habeas Corpus in the States," 251–255. For gubernatorial instructions, see the discussion in Chapter 8.

175. See 21/22 George III, c. 11 (Ireland). For an account of these many bills and the 1782 Act, see Kevin Costello, *The Law of Habeas Corpus in Ireland* (Dublin, 2006), 5–17.

176. *Account of Some Proceedings on the Writ of Habeas Corpus* (1781), 17. Emphasis in original.

177. William Blackstone, *Commentaries on the Laws of England* (Chicago, 1979), vol. 1, p. 133.

8. Writ Imperial

1. John Scott, *Berwick-upon-Tweed: The History of the Town and Guild* (London, 1888), 295–298, quotation at 296.
2. The court also demanded the return "immediately" to the chief justice's chambers even though the court would be in its long winter vacation. These orders are at TNA, KB21/2/84v.
3. *Hale's Prerogatives*, 42. Berwick remained an anomaly after the union of the crowns after 1603: it was held by the English king, but not part of his English realm.
4. That this was the substance of Berwick's return is reported in a discussion of Brearley's case during the consideration of the similar case of Richard Bourne, in 1619, in which the issue concerned whether habeas might go to the Cinque Ports. See Cro. Jac. 543, 79 *ER* 465–466.
5. There were two disputes involving Berwick in 1600–1601 concerning debtors who had fled there in hopes that no process could be served against them. When the mayor answered demands of the Council of the North to turn over a prisoner escaped from the Council's custody, he "pretend[ed] to be exempted from the jurisdiction of the council." When the matter was brought to its attention, the Privy Council demanded that Berwick send its charters to London to be inspected. For this and other examples of the conflict between the two Councils and Berwick, see *Acts of the Privy Council* (London, 1906), n.s., xxxi, 80, 108, 143–144, 201, and 285–286.
6. Chief Justice Popham was a member of the Privy Council, and attended some of the meetings in 1600–1601 when these other cases of Berwick's assertion of autonomy were discussed. Conciliar support or involvement, as in the case of the writ to the Marches of Wales on behalf of Walter Witherley five years later, may well explain how Mayor Thomas Parkinson and the bailiffs of Berwick were made to bend. On Witherley's case, see Chapter 1.
7. They were also ordered to amend the return. TNA, KB21/2/87 contains an order for the mayor and two bailiffs of Berwick to be examined on interrogatories for contempt. This was the usual process: those accused of contempt answered questions prepared by the justices and put to them by the clerk of the Crown Office. The order shows that two of the three had to find bail. The order says nothing about imprisonment, though in cases of disobedience, such a punishment was not un-

common. Scott, *Berwick,* 297, reports their commitment, as does the report of Bourne's case in Cro. Jac. 543, 79 *ER* 465. The imprisonment was probably brief, though instructive.

8. TNA, KB21/2/95. Scott, *Berwick,* 298, shows that Brearley was indeed restored in April 1601, after he agreed to pay the fines incurred by the town's leaders in Queen's Bench. This probably did not include the initial £200 fine for nonreturn of the writ, which had apparently been stopped soon after it was imposed: see TNA, KB21/2/84v.

9. TNA, KB15/64/4. This is a report of commissioners of fees in King's Bench of 1736, which described the court's various clerical offices and named its officers.

10. TNA, KB21/124 (unfoliated, but chronologically ordered, to 1714).

11. For the habeas corpus and threat of attachment in Cowle's case, in Easter and Trinity 1757, see TNA, KB21/38/131 and 142. For the report, see 2 Burr. 834, 97 *ER* 587. Mansfield's discussion of Brearley's case, drawn from the orders entered in the Crown Side rulebook, is the only instance I have seen in over 500 manuscript and printed case reports of a justice referring to a specific rulebook entry: see 2 Burr. 856, 97 *ER* 600. The footnotes to the report at this page give the date references to the rulebook entries.

12. See 2 Burr. 853–854 and 855–856, 97 *ER* 598 and 599. King's Bench might not send habeas corpus to Scotland, since Scotland's crown had been distinct from England's before 1707, and its law remained so thereafter. But all those dominions held by right of the English crown might be subject to the king's greatest court's purview by the king's greatest writs.

13. Mansfield criticized Coke's "obiter opinion" in Calvin's case, and said Coke was mistaken in claiming that Berwick was not governed by the laws of England in such matters as this. See 2 Burr. 858–859, 97 *ER* 601–602.

14. Matthew Hale, *The History of the Common Law of England,* ed. Charles M. Gray (Chicago, 1971), 120. The first printed edition appeared in 1713 (xiii).

15. *Hale's Prerogatives,* 19.

16. One of the recurrent difficulties in discussing English law's movement across "the" empire is that we see law in the singular—as "common"—and assume it entered or did not enter a new territory whole. Once we set aside this unitary fiction, we can see how one part of law—such as habeas corpus—might move about among and within the dominions by means quite different from the ways other parts of law might do so. For an excellent reading of Hale on law's territorial movement,

see Ken MacMillan, *Sovereignty and Possession in the English New World: The Legal Foundations of Empire, 1576–1640* (Cambridge, Eng., 2006), 35–37.

17. *Hale's Prerogatives,* 20 and 204, and chapter 19, especially 208–213.

18. Ibid., 42.

19. Ibid., 26 and 41; Hale, *History of the Common Law,* 118–121.

20. *Hale's Prerogatives,* 32–35. Much the same concerning the desires of Englishmen moving into conquered lands has been suggested for Wales by R. R. Davies, who also discusses language of "dependent" places: *"terrae,"* in contemporary usage. See his *The First English Empire: Power and Identities in the British Isles, 1093–1343* (Oxford, 2000), 81–83, 87–88, 106, and 157–162.

21. This from Hale's manuscript on the rights of the crown, quoted in *Hale's Prerogatives,* 43n. Hale makes much the same point in *Prerogatives:* "English laws are not settled there, or at least are only temporary till a settlement made" (43).

22. Ibid., 42–44.

23. For concepts of subjecthood, see Chapter 6.

24. This is from the patent to Sir Humphrey Gilbert and Sir Walter Ralegh, quoted in MacMillan, *Sovereignty and Possession,* 92. It was standard language in colonial charters. Similar language was in the royal proclamation that Lord Windsor took to Jamaica in 1661: "that all children of our natural-born subjects of England, to be born in Jamaica, shall from their respective births, be reputed to be, and shall be, free denizens of England, and shall have the same privileges to all intents and purposes as our free-born subjects of England." See Edward Long, *The History of Jamaica. Or, General Survey of the Antient and Modern State of that Island . . .* (1774), vol. 1, p. 218.

25. *Charters Granted to the East-India Company, from 1601. . .* (1773?), 370.

26. For an excellent treatment of theories of imperial expansion and possession as manifested in charters in all their variety, see MacMillan, *Sovereignty and Possession,* especially chapters 1 and 3. On urban corporations and their charters, and Hale's view of corporations, see Paul D. Halliday, *Dismembering the Body Politic: Partisan Politics in England's Towns, 1650–1730* (Cambridge, Eng., 1998), chapter 2, especially 30–33.

27. William Blackstone, *Commentaries on the Laws of England* (Chicago, 1979), vol. 1, pp. 104–105. For a summary of these, see Mary S. Bilder, *The Transatlantic Constitution: Colonial Legal Culture and the Empire* (Cambridge, 2004), 35–40. On Coke, see Daniel Hulsebosch, *Constituting Empire: New York and the Transformation of Constitutionalism in the Atlantic*

World, 1664–1830 (Chapel Hill, 2005), 20–28. See also David Lieber-
man, *The Province of Legislation Determined: Legal Theory in Eighteenth-
Century Britain* (Cambridge, Eng., 1989), 32–38.

28. For a critique of modern reliance on Blackstone, and an approach
to early modern legal thought that recovers the more historically
nuanced view of Hale, see Bernadette Meyler, "Towards a Common
Law Originalism," *Stanford Law Review* 59 (2006/2007): especially 560–
562, 580–584, and 589–592. On Hale's influence, see Michael Lobban,
"Blackstone and the Science of Law," *Historical Journal* 30 (1987): 311–
335.

29. YLS, GR 29.23, f. 166 and CUL, Ll.3.13, f. 170v. (Harrison, 1626); and
Latch 160, 82 *ER* 325 (misnamed Jobson's case). This dispute over the
bishop's jurisdiction seems to have provoked an investigation of his
claimed privileges by quo warranto during the same term, but nothing
appears to have come of it: see TNA, KB21/8/65v. A more sensational
struggle blew up in 1641 in the case of indicted murderer William
Rickaby. Though the bishop again objected, the justices just as energetically rejected his complaints and issued habeas for Rickaby's body and
certiorari for the indictment. "Otherwise," the justices said, "there will
be a failure of justice" (HLS, MS 1166, f. 273). Hale's comments on
Rickaby's case are part of his larger discussion of the way in which writs
like certiorari and habeas corpus might enter otherwise autonomous
franchises: see *Hale's Prerogatives,* 207–209. See also March 165 and 213,
82 *ER* 459 and 480–482.

30. HLS, MS 5016, f. 80. Dodderidge says here that habeas was issued to
Berwick in 1 James I (1603–1604), but no sign of this survives. This is
probably a mistaken reference to Brearley.

31. CUL, Gg.2.19, f. 63. Chester presented similar problems solved by the
same analogical means, it being "distinct of the government of the
king, like Wales and Ireland." Nonetheless, habeas corpus might go
there, enforced by the same penalties as used against Berwick; see
HLS, MS 113, p. 123. This was in the case of John Lloyd in 1641–1642.
Ralph Metcalf, the constable of Chester Castle, returned the writ, but
with the claim that process did not run there from Westminster owing
to its palatine privileges. For this return, attachment process issued
against Metcalf. That no result survives after a second writ issued in
early 1642 is probably explained by the fact that the Civil War broke
out in earnest soon after. See TNA, KB145/15/17 (7 June 1641) and
KB32/10 (4 February 1642); KB21/12/171v., 176, and 179v., and
KB21/13/5, 5v., 15, 18, 18v., and 21.

32. "The claim to judge and to actualize law and justice is never separate

from the institutional force necessary to transform the contingent action into a meaningful event." On technologies of jurisdiction, see Shaunnagh Dorsett and Shaun McVeigh, "Questions of Jurisdiction," in McVeigh, *Jurisprudence of Jurisdiction* (New York, 2007), 3–18, quotation at 6.

33. TNA, KB21/16/108v. and 114v., and KB21/17/5v. and 24v. Orders for Overton's writ are at KB21/16/101v. and 107. See also 2 Keble 450, 84 *ER* 282. 1 Sid. 386, 82 ER 1173. Once a major-general and commander in Scotland, Overton was first detained in December 1660. He was released, then imprisoned again in 1663. In January 1664, he was sent to Jersey. He was only released in 1671. See *ODNB*, s.v. Robert Overton. See also Richard L. Greaves, *Deliver Us from Evil: The Radical Underground in Britain, 1660–1663* (Oxford, 1986), 36–37, 78–80, and 184.

34. TNA, KB145/17/31 (21 June 1679) and KB21/19/201; Greaves, *Deliver Us from Evil*, 27–28.

35. Hale, *History of the Common Law*, 120.

36. TNA, KB21/17/103 (Thomas Meade, 1672).

37. See 31 Charles II, c. 2.

38. Remarkably, courts in the Channel Isles continued fitful resistance to the writ from Westminster as late as 1849, when they refused to permit the publication of the 1679 and 1816 Habeas Corpus Acts there. See TNA, HO/45/2843.

39. Richard Ligon, *A True & Exact History of the Island of Barbados . . .* (1657), 20–21. The first edition of Thomas Hobbes's *Leviathan* appeared in 1651, while Ligon was in prison. See *ODNB*, s.v. Richard Ligon.

40. Larry Gragg, *Englishmen Transplanted: The English Colonization of Barbados, 1627–1660* (Oxford, 2003), 29.

41. Robert Cover, "Nomos and Narrative," *Harvard Law Review* 97 (1983–1984): 4–68.

42. *Some Memoirs of the First Settlement of the Island of Barbados and other the Carribbee Islands. . .* (Barbados, 1741), 6–8.

43. Ibid.

44. "An Act Declaring the Negro-Slaves of this Island to be Real Estates," 1668, in Richard Hall, *Acts, Passed in the Island of Barbados, from 1643, to 1762 . . .* (1764), 64–65.

45. Here I mean to reverse the polarity in Cover's juxtaposition of "jurisgenerative" communities and "jurispathic" courts. The lay *nomoi* carried to Barbados seemed to require the jurispathic function against the dangerous jurisgenesis of a governor and his political allies. See Robert C. Post, "Who's Afraid of Jurispathic Courts? Violence and Public Rea-

son in *Nomos and Narrative,*" *Yale Journal of Law and Humanities* 17 (2005): 9–16.

46. LI, MS Hill 49, f. 151. The report is titled "anonymous." Given the presence of an order in the rulebook to send the writ to Barbados on behalf of William Moore in the same term, we can infer that this reports the hearing on the petition for Moore. See TNA, KB21/24/151.

47. Imprisoned sometime in 1691 for allegedly supporting the French, Moore's petition to the council in Barbados to be released or to be tried quickly was initially rejected for fear that he might run off to the French, in Martinique. In February 1692, the council of Barbados reconsidered, and bailed him. This probably explains why his writ—ordered on 11 June 1692—was never returned. See *CSPC* 1689–1692, 573 and 605.

48. Quoted in Davies, *First English Empire,* 158. For discussion of English law in Ireland, see 15–19 and 157–160.

49. Sadly, the fire that destroyed most of Ireland's judicial archive in 1922 precludes learning much about this. For an excellent reconstruction from nonjudicial materials, see Kevin Costello, *The Law of Habeas Corpus in Ireland* (Dublin, 2006), 1–17.

50. "An Act for the Regulating . . . of Fees of . . . Courts of this Island" (1640s); "An Act Establishing Courts" (1661); and "An Act Authorizing the Governor . . . to Appoint a Provost" (1667). Another act of 1668 further regulated fees of court officers and the provost marshal. See Hall, *Acts of Barbados,* 8–11, 27–33, 59, 65–69; Gragg, *Englishmen Transplanted,* 59–60.

51. On the "Court of Grievance" and the practice of the governor and council in hearing error and complaints in equity, see "An Act [for] the Bringing Writs of Error . . . before the Governor and Council" (1655), in Hall, *Acts of Barbados,* 22–23. See also Frederick G. Spurdle, *Early West Indian Government: Showing the Progress of Government in Barbados, Jamaica, and the Leeward Islands, 1660–1783* (Palmerston North, 1960), 51–52.

52. The potential for a conflict of interest in such an arrangement probably explains the use of a separate oath that he and others would take when sitting as a Court of Grievance. See "An Act Appointing an Oath . . ." (1692), in Hall, *Acts of Barbados,* 128–129.

53. In London, the Lords of Trade and Plantations expressed their approval that the bill "was timely prevented" again. See *CSPC* 1677–1680, 446, 454, and 534; and *CSPC* 1681–1685, 83, 90, and 116.

54. The governor and his council also constituted the courts of King's Bench and of Chancery for the island; see *CSPC* 1681–1685, 123. As

Dutton explained of his work as a justice of King's Bench, "I dispose of all causes there myself, which is not the practice in any other colony" (179).

55. Ibid., 390 and 552–553. Dutton responded, in part, by explaining that some had tried to bribe him to approve the habeas corpus bill, and that he had imprisoned one of his chief foes, Thomas Hyatt, "not under an English but under a local statute" (559–561).

56. For proceedings against Witham, see ibid., 695–697, 711–713, and 774. For Lords of Trade and Plantations proceedings, see 760–762. For Witham's depositions, see *CSPC* 1685–1688, 61–63, 68–70, and 90.

57. *CSPC* 1685–1688, 113. For hearings of the case before the Lords of Trade and Plantations, see 105, 109, and 111–113. For the order to restore him and to remit fines against him, see 126. The judgment was later reversed in the Lords; see 3 Mod. 159, 87 *ER* 103–104. For an account of the episode used as a partisan critique of Dutton, see John Poyer, *The History of Barbados* (London, 1808), 121–125.

58. *CSPC* 1696–1697, 573, 629, and 675. The approved version was printed as Act 438, in *An Abridgement of the Laws in Force and Use in Her Majesty's Plantations. . .* (1704), 218–221. By the time this had appeared, the act had been voided by order in council. See *CSPC* 1702, 194–195 and 457.

59. *CSPC* 1702, 532–533. The instructions required the jailer to return "the true cause of the imprisonment" within three days.

60. See [George Frere], *A Short History of Barbados, from its First Discovery and Settlement to the Present Time* (1768), 99–100 and 109; *CSPC* 1706–1708, 408.

61. *The State of the Island of Jamaica . . . Address'd to a Member of Parliament* (1726), 35. Act 19, in *Acts of Assembly, Passed in the Island of Jamaica, From 1681 to 1754* (1756). On nonrepugnancy, see Bilder, *Transatlantic Constitution*, 2–4 and 40–46.

62. *State of Jamaica*, 36. Emphasis in original. For discussion of the allowance of habeas corpus statutes in each of the mainland colonies, see William F. Duker, *A Constitutional History of Habeas Corpus* (Westport, 1980) chapter 2, and A. H. Carpenter, "Habeas Corpus in the Colonies," *American Historical Review* 8 (1902): 18–27.

63. The quotation at the head of the section is from *The Case of Peter du Calvet, Esq. of Montreal in the Province of Quebeck . . .* (1784), 273.

64. Francis Masères, *Collection of Several Commissions, and other Public Instruments . . . Relating to . . . Quebec* (1772), 2. See also F. Murray Greenwood and Barry Wright, eds., *Law, Politics, and Security Measures, 1608–1837*, vol. 1 of *Canadian State Trials* (Toronto, 1996), 31–32 and 132.

65. Masères, *Collection*, 40.

66. See 14 George III, c. 83. *Observations and Reflections, on an Act . . . for the Settlement of the Province of Quebec . . .* (1782), 13–16; [Francis Masères], *An Account of the Proceedings of the British, and other Protestant Inhabitants, of the Province of Quebeck. . .* (1775), 228–230.

67. *An Appeal to the Public; Stating and Considering the Objections to the Quebec Bill* (1774), 32–33.

68. See, for instance, the 1772 opinion of the British solicitor general Alexander Wedderburn, discussed in Jean-Marie Fecteau and Douglas Hay, "Military Justice and the Legal System in Quebec, 1775–83," in Greenwood and Wright, *Law, Politics, and Security Measures,* 147.

69. Much of what follows is narrated in F. Murray Greenwood, *Legacies of Fear: Law and Politics in Quebec in the Era of the French Revolution* (Toronto, 1993), 24–27, and Fecteau and Hay, "Military Justice," 150–159.

70. *Case of du Calvet,* 241 and 280–281; Douglas Brymner, *Report on Canadian Archives, 1888* (Ottawa, 1889), xv–xxv.

71. Hay's counsel was Robert Russell, who was also assigned to help du Calvet. According to du Calvet, Russell's arguments were widely admired and generally accepted by all but the judges who decided the matter: see *Case of du Calvet,* 237–240. Mary Hay's petition is in Greenwood and Wright, *Law, Politics, and Security,* 626–30, quotation at 629.

72. Pierre Du Calvet, *Appel à la justice de l'Etat; ou recueil de lettres, au roi, au Prince de Galles, et aux ministres; avec une lettre à messieurs les canadiens. . .* (1784), 186–190, 192, and 232.

73. *The Pennsylvania Packet,* 5 September 1785, 2; *The Pennsylvania Mercury,* 10 March 1786, 3; *Massachusetts Gazette,* 13 March 1786, 2; and *Essex Journal,* 15 March 1786, 3. See also Brymner, *Canadian Archives,* containing the *Calendar of the Haldimand Collection,* vol. 3, p. 51, B.206: Papers relating to Pierre Roubaud.

74. *The Times* (London), 9 June 1787, 3; and *The Pennsylvania Herald,* 29 September 1787, 2. Numerous newspapers advertised pamphlets of the trial: see, e.g., *The New York Journal,* 13 February 1788, 1.

75. See 24 George III, c. 3 (Quebec), in *Observations on a Pamphlet, entitled A State of the Present Form of Government of the Province of Quebec. . .* (1790), 16 and 33–47. See also Hilda Neatby, *Quebec: The Revolutionary Age, 1760–1791* (Toronto, 1966), 190–192.

76. Richard Burn, trans. Joseph F. Perrault, *Le Juge à Paix, et Officier de Paroisse, Pour la Province de Quebec* (Montreal, 1789), 302–313 and 328–331.

77. Greenwood, *Legacies,* 27 and 29. For slaves released from imprisonment for fleeing masters—though not necessarily released from slavery itself—see *Memoires et Documents relatifs a L'Histoire du Canada,*

publiés par La Societé Historique de Montréal (Montreal, 1859), 31–36 and 56–63.

78. See 34 George III, 2nd sess., c. 5 (Lower Canada).

79. This by multiple acts "for Better Preservation of his Majesty's Government" (37 George III, c. 1 and 43 George III, c. 6), the last of which was passed in March 1811 and lapsed the following year: 51 George III, c. 7 (Lower Canada). See also Greenwood, *Legacies*, 25–27, 116–131, 172–174, and 197–198.

80. This account of events is based on J.-M. Fecteau, "Mesures d'exception et règle de droit: Les conditions d'application de la loi martiale au Quebec lors des rébellions de 1837–1838," *McGill Law Journal* 32 (1986–1987): 465–495, quotation at 480. See also Beverley Boissery, *A Deep Sense of Wrong: The Treason, Trials, and Transportation to New South Wales of Lower Canadian Rebels after the 1838 Rebellion* (Toronto, 1995), chapter 1.

81. See 1 Victoria, c. 9: An Act to Make Temporary Provision for the Government of Lower Canada (UK).

82. See 1 Victoria, c. 4 (Lower Canada); Fecteau, "Mesures d'exception," 483–485; Douglas Brymner, *Report on Canadian Archives, 1901* (Ottawa, 1902), 1059, 1076, and 1089.

83. The account in this paragraph is based on Boissery, *Deep Sense of Wrong,* 38–44.

84. See 2 Victoria, cc. 3 and 4 (Lower Canada), in *Report of the State Trials before a General Court Martial held at Montreal in 1838–9* (Montreal, 1839), vol. 1, pp. 3–9.

85. Brymner, *Canadian Archives, 1901,* 1101–1103.

86. *Judicial Decisions on the Writ of Habeas Corpus ad Subjiciendum and on the Provincial Ordinance, 2d Victoria, Chap. 4, Whereby the Habeas Corpus Ordinance of 1784 has been Suspended* (Three Rivers, 1839), 4.

87. In the wake of these troubles, the attorney and solicitor general gave their joint opinion that a colonial governor might proclaim, "in any district in which large bodies of the inhabitants are in open rebellion, that the Executive government will proceed to enforce martial law"— an authority "arising from and limited by the necessity of the case." The one clear factor pointing against use of martial law was that civilian courts continued to operate. See William Forsyth, *Cases and Opinions on Constitutional Law* (London, 1869), 198–199, quoted in R. W. Kostal, *A Jurisprudence of Power: Victorian Empire and the Rule of Law* (Oxford, 2005), 204, and generally chapter 5.

88. On the courts martial and selection of those pardoned and transported, see Boissery, *Deep Sense of Wrong,* chapter 7. While in transit to

Australia and then at Liverpool, some of these prisoners sued habeas corpus from Queen's Bench, occasioning a lengthy discussion of the imperial elements in the case, before concluding in the prisoners' remand. See 9 Ad. and El. 731, 112 *ER* 1389–1420 (Watson et al., 1839).

89. The charter, dated 31 December 1601, is in *Charters Granted to the East-India Company from 1601.* . . (1773?), 6 and 14. The imprisonment provision is at 13–14.

90. A 1669 charter granting the island of Bombay to the Company made the usual grant of powers to make laws "not repugnant to" English law, and added a power to establish forms of judicature "like those established in England." See *A Collection of Statutes . . . And an Abridgement of the Company's Charters* (1794), appendix [2d pagination], ix. On Company generation of law in India from the seventeenth century onward, see Philip J. Stern, "'One Body Corporate and Politic': The Growth of the English East India Company in the Later Seventeenth Century," Ph.D. diss., Columbia University, 2004, chapter 2. One pamphleteer claimed that as early as 1681 Company members were "in effect our own law makers, and can arrest and imprison any natives that deal with us." See Philopatris, *A Treatise Wherein is Demonstrated that the East-India Trade is the Most National of Foreign Trades* (London, 1681), 35, quotation on 117.

91. The 1726 charter is in *Charters Granted to the East-India Company*, 368–399. For discussion, see M. P. Jain, *Outlines of Indian Legal History*, 5th ed. (Bombay, 1990), 35–44. The 1753 charter is in *Collection of Statutes*, appendix [2d pagination], xxxiii–xxxix.

92. P. J. Marshall, "The British in India," in Marshall, ed., *The Eighteenth Century*, vol. 2 of *The Oxford History of the British Empire* (Oxford, 1998), 502–503.

93. This from the treaty's Article I: see Clive Parry, ed., *The Consolidated Treaty Series* (Dobbs Ferry, 1969), vol. 43, p. 189. Robert Clive, the victor of Plassey, thought that the treaty made the Company "the sovereigns of a rich and potent kingdom." Quoted in Bernard Cohn, "Law and the Colonial State in India," in Cohn, ed., *Colonialism and Its Forms of Knowledge: The British in India* (Princeton, 1996), 59. But as Cohn notes, "a dual principle of sovereignty had been established" (58).

94. Philip Stern calls this composite body, with features disrupting modern notions of unitary sovereignty, a "company-state." On simultaneous British and Mughal authority undergirding Company action long before 1765, see Stern, "'A Politie of Civill & Military Power': Political Thought and the Late Seventeenth-Century Foundations of the East

India Company," *Journal of British Studies* 47 (2008): 253–283. Robert Travers refers to what he calls a "negotiated empire" of fluid ideas about sovereignty following 1765: see his *Ideology and Empire in Eighteenth-Century India: The British in Bengal* (Cambridge, Eng., 2007), especially 43–47. See also Sudipta Sen, *Distant Sovereignty: National Imperialism and the Origins of British India* (London, 2002), introduction and chapter 1; and Lauren Benton, "Colonial Law and Cultural Difference: Jurisdictional Politics and the Formation of the Colonial State," *Comparative Studies in Society and History* 41 (1999): 563–574.

95. Quoted in Rajat Kanta Ray, "Indian Society and the Establishment of British Supremacy, 1765–1818," in P. J. Marshall, ed., *Oxford History of the British Empire,* vol. 2, p. 510; see also 508–513. On events in the 1750s and 1760s, see P. J. Marshall, "The British in India" (491–507). On the *diwani* and lingering Mughal allegiance after 1765, see Marshall, *Bengal: The British Bridgehead* (Cambridge, Eng., 1987), 49–52, 77–79, and 89–90.

96. Travers, *Ideology and Empire,* 117. On the political contexts of these regulations, see 115–138. On the ostensible revival of Islamic criminal law in 1772, see Radhika Singha, *A Despotism of Law: Criminal Justice in Early Colonial India* (New Delhi, 1998), chapter 1, especially 1–6 and 26–32.

97. "Charter for erecting a Supreme Court of Judicature at Fort William, in Bengal" (1774), in *A Collection of Statutes,* appendix [2d pagination], xlv–liv. In keeping with persistent ideas concerned with the delegation of franchises to others, only the king, not Parliament, could create a corporation. The most important discussion of the difference between a statute that advised making a corporation, and the monarch's act by which it was created, occurred in the 1615 case of Sutton's Hospital: see 10 Co. Rep. 1a, 77 *ER* 937. For discussion, see Halliday, *Dismembering the Body Politic,* 32–33.

98. See 13 George III, c. 63, §1: Regulating Act.

99. *A Collection of Statutes,* appendix [2d pagination], xlv and l.

100. See 13 George III, c. 63, §14.

101. *A Collection of Statutes,* appendix [2d pagination], l.

102. Rex v. Warren Hastings et al., in T. C. Morton, *Decisions of the Supreme Court of Judicature at Fort William in Bengal* (Calcutta, 1841), 207–208.

103. Morton, *Decisions of the Supreme Court,* 209.

104. Rex v. Ramgovind Mitter et al., in ibid., 211.

105. BL, Add. 38,401, f. 20 (Chambers to Charles Jenkins, 1 February 1778).

106. BL, Add. 16,265, f. 128 (Impey to Lord Chancellor Bathurst, 20 September 1776).

107. BL, Add. 16,265, ff. 29v.–30 (Impey to governor and Council, 25 May 1775).
108. *Report from the Committee to whom the Petition of John Touchet and John Irving, Agents for the British Subjects residing in the Provinces of Bengal, Bahar, and Orissa . . .* (1781), General Appendix no. 9 (unpaginated, at rear).
109. BL, Add. 16,259, f. 195, quoted in P. J. Marshall, *Making and Unmaking of Empires: Britain, India, and America c. 1750–1783* (Oxford, 2005), 268.
110. BL, Add. 38,401, f. 19v. (Chambers to Charles Jenkins, 1 February 1778).
111. BL, Add. 38,400, f. 84 (opinion in Kamal v. Goring [1777]). Emphasis in original.
112. Quoted in Thomas M. Curley, *Sir Robert Chambers: Law, Literature, and Empire in the Age of Johnson* (Madison, 1998), 593n.
113. BL, IOR/H/121, 160 (Impey to East India Company Court of Directors, 19 September 1775).
114. BL, IOR/H/121, 109 (provincial council of Calcutta to Warren Hastings, 2 November 1775). For Chambers' discussion of Kemaluddin's case, see BL, Add. 38,401, ff. 30–36 (Chambers to Charles Jenkinson, 1 February 1778). The case is recounted in B. N. Pandey, *The Introduction of English Law into India: The Career of Elijah Impey in Bengal, 1774–1783* (Bombay, 1967), 111–117; Jain, *Indian Legal History,* 87–88; and B. B. Misra, *The Judicial Administration of the East India Company in Bengal, 1765–1782* (Delhi, 1961), 217–221.
115. BL, Add. 38,401, ff. 28 (Chambers to Charles Jenkins, 1 February 1778); Walter Firminger, "Selections from the Note Books of Justice John Hyde, I," *Bengal Past and Present* 3 (1909): 31. Emphasis in original. On the *faujdars'* criminal jurisdiction, see Travers, *Ideology and Empire,* 118 and 136–138, and Singha, *Despotism of Law,* 26–27.
116. BL, Add. 38,401, f. 29. Lemaistre's broader view of his authority on habeas corpus would be evident in his discussion of the case of Seroop Chund, in 1777: see *Touchet Report,* General Appendix no. 9 (unpaginated, at rear).
117. Travers, *Ideology and Empire,* chapters 3 and 5.
118. *Touchet Report,* General Appendix no. 13 (unpaginated, at rear), ¶¶ 15 and 21, and generally, 68–69 in the main text of the report.
119. [Anonymous], *Observations upon the Administration of Justice in Bengal; Occasioned by some late Proceedings at Dacca* [1778], 4 and 6.
120. *Considerations on the Administration of Justice in Bengal, extracted from a Pamphlet intitled Thoughts on Improving the Government of the British Territo-*

rial Possessions in the East-Indies (1780?), 2. See the comment that the Court had "been found in experience as oppressive to the natives of the country as it certainly is adverse to the interests of the Company": BL, IOR/H/148, 223. On the idea of a Mughal "ancient constitution," see Travers, *Ideology and Empire,* 19–30.

121. BL, IOR/H/148, 299 (Hastings, Francis, and Wheeler, to Company Directors, 14 March 1780).

122. Habeas use narrowed in the decades after 1781, and especially in the first half of the nineteenth century. See Jain, *Indian Legal History,* 106–108.

123. See 21 George III, c. 70, §§3 and 19: Judicature Act.

124. Quoted in Curley, *Chambers,* 464. Emphasis in original.

125. Manickram Chattopadhia v. Meer Conjeer ali Khan, in Morton, *Decisions of the Supreme Court,* 126, emphasis in original. For "British European subject," see 21 George III, c. 70, § 16.

126. Jain, *Indian Legal History,* 74. This fragmentation of subjecthood would be furthered by the codification effort launched by the grant of a new charter to the East India Company in 1833. For a thoughtful discussion, in part employing Partha Chatterjee's notion of the "rule of colonial difference," see Elizabeth Kolsky, "Codification and the Rule of Colonial Difference: Criminal Procedure in British India," *Law and History Review* 23 (2005): 631–683.

127. See 37 George III, c. 142: Act for Better Administration of Justice at Calcutta, Madras, and Bombay. For discussion, see Travers, *Ideology and Empire,* chapter 6, especially 211–213 and 233–236, and Jain, *Indian Legal History,* 100–102, 161, and 429–430.

128. For Regulation III and other early nineteenth-century regulations limiting habeas in Bengal, see BL, IOR/V/18 "Bengal regulations, 1815–1819," v. 4 (unpaginated).

129. For a protest against restrictions on the use of habeas corpus in Bombay, see *Proceedings of the Governor and Council of Bombay towards His Majesty's Supreme Court of Judicature* (1828), in TNA, TS/11/345. This provides a history of the debates over the Supreme Court in Calcutta in the 1770s and 1780s, and of the establishment of the Supreme Court in Bombay, followed by an account of contests over the writ's use there in 1828.

130. See §82 of the 1801 charter, printed in *A Collection of Legislative Acts of the Ceylon Government, from 1796* (Colombo, 1853), vol. 1, p. 45; also T. Nadaraja, *The Legal System of Ceylon in Its Historical Setting* (Leiden, 1972), 57–61 and 73n.

131. C. U. Aitchison, *A Collection of Treaties, Engagements, and Sanads Relating to India and Neighbouring Countries* (Calcutta, 1892), viii, 248 and 250–262; Nadaraja, *Legal System of Ceylon,* 65–67.

132. P. Rama-nathan, ed., *The Judgments of the Supreme Court of Judicature . . . of Ceylon . . . 1820–1833* (Colombo, 1877), 80–89, especially 81–82.

133. G. C. Mendis, ed., *The Colebrooke-Cameron Papers: Documents on British Colonial Policy in Ceylon, 1796–1833* (Oxford, 1956), vol. 2, pp. 48–49; *Legislative Acts of Ceylon,* vol. 1, p. 303.

134. Mendis, *Colebrooke-Cameron Papers,* vol. 1, p. 144; see also vol. 2, pp. 45–48, and Nadaraja, *Legal System of Ceylon,* 80n.

135. Mendis, *Colebrooke-Cameron Papers,* vol. 1, p. 341, and vol. 2, pp. 51–53.

136. Nadaraja, *Legal System of Ceylon,* 98–99.

137. Quoted in ibid., 112n.

138. Kostal, *Jurisprudence of Power,* 202–203; ibid., 132n.

139. See 31 Charles II, c. 2, §12.

140. See 19 George III, c. 74, §1 (An Act to Amend the Laws Relating to Transportation), and 24 George III, sess. 2, c. 56 (An Act for the Effectual Transportation of Felons). The terms of transportation were extended to include Scottish convicts by 25 George III, c. 46.

141. David Clark and Gerard McCoy, *Habeas Corpus: Australia, New Zealand, the South Pacific* (Leichhardt, 2000), 7.

142. See 27 George III, c. 2: An Act to Enable his Majesty to Establish a Court of Criminal Judicature in New South Wales; Alex C. Castles, *An Australian Legal History* (Sydney, 1982), chapters 4 and 5.

143. Quoted in Clark and McCoy, *Habeas Corpus,* 20.

144. See 4 George IV, c. 96: An Act for the Better Administration of Justice in New South Wales and Van Dieman's Land. The new Supreme Courts' powers were confirmed and extended by the Australian Courts Act of 1828: see 9 George IV, c. 83. See also Bruce Kercher, *An Unruly Child: A History of Law in Australia* (St. Leonards, 1995), 67–75.

145. Castles, *Australian Legal History,* 182–186; C. H. Currey, *Sir Francis Forbes* (Sydney, 1968), 115–116.

146. In re King, reported in *The Australian,* 16 and 23 December 1824, at http://www.law.mq.edu.au/scnsw/html/in_re_king__1824.html (accessed July 21, 2009).

147. In re Warton, reported in *The Hobart Town Gazette,* 29 October 1824, at http://www.law.mq.edu.au/sctas/html/in_re_warton__1824.htm (accessed July 21, 2009).

148. Dowling, Select Cases, v. 2, Archives Office of N.S.W., 2/3462 (1829), at http://www.law.mq.edu.au/scnsw/Cases1829-30/html/in_re_jane_new__1829.html (accessed July 21, 2009).

149. Michael Quinlan, "Australia, 1788–1902: A Workingman's Paradise?" in Douglas Hay and Paul Craven, eds., *Masters, Servants, and Magistrates in Britain and the Empire, 1562–1955* (Chapel Hill, 2004), 219–250. On Legislative Councils, see Castles, *Australian Legal History,* 129–131 and 252–253.

150. See 5 Elizabeth, c. 4: Statute of Artificers (1563). In England, habeas corpus had been used to test imprisonment according to that statute's terms. In the eighteenth century, this included use of the writ apparently to test the validity of apprenticeship indentures. See TNA, KB16/13/7 (4 November 1749), and KB21/36/482 and 489: writ to George Rogby, returning his custody of John Langlands as his apprentice, no result. The 1634 writ for Eusebius Skerce issued to Clerkenwell, where he had been put after illegally leaving his master, spurrier Thomas Hinson, without a result on record: see KB29/283/75d.

151. Thus see the case of Thomas M'ara (1825), who had been imprisoned after fleeing his master. Although questions arose regarding the form of the commitment, the court refused to release him, because "it could not enquire into the propriety of the conviction." See *Sydney Gazette,* 11 August 1825, at http://www.law.mq.edu.au/scnsw/html/r_v_m_ara__1825.htm (accessed July 21, 2009).

152. In re John Foster, *Sydney Gazette,* 23 November 1827, at http://www.law.mq.edu.au/scnsw/Cases1827–28/html/in_re_foster__1827.htm (accessed July 21, 2009). See also Clark and McCoy, *Habeas Corpus,* 37.

153. *Hobart Town Advertiser,* 14 February 1843, at http://www.law.mq.edu.au/sctas/html/1843cases/In%20re%20Morgan,%201843.htm (accessed July 21, 2009).

154. This was an order made in reply to a certiorari, issued in anticipation of habeas corpus. See Dowling, Select Cases, v. 1, Archives Office of N.S.W., 2/3461 (1828), at http://www.law.mq.edu.au/scnsw/Cases1827–28/html/in_re_lookaye_alias_edwards__1.htm (accessed July 21, 2009).

155. Quinlan, "Workingman's Paradise?" 222–228 and 239–240.

156. Supreme Court Ordinance of 1841 (NZ); Clark and McCoy, *Habeas Corpus,* 21–22.

157. Thomas Scott-Smith, *Digest of the Reported Cases in the Court of Appeal and Supreme Court of New Zealand, 1861–1885* (Dunedin, 1885), 92–94; Alexander J. Johnston, *The New Zealand Justice of the Peace,* 2d ed. (Wellington, 1870), vol. 1, pp. 188–190 and 437.

158. Printed in Claudia Orange, *The Treaty of Waitangi* (Wellington, 1987), 255–256.

159. The treaty is in ibid., 257–259. For discussion, see especially chapters 1–3.

160. House of Commons, Parliamentary Papers, New Zealand, *Papers Relative to the Affairs of New Zealand* (14 March 1845), 4–5, in *Accounts and Papers: Twenty-Five Volumes, New Zealand,* xxxiii [*sic*] (1845).

161. Suppression of Rebellion Act, 1863 (NZ); Clark and McCoy, *Habeas Corpus,* 181 and 183–185; Orange, *Waitangi,* 169–170.

162. Katherine Sanders, "Parihaka and the Rule of Law," *Auckland University Law Review* 11 (2005): especially 178–188.

163. Ibid., 189–190. One man did sue habeas corpus on his son's behalf in 1880, though the detainee refused release in order to show solidarity with his fellows. See Clark and McCoy, *Habeas Corpus,* 184.

164. See 28/29 Victoria c. 63; Castles, *Australian Legal History,* 408–412, and Kercher, *Unruly Child,* 98–102.

165. See 46 Victoria no. 5 (NZ); Virginia Crossman, *Politics, Law, and Order in Nineteenth-Century Ireland* (Dublin, 1996), 20–27, 121–122, 205–206, and 218–221.

166. Great Britain, House of Commons, Parliamentary Papers: *Accounts and Papers, forty-eight vols., Colonial and British Possessions . . . Session 15 February–25 August 1883,* vol. 47 (1883), containing *Further Correspondence Respecting Native Affairs in New Zealand* (1883), 8–9 and 22–25.

167. Sanders, "Parihaka," 192.

168. I have largely followed the account provided in Patrick Brode, *The Odyssey of John Anderson* (Toronto, 1989).

169. *Freeman's Journal and Daily Commercial Advertiser,* 4 January 1861; ibid., 59–61.

170. Brode, *Anderson,* 70–71. The abolitionists were advised by Frederick Solly-Flood. His role is noteworthy because he would later write the most important treatise on habeas corpus of the nineteenth century. It has never been published. The manuscript remains in the library of the Royal Historical Society, London.

171. See 3 El. and El. 487, 121 *ER* 525–526.

172. See ibid., 525–528; Brode, *Anderson,* 71–75. After news broke of the English writ—which provoked a furor in many quarters of Canada's legal community—a further habeas issued from Common Pleas in Toronto, on which Anderson was actually released. While the Canadian writ was pending, the English writ was served, but never returned (Brode, *Anderson,* 87–100). Habeas corpus had issued from Queen's Bench to St. Helena in 1858–1859 to bring Captain Charles Lees, convicted there of an assault, to England to pursue process on error: see TNA, TS18/159.

173. See 25/26 Victoria, c. 20: An Act respecting the Issue of Writs of Habeas Corpus out of England.

174. See 4 Cranch 93–94. Scholars of habeas corpus in the years between the passage of the first Judiciary Act in 1789 and the Bollman case are agreed in finding that Marshall's surmise here was without serious foundation. See Eric M. Freedman, *Habeas Corpus: Rethinking the Great Writ of Liberty* (New York, 2001), 25–26; Francis Paschal, "The Constitution and Habeas Corpus," *Duke Law Journal* (1970): especially 627–632; and Paul D. Halliday and G. Edward White, "The Suspension Clause: English Text, Imperial Contexts, and American Implications," *Virginia Law Review* 94 (2008): 686–699.

9. The Palladium of Liberty in Law's Empire

1. James Luttrell, in the same debate, condemned this "iniquitous and daring attack upon the palladium of English liberty." See *Parl. Hist.*, vol. 19, pp. 11, 30, and 40.

2. Francis Pomey, *The Pantheon, Representing the Fabulous Histories of the Heathen Gods and Most Illustrious Heroes. . .*, 6th ed. (1713), 113–115.

3. A. V. Dicey, *Introduction to the Study of the Law of the Constitution* (1885; Indianapolis, 1982, from the 8th ed. of 1915), 133–135.

4. Ibid.

5. Ibid., 145. As Brian Simpson notes, Dicey's work appears simple at first, then "becomes increasingly obscure on rereading, and this problem gets worse and worse." This culminates in "Dicey's simplistic and impoverished discussion of the domestic protection of rights." See A. W. Brian Simpson, *Human Rights and the End of Empire: Britain and the Genesis of the European Convention* (Oxford, 2001), 33 and 37.

6. *The Pall Mall Gazette,* 4 April 1887; *ODNB,* s.v. Frederic Harrison.

7. *Jackson's Oxford Journal,* 8 December 1860.

8. These include New Brunswick, 1856; Quebec, 1861; Nova Scotia, 1864; and Ontario, 1866. See D. A. Cameron Harvey, *The Law of Habeas Corpus in Canada* (Toronto, 1974), 192–217.

9. See 30/31 Victoria, c. 3: British North America Act (UK).

10. On federal issues in Canadian habeas practice, see Harvey, *Habeas Corpus,* chapter 3, and David Clark and Gerard McCoy, *The Most Fundamental Legal Right: Habeas Corpus in the Commonwealth* (Oxford, 2000), 165–167. In Australia, rather than make their own habeas statutes, most states and territories incorporated or presumed the incorporation of the major English and British statutes into their own law. As in Canada,

it would be principally for the descendants of the original state Supreme Courts to use the writ. It remains an open question for which cases Supreme Court justices in one state may send the writ into other states. See David Clark and Gerard McCoy, *Habeas Corpus: Australia, New Zealand, the South Pacific* (Leichhardt, 2000), chapter 2 and 176–179.

11. *Laws of St. Vincent* (London, 1864), Act no. 184, 551–553.

12. As R. W. Kostal puts it, the parliamentary debate over the Ceylon crisis in the three years after 1848 "exposed the . . . tension between British constitutional ideals and the grittier exigencies of imperial rule." From Kostal, "A Jurisprudence of Power: Martial Law and the Ceylon Controversy of 1848–51," *Journal of Imperial and Commonwealth History* 28 (2000): 2.

13. R. W. Kostal, *A Jurisprudence of Power: Victorian Empire and the Rule of Law* (Oxford, 2005), 200–202, and generally, chapter 4.

14. Diana Paton, *No Bond But the Law: Punishment, Race, and Gender in Jamaican State Formation, 1780–1870* (Durham, 2004), especially chapters 4 and 5.

15. Quoted in Kostal, *Jurisprudence of Power,* 7. I rely here on Kostal's careful narrative and analysis of the rebellion and the debates following.

16. *Birmingham Daily Post,* 29 December 1866. The actions of Governor Edward Eyre in Jamaica provoked an enormous debate in English newspapers, which would come to be tied to domestic calls for political reform. On the role of the press, see Kostal, *Jurisprudence of Power,* especially chapter 1, and Bernard Semmel, *Democracy versus Empire: The Jamaica Riots of 1865 and the Governor Eyre Controversy* (New York, 1969), especially chapters 1 and 6.

17. Kostal, *Jurisprudence of Power,* 100–104.

18. This pervasiveness of suspensive norms prompts questions about the utility of approaching the history of emergency state powers through theoretical constructs offered by thinkers like Carl Schmitt. See Nasser Hussain, *The Jurisprudence of Emergency: Colonialism and the Rule of Law* (Ann Arbor, 2003), especially 20–22. A historical approach to liberal legal regimes' attempts to legitimate emergency powers is more illuminating than a theory in which emergencies are conceived as those circumstances that generate exceptions to norms. This is one of the lessons of the legislative history of empire, in which legislation that provided for the suspension of habeas corpus and other emergency measures often did so by anticipation, having been crafted when such emergencies did not exist. The exception was so deeply embedded in the norm, both in thought and in practice, that it was indistinguish-

able from it. Statutes made in Westminster (for instance, that for Canada, in 1837) and in colonial assemblies (like the Jamaican statute of 1681, or the Irish habeas statute of 1781–1782) did just that: they normalized the persistent position from which emergency action, and the legitimation of it, could arise as needed. Such statutes created a "prior authority" for emergency powers, which should make it difficult to see such powers as exceptions, all of Dicey's insistence to the contrary notwithstanding. Britons' imperial law-making through the eighteenth and nineteenth centuries shows the limited ways in which they lived according to the ideological presuppositions they ordinarily expressed. In writing that the norm contained the legitimation of various forms of emergency action, I do not mean to approve of those actions. I do so only to highlight the ways in which liberal democratic order historically has been able to accommodate in its norms modes of action antithetical to formal statements about itself. For a discussion of the tension between liberal argument and constitutional norms on the one hand, and the exercise of colonial power on the other, see Kostal, "Jurisprudence of Power," 1–2, and the works cited there.

19. See 29/30 Victoria, c. 1; Virginia Crossman, *Politics, Law, and Order in Nineteenth-Century Ireland* (Dublin, 1996), 111–113 and 219. After this round of suspension lapsed, magistrates in Ireland continued to call for further suspensions, at least targeted at certain locales (117–127). See also Charles Townshend, *Political Violence in Ireland: Government and Resistance since 1848* (Oxford, 1983), 61 and 88–101.

20. See 24/25 Victoria, c. 104.

21. See ibid., c. 67; Hussain, *Jurisprudence of Emergency*, 89.

22. Cary Federman, *The Body and the State: Habeas Corpus and American Jurisprudence* (Albany, 2006), introduction and chapter 1, especially 23–36.

23. Act 19, in *Acts of Assembly, Passed in the Island of Jamaica, from 1681 to 1754, Inclusive* (London, 1756), 28.

24. Clark and McCoy, *Fundamental Legal Right*, 49–54.

25. See 34/35 Victoria, c. 25; Townshend, *Political Violence*, 63–64; Crossman, *Politics, Law, and Order*, chapter 4, especially 121–127 and 221–222.

26. Townshend, *Political Violence*, 131–137; Simpson, *Human Rights*, 78–80.

27. See Act 27 in H. T. Rivaz, *The Bengal Regulations, the Acts of the Governor-General in Council . . . Punjab*, 4th ed. (1889), vol. 1, pp. 586–591; Simpson, *Human Rights*, 83–84.

28. Clare Anderson, *Legible Bodies: Race, Criminality, and Colonialism in South Asia* (New York, 2004), 4–7, 25–30, and 114–119.

29. For an overview of scholarship on these camps, see Elizabeth van Heyningen, "The Concentration Camps of the South African (Anglo-Boer) War, 1900–1902," *History Compass* 7 (2009): 22–43.

30. Throughout I rely on Caroline Elkins, *Imperial Reckoning: The Untold Story of Britain's Gulag in Kenya* (New York, 2005): on oath taking, see 25–28.

31. Ibid., chapters 3 and 7, especially 217–219; A. W. B. Simpson, "Round Up the Usual Suspects: The Legacy of British Colonialism and the European Convention on Human Rights," *Loyola Law Review* 41 (1995–1996): 665–668; Simpson, *Human Rights,* 834–835, on the Convention, 96–101 and 314–315. On Regulation 18B and its use, see A. W. Brian Simpson, *In the Highest Degree Odious: Detention without Trial in Wartime Britain* (Oxford, 1992), especially 44–45 and chapters 5 and 9.

32. Simpson, *Human Rights,* 874–881 and 1065–1070, including a discussion of similar measures taken in Nyasaland. On the detention camps, see Elkins, *Imperial Reckoning,* xii–xiv, and chapters 5 and 6.

33. See 4 and 5 George V, cc. 21 and 63, and 5 George V, c. 8. On these acts see Simpson, *Highest Degree Odious,* 5–7, and on Regulation 14B, 12–14.

34. On Pitt's India Act, Quebec, and New Zealand, see Chapter 8.

35. On Sir Frederick Loch Halliday and his grandfather, Sir Frederick James Halliday, see *ODNB,* s.v. Sir Frederick James Halliday. To the best of my understanding, these men are not related to my family.

36. On Rex v. Halliday, ex part Zadig, see Simpson, *Highest Degree Odious,* chapter 2, especially 16–17 and 24–25, quotation at 25.

37. *Judicial Decisions on the Writ of Habeas Corpus ad Subjiciendum and on the Provincial Ordinance, 2d Victoria,* chapter 4: "Whereby the Habeas Corpus Ordinance of 1784 Has Been Suspended" (Three Rivers, 1839), 5 and 11.

38. Ibid.

39. INS v. St. Cyr, 533 U.S. 289, 301 (2001), quoting Felker v. Turpin, 518 U.S. 651, 663–664 (1996).

40. On the Suspension Clause and the Judiciary Act in this regard, and on Bollman, see Eric M. Freedman, *Habeas Corpus: Rethinking the Great Writ of Liberty* (New York, 2001), part 1. For debates over the making of the Suspension Clause—which some hoped would contain a more positive statement about the writ's presence in U.S. law—see chapter 2, especially 12–13. On early state suspensions, see Dallin H. Oaks, "Habeas Corpus in the States—1776–1865," *University of Chicago Law Review* 32 (1965): 250–251.

41. On Bollman's case, see Paul D. Halliday and G. Edward White, "The

Suspension Clause: English Text, Imperial Contexts, and American Implications," *Virginia Law Review* 94 (2008): 683–699.

Appendix

1. This number corrects slightly the number reported in Paul D. Halliday and G. Edward White, "The Suspension Clause: English Text, Imperial Contexts, and American Implications," *Virginia Law Review* 94 (2008): 591, n36. This correction was the result of a final exhaustive review of all the survey data. The addition of five previously misdated writs had no effect on the data presented in that article or on the validity of the conclusions drawn from it.
2. Narcissus Luttrell, *A Brief Relation of State Affairs, from September 1678 to April 1714* (Oxford, 1857).
3. To correct for the small sample size—only one survey year (1614) falling within Coke's tenure—this figure is derived from all writs between Michaelmas 1613 and Trinity 1616. For more detailed information on release rates in this period, see Chapter 1.
4. For more detailed information on release rates in this period, see Chapter 1.

Manuscript Sources

Items marked below with an asterisk are also available in the microfiche collection compiled by J. H. Baker, *English Legal Manuscripts* (Leiden, since 1975).

Bodleian Library, Oxford

*North.f.16: reports of Francis North, t. Charles II
Rawl.A.477: Court fees, ca. 1600
*Rawl.C.382: reports, t. Elizabeth and James I
*Rawl.C.719: reports, t. Charles II

British Library, London

Additional Manuscripts:
    10,619: Thomas Twisden, reports, t. Charles II
    16,259: Sir Elijah Impey, vol. 1: Answers and Letters from Europe, 1774–1780
    16,265: Letter Book of Sir Elijah Impey, 1774–1776
    29,137: Warren Hastings Papers, Correspondence, 1776
    32,518; 32,519; 32,520: papers of Sir Francis North, Lord Guilford
    32,521: Court notebooks of Sir Francis North, 1670s
    32,527: Roger North, reports, 1670s
    36,081: Hardwicke papers, legal treatises
    38,161: Hardwicke papers, notes of speeches in Parliament
    38,400–38,401: Liverpool Papers, East India Papers, 1776–1779
Egerton 3376: James Morice, reading on the prerogative, 1578

Hargrave 48: reports, 1652–1657

Hargrave 64: reports, t. Charles II

Hargrave 65: reports, t. Charles II

Hargrave 66: reports, 1702–1704

Hargrave 411: note book of Sir John Turton, t. William III

Harleian 4841: reading on Magna Carta, c. 29, by Francis Ashley, Middle
   Temple, 1616

Harleian 5220: treatise on the prerogative, Sir John Dodderidge

Stowe 1011: commonplace book, John Fortescue Aland, vol. 1

India Office Records:

   IOR/H/64: parliamentary Papers on East India Company Jurisdiction

   IOR/H/121: correspondence on Indian affairs, 1775–1776

   IOR/H/148: correspondence on Indian affairs, 1779–1781

   IOR/H/207: Bengal revenue papers, 1778–1783

   IOR/V/18: Bengal regulations, 1815–1819, vol. 4

Cambridge University Library, Cambridge

*Gg.2.5: reports, t. Henry VIII to Charles I

*Gg.2.19: reports, 1629–1634

*Gg.2.20: reports, 1634–1638

Gg.2.29: King's Bench entries, ca. 1660

*Gg.2.30: reports, 1621–1627

*Ii.5.32: reports, 1616–1632

*Ll.3.13: reports, 1625–1628

Mm.6.57: Littleton Papers

Mm.6.65: miscellanea, sixteenth and seventeenth centuries

Essex Record Office, Chelmsford

D/Y2/7: Morant Collection, Colchester Letters

Folger Library, Washington, D.C.

MS.V.b.6: reports, 1650–1659

Gray's Inn, London

*GI 25: reading on Magna Carta, c. 29, by Robert Chaloner, Gray's Inn, 1522

*GI 34: reports, 1657–1663

*GI 35: reports, 1664–1676

Harvard Law School, Cambridge

*13: reading on Magna Carta, anonymous, ca. 1500
*105: reports, t. Elizabeth and James I
*109: reports, 1611–1619
*113: reports, 1639–1646
*118: reports, t. Elizabeth and James I
*145: reports, 1646–1648
1023: Lord Ellesmere, observations on Magna Carta
*1058: reports, t. Henry VIII to James I
*1071: reports, 1685–1702
*1124: reports, 1697–1702
*1128: Star Chamber Reports, 1624–1640
*1166: reports, 1628–1645
*1167: reports, 1633–1640
*1180: reports, t. Elizabeth and James I
*2069: reports, 1604–1613
*2076: reports, 1600–1602
*2077: reports, 1611–1612
*2080: reports, 1604–1624
*4071: reports, 1687–1702
5016: Commonplace book of Thomas Twisden, ca. 1650
5093: Earl of Nottingham, treatise on pardons, ca. 1680
*Fullwood Reports, 1695–1697

Leicestershire Record Office, Wigston Magna

DG7/Box XI/pp60, i: Finch Papers
DG7/Box XVIII/Law 17: Finch MSS, Heneage Finch fee book, 1656–1672

Lincoln's Inn, London

*Coxe 93: reports, 1628–1641
*Hill 49: reports, 1684–1696
*Hill 83: Sir Edward Northey's reports, 1661–1672
*Hill 84: Sir Edward Northey, notebook, 1671–1672
*Hill 122: reports, 1605–1610
*Maynard 9: reports, 1629–1633
*Maynard 18: reports, 1622–1625
*Maynard 21: reports, t. James I and Charles I
*Maynard 22: reports, 1612–1623
*Maynard 66: reports, t. Elizabeth and James I

*Misc. 9(1): Melmoth MS, reports, 1695–1701
*Misc. 375: reports, 1683–1688
*Misc. 386: reports, 1668–1676
*Misc. 488: reports, t. Elizabeth and James I
*Misc. 492: reports, 1600–1604
*Misc. 499: reports, 1646–1668
*Misc. 500: reports, 1669–1678
*Misc. 713: Sir Peter King's Reports, 1692–1702

National Library of Wales, Aberystwyth

Coedymaen Manuscripts: papers of Sir William Williams

The National Archives, London (Kew)

King's Bench Records:
    KB1 and 2: affidavits
    KB11/14: Crown Side, recorda files, strays, 1689–1690
    KB15/40–51: Crown Side, precedent books, sixteenth–eighteenth centuries
    KB15/55: Crown Office, fees, 1637/1638
    KB15/57: Fees in the Capital Office of the Upper Bench, 1650s
    KB15/59–60: precedents of rules
    KB15/64: Report of Commissioners of Fees in King's Bench, 1736/1737
    KB16: Crown Side, recorda files, main series, after 1689
    KB21: Crown Side, rulebooks
    KB29: Crown Side, controlment rolls
    KB32/5: docket rolls of bails
    KB32/7, part 2: Crown Side, recorda files, strays, 1641–1642
    KB32/10, parts 1 and 2: Crown Side, recorda files, strays, 1630–1649
    KB33/1/1: records in cases of treason, from 1600
    KB39: Indexes to Crown Side affidavits
    KB140: Plea Side, miscellanea
    KB145: Crown Side, recorda files, main series, before 1688
    KB164: Plea Side, habeas corpora rolls
Other Records:
    ADM1: Admiralty, correspondence, including captains' and Admiralty solicitors' letters
    ADM6/67, pt. 1: Entry book of men demanded by habeas corpus, Plymouth, 1812–1815
    ADM7/185: Expenditures for wounded seamen and prisoners of war

ADM7/298–304: Law officers' opinions

ADM97/114/2 and 119: Office of commissioners of wounded seamen, prisoners of war, petitions

CP45: Common Pleas, remembrance rolls

E215/820–21, 860, 868, 872, 875, 883/2–3, 883/5, 889, 944, 952, 961, 963, 970A, 983, 994, 998: Notes of the commissions of fees, 1628, concerning fees of court clerks and prisons

E101/109/16; E101/110/1–5; E101/124/2; and E101/616/28: Exchequer, fines and amercements

HO45/2843: Home Office papers, concerning habeas corpus to Isle of Jersey, 1849

PC2: Privy Council, registers

SP: State Papers

TS: Treasury Solicitors' Papers

Yale Law School, New Haven

*GP72.1: reports, t. James I and Charles I

*GR29.6: reports, ca. 1580–1590

*GR29.8: reports, 1588–1595

*GR29.9: reports, t. Elizabeth and James I

*GR29.14: reports, t. Elizabeth and James I

*GR29.18: reports, 1603–1612

*GR29.19: reports, 1609–1612

*GR29.23: reports, t. James I and Charles I

Table of Cases

This chronologically ordered list covers most cases on habeas corpus discussed in the text, with page references. It does not include references to cases made only in passing when discussing specific aspects of process, nor does it include cases on other forms of process, such as writs of mandamus or certiorari. All writs issued from King's Bench, in Westminster Hall, unless parenthetically noted by the case name as issuing from another court. Cases known from the *English Reports* by a name that is shown to be incorrect by comparison with the record are listed by the name in the record, with the case name used in the reports placed in parentheses.

The following abbreviations are used in the table:

Bail: Those released, usually on giving surety to be of good behavior or to appear in King's Bench or another court for further process. Many of those who were bailed were later discharged.

Comm.: Commissioners or committees, including commissioners of accounts, bankruptcy, the hearth tax, etc., and parliamentary committees of the 1640s, such as those for accounts.

Disch.: Those excused from custody altogether, including those who were first bailed, appeared on their recognizances, and were then discharged. Many such cases of discharge can only be detected from studying the rulebooks, because the only notation made on the writ or roll regards bail.

High Comm.: High Commission

JP(s): Justice(s) of the Peace

PC: Privy Council; if ordered by one councilor: (individual)

Principal Sec.: Principal secretary or secretary of state

Remand: Those returned to the prison whence they came, or committed to the marshal of King's Bench for arraignment or other process in that court.

Self-determ.: Self-determination of custody, allowed in family custody cases.

Unknown: Those for whom information is unknown owing to record damage, loss, or incompleteness.

Unperformed: Writs that were not returned, or to which a return without a body was made owing to the prisoner's death or illness.

Unspec.: Those for whom no information about the alleged wrong or the jailing authority appears on what is otherwise a complete return of the writ.

Viol.: Violate/violation of a by-law, custom, privilege, or proclamation.

Date	Case name	Issue	Detained by	Result	Pages
1429	Rose et al.	Felony	Unspec.	Bail	340n23
1430	White et al.	Felony	Unspec.	Remand	340n23
1450	Joly et al.	Felony	JP	Bail	358n102
1450	Blak	Private suit	Sheriff	Bail	358n107
1450	Brugeys	Felony	Unspec.	Bail	358n107
1506	Hymmerford et al.	Felony	Unspec.	Unknown	357n98
1506	Humpton	Burglary	Assizes	Disch./pardon	382n100
1506	Worley	Unspec.	JP	Remand	373n14
1510	Sage	Felony	Unspec.	Remand	410n23
1514	Warner	Felony	PC	Bail	410n23
1514	Bykkeley	Unspec.	Unspec.	Bail	353n60
1518	Aleyn et al.	Felony	PC	Remand	398n68
1518	Sheffield	Unspec.	PC	Remand	155
1518	Apryse	Unspec.	Chancellor	Disch.	157, 399n76
1522	Dune	Felony	PC	Bail/pardon	398n66
1522	Banaster	Murder	PC	Remand	398n66
1538	Littleford	Unspec.	PC (individual)	Remand	399n77
1539	Becher	Felony	Unspec.	Bail/pardon	358n104
1541	Foster	Unspec.	PC (individual)	Bail	399n78
1542	Leper et al.	Unspec.	King	Remand	155, 398n69, 399n79
1546	Hodges et al.	Unspec.	PC	Remand	157, 399nn75,76
1546	Hychborne	Felony	Unknown	Disch.	383n107
1546	Walker	Felony	Assizes	Bail	117–118
1554	Gray	Unspec.	Queen	Remand	399n79
1554	Robynson et al.	Treason	2 judges	Remand	323, 343n54
1554	Rydwyn et al.	Treason	PC	Remand	323, 343n54
1558	Bennett	Murder	Unspec.	Remand	347n7
1558	Pollard et al.	Treason	PC	Disch. 2; Rem. 4	398n67
1560 CP	Scroggs	Unspec.	Royal comm.	Disch.	363n47
1565	Frank	Homicide	JPs	Bail	382n99
1566	Baker	Forcible entry	Unspec.	Bail/pardon	384n115
1566	Lawrence	Unspec.	PC	Bail/pardon	347n4
1567 CP	Lee	Religion	High Comm.	Disch.	363n47
1573	Suckerman	Unspec.	JP	Bail/pardon	373n13

Date	Case name	Issue	Detained by	Result	Pages
1573	Hyckeford	Unspec.	JP	Bail/pardon	373n13
1573	Howkyns	Robbery	Assizes	Remand/ pardon	356n83, 382n100
1574	Rochester	Unspec.	JP	Bail/pardon	373n13
1574	Miller	Unspec.	PC	Remand	347n4
1574	Grange	Unspec.	King's Bench	Bail/pardon	354n68
1576 CP	Hinde	Unspec.	Lord Treasurer	Unknown	363n47, 375n32
1582	Jerman	Murder	JP	Unknown	352n54
1587 CP	Searche	Viol. privilege	Marshal queen's household	Disch.	363n47
1587 CP	Hellyard	Unspec.	Principal Sec.	Unknown	363n47
1587 CP	Howel	Unspec.	Principal Sec.	Unknown	363n47, 375n32
1590	Packington et al.	Unspec.	Lord Lt.	Unperformed	366n85
1592	Agmondesham	Viol. privilege	Lord Chamberlain	Unperformed	157–158, 399n80
1594	Lopez et al.	Treason	Unspec.	Remand	205, 416n92
1594	Nelson	Unspec.	Unspec.	Unperformed	350n32
1594	Wheeler	Felony	JP	Remand	353n60
1594	Smyth	Homicide	Unspec.	Bail	355n72
1594	Taylor	Forgery	Unspec.	Bail	355n72
1594	Markendall	Treason	JP	Bail	352n51
1594	Robicut	Murder	Unspec.	Remand	352n51
1594	Kelly	Unspec.	PC	Remand	399n84
1594	Kedway	Unspec.	JP	Bail	104, 373n17
1597	Manock	Unspec.	PC	Bail	24–26, 104
1598	Harcourt	Unspec.	PC	Bail	158–159
1598	Barnes	Unspec.	PC	Remand	159
1599 CP	Deane	Words	London JPs	Disch.	363n47
1601	Gardiner	Firearms	JP	Disch.	110, 111, 377n54
1601	Brearley	Contempt	Berwick corp.	Unperformed	117, 259–262, 267, 268, 280, 375n33, 433nn3,4, 434nn8,11, 436n30
1601	Robson et al.	Riot	PC	Bail	351n44, 379n71
1602	Acres	Defamation	Church court	Remand	384n121
1602	Fludd	Defamation	Church court	Remand	384n121
1602	Barrett	Defamation	Church court	Disch.	384n121
1602	Sparrow	Unspec.	JP	Bail	104
1602	Crompton	Firearms	JP	Bail	105
1602	Mady	Unspec.	JP	Bail	374n18
1602	Leaver	Bastardy	JP	Bail	353n59
1603	Thomas	Unspec.	PC	Remand	400n84
1604	Curtys	Alehouse	Quarter sessions	Disch.	384n117
1604	Clark	Malpractice	Coll. physicians	Disch.	105, 152
1604	Brooksby	Treason	PC	Pardon	73–74

Date	Case name	Issue	Detained by	Result	Pages
1605	Broughton	Bigamy	High Comm.	Bail	385n125
1605	Price	Alehouse	Bailiffs	Bail	384n117
1605	Witherley	Contempt	Marches Wales	Disch.	11–14, 26, 27, 28, 81, 82, 215, 280, 337n1, 338nn3–5, 433n6
1605	Farley et al.	Contempt	Marches Wales	Disch.	338n5
1605	Lowe	Illegal Trade	London corp.	Disch.	39–41, 45, 48, 349n28, 379n70
1605	Hyett	Marital	High Comm.	Bail	122–123
1605 CP	Thomlinson	Contempt	Admiralty	Disch.?	363n47
1605–1607	Ladd et al.	Contempt	High Comm.	Unknown	336n1, 342n48, 360n23, 363n47, 410n31
1606	Edwards	Bastardy	Sheriff/constable	Disch.	151
1606	Tooker	Burglary	Unknown	Bail	118
1606	Newman	Contempt	High Comm.	Bail	354n70
1606	Williams	Words	High Comm.	Disch.	375n36
1606	Tompson	Contempt	Cambridge corp.	Disch.	78–79, 87, 365nn64–66
1607	Wyer	Enforce judgmt.	Admiralty	Remand	142, 393n15
1607	Eyre	Marital	High Comm.	Bail	385n126
1607	Kiteley	Unspec.	JP	Disch.	374n18
1607	Osborne	Plague orders	JP	Bail	353n59
1608	Scadding	Aid escape	Admiralty	Remand	142
1608	Rooper	Contempt	Church court	Disch.	384n121
1608	Farndon	Words	London corp.	Disch.	76–77, 78, 79, 363n52, 365n66
1608? CP	Wharton	Religion	High Comm.	Remand	376n42
1609	Edwards	Marital	High Comm.	Bail	123–124
1610	Vaughan et al. (Thames fishermen)	Fishing	Admiralty	Disch.	87, 368n108
1610	Anderson	Unspec.	JP	Bail	373n18
1610	Lant	Forcible entry	JPs	Bail	150, 396n43
1610	Harling	Words	JP	Bail	52, 353n58
1611	Stainforth et al.	Disturb church	JPs	Bail	110, 372n4, 381n91
1612	Vaux	Unspec.	PC	Remand	159, 400n87
1612	East	Bastardy	Quarter sessions	Remand	384n124
1613	Hetley	Contempt	Sewer comm.	Disch.	151
1613	Doake et al.	Disturb church	JPs	Disch.	372n4
1613	Tenant	Malpractice	Coll. physicians	Disch.	152, 397n55

Date	Case name	Issue	Detained by	Result	Pages
1628	Chambers	Contempt	PC	Disch.	106
1628	Melvyn	Treason	Principal sec.	Remand	107, 375n37
1628	Billingsley	Viol. privilege	King's chamberlain	Bail	352n56
1629	Holles et al.	Unspec.	PC	Remand	224
1629	Chambers	Contempt	Star Chamber	Disch.	106
1629	Melvyn	Treason	Principal sec.	Bail	107, 375n37
1629	Symonds	Disturb church	JPs	Disch.	99–101, 136, 316
1630	Bullman	Alehouse	Quarter sessions	Bail	396n46
1630	Eve	Homicide	Assizes	Pardon	383n106
1630–1631	Jones	Viol. privilege	Earl Marshal	Disch.	93–95, 370nn132,133, 371nn135,136
1631	Broadway	Unspec.	PC	Remand	411n36
1631	Brigham	Contempt	Ct. of Requests	Remand	188, 411n37
1631	Gresham	Unspec.	JP	Remand	373n15
1633	White	Words	Earl Marshal	Remand	371n136
1634	Ayres	Bankruptcy	Comm.	Disch.	105, 374n23
1634	Leachford	Unspec.	PC	Remand	421n35
1634	Courtney	Unspec.	PC	Remand	421n35
1634	East et al.	Tax	Treas. king's household	Remand	371n136
1634	Skerce	Apprenticeship	Quarter sessions	Unknown	447n150
1634	Nightengale	Murder	Treas. king's household	Remand	371n136
1635	Barfoote	Burglary	Unknown	Pardon	382n101
1637	Fisher	Trade regulation	JPs/Pinners' Co.	Disch.	185–187, 410n28
1637	Gibson et al.	Robbery	Assizes?	Remand	357n93
1637	Blanck	Malpractice	Coll. physicians	Remand	152, 397n56
1637	Jennings	Unspec.	PC	Remand	422n42
1638	Jennings	Sedition	PC	Remand	422n42
1638	Rawson	Unspec.	PC	Bail	421n35
1638	Barkham	Unspec.	PC	Bail	421n35
1638	Stanlake	Plague relief	JPs?	Bail	396n47
1640	Plowden	Marital	High Comm.	Remand	188–189, 386n131
1640	Brice	Unspec.	Earl of Denbigh	Disch.	104
1641	Rickaby	Murder	Assizes/Durham	Remand	393n20, 436n29
1641	Lloyd	Attachment	Chester Excheq.	Unperformed	185, 373n10, 410n27, 436n31
1641	Thompson	Unspec.	JP	Unperformed	366n87
1642	Langham and Andrews	Refuse office	London corp.	Remand	189–191, 192, 194, 411nn34,41,42
1642	Hayward	Viol. proclamation	London mayor	Disch.	162
1642	Davys	Sedition	London mayor	Disch.	162

Date	Case name	Issue	Detained by	Result	Pages
1642	Cooke	Unspec.	London mayor	Disch.	162
1642	Mason et al.	Viol. procla-mation	Parliament	Bail	162, 226, 401n101, 422n44
1643	Ridyard	Unspec.	London mayor	Disch.	31, 344n59
1643	Roane	Unspec.	Army officer	Bail	402n114
1643	Hudson	Unspec.	Army officer	Bail	402n114
1643	Bower	Unspec.	Parliament	Unknown	162–163
1645	Chambers et al.	Disturb election	London corp.	Bail	190–191, 376n47, 411n42
1646	Hacker et al.	Accounts	Comm.	Disch.	375n35, 401n103
1646	Rawson et al.	Accounts	Comm.	Bail	401n103
1647	Huxley	Viol. procla-mation	Parliament	Disch.	422n45
1647	Payne	Sedition	Parliament	Bail	164
1647	Easton et al.	Accounts	Army com-mittee	Bail	402n105
1647	Vandowall et al.	Preaching	Harwich mayor	Disch.	401n104
1647	Brouncker	Words	JPs	Bail	351n44
1647	Browne	Disturb sewer	Sewer comm.	Disch.	396n50
1647	Albany	Sedition	Parliament	Bail	164
1647	Bruce et al.	Disturb church	JPs	Disch.	372n4
1648	Stawell	Treason	Parliament	Remand	226, 422n46
1648	Lilburne	Sedition	Parliament	Remand	193–197, 409n21, 412nn52,53, 413nn56,57,60, 66
1648	Armiger	Accounts	Comm. plun-dered min-isters	Disch.	402n104
1648	Anon.	Murder	Unknown	Bail	377n57
1648	Brunge	Contempt	Sewer comm.	Disch.	105, 396n50
1649	Hudson	Tithes	Comm. plun-dered min-isters	Disch.	164
1649	London et al.	Blasphemy	JPs	Disch.	402n110
1649	Collier	Contempt	Indemnity comm.	Bail	402n111
1649	Anon.	Coining	Unknown	Unknown	350nn31,37
1650	Chetwynd	Unspec.	Parliament	Remand	113, 379n73, 422n46
1650	Creed	Contempt	Unknown	Unknown	347n9
1651	Gotely	Contempt	Militia comm.	Bail	164
1653–1654	Streater	Sedition	PC/Parl.	Commit	227–229, 389n109
1654	Lilburne	Unspec.	PC	Unperformed	227–228, 422nn48–50
1655	Anon.	Felony	Unknown	Unknown	350n37
1656	Green	Accounts	Tax comm.	Unknown	84, 367n90

Date	Case name	Issue	Detained by	Result	Pages
1657	Blashfield	Disturb church	JPs	Disch.	372n4
1658	Biddle	Unspec.	PC	Unperformed	229
1658	Biddle	Unspec.	PC	Disch.	229
1660	Ld. Willoughby	Unspec.	Military officer	Bail	165, 402n115
1660	Blackwell et al.	Forcible entry	JPs	Disch.	149–150
1661	Baily	Murder	Unknown	Disch.	357n94
1662	Marq. de Brabant	Murder	Assizes	Bail	205
1662	Smith	Sedition	PC	Bail	357n92
1662	Crofton	Treason	PC	Remand	357n94, 378n64
1662	Harrington	Unspec.	PC	Unperformed	231, 423n66
1662	Vane	Unspec.	PC	Remand	162, 230–231, 423n63
1666	Huggett	Murder	Assizes	Disch./settled	118, 383n106
1666	Whitamore	Poaching	Quarter sessions	Remand	356n82
1666	Swallow	Refuse office	London corp.	Disch.	111, 378n63
1667	Fenner	Unspec.	PC	Unperformed	231, 351n44
1667	Daberon	Treasonable practices	Unknown	Bail	356n85
1667	Careswell	Treason	PC	Bail	231, 424n68
1667	Brown	Barratry	Quarter sessions	Bail	356n82
1668	Overton	Unspec.	PC	Unperformed	231, 267–268, 437n33
1668	Parker	Illegal armorial bearings	Earl Marshal	Remand	142, 393n18
1669	Salmon	Unspec.	PC	Unperformed	231, 267–268
1669	Grafton	Refuse office	Drapers' Co.	Disch.	191
1669 CP	Baxter	Religion	JPs	Disch.	235, 353n62, 363n48
1670	Cole	Market regulation	London corp.	Disch./settled	84, 367n91
1670	Walford	Accounts	Comm.	Disch.	379n70
1670	Franklyn	Religion	JPs	Bail	345n64
1670 CP	Rudyard	Religion	JPs	Disch.	235, 353n62, 425n84
1670 CP	Bushel	Contempt	Assizes	Disch.	235–236, 425n84
1671	Maddy	Murder	Assizes	Unknown	118, 383n105
1671	Howard	Marital	Husband	Unknown	43–44, 47, 124
1671?	Anon.	Insanity	Unknown	Unknown	386n144
1671? CP	Anon.	Tithes	Church Ct.	Unknown	354n63
1671–1672	Harwood	Viol. custom	London corp.	Remand	191, 411n44
1672	Broadney	Viol. by-law	London corp.	Unknown	191–192
1672	Meade (Jamaica)	Unknown	Unknown	Unperformed	357n97, 386n139, 437n36
1673	Walcott	Treason	Unknown	Bail	381n91
1674	Leigh	Marital	Husband	Settled	350n38, 386n135
1675	Evans	Unspec.	JP	Bail	356n87, 374n19

Date	Case name	Issue	Detained by	Result	Pages
1675	Hyde (Emerton)	Family custody	Step-father	Self-determ.	124–125, 126, 127–128, 129
1675	Sedden	Religion	JPs	Bail	344n62
1676	Anon.	Child custody	Guardian	Writ denied	387n148
1676	Richardson	Sedition	Quarter sessions	Bail	356n87
1676	Jenks	Sedition	PC	Writ denied	236–237
1677	Murray	Sedition	Sec. of State	Bail	236, 425n89
1677	Murray	Unspec.	PC	Bail	236, 425n89
1677	Harrington	Sedition	PC	Bail	235, 236, 425n89
1677	Nichols et al.	Disturb church	JPs	Bail	372n4, 383n110
1677	Earl of Shaftes-bury	Contempt	Parliament	Remand	215–217, 418n1
1677 CP	Jones	Religion	JP	Remand	347n9
1678	Weller	Unknown	Unknown	Disch./settled	382n96
1678	Stayley	Treason	Unknown	Remand	425n92
1678	Coleman	Treason		Remand	45–46, 425n92
1679	Beaumont	Contempt	Quarter sessions	Disch.	107, 375n39
1679	Spalding	Unspec.	Parliament	Bail	425n93
1679	Price	Unspec.	Parliament	Bail	425n93
1679	Milbourne	Treason	Parliament	Bail	425n93
1679	Earl of Castle-maine	Treason	PC	Bail	425n93
1679	Mannock and son	Treason	Justice KB	Bail	425n93
1679	Crumpe	Convert to Catholicism	PC	Bail	425n93
1679	Arthur	Treason	Justice KB	Disch.	425n93
1679	Sheldon	Treason	Justice KB	Disch.	425n93
1679	Curson	Harboring priest	JP	Bail	425n93
1679	Lord Brudnell	Treason	Justice KB	Bail	425n93
1679	Preston	Treason	Parliament	Remand	425n93
1679	Griffin	Treason	Justice KB	Disch.	425n93
1679	Creed	Unspec.	PC	Bail	240, 267–268, 426n103
1681	Sheridan	Unspec.	Parliament	Bail	243, 244
1681	Moone	Disturb church	JPs	Remand	372n4
1682	Earl of Danby	Unspec.	Parliament	Remand	237, 238, 242
1682	Cater	Religion	Quarter sessions	Disch.	120, 384n119
1682	Lloyd	Homicide	Unknown	Bail	383n104
1682	Thompson et al.	Sedition	PC	Bail	242, 427n111
1682	Burke	Accounts	Quarter sessions	Disch.	110
1686	Curslowe	Unknown	Unknown	Disch.	357n95
1686	Selick	Child custody	Unknown	Writ denied	387n149
1686	Alborough	Robbery	Assizes	Transportation	119, 383n113
1687	Tilly	Illegal armorial bearings	Earl Marshal	Remand	393n18
1689	Fitzherbert et al.	Treason	Justice KB	Disch.	391n180

Date	Case name	Issue	Detained by	Result	Pages
1689	Canning	Sedition	Sec. of State	Bail	391n180
1689	Saxton	Treason	Sec. of State	Remand	391n178
1689	Guilstrop	Treason	PC	Remand	391n178
1690	Lundy	Treasonable practices	Sec. of State	Disch.	426n104
1690	Lowthorpe	Treason	Chief Justice KB	Remand	391n178
1690	Williamson	Treasonable practices	Sec. of State	Disch.	391n180
1690	Kattony	Sedition	JP	Disch.	391n181
1690	Bythwood	Sedition	Sec. of State	Disch.	391n181
1690	Cross	Treason	PC	Remand	391n178
1690	Vaughan	Child custody	Guardian	Settled	128
1690	Monson	Unspec.	JP	Disch.	374n19
1690	Thredder et al.	Accounts	JPs	Disch.	117, 396n47
1690	Fuller	POW	Admiralty comm.	Disch.	169–170, 171
1690	Read	Desertion	Army officer	Remand	403n117
1690	Depremont et al.	Alien enemies	PC	Remand/POW exch.	171
1691	Oldfield?	Insanity	Unknown	Unknown	387n145
1692	Moore (Barbados)	Unknown	Unknown	Unperformed	271, 357n97, 438nn46,47
1693	Golding	POW	Naval officer	Bail	170, 171
1694	Greven	Insubordination	Army officer	Disch.	165
1694	Acman	Insubordination	Army officer	Bail	403n117
1694	Darby	Poaching	JP	Bail	396n47
1694	Clarke	Poaching	JP	Disch.	105–106
1694	Phillips	Unspec.	JP	Disch.	374n19
1694	Lock et al.	Impressment	Admiralty comm.	Disch.	117
1695	Grascot	Viol. privilege	London corp.	Disch.?	198–199, 414n71
1695	Dupuis	Spy	PC	Remand/POW exch.	171, 206, 405n145
1695	Bethel	Clipping coin	Assizes	Remand	354n64, 411n35
1696	Ridley	Treason	PC	Bail	250, 429n146
1696	Hunt	Treason	Sec. of State	Bail	249, 429n141
1697	DuCastre et al.	Alien enemy	Sec. of State	Disch.	28–29, 171, 206, 242, 416n96
1697	Cumberford	POW	Admiralty comm.	Bail	170, 405n140
1697	Greenwell	Malpractice	Coll. physicians	Disch.	365n69, 383n112
1698	Knightley	Treason	JP	Disch./pardon	119, 383n113
1700	Fowler	Tithes	Church court	Disch.	348n19
1701	Archer	Child custody	Father	Self-determ.	128, 387n151
1701	Claxton	Lewd	JP	Remand	377n57
1702	Swanson	Forced marriage	JP?	Remand	416n94

Date	Case name	Issue	Detained by	Result	Pages
1702	Keach	Unknown	Admiralty	Remand	393n17
1704	Estwick	Viol. privilege	London corp.	Disch.?	414n71
1706	Alexander	Desertion	Army officer	Disch.	166
1706	Mendel	Disturb church	JPs	Disch.	372n4
1706	Hames	Treasonable practices	Sec. of State	Bail	85, 367n99
1710	Lady Annesley	Child custody	Guardian	Self-determ.	128–130, 131, 387n152
1714	Green	Poaching	Unknown	Disch.	374n29
1714	Whitten	Poor law	JPs	Unknown	85, 368n102
1715	Gibson	Accounts	JPs	Bail	382n96
1717	Wilkins	Conscription	Army officer	Disch.	109, 376n48, 402n116
1718	Green	Insanity	Robert Norris	Unknown	387n145
1718	Jackson	Mutiny	JP	Bail	377n60
1720	Turberville	Marital	Guardian	Self-determ.	126, 386n140
1721	Lister (Rawlinson)	Marital	Husband	Disch.	177–179, 187, 192, 198, 199, 200, 201, 207, 316
1722	Layer	Treason	Sec. of State	Remand	429n142
1722	Marsden	Marital	Husband	Unknown	46–47, 450nn36,38
1724	Howland	Child custody	Guardian	Custody re-assigned	128–129, 130, 387nn153–155
1729	Kimberley	Marital	JP	Remand	426n104
1730	Nathan	Bankrupt	Comm.	Disch.	374n20
1730	Strudwick	Private suit	Common Pleas	Remand	110–111, 377n58
1730	Wonters	Murder	Assizes	Pardon	362n39
1731	Anon.	Petty treason	Coroner	Remand	366n84
1732	Cartor	Disorderly	JP	Bail	174
1733	Harper	Vagabond	JP	Disch.	116–117, 381n92
1733	Crisp (Crest)	Robbery	JP	Bail	111, 377n59
1734	Smith	Child custody	Guardian	Self-determ.	129–130, 131
1738	Lacy	Vagabond	JPs	Remand	381n92
1745	Reynolds	Conscription	Army officer	Bail	167, 404n129
1746	Ratcliffe	Treason	Sec. of State	Remand	429n142
1746	Purser	Treasonable practices	Sec. of State	Bail	249
1749	Langlands	Apprenticeship	Master	Unknown	447n150
1751	Hinson	Marital	Husband	Unknown	45
1756	Backas	Impressment	Naval officer	Disch.	33, 114
1757	Parkin	Desertion	Army officer	Disch.	167–168, 404n131
1757	Ferrers	Marital	Husband	Self-determ.	44–45, 349nn24,25
1757	Winter	Desertion	Army officer	Disch.	403n122
1758	Wilkes	Marital	Mother	Self-determ.	199–200, 414n72

Date	Case name	Issue	Detained by	Result	Pages
1786	Airey	Insanity	Dr. Hall	Unknown	387n147
1786	Bowes	Marital	Husband	Self-determ.	349n25
1789	Lintot	Child custody	Mother	Unknown	132
1789	Edgar	Marital	Husband	Self-determ.	386n143
1790	Boutcher et al.	Impressment	Naval officer	Remand	381n90
1793	Stallwood	Marital	Father	Self-determ.	126–127
1793	Soper	Child custody	Father	Mother's custody	389n170
1794	Murray	Child custody	Mother	Father's custody	132
1794	Holland	Sedition	Quarter sessions	Remand	390n174
1794	Pennyman et al.	Impressment	Naval officer	Unknown	380n82
1798	Browne	Rogue	JP	Disch.	390n175
1798	Jordan	Sedition	Assizes	Remand	390n174
1798	Keighley	Child custody	Father	Mother's custody	389n170
1798	Fretus et al.	Impressment	Naval officer	Disch.	206, 346n69, 416n95
1799	Merrin et al.	Theft	Naval officer	Unknown	166, 403n119
1801	Suddis	Stolen goods	Army officer	Remand	166
1804	De Manneville	Child custody	Father	Father's custody	389nn169,170
1810	Baartman	Contract	Private indivs.	Remand	207–208, 417nn101,102
1814	Blake	Insubordination	Army officer	Remand	165–166, 403n118
1824	King (Sydney)	Desertion	Local magistrate	Remand	294, 446n146
1824	Warton (Hobart)	Felony	Local magistrate	Disch.	294, 446n147
1825	M'ara (Sydney)	Left service	Local magistrate	Remand	447n151
1826	Siva Poonian (Colombo)	Debt	Unknown	Disch.	291–292, 446n132
1827	Foster (Sydney)	Theft	Local magistrates	Nisi rule to disch.	447n152
1828	Lookaye (Sydney)	Left service	Local magistrate	Remand	296, 447n154
1829	New (Sydney)	Felony	Supr. Ct. NSW	Remand	295, 366n76
1838	Teed (Quebec)	Unspec.	Unspec.	Court closed	279–280
1839	Houde (Quebec)	Unspec.	Unspec.	Court closed	280
1843	Morgan (Hobart)	Neglect of work	Local magistrates	Disch.	295
1859–1860	Lees	Assault	Ct. martial	Brought from St. Helena	448n172
1860	Anderson (Toronto)	Extradition	Local magistrates	Remand	299–301, 448nn168,172
1860	Anderson	Extradition	Local magistrates	Disch.	299–301, 448nn168,172
1865	Leivens (Jamaica)	Sedition	Governor	Remand	307
1917	Zadig	Public safety	Military officer	Remand	313, 452n36

Table of Statutes

This chronological list of statutes is organized according to traditional regnal year form of citation and includes both a short title or description as well as the pages on which each statute is discussed. All statutes were made by the Parliament of England (to 1707), Great Britain (1707–1801), or the United Kingdom (after 1801), unless a colonial legislature or legislative council is noted as the creator.

Statute	Subject	Pages
3 Edward I, c. 15	Mainprise	156, 398n73
5 Richard II, c. 7	Forcible entry	149, 395n40
13 Richard II, c. 2	Constable and earl marshal's court	94, 371n135
15 Richard II, c. 2	Forcible entry	149, 395n40
14 Henry VIII, c. 5	Physicians	151, 397n52
23 Henry VIII, c. 5	Commissions of sewers	151, 396n49
32 Henry VIII, c. 16	Strangers (foreigners)	211, 418n111
33 Henry VIII, c. 6	Crossbows and handguns	105, 374n27
5/6 Edward VI, c. 25	Alehouses	150, 396n45
1 Mary, sess. 2, c. 3	Disturbing preachers	99–101, 372n4
1 Mary, sess. 2, c. 9	Physicians	151, 397n53
1/2 Philip and Mary, c. 13	JPs bailing prisoners	63, 148, 359n109, 395n37
2/3 Philip and Mary, c. 10	Examination of prisoners	148, 395n37
1 Elizabeth, c. 1	Supremacy (religious)	122, 147, 384n122, 395n32
1 Elizabeth, c. 2	Uniformity (religious)	19, 99–100
5 Elizabeth, c. 4	Artificers	295, 447n150
35 Elizabeth, c. 14	Pardon	221, 420n21
39 Elizabeth, c. 28	Pardon	221, 420n21

Index

Names of persons using habeas corpus may be found in the Table of Cases; names of other individuals will be found here. Most statutes should be searched in the Table of Statutes.

Felony. *See* Wrongs alleged against prisoners: felony
Fielding, Viscount, 255–256
Filmer, Robert, 178
Finch, Heneage, 84, 239, 361n37, 367n91
Finch, Henry, on liberty of the subject, 187, 410n31
Fines, 83–84, 106, 151, 225, 259, 261–262, 269, 364n54, 366nn82,86,87, 373n11, 378nn68,69, 385n128, 434n8
Firearms regulation, 29, 40, 105, 110, 120, 328
Fitzherbert, Anthony: *Natura Brevium,* 364n59, 365n63
Five Knights' case, 137–139, 215, 391n1, 392n3, 400n89; and Privy Council imprisonment orders, 26, 50, 138–139, 159–160, 163; and Heath, 50–51, 138, 139, 149; and Bramston, 137–138, 139, 152, 222, 225, 411n41; and Coke, 138–139
Fleetwood, William (MP), 221–222
Fleming, Thomas (chief justice), 5, 35, 135, 294, 315, 354n66; as solicitor general, 22, 24–25, 341n40, 342n45; as recorder, 22–24; and Manock's case, 25; and Privy Council, 26, 27; release rates under, 30, 332–333, 343n57; return of writ under, 53, 54; on king's prerogative, 64–65, 68–69, 280; and jurisdiction of Queen's Bench, 64–65, 81, 88, 94, 363n45; and Calvin's case, 70; on relationship of subject to king, 70; on Queen's Bench, 75; and Farndon's case, 76–77; and Thames fishermen's case, 87, 88; and equity, 92
Floyd, Edward, 219–220, 221, 233, 244, 419n11
Forbes, Francis (chief justice, New South Wales), 315; on habeas corpus, 82, 294, 299; and Lookaye's case, 296
Forced resettlement, 298. *See also* Deportation and transportation
Forsett, Edward, 69
Fortescue Aland, John (justice), 66–67; on equity, 88
Fox, Charles James (MP), on habeas corpus, 303–304

France, 247; Louis XIV, 31, 170, 237; revolutionary regime in, 102, 133, 253–254, 255, 315, 324, 414n66, 431n168; Napoleon, 256, 298
Franchise: legal liberties as, 23, 24, 35, 42, 86, 184–187, 192; and writ of quo warranto, 34, 42, 74–75; custodian's franchise, 41–43, 44, 45, 74, 88, 184–187, 205, 258, 285, 286, 407n165; and sanctuaries, 72, 185; Spelman on franchises, 74–75, 348n14, 410n22; Hale on franchises, 262, 266–267, 269, 286, 348nn13,14; and colonial charters, 283, 443n97
Franks, Frederick, 36, 346n74
Franks, Mary, 36
Fretus, Peter, 206, 346n69
Frodesham, Humphrey, 366n86
Fuller, Nicholas, 336n1
Fyneux, John (chief justice), 69

Gardiner, Thomas, 190
Gawdy, Francis (justice), 350n32
Geographical diffusion of habeas corpus: to dominions, 8, 12–14, 18, 34–35, 60, 63, 71, 75, 81–82, 85–87, 135–136, 137, 140, 143–144, 185, 212, 213, 239, 259–302, 305–309, 313, 396n51, 434nn12,16, 435n24; and king's prerogative, 35, 69, 75, 85–87, 185, 258, 280, 286, 299, 309; and Habeas Corpus Act, 69, 256–258, 280, 298–299; and allegiance to the king, 203; role of common law in, 213, 217, 236, 239, 274, 275, 278, 281, 283, 288, 290, 292, 293, 299, 301. *See also* Australia; Barbados; Berwick-upon-Tweed; Calais; Ceylon; Colonial assemblies; Colonial courts; Empire, impact of, on habeas corpus; Hale, Matthew; India; Ireland; Jamaica; Jurisdiction of King's Bench; Law of the land; New Zealand; Nonrepugnancy principle; Palatinates; Quebec
Gheeraerts, Marcus (painter), 359n1
Glanvill, Richard, 369n123
Glorious Revolution. *See* Revolution of 1688–89
God: and the king, 66, 67–68, 69, 73, 360n12; miracles of, 67–68, 69, 202;

Return to habeas corpus (continued)
returns, 103–105, 106, 107, 110, 120,
123, 149–150, 174, 175, 185, 235,
373n11; amendments of returns,
106–107, 112, 113, 296, 374n23,
375nn32,34,36,38, 378n69, 433n7;
rule against controverting returns,
108–112, 113, 114–115, 245, 246,
376n41, 378n63; delays in, 239; and
Brearley's case, 259–262. See also Judgments on habeas corpus
Revolution of 1688–89, 3, 31, 154, 165,
327, 331
Richardson, Thomas (chief justice),
353n62, 371n136
Robinson, Benjamin, 372n4
Rochford, Lord, 250–251
Rogby, George, 447n150
Rokeby, Thomas (justice), 429n146
Rolle, Henry (chief justice), 164, 194,
227, 229, 338n3, 350n31
Roman law, 20, 209, 377n56
Rousseau, Jean-Jacques, 183
Royal imprisonment orders, 221, 234,
237, 399n79; and jurisdiction of
King's Bench, 155–156, 157–158, 159–
160; of Charles I, 228, 244. See also
Five Knights' case; Privy Council
Rudyard, Benjamin (MP), 67–68, 69
Rules, 374n26, 389n166, 395n36,
400n93; vs. principles, 4, 97, 100–101,
109–110, 160, 372n5, 378n68, 395n36,
400n93; procedural rules, 6; concept
of, 67–68, 72, 87–89, 91, 100–101,
102, 105, 155; vs. discretion, 91, 147,
155, 156–157; rule against controverting returns, 108–112, 113, 114–115,
245, 246, 376n41, 378n63; as guides
for judges vs. orders made by judges,
378n68. See also Nisi orders or rules
Russell, Robert, 440n71
Rye, 366n87, 368n103

Salisbury, Robert Cecil, Earl of, 11–12
Salus populi. See Public good
Sanctuary, 72, 185
Sandwich, 368n103
Sawyer, Geoffrey, 61–62

Scotland, 18, 22, 161, 202, 204–205, 236,
260, 424n77, 434n12, 437n33; Jacobites in, 134, 248, 249
Scudamore, Rowland (jailer), 337n1
Secretaries of state, 11, 64, 107, 115,
154, 157, 248, 249, 254, 330, 428n137,
432n168,170
Seddon, Samuel, 36, 37, 55, 115–116,
346n80, 355n76, 356n89, 381n88
Seditious libel. See State wrongs: seditious libel
Selden, John, 15, 50, 138, 139, 149, 178,
222–223, 224
Seven Years' War, 32, 113–114, 169
Shaftesbury, Anthony Ashley Cooper,
Earl of, 227, 230, 425n89; imprisonment of, 215–217, 234, 236, 237, 243,
418n1; and Habeas Corpus Act, 239
Sharp, Granville, 314, 407n167,
417n104; and slavery, 7, 174, 210–
212, 407n167, 418n111; and naval im-
pressment, 7, 212; vs. Lilburne, 179,
209, 210, 316; views on English law,
208–210, 277; on suspension of habeas corpus, 252, 312, 430n154
Sheppard, William, 383nn108,109
Sheriffs, 2, 16, 17, 43, 61–62, 339n20,
353n61
Shirley, Thomas, 219, 221
Shower, Bartholomew, 206
Signatures on writs, 63, 359n109
Silvy, Joseph, 206, 346n69
Simpson, John, 401n103
Skinner, Quentin (historian): Regarding
Method, 336n5, 337n7, 421n29; on republican liberty, 408n7, 409n14
Slavery, 101, 120, 241, 278, 406n158,
407nn164,165,168, 440n77, 448n170;
and Sharp, 7, 174, 210–212, 407n167,
418n111; and colonial statutes, 8, 34,
306–307; and subjecthood, 69, 208–
212; Somerset's case, 174–176, 207,
208, 211, 316, 406n157; and republican liberty, 180, 408n7; in Barbados,
263, 274; Anderson's case, 299–301,
305, 316, 448nn168,172
Smith, John, 129–130
Smith, Penelope, 129